HANDBOOK OF COMMUNICATION AND PEOPLE WITH DISABILITIES
Research and Application

LEA's COMMUNICATION SERIES
Jennings Bryant/Dolf Zillmann, General Editors

Selected titles in Applied Communications (Teresa L. Thompson, Advisory Editor) include:

Beck/Ragan/du Pre • Partnership for Health: Building Relationships Between Women and Health Caregivers

Elwood • Power in the Blood: A Handbook on AIDS, Politics, and Communication

Harris • Health and the New Media: Technologies Transforming Personal and Public Health

Ray • Communication and Disenfranchisement: Social Health Issues and Implications

Socha/Diggs • Communication, Race, and Family: Exploring Communication in Black, White, and Biracial Families

Street/Gold/Manning • Health Promotion and Interactive Technology: Theoretical Applications and Future Directions

Whaley • Explaining Illness: Research, Theory, and Strategy

Williams/Nussbaum • Intergenerational Communication Across the Life Span

For a complete list of other titles in LEA's Communication Series, please contact Lawrence Erlbaum Associates, Publishers

HANDBOOK OF COMMUNICATION AND PEOPLE WITH DISABILITIES
Research and Application

Edited by

Dawn O. Braithwaite
University of Nebraska–Lincoln

Teresa L. Thompson
University of Dayton

LEA LAWRENCE ERLBAUM ASSOCIATES, PUBLISHERS
2000 Mahwah, New Jersey   London

Lawrence Erlbaum Associates, Inc., Publishers
10 Industrial Avenue
Mahwah, NJ 07430

Cover design by Kathryn Houghtaling Lacey

Library of Congress Cataloging-in-Publication Data

Handbook of communication and people with disabilities : research and
    application / edited by Dawn O. Braithwaite, Teresa L. Thompson.
        p.   cm. – (LEA's communication series)
    Includes bibliographical references and index.
    ISBN 0-8058-3059-6 (cloth : alk. paper)
    1. Handicapped–Means of communication–United States.
2. Sociology of disability–United States.   3. Communication in
services for the handicapped–United States.   4. Communication
devices for the disabled–United States.   I. Braithwaite, Dawn O.
II. Thompson, Teresa L.   III. Series.
HV1568.4.H35   2000
362.4'048–dc21   99-29094
                                                  CIP

Books published by Lawrence Erlbaum Associates are printed
on acid-free paper, and their bindings are chosen for strength
and durability.

Printed in the United States of America
10 9 8 7 6 5 4 3 2 1

To my cousin, Greg
—D.O.B.

To my brother, Steve
—T.L.T.

In Tribute to Irv Zola

Contents

Preface

Over the last 25 years the field of communication has seen an important proliferation of studies on how the presence of a physical disability affects communication among individuals. Much of this research has been prompted by personal experiences of scholars who are themselves disabled or who have a close family member who is disabled. Scholars have typically started their research efforts because of perceived concerns about difficult or awkward interaction between individuals with and without disabilities. Both disabled and ablebodied individuals often are affected by the discomfort, avoidance, and uncertainty characterizing such interactions. The goal of disability research in communication has been to illuminate these experiences and to ultimately improve communication in both personal and professional relationships.

Until recently, disability studies in communication had been scattered efforts conducted by a few individuals at various points in their academic careers. In the last few years, however, research in this area has begun to burgeon. This growth can be traced to the passage of the Americans with Disabilities Act, as evidenced by the launching of the Caucus on Communication and Disability of the National Communication Association (NCA).

Prior to the formation of the caucus, over 400 individuals at universities around the country signed petitions reflecting their interest in communication and disability research.

Although much more research is now being conducted in this area, to date there has been no vehicle for the dissemination of research findings outside of such broad journal outlets as *Disability and Society* and the *Journal of the Association for Persons with Severe Handicaps*. The study of communication and disability does not fit neatly into any traditional academic subspecialization. Thus, most research has been haphazardly published in a myriad of outlets and has frequently been difficult for other scholars to find. The most consistent publication outlet has been *Disability Studies Quarterly*, a stapled, off-set produced, nonreferred publication that is notoriously difficult to find and presents few full-length articles. Therefore, the goal of the present volume has been to gather original essays and literature reviews on communication and disability to facilitate the efforts of future researchers and practitioners in this area. The chapters thoroughly summarize and critique past research, report new research findings, reconceptualize work within their respective domains, and provide policy recommendations. Each chapter features a central focus on the role of communication processes in constructing "disability." This book will be a helpful resource for communicators both with and without disabilities.

The target audience for the present volume extends far beyond the new NCA caucus or communication scholars. Interest in the social construction of disability is now reflected in all of the social sciences, with particularly notable appeal in such fields as psychology, social work, sociology, special education, anthropology, gerontology, nursing, and rehabilitation. It is hoped that this book will be useful to scholars with interests in disability in all of those areas.

The Personal Side

We have been working on issues related to communication and disability independently since the 1970s. Although we have been on conference panels together, we have never collaborated on any research projects. Each of us came up with the idea for the present volume individually, as well. John Ferris' initiation of NCA's Caucus on Communication and Disability was one catalyst. Shortly after the development of a panel proposal that helped inaugurate the caucus, Teri received an E-mail from Bryan Whaley suggesting a book such as this. This arrived at about the same time that she had been thinking that there might finally be enough work available in the area to warrant such an effort. She E-mailed Dawn, who had already had the same idea. We decided to work together on the project and set about contacting potential authors. The problem, we found, was that there were too many good proposals to fit into a manageable-size book. There are many excellent scholars, both established and up-and-coming, who are now doing research on issues related to communication and disability. We were delighted with the number and quality of the proposals received; selecting among them was a difficult task. Although unable to include all of the chapters we would have liked, we finally settled on an excellent corpus of chapters, and are confident that the reader will find the volume helpful, informative, and insightful. The chapters are previewed in the introduction.

As with all books, there are many people who contributed to the development of the present volume and without whose efforts it would not have been possible. We would like to thank Dr. Anneliese Harper of Scottsdale Community College for her assistance and especially Nancy Eckstein, doctoral student at the University of Nebraska-Lincoln, for her invaluable research and editorial assistance on the final manuscript. Deep appreciation is also extended to Dr. Jennings Bryant, Ronald Reagan Chair of Communication at the University of Alabama, and Linda Bathgate of LEA for their incredible support, creativity, and flexibility. We also thank all of the authors for their hard work and fine scholarship.

Teri would like to thank Dawn for carrying the burden of most of the book through a very difficult time of transition for the Braithwaites, and her children Alyse and Tony for keeping her laughing and loving during the project. She would particularly like to thank her 11-year-old daughter Alyse for showing her how to use their new computer and helping her edit and her 7-year-old son Tony for always being a character. Her love and deep thanks are especially extended to Lou Cusella (her idea man!) for his passion, support, love, and sense of humor.

Dawn would like to thank all of the people with disabilities who have shared their experiences and wisdom with her over the years in research interviews and those who have read her work and given her their impressions of the findings. She would like to thank Teri for many years of collegiality and friendship. Most importantly, Dawn would like to thank Dr. Charles Braithwaite, her partner in life, her closest colleague, and her best friend.

—D.O.B.
—T.L.T.

Contributors

Richard Y. Bourhis (PhD, University of Bristol, 1977) is professor of psychology at the Université du Quebec à Montreal.

Dawn O. Braithwaite (PhD, University of Minnesota, 1988) is an associate professor of Communication Studies and an affiliate faculty member in the Family Research and Policy Initiative at the University of Nebraska-Lincoln.

Adrian Bennett Cairns III (MA, University of Georgia, 1995) is a rehabilitation counselor in Chattanooga, Tennessee.

Rebecca J. Cline (PhD, The Pennsylvania State University, 1975) is an associate professor in the Department of Health Sciences Education, University of Florida.

Audra L. Colvert (MA, Bowling Green State University, 1991) is an assistant professor of communication at Towson University.

Thuy-Phuong Do (MA, San Diego State University, 1997) is a lecturer in the School of Communication at San Diego State University.

Olan Farnall (PhD, University of Alabama, 1995) is an assistant professor in the School of Communication, California State University-Fullerton.

Susan Anne Fox (PhD, University of California, Santa Barbara, 1994) is an assistant professor of communication at Western Michigan University.

Patricia Geist (PhD, Purdue University, 1985) is a professor in the School of Communication, San Diego State University.

Howard Giles (PhD, University of Bristol, 1971) is a professor of communication at the University of California, Santa Barbara.

Mindi Ann Golden (MA, San Jose State University, 1995) is a doctoral student in the Department of Communication, University of Utah.

Beth Haller (PhD, Temple University, 1995) is an assistant professor of journalism, Towson University.

Nancy Grant Harrington (PhD, University of Kentucky, 1992) is an associate professor of communication at the University of Kentucky.

Lynn M. Harter (PhD, University of Nebraska, 2000) is an assistant professor of speech communication at Moorhead State University.

Kelly P. Herold (PhD, University of Southern Mississippi, 1995) is an assistant professor of communication studies at Winona State University.

Miho Iwakuma (MA, University of Oklahoma, 1994) is a doctoral student in the Department of Communication, University of Oklahoma.

Krishna Prasad Kandath (MA, Bowling Green State University, 1997), is a doctoral student, School of Communication Studies, Ohio University.

Joachim Knuf (DPhil, Oxford University, 1986) is an associate professor of communication at the University of Kentucky.

Gary L. Kreps (PhD, University of Southern California, 1979) is chief of the Health Communications and Informatics Research Branch of the National Cancer Institute at the National Institutes of Health, Bethesda, MD.

Ida Malian (PhD, The University of Michigan, 1977) is coordinator and associate professor of special education at Arizona State University West.

Cynthia K. Matthews (MA, New Mexico State, 1994) is a doctoral candidate in communication, University of Kentucky.

Nelya J. McKenzie (PhD, University of Florida, 1994) is an associate professor in the Department of Communication, Auburn University.

Anne McIntosh (PhD, University of Texas at Austin, 1995) is an instructor at Central Piedmont Community College, a consultant with Communication Connection, Inc., and a board member with Steve Hodges Foundation.

Gerianne Merrigan (PhD, University of Washington, 1992) is an associate professor in the Department of Speech & Communication Studies, San Francisco State University.

Sally A. Nemeth (MA, The University of Dayton, 1990) works as the education coordinator/liaison for The Central Ohio Lions Eye Bank, Columbus, Ohio.

Ann Nevin (PhD, University of Minnesota, 1977) is professor of special education at Arizona State University West.

Martin F. Norden (PhD, University of Missouri-Columbia, 1977) is a professor in the Department of Communication at the University of Massachusetts-Amherst.

Jon F. Nussbaum (PhD, Purdue University, 1981) is a professor in the Department of Speech Communication at The Pennsylvania State University.

Mark P. Orbe (PhD, Ohio University, 1993) is an assistant professor of communication at Western Michigan University.

Roxanne Parrott (PhD, University of Arizona, 1990) is an associate professor of speech communication, University of Georgia-Athens.

Michael E. Roloff (PhD, Michigan State University, 1975) is a professor in the Department of Communication Studies, Northwestern University.

Mary Ann Romski (PhD, University of Kansas, 1981) is a professor in the Departments of Communication, Psychology, and Education Psychology & Special Education at Georgia State University.

Heidi M. Rose (PhD, Arizona State University, 1992) is associate professor in the Department of Communication, Villanova University.

Rose A. Sevcik (PhD, Georgia State University, 1989) is an assistant research professor in the Department of Psychology at Georgia State University.

Kara Shultz (PhD, University of Denver, 1991) is an associate professor of communication studies and theatre arts at Bloomsburg University.

Andrew R. Smith (PhD, Southern Illinois University, 1989) is an associate professor of communication studies at Edinboro University of Pennsylvania.

John W. Smith (PhD, Wayne State University, 1989) is an associate professor in the School of Interpersonal Communication, Ohio University.

Kari P. Soule (MA, Northwestern University, 1998) is a doctoral candidate in the Department of Communication Studies, Northwestern University.

Tricia Stuart (BA, University of Georgia, 1997) is an editorial assistant, University of Georgia Press.

Teresa L. Thompson (PhD, Temple University, 1980) is professor of communication at the University of Dayton.

Al Weitzel (PhD, University of Southern California, 1973) is a professor in the School of Communication, San Diego State University.

S. Marie Westhaver (MA, University of Maine, 1995) is a graduate student in the School of Social work at Carleton University of Ottawa.

Bryan B. Whaley (PhD, Purdue University, 1991) is an associate professor, Department of Communication, University of San Francisco.

Kim Wolfson (PhD, University of Massachusetts-Amherst, 1987) is a communication consultant based in Amherst, Massachusetts.

David W. Worley (PhD, Southern Illinois University, Carbondale, 1996) is an assistant professor at Indiana State University.

Introduction

A History of Communication and Disability Research: The Way We Were

Teresa L. Thompson
University of Dayton

Research on communication and disability issues is different in some important ways from research on other communicative issues. All research interests are prompted by some of the same things. People choose to study the things they do because of aptitudes and abilities in certain areas and because certain ways of thinking about things make more sense to them than do other approaches. Communication scientists study phenomena because they help them understand more general communicative processes or because of the relevance of communication theory or concepts to the phenomena. They also choose topics to study because of personal experiences. It seems likely that the role of personal experiences in creating interest in the study of communication and disability is, however, even more important than it is in most other areas of study. And it may be that the reason for this increased importance is the power of the personal experiences that prompt research.

Many researchers come to the study of communication and disability through personal experiences either as individuals with a disabilities or through observing how loved ones who have disabilities are treated by others. Personal experiences are, of course, important determinants of many individuals' research agendas. Work experiences may determine interests in various aspects of organizational communication; relational experiences may influence research in interpersonal communication. Experiences participating in the media as viewer or producer may prompt research interests in mass communication. But it seems that there is a more consistent and stronger influence of personal experiences in the lives of those who study communication and disability than in these other areas. Almost everyone I know who studies this area has a strong personal reason for doing so.

It may be that personal experiences are particularly strong determinants of interests in communication and disability because of the strength or force of those experiences. Disability is socially constructed as a defining characteristic of an individual. Scholars who are or become disabled find that they are treated as disabled individuals, rather than as individuals who have a number of characteristics, only one of which happens to be a disability. The disability is frequently not really relevant to most interactions in which the individual participates, but it still becomes the defining characteristic. This happens to others who have characteristics that are different from the majority, whether it be height, ethnicity, or level of intelligence. Societally, everything seems to revolve around the person's disability. More importantly, the disability is a negatively valenced characteristic (Goffman, 1963). It is seen as a limitation and is defined as stigmatizing. Because of one characteristic, everything about how that individual is seen changes, and in a rather negative fashion. The negative valence spreads, and the individual is also seen as less competent in other ways.

Perhaps the power of this type of experience is obvious. It is a world-shattering change for an individual who has not previously been disabled, and a world-defining experience for all concerned. This kind of powerful experience is certainly likely to influence one's research agenda. Most individuals who study communication and disability, if they do not themselves have a disability, as one quarter of the authors in this book do, have a loved one who does. While they may not have experienced this world-defining stigmatization targeted toward themselves, they have still seen such experiences at close range. To see a loved one treated as a less-than-human being is also a devastating experience. This, too, prompts such a strong reaction that it is likely to guide a researcher's work if given the chance.

PERSONAL STORIES

My own experience in this area came through my brother, Steve, who has cerebral palsy and a severe hearing loss. Because he is 9 years younger than I am, I was able to observe, as he was growing up, the differences between how he was treated by others and the treatment my other siblings and I received. I remember such experiences as a slumber party when I turned 14, when Steve, who had never been able to walk, pulled himself on the floor into the family room, laughing and smiling. Judy Carson, the most popular girl in the eighth grade, turned to me and disdainfully asked, "What's wrong with him?" Those kinds of experiences impress themselves on one's heart—they influence the kind of person you become and the types of things you find worthy of study.

With this basis of personal experience, my interest was drawn to such issues. However, I didn't know that the topic could be a legitimate area of study until I came across references to Robert Kleck's (1966, 1968, 1969) work on how individuals respond to those with disabilities in Hastorf, Schneider, and Polefka's (1970) *Person Perception*. It was a life-defining moment. I started conducting research on communication and disability that semester and continued for the next 12 years.

My coeditor, Dawn Braithwaite, had similar personal experiences leading to her interest in communication and disability. Growing up, she had a good friend who was deaf. As a freshman at Goldenwest College, which at the time had the largest deaf student population outside of Gallaudet College, she worked as a note taker for deaf students and got to know a group of deaf people, making some close friends among them. A turning point, however, occurred not long before she began her doctoral studies, when a cousin in Missouri had a terrible car accident and became paraplegic. She was concerned about what she would do and say when she saw him— should she mention his accident? Not say anything? Would it upset him to talk about it? She thought about it a lot from a communication perspective and decided to do a project on communication with disabled people during her first year of doctoral study. When she began looking at the literature, she was shocked to find that most of the research was from the perspective of the ablebodied person—their attitudes toward people with disabilities, how disabled people should communicate to make ablebodied people more comfortable, and so forth. None of this addressed the issues about which she had been concerned. She knew then what she wanted to study: communication of people with disabilities from their own perspective.

My experiences and Dawn's are not unique. Most individuals who study communication and disability have similar, many more powerful, stories to tell. It is those kinds of experiences that have prompted the research that has been conducted on this topic over the years, and that led to this book on communication and disability. The power of those personal experiences is a reflection of the nature of the phenomenon that is our focus.

EARLY RESEARCH

As research began in the early years, there was, of course, no body of knowledge in the field of communication on which to draw. I began looking at this research in the early 1970s, so some reflection of the social consciousness created in the 1960s was seen in the available literature. Work was prompted by a sense of moral injustice about the treatment of those with disabilities. Research using an experimental paradigm, manipulating whether an experimental confederate appeared to have a disability or to be ablebodied, was published in psychology journals. Attitudinal variables (Yuker, Block, & Campbell, 1966), nonverbal indicators of attitudes, avoidance, and stereotypes were the most common dependent variables. Findings from this era included Farina, Sherman, and Allen's (1968) conclusion that people with disabilities are evaluated as not well-adjusted and Farina and Ring's (1965) results that stigmatized people are avoided. Richardson, Hastorf, Goodman, and Dornbusch (1961) reported uncertainty and discomfiture during interactions with people with disabilities, while Richardson (1970) noted that those with disabilities are unlikely to be selected as friends or colleagues. Other evidence of lack of attraction to and avoidance of people with disabilities was provided by Barker (1948); White, Wright, and Dembo (1948); Bord (1976); and Langer, Fiske, Taylor, and Chanowitz (1976). Kleck, Ono, and Hastorf (1966) noted greater interpersonal distance and distortion of verbalized opinions in ablebodied individuals interacting with those with disabilities. Wright (1960) and Titley (1969) concluded that those with physical stigmas are perceived as more reserved, alienated, introverted, and defensive than are the ablebodied. Concern about the impact of these behaviors and attributions on the self-concepts of individuals with disabilities was expressed and documented by Curra (1975); Meissner, Thoreson, and Butler (1967); Scheff (1974); Siller, Chapman, Ferguson, and Vann (1967); and Wright (1960). A survey of current research indicates that little has changed since this era.

Special education research at this time sometimes covered disability issues, but focused almost exclusively on educational concerns related to children and the classroom. I do not mean to imply that these concerns are not important. To the contrary, they are key issues. But they are not primarily communicative concerns.

Qualitative research, typically framed from a deviance perspective, was occasionally found in sociology outlets. Books were more common than research reports. The most influential of all sources came from this tradition: Erving Goffman's (1963) *Stigma: Notes on the Management of*

Spoiled Identity. Everyone cited it. I poured over Goffman's book, searching for communication-related hypotheses to guide my early work. Because Goffman was a symbolic-interactionist, of course, it was replete with such propositions. It was that work, combined with the strongly social-scientific training that I had received, that guided the directions taken by my early work. Thus, it also limited the directions taken by my early work. Goffman's work, and all other early research, focused on how the stigmatized are communicated to by others. That emphasis turned research to the perspective of the ablebodied interactant, rather than taking a more dyadic view or looking at the perspective of the interactant with a disability. Notice that this is consistent with what Dawn found when she began doing research in this area somewhat later. The perspective was useful for me, however; I already knew how my brother felt about his disability—I wanted to know what he could do to change how others treated him.

Thus, I continued doing research on this aspect of the interaction. My first three studies and one later article (see Thompson, 1982a; Thompson & Seibold, 1978) focused on a suggestion made by Goffman that an individual with a disability might be able to alleviate some of the uncertainty and anxiety experienced by ablebodied individuals with whom he or she comes in contact by disclosing some information about the disability. Ablebodied interactants frequently have questions about the nature and cause of the disability, how the disability limits behavior, and so forth. Addressing this uncertainty, argued Goffman, allows the individual with a disability to eventually remove the disability as the focus of attention and permit it to recede into the background. Empirical evidence did provide some support for this hypothesis. This direction guided my early research.

Later research turned to the communicative competence dimensions of the experience for individuals with disabilities. Research in other areas of the social sciences and in special education was also beginning to turn to the effects of differential, stereotypical treatment on persons with disabilities. If individuals with disabilities are avoided by others and experience atypical reactions when contact does occur, do they have the opportunities necessary for the development of effective communication skills that nondisabled individuals have? This issue had earlier been raised by Kelley, Hastorf, Jones, Thibaut, and Usdane (1960) and was again argued by Kitano, Stiehl, and Cole (1978). Public Law 94–142, the Education for All Handicapped Children Act of 1975 (20 *u.s.c.* §§1401 *et seq.*, 1976), had just been passed, mandating that all children be placed in the "least restrictive environment" appropriate for that child. For many children with disabilities, this meant placement in "mainstreamed" classrooms with ablebodied children for the first time. This provided potential for new opportunities and increased interaction. My next several studies focused on determining whether children with disabilities were as effective as their peers in adapting their communication to a specific listener and whether mainstreaming improved this. Concomitantly, of course, it was necessary to study whether children with disabilities were actually a part of communication networks and whether mainstreaming impacted the abilities of ablebodied children to adapt their communication to their peers with disabilities. Thus began a 5-year study (see Thompson, 1981a, 1982b, for examples).

At this time, little research was being conducted on communication and disability issues outside of the classroom context. Except for those working in rehabilitation, psychologists had mostly lost interest in the topic. The social consciousness of the 1960s had lost influence to the narcissistic 1970s and 1980s. Symbolic-interactionists were not in a time of prime influence in sociology. Research did continue in special education, however, in some of the same directions that my work was taking. But these researchers were concerned with other implications of mainstreaming, not communicative ones.

DISABILITY STUDIES QUARTERLY

In the 1980s, disabled sociologist Irv Zola began producing *Disability Studies Quarterly* (*DSQ*). This was a stapled, off-set produced publication that included few full-length research pieces, and was notoriously difficult to find. But at least it was something. Actually started by Natalie Allon and Margaret Zahn in 1980, it was originally called *The Disability and Chronic Disease Newsletter. DSQ* included commentary from researchers, announcements of meetings, paper calls, funding announcements, brief reviews of ongoing research, book notes, and mentions of dissertations on relevant topics. As *DSQ* expanded in later years, many issues focused on a particular topic, such as the media and disability, frequently including extensive bibliographies. Other special themes included women and disability, mental disabilities, cross-cultural concerns, handicapped newborns, independent living, deafness, chronic illness, political issues, disability demographics, the Americans with Disabilities Act (ADA), personal assistance and caregiving, bioethics, genetics, disability rights, technology, spirituality, AIDS, and disability culture. As this incomplete list indicates, some of these topics have more relevance to the study of communicative phenomenon than do others. Nonetheless, *DSQ* served as an interesting and important resource for communication and disability researchers.

DAWN'S RESEARCH

In the meantime, Dawn and some colleagues had begun researching from a very different but complementary perspective, focusing on the perspective of the disabled individual rather than the perspective of the ablebodied participant. The literature indicated that people with disabilities were relatively unsophisticated communicators, often lacking in basic social skills. So her first studies (Braithwaite, 1985; Braithwaite, Emry, & Wiseman, 1984) were exploratory, looking at some of the problematic issues for people with disabilities when they communicate with ablebodied persons they do not know well. From these telephone interviews, Dawn began describing their experiences communicating with ablebodied others and began deriving some of the impression management strategies they used to overcome the effects of being stigmatized. After gaining experience from the first study, she moved on to a larger research effort, using in-depth, face-to-face interviews with people who were visibly disabled. She found that there were three main communication issues people with disabilities coped with, and she wrote about these in various venues: dealing with violations of privacy and demands (or expectations) for self-disclosure (Braithwaite, 1991), dealing with ablebodied persons' discomfort and uncertainty (Braithwaite, 1990, 1992), and dealing with issues involving helping (Braithwaite, 1987). In all these studies, people with disabilities described how ablebodied persons treated them and the communication strategies they enacted as a result. What Dawn found, contrary to conceptions in the literature, was that many people with disabilities are sophisticated communicators. They know that nondisabled people are often uncomfortable or uncertain with them, and they take positive steps to communicatively manage those feelings and to attempt to create a positive impression of self. In all the studies, Dawn discovered that the main goal of these disabled communicators has been to be seen and treated as a "person first" (Braithwaite, 1996). She also saw in the interviews that people with disabilities experience communication from a minority perspective and face many of the issues that other persons of minority status face. Thus, she started making the argument that people with disabilities constitute a culture (Braithwaite, 1991, 1996; Braithwaite & Braithwaite, 1997). Around the same time, she and Denise Labrecque (Braithwaite & Labreque, 1994) wrote about what the communication discipline could contribute to the enactment of the Americans with Disabilities Act, concluding that understanding social barriers and helping people with disabilities enact fruitful communication strategies is one area in which communication researchers can provide insight. Two of Dawn's recent projects have looked at social support and people with disabilities. She has been fascinated with the idea of helping as a communication issue and has framed this as instrumental social support. Her team did another round of interviews with people who are disabled on how they communicate to manage too little and more commonly too much help. In another study, she and two colleagues, Vince Waldron and Jerry Finn (1999), studied the incidence of different types of social support exchanged between disabled people in Internet-based support groups and talked about the positive benefits that Internet-based interactions can potentially bring to people with disabilities. Her most recent work, with doctoral candidate Lynn Harter, is included in the present volume—a look at the personal relationships of people who are disabled from a dialectical perspective.

RELATED RESEARCH

The only early attempt to tie the work in communication and disability together was Gordon Dahnke's (1982) model in *Communication Yearbook 6*. Dahnke's model was not unlike a causal process theory I had once proposed but never published, feeling that it was not yet complete. Unfortunately, neither was Dahnke's. It ignored much other relevant work in related fields. Dahnke's model focused on uncertainty and information transfer as key variables. This focus on uncertainty in communicative processes was not, of course, unique to the study of interaction between ablebodied individuals and those with disabilities, as can be seen in Berger and Calabrese's (1975) work and the line of research emanating from that.

In the years since Dawn and I began our work, research efforts have been scattered here and there in various publication outlets. For instance, there has been work on communicative aspects of blindness (Sharkey & Stafford, 1990; Velcic, 1989); on media issues as they relate to disability (Austin, 1980; Bonnstetter, 1986; Clogston, 1993a, 1993b; Dahl, 1993; Haller, 1993); on interpersonal communication and disability (Stromer, 1983); on disability and marital relationships (Thompson, 1981b); on communication-handicapped students (Hurt & Cook, 1979); on communication apprehension and self-disclosure in hearing-impaired people (Hurt & Gonzalez, 1988); on communication anxiety and signing effectiveness (Booth-Butterfield & Booth-Butterfield, 1994); on the visual rhetoric of signing (Brueggeman, 1995); on helping behavior (Thompson & Cusella, 1988); on instructional issues related to disability (Hart & Williams, 1995);

on imposed inequality and miscommunication (Hardaway, 1991); and on hemophiliacs (Scheerhorn, 1990; Scheerhorn, Warisse, & McNeilis, 1995). Grove and Werkman (1991) tested the relative predictive strength of two theoretical frameworks that have been used to help explain conversations between the ablebodied and disabled. These are just examples of the work that has been done; this is certainly not an exhaustive list.

The difficulty for all of us studying communication and disability became finding a "home" for such research. Our training was in interpersonal communication, so we saw our work as a subset of interpersonal interaction. We joined the appropriate divisions of our associations and published our work in outlets that publish interpersonal studies. Dawn presented and published some of her early work in intercultural communication venues, as they were more open to qualitative methods. But we were always outliers. As health communication began emerging as an area of study within our field, others identified us in that specialization. "Okay," we said, "we guess it seems somewhat closer to our focus than just general interpersonal communication." But both Dawn and I remember whispering to each other at the initial meeting of the new Speech Communication Association Commission on Health Communication in 1986, "Do we belong here?" We were both unsure. Disability is not in and of itself a health issue in the same way as are illnesses. But we stayed there, because we had no other academic home. Eventually, requests for articles and books, editorial demands, administrative requests, and the interests of grad students moved us into more "mainstream" health communication or gerontological research.

The lack of uniqueness of our feelings of "homelessness" in those early days is reflected in the institution of the National Communication Association's (NCA; formerly the Speech Communication Association) Caucus on Communication and Disability; our feelings were shared by other authors in this book and readers of this book. The NCA caucus, like the Interest Group on Media and Disability of the Association for Education in Journalism and Mass Communication, provides a home for researchers and an outlet through which to disseminate and promote research on communication and disability. The goal of our research has been to address an important societal concern. As social scientists and scholars, we think that research should provide information to help alleviate social problems. Communication issues are problematic for those with disabilities. This book provides a forum through which such research can be encouraged and disseminated. Many young scholars are studying disability and communication; many of these scholars are themselves disabled.

AN OVERVIEW

With that frame, the chapters within this volume were designed to accomplish several goals. Each summarizes relevant research and provides policy and practical suggestions. Many present new research findings. All provide information to promote more effective interaction between disabled and ablebodied individuals. Additionally, all are designed to provoke future research in this area.

The book begins with an emphasis on interpersonal issues as they relate to communication and disability. Dawn Braithwaite and Lynn Harter begin this section with a dialectical perspective on the personal relationships of people with disabilities. Sally Nemeth continues this theme as she discusses the concepts of power, the body, and identity. Do and Geist provide an extension of this analysis with a chapter titled "Othering the Embodiment of Persons with Physical Disabilities." The important problem of helping behavior is addressed in Kari Soule and Michael Roloff's chapter, which uses a resource theory perspective. Then Marie Westhaver describes the contributions that a feminist phenomenological perspective can provide to our understanding of women's experience with disability. She focuses on societal constructions of the body and the impact of those constructions.

The next section of the book provides a discussion of organizational issues related to disability and communication. Malian and Nevin outline communication issues in special education. Still focusing on the educational context, David Worley emphasizes communication concerns facing students with disabilities on college campuses. The conflict management techniques particularly relevant to persons with physical disabilities are discussed by Audra Colvert and John Smith, who tie this concept to the organizational problems likely to be experienced in light of the ADA. Kelly Herold then discusses communicative strategies useful for disabled applicants in interview contexts, noting the 70% unemployment rate of the disabled. Ending this section is Gary Kreps' analysis of other organizational issues raised by the ADA; he focuses on multicultural relations in modern organizations.

Disability and culture are the focus of the next section. Key theoretical perspectives relevant to our understanding of interability communication are discussed in a chapter by Susan Fox, Howard Giles, Mark Orbe, and Richard Bourhis. Geri Johnson continues this theme in her chapter on negotiating personal identities. She relates accounts and identity management theory in her discussion of the treatment of people with disabilities. Reactions to disabilities in different cultures is then offered by Miho Iwakuma and Jon Nussbaum. The conclusion of this section is provided by Kara Shultz' discussion of social movements of persons with disabilities, with a particular focus on Deaf Power.

The next major section of the book emphasizes media and technology as they relate to disability. Both Beth Haller and coauthors Kim Wolfson and Martin Norden discuss images of the disabled, Haller in the media in general and Wolfson and Norden in film in particular. Olan Farnall analyzes people with disabilities in advertising, arguing that they are "invisible no more." The section culminates with Susan Fox's examination of computer-mediated communication as it is used by people with disabilities.

Several specific disability cultures are then discussed. An application of uncertainty reduction theory is provided in Roxanne Parrott, Tricia Stuart, and Adrian Cairns' chapter on communication during adjustment to spinal cord injury. Anne McIntosh discusses the interactions that occur between those who are deaf and those who are hearing. This theme is continued in the chapter by Heidi Rose and Andrew Smith, who discuss the "violence" of deaf-hearing communication. John Smith and Krishna Kandath next offer an analysis of what the field of communication can offer to our understanding of blindness. Cynthia Matthews and Nancy Grant-Harrington then focus on people with nonvisible disabilities. An emphasis on stuttering and its social implications is offered by Brian Whaley and Mindi Golden, while the communication of those who have difficulty speaking is discussed by Mary Ann Romski and Rose Sevcik. Related issues are addressed in Al Weitzel's chapter on communication and voicelessness. Rebecca Cline and Nelya McKenzie identify the communication issues facing individuals who are HIV-positive or who have AIDS. Their discussion emphasizes HIV/AIDS as a disability. A novel and positive focus on disability is provided by the last chapter in this section. Joachim Knuf writes about "The Margins of Communication," in his discussion of Alzheimer's disease. He argues that a broader perspective on communication, rather than a strict language focus, can improve our interactions with those with Alzheimer's. His analysis has implications for all types of disabilities.

Braithwaite and Thompson end the book with a chapter that summarizes and critiques the research conducted so far and offers some directions for future research and discussion.

As mentioned earlier, one goal of this book is to provide a resource for communication and disability researchers. Even more importantly, however, we hope that the information offered herein can be used on a very practical level to address the communicative issues that are sometimes problematic for persons with disabilities and others with whom they interact.

REFERENCES

Austin, B. A. (1980). The deaf audience for television. *Journal of Communication, 30*, 25–30.

Barker, R. (1948). The social psychology of physical disability. *Journal of Social Issues, 6*, 34–43.

Berger, C. R., & Calabrese, R. J. (1975). Some explorations in initial interaction and beyond: Toward a development theory of interpersonal communication. *Human Communication Research, 1*, 99–112.

Bonnstetter, C. M. (1986). Magazine coverage of the mentally handicapped. *Journalism Quarterly, 63*, 623–626.

Booth-Butterfield, M., & Booth-Butterfield, S. (1994). Communication anxiety and signing effectiveness: Testing an interference model among deaf communicators. *Journal of Applied Communication Research, 22*, 273–286.

Bord, R. J. (1976). The impact of imputed deviant identities in structuring evaluations and reactions. *Sociometry, 39*, 108–116.

Braithwaite, D. O. (1985, November). *Impression management and redefinition of self by persons with disabilities.* Paper presented at the annual meeting of the Speech Communication Association, Denver, CO.

Braithwaite, D. O. (1987, November). *"If you push my wheelchair, don't make car sounds": On the problem of 'help' between disabled and ablebodied persons.* Paper presented at the annual meeting of the Speech Communication Association, Boston, MA.

Braithwaite, D. O. (1990). From majority to minority: An analysis of cultural change from ablebodied to disabled. *International Journal of Intercultural Relations, 14*, 465–483.

Braithwaite, D. O. (1991). "Just how much did that wheelchair cost?": Management of privacy boundaries and demands for self-disclosure by persons with disabilities. *Western Journal of Speech Communication, 55*, 254–274.

Braithwaite, D. O. (1992). "Isn't it great that people like you get out?" Communication between disabled and ablebodied persons. In E. B. Ray (Ed.), *Case studies in health communication* (pp. 149–159). Hillsdale, NJ: Lawrence Erlbaum Associates.

Braithwaite, D. O. (1996). "I am a person first." Different perspectives on the communication of persons with disabilities. In E. B. Ray (Ed.), *Communication and disenfranchisement: Social health issues and implications* (pp. 257–272). Mahwah, NJ: Lawrence Erlbaum Associates.

Braithwaite, D. O., & Braithwaite, C. A. (1997). Understanding communication of persons with disabilities as cultural communication. In L. A. Samovar & R. Porter (Eds.), *Intercultural communication: A reader* (8th ed., pp. 154–164). Belmont, CA: Wadsworth.

Braithwaite, D. O., Emry, R. A., & Wiseman, R. L. (1984, February). *Ablebodied and disablebodied persons' communication: The disabled person's perspective.* Paper presented at the annual meeting of the Western Speech Communication Association, Seattle, WA. (ERIC Document Reproduction Service, No. ED 264 622)

Braithwaite, D. O., & Labrecque, D. (1994). Responding to the Americans with Disabilities Act: Contributions of interpersonal communication research and training. *Journal of Applied Communication Research, 22*, 287–294.

Braithwaite, D. O., Waldron, V., & Finn, J. (1999). Communication of social support in computer-mediated groups for persons with disabilities. *Health Communication, 11*, 123–152.

Brueggeman, B. L. (1995). The coming out of deaf culture and American sign language: An exploration into the visual rhetoric and literacy. *Rhetoric Review, 13*, 409–420.

Clogston, J. (1993a). Changes in coverage of patterns of disability issues in three major American newspapers: 1976–1991. *Journal of Mediated Communication, 9*, 69–82.

Clogston, J. (1993b). Fifty years of disability coverage in the *New York Times. News Computing Journal, 8*, 39–50.

Curra, J. (1975). *The sociology of social deviance, social behaviorism, and the concept of consensus: Labeling theory and "behind."* Unpublished doctoral dissertation, Department of Sociology, Purdue University, Lafayette, IN.

Dahl, M. (1993). The role of the media in promoting images of disability—disability as metaphor: The evil crip. *Canadian Journal of Communication, 18*, 75–80.

Dahnke, G. (1982). Communication between handicapped and nonhandicapped persons: Toward a deductive theory. In M. Burgoon (Ed.), *Communication Yearbook 6* (pp. 92–135). Beverly Hills, CA: Sage.

Farina, A., & Ring, K. (1965). The influence of perceived mental illness on interpersonal relations. *Journal of Abnormal Psychology, 70*, 47–51.

Farina, A., Sherman, M., & Allen, J. G. (1968). Role of physical abnormalities in interpersonal perception and behavior. *Journal of Abnormal Psychology, 73*, 590–593.

Goffman, E. (1963). *Stigma: Notes on the management of spoiled identity.* Englewood Cliffs, NJ: Prentice-Hall.

Grove, T. G., & Werkman, D. L. (1991). Conversations with ablebodied and visibly disabled strangers: An adversarial test of predicted outcome value and uncertainty reduction theories. *Human Communication Research, 17*, 507–534.

Haller, B. (1993). Paternalism and protest: Deaf persons in the press, 1986–1990. *Mass Communication Review, 20*, 169–179.

Hardaway, B. D. (1991). Imposed inequality and miscommunication between physically impaired and physically nonimpaired interactants in American society. *Howard Journal of Communications, 3*, 139–148.

Hart, R. D., & Williams, D. E. (1995). Able-bodied instructors and students with physical disabilities: A relationship handicapped by communication. *Communication Education, 44*, 140–150.

Hastorf, A. H., Schneider, D. J., & Polefka, J. (1970). *Person perception.* Reading, MA: Addison-Wesley.

Hurt, H. T., & Cook, J. A. (1979). The impact of communication-handicapped students on high-school teachers' expectancies, interaction anxiety, and interpersonal perceptions in regular education classes. *Communication Quarterly, 27*, 38–46.

Hurt, H. T., & Gonzalez, T. (1988). Communication apprehension and distorted self-disclosure: The hidden disabilities of hearing-impaired students. *Communication Education, 37*, 106–117.

Kelley, H. H., Hastorf, A. H., Jones, E. E., Thibaut, J. W., & Usdane, W. M. (1960). Some implications of social psychological theory for research on the handicapped. In L. H. Lofquist (Ed.), *Psychological research and rehabilitation* (pp. 172–204). Washington, DC: American Psychological Association.

Kitano, M. R., Stiehl, J., & Cole, J. T. (1978). Role taking: Implications for special education. *Journal of Special Education, 12*, 59–74.

Kleck, R. (1966). Emotional reactions in interactions with the stigmatized. *Psychological Reports, 19*, 1236.

Kleck, R. (1968). Physical stigma and nonverbal cues emitted in face-to-face interaction. *Human Relations, 21*, 19–28.

Kleck, R. (1969). Physical stigma and task-oriented interaction. *Human Relations, 22*, 51–60.

Kleck, R., Ono, H., & Hastorf, A. H. (1966). The effects of physical deviance on face-to-face interaction. *Human Relations, 19*, 425–436.

Langer, E. J., Fiske, S., Taylor, S. E., & Chanowitz, B. (1976). Stigma, staring, and discomfort: A novel-stimulus hypothesis. *Journal of Experimental and Social Psychology, 12*, 451–463.

Meissner, A. L., Thoreson, R. W., & Butler, A. J. (1967). Relation of self-concept to impact and obviousness of disability among male and female adolescents. *Perceptual and Motor Skills, 24*, 1099–1105.

Richardson, S. A. (1970). Age and sex differences in values toward physical handicaps. *Journal of Health and Social Behavior, 11*, 253–258.

Richardson, S. A., Hastorf, A. H., Goodman, N., & Dornbusch, S. M. (1961). Cultural uniformity in reaction to physical disabilities. *American Sociology Review, 26*, 241–247.

Scheerhorn, D. (1990). Hemophilia in the days of AIDS: Communicative tensions surrounding "associated stigmas." *Communication Research, 17*, 842–847.

Scheerhorn, D., Warisse, J., & McNeilis, K. (1995). Computer-based telecommunication among an illness-related community: Design, delivery, early use, and the functions of HIGHnet. *Health Communication, 7,* 301–326.

Scheff, T. J. (1974). The labeling theory of mental illness. *American Sociology Review, 39,* 444–452.

Sharkey, W. F., & Stafford, L. (1990). Turn-taking resources employed by congenitally blind conversers. *Communication Studies, 41,* 161–182.

Siller, J., Chapman, A., Ferguson, C., & Vann, D. H. (1967). *Attitudes of the nondisabled toward the physically disabled: Vol. 2. Studies in reaction to physical disability.* New York: New York School of Education.

Stromer, W. F. (1983). Disability and interpersonal communication. *Communication Education, 32,* 425–427.

Thompson, T. L. (1981a). The development of communication skills in physically handicapped children. *Human Communication Research, 7,* 312–324.

Thompson, T. L. (1981b). The impact of a physical handicap on communicative characteristics of the marital dyad. *Western Journal of Speech Communication, 45,* 227–240.

Thompson, T. L. (1982a). Disclosure as a disability-management strategy: A review and conclusions. *Communication Quarterly, 30,* 196–202.

Thompson, T. L. (1982b). "You can't play marbles—You have a wooden hand": Communication with the handicapped. *Communication Quarterly, 30,* 108–115.

Thompson, T. L., & Cusella, L. P. (1988). Help between disabled and ablebodied persons: An exploratory observational study of a feedback system. *Journal of Applied Communication Research, 16,* 51–68.

Thompson, T. L., & Seibold, D. R. (1978). Stigma management in "normal"-stigmatized interactions: Test of the disclosure hypothesis and a model of stigma management. *Human Communication Research, 4,* 229–242.

Titley, R. W. (1969). Imaginations about the disabled. *Social Science and Medicine, 3,* 29–38.

Velcic, M. (1989). The blind side of rhetoric. *Semiotics, 74,* 165–171.

White, R. W., Wright, B. A., & Dembo, W. (1948). Studies in adjustment to visible injuries: Evaluations of curiosity by the injured. *Journal of Abnormal and Social Psychology, 53,* 13–28.

Wright, B. A. (1960). *Physical disability: A psychological approach.* Evanston, IL: Harper & Row.

Yuker, H. E., Block, J. R., & Campbell, W. J. (1966). *A scale to measure attitudes toward disabled persons.* Human Resources Study, #7.

I

Interpersonal and Relationship Issues

1

Communication and the Management of Dialectical Tensions in the Personal Relationships of People With Disabilities

Dawn O. Braithwaite
University of Nebraska-Lincoln

Lynn M. Harter
Moorhead State University

Keywords: Personal relationships, dialectical theory, relationship maintenance, relationship remodeling

Scholars studying personal relationships have rightly pointed out that relationships are central to happiness and also present people with some of the greatest challenges in life (Duck & Wood, 1995). In this chapter, we highlight both the strengths and hazards of the personal relationships of people who are disabled. Following a search of the literature about the personal relationships of people who are disabled, we made two initial observations. First, as has been seen in the past, there has been a relatively limited amount of research focused on the communication of people with disabilities, especially from their own perspective rather than the perspective of ablebodied people (Braithwaite, 1990, 1996; Braithwaite & Braithwaite 1997; see also Thompson, introduction, this volume). Additionally, in the existing literature, people who are disabled are often positioned as passive and reactive rather than as active participants in their own communicative and relational encounters (Braithwaite, 1996). This is one area in which this volume will help move forward understanding, research, and practice.

Second, the majority of the available literature deals with communication of people who are disabled as they interact with strangers or people they are just getting to know. However, like people everywhere, persons who are disabled live their lives in a web of personal relationships—family, friendship, work, community, and romantic. Yet, very little is known about communication in personal relationships of people who are disabled and the unique challenges being disabled brings to personal relating for them and their relational partners. Although disability and chronic illness may strike one person, the conditions affect everyone else with whom they relate—relational partners, family, and friends (Lyons, Sullivan, Ritvo, & Coyne, 1995; Morse & Johnson, 1991). Although close personal relationships are difficult to maintain in the best of circumstances, illness and disability can cause even greater challenges:

> Superimpose the additional complexities of illness, and people must navigate carefully over particularly strange and foreboding relational terrain . . . threats to social identity, performance of roles, and hopes for the future . . . each party in the relationship asks, "What will life be like for me in this relationship and for us?" (Lyons & Meade, 1995, p. 186)

Although there is a need to understand the effects of disability on relationship partners, Lyons et al. (1995) pointed out that "there is as yet no comprehensive model that details the stresses, strategies, and outcomes of relationship focused coping" (p. 85). Thus, the purpose of this chapter is to review the literature and to report what is known about communication in the personal relationships of people who are disabled, and to discuss where researchers need to go from here to advance both knowledge and practice.

EARLY RESEARCH

Most of the earlier research on people with disabilities did not present a very flattering picture of their social abilities. Scholars presented persons with disabilities as possessing poorer social skills than ablebodied others, arguing that they had less opportunity to develop role-taking skills and interpersonal sensitivity (e.g., Gresham, 1983; Ingwell, Thoreson, & Smits, 1967; Kelley, Hastorf, Jones, Thibault, & Usdane, 1960). As a result, disabled persons were often presented as poorer communicators and socially isolated (Clark, Weiman, & Paschall, 1983; Thompson, 1981). Coleman and DePaulo (1991) identified some of the stereotypes that were typically presented in the literature concerning disabled people "as dependent, socially introverted, emotionally unstable, depressed, hypersensitive, and easily offended, especially with regard to their disability" (p. 69).

However, after many years of interviewing and interacting with people who have visible physical disabilities, we have not come away with these same impressions. Just the opposite, we argue that people who are disabled need to develop a wider repertoire of communication abilities in a world where many people will misunderstand them, feel uncomfortable around them, and not know how to talk with them (Braithwaite, 1996). People with disabilities need to be able to interact with higher levels of communicative competence, including greater motivation, knowledge, and skills (Spitzberg & Cupach, 1984, 1989), than will their nondisabled counterparts. In fact, the many disabled people who have participated in some previous research interviews (e.g., Braithwaite, 1987, 1990, 1991) seem quite observant about their communication with ablebodied people and have developed very sophisticated sets of communication strategies to deal with a wide variety of exigencies, as chapters by other authors in this volume also demonstrate. Perhaps, in earlier times when people with disabilities were more often sequestered and isolated from other people, they were not able to develop socially. In today's world, however, people with disabilities are increasingly present and active in the workplace, on college campuses, in churches, at sporting events—literally any place one would encounter ablebodied people.

There is no reason to expect that people with disabilities would be anything but interested in forming close personal relationships in their lives. It is important, then, that scholars understand the personal relationships of people who are disabled and provide as much information as possible to help them and their relational partners understand and develop close and satisfying personal relationships. Studying the relationships of people with disabilities is more important than ever as the number of disabled persons is rising as medical technology has enabled the average life expectancy to increase to more than 75 years (Coyne & Fiske, 1992).

Furthermore, studying the relationships of people with disabilities is important as disability affects not only the individual disabled person but his or her relational partners. For example, data from both Canada and the United States indicates that disabled people are more likely to be divorced than their ablebodied counterparts (Crewe & Athelstan, 1985; Crewe, Athelstan, & Krumberger, 1979; Franklin, 1977; Social Trends Directorate, 1986; Trieschmann, 1987). Although close personal relationships are important for all human beings, they are perhaps even more critical for people with disabilities. Lyons et al. (1995) pointed out the simple validation that relationships bring to people with disabilities. Friendships are especially important because, unlike nonvoluntary relationships of the family, the voluntary nature of friendships can be taken as an indication of "true caring" versus obligation.

A DIALECTICAL PERSPECTIVE

As we sought to organize and understand the literature on the personal relationships of people who are disabled, we were struck with the experiences of disabled people as an ongoing "balancing act." In fact, people with disabilities are well aware of the sense of balancing membership in the disabled and ablebodied cultures (Braithwaite, 1990, 1996; Braithwaite & Braithwaite 1997; Fox & Giles, 1997; Padden & Humphries, 1988). Along with the challenges associated with maintaining any personal relationship, being disabled necessitates balancing all of the changes becoming disabled brings with the stability necessary to maintain relationships (Braithwaite, 1990). People with disabilities and their relational partners face even more challenges to issues of independence and dependence in their relationships. Also, people with disabilities experience the continual need to balance how much to reveal about their disability and how much to keep private (Braithwaite, 1991; Thompson, 1982; Thompson & Seibold, 1978). Framing communication in the relationships of people with disabilities dialectically helped us better understand the unique characteristics and challenges of these relationships.

Scholars taking a dialectical perspective begin with the assumption of constant change as partners manage oppositional forces and tensions that are inevitable within relationships (Baxter, 1993; Baxter & Montgomery, 1996; Montgomery & Baxter, 1998). Rather than a single, unified theory, dialectical scholars present a family of perspectives that share a commitment to the view that oppositional forces are ever present in relationships (Montgomery, 1993; Montgomery & Baxter, 1998). According to Montgomery and Baxter, dialectical theorists view persons in relationships as constantly adjusting to contradictions, "the dynamic interplay between unified opposites [which are] interdependent with one another, and it is this interplay between opposites that creates a relational system characterized by contingency, fluidity, and change" (p. 4). The presence of these oppositional forces is not a negative force, but rather an "ongoing dynamic interaction between unified oppositions" (Baxter & Montgomery, 1996, p. 10). Baxter (1988, 1993) identified commonly encountered dialectical tensions within interpersonal relationships around three contradictions: integration–separation, stability–change, and expression–privacy. Despite their opposition, the forces are interdependent, and each force defines the other, becoming a force of "both/and" rather than "either/or" (Baxter & Montgomery, 1996; Montgomery & Baxter, 1998). A dialectical perspective, according to Montgomery (1993), "sees the natural state of relationships as change, fluctuation, evolution and movement. Stability is but a momentary transition in a stream of continuous change" (p. 208). Constant change, resulting from ongoing dialectical tensions between contradictory yet desirable forces, is the inherent order of our social realities.

We argue that dialectical theory is ideally suited to help understand and study the personal relationships of people with disabilities as these individuals constantly find the need to strike a balance between living in the ablebodied and disabled worlds and manage ongoing oppositions ever present in their relationships, oppositions that can be heightened by the presence of disability of one of the partners. A dialectical perspective helps us move beyond a focus on the dyad only to look at relationships as embedded in larger webs of social relationships (Baxter & Montgomery, 1996; Braithwaite & Baxter, 1995). Dyadic relationships cannot be understood outside of the influences of family, friendship networks, and organizations to which the pair belong. This is especially critical when looking at the relationships of people who are disabled, as they are so often strongly linked to families, caregivers, and larger organizational systems such as health care and social services. As we looked at the personal relationships of people with disabilities, we arranged the literature around three interrelated, dialectical pairs: autonomy–connection, openness–closedness, and predictability–novelty.

Autonomy–Connection

This dimension is perhaps the most salient for the relationships between persons who are disabled and those who are not, as all parties seek to manage the need to be simultaneously independent and dependent on one another. Baxter (1993) explained, "No relationship can exist unless the parties forsake individual autonomy. However, too much connection paradoxically destroys the relationship because the individual entities become lost. Simultaneously autonomy can be conceptualized only in terms of separation from others" (p. 89). This tension illustrates how relationship partners are always straddling the fence between unity and differentiation (Baxter & Montgomery, 1996). Reviewing the extant literature showed us that the actual and perceived functional limitations of people with disabilities propel and keep this tension prominent in the relationships of people with disabilities and their partners.

One important factor in understanding the negotiation of autonomy and connectedness in the relationships of any particular person who has a disability is the extent and nature of the disability itself. LeClere and Marsteller Kowaleski (1994) argued:

> The functional limitations imposed by chronic health conditions or physical impairments are variable and not always accompanied by poor health . . . they run the gamut from an inability to perform any task of daily living to the need for only occasional assistance with more complex physical or cognitive tasks. Persons with disabilities ranging from the simplest to the most severe, however, require some form of regular aid. (pp. 457–458)

Depending on the nature of their disabilities, then, people with disabilities will need varying amounts of assistance from their relational partners and others. Some people with disabilities will lead very independent lives, whereas others will need direct care from their families or other formal services (LeClere & Marsteller Kowaleski, 1994). In the individually versus communally oriented U.S. culture, where freedom and interdependence are valued, the prospect of being disabled, and thus dependent on others, is bound to have negative connotations.

In terms of family relationships, negotiating the autonomy–connectedness dialectic is extremely difficult for parents. Crewe and Athelstan (1985) described the parental dilemma as follows:

> Stop and consider, however, how difficult it would be for a parent to know when to do things for a disabled youngster and when to insist that he or she cope alone. . . . The functional limitations of disability, transportation problems, architectural barriers, and the social barriers of disability may keep a disabled child close to parents. So the gradual transfer of interest from family to peer group may not occur for such a child. (pp. 49–50)

For parents and children, the management of dependence with the necessary independence for adult independent living is difficult to negotiate (Crewe & Zola, 1983). These tensions are exacerbated when the child reaches adolescence, where issues of independence and dependence are paramount.

When a person is disabled after childhood, the adjustment problems increase as the independent young adult or adult now becomes dependent on others, perhaps for a fixed period of time or, in other cases, permanently. This adjustment has been likened to becoming a member of a different culture (Braithwaite, 1990, 1996). This dependence is determined in large measure by the type of disability experienced. Family members and the disabled persons themselves all go through phases similar to adjustment to death and dying, beginning with shock and grief. The family normally pulls together to support the person who has become disabled, and the disability may even have a unifying effect on the family, albeit temporary (Crewe & Althelstan, 1985).

Coping with challenges associated with a disabled family member affects the relationships of every family member, especially, in the case of a child, the parents' marriage (El Ghatit & Hanson, 1976; Lyons et al., 1995). Additionally, having a family member with a disability potentially impacts independence–dependence tensions in family relationships beyond those with the disabled family member, for example, those of other children and the parents within the family. For example, LeClere and Marsteller Kowaleski (1994) reported that the risk of severe behavioral problems among coresident children were significantly increased by the presence of a disabled family member.

It is important to point out that not all of the effects of childhood disability are negatively related to independence of adults. In fact, Rousso (1988) reported that some disabled women credit their parents with pushing them toward independence by stressing the importance of education and career development. Many of these individuals believed that "had they not been disabled, they probably would not have obtained such a good education or have gone so far in their careers" (p. 251). However, educational and career success may come at the expense of other aspects of life, as disabled children, especially females, were not encouraged to view themselves as sexual, or potential marital partners (Roskies, 1972; Rousso, 1988). Instead, these young women were encouraged to prepare for work, rather than having their own family relationships. Goffman (1963) pointed out that disabled men and women possess limited choices in the formation of personal relationships as a result of an "aesthetic-sexual aversion to disability that permeates society" (p. 44). This is part of what makes it easy for some disabled individuals to experience social isolation and loneliness (Lyons et al., 1995).

In terms of the disabled person him- or herself, managing the autonomy–connectedness dialectic is indeed challenging. Several of the young adults who participated in a series of research interviews reported coming out of long hospital stays only to find that their parents had, of financial necessity in many cases, closed their apartments and the young adults were forced to move back into their parents' homes. In most cases, the adult who is disabled did not have any input into these decisions. In some cases, those who had been dating or even cohabiting found that their relationships had ended while they were in the hospital, but their partners had not discussed this with them for fear of upsetting them. For many, careers or planned college majors were now impossible to pursue. So, these individuals, returned home only to find their independence gone, and regaining it, within the parameters of assistance they would now need from others, would prove to be a great challenge. Weinberg (1988) suggested that part of this problem stems from equating social autonomy with physical independence, and she highlighted this paradox—the only way for a disabled person to achieve autonomy is to become dependent and accept assistance from others.

For adults with predisability, long-term relationships, and especially for those with children, the onset of disability obviously has an enormous impact on all aspects of family life. When one partner becomes disabled, a large majority of their families experience moderate to severe levels of lost income, care of home and children, to profound effects on the marital relationship itself (Crewe & Althelstan, 1985). These effects are complex and are formed within an elaborate set of variables, including gender of the spouse who is disabled, previous roles and levels of dependence among family members, marital satisfaction before the disability, type and severity of the disability, and the psychological and physical adjustment of the disabled spouse (Crewe & Athelstan, 1985; Crewe et al., 1979). Moreover, disability can be especially devastating for women with disabilities enacting traditional caretaker roles and on whom others depend.

When disability enters the picture in an ongoing relationship there will be a need to renegotiate relational roles and responsibilities. Lyons and Meade (1995) referred to this process as "relationship remodeling," using the remodeling metaphor to discuss adjusting relationships to chronic illness and disability. They presented three "central elements" in this process: "the commitment to relationship maintenance, the perception that change could contribute to relationship quality, and the identification of specific adaptation strategies that could result in improvements" (p. 208).

Literature on this topic often stresses the differential experiences of men and women who are disabled. Asch and Fine (1988) reported they found a dearth of materials on the intimate relationships of disabled people, but what they did find was mostly about the intimate relationships of disabled men partnered with nondisabled women. Asch and Fine argued that the perceived functional limitations due to societal stereotypes and stigma of disabled persons are potentially more significant for women than for men with disabilities. For example, disabled women are more likely than men to be undereducated and underemployed (Asch & Fine, 1988; Franklin, 1977). In addition, disabled women are more likely than nondisabled women to be unmarried, and if they marry, to marry later, and then are more likely to be divorced (Crewe & Athelstan, 1985; Crewe et al., 1979; Franklin, 1977; Trieschmann, 1987). Women who became disabled after marriage are much more likely than men to become divorced after disablement (Crewe et al., 1979). Perhaps even more startling is that, while negative stereotypes of people with disabilities are well-documented in the literature, women are viewed much more negatively than men. Asch and Fine also reported that women with disabilities were "virtually never depicted as wife, mother, or worker" (p. 15).

In terms of establishing interdependent relationships, disabled women are "doubly oppressed," according to Asch and Fine (1988, p. 13). They are less likely than men to form intimate relationships and families and, at the same time, are perhaps "'freer' to be nontraditional" than are their nondisabled female counterparts (p. 13). So, whereas ablebodied women, socialized to be caretakers, are more likely to enter relationships with disabled men, nondisabled men are much less likely seek out relationships with women who are disabled. Asch and Fine concluded:

> Men may assume incorrectly that a disabled woman could not contribute to either physical or emotional housekeeping to a spouse and children. If a woman cannot sew on a button because she cannot use her hands, she may be thought unfit to help with the mending of emotional fences as well. (p. 17)

In sum, the autonomy–connectedness dialectic is a complex one for disabled people to manage. On the one hand, they may have trouble establishing their autonomy in relationships with others when they are physically dependent, and at the same time, they may have trouble establishing and maintaining connectedness, especially if they are female. How both disabled women and men communicate to initiate and sustain personal relationships needs to be studied further.

Openness–Closedness

Early work in self-disclosure centered around the view that openness is inherently good, a view later challenged by scholars studying how people maintain privacy boundaries (Derlega, Metts, Petronio, & Marguilis, 1993;

Petronio, 1991, in press; Petronio, Martin, & Littlefield, 1984). Disclosure in personal relationships involves somewhat of a paradox: "On the one hand, open disclosure between relationship parties is a necessary condition for intimacy; but on the other hand, openness creates vulnerabilities for self, other and the relationship that necessitate information closedness" (Baxter, 1993, p. 89). According to Derlega et al., private information is "the material that others do not normally know about us (e.g., opinions, beliefs, and feelings about ourselves, social issues, or relationships with others) but that we might be willing to disclose based on others' need to know" (p. 74). From a dialectical perspective, partners simultaneously manage the need for both revelation and privacy. The question becomes, how do we manage privacy in relationships—just how much information do we reveal to others and when do we reveal it?

When one partner has a disability, the issues surrounding privacy are even more complex and paradoxical and, as Braithwaite (1991) discovered, people with disabilities do live in a world of reduced privacy. Researchers have found that disabled persons most often perceive or experience a demand for information about their disability in the early phases of relationships with ablebodied others (Braithwaite, 1991; Thompson, 1982; Thompson & Seibold, 1978). Stromer (1983) suggested that people with disabilities face continual pressure to disclose information about their disabilities, and that they often

> want more than anything to get through five minutes of conversation without having the subject come up at all. Most disabled persons would like a reference to that part of their life to come up in a conversation as casually as any one might mention the inability to swim or to play a tuba. (p. 427)

However, the issue of revealing information about the disability is ever present for people with disabilities, and is a complex one. Braithwaite (1991) explained that research literature presents openness about the disability as good for the relationship, as ablebodied people do feel more comfortable with disclosure about the disability. Scholars have recommended that people with disabilities disclose their disability to help ablebodied persons feel more comfortable (Goffman, 1963; Hastorf, Wilfogel, & Cassman, 1979; Thompson & Seibold, 1978; White, Wright, & Dembo, 1948). However, Braithwaite (1991) questioned this prescription, saying that little is known about how disclosures are experienced by the disabled individual. In research interviews, Braithwaite (1991) found that individuals with disabilities did disclose at times, but only when they deemed that revealing such information met certain conditions of appropriateness. Petronio et al. (1984), after studying these conditions, found that one does not disclose unless the characteristics of sender, target, relationship, and context, and the potential ramifications deem that disclosure is an appropriate thing.

Early work on privacy and people with disabilities is informative; however, most of the research concerned interactions with strangers or in relationships just beginning to form. Still to be understood is what role the management of privacy boundaries plays in the ongoing relationships of people who are disabled. Adopting a dialectical perspective, one would not advise whether people with disabilities should or should not reveal information about their disabilities. Rather, a dialectical perspective would lead to a focus on disclosure within ongoing relationships as balancing *both* openness and closedness, and on how people with disabilities and their relational partners manage this dialectical tension.

Unfortunately, there is very little information concerning how people with disabilities and their partners manage the openness–closedness dialectic in ongoing relationships. Early on in the relationship, both parties likely struggle with how and when to talk about the disabled partner's disability, and both need to decide when to bring it up and how much to disclose. Braithwaite (1991) pointed out that disclosure about a disability is tricky from the perspective of expectations of self-disclosure reciprocity, if those exist. If one party discloses about breaking his or her neck and living as quadriplegic, with what information will the nondisabled person reciprocate? It is highly likely that the person with the disability will always bear the burden of revealing information about his or her health status and body that the other simply does not have to reveal. How couples manage the ongoing nature of openness and closedness is certainly something scholars need to explore.

In addition, the timing of the disclosures about one's disability may also represent difficult choices. Braithwaite (1991) found that people with disabilities often delayed disclosure to establish themselves as "persons first," that is, they steer the conversation to other topics of mutual interest, such as music or sports, so that they may avoid focusing the developing relationship around being disabled. Yet, at other times they disclose to meet the same goal. When, then, should the subject of the disability be broached? This also brought up the question of what would happen if the topic of the disability was never raised by either partner in the developing relationship. In research interviews, people with disabilities certainly were concerned about talking about their disability too early or too often with a new person, to avoid making it the focus of the relationship (Braithwaite, 1991). Yet, several interviewees also talked about the awkwardness of *not* talking about their disability as well. One man, who was disabled right after high school graduation, discussed seeing his friends after his rehabilitation work and feeling very awkward that absolutely no one mentioned his disability. He maintained that they would have asked him about a new car or bike, yet no one mentioned that he was now using a motorized wheelchair! In another interview, a woman who had polio as a child talked about the first months in her relationship with her husband. One thing that she had really liked about him was that he treated her as "normal" rather than disabled and that her disability had seemingly never been a factor in their relationship. As Nemeth describes later in this volume, this was refreshingly different from her previous dating relationships. However, after a period of months had gone by and they were dating seriously, she kept wondering when "*it* was going to come up." Finally she could stand it no more and blurted out, "Well, are you ever going to ask me about my disability or not?" In both of these examples, issues surrounding timing of revealing or asking about the disability were problematic for the relational partners.

Furthermore, managing the openness–closedness dialectic will be a continual factor in an ongoing relationship. Obviously, at the time severe illness or disability occurs, the disabled partner may have little privacy, as he or she is dependent on others for care and has largely relinquished control in the acute and recovery stages (Morse & Johnson, 1991). However, as the person moves toward wellness, the ability to control private information, along with other aspects of life, will be critical to recovery. In fact, Morse and Johnson defined wellness as "regaining normalcy," as the individual regains control over body, life, and relationships. Lyons and Meade (1995) stressed the importance of "reshaping both the objective and subjective aspects of relationships" (p. 193) and they found that satisfactory maintenance of relationships when one partner is chronically ill depends on "the ability to communicate about important issues" (p. 193). Negotiating issues of privacy will be especially critical to the success of the relationship when one partner has a disability. For example, partners will need to work out how to ask for and/or offer assistance (Braithwaite, 1987; Lyons & Meade, 1995; Soule & Roloff, this volume). Doubtless, partners will need to negotiate continually this openness and closedness dialectic and will need to revisit their implicit and explicit understandings.

In addition to the disabled persons themselves revealing information about their disability, their relational partner(s) will also need to be concerned about revealing information to the larger social networks in which the relationships are embedded. For example, how does an ablebodied partner cope with questions from family and friends about his or her partner's disability? Given the high levels of uncertainty and discomfort associated with interacting with a disabled person (e.g., Deegan, 1977; Hardaway, 1990; Heinemann, Pellander, Vogelbusch, & Wojtek, 1981; Thompson, 1982), it is surprising that some people feel more comfortable asking the nondisabled partner to reveal information about the disabled partner's condition. This will very likely place the nondisabled partner in a bind—how does one manage the private information of another person? Although the simple answer would be to tell the questioner to talk directly to the disabled person, there may be potential benefits from revealing information about a partner's disability in some situations. For example, nondisabled partners might be able to put family members more at ease and smooth developing relationships with their disabled partner, if they are able to answer the family members' questions. Obviously, this will be an issue that disabled and nondisabled relational partners may wish to discuss in advance and they may need to come to some agreements concerning when openness or closedness is in order. Although these issues cannot be resolved here, certainly how partners manage the openness–closedness dialectic, within the dyad and beyond, needs to be explored.

Stability–Change

This last dialectical tension is an important factor in the personal relationships of people who are disabled. "Just as relationships need predictability they also need novelty" (Baxter, 1993, p. 89). This tension is predicated on the assumption that individuals desire stable characteristics in relationships, while at the same time being stimulated by spontaneity, novelty, and change. Thus, tension is created between the comfort of the status quo and the freshness of uncertainty (Baxter & Montgomery, 1996). "From the interplay of certainty with uncertainty, order with disorder, predictability with novelty, relationships sustain a vibrant, alive, and dynamic ongoingness" (Baxter, 1993, p. 106).

Certainly the onset of chronic illness or disability can bring sudden and profound changes to personal relationships and demand change to every aspect of the relational partners' established roles and routines. One important factor in the impact of the disability is the timing of its onset. However, Thompson (1981) found that sharing and autonomy were not significantly different in marriages where one partner had a disability whether they formed their relationship before or after disablement. Relationships are much more challenged when one partner becomes disabled. Dialectical theory would explain this as upsetting the balance of stability and change in the relationship, as disability affects all areas of the disabled person's physical, emotional, and social state, as well as the life of the relationship (Crewe & Athelstan, 1985). Thompson (1981) reflected on the impact of the onset of disability: "Relationships build patterns, and those patterns may be difficult to change. What now needs to be determined is how to best change patterns should the need arise" (p. 240).

Lyons, Sullivan, Ritvo, and Coyne (1995) suggested adopting a relational view for coping with chronic illness. While there is no existing model of relational coping for when a partner develops a chronic illness or disability, they proposed six dimensions of relational coping: (a) reevaluating both self and relationship, (b) containing the impact of the illness on the relationship, (c) network remodeling, (d) relationship adaptation, (e) relationship reciprocity, and (f) communal coping.

First, Lyons et al. (1995) explained that the persons with disabilities must reevaluate themselves and come to terms with their disablement. Braithwaite and Braithwaite (1997) looked at adjusting to disability as a process of redefinition of self and the meaning of disability. Braithwaite (1991, 1996) argued that this process is identifying oneself as part of a disabled culture and developing communication strategies to interact successfully as a member of that culture. Also, the relational partners must reevaluate the relationship, looking at the aspects that will require adjustment as well as recognizing the positive aspects of the changes on the relationship. The latter is important, as not all aspects of disability are negative in relationships. Many disabled people who have been interviewed have expressed some positive outcomes of becoming disabled, such as becoming more outgoing, more socially sensitive, confident, and/or concerned with character over appearance.

Second, partners need to contain the impact of the illness on the relationship (Lyons et al., 1995), keeping the illness or disability from "assuming a dominant place" in the relationship (p. 86). Third, network remodeling refers to "restructuring of the social network to accommodate the limitations of the health problem" (Lyons et al., 1995, p. 87). This may include terminating some relationships and changing the focus of others. For example, individuals or couples may find themselves socializing with different friends who share new interests and/or they may choose to spend more or less time with certain family members and friends. Recent research has also suggested that people with disabilities and members of their social networks may also cope with relational challenges and changes by becoming part of support groups. For example, Braithwaite, Waldron, and Finn (1999) found that they may turn to computer-mediated support groups for social support (Braithwaite, Waldron, & Finn, 1999; see also Fox, this volume). For example, in some states, agencies have been lending computers to families with disabled children and establishing listservs, allowing these families to interact with one another online, providing social support to one another.

The fourth dimension is adapting the relationship and finding new ways to maintain it (Lyons et al., 1995). This process involves both making adaptive changes necessary to maintain the relationship and finding stability following disruptions caused by acute phases of illness or disability. Communication scholarship can make very useful contributions here in the form of relational maintenance strategies (e.g., Canary & Stafford, 1994; Dindia & Baxter, 1990; Montgomery, 1993) and concerning the communication of social support (e.g., Albrecht & Adelman, 1987; Burleson, Albrecht, & Sarason, 1994; Goldsmith, 1992).

Fifth, relationship reciprocity "involves attention to the (emotional and instrumental) well-being of significant others and of the social unit, and the maintenance of social equity" (Lyons et al., 1995, p. 89). Disability changes the roles, contributions, and even balance of power in the relationship. Maintaining the relationship mandates a reevaluation of each member's role and contributions to the relationship.

Finally, partners needs to engage in communal coping (Lyons et al., 1995), taking the position that "illness is '*our* problem,' [italics added] and so they cope with many of the emotional (e.g., anger, frustration, disappointment) and instrumental (e.g., income, treatment, child care) aspects of a health problem together" (p. 89). Lyons and Meade (1995) stressed that relationship remodeling is different from relationship maintenance, which is a strategy to repair the relationship or keep the relationship as it is. In the case of illness and disability, this is not always desirable, or even possible. Rather, relationship remodeling strategies

> imply adaptation and change, as well as the desire for both maintenance and enhancement. . . . As with the process of home remodeling, relationship remodeling can be smooth or rough, but even if smooth it likely contains rough spots. One the one hand, change can be exciting. On the other, it invites potential conflict around the need, nature, and extent of change. (pp. 194, 200)

IMPLICATIONS

Clearly, disability involves a great deal of change and coping for people who are disabled and their family, friends, and relational partners. Existing literature on communication and the personal relationships of people who are disabled is very sparse and there is a serious need for more research and theory. Dialectical theory provides a useful lens with which to explore the complex issues that people who are disabled and their relational partners face as they negotiate issues of connection–autonomy, openness–closedness, and predictability–novelty. We hope that communication researchers will take up the challenge of doing this research and disseminating it to those who work with disability issues.

Although there are no easy answers on how to form and maintain relationships for people who are disabled, current knowledge implies that their understanding of communication issues and their ability to communicate effectively will be key to their successful relationships and their ability to live and work in a world where many people will be uncomfortable around them, at least initially. For people who are disabled; for their current family, friends, and partners; and for potential relational partners, the ability to anticipate challenges to managing issues of interdependence, disclosure, and change will be of paramount importance in their effort to have meaningful long-term relationships with one another. There are many factors that must be taken into account, such as age of onset of disability, type and severity of disability, long-term prognosis for the disabled individual, the relationship type (family, friend, work, or intimate), and the willingness and ability of relational partners to accept and cope with the impact of disability on their relationship. Perhaps of all of these factors, type of disability will be one of the most influential. In this chapter, all experiences with disabilities have been treated as the same; however, there is every reason to believe the experiences of persons who are, for example, deaf, blind, paraplegic, have multiple sclerosis, and those with AIDS would be somewhat, if not significantly, different.

In addition, researchers have not even begun to explore the personal relationships between people who are disabled. Anecdotal evidence suggests that they also may face adjustment issues and that those with later onset disabilities especially may find that they experience discomfort and uncertainty around people who are disabled; after all, many of them did not have experience interacting with disabled others until they became disabled themselves. On the other hand, it may be that they are benefited by having this additional perspective and understanding of the experiences of their relational partners. Researchers can raise many questions; for example, would people who are disabled have a better chance of success in intimate relationships if they choose partners who are also disabled? It is not known how long-term relational partners who are disabled manage these dialectical tensions, and research is needed. As stated at the outset of this chapter, researchers do need to study the strengths as well as the challenges people with disabilities face in their close relationships.

Although there are few easy answers or prescriptions, understanding how relational dialectics play out in developing and ongoing personal relationships, and especially regarding those issues unique to the relationships of people who are disabled, will help both disabled and nondisabled individuals manage the social as well as the physical changes and challenges associated with physical disability.

DISCUSSION QUESTIONS

1. What view does early research literature present of the communication of people with disabilities and of their ability to form and maintain personal relationships? How does this compare with your own experiences of observing how people with disabilities and able-bodied others communicate with one another?
2. What challenges do people who are disabled and their relational partners have in managing issues of both connection and autonomy?
3. What challenges do people who are disabled and their relational partners have in managing issues of both openness and closedness?
4. What challenges do people who are disabled and their relational partners have in managing issues of both predictability and novelty?
5. What concerns would you have about your relationship, if your closest friend or relationship partner became disabled? What relationship remodeling would you have to do to maintain your relationship?

REFERENCES

Albrecht, T. L., & Adelman, M. B. (Eds.). (1987). *Communicating social support.* Newbury Park, CA: Sage.

Asch, A., & Fine, M. (1988). Introduction: Beyond pedestals. In M. Fine & A. Asch (Eds.), *Women with disabilities: Essays in psychology, culture, and politics* (pp. 1–37). Philadelphia: Temple University Press.

Baxter, L. A. (1988). A dialectical perspective on communication strategies in relationship development. In S. Duck (Ed.), *Handbook of personal relationships* (pp. 257–273). New York: Wiley.

Baxter, L. A. (1993). The social side of personal relationships: A dialectical perspective. In S. Duck (Ed.), *Social context and relationships* (pp. 139–165). Newbury Park, CA: Sage.

Baxter, L. A., & Montgomery, B. M. (1996). *Relating: Dialogues and dialectics*. New York: Guilford.

Braithwaite, D. O. (1987, November). *"If you push my wheelchair, don't make car sounds": On the problem of "help" between disabled and ablebodied persons.* Paper presented at the annual meeting of the Speech Communication Association, Boston, MA.

Braithwaite, D. O. (1990). From majority to minority: An analysis of cultural change from ablebodied to disabled. *International Journal of Intercultural Relations, 14*, 465–483.

Braithwaite, D. O. (1991). "Just how much did that wheelchair cost?": Management of privacy boundaries and demands for self-disclosure by persons with disabilities. *Western Journal of Speech Communication, 55*, 254–274.

Braithwaite, D. O. (1996). "I am a person first": Different perspectives on the communication of persons with disabilities. In E. B. Ray (Ed.), *Communication and disenfranchisement: Social health issues and implications* (pp. 257–272). Mahwah, NJ: Lawrence Erlbaum Associates.

Braithwaite, D. O., & Baxter, L. A. (1995). "I do" again: The relational dialectics of renewing marriage vows. *Journal of Social and Personal Relationships, 12*, 177–198.

Braithwaite, D. O., & Braithwaite, C. A. (1997). Understanding communication of persons with disabilities as cultural communication. In L. A. Samovar & R. Porter (Eds.), *Intercultural communication: A reader* (8th ed., pp. 154–164). Belmont, CA: Wadsworth.

Braithwaite, D. O., Waldron, V., & Finn, J. (1999). Communication of social support in computer-mediated groups for Persons with disabilities. *Health Communication, 11*(2), 123–151.

Burleson, B. R., Albrecht, T. L., & Sarason, I. G. (Eds.). (1994). *Communication of social support.* Thousand Oaks, CA: Sage.

Canary, D., & Stafford, L. (Eds.). (1994). *Communication and relational maintenance.* San Diego, CA: Academic Press.

Clark, A. J., Weiman, L. A., & Paschall, K. A. (1983). A preliminary report of an investigation of unwillingness to communicate among physically handicapped persons. *Journal of the Communication Association of the Pacific, 12*, 155–160.

Coleman, L., & DePaulo, B. (1991) Uncovering the human spirit: Moving beyond disability and "missed" communication. In N. Coupland, H. Giles, & J. Weimann (Eds.), *Miscommunication and problematic talk* (pp. 61–85). Newbury Park, CA: Sage.

Coyne, J. C., & Fiske, V. (1992). Couples coping with chronic illness. In T. J. Akamatsu, J. C. Crowther, S. C. Hobfoll, & M. A. P. Stevens (Eds.), *Family health psychology* (pp. 129–149). Washington, DC: Hemisphere.

Crewe, N., & Athelstan, G. (1985) *Social and psychological aspects of physical disability.* Minneapolis: University of Minnesota, Department of Independent Study and University Resources.

Crewe, N., & Athelstan, G., & Krumberger, J. (1979). Spinal cord injury: A comparison of preinjury and postinjury marriages. *Archives of Physical Medicine and Rehabilitation, 60*, 252–256.

Crewe, N. M., & Zola, I. K. (1983). *Independent living for physically disabled people.* San Francisco, CA: Jossey Bass.

Deegan, M. J. (1977). The nonverbal communication of the physically handicapped. *Journal of Sociology and Social Welfare, 4*, 735–748.

Derlega, V., Metts, S., Petronio, S., & Marguilis, S. T. (1993). *Self-disclosure.* Newbury Park, CA: Sage.

Dindia, K., & Baxter, L. A. (1990). Strategies for maintaining and repairing marital relationships. *Journal of Social and Personal Relationships, 4*, 143–158.

Duck, S., & Wood, J. T. (1995). For better, for worse, for richer, for poorer: The rough and the smooth of relationships. In J. T. Wood & S. Duck (Eds.), *Confronting relationship challenges* (pp. 1–21). Thousand Oaks, CA: Sage.

El Ghatit, A. Z., & Hanson, R. W. (1976). Marriage and divorce after spinal cord injury. *Archives of Physical Medicine and Rehabilitation, 57,* 470–472.

Fox, S. A., & Giles, H. (1997). "Let the wheelchair through!": An intergroup approach to interability communication. In W. P. Robinson (Ed.), *Social psychology and social identity: Festschrift in honor of Henri Tajfel* (pp. 215–248). New York: Butterworth.

Franklin, P. (1977). Impact of disability on the family structure. *Social Security Bulletin, 40,* 3–18.

Goffman, E. (1963). *Stigma: Notes on the management of spoiled identity.* New York: Simon & Schuster.

Goldsmith, D. (1992). Managing conflicting goals in supportive interaction: An integrative theoretical framework. *Communication Research, 19,* 264–286.

Gresham, F. N. (1983). Social skills assessment as a component of mainstreaming decisions. *Exceptional Children, 49,* 331–336.

Hardaway, B. (1990). Imposed inequality and miscommunication between physically impaired and physically nonimpaired interactants in American society. *Howard Journal of Communication, 3,* 139–148.

Hastorf, A. H., Wildfogel, J., & Cassman, T. (1979). Acknowledgement of handicap as a tactic in social interaction. *Journal of Personality and Social Psychology, 37,* 1790–1797.

Heinemann, W., Pellander, F., Vogelbusch, A., & Wojtek, B. (1981). Meeting a deviant person: Subjective norms and affective reactions. *European Journal of Social Psychology, 11,* 1–25.

Ingwell, R. H., Thoreson, R. W., & Smits, S. J. (1967). Accuracy of social perception of physically handicapped and non-handicapped persons. *The Journal of Social Psychology, 72,* 107–116.

Kelley, H. H., Hastorf, A. H., Jones, E. E., Thibault, J. W., & Usdane, W. M. (1960). Some implications of social psychological theory for research on the handicapped. In L. Lofquist (Ed.), *Psychological research and rehabilitation* (pp. 172–204). Washington, DC: American Psychological Association.

LeClere, F., & Marsteller Kowaleski, B. (1994). Disability in the family: The effects on children's well-being. *Journal of Marriage and the Family, 56,* 457–468.

Lyons, R. E., & Meade, D. (1995). Painting a new face on relationships: Relationship remodeling in response to chronic illness. In S. Duck & J. T. Wood (Eds.), *Confronting relationship challenges* (pp. 181–210). Thousand Oaks, CA: Sage.

Lyons, R. F., Sullivan, M. J. L., Ritvo, P. G., & Coyne, J. C. (1995). *Relationships in chronic illness and disability.* Thousand Oaks, CA: Sage.

Montgomery, B. M. (1993). Relationship maintenance versus relational change: A dialectical dilemma. *Journal of Social and Personal Relationships, 10,* 205–223.

Montgomery, B. M., & Baxter, L. A. (Eds.). (1998). *Dialectical approaches to studying personal relationships.* Mahwah, NJ: Lawrence Erlbaum Associates.

Morse, J. M., & Johnson, J. L. (1991). *The illness experience: Dimensions of suffering.* Newbury Park, CA: Sage.

Padden, C., & Humphries, T. (1988). *Deaf in America: Voices from a culture.* Cambridge, MA: Harvard University Press.

Petronio, S. (1991). Communication boundary management: A theoretical model of managing disclosure of private information. *Communication Theory, 1,* 311–335.

Petronio, S. (Ed.). (in press). *Balancing the secrets of private disclosure.* Mahwah, NJ: Lawrence Erlbaum Associates.

Petronio, S., Martin, J., & Littlefield, R. (1984). Prerequisite conditions for self-disclosing: A gender issue. *Communication Monographs, 51,* 268–273.

Roskies, E. (1972). *Abnormality and normality: The mothering of thalidomide children.* Ithaca, NY: Cornell University Press.

Rousso, H. (1988). Daughters with disabilities: Defective women or minority women? In M. Fine & A. Asch (Eds.), *Women with disabilities: Essays in psychology, culture, and politics* (pp. 139–171). Philadelphia: Temple University Press.

Social Trends Directorate. (1986). *Profile of disabled persons in Canada.* Ottawa: Statistics Canada.

Spitzberg, B. H., & Cupach, W. R. (1984). *Interpersonal communication competence*. Newbury Park, CA: Sage.

Spitzberg, B. H., & Cupach, W. R. (1989). *Handbook of interpersonal competence research*. New York: Springer-Verlag.

Stromer, W. F. (1983). Disability and interpersonal communication. *Communication Education, 32*, 425–427.

Thompson, T. L. (1981). The impact of a physical handicap on communicative characteristics of the marital dyad. *Western Journal of Speech Communication, 45*, 227–240.

Thompson, T. L. (1982). Disclosure as a disability-management strategy: A review and conclusions. *Communication Quarterly, 30*, 196–202.

Thompson, T. L., & Seibold, D. R. (1978). Stigma management in normal-stigmatized interactions: Test of the disclosure hypothesis and a model of stigma acceptance. *Human Communication Research, 4*, 231–242.

Trieschmann, R. B. (1987). *Aging with a disability*. New York: Demos Publications.

Weinberg, J. K. (1988). Autonomy as a different voice: Women, disabilities, and decisions. In M. Fine & A. Asch (Eds.), *Women with disabilities: Essays in psychology, culture, and politics* (pp. 269–296). Philadelphia: Temple University Press.

White, R. W., Wright, B. A., & Dembo, W. (1948). Studies in adjustment to visible injuries: Evaluations of curiosity by the injured. *Journal of Abnormal and Social Psychology, 53*, 13–28.

2

Society, Sexuality, and Disabled/Ablebodied Romantic Relationships

Sally A. Nemeth
Ohio State University

Keywords: Socialization, sexuality, passing, reciprocity, autonomy, super crip

"It must make you feel really good to know that I could be with anyone I want, and I am here with you." I have to wonder what Joe, my former lover, would think if he knew I introduced a chapter on communication and disabled/ablebodied persons' romantic relationships with the off-hand comment he made to me on a steamy Saturday night some five summers ago. He might be surprised to realize that occasionally I recall his remark with a tinge of enlightened smugness and a smile of amusement at its pomposity and presumption. Yet, there is still a part of me that buys into his assumption, kicking and screaming as my ego might be; this part of myself is trained to believe that as a blind woman I am lucky to find an ablebodied partner. Much as I hate to admit it, it did feel good to have a handsome, ablebodied man who wanted "me."

In this chapter I discuss disabled/ablebodied romantic relationships and some of the disability-related factors that influence their development and maintenance. I begin with a look at the socialization of children with disabilities in terms of the ways in which they become identified with and develop identities through their disabilities. Second, I follow this with a brief discussion of societal messages that demonstrate and/or institutionalize negative attitudes about sexuality and disability. Third, I examine a few specific issues relevant to disabled/ablebodied sexual relationships. In the final section, I review what has been said about how people with disabilities negotiate their relationships and provide some tentative guidelines for partners with and without disabilities.

SOCIALIZATION OF CHILDREN
WITH DISABILITIES

Children with disabilities enter the world with minority status (Braithwaite, Emry, & Wiseman, 1984). Typically the sole disabled family member, they are socialized at home and in the larger society in accordance with the norms and attitudes displayed in both these environments. Generally, attitudes surrounding disability are rigid, negative, and limiting (Braithwaite, 1985; Farina & Ring, 1965; Fish & Smith, 1983; Kleck, Hiroshi, & Hastorf, 1986; Thompson & Seibold, 1978; Zola, 1982b, 1984). Much attention is often lavished on disabled persons' physical needs while social, emotional, and sexual needs are downplayed, disconfirmed, or ignored altogether (Zola, 1982a).

According to Olkin (1997), children with disabilities are likely to witness the stigmatization and ostracization of disabled peers and have few adults with disabilities after which to model themselves. They acquire self-concepts amid a variety of mixed familial, peer, societal, and media messages that question their potential for life relationship success as well as their worth as human beings. They become objectified through politically correct labels and medicalization, wherein health professionals equate who children are with the level of function of their bodies. Olkin further noted that children with disabilities may feel they lack control not only over how their bodies feel and respond but also over who touches their bodies, and when, how, and for whom their "defective parts" are placed on display. Children who are disabled may also come to understand genetic testing and disease prevention strategies to mean that people like themselves should not be born and that a life like theirs is not worth living (Olkin, 1997).

These children discover, through attempts at social interaction and play, that being different adversely affects how other children assess their limitations (Thompson, 1982a) as well as their playmate and/or friendship suitabilities. They soon learn that a disability harnesses them with the burden of responsibility for approaching others and making friends (Asch, 1984; Weinberg, 1982). Ablebodied children learn that, although helping people with disabilities is positive, engaging in friendships with them carries significantly greater social risk (Blackman & Dembo, 1984; Weiserbs & Gottlieb, 1995).

During adolescence, when dating and sexuality are usually explored, disabled youth generally come to realize that the standard norms of attraction and romance do not apply to them. Discussions about romance and sex are often avoided by parents, teachers, health care providers, and sometimes also by ablebodied siblings and/or peers, either in a misguided attempt to shelter children with disabilities from emotional pain, or because they perceive these issues to be irrelevant (Hwang, 1997). Correspondingly, children and adolescents with disabilities are frequently encouraged to focus their energies on goals presumed to be more realistic and attainable than dating, marriage, and childbearing—school being a common point of emphasis (Phillips, 1990). The tendency for messages surrounding their sexuality to be mixed, when mentioned at all, is illustrated well by a respondent in Phillips' study. This blind woman reported that during her childhood, her family alternatively advised her to work hard at becoming self-sufficient, because she would be unlikely to marry, and that she should marry a kind, ablebodied boy to take care of her.

The traditional gender role, taught to virtually all females, holds that girls should be "sugar and spice and everything nice." The song, *At Seventeen,* written and so eloquently sung by Janis Ian, also informs us that it is the pretty girls who get to go on dates. Often, girls with disabilities are not considered marriageable (Simon, 1988; Welner, 1997), which can be devastating to their feelings of self-worth (Hwang, 1997). In fact, girls who are disabled before adolescence rate their parents' expectations for their potential to marry and have children lower than daughters who become disabled during or after adolescence (Rousso, 1988). Emphasis placed on the female as caregiver, learned by both sexes in childhood, has been noted as a primary contributor to divorce when a wife becomes disabled and dependent on her husband (Greengross, 1976; Mairs, 1996).

For disabled boys, the process is similar. Boys learn that, above all, they should not be weak or emotional, like girls (Bem, 1993). They absorb the male myths of sexuality—that sex must always lead to orgasm; men should always be ready and anxious for sex; the penis is the primary instrument of sexuality; that males must be able to always perform and satisfy their partners; and that those who cannot perform are inadequate and unworthy of lovers (Tepper, 1997; Zilbergeld, 1992). Men who are disabled are commonly judged as sexual noncontenders because they may appear limited when observed through the lens of the traditional male gender role, which mandates self-sufficiency, competitiveness (especially in athletics), and physical strength. Phillips (1990) described one young man with a disability who arrived at the front door of his date's home, only to be promptly dismissed by her father with the remark that no daughter of his would be permitted to date someone who was not a whole man.

Disabled children, having formed their identities amid a continual flurry of mixed, often disconfirming messages about their worth as human beings, their physical and/or mental capabilities, and their relationship potentialities, tend to acquire lower self-esteem than ablebodied children (Thompson, 1982a, 1987). They reach adulthood only to face similar types of stigmatization and attitudinal barriers. In the next section, these societal influences that affect disabled/ablebodied persons' communication and relationships are discussed.

SOCIETAL ATTITUDES TOWARD
SEXUALITY AND DISABILITY

It is well established that communication between the disabled and ablebodied is characterized, at least initially, by rigidity, stereotyped perceptions, uncertainty, and discomfort and that having a disability negatively impacts relationships between these groups (Belgrave & Mills, 1981; Braithwaite et al., 1984; Kleck, 1968; Thompson, 1982b). Where possible, ablebodied persons are likely to avoid communication with people with disabilities altogether (Thompson, 1982b).

The vast array of media messages reflect and/or reinforce a presumed dual dimensionality of people with disabilities (Zola, 1984). Messages depicting an outstanding–helpless dichotomy dominate, portraying them either as heroic super crips or as tragic, usually embittered and angry, unfortunates worthy only of pity and charity. They are seldom seen as whole and complex, leading the same kinds of everyday lives as ablebodied people (Kroll & Klein, 1992). As illustration of the helplessness message, Hwang (1997) noted:

> Women with disabilities in soap operas generally tend to languish pathetically at home clad in robes until they have the decency to die poignantly or, they remove themselves from the plot so their husbands can find real women; that is, unless they become miraculously cured and then go on to resume normal lives. (p. 121)

Zola (1983) took issue with the opposite pole of the dichotomy—the super-crip image of people who "overcome" their disabilities, stating that this message is misleading and detrimental. It sets up the presumption that the only admirable or even acceptable way of adapting to disability is to refuse to be limited by it. The life-long work of disability maintenance, and the mundane successes and disappointments of daily living are misconstrued by the super-crip image as giving in and failing to try (Zola, 1983).

Societal messages about sexuality and disability seem to indicate that the American public fails to perceive people with disabilities as sexual beings. Society's narrow definitions of what constitutes sex; for whom romantic relationships are acceptable and natural; and the monumental value it places on health, youth, beauty, and physical perfection keep sexuality and disability taboo (Zola, 1982a). "Sick people" are not expected to have desires or be desired (particularly not by ablebodied people), despite evidence that people with disabilities do engage in and enjoy romantic/sexual relationships (Kroll & Klein, 1992; Mairs, 1996; White, Rintala, Hart, & Fuhrer, 1993; Zola, 1982a, 1982b).

This message, so deeply ingrained, is incorporated into societal structures. Many institutions for people with disabilities are architecturally designed and monitored to prevent "unacceptable" relational behaviors such as romance and sex from occurring (Hwang, 1997). The fact that women with disabilities may need gynecological and/or obstetric care is overlooked by the failure to make office and examination procedures/equipment accessible (Welner, 1997). Additionally, the social security system incorporates major financial penalties for marriage into the rules for its disabled recipients of federal support (Waxman, 1994).

Stigmatization and attitudinal barriers surrounding disability affect the development and maintenance of romantic relationships. In the next section, I explore four issues: passing, equity, emotion, and autonomy as they relate to disability and disabled/ablebodied romantic relationships.

ADULT ROMANTIC RELATIONSHIPS
AND DISABILITY

I remember clearly the first time I went to a restaurant with a romantic partner and was asked, "Would you like a Braille menu?" I was horrified. I had been found out, and I cried over the loss of my ability to "pass"—to pass myself off as ablebodied. For those of us with disabilities, passing is a way to avoid stigmatization (Goffman, 1963). Socially, passing may be perceived as a way of appearing more approachable and, for some people with disabilities, a way to improve chances of attracting an ablebodied romantic partner (Phillips, 1990). Some disabled persons restrict the number of possible relational partners by refusing to befriend and/or date other disabled persons, viewing their decision as an issue of perceived social marketability. That is, "settling" for a disabled partner is tantamount to admitting an inability to compete for the choice goods of the sexual market (Phillips, 1990). Ironically, this attitude may extend to a generalized suspicion of ablebodied people who choose to initiate a relationship, particularly a romantic relationship, with someone who has a disability (Mairs, 1996; Phillips, 1990). Sometimes, ablebodied partners attempt to cloak disability to avoid undue attention, stigma by association, or being judged as strange and/or suspect for dating someone with a disability (Phillips, 1990). Too often, discrimination occurs because of the belief that to associate with a person who has a disability, whether as friend, lover, or acquaintance, must mean there is also something wrong with the ablebodied person (Fisher & Galler, 1988).

At times, people fall into more than one minority group and may attempt to choose in which way they most hope to pass. For example, gays and lesbians with disabilities are doubly stigmatized; some choose to accentuate their sexuality and hide their disability because they view the latter as being more denigrating (Appleby, 1994). This can be especially isolating (Saad, 1997). According to Hillyer (1993), a person who is both homosexual and disabled is usually the only member of a family who is characterized by both of these stigmatizing identities. Unlike the pride instilled by family members and communities surrounding race or ethnicity, families typically train gay disabled members to feel ashamed and to hide these identities. For gays who have AIDS and are asymptomatic, passing is relatively easy because society holds the general presumption that all people are heterosexual and ablebodied unless proven otherwise (Anderson & Wolf, 1986).

Fisher and Galler (1988) interviewed women involved in disabled/ablebodied friendships; because friendship is often a component of romance, perhaps some of their data may also have implications for romantic relationships. Fisher and Galler found reciprocity to be a friendship theme valued by both partners. Respondents discovered through their own friendships that reciprocity is a key element in maintaining a shared sense of relational equity. Years ago, I became extremely offended when people referred to my ablebodied romantic partner as "special" for dating a disabled woman. To me, this attitude implied that my partner was "special" for choosing to be with someone who could not contribute equally to the relationship.

Considering the beliefs that society holds about relationship roles and the limitations of people with disabilities to fulfill those roles, the attitude that disabled/ablebodied relationships are inevitably unbalanced is not very surprising; this may be a barrier through which relational partners need to work.

People with disabilities sometimes feel they have to be especially "good" relational partners to make up for what their lovers are giving up by staying with them—the potential for a "normal" relationship. They sometimes believe they have to compensate for their disability-caused relational limitations by being overly giving, supportive partners (Fisher & Galler, 1988). One way this gets translated into behavior is denial or suppression of any negative or unpleasant emotions. There is the sense that expression of discontent, including anger, implies that they are ungrateful for their kind treatment (Zola, 1982a). If they internalize the anger, it can lead to self-loathing and/or resentment; if they vent the anger, they run the risk of being perceived as the stereotypical bitter cripple with the expectation that the world owes them. There is often a thin line between martyrdom and self-pity, and there is a fear of a rejection that will not only be emotionally damaging but will also leave them with limited assistance. My current partner summed this up by telling a friend, "She thinks that if she pisses me off, she won't get any help."

Emotional strength exhibited by suppression of negative emotions can be part of the air of independence. According to Phillips (1990), most of us have deeply internalized the folk ideas: "stand on your own two feet," "it is better to give than to receive," and "we must help those who cannot help themselves." Thus, the conditions under which one should ask for and/or provide assistance (especially in initial interactions) typically have been clouded by uncertainty (Emry & Wiseman, 1987; Emry, Wiseman, & Morgan, 1986). Over the years, I have heard many ablebodied people say that people with disabilities do not want help, they want to be independent. Thus, to attempt to help a disabled person, they believe, may be interpreted as insulting or paternalistic and lead to negative feelings or interactions. Sometimes this does occur. Likewise, people with disabilities, especially in the era of the Americans with Disabilities Act, are expected to desire independence. For myself, and my friends with disabilities, there is anxiety surrounding the notion of allowing ourselves to become "too" dependent on our romantic partners for fear of greater vulnerability should those relationships end.

Concerns over equity and autonomy are not one-sided. According to Fisher and Galler (1988), ablebodied women feel a sense of responsibility for their disabled friends. They also experience uncertainty about what their own rights are within the relationship. In other words, even though they tend to understand and confirm their disabled friends' rights to emotional and physical support, they seem to be less certain of their own entitlements within the relationship.

In my experience, ablebodied partners sometimes feel they are maneuvering through a relational mine field, moving carefully and waiting for a wrong word or action to blow up in their faces, unsure of the exact amount of empathy or assistance that will prevent accusations of paternalism or indifference. I have been told that they struggle, too, over when to insist on helping and when to let go and believe that if we say we can do something or that we do not want help, we mean it. My partner has found this to be especially difficult when I am angry at him because he knows my instinct is to blast the message "I'll show you that I don't need you around!" This situation has been nicely illustrated on occasions of my insistence on paying $25 to take a taxi home from his house and his insistence on driving me home after we have had a fight; it has always been for me, on some level, a struggle over power and control.

Despite barriers to relationship development and struggles with the issues discussed above, people do come together as romantic couples. Understanding that we come to these disabled/ablebodied relationships with societally imposed disability baggage is perhaps the first step in negotiating relationships that work. The next section is focused on the reported ways in which people who are satisfied with their disabled/ablebodied romantic relationships have negotiated issues and/or roles within them.

NEGOTIATING DISABLED/ABLEBODIED ROMANTIC RELATIONSHIPS

People who have satisfying disabled/ablebodied romantic relationships seem to have successfully stepped beyond their socialization to redefine relational roles and expectations. According to Tepper (1997), part of this negotiation can include the redefinition or complete rejection of traditional gender roles (i.e., who works outside the home and who cares for the house and children). It may also involve attitudinal shifts in definitions of acceptable and fulfilling sex. Because for some disabling conditions, sex can be problematic—in terms of privacy (Heslinga, Schellen, & Verkuyl, 1974), mechanics and positioning (Hwang, 1997; Tepper, 1997), as well as physiological responses to illness (Nichols, 1995) and/or side effects of medications (Schover, 1989)—experimentation and discussion become essential. Many people attribute new value and fulfillment to touch, communication, and pleasuring that may or may not lead to intercourse and/or orgasm (Zola, 1982a).

Relational partners need both autonomy and connection (Baxter, 1993). Therefore, disabled/ablebodied couples need to negotiate satisfying levels and types of reciprocal support. This negotiation could involve agreeing to attribute equal value to physical, emotional, and mental forms of support, deciding to obtain volunteers and/or hire outside help for certain tasks, and may also entail what Baxter referred to as reframing: "transformation of meaning in which the contrasting elements of a given contradiction cease to be regarded as antithetical to one another" (Baxter, 1993, p. 101). For example, a couple might reframe "assistance with bathing" as "bathing together," or they may reframe assistance with transportation to work from "dependency" to "car pooling."

Over time, they may discover circumstances where passing is desirable, and become coconspirators. They may agree that the ablebodied partner should serve as a mediator in certain contexts (i.e., securing appropriate accommodations in a restaurant) or speak for the disabled partner (i.e., defending against stigmatization or discrimination). These actions tend to occur once partners have become comfortable with each other and the disability's place in the relationship, but caution is needed to avoid disconfirming the partner with the disability or crossing boundaries of independence or a disabled person's desire to educate the general public (Fisher & Galler, 1988).

Disabled/ablebodied couples may need to establish boundaries that maintain comfortable levels of dialectical tension not only between autonomy and connection, but also between openness and closedness in their relational communication. The ultimate value of complete openness and honesty in relationships is an interpersonal myth. For married couples, Bienvenu (1970) noted: "Regulating the disclosure of private information has been identified by some as a more productive route to a successful marriage than practicing complete openness" (p. 222). Partners must recognize that disclosure of private information including expression of anger, resentment, and other negative emotions, although important for each, must be balanced within the long-term goals of the relationship. Together, couples can work toward a sense of trust in each other's abilities to both express and receive unpleasant messages (Zola, 1982a). Confirmation and mutual respect are key.

CONCLUSION

Children with disabilities are typically socialized within families and cultures that hold negative attitudes toward and perceptions of disability. Through media representations, family communications, and social interaction, disabled girls and boys are bombarded with messages that they are less desirable or outright unfit as romantic partners. In adulthood, these internalizations can result in struggles over issues of passing, autonomy, reciprocity, and validity in establishing and maintaining romantic relationships. Disabled/ablebodied couples satisfied with their relationships are likely to redefine roles and expectations, reframe dialectical tensions, and develop trust in their abilities to communicate effectively.

DISCUSSION QUESTIONS

1. How does the socialization of children with disabilities affect how they view their relationship potentialities? How might it affect their communication with potential romantic partners?
2. Think of societal messages you have received about people with disabilities over your lifetime. Choose three and discuss how these have helped and hindered you in communicating with others who have disabilities.
3. Discuss the potential advantages and disadvantages of passing for both disabled and ablebodied partners in a relationship. What might be some circumstances when couples would agree to try and pass? How could this be negotiated?

REFERENCES

Anderson, B. J., & Wolf, F. M. (1986). Chronic physical illness and sexual behavior: Psychological issues. *Journal of Counseling and Clinical Psychology, 54*, 168–175.

Appleby, Y. (1994). Out in the margins. *Disability and Society, 9*(1), 19–32.

Asch, A. (1984). Personal reflections. *American Psychologist, 39*, 551–552.

Baxter, L. A. (1993). Dialectical contradictions in relationship development. In S. Petronio, J. K. Alberts, M. L. Hecht, & J. Buley (Eds.), *Contemporary perspectives on interpersonal communication* (pp. 88–102). Madison, WI: Brown & Benchmark.

Belgrave, F., & Mills, J. (1981). Effect upon desire for social interaction with a physically disabled person of mentioning the disability in different contexts. *Journal of Applied Social Psychology, 11*, 44–57.

Bem, S. L. (1993). *The lenses of gender: Transforming the debate on sexual inequality.* New Haven, CT: Yale University Press.

Bienvenu, M. (1970). Measurement of marital communication. *Family Coordinator, 19,* 26–31.

Blackman, A. A., & Dembo, M. H. (1984). Prosocial behaviors in a main stream preschool. *Child Study Journal, 14,* 205–209.

Braithwaite, D. O. (1985, November). *Impression management in redefinition of self by persons with disabilities.* Paper presented at the annual convention of the Speech Communication Association, Denver, CO.

Braithwaite, D. O., Emry, R. A., & Wiseman, R. L. (1984, February). *Ablebodied and disablebodied persons' communication: The disabled person's perspective.* Paper presented at the Western Speech Communication Association conference, Seattle, WA. (ERIC Document Reproduction Service, No. ED 264 622).

Emry, R., & Wiseman, R. L. (1987, November). *When helping may not be helpful: The development of learned helplessness in the physically disabled.* Paper presented at the annual convention of the Speech Communication Association, Boston, MA.

Emry, R., Wiseman, R. L., & Morgan, D. (1986, November). *Disabled students in an academic setting.* Paper presented at the annual convention of the Speech Communication Association, Chicago, IL.

Farina, A., & Ring, K. (1965). The influence of perceived mental illness on interpersonal relations. *Journal of Abnormal Psychology, 70,* 47–51.

Fish, G., & Smith, S. M. (1983). Disability: A variable in counselor effectiveness and attitudes toward disabled persons. *Rehabilitation Counseling Bulletin, 27,* 120–123.

Fisher, B., & Galler, R. (1988). Friendship and fairness: How disability affects friendship between women. In M. Fine & A. Asch (Eds.), *Women with disabilities: Essays in psychology, culture, and politics* (pp. 172–194). Philadelphia: Temple University Press.

Goffman, E. (1963). *Stigma: Notes on the management of spoiled identity.* Englewood Cliffs, NJ: Prentice-Hall.

Greengross, W. (1976). *Entitled to love.* London: Malaby.

Heslinga, K., Schellen, A. M. C. M., & Verkuyl, A. (1974). *Not made of stone: The sexual problems of handicapped people.* Springfield, IL: Charles C. Thomas.

Hillyer, B. (1993). *Feminism and disability.* Norman: University of Oklahoma Press.

Hwang, K. (1997). Living with a disability: A woman's perspective. In M. Sipski & C. Alexander (Eds.), *Sexual function in people with disability and chronic illness* (pp. 119–130). Gaithersburg, MD: Aspen.

Kleck, R. (1968). Physical stigma and nonverbal cues emitted in face-to-face interaction. *Human Relations, 21,* 19–28.

Kleck, R., Hiroshi, O., & Hastorf, A. H. (1986). The effects of physical deviance upon face-to-face interaction. *Human Relations, 19,* 425–438.

Kroll, K., & Klein, E. L. (1992). *Enabling romance: A guide to love, sex, and relationships for the disabled and the people who care about them.* New York: Harmony.

Mairs, N. (1996). *Waist-high in the world: A life among the nondisabled.* Boston: Beacon.

Nichols, M. (1995). Sexual desire disorder in a lesbian-feminist couple: The intersection of therapy and politics. In R. C. Rosen & S. R. Leiblum (Eds.), *Sex studies in sex therapy* (pp. 163–175). New York: Guilford.

Olkin, R. (1997). The human rights of children with disabilities. *Women and Therapy, 20*(2), 29–42.

Phillips, M. J. (1990). Damaged goods: Oral narratives of the experience of disability in American culture. *Social Science and Medicine, 30,* 849–857.

Rousso, H. (1988). Daughters with disabilities: Defective women or minority women? In M. Fine & A. Asch (Eds.), *Women with disabilities: Essays in psychology, culture, and politics* (pp. 139–170). Philadelphia: Temple University Press.

Saad, S. C. (1997). Disability and the lesbian, gay man, or bisexual individual. In M. L. Sipski & C. J. Alexander (Eds.), *Sexual function in people with disability and chronic illness* (pp. 413–428). Gaithersburg, MD: Aspen.

Schover, L. R. (1989). Sexual problems in chronic illness. In S. R. Leiblum & R. C. Rosen (Eds.), *Principles and practice of sex therapy* (pp. 319–351). New York: Guilford.

Simon, B. L. (1988). Never-married old women and disability: A majority experience. In M. Fine & A. Asch (Eds.), *Women with disabilities: Essays in psychology, culture, and politics* (pp. 215–226). Philadelphia: Temple University Press.

Tepper, M. S. (1997). Living with a disability: A man's perspective. In M. Sipski & C. Alexander (Eds.), *Sexual function in people with disability and chronic illness* (pp. 131–146). Gaithersburg, MD: Aspen.

Thompson, T. L. (1982a). You can't play marbles—you have a wooden hand: Communication with the handicapped. *Communication Quarterly, 30*, 108–115.

Thompson, T. L. (1982b). Disclosure as a disability-management strategy: A review and conclusions. *Communication Quarterly, 30*, 196–202.

Thompson, T. L. (1987, November). *Communication between the disabled and ablebodied: A three phase study of disconfirmation and its effects.* Paper presented at the annual convention of the International Communication Association, Montreal, Canada.

Thompson, T. L., & Seibold, D. R. (1978). Stigma management in normal-stigmatized interactions: Test of the disclosure hypothesis and a model of stigma acceptance. *Human Communication Research, 4*, 231–242.

Waxman, B. F. (1994). It's time to politicize our sexual oppression. In B. Shaw (Ed.), *The ragged edge: The disability experience from the pages of the first fifteen years of the Disability Rag* (pp. 82–87). Louisville, KY: Advocado.

Weinberg, (1982). Growing up physically disabled: Factors in the evaluation of disability. *Rehabilitation Counseling Bulletin, 25*, 219–227.

Weiserbs, B., & Gottlieb, J. (1995). The perception of risk over time as a factor influencing attitudes toward children with disabilities. *Journal of Psychology, 129*, 689–699.

Welner, S. L. (1997). Gynecologic care and sexuality issues for women with disabilities. *Sexuality & Disability, 15*(1), 33–40.

White, M. J., Rintala, D. H., Hart, K. A., & Fuhrer, M. J. (1993). Sexual activities, concerns and interests of women with spinal cord injury living in the community. *American Journal of Physical Medicine and Rehabilitation, 72*, 372–378.

Zilbergeld, B. (1992). *The new male sexuality.* New York: Bantam.

Zola, I. K. (1982a). Denial of emotional needs to people with handicaps. *Archives of Physical Medicine and Rehabilitation, 63*(2), 63–67.

Zola, I. K. (Ed.). (1982b). *Ordinary lives: Voices of disability and disease.* Cambridge, MA: Applewood.

Zola, I. K. (1983). Developing new self-images and interdependence. In N. M. Crewe, I. K. Zola, & Associates (Eds.), *Independent living for physically disabled people* (pp. 49–59). San Francisco: Jossey-Bass.

Zola, I. K. (1984). Communication barriers between "the ablebodied" and "the handicapped." In R. P. Marinelli & A. E. Dell Orto (Eds.), *The psychological and social impact of physical disability* (2nd ed., pp. 139–148). New York: Springer.

3

Embodiment and Dis-Embodiment: Identity Trans-Formation of Persons With Physical Disabilities

Thuy-Phuong Do
Patricia Geist
San Diego State University, CA

Keywords: Embodiment, dis-embodiment, trans-formation, identity, stereotypes, dys-appearance, compassion

Excavation

Tonight, when I take off my shoes:
three toes on each twisted foot
I touch the rough skin. The holes
where pins were. The scars.
If I touch them long enough will I find
those who never touched me? or those
who did? Freak, midget, three toed
bastard. Words I've always heard.
Disabled, crippled, deformed, Words
I was given. But tonight I go back
farther, want more, tear deeper into
my skin. Peeling it back I reveal
the bones at birth I wasn't given—
the place where no one speaks a word.

—Fries (1994, p. 91)

49

From childhood through adulthood, everyone has internalized or ignored messages communicated to them about their physical bodies. Sometimes these messages empower and make people feel whole or strong. Other times, these messages deeply wound the sense of self, so much so that individual may question their worthiness. They may feel weakened or devalued by a message, even though it focuses only on one physical part of them. Not surprisingly, over time, hearing the same messages repeatedly devaluing their physical presence, they begin to communicate these messages to themselves. The painful sound they hear then, is often their own voices reverberating in shame, regret, embarrassment, and retreat.

Imagine for a moment what persons born with a physical disability experience in communication during their lifetime when they are stereotyped as "mentally handicapped" (Do, 1997; Kleinfield, 1977; Morris, 1991; Shapiro, 1993); when they are referred to as "victims," "sufferers," and "handicapped" (Braithwaite, 1996); when they are verbally accepted, but nonverbally rejected (Braithwaite, 1990; Braithwaite & Braithwaite, 1997; Emry & Wiseman, 1987; Thompson, 1982); when they are perceived to be damaged and defective (Phillips, 1990); when they receive less empathic and appropriate communication (Thompson, 1981, 1982; Thompson & Cusella, 1987); when they feel an obligation to develop strategies to reduce the discomfort of ablebodied persons (Belgrave & Mills, 1981; Braithwaite, 1986, 1991; Braithwaite, Emry, & Wiseman, 1984; Hastorf, Wildfogel, & Cassman, 1979; Mills, Belgrave, & Boyer, 1984; Thompson, 1982); when they are routinely asked by strangers to reveal private information about their health, bodies, sexuality, or personal habits (Braithwaite, Emry, & Wiseman, 1984; Braithwaite, 1991); and when they realize it is simply better to avoid communication than to be disrespected or degraded (Braithwaite & Labrecque, 1994).

This chapter provides insight into the concept of *trans-formation*, which is the process of communicating in ways that transcend stereotypes. It is the process of resisting messages that make people feel apart from, invisible, absent, or othered and of communicating in ways that enable people to feel included, visible, present, and welcomed. We provide a window into the emotional lives of three persons who have lived their lives, from birth to the present, with visible, physical disabilities. Readers are encouraged to reflect on their own lives and perhaps experience their own trans-formations as they learn about messages that have embodied and dis-embodied these three individuals. Their stories reveal processes of trans-formation, communicating with others from childhood to adulthood.

The chapter begins with a discussion of literature about embodiment and dis-embodiment, including a description of trans-formation as a communicative process of embracing and resisting the messages about embodiment. Next, the significance of stories as a vehicle for understanding trans-formation, embodiment, and dis-embodiment is described. The stories of three persons born with visible, physical disabilities and the messages they have heard that contribute to their feelings of embodiment and disembodiment are presented next. In the process, they account for their own processes of trans-formation. Finally, the chapter concludes with a description of strategies for facilitating trans-forming communication among persons with and without physical disabilities and a discussion of what the future may bring for this area of scholarly inquiry.

EMBODIMENT AND DISEMBODIMENT

Our bodies are with us, though we have always had trouble saying exactly how. We are, in various conceptions or metaphors, in our body, or having a body, or at one with our body, or alienated from it. The body is both ourselves and other, and as such the object of emotions from love to disgust.... Most of the time, the body maintains an unstable position between such extremes, at once the subject and object of pleasure, the uncontrollable agent of pain and the revolt against reason—and the vehicle of mortality. As such, it is always the subject of curiosity, of an ever-renewed project of knowing. (Brooks, 1993, p. 1)

Our sense of self is decidedly a process and product of our experience of life and the cultural systems we inhabit (Bordo, 1989; Shilling, 1993). Through our bodies, we are enabled, constrained, managed, disciplined, accepted, and rejected by ourselves and others. Not surprisingly, bodies have occupied a central place in theory in a variety of disciplines, including sociology, political science, psychology, literature, theology, and communication (Brooks, 1993; Foster, 1994; Foster, Siegel, & Berry, 1996; Jaggar & Bordo, 1989; Leder, 1990; Shilling, 1993). Yet, as Brooks (1993) pointed out, "we still don't know the body. Its otherness from ourselves, as well as its intimacy, make it the inevitable object of an ever-renewed writing project" (p. 286).

When we view our bodies as a site of struggle, the physical body becomes embodied as the referent point by which we as humans define ourselves and are defined by others (Bordo, 1989). Central to the struggle is the duality of meaning where the same situations experienced on one level as constraining or enslaving also can be experienced on another level as liberating and transforming. The intimacy and otherness of our bodies is represented in the duality of embodiment and disembodiment and the duality of presence and absence we experience in wellness and illness, in ability and disability. Essentially, everyone experiences the duality of embodiment and disembodiment. We see this clearly in *Minding the Body* (Foster, 1994), where authors "probe what seemed disturbing or exhilarating in their personal lives, what had snagged, invalidated, buoyed, or surprised them about their bodies" (p. 8).

It becomes clear how, in our everyday lives, we move within these dualities frequently, and at times experience both simultaneously. As an embodied self, we may be conscious of our body, looking at it, sensing it, but at the same time feel disembodied by the alien nature of novel sensations in illness, cyclical body changes, and dysfunction (Leder, 1990). Leder captured these dualities in his book, *The Absent Body*, when he stated:

> Insofar as the body tends to disappear when functioning without problems, it often seizes our attention most strongly at times of dysfunction; we then experience the body as the very *absence* of a desired or ordinary state, and as a force that stands opposed to the self. (p. 4)

Leder suggested that at moments of breakdown we experience what he termed *dys-appearance*. That is, in contrast to the disappearances that characterize ordinary functioning, in dys-appearance we experience both a limit on vital functioning and also an affective disturbance arising from or giving rise to self-consciousness. Leder explained dys-appearance in this way:

> *Dys* is from the Greek prefix signifying "bad," "hard," or "ill" and is found in English words such as "dysfunctional".... However, *dys* is also a variant spelling, now somewhat archaic, of the Latin root *dis*. This originally had the meaning of "away," "apart," or "asunder".... The body in dys-appearance is marked by being away, apart, or asunder. (Leder, 1990, p. 87)

Essentially, our bodies in dys-appearance or dis-embodiment can be experienced in two ways: (a) as a reversal of a normal or desired state, and (b) as away, apart from self, as an alien thing or painful prison or tomb in which we are trapped (Leder, 1990).

Scheman (1993) stated that the root of disembodiment lies in the process of defining our own or others' self-identities solely by the physical body. In this way, those persons who do not possess what the culture has defined as the "ideal body" are the ones who are subordinated, othered, and considered less than or inferior to the ideal (Bordo, 1989; Foucault, 1978; Said, 1978). For persons who are disabled, the unobtainable body image becomes even more impossible because their bodies are defined as damaged (i.e., bad, ugly, weak), which implies that they will never be whole (i.e., good, pretty, strong). Their visible flaws become scars for the world to see and the basis on which to reject their bodies as different, and to alter our communication in ways that intensify dys-appearance and dis-embodiment.

Embodiment and dis-embodiment are natural processes that operate everyday, habitually, often unconsciously. However, others' communication can intensify self-consciousness to the point that our dys-appearance is uncomfortable:

> The other person transforms me into an object and denies me, I transform him [or her] into an object and deny him [or her], it is asserted. In fact the other's gaze transforms me into an object, and mine him [or her], only if both of us withdraw into the core of our thinking nature, if we both make ourselves into an inhuman gaze, if each of us feels his [or her] actions to be not taken up and understood, but observed as if they were an insect's. This is what happens, for instance, when I fall under the gaze of a stranger. But even then, the objectification of each by the other's gaze is felt as unbearable only because it takes the place of possible communication. A dog's gaze directed towards me causes me no embarrassment. The refusal to communicate, however, is still a form of communication. (Merleau-Ponty, 1962, p. 361)

Leder (1990) suggested that this uncomfortable intensification of self-consciousness often relates to a rupture in mutuality or a discrepancy in power. It is compassion, in the sense of experiencing and sharing another's perspective, which allows us each to become trans-formed into real, dimensional, embodied selves, and not defined solely by a physical characteristic (pp. 161–162).

Communication can be a vehicle for trans-formation, for experiencing compassion, for crossing the boundaries between embodied and dis-embodied selves. Resisting dis-embodiment through communication can trans-form interaction in ways to construct understanding and compassion. Trans-formation from dis-embodiment to embodiment may ease tensions of difference/indifference, stimulate interest in understanding, and transcend the othering that routinely occurs for persons with disabilities.

One step toward trans-formation is to listen to the voices of people who were born with a physical disability. Their narratives provide an opportunity to learn a great deal about the everyday processes of embodiment and dis-embodiment. And we can begin to understand the significant role communication plays in either intensifying or trans-forming the debilitating self-consciousness that restricts compassion.

STORIES OF EMBODIMENT AND DISEMBODIMENT: COMMUNICATING TRANS-FORMATION

The power of a story to affect and reflect people's lives should never be underestimated (Bochner, Ellis, & Tillmann-Healy, 1996; Do, 1997; Ellis, 1993, 1997; Fisher, 1989; Varallo, Ray, & Ellis, 1998). Narratives give voice to the localized concerns of persons with disabilities who are usually not heard due to the hierarchical structure of our society. More often than not, society privileges those who have undamaged bodies to speak with a stronger voice than "others" (Burawoy et al., 1991; Foss, Foss, & Trapp, 1991; Morris, 1991; Rosenau, 1992; Shapiro, 1993). Most issues that affect persons with disabilities have been unarticulated throughout history because other dominant master narratives have rendered persons with disabilities a marginalized group (Deegan & Brooks, 1985; Morris, 1991; Rosenau, 1992).

Narratives, in addition to allowing the reader to glimpse the experiences and emotions of persons with disabilities, also allow the reader to reflect on themselves and their own experiences. For instance, Ellis (1996) reflected on Tolstoy's "Death of Ivan Ilych" by writing that:

> The story made me think about how I was living my life and working my work. I thought further about the role of family relationships, career, and social support in one's life, and even more abstractly about mortality, meaning, and life after death. This cognitive awareness was accompanied by emotional, bodily, and spiritual reactions. (p. 3)

Through narrative, Ellis was able to reflect on her own relationships and experiences. For Ellis and others, narrative is a way of understanding and making sense of our lives (Bochner et al., 1996; Ellis, 1993, 1996, 1997).

Encouraging persons with disabilities to share their accounts will ensure that someone else does not speak for them. The personal narratives of persons with disabilities reveal their perspectives on resistance, transformation, embodiment, and dis-embodiment (Do, 1997; Kleinfield, 1977;

Michaux, 1970; Morris, 1991; Sparkes, 1996; Zola, 1982). For instance, in his book on persons with disabilities, Kleinfield (1977) constructed an extensive and well-articulated story that portrayed the marginalized voice of the disabled culture. Morris (1991) described life after acquiring a disability as a woman who was once a university professor. Zola (1982) chronicled his life from the point of disability on to enrich understanding of life. Do (1997) narrated the story of growing up as a child with polio and the achievements she made in spite of the messages she received.

Narratives speak words that humanize persons with disabilities. They provide opportunities to deconstruct and trans-form the dominant narratives that portray persons with disabilities as poor, uneducated, handicapped, underemployed shut-ins (Burawoy et al., 1991). Stories told by the members of the disabled culture trans-form stereotypes and allow persons with disabilities to become "selves," making them persons and not "others" (Fine, 1994).

TRANS-FORMING COMMUNICATION

Mike, Thuy, and Amy tell their stories of trans-formation, revealing communication surrounding embodiment and dis-embodiment. All three were congenitally disabled from birth. Mike has cerebral palsy, Thuy has polio, and Amy has a spinal cord injury. Each of their stories provides understanding of the duality of embodiment and disembodiment in a compliment, in the past and present, and in absence and presence. In each situation, communication influences trans-formation of identity as compliments, encouragement, and assistance are embraced, resisted, or challenged.

The Duality of Complimenting: Mike's Story

Throughout their lives, people with disabilities receive messages that affect them at different levels. Mike, a 27-year-old who has cerebral palsy, recounts his experience with the way others talk about his body. Mike's story illustrates how messages serve to fragment a person's identity, often dis-embodying a person by complimenting his or her isolated physical strength.

> In terms of my body image, I am okay with my upper body, I think I am pretty buff. The lower body, I don't know, I have some reservations about

it but there's really not much I can do about it. I think my body is okay. One woman I knew said she liked my upper body, she liked my muscles. That was about it. And I have gotten a lot of compliments about my arms. But there's more to me than the arms. That's what I usually tell people. On a couple of occasions people tell me "oh you must have strong arms." That's where the conversation ends. When I first meet somebody I might be defined with what they see of me from the outside. That has not always been the case. I have met some people that once they got to know me they do not even think of me as being disabled. And they have told me that too. They say "we don't even think of you as being disabled."

Mike's narrative provides two insights about dis-embodiment and identity trans-formation. First, the narrative illustrates how communication intended to compliment can function in ways that dis-embody a person's identity. How can communication intended to compliment function to dis-embody? Why does the conversation end as soon as Mike is complimented on his arms? Often, we assume that a compliment is positive communication that should be accepted graciously by the receiver, because it is offered with good intent on behalf of the sender. However, as we see in Mike's account, he does not want his identity to be connected only to his "upper body," his "arms," or his "muscles." He tells people, "there's more to me than my arms." He wants other strengths, for instance, his intellect or his talents, to be something that a stranger, acquaintance, or friend would compliment more than "what they see of me from the outside."

The second insight gained from Mike's narrative is that when a particular part of a person's body is repeatedly focused on in communication, that person can easily begin to internalize an identity that reinforces and intensifies a fragmented, disembodied self. When Mike says, "I have gotten a lot of compliments about my arms," we see that Mike has received messages about his arms repeatedly. What impact does this have? Consider what Mike states at the beginning of his narrative:

> In terms of my body image, I am okay with my upper body, I think I am pretty buff. The lower body, I don't know, I have some reservations about it but there's not much I can do about it.

Mike's talk indicates the duality of embodiment and disembodiment in communication. Receiving compliments about characteristics other than his body may contribute to a trans-formation, but at the same time Mike is working internally to trans-form his identity by communicating to himself that "there's not much I can do about it."

Mike's trans-formation from a dis-embodied self is facilitated when people "do not even think of me as disabled." As he points out, people have said to him, "we don't even think of you as being disabled." Mike indicates that once people get to know him he is not stereotyped, fragmented, or disembodied as he so often is when he receives repeated compliments on one isolated physical characteristic.

Compliments often reflect dis-embodiment because what is not communicated often becomes more important than what is communicated. For Mike, the conversation ends when he feels that a person who has a choice about what they can say to him, chooses to talk about his arms rather than another one of his true strengths. Trans-formation occurs when communication does not stereotype or fragment his identity.

In the next narrative, Thuy focuses on her initial resistance to communication that eventually facilitates her embodiment and transformation.

The Duality of Past and Present: Thuy's Story

Thuy, who contracted polio at the age of 2, recounts one of her early childhood experiences growing up with a disability. Thuy's story illustrates how one key message early in the life of a person with a disability can greatly impact trans-formation by contradicting other messages of dis-embodiment.

The most vivid memory I have was of my teacher, Mrs. Austin [in kindergarten]. She did something for me that was a key event in shaping my attitude of myself and my disability. It happened during break time, when we would get a snack of graham crackers and a carton of milk. We had to form a line, pick up a carton of milk from a bucket and grab two graham crackers. I always tried to be first in line because every time I was last, the milk would be at the bottom of the bucket and I would have to ask one of the students to bend down and grab it for me. One day, the teacher observed this and told me that I could get the milk myself. She told me to lean on one of my crutches and put the other one against the wall, freeing one hand so I could grab the milk. I hated her for this. I cried. I hated the fact that she made me do it myself in front of all the other kids. But I thank her for it now. That was the first day I learned to get an attitude about my difference. She showed me that I may have been different, but my difference did not limit me, only I limited me. God bless her. (Do, 1997, p. 133)

Thuy's narrative provides insights into the process of embodiment and identity trans-formation. First, similar to Mike's trans-formation of taking compliments at their face value, Thuy was taught to look deeper into society's prevalent norm of "helping" people with disabilities to see how that norm could make her feel if she had to be dependent on others.

How is helping a person with a disability harmful? In our society, we are taught to offer help to a person with a disability. We automatically open doors for them or help them carry something if they look as though they may be having difficulty carrying it themselves. Many of us do this routinely, often forgetting to ask whether the assistance is needed in the first place. What happens is that persons with disabilities are constantly given help doing things that most ablebodied people do themselves everyday. If a person with a disability needs help doing things that most take for granted, how can they do things that are really important? How can they work? How can they own their own businesses if they cannot even open their own doors? Thuy's story illustrates this norm. At first, she exhibits disability management skills by moving to the front of the line to be able to get the milk carton herself. However, realizing she could not always be in front, she decides to ask other children for help. What was insightful on Mrs. Austin's part was communicating to Thuy that she needed to learn to do it for herself. Mrs. Austin acted contrary to the norm that many ablebodied adults would have followed. She decided not to protect Thuy and, instead, she showed Thuy that she was perfectly able do it on her own. Further, she communicated this message to Thuy in front of the other children, which possibly facilitated their trans-formations by helping them to understand two important ideas: one, that a disability does not prevent a person from doing everyday things that ablebodied people can do, and two, that it is not automatically necessary to help a person with a disability; rather, asking whether they need the assistance respects their identity. Although Thuy's trans-formation did not occur at that point in her past, she learned a valuable lesson through Mrs. Austin's communication, a message she has never forgotten.

The second insight Thuy's narrative illustrates is that a message intended to embody another person does not guarantee that trans-formation will occur. Thuy's story indicated that Mrs. Austin's message ended up holding a very powerful meaning to Thuy later in life. However, when the message was first communicated to her, she rejected it. Thuy says, "I hated her for this. I cried. I hated the fact that she made me do it myself in front of all the other kids." She then goes on to say, "But I thank her for it now. That was the first day I learned to get an attitude about my difference." In this narrative we see how Thuy's body is a site of struggle, as her disability became the referent point for a message that was interpreted initially by Thuy as dis-embodiment, but later was reinterpreted as embodiment. The duality of meaning is exemplified in this one message interpreted differently based on the trans-formed identity Thuy embraces today. Due to the mystery that our body holds not only for others, but for ourselves, we are constantly redefining our embodiment through the way we and others talk about our bodies. Therefore, messages that may be intended to embody may be resisted and interpreted as dis-embodying.

In the following narrative, Amy, a mother of two children who has a spinal cord injury, recounts her experience with being physically absent throughout high school.

The Duality of Absence and Presence: Amy's Story

Amy's story is an example of how disembodiment is manifested in the myth that a person's mind is absent—ill or damaged—because of a physical disability. The duality of absence and presence is literally represented in being physically absent but mentally and emotionally present. The duality becomes complicated by latent disembodiment: (a) stereotyping of the physically disabled as persons who are also mentally disabled, and (b) compensating for "the handicap" by assigning passing grades.

> One thing I regret, though, is that because I was so ill, I was given a lot of grades that I really didn't earn. They just passed me through with C's or whatever to get me through. Because I had so many surgeries, I was very ill as a child, I had lots of surgeries. I was out half of tenth and half of eleventh grade, I had two sclerosis surgeries. So by the time I went to twelfth grade I was basically just graduated. The problem with that was that when I was ready to go to college, I wasn't ready to go to college. I had to start at a junior college in order to catch up to learn everything I needed to transfer to the university. But that's kind of the name of the game. It's the realm of disability and it's the realm of a child with disability.

Amy's narrative clearly demonstrates dis-embodiment as others' actions communicate to her that they embrace the myth that people with physical disabilities also possess mental disabilities. Amy's story indicates that she is not expected to function in school as well as the ablebodied students and that teachers "just passed me through with C's or whatever to get me through." The actions of Amy's teachers may have been intended as communicating caring and assistance by not adding schoolwork to her strain of having to cope with the numerous surgeries. However, Amy's

teachers did not require her to earn her grades like the other students because of her disability. In this way, Amy received the message that it was
acceptable for her to get by with doing less than other children because she
had a disability. As Amy pointed out, passing her only harmed her later
when she "wasn't ready to go to college," and she had to go back and learn
what she did not learn in high school.

The impact of being dis-embodied in this way made it difficult for Amy
to trans-form and embrace an embodied identity that was present even
when she was absent from school. It is difficult to transcend messages
that implicitly train a person with a disability to set lower expectations for
themselves and difficult for them to resist others' attempts to compensate
for their absence or what they perceive as self that has disappeared or
become dis-embodied.

COMMUNICATING TRANSFORMATION: EMBODYING IDENTITY

Everyone is othered to some extent; we all possess disabilities, whether
visible or invisible. Trans-formation implies communicating new messages
that resist stereotyping and othering. It is not a process that is negative or
positive, good or bad; rather it is a process of finding a personal middle
ground between extremes through inventing and reinventing one's identity.
Importantly, persons who are abled or disabled can be part of the trans-
formations that communicate embodiment.

Along with breaking away from the label of the "silent majority" comes
the redefinition of disability. The attempt to define persons with disabilities as a culture more than ever before comes from an effort to unify
the fragmented disabled community and to understand the repertoire of
strategies they must develop to function in an ablebodied society (Braithwaite, 1996). The call for persons with disabilities to judge themselves by
their own standards and not the "normal" ablebodied standard helps define
persons with disabilities as a culture (Braithwaite, 1990; Braithwaite &
Braithwaite, 1997; Deegan, 1977; Emry & Wiseman, 1987; Morris, 1991;
Shapiro, 1993). By viewing disability as a characteristic of individuals of
a particular culture we begin to understand the possibilities for communication that may be different, but not inferior to behaviors of people who
are ablebodied (Braithwaite, 1996).

One strategy for communicating alluded to by Mike, Thuy, and Amy
either implicitly or explicitly is for others to treat the person as primary and

the disability as secondary (e.g., Braithwaite, 1996). Instead of entering a communicative situation with a picture of persons with disabilities as embodied or dis-embodied based on the strengths or weaknesses of their physical bodies, come to the interaction picturing a person who has varied interests and talents that should be considered in conversation. In other words, place no limits on the person because of a label or a stereotype.

A second strategy revealed in the three stories is mirroring. When an ablebodied person communicates in a way that dis-embodies by focusing on some aspect of the person with a disability, then the person with a disability immediately responds by communicating specifically in a manner that emphasizes the stereotype being used. This strategy is exemplified by Mike's statement in another part of his interview:

> I am so sick and tired of being an inspiration to people. Can't I be somebody's husband?! I am sick of being a stinking inspiration! So I got out of bed this morning, so what?! I'm just a guy. If you want to look for inspiration, look to Martin Luther King. I'm just a guy who uses a couple pieces of aluminum to get around.

Mike's "voice" clearly becomes animated when he considers how dis-embodying it feels to have others see him as some type of inspiration. By communicating about his take on someone's characterization of him as an "inspiration," Mike strategically reveals how disembodying such a statement can be. His communication is designed to broaden what he sees as a very limited view of what it means to be an inspiration.

A third strategy the participants learned to use as they gained experience with their disabilities later in life is that of screening the messages they receive. A positive identity is difficult to maintain when others have communicated negative messages all of one's life. However, people with a disability who function in a society that has deep-rooted stereotypes of the culture of disability learn to screen out messages that have no bearing on their identity and embodiment. For instance, if Amy had not resisted the "passing through" that repeatedly occurred in her education, she would not have become a successful college student. But at the same time, it is important to recognize that a message that at first can be interpreted as dis-embodying may later be interpreted as embodying. Thuy at first screened out her teacher's message but later recognized how embodying and empowering it was, so much so that it reverberates in her identity today. Screening the messages that embody and dis-embody one's identity is an essential skill for a person with a disability.

Unfortunately, it is not always the case that a person with a disability develops the ability to screen out limiting messages, especially messages they hear day after day. Mike had this experience when trying to date:

> I get these messages from women that I'm asexual . . . I feel as an adult that I did not have the proper experience to feel really secure about relationships. Because even though now I'm in my thirties, I'm still going through what people go through in their twenties.

If we listen carefully to the messages Mike has received and imagine ourselves receiving these messages time and time again, it becomes easier to imagine why Mike feels the way he does.

WHAT THE FUTURE MAY BRING

The direction of future research on persons with disabilities, embodiment, and communication is wide open. Considering the experiences of Mike, Thuy, and Amy, one possible avenue of exploration is that of children with disabilities and the messages they receive growing up, at home and at school. Much of what was taught and learned at an early age impacted the participants' identities deeply. In childhood there were critical moments that helped the participants develop an "attitude" about their self-image or limited the participants by telling them that they "could not" do many things. Research needs to explore the process of acquiring a disability in childhood and denying or incorporating the disability into one's adult identity. There simply is not much research on children and disability, even though childhood can be a crucial time to develop a healthy identity, as illustrated by all of the participants' experiences.

As the first author of this chapter, I have found that the scars that once made me angry every time I looked at my feet have disappeared. My feet are not worse or better than any other feet. However, I still do not wear shorts or dresses in public because the attention I will receive will only focus on one thing, my disability. What is the trans-formation process that will lead to the acceptance of the visibly disabled body? When will persons with disabilities be able to talk about their bodies comfortably and feel embodied even when the normally covered scars or "abnormal" limbs are completely exposed, instead of hidden?

People with disabilities believe that the answer lies in treating them as humans first. Yet, this suggestion is more easily spoken than acted upon.

It is a matter of training the perception, especially of young children. What one may perceive as ugly, another will see as beautiful and yet another will perceive as in-between. The training of our young to see the similarities instead of the differences will be vital to trans-formation.

Critical to facilitating people talking to one another as human beings is to listen to the stories of persons with disabilities. We should encourage them to speak and tell their stories of being silenced, discredited, excluded, and stigmatized as well as to tell their stories of being heard, encouraged, and included (Perry & Geist, 1997; Ray, 1996a, 1996b; Varallo et al., 1998). A sincere desire on all our parts to learn about and understand another's experience will be vital to this trans-formation.

DISCUSSION QUESTIONS

1. What types of messages about your body have people communicated to you? Have these messages contributed to or detracted from your sense of embodiment?
2. Do you believe that you have been stereotyped in any way based on one of your physical characteristics? If so, how did you become aware of being stereotyped? Do you believe your communication with others is affected by being stereotyped in this way?
3. Consider a time when you believe your communication dis-embodied someone else. What did you say? How did the person respond? When did you become aware that your message had dis-embodied this person? If you were to have a chance to go back to that situation, how might you communicate differently?
4. What do you believe to be some of the stereotypes people in our society have about persons with visible physical disabilities?
5. What can we say or do to educate people who habitually communicate in ways that dis-embody others? How should we, as parents and teachers, communicate with children not only to facilitate their own sense of embodiment but also to teach them to communicate with others to facilitate others' embodiment?

REFERENCES

Belgrave, F. Z., & Mills, J. (1981). Effect upon desire for social interaction with a physically disabled person of mentioning the disability in different contexts. *Journal of Applied Social Psychology, 11*, 44–57.

Bochner, A. P., Ellis, C., & Tillmann-Healy, L. M. (1996). Relationships as stories. In S. Duck (Ed.), *Handbook of personal relationships* (pp. 307–324). Sussex, England: Wiley.

Bordo, S. R. (1989). The body and the reproduction of femininity: A feminist appropriation of Foucault. In A. M. Jaggar & S. R. Bordo (Eds.), *Gender/body/knowledge* (pp. 13–33). New Brunswick, NJ: Rutgers University Press.

Braithwaite, D. O. (1986, February). *Redefinition of disability and identification as a subculture by persons with physical disabilities.* Paper presented at the annual meeting of the Western Speech Communication Association, Tucson, AZ.

Braithwaite, D. O. (1990). From majority to minority: An analysis of cultural change from ablebodied to disabled. *International Journal of Intercultural Relations, 14,* 465–483.

Braithwaite, D. O. (1991). Just how much did that wheelchair cost? Management of privacy boundaries by persons with disabilities. *Western Journal of Speech Communication, 55,* 254–274.

Braithwaite, D. O. (1996). Persons first: Exploring different perspectives on communication with persons with disabilities. In E. B. Ray (Ed.), *Communication and disenfranchisement: Social health issues and implications* (pp. 449–464). Hillsdale, NJ: Lawrence Erlbaum Associates.

Braithwaite, D. O., & Braithwaite, C. A. (1997). Understanding communication of persons with disabilities as cultural communication. In L. A. Samovar & R. E. Porter (Eds.), *Intercultural communication* (8th ed., pp. 154–164). San Francisco: Wadsworth.

Braithwaite, D. O., Emry, R. A., & Wiseman, R. L. (1984). *Ablebodied and disablebodied persons' communication: The disabled persons' perspective.* (ERIC Document Reproduction Service No. ED 264 622).

Braithwaite, D. O., & Labrecque, D. (1994). Responding to the Americans with Disabilities Act: Contributions of interpersonal communication research and training. *Journal of Applied Communication Research, 22,* 287–294.

Brooks, P. (1993). *Body work: Objects of desire in modern narrative.* Boston: Harvard University Press.

Burawoy, M., Burton, A., Ferguson, A. A., Fox, K. J., Gamson, J., Gartrell, N., Hurst, L., Kurzman, C., Salzinger, L., Schiffman, J., & Ui, S. (1991). *Ethnography unbound: Power and resistance in the modern metropolis.* Berkeley: University of California Press.

Deegan, M. J. (1977). The non-verbal communication of the physically handicapped. *Journal of Sociology and Social Welfare, 4,* 735–748.

Deegan, M. J., & Brooks, N. A. (Eds.). (1985). *Women and disability: The double handicap.* New Brunswick, NJ: Transaction.

Do, T. P. (1997). In my shoes for life: A disabled woman's journey. In L. A. M. Perry & P. Geist (Eds.), *Courage of conviction: Women's words, women's wisdom* (pp. 129–143). Mountain View, CA: Mayfield.

Ellis, C. (1993). "There are survivors": Telling a story of sudden death. *The Sociological Quarterly, 34,* 711–730.

Ellis, C. (1996). On the demands of truthfulness in writing personal loss narratives. *Journal of Personal and Interpersonal Loss, 1,* 157–177.

Ellis, C. (1997). Evocative autoethnography: Writing emotionally about our lives. In Y. Lincoln & W. G. Tierney (Eds.), *Voice in text: Reframing the narrative* (pp. 115–139). Thousand Oaks, CA: Sage.

Emry, R., & Wiseman, R. L. (1987). An intercultural understanding of ablebodied and disabled persons' communication. *International Journal of Intercultural Relations, 11,* 7–27.

Fine, M. (1994). Working the hyphens: Reinventing self and other in qualitative research. In N. K. Denzin & Y. S. Lincoln (Eds.), *Handbook of qualitative research* (pp. 70–82). Thousand Oaks, CA: Sage.

Fisher, W. R. (1989). *Human communication as narration: Toward a philosophy of reason, value, and action.* Columbia: University of South Carolina Press.

Foss, S. K., Foss, K. A., & Trapp, R. (1991). *Contemporary perspectives on rhetoric* (2nd ed.). Prospect Heights, IL: Waveland.

Foster, P. (Ed.). (1994). *Minding the body: Women writers on body and soul.* New York: Doubleday.

Foster, T., Siegel, C., & Berry, E. E. (Eds.). (1996). *Bodies of writing, bodies in performance.* New York: New York University Press.

Foucault, M. (1978). *The care of the self: The history of sexuality* (Vol. 3). New York: Random House.

Fries, K. (1994). Excavation. In B. Shaw (Ed.), *The ragged edge* (p. 91). Louisville. KY: Advocado Press.

Hastorf, A. H., Wildfogel, J., & Cassman, T. (1979). Acknowledgment of handicap as a tactic in social interaction. *Journal of Personality and Social Psychology, 37,* 1790–1797.

Jaggar, A. M., & Bordo, S. R. (Eds.). (1989). *Gender/body/knowledge: Feminist reconstructions of being and knowing.* New Brunswick, NJ: Rutgers University Press.

Kleinfield, S. (1977). *The hidden minority: A profile of handicapped Americans.* Boston: Little, Brown.

Leder, D. (1990). *The absent body.* Chicago: University of Chicago Press.

Merleau-Ponty, M. (1962). *Phenomenology of perception* (C. Smith, Trans.). London: Routledge.

Michaux, L. A. (1970). *The physically handicapped and the community: Some challenging breakthroughs.* Springfield, IL: Thomas.

Mills, J., Belgrave, F. Z., & Boyer, K. M. (1984). Reducing avoidance of social interaction with a physically disabled person by mentioning the disability following a request for aid. *Journal of Applied Social Psychology, 14,* 1–11.

Morris, J. (1991). *Pride against prejudice: Transforming attitudes to disability.* Philadelphia: New Society.

Perry, L. A. M., & Geist, P. (1997). *Courage of conviction: Women's words, women's wisdom.* Mountain View, CA: Mayfield.

Phillips, M. J. (1990). Damaged goods: Oral narratives of the experience of disability in American culture. *Social Science and Medicine, 30,* 849–856.

Ray, E. B. (Ed.). (1996a). *Communication and disenfranchisement: Social health issues and implications.* Mahwah, NJ: Lawrence Erlbaum Associates.

Ray, E. B. (Ed.). (1996b). *Case studies in communication and disenfranchisement: Applications to social health issues.* Mahwah, NJ: Lawrence Erlbaum Associates.

Rosenau, P. M. (1992). *Post-modernism and the social sciences: Insights, inroads, and intrusions.* Princeton, NJ: Princeton University Press.

Said, E. W. (1978). *Orientalism.* New York: Random House.

Scheman, N. (1993). *Engenderings: Constructions of knowledge, authority, and privilege.* New York: Routledge.

Shapiro, J. P. (1993). *No pity: People with disabilities forging a new civil rights movement.* New York: Random House.

Shilling, C. (1993). *The body and social theory.* Newbury Park, CA: Sage.

Sparkes, A. C. (1996). The fatal flaw: A narrative of the fragile body-self. *Qualitative Inquiry, 2,* 463–494.

Thompson, T. L. (1981). The development of communication skills in physically handicapped children. *Human Communication Research, 7,* 313–324.

Thompson, T. L. (1882). "You can't play marbles—you have a wooden hand": Communication with the handicapped. *Communication Quarterly, 30,* 108–115.

Thompson, T. L., & Cusella, L. P. (1987, November). *Communicating help between disabled and ablebodied persons: An exploratory observational study.* Paper presented at the annual meeting of the Speech Communication Association, Boston, MA.

Varallo, S. M., Ray, E. B., & Ellis, B. H. (1998). Speaking of incest: The research interview as social justice. *Journal of Applied Communication Research, 26,* 254–271.

Zola, I. K. (1982). *Missing pieces: A chronicle of living with a disability.* Philadelphia: Temple University Press.

4

Help Between Persons With and Without Disabilities From a Resource Theory Perspective

Kari P. Soule
Michael E. Roloff
Northwestern University

Keywords: Appropriate help, ego-threat, resource theory, services, status, unnecessary help, unsolicited help

Individuals who have physical, cognitive, or emotional disabilities must not only cope with the challenges imposed by their disability, but often contend with job and educational discrimination as well (Braithwaite, 1990; Dahnke, 1982; Emry & Wiseman, 1987a; Gliedman & Roth, 1980; Wertlieb, 1985). Furthermore, persons with disabilities sometimes confront challenges in their everyday interactions with the nondisabled, or ablebodied persons. Sadly, problematic interactions even occur during episodes in which ablebodied people provide assistance to persons with physical disabilities. Indeed, Braithwaite and Labrecque (1994) noted that helping "is one of the most difficult challenges both disabled and ablebodied persons face" (p. 291).

Support from ablebodied people can be a necessary and/or valuable resource for a person who is disabled, and can range from providing physical assistance to expressing emotional support (Ladieu, Hanfmann, & Dembo, 1947). However, help from the ablebodied can become problematic when those with disabilities view it as patronizing and condescending (Braithwaite, 1987, 1990; Buscaglia, 1983). Although assisting persons who are disabled can be motivated by a desire to be supportive, it can also communicate to disabled people that they are inferior and unable to take care of themselves. Such an interpretation may unduly reduce the independence of individuals with disabilities and lower their self-esteem. Furthermore, the responses of persons with disabilities to unwelcome assistance may also be problematic. A choice on the part of a person with a disability to reject help that is perceived as debasing may be viewed as inconsiderate and ungrateful by a helper (e.g., Buscaglia, 1983).

To shed light on why helping episodes between those with and without physical disabilities can be problematic, this chapter discusses helping as a form of resource exchange. It begins by providing an in-depth look at help between persons with and without disabilities. It then examines the central tenets of resource theory (Foa & Foa, 1974) and illustrates how this perspective relates to helping interactions between persons with and without disabilities. Finally, it suggests communication strategies that both persons with and without disabilities can use to forestall potential problems when the issue of help arises, and suggests future research in communication relating to this topic.

HELP BETWEEN ABLEBODIED AND DISABLED PERSONS

As a result of the experiences of her brother David, the first author became interested in communication between those with and without disabilities. During David's first year of college, he was in a car accident, causing him to become a paraplegic. Not only did he have to become physically adjusted to his disability, but he also had to make social adjustments as well, especially with regard to receiving help. Not having much experience with persons with physical disabilities, the first author's initial response was to try to do everything for her brother, from pushing his wheelchair to bringing him anything he needed. David soon let her know that he valued his independence and needed to learn to do things on his own. As a result, she began to notice that family members and strangers alike were being overly helpful to David. Often, David would grit his teeth and accept this "help" with a smile and gratitude, but at other times he looked enraged. To understand why receiving problematic assistance arises so often in interactions between those with and without disabilities, this author began investigating theory and research related to helping episodes.

Because a norm in Western culture dictates that the ablebodied should "help the handicapped" (Braithwaite, 1990; Heinemann, Pellander, Vogelbusch, & Wojtek, 1981), and persons with disabilities are stereotypically perceived as dependent (Longmore, 1985) and in need of help (Weinberg, 1978), disabled individuals often are given help by well-meaning ablebodied communicators (Braithwaite, 1987, 1990; Braithwaite & Labrecque 1994; Edelmann et al., 1984; Thompson & Cusella, 1988). For the purposes of this chapter, a helping episode is defined as an interaction in which an ablebodied person provides some sort of assistance to an individual with a disability, who then responds in some manner to this assistance. This aid might arise from an explicit request for assistance from the person with the disability, such as "Could you please get that door for me?", or might be unsolicited, in that it was prompted by an ablebodied person's inference that an individual with a disability required assistance (Braithwaite, 1987, 1990). Responses of persons with disabilities to unsolicited help could include expressions of genuine gratitude, polite but feigned appreciation, silent begrudging acceptance of the help, or outright rejection and even condemnation of the assistance (Ladieu et al., 1947).

Assistance may also vary according to how necessary or unnecessary it is. Unnecessary assistance involves giving persons with disabilities help with a task that they could have done by themselves, whereas necessary assistance refers to giving someone help with an action that he or she could not have performed alone (Braithwaite, 1987; Ladieu et al., 1947). Although many helping episodes between those with and without disabilities that involve the above types of help proceed without conflict (Braithwaite, 1987; Thompson & Cusella, 1988), some do not. We next turn to the problematic ones.

The Effect of Unsolicited Help on Persons With Disabilities

Unsolicited help, as opposed to help that is solicited, may cause many of the problems that can occur in helping episodes between those with and without disabilities. If a person with a disability asks for or solicits help, he or she remains in charge of his or her own needs and wants. However, when a disabled person receives unsolicited help, an ablebodied individual has unilaterally decided what this person with a disability can and cannot do. Although unsolicited help can be a valuable resource and could serve as a way to build intimacy with another, some persons with disabilities may see this help as patronizing, condescending, and overcompensating (Braithwaite, 1987, 1990), as a deprecating way of indicating their inferior position (Schneider, Major, Luhtanen, & Crocker, 1996), or as illustrating rejection of them as human beings (Buscaglia, 1983). Unsolicited assistance may also imply that persons with disabilities must rely on ablebodied others, and therefore is "a permanent denial of . . . [the disabled's] rights and dignity as human being[s]" (Gliedman & Roth, 1980, p. 4). Furthermore, unsolicited help may be dangerous to persons with disabilities if they are not expecting it or it is not given properly (Braithwaite, 1987; Ladieu et al., 1947). For example, pulling up a person with a mobility disability who has fallen might hurt him or her physically if not done correctly. Finally, some persons with disabilities report that if an ablebodied interactant does not stop giving them unwanted, unsolicited assistance, especially when it has been rejected, it is likely that any relationship with this person will end (Braithwaite, 1987).

The potential negative effects of unsolicited help on persons with disabilities may be exacerbated if the assistance given was unnecessary. Receiving unsolicited and unneeded assistance prompts greater tension in the recipient, less liking for the helper, and less indebtedness toward the helper than does receiving needed assistance (DePaulo, Brittingham, & Kaiser, 1983). Similarly, unsolicited, unnecessary help can cause a person with a disability to feel embarrassed, inadequate, dependent, or even angry (Braithwaite, 1987), because it may seem that an ablebodied helper automatically assumed the person with a disability was dependent and helpless. However, if the help given was necessary, a person with a disability may be less likely to experience these negative feelings, because he or she would not have been able to perform an action without this help and may have feelings of gratitude or charity toward a helper. Indeed, some individuals with disabilities appreciate unsolicited, necessary help because they are able to avoid the burden and potential embarrassment of having to ask for aid (Braithwaite, 1987). Unfortunately, it may not always be clear to an ablebodied person whether assistance is necessary, and well-meaning, unsolicited help could be unappreciated and even lead to conflict.

The Effect of Unsolicited Help on Conflict

During helping episodes, some persons with disabilities report that they develop negative emotions in response to unsolicited help (Alger & Rusk, 1955; Braithwaite, 1987), and although rare, may even verbalize feelings of anger and resentment to a helper (Braithwaite, 1987). Although such negative disclosures might reflect the desire of a person with a disability to be afforded the same treatment as an ablebodied person, such responses may cause the ablebodied helper to see him or her as ungrateful (e.g., Buscaglia, 1983).

If assistance is refused in an assertive manner, an ablebodied helper may also perceive a person with a disability to be angry, emotionally unstable, and maladjusted (Emry & Wiseman, 1987b). Furthermore, after such a refusal, the ablebodied person may become reluctant to provide future help to persons with disabilities, even if the help was requested (Moss & Page, 1972; Tipton & Browning, 1972). One reason for this reluctance is that in addition to being viewed as dependent and helpless, individuals with disabilities are stereotypically perceived as easily offended and highly sensitive about their disability (Belgrave & Mills, 1981). When a person with a disability refuses help, this stereotype may seem to be confirmed, especially since few instances are required to confirm that an unfavorable trait describes a group (Rothbart & John, 1985). Moreover, even less aggressive responses may be problematic. Ablebodied persons may become angry if persons with disabilities instruct them about how to provide better help (Ladieu et al., 1947). For example, one woman with a visual impairment reports that some ablebodied people become offended if she tells them how best to guide her down a set of stairs or across a street (Shearer, 1981).

Therefore, some episodes between persons with and without disabilities involving unsolicited help may be characterized by miscommunication, which occurs when efforts to communicate something to another person are misinterpreted (Emry & Wiseman, 1987a). Both those with and without disabilities may initially misinterpret the communicative efforts of the other, which results in further misinterpretations on both sides. To examine why this breakdown in communication may occur, we explore helping episodes within the context of resource theory.

RESOURCE THEORY

Looking at helping episodes between persons with and without disabilities from the viewpoint of a social exchange may provide a clear picture of the dynamics involved in such interactions (Braithwaite, 1987). Foa and Foa's (1974) resource theory is based on the principles of social exchange and allows us to understand the viewpoints of both those with and without disabilities in helping interactions. Essentially, this perspective assumes that individuals have cognitive filters that are used to interpret the actions of others. Three of these resources—love, services, and status—are particularly relevant for our analysis. Love constitutes expressions of affection toward another (Foa & Foa, 1974). Services are nonmaterial actions performed for a recipient such as running an errand, holding open a door, or helping a wheelchair user over a curb (Foa & Foa, 1974). Status refers to actions that illustrate that another has done something well, is competent, or whose presence is to be honored (Foa & Foa, 1974). Moreover, resource theory posits that there are two fundamental types of exchanges. In the first, resources are provided to another, but in the second they are denied or taken away. Since resources are perceived entities rather than firmly grounded in the physical characteristics of objects, two individuals may differ as to which resources best describe a given action and as to the type of resource exchange that occurred (Foa & Foa, 1974).

This analysis may be especially useful for understanding helping episodes. When a person with a disability successfully solicits assistance from an ablebodied helper, resources are exchanged. Specifically, when asking for help, a person with a disability acknowledges from the outset his or her lesser competency pertaining to performing an action. Therefore, the helper does not appear to be illegitimately denying the other's status by giving what he or she perceives to be a service. In this case, the help provider probably receives gratitude (status) or affection (love) in return for providing this assistance.

However, the offer or giving of unsolicited help by an ablebodied person may be perceived quite differently by persons with disabilities as opposed to those without. When ablebodied persons give unsolicited help to individuals with disabilities, they perceive themselves to be performing a needed service and perhaps showing their affection toward a person with a disability. After all, they are spontaneously offering assistance rather than waiting for a request. This perception of unsolicited help may explain why ablebodied people often do not realize that some persons with disabilities do not like receiving it (Braithwaite, 1987). Thus, ablebodied helpers expect that their good deed will at least be acknowledged and accompanied by a sign of gratitude (status) or affection (love) from a partner with a disability. They are hurt if such positive responses are not forthcoming. For example, in Braithwaite's study, a person with a disability reports that when she tried to convince an ablebodied helper that she did not need the unsolicited assistance he gave, this help provider "seemed very hurt that I wasn't just very appreciative and (did not) just thank him profusely for doing that" (p. 15). She then said that "we (persons with disabilities) are supposed to be forever thankful to all the wonderful nondisabled people in the world that make our lives miserable in the name of helping us" (Braithwaite, 1987, p. 15).

As this example shows, individuals with disabilities may perceive things differently. Although the ablebodied view themselves as performing a service, or giving to the person with a disability, they may actually be taking status away from them (Foa & Foa, 1974). Thus, rather than characterizing the unsolicited assistance as providing love or a service, some persons with disabilities may interpret it as a denial of status (Ladieu et al., 1947), in that it communicates inferiority and helplessness. This loss of status makes them feel pitied (Braithwaite, 1987; Ladieu et al., 1947). Moreover, some individuals with disabilities may characterize unsolicited assistance as an intense and unpleasant reminder of the limitations placed on them by a physical disability (Nadler, Sheinberg, & Jaffe, 1982). Similarly, Fisher, Nadler, and Whitcher-Alagna (1982) theorized, that a recipient's reaction to aid is directly related to the degree to which the help constitutes a threat to his or her self-esteem. Because societal norms dictate that individuals should be self-reliant, especially within specific domains (e.g., sex role), receiving even needed help may adversely impact a person's feelings of self-worth. Hence, receiving assistance that lowers self-worth should prompt defensive reactions such as refusing help, attributing negative motives for providing assistance, and negatively evaluating the quality of the help (Fisher et al., 1982).

A disabled person's expressed disapproval of unsolicited help may in turn cause the ablebodied person to feel that he or she has actually been denied love or status. Persons with disabilities do, however, realize that an ablebodied helper may want rewards for giving assistance (Ladieu et al., 1947), and will confer these rewards if the emotional and psychological costs of the help are not too high for them (Braithwaite, 1987). These rewards may be bestowed when the person with a disability acts humble and thankful to a benefactor, even although he or she does not truly feel that way (Shearer, 1981). Hiding their true emotions avoids alienating or angering ablebodied persons, which could result in negative relational consequences (Shearer, 1981). However, when persons with disabilities perceive the help to be degrading or a severe denial of status, these costs may become too high, and rewards such as gratitude and affection are not given to a help provider.

The degree to which a person with a disability experiences unsolicited help as a loss of status may depend on characteristics of the helper. Individuals are thought to be most defensive when they receive aid from someone who is either similar or inferior to them. In effect, people feel that they should be able to perform as well or better than the aforementioned individuals and if not, they suffer from "comparison stress" (Nadler & Fisher, 1986). Consistent with this view, individuals are more reluctant to seek help on ego central tasks (e.g., those reflecting intelligence, creativity) from similar rather than dissimilar others (Nadler, 1987). Furthermore, although frequent assistance from a friend on a task not central to ego (e.g., those determined by luck or mood) is responded to quite positively, the opposite is true when the task is central to the recipient's ego (Nadler, Fisher, & Itzhak, 1983). On tasks that are central to the ego, assistance from strangers is less threatening than is that from friends (Nadler et al., 1983).

Another factor that may impact a disabled person's refusal of unwanted help is the age of a helper. People with disabilities report that older people are more likely to give them help than are younger persons (Braithwaite, 1987). In contexts in which advanced age carries with it greater status, receiving help from an older person, who might be viewed as superior, might not create as much defensiveness as would receiving assistance from someone who is younger. Indeed, Searcy and Eisenberg (1992) found the least defensiveness among siblings when they received help from an older, as opposed to a younger, brother or sister.

Possibly, role expectations might attenuate feelings of lost status. Some people with disabilities report that women, as opposed to men, are more likely to give them help (Braithwaite, 1987; Shearer, 1981). Because women are stereotypically viewed as nurturing (Tarvis, 1977), those with disabilities may be more accepting of their help than that of men because such behavior is congruent with their sex role. For example, siblings report being less defensive when receiving assistance from sisters than from brothers, and the least defensive when aid comes from an older sister (Searcy & Eisenberg, 1992).

In summary, the two different views of persons with and without disabilities concerning unsolicited help may result in a communication problem between them. Ablebodied persons perceive themselves to be performing a worthwhile service or even expressing affection to a partner with a disability when giving him or her unsolicited help. Some persons with disabilities, however, may view certain ablebodied helpers as taking away or denying their status through this assistance, and do not reward these helpers for giving it to them. The lack of rewards, such as gratitude or affection, may cause help providers to feel unappreciated and worthless, producing negative feelings toward interactants with disabilities. As a result, both interactants leave the helping episode with negative feelings toward the other.

MANAGING HELPING EPISODES

Communication Strategies for Persons With Disabilities

Braithwaite (1987) found that individuals with disabilities enact four different strategies when they are given or offered unwanted, unsolicited help. The first strategy involves explaining to the helper that he or she has given unwanted aid and why it is unnecessary or not wanted. A second strategy that may be used in a helping situation is for a person with a disability to make a joke of a refusal of help. For example, one man recalls jokingly telling an ablebodied person trying to give him help, "What are you trying to do, steal my glory?" (Braithwaite, 1987, p. 25). A third strategy involves persons with disabilities doing for themselves any action that they perceive a helper is about to perform for them. An example of this strategy might include a person with a disability trying to open a door at a supermarket, and seeing a helper rush toward the door with the obvious intention of assisting him or her to open it. In response, the person with the disability may hurry to open the door before this "helper" can. The fourth strategy includes getting angry with a helper, although this reaction is rare and usually occurs only when other attempts to stop this person from giving aid have failed (Braithwaite, 1987).

From a resource theory perspective, two of the strategies identified by Braithwaite may be particularly useful in unwanted helping episodes. If persons with disabilities can show that this help was not a service by explaining to ablebodied helpers why they did not want or need help with this task, and/or by performing this task by themselves, then the refusal may not be problematic. To examine why these two strategies may be particularly relevant in this context, we look at disabled persons' rejections of unwanted help using these two strategies as social confrontations.

A social confrontation "is a particular kind of communication episode initiated when one actor signals another actor that his or her behavior has violated a rule or expectation for appropriate conduct within the relationship or situation" (Newell & Stutman, 1988, p. 266). In the context of help between persons with disabilities and those without, a disabled interactant's rejection of unwanted help signals to an ablebodied person that this behavior is not appropriate, and the episode between the two partners will continue until the issue of help is dropped. The first step in resolving a social confrontation episode is to establish the legitimacy of the confronter's expectation. Therefore, when a person with a disability does not want unsolicited help, he or she may need to convince an ablebodied helper of the legitimacy of the refusal of assistance so that the relationship is left undamaged. For example, he or she might say "That's all right. I can get it," without undue animosity (Thompson & Cusella, 1988). Such a refusal may communicate to an ablebodied person that the individual with a disability recognizes the offer of help, but can and wants to perform this action unassisted.

Moreover, if the legitimacy of the refusal is established, a relational rule can be developed by these communicators which dictates that unwanted, unsolicited help is unacceptable. An ablebodied helper, however, may not realize the legitimacy of a disabled person's refusal because he or she stereotypically views persons with disabilities as dependent and helpless (Longmore, 1985), and in need of this assistance (Weinberg, 1978). Persons with disabilities may prove that a refusal is legitimate and also illustrate that the help does not constitute a service by (a) taking the time to explain to an ablebodied helper that the help was not needed and they value their independence, and/or (b) showing a helper that they can accomplish this action through physically performing it by themselves. For example, if an ablebodied helper pushes a wheelchair user's chair over a curb, the person with a disability could explain that he or she can perform this action without help and enjoys the independence of doing so. Then he or she could actually push the wheelchair over the curb to prove this point. However, when illustrating the legitimacy of a refusal of help, the nonverbal behaviors of the person with a disability also need to be considered. If the person explains why the help is unnecessary to an ablebodied helper in a sarcastic or angry tone, it could communicate to this helper that he or she is socially incompetent and disliked by the individual with a disability. In addition, if a person with a disability acts offended and makes a grandiose production of performing the action in question him or herself, a helper could again feel disliked and incompetent. Thus, when proving that a refusal of unwanted help is legitimate, persons with disabilities need to ensure that their nonverbal actions are natural and polite to avoid negative repercussions in their relationships with ablebodied helpers.

The above communication strategies, however, assume that a person with a disability can perform the action without help. Even though the person may actually need help performing a particular task, such as a quadriplegic needing assistance to carry a cup of coffee to a table in a coffee shop, we would argue that he or she probably values being able to control when and how this assistance occurs by asking for help. Thus, it may be useful for a person who was given necessary, unsolicited assistance to both let a helper know that (a) this aid did provide a useful service by giving the helper rewards, such as gratitude or affection, and (b) to explain that he or she prefers to ask for help rather than have it be given without warning. Another strategy may include persons with disabilities trying to prevent misunderstandings concerning aid by communicating, in the initial stages of a relationship with an ablebodied person, what kinds of help they consider to be appropriate (Braithwaite, 1987). Alhough this strategy cannot be used if a stranger gives a person with a disability unwanted help, it could be useful in preserving positive interactions and setting up clear expectations at the outset of a new relationship.

Communication Strategies for Ablebodied People

Unfortunately, it is not always clear what an ablebodied person should do if he or she believes a person with a disability needs help. Some persons with disabilities report that it is acceptable for ablebodied individuals to ask them for permission to give help before bestowing it, and others report that ablebodied people should not ask and need to wait to give help until a disabled communicator requests they do so (Braithwaite, 1987, 1990; Braithwaite & Labrecque, 1994). Thus, the decision as to whether to ask for permission to give assistance is often left to the judgment of an ablebodied interactant. However, Braithwaite and Labrecque say that one "rule" an ablebodied person should follow is that if he or she does ask for permission to give help and it is denied, this refusal should be respected and the help in question not given.

Something else the ablebodied should keep in mind is that giving unsolicited help may not be acceptable. However, giving help is generally acceptable if it is indicative of simple politeness (Braithwaite, 1987; Ladieu et al., 1947). For example, it is common courtesy in the United States that when opening a door, you should also hold it open for the person behind you. In this situation it would not appear to be objectionable to give unsolicited help to a person with a disability by keeping the door open for him or her. One rule of thumb that may be useful in determining whether giving an individual with a disability unsolicited help is acceptable, is to ask yourself whether you would give this help to an ablebodied person (Braithwaite, 1987). If the answer is "yes," then this help will probably be agreeable to most people who are disabled.

FUTURE DIRECTIONS FOR RESEARCH EXAMINING HELP

Finally, there are many unanswered issues concerning helping interactions. Future research should focus on three issues.

Determinants of Appropriate Assistance

Researchers must study the nature of "appropriate assistance" more fully. It seems counterproductive and overly simple to urge ablebodied persons to be reluctant to offer or provide assistance to individuals with disabilities (Ladieu et al., 1947). Instead, researchers should help ablebodied individuals discern under what conditions assistance will most likely be appropriate. Within the context of resource theory, it is thought that persons with disabilities perceive help as either a service or a denial of status. Into which of these two categories a person with a disability places this help, however, depends on how he or she evaluates it.

Researchers working within the framework of resource theory often assess the quality of a service by asking individuals the extent to which their partners provide help when it is needed, and the degree to which their partners check their need for resources (Rettig, Danes, & Bauer, 1993). This implies that appropriate aid should match the level of recipient need. Similarly, DePaulo et al. (1983) assert that appropriate help is that which is relevant to a recipient's needs. Indeed, their research indicates that individuals respond more positively to necessary than to unnecessary assistance. However, as noted earlier, it may not be easy to determine the extent to which assistance is required. A person with a disability may be struggling to complete a task, but his or her struggle may not be an indirect request for assistance. Rather, it may simply be a sign that he or she is determined to complete the task. Hence, help from others might be unwelcome.

As mentioned earlier, a second standard that may be used to determine appropriateness is the degree to which the help is ego-threatening, or pertains to a task that is central to the recipient's ego. Presumably, parts of the self-concept are more important to individuals than others and hence, even needed assistance in those areas may be extremely threatening. Just as it may be difficult to determine whether assistance is truly needed, it may be equally difficult to determine the degree to which assistance may be ego-threatening.

Unfortunately, there is limited research concerning how the aforementioned standards are used to determine the appropriateness of help. It is possible that individuals can employ both need and ego-threat when evaluating resources, but in most cases, people use only one of these standards. Perhaps most help providers are primarily fixated on the recipient's apparent need for a service, and they are unaware of the status implications of the assistance. As such they are insensitive to the ego-threat that might result. Conversely, some persons with disabilities may be more aware of their relative status, and hence they are more sensitive to the ego-threat involved with accepting a resource than they are to their apparent need for a service. Regardless, researchers need to validate the differential categorization of resources and evaluation criteria used by persons with and without disabilities.

Means of Providing Nonthreatening Assistance

By recognizing that needed assistance may be perceived as ego-threatening and inappropriate, a second important question is raised for future research. How can the ablebodied provide needed assistance that will not diminish a disabled person's self-worth and stimulate defensiveness? In effect, what can be done to decrease the possibility that giving a service will be perceived as taking away status? Helping research suggests several possible mechanisms that deserve attention. One is the source of assistance. Although intimates are frequent sources of valuable support, in some cases their assistance becomes counterproductive. This implies that the offer of a service might be perceived as a denial of status when made by one person but not when made by another. Clearly, this research suggests that the source of assistance should be adapted to the type being provided.

Scholars have long noted that requests can threaten the face or image of the target (Brown & Levinson, 1978). Similarly, Fisher et al. (1982) speculate that the messages that accompany assistance may signal the help provider's lack of respect for the recipient, and therefore cause the recipient to perceive that the help diminishes his or her status. A number of communication cues might exacerbate feelings of lost status. For example, imperatives (e.g., "From now on, I will take you to rehab") may be inherently more threatening to the disabled person's need for autonomy than indirect offers of assistance (e.g., "Would you like me to take you to rehab?"). Even offers of assistance may become ego-threatening when expressed in a patronizing or condescending tone which implies that the person with a disability is childlike and incompetent. Therefore, identifying nonthreatening ways of offering needed assistance is a critical area of research. Unfortunately, there is limited research that informs as to the possible effects of linguistic and nonverbal cues on how assistance is perceived by persons with disabilities.

Conflict Management Strategies for People With Disabilities

Regardless of efforts to inform ablebodied individuals as to the best means of providing assistance to persons with disabilities, inappropriate assistance will sometimes result. As a result, researchers should identify the best means of managing such conflicts. For example, under what conditions should a person with a disability overlook inappropriate assistance and when should he or she confront the help provider? Because help providers may perceive their assistance to be legitimate and altruistically motivated, the rejection may cause them to feel that their own status has been denied, prompting conflict escalation. If so, what kinds of messages might be used by persons with disabilities that will prevent the inappropriate assistance from occurring again and, at the same time, not threaten the help provider's image? For example, Kubany, Richard, Bauer, and Muraoka (1992) found that "I messages" (e.g., "I am angry") are perceived to be less stigmatizing and aggressive and to provoke less negative emotions than do "you messages" (e.g., "You really make me angry").

Such examples highlight the importance of conducting research on the interactions between individuals with disabilities and the ablebodied persons who wish to provide assistance to them. The analysis discussed in this chapter points to a failure in resource exchange as a fundamental problem for such interactions. Problems often result because persons with disabilities and those without have different perspectives on which resources are being exchanged and whether they are being provided or taken away. Communication can play a central role in reducing the impact of these perceptual differences and resolving the conflicts they stimulate.

DISCUSSION QUESTIONS

1. Think of a situation in which a person with a disability is trying to refuse unnecessary, unsolicited help from an ablebodied individual. How could he or she best phrase this refusal without alienating

the helper? Are there any other strategies this person could use? Why?

2. This chapter discussed how the decision of whether to ask a person with a disability for permission to give help can often be left to the judgment of an ablebodied communicator. How would you make this decision and what criteria would you use to justify it? How would the situation surrounding this helping episode affect your situation?

3. Imagine that you have just asked a disabled person's permission to give him or her assistance, and he or she curtly refused your offer. How would you react (be honest)? What could you do or say to this person so that you could have (or continue to have) a positive interaction with him or her? What would you do the next time this situation arises?

4. Can intimacy between a disabled person and an ablebodied helper (such as a close friendship or a romantic relationship) affect helping episodes? If so, how?

REFERENCES

Alger, I., & Rusk, H. A. (1955). The rejection of help by some disabled people. *Archives of Physical Medicine and Rehabilitation, 36*, 277–281.

Belgrave, F., & Mills, J. (1981). Effect upon desire for social interaction with a physically disabled person on mentioning the disability in different contexts. *Journal of Applied Social Psychology, 11*, 44–57.

Braithwaite, D. O. (1987, November). *"If you push my wheelchair, don't make car sounds": On the problem of "help" between disabled and ablebodied persons.* Paper presented at the annual meeting of the Speech Communication Association, Boston, MA.

Braithwaite, D. O. (1990). From majority to minority: An analysis of cultural change from ablebodied to disabled. *International Journal of Intercultural Relations, 14*, 465–483.

Braithwaite, D. O., & Labrecque, D. (1994). Responding to the Americans with Disabilities Act: Contributions of interpersonal communication research and training. *Journal of Applied Communication Research, 22*, 287–294.

Brown, P., & Levinson, S. (1978). Universals in language usage: Politeness phenomena. In E. N. Goody (Ed.), *Questions and politeness: Strategies in social interaction* (pp. 56–311). Cambridge, UK: Cambridge University Press.

Buscaglia, L. (1983). *The disabled and their parents.* Thorofare, NJ: Slack Inc.

Dahnke, G. L. (1982). Communication between handicapped and nonhandicapped persons: Toward a deductive theory. In M. Burgoon (Ed.), *Communication Yearbook 6* (pp. 92–135). Beverly Hills, CA: Sage.

DePaulo, B. M., Brittingham, G. L., & Kaiser, M. K. (1983). Receiving competence-relevant help: Effects on reciprocity, affect, and sensitivity to the helper's nonverbally expressed needs. *Journal of Personality and Social Psychology, 45*, 1045–1060.

Edelmann, R. J., Scott, A., Scott, J., Singh, E., Trotter, R., & Wright, M. (1984). Disablement and helping. *Psychological Reports, 54*, 453–454.

Emry, R., & Wiseman, R. L. (1987a). An intercultural understanding of able-bodied and disabled persons' communication. *International Journal of Intercultural Relations, 11*, 7–27.

Emry, R., & Wiseman, R. L. (1987b, November). *When helping may not be helpful: The development of learned helplessness in disabled persons.* Paper presented at the annual meeting of the Speech Communication Association, Boston, MA.

Fisher, J. D., Nadler, A., & Whitcher-Alagna, S. (1982). Recipient reactions to aid. *Psychological Bulletin, 91*, 27–54.

Foa, U. G., & Foa, E. B. (1974). *Societal structures of the mind.* Springfield, IL: Charles C. Thomas.

Gliedman, J., & Roth, W. (1980). *The unexpected minority: Handicapped children in America.* New York: Harcourt Brace.

Heinemann, W., Pellander, F., Vogelbusch, A., & Wojtek, B. (1981). Meeting a deviant person: Subjective norms and affective reactions. *European Journal of Social Psychology, 11*, 1–25.

Kubany, E. S., Richard, D. C., Bauer, G. B., & Muraoka, M. Y. (1992). Impact of assertive and accusatory communication of distress and anger: A verbal component analysis. *Aggressive Behavior, 18*, 337–347.

Ladieu, G., Hanfmann, E., & Dembo, T. (1947). Studies in adjustment to visible injuries: Evaluation of help by the injured. *Journal of Abnormal and Social Psychology, 42*, 169–192.

Longmore, P. K. (1985). A note on language and the social identity of disabled people. *American Behavioral Scientist, 28*, 419–423.

Moss, M. K., & Page, R. A. (1972). Reinforcement and helping behavior. *Journal of Applied Social Psychology, 2*, 360–371.

Nadler, A. (1987). Determinants of help seeking behavior: The effects of helper's similarity, task centrality and recipient's self esteem. *European Journal of Social Psychology, 17*, 57–67.

Nadler, A., & Fisher, J. D. (1986). The role of threat to self-esteem and perceived control in recipient reaction to help: Theory development and empirical validation. In L. Berkowitz (Ed.), *Advances in experimental social psychology* (Vol. 19, pp. 81–122). New York: Academic Press.

Nadler, A., Fisher, J. D., & Itzhak, S. B. (1983). With a little help from my friend: Effect of single or multiple act aid as a function of donor and task characteristics. *Journal of Personality and Social Psychology, 44*, 310–321.

Nadler, A., Sheinberg, L., & Jaffe, Y. (1982). Coping with stress in male paraplegics through help seeking: The role of acceptance of physical disability in help-seeking and -receiving behaviors. In C. D. Spielberger, I. G. Sarason, & N. A. Milgram (Eds.), *Stress and anxiety* (Vol. 8, pp. 375–384). Washington, DC: Hemisphere.

Newell, S. E., & Stutman, R. K. (1988). The social confrontation episode. *Communication Monographs, 55*, 266–285.

Rettig, K. D., Danes, S. M., & Bauer, J. W. (1993). Gender differences in perceived family life quality among economically stressed farm families. In U. G. Foa, J. Converse, Jr., K. Tornblom, & E. B. Foa (Eds.), *Resource theory: Explorations and applications* (pp. 123–156). San Diego: Academic Press.

Rothbart, M., & John, O. P. (1985). Social categorization and behavioral episodes: A cognitive analysis of the effects of intergroup conflict. *Journal of Social Issues, 41*, 81–104.

Schneider, M. E., Major, B., Luhtanen, R., & Crocker, J. (1996). Social stigma and the potential costs of assumptive help. *Personality and Social Psychology Bulletin, 22*, 201–209.

Searcy, E., & Eisenberg, N. (1992). Defensiveness in response to aid from a sibling. *Journal of Personality and Social Psychology, 62*, 422–433.

Shearer, A. (1981). *Disability: Whose handicap?* Oxford: Basil Blackwell.

Tarvis, C. (1977). Stereotypes, socialization, and sexism. In A. Sargent (Ed.), *Beyond sex roles* (pp. 178–187). St. Paul, MN: West.

Thompson, T. L., & Cusella, L. P. (1988). Help between disabled and ablebodied persons: An exploratory observational study of a feedback system. *Journal of Applied Communication Research, 16*, 51–68.

Tipton, R. M., & Browning, S. (1972). Altruism: Reward or punishment? *Journal of Psychology, 80*, 319–322.

Weinberg, N. (1978). Modifying social stereotypes of the physically disabled. *Rehabilitation Counseling Bulletin, 22*, 114–124.

Wertlieb, E. C. (1985). Minority group status of the disabled. *Human Relations, 38*, 1047–1063.

5

Opening Up Spaces for Difference Via a Feminist Phenomenological Approach to Disability

S. Marie Westhaver
Carleton University

Keywords: Communication, disability, feminism, phenomenology, embodiment

Communication scholars have long recognized that differences between people are frequently experienced as sources of difficulty in maintaining relationships. However, they have only recently begun to examine what happens to relationships when those differences are narrowed to those who are physically differentiated. Research on disability has traditionally focused on barriers created by physical variance to be overcome to further integration of persons with disabilities into society. These persons are seen as the source of much anxiety and discomfort for ablebodied strangers who encounter them (Braithwaite, 1996; Coleman & DePaulo, 1991; Wright, 1960).

Communication researchers are still in the early stages of revealing the nature of overlapping personal, sociocultural, and historical structures and their impact on the abilities of ablebodied and, to a greater extent, differently abled individuals to express the full nature of their gendered identities. As Fine and Asch (1981) note, women with disabilities are economically, socially, and psychologically significantly more disadvantaged than either

ablebodied women or men with disabilities. I argue that a feminist phenomenological approach (also in an early stage of development) enables
us to explore the tensions that exist at the most commonplace levels of
relationships experienced by women with disabilities.

A feminist phenomenological approach reveals the ways in which the
everyday experiences of women with disabilities connect to the larger social and cultural levels to either open up new spaces for differentiation or
to maintain and perpetuate inequalities based on difference. Thus, the purpose of this chapter is to show, through an analysis of the "body talk" of
women with disabilities, how this perspective provides the critical linchpin
in revealing how women with disabilities accept, maintain, contest, and
transform societal meanings of disability within the parameters of their
lived everyday experiences.

A three-step phenomenological process (description, reduction, and interpretation) is explicated and applied in analyzing themes emerging from
women's personal experiences of disability. Five participants in an earlier
study are women born with physical disabilities who range in age from
21 to 36 years. One of the participants is paraplegic, and another has a
differentiated gait. Of the three remaining participants, who are visually
impaired, one has congenital albinism causing her hair to appear white in
color. All are white, middle class, and heterosexual. Thus, issues of race
and class did not emerge in the interviews.

Open-ended questions were asked of the participants during face-to-
face audiotaped qualitative interviews. The questions were designed to
help access their lived experiences of inhabiting differentiated physiques.
For example, they were asked: "How do you see yourself as a woman
with a disability?" Other questions included asking for their descriptions
of times when they felt especially accepted as women with disabilities
as well as times when they felt especially threatened. An analysis of the
themes emerging from their responses constitutes the basis for understanding how a feminist phenomenological perspective allows access to the impact of communication in connecting women with disabilities to the public
world.

Before I begin this exploration of women's lived experiences of disability, I want to address my position as a researcher within the research
process. Researchers need not conduct studies from a detached, disinter-
ested, and objective stance but as passionately involved participants who
acknowledge personal and social change as goals of the study (Treichler,
Kramarae, & Stafford, 1985). Hence, it is important that I acknowledge my
position with respect to my own lived experiences of physical disability.

Having been born with one arm, my earliest childhood memories are punctuated by reflective moments when I considered the responses of others to my differentiation. My responses to inquiries about my "arm" entail assuring people who assume that life must be quite a struggle for me that I am managing very well. Although manageable, my limitations emerge more from my scoliosis (curvature of the spine) and a back injury I experienced as a runner in my early twenties. But it is my visible disability that most draws attention and elicits curiosity.

A lifelong interest in hearing others' stories of disability has led me to realize just how rich and varied our narratives are as well as the fact that we share many commonalities. I am a white, middle class, heterosexual woman who is striving to broaden my horizons of exposure. As a researcher with disabilities, I am struck by the fact that women indicate how rarely they have a chance to talk about their thoughts and feelings about disability.

As women narrate their experiences of disability, they challenge and transform the presuppositions attached to problems they encounter every day. The personal is political. The political is personal.

PHENOMENOLOGY AND THE LIVED BODY

Recently I invited a group of communication scholars to close their eyes and I asked them: "What do you think of and what do you 'see' when you hear the words 'physical disability'?" As expected, their responses entailed taken-for-granted images of disability—"wheelchairs," "handicaps," and "visually impaired persons." Indeed, it is the exterior of the differentiated body that most draws attention in the dominant societal discourse surrounding disability.

Communication scholars have traditionally followed Goffman's (1963) theory that physical variance is a stigmatizing marker which negatively influences interactions between individuals with a disability and the ablebodied. The question for communication researchers following a phenomenological approach is one of introducing thoughts and feelings surrounding the meanings of disability to bring the participants closer to their descriptions of their lived experiences. This must be done in such a way so as not to deepen the divide between the exterior and the interior of the body in order to comprehend their intimate relationship.

Phenomenologists acknowledge that the body is not an object or machine within which the body and mind are divided. Humans are embodied.

This means that the body and mind are one fully present and indivisible unity referred to as the lived body. As Trinh Minh-ha (1989) pointed out: "We don't have bodies. We are body" (p. 34). For phenomenologists, knowledge of disability is grounded in the lived experiences of inhabiting a variant body which is problematized as a site of struggle over the meanings of differentiation. Individual notions of difference, then, are multiple, conflictual, and filled with tensions surrounding the sociocultural–political situations undergirding them.

A founder of phenomenology, Husserl, directed us to "go to the things themselves" (1900/1970, p. 270). This theme guides the phenomenologist who is interested in disability and the manner in which it appears to consciousness, thereby providing the access to experience. Phenomenology as a method is a rigorous and systematic means of explaining the meanings of experiences as they are lived. The researcher follows a three-step process (description, reduction, and interpretation) that is synergistic in nature, meaning that the methodology entails each step as a part in a whole. The very entailment makes the whole larger than the sum of its parts (Lanigan, 1988, p. 8). For communication theorists, one interpretation of Husserl's directive is to go to the everyday worlds of individuals to faithfully describe their experiences of living with physical variance.

WHAT FEMINISM AND PHENOMENOLOGY DO FOR DISABILITY RESEARCH

Both phenomenology and feminism situate the personal in the research process. They take as foundational the primacy of lived experience (our being-in-the-world) as the data of the human realm (Langellier & Hall, 1989, p. 195). Feminism extends phenomenology in that it seeks to empower women and thereby honors the validity and primacy of women's lived experiences in their everyday lives as a resource for knowledge. The feminist perspective establishes gender as a major element studied—a lens through which all other perceptions pass.

Nelson (1989) argued that "the ultimate task of phenomenology is to describe, define, and interpret both the personal and political not as different kinds of experience, but as the experience of different levels of consciousness" (p. 227). Where feminism and phenomenology intersect, they mutually enhance the conduct of this research because, as Langellier (1994) asserted, feminism "situates phenomenology within numerous critical, consciousness-raising discourses about gender, race, class, and other social hierarchies" (p. 66).

Probyn (1991) argued that we can find "ways of speaking our bodies" wherein we "use the body with attitude, to defiantly put the body forward as an image within discourse" (pp. 110–111). In other words, we can speak our bodies in ways that empower us from places within the societal terrain as varied as they are unique. We can fully introduce the lived body into the research process to arrive at a sense of how women with disabilities respond to the shifting discourse of disability—how it influences their bodily styles.

In a moving phenomenological investigation of Diane DeVries, a woman born without limbs, Frank (1988) described the relationship of a woman with her body and her use of it while exposing gaps in evaluations of her adjustment. "For me," Frank said, "the encounter with Diane challenged my adherence to the conventional linkages among physical normalcy, beauty, sexuality, and social integration" (p. 67). Frank also recalled that "The encounter with Diane further evoked an image of mythic beauty, the Venus de Milo, which it should be remembered, is the portrait of a goddess" (p. 67). This study serves as a stepping stone for communication scholars not only to extend and challenge our understanding of preformed notions of adjustment under the rubric of embodiment but also, as Frank suggested, to frame a feminist discourse on the experiences of disability that are taken for granted.

SKETCH OF A FEMINIST PHENOMENOLOGICAL APPROACH

The following section provides a very brief sketch or outline of the major steps of the feminist phenomenological approach which, as stated earlier, entails contextualizing a phenomenological methodology within a feminist framework of being true to the phenomenon of women's experience. Data from a previous investigation is used to explain the three stages (description, reduction, and interpretation) in the order that they can be followed in explicating lived experience through a phenomenological study. A summary is given of part of the data from the study to show how the stages are rigorously followed.

Description

In the first stage, known as description, it is critical that through a process known as bracketing (epoché) the researcher suspends all prejudgments about the lived experience of disability to describe the phenomena as they are lived. Phenomenological description focuses on the phenomena and how they show themselves (Langellier, 1994, p. 78).

Description allows us to "hear" the voices of the participants through a reporting of the talk itself. We are interested in researching the gendered phenomenon of disability so, for example, interviews conducted for the purpose of this study pose questions that enable us to obtain descriptions of living as a woman with disability. The questions open doors to new worlds rich with meanings, and the text of the body talk of the participants is, in turn, grouped into units of meaning or nonrepetitive thematic topics with many variations in the themes. For example, several themes emerge in this study, some of which include conflict over self-identification as a person with a disability as well as conflict surrounding acceptance of the differentiated body in relationships with romantic partners.

A powerful theme that emerges in studies of disability in the field of communication is that of identity. There is much to learn about how multiple and volatile the issue of identity is—how fluctuating and conflictual it can be not only for women with disabilities but also for those closest to them on a deeply personal level. In this chapter I briefly explore the themes surrounding difference, embodiment, and relationships with romantic partners while contextualizing them within the broader scope of the study. No real names are used in the themes. I use ellipses to indicate the removal of talk that does not contribute to the meaning of the statement.

Theme 1: Not Different. In this theme, the participant describes herself as a person with a disability.

> Normal. Normal. There's nothing different. I really don't think there's anything different about me. . . . When you think about it, everybody is different in some way whether they have a disability or not. Everyone looks different but we're all the same you know. That's the way I feel. I'm just sitting down all the time. That's it.

Theme 2: Different. Another female participant who has a differentiated gait recalls the first time she saw herself on video in her early adulthood.

> It was shocking. It was surprise. Disappointment I guess where I always thought I didn't look half-bad. I was kind of disappointed when I first saw myself walk because the reality hit. Wow! Are you that different and didn't know it? I mean I didn't feel any different inside, but it was like I knew I was different then. Before that I had no idea. . . . I had never really considered myself 'a disabled person'. . . . It was like wow! You are different. You are

definitely a disabled person.... It was like wow! There goes some of my self-confidence. I don't feel as good about myself as I used to.

Theme 3: Rejection.

I was the class joke.... Any guy that dated me was going to take crap for it and he did—boy did he. He got in more than one fight over me.... Somebody wrote in the coat room behind his jacket... "Love is blind and so is Anna.".... Joe beat the guy up for it and back then it did hurt me. I took it as an insult.

I think a few of his friends were like well "Well what are you doing with her?" type thing.... He just basically you know—"You don't judge a book by it's cover" he said and "You just don't look at their outside," he said "because if anybody judged yous [*sic*] guys by your outlook yous [*sic*] would have nobody."

Theme 4: Acceptance. The participants speak of their relational partners' expressed acceptance of them, which they in turn interpret as being confirming of them to differing degrees. One participant describes her relational partner as not privileging the exterior of the body ("He's the kind of person who looks beyond the physical with people and he's great, he looks at people the same way I do... which is who they are not what they look like"). She considers her partner's concept of beauty "relative" ("I knew I was the homeliest girl on the planet") and qualifies his judgments as singularly different from others by indicating that he overlooks her differentiation ("To him—it didn't matter") in favor of qualities essential to identity that others refuse to see.

A second participant says that she is valued as beautiful by her partner:

He makes me feel that I'm actually satisfying someone out there but he's not you know—somebody out there—that he's not settling like himself [*sic*] for second best or just for what he can get.... He always tells me that I'm beautiful—pretty.

Another participant observes:

He doesn't make me feel different at all. He doesn't notice the chair except when he has to put it in the car. He makes me feel beautiful and sexy—all of those things. It's just my whole person is just so wonderful.... Just finally there's a man out there who's going to accept me for what I am and I don't have to change anything.

Theme 5: Skepticism. The participants remain skeptical of their desirability on an ongoing basis. One compares herself unfavorably with the "really good lookers." ("I wonder to myself... you know... am I deserving? Like... am I what he wants in a woman?") Another questions her partner's judgment. ("What did he see in me? What's he even doing with me?"). She wonders whether he would rather be with another woman who belonged to "the normal population."

One participant describes an encounter with one of the most popular boys in high school, who put his arm around her while walking her home from school.

> I thought that he was just being a jerk.... That he was kidding around with me... and he even asked me out. I thought yeah right.... I didn't believe someone like that.... I thought if anyone is interested in me it's a joke.

Reduction

In the second or reduction stage of this study the researcher identifies and explicates the essential features or underlying organizing structures that help make sense of the five thematic topics found in the description stage. Through the technique of free variation the researcher reflects on the themes and imagines their features "as present or absent within the context of the whole to determine which are essential and which belong together as variations of the phenomena" (Langellier, 1994, p. 78). It is most important to note the impossibility of a complete reduction that identifies all variations of the phenomenon being analyzed.

Reduction reveals two essential features (sites of resistance and sites of acquiescence) undergirding the participants' body talk, which center around difference. All of the participants focus on societal categories of difference with respect to their visible, exterior qualities and their invisible, interior qualities associated with the mind. We can never completely separate ourselves as relational individuals from a dominant social code. But as the participants speak their bodies on an individual level, sites of resistance and acquiescence to the societal code of disability are evident.

Sites of resistance are evident in Themes 1 (Not Different), 4 (Acceptance), and 3 (Rejection). In these three themes the participants and their relational partners express a willingness to conceptualize their bodies on their own terms at the individual level rather than that of a social collectivity. But where negative societal attitudes toward the differentiated body are assumed on individual levels to varying degrees, as in Themes 2 (Different), 3 (Rejection), and 5 (Skepticism), sites of acquiescence are evident.

For example, where sites of resistance can be identified in Themes 1 (Not Different) and 4 (Resistance), the participants define and conceptualize their differences so that there is a leveling out of differences. In Theme 1, disability is seen as being one marker within a multiplicity of markers which is, in turn, shared by most people ("I'm not different"). The participant describes herself in terms of activity ("I'm just sitting down all the time") rather than in terms of deficient body parts. In this way she reclaims her body discursively, giving new meanings to disability that privilege rather than devalue her.

Similarly, in Theme 4 (Acceptance) the participants speak their bodies so as to gain control of their positioning on a social level while collapsing the boundaries between disability and ableism. They indicate that their relational partners find their differentiated physiques aesthetically pleasing ("He always tells me that I'm beautiful") while privileging both interior and exterior qualities ("It's just my whole person is just so wonderful"). Restrictions are overlooked ("He doesn't notice my chair"). Her partner's assurance that he does not find her physical qualities "different" bolsters the confidence of one participant that he is not settling for second best.

Another unit of meaning emerges in Theme 4 (Acceptance) that appears at once to be both a site of resistance and acquiescence. One participant states that, like herself, her partner "looks beyond the physical" in considering her to be beautiful. She acknowledges people for "who they are," which is based on interior features. Resistance to essentializing normalcy based on cultural standards of physicality is shown but at the expense of showing regard for the exterior of the body. Looks do not count—seemingly at all. This devaluing of physical attributes as important can be seen as acquiescing to an extent to assumed societal devaluing of the differentiated body ("I knew I was the homeliest girl on the planet").

Moreover, where sites of resistance are evident in Themes 3 (Rejection), 2 (Different), and 5 (Skepticism), a very strong sense of judgment prevails whereby differentiated bodies are rejected outright—cast away bodies. For example, in Theme 3, negative responses to the participants' bodies ("What are you doing with her?") elicit a felt need to establish authority over critics by turning the tables on them. One relational partner retaliates ("You don't judge a book by its cover") while suggesting to them that they are critically lacking in their outlook—an interior quality. Yet in privileging the interior body in this way at the expense of the outside, he appears to acquiesce to an extent in his friends' denigration of her body. In another instance, the verbal violence of the opposition ("Love is blind and so is Anna") is silenced by using physical violence ("Joe beat the guys up for it").

Issues of authority over the variant body also emerge in Theme 2 (Different). This is a theme of profound loss wherein the participant abandons her previous views of her body when she sees herself on video for the first time. She conceptualizes her body for the first time from a stigmatizing dominant societal stance. Her newly found categorization of her body as "disabled" results in a loss of her self-confidence and self-esteem.

In much the same way, the participants in Theme 5 (Skepticism) cast themselves in an unfavorable light of differentiation. Seeing themselves in contrast to "the really good lookers," the "two percent of the normal population," "the norm," they assume their relational partners may also see them as inferior. They acknowledge that their partners could do better than to be with them ("It must be a joke") ("What does he see in me?"). Lacking in self-confidence they question their worthiness to be chosen as partners.

Interpretation

Langellier (1994) described the task of phenomenological interpretation as being "to reflect on the description and reduction in order to explicate meanings not immediately apparent in the phenomenon" (p. 70). Interpretation, therefore, requires reflection in this way on the body talk of the participants surrounding disability. The central signifiers "I felt different/I felt disabled" and "I'm not different/I'm not disabled" emerge within the meanings they attach to the dominant discourse of difference. In this third stage, the researcher identifies underlying multiple pairs of binary oppositions or oppositional clusters of meanings. They represent hidden cultural codes that "organize the flow of value and power" (Scholes, 1985) in the body talk of the participants.

In this section, four of these binaries are explicated against the larger context of feminist theory as well as other communicative and cultural discourses. I show how they influence the bodily styles of the participants as they define themselves in terms of their exterior qualities or in terms of their intellects and emotions and at other times as a composite of both mind and physicality. These four binaries that are particularly relevant to the lived experiences of the participants are ability–disability, mind–body, masculinity–femininity, public world–private world. These polarities are not clearly defined but overlap and are rather blurred and inconsistent.

Fine and Asch (1992) asserted that the social construction of femininity and disability entails that the biological can only be understood within those contexts and relationships that shape and give meaning to femaleness and disability (p. 144). Interwoven throughout the body talk of the participants are notions of how they are situated in relation to regulatory cultural codes of femininity and ableism. The power dynamics inherent in those codes determine which bodies are discursively sustained and therefore seen and to what degrees they are present in their discourse.

For example, within all of the themes is found an emphasis on a hierarchical mind–body division familiar in Western culture. This duality is gender-based, in that the devalued outer body is associated with women and is subordinate to the privileged mind, which is aligned with masculinity (Currie & Raoul, 1992). Spitzack (1993) contended that women's bodies are under constant surveillance not only by men but also by women who critique the feminine form for its lack of conformity to cultural standards.

Gayle (1992) reflected on the objectification of marginalized women thusly: "As objects, one's reality is defined by others, one's identity created by others, one's history named only in ways that define one's relationship to those who are subject" (p. 238). Moreover, Lonsdale (1990) asserted that women with disabilities are defined primarily by their physical conditions (p. 82). The participants in the study discussed earlier in this chapter indicate that their physical variance was a focal point of attention marking them as "disabled." What is at stake for them in being defined and hence objectified as "disabled" is that outside of this label they are not "seen" as whole human beings.

As body–object, Young (1990) observed, the body is looked at and acted on (p. 150). The participants' narratives in Themes 1 (Not Different), 2 (Different), 3 (Rejection), 4 (Acceptance), and 5 (Skepticism) reveal their awareness of being gazed on and responded to as body–objects. They indicate a learned sensitivity to being categorized as different so that their variant physiques are seen as barriers to what is authentically their essence— their minds. But in Theme 4 (Acceptance) is also found descriptions of the body–subject wherein the mind, body, and self are a unified entity—a lived body. Here self-affirmations are used to describe positive evaluations of their lived bodies.

Where notions of body–object undergird the body talk of the participants, it is replete with commentaries on rejection and alienation. For example, in Themes 2, (Different), 4 (Acceptance), and 5 (Skepticism), there is a sense of the participants experiencing masculine judgment of their aesthetic worthiness in a cultural courtroom filled with female defendants ("I knew I was the homeliest girl in the school"). The most central aspects of their relationships both intrapersonally ("I wonder . . . what does he see in me") and with others ("I thought if anyone is interested in me it's a joke") indicate an awareness of the public character of their differentiated bodies, and they respond with a kind of discrediting self-assessment.

Particularly in Theme 2 (Different) the description of the experience of difference is shocking in its distortion of the history of the body of the participant and subsequent self-alienation. As body–object, the participant subsumes her identity into a category called "disabled." Suddenly, her ways of knowing herself are informed by deeply rooted social values assumed when she sees herself from a dominant cultural view. Similarly, in Theme 4 (Acceptance), there is a kind of concealment of an integral part of the body ("He looks beyond the physical"), and although the physique is not overtly rejected, what is essentially meaningful about the body is located in the mind.

Moreover, Schwictenberg (1989) observed that a specific ideology of beauty represents certain abstract properties as constants in various concrete ways, for example, through various kinds of beauty culture data. Value is placed on achieving a certain "look," often that of an "ideal image" such as that of a movie star. Although women know full well the look is manufactured, they continue to invest in it.

Indeed, it is the emotional investment of the participants in the notion of satisfying societal criteria of their attractiveness that limits and restricts their possibilities for loving and enjoying their bodies. Wolf (1991) spoke of societal censorship of "real women's faces and bodies" (p. 17). Wherever overriding assumptions of variance are expressed as negative, an integral part of the body is concealed—its energy is depleted and diverted into an ongoing struggle with rejection and alienation.

An integral component of the narratives of the participants is the multiple indications of their positioning, as women with disabilities, even within the private world of intimate relationships, in a dimension of shared disempowerment that erodes their beliefs that their bodies count. Wendell (1989) contended that careful study of the lives of the disabled will reveal the artificiality of the line drawn between the biological and the social because much of what is disabling about physical conditions is socially constructed. The world is structured to support the ideally shaped—the ablebodied—such that there exists a split between the public and private worlds. Women, children, the disabled, sick, and the old are relegated to the private world. The ablebodied (the positive, valued body) youth, performance, and production all comprise the public world, the world of strength (p. 111).

The tensions between the private and public worlds of which Wendell (1989) spoke are evident in Theme 3 (Rejection). Here the variant body is acted on ("What are you doing with her?") where a need exists to put the differentiated body in its place (the private). Measured against a yardstick of ableism, the participants fall short of the ideal and are reminded that they represent a failure to achieve normalcy. Furthermore, the violence evident in the responses of others to their selection as partners is profoundly striking and disturbing.

Attempts are made to reposition the women, to keep them outside the boundaries of normalcy as though they are both an affront to masculinity and also the ideal. Also unsettling is the retaliatory physical violence ("Joe beat the guys up for it") and insults conveyed by friends to the women's partners. Issues remain unresolved, whereas the overriding prejudice associated with categories of difference is not alleviated.

Where the differentiated body is seen as body–object in Themes 2 (Different), 3 (Rejection), and 5 (Skepticism), the participants respond to competing discourses of disability in ways that restrict the parameters of their embodied existence. But in Themes 1 (Not Different) and 4 (Acceptance), these parameters expand where the view of the body–subject undergirds the body talk of the participants. For example, the Theme 1 participant describes herself as "just sitting down all the time" and thus reframes the marginalizing frame of reference characterizing individuals as "different." or "disabled." In this way she places herself closer to the center, where her experience of difference would be culturally acceptable and she would be "seen" more holistically.

Similarly, in Theme 4 (Acceptance) the participants describe their relational partners as not differentiating between visible and invisible qualities in expressing appreciation of them ("He tells me that I'm beautiful"). Where notions of "beauty" become part of the corporeal text in this theme, the cultural boundaries between ableism and disability appear more fluid and inconsistent. Also, the participants see their partners' response to them ("He always tells me you know like that I'm beautiful—pretty"), ("He makes me feel beautiful and sexy—all of those things") as validation of their bodily attractiveness. For the partners of both participants, notions of beauty based on regulatory, normative ideals that denigrate difference are resisted as physical differences are positively valued, thereby rendering their differentiated physiques equal status to that of other women.

CONCLUSION

As women with disabilities speak their bodies, new sites of spoken discourse give rise to an understanding of the lived experience of inhabiting a differentiated body as conflicting and multidimensional. Within the everyday lives of women with disabilities are constant reminders of their position as outsiders in the discursive arenas within which ableism and femininity are ideals. Their bodies are under siege aesthetically as they pursue the most ordinary activities taken for granted by other women such as courtship and marriage. Even within loving, caring relationships these women struggle to maintain their ground as it continues to be eroded by their internalization of cultural standards of the ideal.

Where victories over negative societal attitudes are won in reframing the discourse of disability, possibilities are presented for creating new and transformative meanings of physical disability. The interpretation of the participants' body talk in this chapter links oppositional practices of "speaking the body" to empowerment. However, as Langellier (1994) observed: "Oppositional practice is not revolutionary movement; personal empowerment may not be matched by structural, institutional change" (p. 71). But as women courageously share their stories of living in differentiated bodies, the possibilities for more differently abled women to affirm themselves as whole biological and social beings become even greater. Communication researchers can help to slay the discursive dragons.

Further communication research in this area needs to uncover ways to further the understanding of how issues of class, race, gender, and ability intersect to challenge women with disabilities in their everyday lives. Also, there is an urgent need for communication scholars to respond to support women with disabilities in their everyday lives by offering them communicative strategies for response to negative and devaluing remarks conveyed to them.

In my research I have found that women with disabilities not only describe very limited opportunities to talk about their lived experiences of inhabiting a variant physique but also little reflection on how they and others talked about their bodies. Those of us in the field of communication, as well as women with disabilities in general, must open up spaces for difference wherever possible by initiating discussion of the conflicts and gains of living with disability. We are in a position to heighten sensitivity toward differentiation and increase respect for and acceptance of the same for both men and women with and without disabilities.

At the same time, women in general and particularly women with disabilities must not await permission from others to love and accept their bodies. We who live with variance must give ourselves approval from within while living in a society that tends to turn away from difference in various discursive arenas particularly in the public world. In speaking our bodies, we help to build ripple effects of positive body talk that contribute overall to a more sustaining discourse of disability. By inhabiting our variant bodies with attitude, we help to assist other women with disabilities to express their wholeness and their authenticity while creating a discursively nourishing oasis for the world in which we all must live.

DISCUSSION QUESTIONS

1. What comes to mind when you think of "disability"? Take a moment to think. Close your eyes and see the word "disability" in print. What thoughts and feelings emerge during your reflection? What meanings underlie your responses?
2. If the dominant societal attitude toward disability were to become positive overall, how would this affect the lives of women with disabilities?
3. How do our assumptions about the relationship between our minds and bodies influence our attitudes toward disability?

REFERENCES

Braithwaite, D. O. (1996). Understanding communication of persons with disabilities as cultural communication. In L. A. Samovar & R. E. Porter (Eds.), *Intercultural communication: A reader* (pp. 148–154). Belmont, CA: Wadsworth.

Coleman, L. M., & DePaulo, B. M. (1991). Uncovering the human spirit: Moving beyond disability and "missed" communications. In N. Coupland, H. Giles, & J. M. Weimann (Eds.), *"Miscommunication" and problematic talk* (pp. 44–61). Newbury Park, CA: Sage.

Currie, D., & Raoul, V. (1992). The anatomy of gender: Dissecting sexual difference in the body of knowledge. In D. H. Currie & V. Raoul (Eds.), *Women's struggle for the body* (pp. 1–36). Ontario: Oxford University Press.

Fine, M., & Asch, A. (1981). Disabled women: Sexism without the pedestal. *Journal of Sociology and Social Welfare, 8,* 223–48.

Fine, M., & Asch, A. (1992). *Disruptive voices: The possibilities of feminist research.* Ann Arbor: University of Michigan Press.

Frank, G. (1988). On embodiment: A case study of congenital limb deficiency in American culture. In M. Fine & A. Asch (Eds.), *Women with disabilities: Essays in psychology, culture, and politics* (pp. 41–72). Philadelphia: Temple University Press.

Gayle, N. A. (1992). Black women's reality and feminism: An exploration of race and gender. In D. H. Currie & V. Raoul (Eds.), *Women's struggle for the body* (pp. 232–242). Ontario: Oxford University Press.

Goffman, E. (1963). *Stigma: Notes on the management of spoiled identity.* Englewood Cliffs, NJ: Prentice-Hall.

Husserl, E. (1970). *Logical investigations* (Vol. 1; J. N. Finley, Trans.). New York: Humanities Press. (Original work publihsed, 1900)

Lanigan, R. L. (1988). *Phenomenology of communication: Merleau-Ponty's thematics in communicology and semiology.* Pittsburgh, PA: Duquesne University Press.

Langellier, K. M. (1994). Appreciating phenomenology and feminism: Researching quilt making and communication. *Human Studies, 17*, 65–80.

Langellier, K. M., & Hall, D. (1989). Interviewing women: A phenomenological approach to feminist communication research. In K. Carter & C. Spitzack (Eds.), *Doing research on women's communication: Perspectives on theory and method* (pp. 193–220). Norwood, NJ: Ablex.

Lonsdale, S. (1990). *Women and disability: The experience of physical disability among women.* New York: St. Martin's Press.

Nelson, J. L. (1989). Phenomenology as feminist methodology: Explicating interviews. In K. Carter & C. Spitzack (Eds.), *Doing research on women's communication: Perspectives on theory and method* (pp. 221–242). Norwood, NJ: Ablex.

Probyn, E. (1991). The body which is not one: Speaking an embodied self. *Hypatia, 6,* 116–122.

Schwictenberg, C. (1989). The "mother lode" of feminist research: Congruent paradigms in the analysis of beauty culture. In B. Derwin, L. Grossberg, B. J. O'Keefe, & E. Wartella (Eds.), *Rethinking communication: Paradigm exemplars* (pp. 291–306). London: Sage.

Scholes, R. (1985). *Textual power.* New York: Vail-Ballou.

Spitzack, C. (1993). The spectacle of anorexia nervosa. *Text and Performance Quarterly, 13,* 1–20.

Treichler, P. A., Kramarae, C., & Stafford, B. (1985). Section 3: On boundaries. In P. A. Treichler, C. Kramarae, & B. Stafford (Eds.), *For alma mater: Theory and practice in feminist scholarship* (pp. 197–198). Urbana: University of Illinois Press.

Trinh, T. M. (1989). *Women, nature, other. Writing postcoloniality and feminism.* Bloomington: Indiana University Press.

Young, I. M. (1990). *Throwing like a girl and other essays in feminist philosophy and social theory.* Bloomington: Indiana University Press.

Wendell, S. (1989). Feminism, disability and transcendence of the body. *Canadian Woman Studies, 13*(4), 116–122.

Wolf, N. (1991). *The beauty myth.* New York: Doubleday.

Wright B. A. (1960). *Physical disability: A psychological approach.* New York: Harper & Row.

II

People With Disabilities in Organizational Settings

6

Effective Communication to Enhance Special Education

Ida Malian
Ann Nevin
Arizona State University West

Keywords: Individualized Education Plan (IEP), Education of All Handicapped Children Act (EHA), Individuals with Disabilities Education Act (IDEA), mediation, collaboration, consultation, Life Space Interview

One out of every five people with whom we communicate is likely to be a person with a disability. What does this mean for effective communication between adults? We should expect that our communication with the ordinary American public will involve a person with a disability on a relatively frequent basis. In fact, about 20% of the total U.S. population recently reported that they had a disability (President's Committee, 1994). *Disability* was defined by the Bureau of the Census as having difficulty in performing one or more functional or daily living activities, or one or more socially defined roles or tasks.

People who work in educational settings encounter children with disabilities. According to the *Sixteenth Annual Report to Congress on the Implementation of the Individuals with Disabilities Education Act* (1990), there were over 4 million disabled children between the ages of 5 and 21 who were educated during the 1992–1993 academic year. Of these 4 million children, the types of disabilities with the highest incidence included students with specific learning disabilities (51.3%); students with speech or language impairments (22.9%); students with mental retardation (11.6%); and students with serious emotional disturbance (8.4%).

Where were these students enrolled? The predominant placement for these students was in the resource room (36.5%) and the regular classroom (32.8%), which means that 69.3% of the students with disabilities were in settings with students without disabilities. A "resource room" is defined as a specially equipped and managed setting where a teacher with special training instructs students who are assigned to go there at designated times for assistance in some aspect of learning or guidance (Kelly & Vergason, 1978). Approximately 25% of students with disabilities were enrolled in separate classes and less than 6% were enrolled in separate schools or residential facilities (U.S. Department of Education, 1994).

What does this mean for effective communication? Most educators know that they must adapt their language to communicate effectively with children at various stages of cognitive development. That is why the first-grade teacher talks a little slower, uses simpler vocabulary and syntax, and includes gestures and facial expressions more often than the high school teacher. However, when educators communicate with students with disabilities like learning disabilities, speech or language impairments, mental retardation, or emotional disturbance, more elaborate adaptations and accommodations must be made. This also means that students without disabilities will be communicating with students with disabilities, given that nearly 70% of the students with disabilities are enrolled in either resource rooms or regular classrooms. Systematic practice in effective communication skills is required for all students.

The purpose of this chapter is to introduce the reader to the underlying laws, legislation, and litigation that guide much of the formal and informal communication among educators and students, parents, and professionals alike. In addition, a framework for creating a community of psychodynamic communication is described, followed by examples of research on the best practices. These practices yield more effective communication, which enhances the outcomes for students with special education needs.

LAWS, LEGISLATION, AND LITIGATION REGARDING COMMUNICATION MANDATES

The field of special education has both the advantage and the disadvantage of being governed by federal, state, and local school district mandates. The advantage is that there are overarching federal guidelines that mandate specific procedures, processes, and rights to be provided to students eligible for special education by and through the parents. The disadvantage is the national data indicating that paperwork is the prominent cause of burnout in teachers (Fimian, 1988). With the mandates come paperwork documenting the processes for all agencies, teachers, and parents.

Through a series of federal legislation targeting educational reform for exceptional students, a culminating law was passed in 1975: Public Law 94-142—the Education of All Handicapped Children Act (EHA). Much of the momentum of the act evolved during the Kennedy administration, when a greater awareness of individuals with handicaps was present than had been the case in the past. Consequently, the 94th Congress' 142nd bill was passed in 1975 providing, for the first time, sanctions against school districts that do not provide free and appropriate public education for students with disabilities. The federal law also provided some nationwide consistency in terms of planning for services for students with disabilities. The EHA and its reauthorization, the Individuals with Disabilities Education Act (IDEA), provide for direct communication between parents, teachers, and other professionals involved in the education of the student. The continued active involvement of parents in the identification, instructional, and evaluation process of their students is highlighted in the law. The district must communicate all intents to change the educational program of students in special education. Further, informed consent is underscored at all junctures of the special education process.

A critical concept is that of an appropriate education. The concept of "appropriateness" and how it is communicated has led to controversy and litigation. The law has been interpreted to mean than an appropriate education is one that is in accordance with an individual education plan (IEP) that is agreed to by parents, educators, and other specialists. Others interpret it to mean "best." Consequently, many disputes concern communication and interpretation of private school (best) versus public school (appropriate) special education. Thus, the essence of communication in special education can be achieved by following the mandated IEP format.

The IEP as a Communication Tool

In essence, communication between school district personnel and parents can be achieved by the mandated IEP format. This communication should include (a) understanding of the present level of academic and nonacademic capabilities of both the student and the school; (b) determination of the goals of the conversation; (c) listing of related data that will serve as the foundation for communication; and (d) a review to check for understanding among parents and district.

Communication should begin with an understanding of the present level of academic and nonacademic capabilities of both the student and the school. By focusing communication on the perspectives of the parents (e.g., possible anxiety about the team meeting or anger about the timelines), positive communication can be established by district personnel who suggest that the parents bring a friend to the meeting. Similarly, if district personnel are anxious that parents may be making "unreasonable" demands or are angry that several other meetings have been postponed, then it may be advantageous to hold a session prior to the IEP meeting where problems between both parties and possible solutions are clearly identified.

Using the goals and objectives mandate of the IEP can create a focused purpose for communication. A brief list of what might be accomplished at the team meeting may facilitate the interaction, particularly if both parties share the list. Both parents and district personnel must determine what ancillary data each needs to bring to the conversation. Specific examples of student work (both at home and at school), direct classroom and home observations of behaviors, and verbatim listing of student comments will facilitate a more objective conversation. Finally, a review of the major points of the conversation should occur to check for understanding, clarify if necessary, and to develop action steps for future discussion.

Using the IEP mandates as benchmarks for communication can establish an immediate linkage and common language for the parents and district. Eventually this can lead to more informed team meeting participation on the part of the parents (Thousand, Villa, & Nevin, 1997).

CREATING A COMMUNITY OF PSYCHODYNAMIC COMMUNICATION

In this section we discuss five concepts from the psychodynamic field that promote an understanding of what is needed for effective communication in the special education context: stages of communication, problem solving, collaboration, consultation, and mediation.

Stages of Communication

Erikson (1963) proposed a theory of development that highlights the psychodynamic elements influential in learning and communication. Erikson considered all aspects of the individual as contributing to understanding. Communication between individuals and professionals involved in the education of students with disabilities parallels Erikson's theory. Progress through each stage is sequential and serves as the foundation for the next stage. Each stage represents a polarity with specific issues to be resolved if the communication interaction is to proceed effectively to the next stage.

The first stage or polarity to be resolved is acquiring a sense of trust while overcoming a sense of mistrust. Overcoming mistrust can be accomplished through predictability of actions and communication. The laws mandating written notice and parental involvement at all stages of the special education process facilitate this predictability.

The second stage presents the communication task of acquiring a sense of autonomy while overcoming a sense of shame and doubt. Parents at various stages of grieving the "loss" of a "normal" child may experience a sense of shame. This perception can affect communication with professionals. Furthermore, parents may doubt their communicative abilities and sense professional intimidation.

Attaining a sense of responsibility while overcoming a sense of guilt may present an additional challenge in communication. Parents may assume a great deal of guilt for the disabilities of their child. They may reflect on their school years and remember many of the disabilities that they may feel then went unnoticed. Team meetings with parents emphasizing joint educational responsibility to implement the developed educational plan for the students may establish a foundation for collaboration and individual responsibility at school and at home.

Acquiring a sense of industry and overcoming inferiority presents another challenge for communication. Parents may feel inferior to the professionals, who have various educational degrees. Acknowledging that the parents know the child best and that all parties have the best educational interest in mind will allow the industry of the educational planning to flourish.

Establishing a sense of identity while overcoming a sense of identity diffusion presents a challenge of acknowledging the parent and district personnel as equal team members with unique contributions according to their roles on the team. The clear delineation of identities while communicating will result in a more collaborative exchange.

Problem Solving

Problem-solving communication skills are foremost in the repertoire of professionals involved with the education of students with disabilities. It is especially important for students to learn that there is more than one solution to each problem, as they tend to choose repeatedly the same solution no matter what the nature of the problem. To avoid this tendency, parents and professionals alike need to explore a variety of instructional design and behavioral management solutions and to model effective problem-solving skills for students.

Educators have made frequent use of Gordon's (1980) six-step model of problem solving, adapted from Dewey's reflective thinking process (e.g., Bormann & Bormann, 1996). This six-step model suggests that participants (a) identify the problem (analyze the issues in objective terms); (b) generate all solutions (brainstorm as many ideas as possible without evaluation); (c) evaluate the consequences of the solutions (discuss and prioritize positive and negative aspects of each solution); (d) select a mutually agreed on solution (find the best possible solution acceptable to all parties); (e) implement the solution (develop a very specific implementation plan); and (f) evaluate the solution (plan a date to check back and evaluate the solution implemented. If the solution is not working, go back to the list of possible solutions or generate a new solution and implement).

Special communication Challenges When Using the Problem-Solving Approach.   Communication challenges exist in the problem-solving model, particularly in the first two steps. At the problem definition step, the actual problem must be identified through an open and honest process. If this critical hurdle is not overcome, the wrong problem or a fictitious problem may be posed. This will not solve the existing problem and may create new layers of problems.

At the second step (solution generation), there may be preconceived solutions that individuals have implemented and found effective for them in the past. This retrofitting of a solution to a problem negates the existing problem. New solutions may be difficult to generate, possibly leading parties to believe that there was not a problem after all. The discomfort and angst regarding the process needs to be addressed.

Solution redundancy may also occur. Many students with emotional and behavioral disabilities tend to have one solution in their repertoire, which they use for all problems. Examples include running away, hitting, or fighting when faced with a conflict. This pattern eventually will result in the same unacceptable consequence for the student, such as loss of privileges. At this step of generating all possible solutions, it is necessary to be innovative and creative and to look at problems from new perspectives that do not rely on the familiar solution. The next step allows for evaluation of the proposed solutions.

Still another challenge is provided when some parties come to premature closure. Once a particular solution is suggested that is acceptable to the party, the remainder of the steps are seen as superfluous.

Consultation

Consultation is a form of communication in which a person with specialized knowledge or expertise provides information and advice to another person who needs that knowledge. In educational settings, consultation communication can occur between teachers and psychologists, speech/language therapists, administrators, rehabilitation counselors, social workers, and so on.

In an educational context, consultation generally follows a series of steps similar to the six-step problem-solving process described here: entry into the consultation situation, problem identification, problem analysis, plan implementation, plan evaluation, and termination of the consultation relationship (Heron & Harris, 1993). Educational consultation can be characterized as relying on a one-way, expert-to-novice communication pattern.

Programmatic and conceptual barriers that affect school-based consultation have been identified by Johnson, Pugach, and Hammittee (1988). Programmatic barriers to effective consultation include lack of time to consult or lack of administration support. Conceptual barriers include lack of credibility of the specialist, a misperceived hierarchical relationship, and knowledge/skills differences between professionals and parents. Overcoming barriers takes effective collaboration skills that are discussed next.

Collaboration

West and Idol (1987) compared various consultation models (expert, advocacy, mental health, and medical) and found that teachers prefer a more collaborative model. Collaboration is a form of communication in which each person is considered to possess unique knowledge and expertise that is of value to all others in the interaction; this includes teachers, parents, students, advocates, and the like. In a collaborative communicative interaction, each person can serve in the "expert" role at one time or another.

Collaboration relies on the concept of *parity*, a condition in which each person is perceived to be an equal and is treated with respect. The communication interactions are reciprocal, multidimensional as distinguished from the typically one-way unidimensional patterns found in consultation.

Within a special education context, collaborative models emphasize a dynamic interactive partnership process comprised of six basic elements (Idol, Nevin, & Paolucci-Whitcomb, 1994; Nevin, Thousand, Paolucci-Whitcomb, & Villa, 1990). Team members (e.g., IEP team members such as classroom teachers, parents, specialists) (a) view each other (including students) as having unique, valuable expertise; (b) meet each other often; (c) take turns in leadership roles and agree to meet commitments; (d) practice the important skill of reciprocity (equal give and take); (e) focus on interpersonal communication skills, such as paraphrasing and encouraging contributions, that help the team achieve their tasks and maintain positive interactions among the team members; and (f) agree to consciously learn social interaction and communication skills, such as conflict management and public agenda building, to make the consensus-building process more effective.

The results of a more collaborative approach to problem solving have been well documented at the administrative level (Villa & Thousand, 1996) and the instructional level (Thousand, Villa, & Nevin, 1994). Benefits include shared ownership of problem definitions and solutions that come from participatory decision-making processes; shared knowledge and expertise as specialists and generalists interact with each other (sometimes called "role release"); increased cohesiveness and willingness to work together on future projects because of a past history of working together (even if the previous project was not a total success); and new conceptualizations or more inventive solutions because of mutual stimulation of higher level thinking processes. The result is improved services to students with disabilities. Parents who participate on teams where these elements are present report similar improvements (Thousand et al., 1997).

Mediation

Mediation is a form of interaction where an impartial person attempts to identify issues between others with the goal of deriving a mutually agreeable resolution. Mediation typically occurs during ceased negotiations, such as strikes, or when parents and school personnel cannot communicate effectively. In a typical special education communication conflict (e.g., a disagreement between parents and a specialist about a particular method of instruction or a disciplinary–behavior management approach), an impartial individual may be helpful in mediating the conflict. The key to mediation is that both communicators agree to find a mutually agreeable resolution. At times this may be a solution that both parties can "live with" rather than the "ideal" solution. No value judgments or decisions are rendered by the mediator. However, the option of having mediators is not always possible. Therefore, using a mediation approach toward understanding the other party and considering alternative solutions can facilitate conflict resolution when communication problems occur. Formally, mediation is an alternative to due process procedures that parents and advocates may invoke when unresolved issues remain regarding IEP details (Arizona Department of Education, 1992).

PRACTICAL APPLICATIONS

In this section we describe current practices that promote effective communication between various communicators in educational settings: teacher to student, student to student, professional to professional, parent (and advocate) to professional, and parent to student.

Teacher–Student

Jones (1987) developed a model that stresses individual responsibility and student self-control. Many theorists previously had emphasized the importance of verbal communication, but Jones was the first to highlight nonverbal communication within the context of classroom management. Jones' key elements are the effective use of body language, providing incentives that motivate target behaviors, and efficiency in individual assistance for students. The focus here is on nonverbal communication.

Jones (1987) defined body language as including eye contact, physical proximity, body carriage, facial expressions, and gestures. Using these nonverbal behaviors appropriately can facilitate or hinder communication between teachers and students. They take on a greater significance for children with mental retardation and children with learning disabilities, who may not be as sophisticated in picking up on nonverbal gestures as students with behavior disorders or students with emotional disabilities.

Mutual eye contact is the key to communicating with students with disabilities. Effective teachers develop a "roving eye" to periodically scan the classroom for pockets of problems. Typically, the teacher can identify quadrants in the room to scan and will engage select students with eye contact. Students who are off task or confused often tend to avoid eye contact, but once they know that the teacher has "locked in" on them and that their behavior is being observed, they will often unconsciously begin to behave more appropriately. Of course, teachers must also be sensitive to the possible influences of cultural heritage and ethnic differences where avoiding eye contact can be a sign of respect for elders (Thomas, Correa, & Morsink, 1995).

Similar to eye contact, physical proximity to the student demonstrates the immediacy of the situation and need for communication. Being close to the student can facilitate more personal exchange (Charles, 1996; Redl, 1959). Depending on the distance between the teacher and the student, the nature of the communication can change from public reprimand, which may lead to humiliation, to a more respectful, private (even silent, due to proximity) cue to redirect behavior.

Facial expressions convey enthusiasm, disappointment, excitement, and also lack of comprehension of communication. Communicators who are engaged in eye contact search the face for other clues to an understanding of the conveyed conversation. Students, teachers, and professionals need to be aware of subtle clues in the facial expressions of the other person in order to stop and clarify if necessary; to provide an opportunity to inquire; and to express a direct opinion regarding the immediate topic. Some students with behavioral disabilities are adept at "reading" teachers' facial expressions and then inferring the gesture as a positive or negative reinforcer.

Finally, gestures can represent signals for the student to gain self control without direct behavioral encounter. A finger snap, a hand up, or a wave can constitute what Redl and Wattenberg (1959) called "signal interference." This is a signal to interfere with the escalation of negative behaviors or inappropriate conversation.

The recognition of nonverbal communication patterns within special education settings can enhance or inhibit communication between teachers and students with disabilities and with their parents and other professionals. Another example of using a nonverbal communication system with special education students is reported by Hodgson (1997), who incorporated sign language and gestures for classroom management of students with autism. Pictorial and color-coded representations of all aspects of classroom management appeared to facilitate the transitions of students from one activity to another.

The Life Space Interview (Morse, 1963, 1965; Redl, 1959) is a classic alternative used to improve teacher-student communication. Basically, the Life Space Interview occurs between the student and teacher who explore factors involved in a conflict. The Life Space Interview is not punitive but rather corrective of future behaviors. The Life Space Interview has been found to be effective in improving communication with students with emotional disturbance and behavior disorders. Because the principles of Life Space Interview seem to transcend disabilities and age, it is a valuable communication tool for special education teachers. Brenner (1967) identified 10 tenets of the Life Space Interview process.

1. Be polite, because often when individuals are faced with a conflict, they behave defensively. Basically, extend the same courtesy to the child that would be extended to an adult. For some students with disabilities, this may be their first encounter with an adult communicator who is respectful of their special needs.
2. Don't tower over the child. Speak to the child at eye level so that a perception of authority or intimidation does not exist and one of mutuality does.
3. At the appropriate time confront the child with the misdeed. This involves an objective statement of what happened. If possible, delineate the antecedents to the event, the exact behavior in response, and the consequence that logically resulted.
4. Use "why" sparingly. It is difficult to explore the actual reasons a behavior occurred and often the student will say "I don't know." This may be an accurate response for a student who has hyperactivity, emotional problems, or otherwise acts impulsively.
5. Listen to the student. Nonverbal as well as verbal acknowledgments of the student's feelings and disclosures facilitate continued communication.
6. If the child is overwhelmed, statements referring to the commonality of misbehaviors among students may divert the immediate pressure from the student.
7. Paraphrase what the student is saying and bring the conversation to the next more meaningful level. Interjection of values such as "you are feeling disappointed" may be appropriate with select students.
8. Avoid "wishful thinking," which Almy (1961) classically described as projecting adult thoughts of positive resolution onto the student. For example, a teacher might think, "Of course this child can figure it out; after all I've taught him the basic skills."
9. Help the student develop positive steps to improve the situation.
10. At some point, give the student the opportunity to ask questions.

An example of using a similar approach in an instructional context is provided by Echevarria and McDonough (1995), who researched an instructional model that relies on conversation. These researchers documented the benefits of using an interactive instructional conversation approach to improve the reading skills of students in a bilingual special education setting. Rather than focusing solely on remediation of deficit areas, "the instructional conversational approach does appear to provide additional learning opportunities within a meaningful context" (p. 108). The elements of an instructional conversation include (a) focus on themes rather than discrete decoding; (b) invitation to elaborate (e.g., "Tell me more about __" rather than "What color is the coat in the story?"); (c) connected discourse between student and teacher (rather than one way from teacher to student); and (d) a challenging but positive affective atmosphere. The researchers found increases in oral participation and student-to-student interactions during reading lessons (e.g., turn taking, increased oral expression, and initiation of conversations).

Student–Student

One of the most annoying challenges faced by teachers is student-to-student communication. Teachers often overhear less than desirable communicative interactions between students, or students often come to their teachers with problematic situations. These are not just annoying problems like tattling or complaints about who said what to whom. The communication problems after school or at recesses often result in violent interactions, such as intimidation, bullying, assault, and drive-by shootings. Johnson and Johnson (1995) reported that "violence is becoming so commonplace in many communities and schools that it is considered the norm rather than the exception" (p. 3). Such negative interactions are exacerbated when students communicate with peers who have disabilities. Without explicit interventions and guided practice, students with disabilities can become social isolates, outcasts, or scapegoats. For example, Love and Malian (1997), in a statewide study of graduates of special education programs, found that many graduates and their parents reported incidents of scapegoating and ridicule.

There are two major methods of improving communication among students. The first method is comprehensive, in that it deals with schoolwide policies that result in all teachers, staff, students, and community members creating a safe environment wherein problem-solving methods are used to negotiate conflict. Peer mediation programs, such as *Teaching Children to Be Peacemakers* by Johnson and Johnson (1991), are examples of a comprehensive intervention. Another example is *The Bullying Prevention Handbook* by Hoover and Oliver (1997). These comprehensive curricula have several features in common: step-by-step strategies for understanding the nature of conflict; role playing for guided practice of communication skills for smoothing, compromising, and confronting; and counseling for handling anger and other emotions before, during, and after conflicts.

An example of a comprehensive classroomwide curriculum is reported by Kelly (1994), who used class meetings as a way of improving student-student communication. The disruptive behaviors of students with disabilities (e.g., those with emotional disturbance, behavior disorders, and/or attention deficit hyperactivity disorder) can often be inadvertently reinforced by the reactions of classmates. Class meetings provide a forum for the teacher and students to discuss how any student's behavior is affecting them and the constructive actions that can be taken. Through skillful direction of the conversation, the teacher and students avoid focusing only on negative behaviors or attributes. The alternative responses students learn include (a) expressing concern and empathy, (b) being consistent in responding to inappropriate behavior, and (c) being coached and reinforced to express appropriate responses to undesired behaviors. As Kelly noted, "Class meeting problem solving is premised on the notion that a solution does not necessarily make a problem 'go away.' Instead, a solution is a temporary accommodation and adjustment in how the school system can meet the needs of the individual child" (p. 108).

The second method is individualistic, in that it focuses on explicit teaching of the communication skills needed by students with and without disabilities to negotiate conflict. The classroom management strategy of cooperative group learning can be helpful in explicit teaching of social skills along with academic skills. For example, Brewster (1990) developed a lesson plan to teach "friendly disagreeing" skills as part of a social studies lesson. The children are taught that there are at least five ways to disagree in a friendly way: to ask for a different opinion, to ask others to explain why, to add on or to modify another person's ideas, to offer alternatives, and to state the nature of the disagreement. In addition, children are explicitly taught that the tone of voice, gestures, and facial expression are as important as the cognitive content of their message. Using these ideas, Conn-Powers (1994) integrated a fifth-grade boy with gifts, talents, and challenging interpersonal behaviors into a mathematics lesson by teaching him to disagree in a friendly way. For example, all the children were taught to ask for a different opinion by saying with a happy face and an interested tone of voice, "Can you give me another idea?" Another example that all the children learned was to add on or to modify a classmate's ideas by showing a questioning face and tone of voice and asking, "How about if we added this idea?" The most challenging example (one that took longer for the children to use) is to learn to state the disagreement clearly, using a neutral tone of voice and friendly face by saying, "Here's why I think this way." Not only did the boy participate meaningfully during a class discussion but also he used the friendly disagreeing skills in a tether-ball dispute at recess.

Professional–Professional

Professionals need to constantly reflect on their beliefs and values regarding the education of students with disabilities. Idol et al. (1994) suggested that, because the attitudes and feelings people have about themselves tend to determine the nature of a personal and/or professional relationship, a prerequisite to positive and effective communication is an awareness of one's own attitudes about individuals with disabilities, their families, the services that are needed, and other professionals that are involved in the team.

Professionals can share in the use of IEP terminology, which forms a common ground for discussions about goals and objectives, to build on the strengths identified in the assessments to remediate need areas. The IEP, therefore, facilitates communication because (a) everyone is using the same terminology (e.g., resource room, goals, objectives); (b) everyone is using common timelines (e.g., annual reviews); and (c) everyone describes strengths and weaknesses across the various disciplinary assessments.

Villa and Thousand (1994) described a cooperative team approach that involves explicit communication between special educators and classroom teachers who practice the new role of "team teaching" to accommodate students with special needs. A 30-minute agenda for coteaching team members takes participants through each of the stages of group development. It provides a structure for the participants to engage in specific communication skills that are designed to facilitate task achievement (such as public recording of decisions or coordinating the agenda) as well as maintenance of positive personal relationships (e.g., encouraging contributions or celebrating small steps toward task achievement). Villa and Thousand (1994) remind us that it may take a cooperative education team some time to become as effective and efficient as it would like to be:

> The task of educating an increasingly diverse student population can be overwhelming. No one teacher is capable of successfully meeting this challenge alone. We propose that collaboration among students (through cooperative learning structures) and adults (through cooperative education teams) is a key to meeting the challenge of educating a heterogeneous student population. (Villa & Thousand, 1994, p. 100)

Parent–Professional

Communication among parents and professionals takes many forms. For example, parents often participate in informal classroom activities such as birthday celebrations or formal activities such as tutorials. Parents and teachers communicate formally during parent–teacher conferences or more informally at after-school activities. Parents of students with differing abilities, however, must face the sometimes intimidating challenge of communicating with a variety of professionals during IEP meetings. The research on parent participation during IEP meetings leads to the dismal conclusion that parents are typically on the receiving end of one-way communication from the professional to the parent (Thousand et al., 1997). There are several variables that can positively influence the quality, efficacy, and satisfaction of parent–professional communication.

First, the prevailing professional perceptions of the primarily passive role of parents can be changed to the perception of an active role for parents when a more collaborative communication model is used. Second, professional assumptions about the essentially subordinate or dependent nature of parental participation can be changed to the assumption of a partnership nature with explicit training. Third, professional decisions about working "for" parents can be changed via awareness training to a decision about working "with" parents. This change can also lead to decreased labeling of parents as disabled or blaming parents as ineffective just because one of the children has a disability. Fourth, the professional emphasis on the similarities between families with and without children with disabilities can be encouraged, with the resulting effect of a more inclusive sense of community. Fifth, parent perceptions that professionals have all the power can be changed to a partnership relationship.

Parents and professionals working in special education settings are setting new standards for achieving more active and meaningful parental involvement, especially when they (a) agree to work in a problem-identification/solution-generation atmosphere; (b) consciously learn and practice communication skills; and (c) use strategies explicitly designed to include parents. There is scant research about increasing participation and partnerships among parents of students with disabilities from ethnically and linguistically diverse cultures.

Another limited research area is inclusion of students with disabilities themselves in the communication loop. Although it is required by legal mandate to include students who are 16 or older, it is permissible, where appropriate, to include younger students. Indeed, there are some brave IEP teams who include students with disabilities and their ablebodied peers in the decision-making processes. Villa and Thousand (1996) described various communication roles that students might practice: (a) plan and deliver peer tutorials, (b) serve as a student voice on school committees, (c) plan instruction with specialists so that a more normal experience is provided, and (d) help others to make friends. An example of what can happen when students are included comes from Countryman and Schroeder (1996), who reported how middle school teachers included students when holding parent–teacher conferences. Evaluation data were so supportive they decided to maintain the practice. Improvements included honesty in reporting, empowerment for students to own their educational programs, and improved student–teacher, student–parent, and parent–teacher relationships.

Parent–Student

Two models highlighting parent–student communication that have direct and positive impact on students with disabilities and their parents are the congruent communication process (Ginott, 1965) and Parent Effectiveness Training (Gordon, 1975). Ginott's model is based on congruent communication or communication that addresses the child's situation rather than his or her character and personality. For example, a parent would say, "I did not like what you did" (focusing on the action) instead of saying, "I think you're being hateful" (focusing on the character of the child). The definitive parent–child communication text by Ginott refers to "sane" messages as communication that relates to actions of the child. Therefore, the sane message would communicate a statement of the appropriate behavior rather than anger with the student. This is critical to students with disabilities, whose behaviors are often impulsive. The sane message would underscore the behavior, coupled with a corrective statement for future behaviors. For example, "I would prefer you to play the music more quietly" rather than "You are inconsiderate."

Students with disabilities often perceive situations differently from their parents. Ginott suggests that acceptance and acknowledgment of students' feelings and perception is a critical first step to effective communication. Paraphrasing a student's feelings and accepting those feelings as real for the student is an effective way to build trust and communicates acceptance. For example, a parent might say, "I know Ann was your best friend, and I know you are going to miss her" instead of saying, "What do you care that she's moved? You are good at making new friends."

Ginott also discussed the concept of conferring dignity on students. Usually effective during a stressful situation, conferring dignity acknowledges and supports the efforts of students in their work. The fact that a student failed an examination yet came to school during a traumatic period can be acknowledged as a tremendously brave effort, rather than magnifying the failed exam.

Ginott's recommendations are supported by the objectivity principle, which is a hallmark of Gordon's (1975) Parent Effectiveness Training. Gordon stressed the importance of active listening, which requires both parent and student to be active participants in the relating and listening process. For example, an active listening substitute to, "I don't care what other parents do, you have to clean your room" could be "I understand that other parents are different; however, we all have responsibilities here." Gordon discussed three structures for communication between parents and children. The first is represented as an authoritarian structure, where parents are the sole communicators of decisions to their children. The second structure is the antithesis; the laissez-faire model suggests a passive style of communication on the part of the parents, where the majority of decisions are made by the children. The model of choice is the democratic structure, where parents and children are mutual communicators and problem solvers.

ISSUES IMPACTING EFFECTIVE COMMUNICATION IN SPECIAL EDUCATION

Communication researchers and other professionals can provide many contributions to empower more effective communication among those who work in educational settings. The communication potential of many students and adults with disabilities can be enhanced through technology itself. Such devices as print-to-voice readers for the blind and reading disabled, telecommunication for the deaf and hearing impaired, and voice-activated computer-assisted writing systems can transform the communicative interactions of people who have previously been noncommunicative. However, technology-enhanced communication presents challenges for those teachers, students, parents, and others who are technophobes or those who do not have access to the technology itself.

The changing functions of schooling also present exciting challenges to communication professionals. Special education has heretofore been characterized as providing a continuum of placement options ranging from general education classroom with support from specialists, to resource room, to special class, to special school, to residential and homebound (or other forms of institutions like prisons) settings. Nevin, Villa, and Thousand (1992) proposed the creation of a constellation of services, in which individualized supports and special services are brought to the child and family rather than the child and family having to go to the services. Social service agencies set up accessible offices in the local schools to provide welfare distribution, health care, probation officers, rehabilitation counseling, job training, parent training, and postsecondary education screening and learning opportunities. Imagine the communication demands that such a constellation of service providers presents to the layperson: specialized vocabulary, unique interview and data collection guidelines, arcane eligibility requirements, and overworked professionals trying to communicate with clients who are often fatigued, stressed, anxious, and distrustful of the professional. What can communication professionals offer those who want to establish an effective constellation of services?

Teacher education programs present a unique challenge to communication researchers and practitioners. Most teacher education programs omit explicit preparation for teachers in the area of communication, with the exception of speech classes. Think of the typical 6-hour school day during which one teacher communicates with 30 students without benefit of training in the most effective ways to enhance that communication. Specifically, teacher education programs need to require candidates to complete courses in the curriculum that allow knowledge, skills, and practice in the area of communication, infuse communication skills throughout the curriculum, and develop required evaluation of effective communication skills during directed internships prior to teacher certification.

Students with and without disabilities in those classrooms represent the future of our world. They will mature to take their places in government as senators and representatives, judges and bureaucrats, presidential staffers and diplomats. They will become attorneys, physicians, teachers, sanitation engineers, prison guards, and inmates alike. In addition, they will become parents of the future generation of school children. In short, they represent both the future recipients and beneficiaries of effective communication in special education. Educational personnel in general and special educators in particular need a viable active partnership with communication researchers and other professionals to ensure an enhanced future for all.

DISCUSSION QUESTIONS

1. Why is the IEP "a communication tool" between school professionals and parents?
2. What are two problem-solving processes that might facilitate the IEP process? Discuss at least three interactions that facilitate these IEP processes.
3. When might "mediation" be used to facilitate improved communication (a) between professionals; (b) between students with and without disabilities; and (c) between parents and professionals?
4. What are two major methods for improving communication among students with and without disabilities? Why are both methods needed?
5. Choose two of the five variables that can positively influence the quality, efficacy, and satisfaction of parent–professional communication. Delineate how you will use these variables to create communication that results in "more active and meaningful parental involvement."

REFERENCES

Almy, M. (1961). Wishful thinking about children's thinking? *Teacher's College Record, 62*, 396–406.

Arizona Department of Education. (1992). *Arizona mediation handbook*. Phoenix, AZ: Author.

Bormann, E. G., & Bormann, N. C. (1996). *Effective small group communication* (6th ed.). Minneapolis, MN: Burgess.

Brenner, M. (1967). Life Space Interview in the school setting. In H. Clarizio (Ed.), *Mental health and the educative process: Selected readings* (pp. 238–243). Chicago: Rand McNally.

Brewster, D. (1990). Friendly disagreeing. In D. Johnson & R. Johnson (Eds.), *Creative controversy: Intellectual challenge in the classroom* (pp. 543–547). Edina, MN: Interaction.

Charles, C. (1996). *Building classroom discipline: From models to practice* (4th ed.). New York: Longman.

Conn-Powers, C. (1994). Upper elementary mathematics for a student with gifts and talents. In J. Thousand, R. Villa, & A. Nevin (Eds.), *Creativity and collaborative learning: A practical guide for empowering students and teachers* (pp. 143–152). Baltimore: Paul H. Brookes.

Countryman, L., & Schroeder, M. (1996). When students lead parent-teacher conferences. *Educational Leadership, 53*, 64–68.

Echevarria, J., & McDonough, R. (1995). An alternative reading approach: Instructional conversations in a bilingual special education setting. *Learning Disabilities Practice, 10*, 108–119.

Erikson, E. (1963). *Childhood and society* (2nd ed.). New York: W. W. Norton.

Fimian, M. (1988). *A longitudinal study of teacher trainee and teacher stress and burnout: Project summary*. (ERIC Document Reproduction Service No. ED 215 489).

Ginott, H. (1965). *Between parent and child*. New York: Avon.

Gordon, T. (1975). *Parent effectiveness training*. New York: Plume.

Gordon, T. (1980). *Teacher effectiveness training*. New York: Plume.

Heron, T., & Harris, K. (1993). *The educational consultant: Helping professionals, parents and mainstreamed students* (3rd ed.). Austin, TX: Pro-Ed.

Hodgson, L. (1997). *Improving communication: Providing supports for school and home*. Troy, MI: Quire.

Hoover, J., & Oliver, R. (1997). *The bullying prevention handbook*. Bloomington, IN: National Educational Service.

Idol, L., Nevin, A., & Paolucci-Whitcomb, P. (1994). *Collaborative consultation* (2nd ed.). Austin, TX: Pro-Ed.

Individuals with Disabilities Education Act. (1990) 20 U.S.C. 1400 *et seq*.

Johnson, D., & Johnson, R. (1991). *Teaching children to be peacemakers*. Edina, MN: Interaction.

Johnson, D., & Johnson, R. (1995). *Reducing school violence through conflict resolution*. Alexandria, VA: Association for Supervision and Curriculum Development.

Johnson, L., Pugach, M., & Hammittee, D. (1988). Barriers to effective special education consultation. *Remedial and Special Education, 9*, 41–47.

Jones, F. (1987). *Positive classroom discipline*. New York: Macmillan.

Kelly, B. (1994). Student disruptions in the cooperative classroom: Experiences in a New Brunswick, Canada, School District. In J. Thousand, R. Villa, & A. Nevin (Eds.), *Creativity and collaborative learning: A practical guide to empowering students and teachers* (pp. 103–114). Baltimore: Paul H. Brookes.

Kelly, L., & Vergason, G. (1978). *Dictionary of special education and rehabilitation*. Denver, CO: Love.

Love, L., & Malian, I. (1997). What happens to students leaving secondary special education services in Arizona? Implications for educational program improvement and transition services. *Remedial and Special Education, 18*, 261–269.

Morse, W. (1963). Training teachers in Life Space Interviewing. *American Journal of Orthopsychiatry, 33*, 727–730.

Morse, W. (1965). The mental hygiene viewpoint on school discipline. *High School Journal, 48*, 396–401.

Nevin, A., Thousand, J., Paolucci-Whitcomb, P., & Villa, R. (1990). Collaborative consultation: Empowering public school personnel to provide heterogeneous schooling for all, or, who rang that bell? *Journal of Educational and Psychological Consultation, 1*, 41–67.

Nevin, A., Villa, R., & Thousand, J. (1992). An invitation to invent the extraordinary: A response to Morsink. *Remedial and Special Education, 13*, 44–46.

Education for All Handicapped Children Act. (1976). 20 U.S.C. §§1401 *et seq*.

President's Committee on Employment for Persons with Disabilities. (1994). *Americans with Disabilities*. Washington, DC: Author.

Redl, F. (1959). The strategy and techniques of the Life Space Interview. *American Journal of Orthopsychiatry, 29*(1), 1–18.

Redl, F., & Wattenberg, W. (1959). *Mental hygiene in teaching* (Rev. ed.). New York: Harcourt Brace.

Thomas, C., Correa, V., & Morsink, C. (1995). *Interactive teaming: Consultation and collaboration in special programs* (2nd ed.). Englewood Cliffs, NJ: Prentice Hall.

Thousand, J., Villa, R., & Nevin, A. (1994). *Creativity and collaborative learning: A practical guide to empowering students and teachers*. Baltimore: Paul H. Brookes.

Thousand, J., Villa, R., & Nevin, A. (1997). Including all the experts: Effective collaborations for student success. *Reaching Today's Youth, 1*, 13–17.

U.S. Bureau of the Census. (1992). *Population report*. Washington, DC: U.S. Government Printing Office.

U.S. Department of Education. (1994). *Sixteenth annual report to congress on the implementation of the Individuals with Disabilities Education Act.* Washington, DC: Division of Innovation and Development, Office of Special Education Programs.

Villa, R., & Thousand, J. (1994). One divided by two or more: Redefining the role of a cooperative education team. In J. Thousand, R. Villa, & A. Nevin (Eds.), *Creativity and collaborative learning: A practical guide to empowering students and teachers* (pp. 79–102). Baltimore: Paul H. Brookes.

Villa, R., & Thousand, J. (1996). *Restructuring for diversity: The inclusive school.* Alexandria, VA: Association for Supervision and Curriculum Development.

West, F., & Idol, L. (1987). School consultation (part 1): An interdisciplinary perspective on theory, models, and research. *Journal of Learning Disabilities, 20,* 474–494.

7

Communication and Students With Disabilities on College Campuses

David W. Worley
Indiana State University

Keywords: Nonverbal teacher immediacy, college students with disabilities, ADA compliance, student services, physically disabled, handicapped students, learning disabled students, heath resource center

Sandra sat in her wheelchair and talked with me about her college experience while Zorba, her canine companion and aide, sat protectively nearby. As she told of her encounters with an English teacher, her slurred words were punctuated with quick grimaces and erratic eye movements. At the close of the story, she particularly noted how the teacher avoided eye contact with her and concluded, "I realized that the reason he didn't look at me was because he couldn't stand to look at my face."

This vignette poignantly demonstrates the experiences of persons with disabilities. It also highlights the prejudicial, stereotypical treatment of persons with disabilities common to U.S. society (Hardaway, 1991) and the college campus. In this way the college campus serves as a microcosm representing, to a degree, the social beliefs and behaviors of the larger society. By focusing on the attitudes and behaviors of the nondisabled with persons who are disabled on the college campus, researchers have an opportunity to understand these dynamics better. In addition, social change may be effected through the process of education, since perspectival shifts within the academy have the potential to impact both immediate and future attitudes and behaviors toward persons with disabilities. But to affect this change the lives of students with disabilities on college campuses must be understood. This chapter summarizes such information by first discussing a theoretical model, then reviewing the literature and, finally, concluding with suggestions for future research, key terms, and questions for reflection.

THE DUNKIN AND BIDDLE MODEL

This chapter is organized around three variables drawn from Dunkin and Biddle's (1974) study of teaching: (a) preoperational or presage variables, which include the experiences and the characteristics of teachers before they enter the classroom; (b) context variables, which refer to the formative experiences and characteristics of pupils before entering the classroom; and (c) process variables, which identify those behaviors that both teacher and pupil manifest in the classroom and that bear most directly on the immediate learning environment.

This model is particularly appropriate for the present chapter in view of extant disability research, which focuses on selected variables that influence the general attitudes of others toward persons with disabilities both on and off the college campus. These include: "(a) nondisabled person characteristics, particularly information and contact; (b) perceived disabled person characteristics such as type and severity, and nondisability characteristics such as social skills and intelligence; and (c) other variables such as context, group norms, and method variables" (Yuker, 1994, p. 4). Each of these influences interfaces well with the Dunkin and Biddle (1974) variables. Specifically, the characteristics of nondisabled persons, especially degree of contact and information, intersect with Dunkin and Biddle's preoperational variables, while the characteristics of persons with disabilities and group norms directly influence context and process variables. Dunkin and Biddle's context variable directly harmonizes with the last of Yuker's (1994) categories. In view of these clear connections, the Dunkin and Biddle model provides an appropriate structure for this chapter.

A REVIEW OF LITERATURE

Preoperational Variables

Studies related to preoperational variables report teacher attitudes, contact, and training as related to their interactions with students who are disabled.

Teacher Attitudes. Over a decade ago, Hannah (1988) asserted that "teachers of varying types and stages of professional development hold beliefs about disabled persons similar to those held by the general public" (p. 156). Specifically, studies of university instructor attitudes toward students with disabilities, summarized in the following sections, reveal an interesting ambiguity; the majority of instructors in higher education indicate a generally positive response to the inclusion of students with physical disabilities in college programs, although there are some clear reservations when inclusion impacts professors directly. Therefore, as does the general public, instructors express ambivalence in their interactions with persons who are disabled (Braithwaite & Labrecque, 1994).

For example, Newman (1976) and McCarthy and Campbell (1993) reported that a majority of faculty favor unrestricted admission of students with disabilities whereas a minority prefer admitting students with disabilities on a "restricted basis" (p. 195). However, even those favoring unrestricted admission prefer limited admission or limited academic accommodation when students with disabilities are to be admitted to their particular departments. Wiseman, Emry, and Morgan (1988) attributed this ambiguity to faculty uncertainty in dealing with students who are disabled both personally and pedagogically. This is particularly likely if the faculty lack prior contact with students who are disabled (Fitchen, Amsel, Bourdon, & Creti, 1988).

Consistent with Newman (1976) and Fitchen et al. (1988), Schoen, Uysal, and McDonald (1987) reported that professors respond differently to students with disabilities based on the type and severity of the disability. Although some prefer to interact with students who are blind or orthopedically disabled, most professors expressed concern about teaching deaf students given the communicative challenges. Moreover, Esses and Beaufoy (1994) noted that a similar hierarchy impacts the attitudes of nondisabled individuals in the general public toward persons with disabilities. Notably, those considered more personally responsible for their disability (e.g., persons with AIDS) are perceived less positively than people who are perceived as less responsible. Therefore, the type, severity, and cause of the disability significantly impact nondisabled persons' attitudes toward people with disabilities.

Additionally, Fonosch and Schwab (1981) found that key characteristics, most notably gender and academic discipline, impact teachers' attitudes toward students with disabilities. In particular, they discovered that females and teachers in the social sciences and education have more positive attitudes. Given the cultural and educational socialization that occurs in the lives of females and those specializing in social science and education, one might anticipate such a finding. However, this conjecture is not fully supported by other research (Yuker, 1994).

Teacher Contact.   In addition to teacher attitudes, a second preoperative variable, teacher contact or previous experience teaching students with disabilities, demonstrates a significant impact. In general, those teachers who have prior experience with students who are disabled report a higher incidence of acceptance and comfort than those who have not had such experience. This is also true with the nonteaching public (Yuker, 1994).

Specifically, two studies (Fitchen et al., 1988; Fonosch & Schwab, 1981) confirmed that increased contact and experience with students who are physically disabled "alleviate(s) discomfort and make(s) professors more interested in teaching disabled students" (Fitchen et al., 1988, p. 178). However, McCarthy and Campbell (1993) reported that 25% of their respondents "had no interaction with disabled students during their tenure at the university" (p. 122), which is likely the result of lack of opportunity rather than purposeful exclusion; some level of active avoidance, however, has been verified (Orlansky & Heward, 1981).

While prior contact and previous experience are evidently important influences on the attitudes of both the general public and professors toward students who are disabled, Yuker (1994) asserted that this contact must have particular qualities. Specifically, he noted that contact must include equal status (i.e., educational, social, and occupational similarity); cooperative interdependence (i.e., mutually rewarding and reciprocal interaction); modeling of positive attitudes by authority figures in the contact situation; and the opportunity for nondisabled and disabled persons to become personally acquainted over time to disconfirm stereotypes. These requirements present an interesting dilemma for the college instructor. Given the power differential that exists between professors and students, equal status and cooperative interdependence are difficult, if not impossible, to negotiate.

Furthermore, since faculty often serve numerous students each semester, individualization is equally difficult.

Still further, relational development is often based on self-disclosure. Studies reveal that, although disclosure by persons with disabilities about their disability proves beneficial to the interaction of the nondisabled and disabled (Royse & Edwards, 1989; Thompson, 1982a), not all persons with disabilities are comfortable disclosing such information since the disclosure tends to highlight the disability rather than the person (Braithwaite, 1991; Zola, 1982). Therefore, even though contact does assist professors' reported interaction with students who are physically disabled, the level and degree of contact may be less than constructive due its inherent limits.

These issues are made all the more problematic by the fact that the average faculty member teaches only three students with physical disabilities (Fitchen et al., 1988) thereby limiting both the frequency and amount of contact. Furthermore, both Newman (1976) and Buckrop (1993) reported that most faculty have little or no experience teaching students with disabilities. Fundamentally, then, "actual experience of faculty readiness for working with handicapped students raises some doubt about the quality of the instruction and guidance they provide handicapped students"(Walker, 1980, p. 54).

Teacher Behavior. Teacher behavior, particularly communicative behavior, acts as a third preoperational variable. Although little study of actual teacher behavior toward students with disabilities exists, Hart and Williams (1995) identified four types of instructors: "the avoider, the guardian, the rejecter, and the nurturer" (p. 144). Avoiders, as the name indicates, remain physically and communicatively separated from disabled students and refrain from any discussion of disability. They manifest avoidance characteristics including "nervous nonverbal behavior, such as feet shuffles, vocal fillers, stuttering, pauses, and limited eye contact" (p. 144).

The guardians, on the other hand, engage in protective behavior toward students with disabilities and act as advocates for them. However, these teachers "prevented students from discussing their disabilities, reduced their interaction with ablebodied students or changed academic standards and policies" (p. 147), which resulted in a perception of unequal treatment by both nondisabled and disabled students.

The rejecters "destroyed the student's confidence or simply frustrated the student into withdrawing emotionally and academically" (p. 147) through ignoring, verbally abusing the disabled students, or reducing nonverbal attention (e.g., avoiding eye contact) so that it was clear to the class that disabled students were discriminated against. On the other hand, the nurturer included students with disabilities in the classroom by practical accommodation, warmth, humor, nonverbal immediacy, open discussion of disability issues, and by encouraging contact and communication between nondisabled students and the disabled student. Essentially, these behaviors indicate to all students, whether disabled or nondisabled, that they are capable and responsible for their learning. To encourage more nurturing behavior, Hart and Williams recommended additional teacher training to develop sensitivity and skill in pedagogical interaction with students who are disabled.

Teacher Training. The training of teachers to interact more effectively with students who are disabled acts as a fourth important preoperational variable. Few faculty members receive any significant training regarding such interaction (Buckrop, 1993). Even though training is recommended by both researchers and students with disabilities (Hart & Williams, 1995; Moore, Newlon, & Nye, 1986), and even though effective models for training exist (Cortez, 1983; Donaldson, 1980), only 50% of educators actually enroll in training when it is offered (McCarthy & Campbell, 1993). A variety of global factors common to the general population may explain this reluctance, including childhood socialization regarding persons with disabilities, a combination of extreme personality factors (e.g., dogmatism, anxiety, intolerance of ambiguity, level of ego strength), and perceived deviation of persons with disabilities from social norms (Cloerkes, 1979). However, professors note that their anxieties about teaching students with disabilities (Wiseman et al., 1988) and the demands on their already limited time (McCarthy & Campbell, 1993) most strongly influence their reluctance to participate in training. However, training has been shown to help reduce anxiety and may well be worth the investment of instructors' time (Wiseman et al., 1988). Consequently, active recruiting techniques along with meaningful compensation in money or time may help professors to be more responsive to training. Furthermore, as professors meet students with disabilities in their classes, which they are likely to do given the 9% increase in the enrollment of students with disabilities in 1995 (HEATH, 1996), there is hope that their need for additional information will spur them to become involved in training programs.

Context Variables on the College Campus

The success of college students with disabilities is a complex issue. However, the academic and social climate in which students with disabilities live remains a critical factor in their retention and success (Wiseman et al.,

1988). Contextual variables, including political climate, interaction with college personnel, and interaction with college peers are essential aspects of the experience of college students with disabilities.

Political Climate. The first context variable examined in the literature concerns the political climate, which includes the institutional programs and policies that affect students with disabilities as well as their responses to these initiatives (Jaschik, 1994; Stubbins, 1988). While the Rehabilitation Act of 1973 (Perry, 1981) and the Americans with Disabilities Act (Jarrow, 1993; Wehman, 1993) mandate equal access and accommodations for students who are disabled, colleges face significant barriers implementing these legal mandates. The increasing number of disabled students, which totaled over 880,000 in 1993 (Henderson, 1995); the array and costs of services these students require; and the increased litigation by students with disabilities all add to the already heavy financial and administrative burdens colleges bear (HEATH, 1996). Moreover, students who are disabled must volunteer for campus services, which tends to further stigmatize them (Braithwaite, 1996), and an additional barrier is created as campuses struggle to provide the mandated services. Together, these factors create a political climate on campuses unsettled by legal, financial, and administrative problems punctuated by the efforts of a contingent of politically active students with disabilities who seek to make the mandates a reality.

Interaction With College Personnel. A second context variable concerns the interaction of college students who are disabled with nonfaculty college personnel. Although limited research has considered this interaction, four studies dealing with context variables provide some insights (Dequin, Schilling, & Huang, 1988; Kelly, 1984; Palmerton & Frumkin, 1969a, 1969b).

These studies indicate that, for the most part, students with physical disabilities find support from college coordinators, academic librarians, and college counselors, especially if the nonfaculty personnel are female or younger. Evidently, females have a greater sense of identification with persons who are disabled (Fonosch & Schwab, 1981), whereas younger persons may have internalized the increasing tolerance typical of contemporary culture. However, regardless of the generally positive response of nonfaculty personnel toward students with disabilities, these students must actively seek assistance; they may be reluctant to do so because such action further emphasizes their disabilities over their personhood (Braithwaite, 1996). As a result, interaction as well as the delivery of needed services may be inhibited.

Interaction With College Peers.   By far, the most research concerning contextual variables has focused on the third contextual variable:
the interaction of students who are disabled with their peers. This interaction is particularly influenced by the attitudes, interaction/behaviors, and
cognitions of nondisabled college students regarding their disabled peers.

Attitudes.   Stovall and Sedaleck (1983) found that although the attitudes of undergraduate college students were generally positive toward
their disabled peers, their attitudes shifted in accordance with the level of
contact. While nondisabled students were receptive to sitting next to a peer
with a disability in class, most would not consider close personal relationships such as dating or especially marriage (Eisenman, 1986). Thus, a
combination of positive attitudes, lack of contact and ambivalent responses
are found in the attitudes of nondisabled college students just as with college instructors and the general public.

Behavior/Interaction.   Even though college students express generally positive attitudes toward persons with disabilities, given their discomfort, response inhibition, and/or social skill deficit (Fitchen & Bourdon,
1986), they do not seek significant contact with their peers who are disabled
but actually avoid contact (Snyder, Kleck, Strenta, & Mentzer, 1979). That
is, their generally positive attitudes are not actualized in observed behavior.

Cognition.   Cognition researchers have studied the thoughts and attributions nondisabled college students express toward their peers who
are disabled in an attempt to identify precursors to behavior. For example,
Fitchen and Amsel (1988) found that some nondisabled students think more
positively about themselves and others in the presence of a person with a
disability, which may result from feelings and thoughts of sympathy toward
their peers who are disabled (Fitchen & Amsel, 1986). Additionally, when
the thoughts of nondisabled and disabled are compared, the nondisabled
express a greater number of negative thoughts toward themselves and their
peers with disabilities as compared with students with disabilities. In part,
this pattern is related to the aversion of students with disabilities to pity or
depersonalization born of either positive or negative stereotyping (Fitchen
& Amsel, 1986).

Examining the nature of these thoughts, Fitchen and Amsel (1986) found
that nondisabled college students attribute fewer socially desirable traits to
college students with disabilities due to persistent stereotypes born of both
discomfort and social anxiety. At the same time, however, nondisabled

students believe that their peers who are disabled have essentially the same preferences for nonacademic and recreational activities as they do, even in the face of long-standing stereotypes. Belgrave (1984) suggested that students with disabilities can find common ground with their nondisabled counterparts by demonstrating interest in recreational activities typical of nondisabled students. Ostensibly, when students with disabilities express such interest, the nondisabled students feel less strain and conclude that the students with disabilities are not preoccupied with the disability or the attending perceived limitations.

Experiences of Students With Disabilities

A fourth important context variable in the literature reports experiences of students with disabilities on the college campus. Although much of the literature does not address the perspective of the students who are disabled (Braithwaite, 1991), nevertheless, research yields some insights.

Experiences With Instructors.   The literature presents a mixed picture of the perceptions of students with disabilities toward their instructors. Although many believe that their professors hold negative attitudes toward them (Babbit, Burbach, & Iutcovich, 1979), they also find most of the behaviors professors manifest toward them appropriate including offering practical accommodations and requesting that students with the disabilities help define their own needs (Burbach & Babbit, 1988; Fitchen et al., 1988). In another study, however, West et al. (1993) discovered that many respondents felt that instructors lacked understanding and even discriminated against them, particularly by refusing to provide requested accommodations including being offered additional time to complete assignments or allowing the students to take examinations at a testing center especially suited to their needs.

Anecdotal evidence presents an equally mixed picture. Maura Donovan (1990), a quadriplegic, wrote, "In pursuing my education over the years, I had to cope with many mistaken and handicapping assumptions made by others" (p. 379). Such assumptions likely include the belief that some students with disabilities may not be able to adequately engage discipline-specific content (Newman, 1976). Ron Nichols, who is also a quadriplegic, added:

I can speak to both pleasant and unpleasant experiences that I've had in ten years of going to college after my accident. There were two professors—one male and one female—who were totally anti-me. They could not handle me on an emotional or a professional basis, and it severely impacted upon my grades, since I was a student in both their classes. They would antagonize me, go out of their way to ridicule me. They would not answer my questions. (Orlansky & Heward, 1981, p. 56)

Experiences With Peers. For the most part, students who are disabled are comfortable with their nondisabled peers and have a number of nondisabled friends (Fitchen & Bourdon, 1986). However, they frequently encounter stigma, misunderstanding, social isolation, and attitudinal barriers in their interactions with nondisabled peers who are not friends (Burbach & Babbit, 1988; Penn & Dudley, 1980; West et al., 1993). Furthermore, although students who are disabled consider most interactive behavior by their nondisabled peers appropriate (Fitchen & Bourdon, 1986), they also believe that these peers hold more negative attitudes than the peers appear to hold (Babbit et al., 1979) as evidenced by the active withdrawal of many nondisabled students from significant contact with their disabled peers (Thompson, 1982b; Weinberg, 1978).

Process Variables

As preoperational and contextual variables intermingle with classroom dynamics they impact the subsequent process variables or classroom interaction that transpires. From a communication perspective, nonverbal immediacy behaviors provide important cues to the genuine nature of these interactions.

Teacher Immediacy. Teacher immediacy refers to a set of communicative behaviors including increased proxemics, eye contact, touch, and facial animation (Anderson, 1979) that increase the response of students to both the teacher and course content (Gorham, 1988). Teacher immediacy has been found to impact both teacher effectiveness (Andersen & Andersen, 1987; Nussbaum, 1992; Sallinen-Kuparinen, 1992) and student learning (Andersen, 1985; Christophel, 1990; Gorham & Zakahi, 1990; Kelly & Gorham, 1988; Plax, Kearney, McCroskey, & Richmond, 1986; Richmond, Gorham, & McCroskey, 1987).

Immediacy and Disability. In view of the importance of teacher immediacy to learning, immediacy behaviors toward persons who are disabled should be examined. Although little research is available regarding the immediacy behaviors of college teachers toward students with disabilities, one study suggests that university instructors tend to enact fewer and different types of nonverbal, nonoral immediacy behaviors toward students with disabilities as compared with nondisabled students (Worley, 1996). Additionally, a handful of more generalized studies have found that (a) individuals prefer to maintain a further physical distance from persons who are disabled in unplanned, public interactions (Worthington, 1974); (b) persons with disabilities receive less eye contact, increased stares, greater distance, and decreased conversational time during interactions with the nondisabled (Thompson, 1982a, 1982b); and (c) when nondisabled persons write about nonverbal interaction with persons who are disabled they employ less immediate language (Feinberg, 1971).

GENERAL SUMMARY AND CONCLUSION

The classroom is a complex environment, especially as it relates to the learning experiences of students with disabilities. This chapter, organized around three of Dunkin and Biddle's (1974) variables, reveals some important conclusions. A focus on preoperational variables reveals that college teachers express generally positive, although tempered, attitudes toward students who are physically disabled, even though few of them have actually taught students who are disabled and even fewer have received any significant training to facilitate their instructional interaction.

The second set of variables, context variables, reveals an ambiguity in the interaction between students with disabilities and others on the university campus. Although the results indicate generally positive attitudes of personnel and the nondisabled toward students with disabilities, the behavior manifested by these same persons is not always positive.

A number of communication researchers have focused on the process variable of teacher nonverbal immediacy behaviors, although little research has focused on the study of the nonverbal interactions of college instructors with students who are disabled.

To summarize, the preoperational variables of teacher attitude, experience, and training are significant precursors to teacher classroom behavior. The contextual variables of the politics of the college community regarding students with disabilities, as well as the experiences of these students with their professors, college personnel, and peers, shape their perceptions and expectations as they enter the classroom. Together these elements interact with and influence teacher immediacy behaviors, which in turn affect student learning.

It is also important to note that these conclusions, in general, also describe the culture at large. The college campus acts as a microcosm of society. Thus, understandings and interventions on the college campus hold potentially rich insight for enhancing attitudinal and behavioral shifts within the general population toward persons who are disabled.

SUGGESTIONS FOR FUTURE RESEARCH

Future research needs to focus less on attitudes and more on the actual behavior of interactants. Since most of the attitudinal research relies on self-report data without the verification afforded by observing actual behavior (Yuker, 1994), little attention in prior disability studies has been given to how attitudes and behavior interface. Given communication scholars' research focus on teacher nonverbal immediacy and its importance in the classroom, renewed attention to nonverbal communication behavior may well provide important insights into how teachers and the general public actualize their attitudes toward persons with disabilities. Additionally, research focusing on instructional and support services for both learning and physically disabled students, accommodating technologies for students with physical disabilities, and practical strategies for teachers, professional support staff, and both nondisabled and disabled students will assist colleges in providing equitable and appropriate responses to the needs of students with disabilities.

DISCUSSION QUESTIONS

1. How can communication scholars address the need for additional study of the communicative behavior of college instructors and students with disabilities in the classroom? What research methods might be most useful?
2. What strategies and behaviors by both students with disabilities and instructors have been found useful in their interactions? What additional strategies might prove useful?
3. Summarize the experience of students with disabilities on the college campus. What patterns emerge? How reflective are these patterns of the larger society?
4. Evaluate the claim that the college campus is a microcosm of the larger society. How are the responses and behaviors of the general public like and not like those observed on the college campus?

5. What other communication variables, in addition to nonverbal immediacy, might yield important insights into the college experience of students with disabilities in the classroom?
6. What suggestions would you make for identifying and altering the communicative interaction between students who are nondisabled and disabled? How can research help in this endeavor?
7. In what ways could training for both faculty and students assist future interactions on the college campus? What elements would need to be included in this training if it is to be successful?

REFERENCES

Andersen, J., & Andersen, P. (1987). Never smile until Christmas? Casting doubt on an old myth. *Journal of Thought, 22,* 57–61.

Andersen, J. F. (1979). Teacher immediacy as a predictor of teaching effectiveness. In D. Nimmo (Ed.), *Communication Yearbook 3* (pp. 543–560). New Brunswick, NJ: Transaction.

Andersen, P. A. (1985). Nonverbal immediacy in interpersonal communication. In A. W. Siegman & S. Feldstein (Eds.), *Multichannel integrations of nonverbal behavior* (pp. 1–36). Hillsdale, NJ: Lawrence Erlbaum Associates.

Babbit, C. E., Burbach, H. J., & Iutcovich, M. (1979). Physically handicapped college students: An exploratory study of stigma. *Journal of College Student Personnel, 20,* 403–407.

Belgrave, F. Z. (1984). The effectiveness of strategies for increasing social interaction with a physically disabled person. *Journal of Applied Psychology, 14,* 147–161.

Braithwaite, D. O. (1991). "Just how much did that wheelchair cost?" Management of privacy boundaries by persons with disabilities. *Western Journal of Speech Communication, 55,* 254–274.

Braithwaite, D. O., & Labrecque, D. (1994). Responding to the Americans with Disabilities Act: Contributions of interpersonal communication research and training. *Journal of Applied Communication, 22,* 287–294.

Braithwaite, D. O. (1996). "I am a person first": Different perspectives on the communication of persons with disabilities. In E. B. Ray (Ed.), *Communication and disenfranchisement: Social health issues and implications* (pp. 257–272). Mahwah, NJ: Lawrence Erlbaum Associates.

Buckrop, J. (1993, April). *Equal access to learning and the disabled student.* Paper presented at the Central States and Southern States Speech Communication Association Joint Conference, Lexington, KY.

Burbach, H. J., & Babbitt, C. E. (1988). Physically disabled students on the college campus. *Remedial and Special Education, 9,* 12–19.

Christophel, D. M. (1990). The relationships among teacher immediacy behaviors, student motivation and learning. *Communication Education, 41,* 138–151.

Cloerkes, G. (1979). Are prejudices against disabled persons determined by personality characteristics? *International Journal of Rehabilitation Research, 4,* 35–46.

Cortez, D. M. (1983). A study of the effects of an inservice program for postsecondary faculty on mainstreaming handicapped college students (Doctoral dissertation, New Mexico State University, 1983). *Dissertation Abstracts International, 44,* 2732A.

Dequin, H. C., Schilling, I., & Huang, S. (1988). The attitudes of academic librarians toward disabled persons. *Journal of Academic Librarianship, 14,* 28–31.

Donaldson, J. (1980). Changing attitudes toward handicapped persons: A review and analysis of research. *Exceptional Children, 46,* 504–514.

Donovan, M. (1990). How accessible is an education? In M. Nagler (Ed.), *Perspectives on disability: Text and readings on disability* (pp. 377–380). Palo Alto, CA: Health Markets Research.

Dunkin, M. J., & Biddle, B. J. (1974). *The study of teaching.* New York: Holt, Rinehart & Winston.

Eisenman, R. (1986). Social distance ratings toward blacks and the physically disabled. *College Student Journal, 20,* 189–190.

Esses, V. M., & Beaufoy, S. L. (1994). Determinants of attitudes toward people with disabilities. *Journal of Social Behavior and Psychology, 9,* 43–64.

Feinberg, L. B. (1971). Nonimmediacy in verbal communication as an indicator of attitudes toward the disabled. *Journal of Social Psychology, 84,* 135–140.

Fitchen, C. S., & Amsel, R. (1986). Trait attributions about college students with a physical disability: Circumplex analyses and methodological issues. *Journal of Applied Social Psychology, 16,* 410–127.

Fitchen, C. S., & Amsel, R. (1988). Thoughts concerning interaction between college students who have a physical disability and their nondisabled peers. *Rehabilitation Counseling Bulletin, 32,* 22–40.

Fitchen, C. S., Amsel, R., Bourdon, C., & Creti, L. (1988). Interaction between students with physical disabilities and their professors. *Journal of Applied Rehabilitation Counseling, 19,* 13–19.

Fitchen, C. S., & Bourdon, C. V. (1986). Social skill deficit or response inhibition: Interaction between disabled and nondisabled college students. *Journal of College Student Personnel, 27,* 326–333.

Fonosch, G. G., & Schwab, L. O. (1981). Attitudes of selected university faculty members toward disabled students. *Journal of College Student Development, 22,* 229–235.

Gorham, J. (1988). The relationship between verbal teaching immediacy behaviors and student learning. *Communication Education, 37,* 40–53.

Gorham, J., & Zakahi, W. R. (1990). A comparison of teacher and student perceptions of immediacy and learning: Monitoring process and product. *Communication Education, 39,* 354–367.

Hannah, M. E. (1988). Teacher attitudes toward children with disabilities: An ecological analysis. In H. E. Yuker (Ed.), *Attitudes toward persons with disabilities* (pp. 154–170). New York: Springer.

Hardaway, B. (1991). Imposed inequality and miscommunication between physically impaired and physically nonimpaired interactants in American society. *Howard Journal of Communication, 3,* 139–148.

Hart, R. D., & Williams, D. E. (1995). Able-bodied instructors and students with physical disabilities: A relationship handicapped by communication. *Communication Education, 44,* 140–154.

HEATH Resource Center. (1996). ACE HEATH report: Update on disability issues. *Educational Record, 77,* 54–55.

Henderson, C. (1995). Postsecondary students with disabilities: Where are they enrolled? *American Council on Education Research Briefs, 6,* 2–11.

Jarrow, J. (1993). Beyond ramps: New ways of viewing access. In S. Kroeger & J. Schuck (Eds.), *New directions for student services: Responding to disability issues in student affairs* (Vol. 64, pp. 5–16). San Francisco: Jossey-Bass.

Jaschik, S. (1994). Colleges and the disabled. *Chronicle of Higher Education, 40*(33), A38.

Kelly, B. A. (1984). Attitudes toward disabled persons of selected collegiate coordinators for disabled students. *Journal of College Student Personnel, 25,* 255–259.

Kelly, D. H., & Gorham, J. (1988). Effects of immediacy on recall of information. *Communication Education, 37,* 198–207.

McCarthy, M., & Campbell, N. J. (1993). Serving disabled students: Faculty needs and attitudes. *NASPA Journal, 30,* 120–125.

Moore, C. J., Newlon, B. J., & Nye, N. (1986). Faculty awareness of the needs of physically disabled students in the college classroom. *AHSSPPE Bulletin, 4,* 136–145.

Newman, J. (1976). Faculty attitudes toward handicapped students. *Rehabilitation Literature, 37,* 194–201.

Nussbaum, J. F. (1992). Effective teacher behaviors. *Communication Education, 41,* 167–180.

Orlansky, M. D., & Heward, W. L. (1981). *Voices: Interviews with handicapped people.* Columbus, OH: Merrill.

Palmerton, K. E., & Frumkin, R. M. (1969a). Type of contact as a factor in attitudes of college counselors toward the physically disabled. *Perceptual and Motor Skills, 28*, 489–490.

Palmerton, K. E., & Frumkin, R. M. (1969b). College counselor knowledge about and attitudes toward disabled. *Perceptual and Motor Skills, 28*, 657–658.

Penn, J. R., & Dudley, D. H. (1980). The handicapped student: Problems and perceptions. *Journal of College Student Personnel, 21*, 354–357.

Perry, D. C. (1981). The disabled student and college counseling centers. *Journal of College Student Personnel, 22*, 533–538.

Plax, T. G., Kearney, P., McCroskey, J. C., & Richmond, V. P. (1986). Power in the classroom VI: Verbal control strategies, nonverbal immediacy, and affective learning. *Communication Education, 35*, 43–55.

Richmond, V. P., Gorham, J. S., & McCroskey, J. C. (1987). The relationship between selected immediacy behaviors and cognitive learning. In M. L. McLaughlin (Ed.), *Communication Yearbook 10* (pp. 574–590). Beverly Hills, CA: Sage.

Royse, D., & Edwards, T. (1989). Communicating about disability: Attitudes and preferences of persons with physical handicaps. *Rehabilitation Counseling Bulletin, 32*, 203–209.

Sallinen-Kuparinen, A. (1992). Teacher communicator style. *Communication Education, 41*, 153–166.

Schoen, E., Uysal, M., & McDonald, C. D. (1987). Attitudes of faculty members toward treatment of disabled students reexamined. *College Student Journal, 21*, 190–193.

Snyder, M. I., Kleck, R. E., Strenta, A., & Mentzer, S. J. (1979). Avoidance of the handicapped: An attributional ambiguity analysis. *Journal of Personality and Social Psychology, 37*, 2297–2306.

Stovall, C., & Sedaleck, W. E. (1983). Attitudes of male and female university students toward students with different physical disabilities. *Journal of College Student Personnel, 24*, 325–330.

Stubbins, J. (1988). The politics of disability. In H. E. Yuker (Ed.), *Attitudes toward persons with disabilities* (pp. 22–32). New York: Springer.

Thompson, T. (1982a). Disclosure as a disability-management strategy: A review and conclusions. *Communication Quarterly, 30*, 196–202.

Thompson, T. (1982b). Gaze toward and avoidance of the handicapped: A field experiment. *Journal of Nonverbal Behavior, 6*, 188–196.

Walker, M. L. (1980). The role of faculty in working with handicapped students. In H. Z. Sprandel & M. R. Schmidt (Eds.), *New directions for student services: Serving handicapped students* (Vol. 10, pp. 53–62). San Francisco: Jossey-Bass.

Wehman, P. (Ed.). (1993). *The ADA mandate for social change*. Baltimore: Paul H. Brookes.

Weinberg, N. (1978). Modifying social stereotypes of the physically disabled. *Rehabilitation Counseling Bulletin, 22*, 114–124.

West, M., Kregel, J., Getzel, E., Zhu, M., Ipsen, S. M., & Martin, E. D. (1993). Beyond section 504: Satisfaction and empowerment of students with disabilities in higher education. *Exceptional Children, 5*, 456–467.

Wiseman, R. L., Emry, R. A., & Morgan, D. (1988). Predicting academic success for disabled students in higher education. *Research in Higher Education, 28*, 255–269.

Worley, D. W. (1996). An investigation of the nonverbal, non-oral immediacy behaviors of a SIUC instructor toward a student with an orthopedic disability. (Doctoral dissertation) *Dissertation Abstracts International, 57*(06), 2274.

Worthington, M. E. (1974). Personal space as a function of the stigma effect. *Environment and Behavior, 6*, 289–294

Yuker, H. E. (1994). Variables that influence attitudes toward people with disabilities: Conclusions from the data. *Journal of Social Behavior and Personality, 9*, 3–22.

Zola, I. K. (1982). *Missing pieces: A chronicle of living with a disability*. Philadelphia: Temple University Press.

8

What Is Reasonable? Workplace Communication and People Who Are Disabled

Audra L. Colvert
Towson University

John W. Smith
Ohio University

Keywords: Communication plans, natural supports, statement of integrity, ergonomic interventions, reasonable accommodation

Many disability rights advocates consider the passage of the Americans with Disabilities Act (ADA) to be the most sweeping civil rights legislation passed since 1964 (Olsheski & Breslin, 1996). This legislation provides access to programs, goods, services, and employment that were previously inaccessible for approximately 49 million Americans with disabilities. Through the process of "reasonable accommodation," adjustments or modifications are made to the physical environment, job descriptions, or the performance of the job for persons with disabilities (West, 1996). Not only has the ADA required changes in the physical environment, it also necessitates adjustments in organizational cultures. The ADA directs businesses and government agencies to take proactive steps toward offering equal opportunities to persons with disabilities and to cease discriminatory practices. Changes in routines and the development of new methods of communication are changing the way work is done.

In this chapter, we explore the importance of communication between applicants/employees with physical disabilities and their interviewers/ employers in the workplace. This first section establishes the need for, and significance of, the ADA. The second section focuses on employer concerns about reasonable accommodation, and the third section links those concerns to those of applicants and employees. Finally, we discuss how corporate communication strategies and informal employee relations are working to alleviate these concerns.

THE NEED FOR THE ADA

To understand the changes in organizational cultures that have emerged in the workplace as a result of the ADA, it is necessary to briefly review why the ADA was created. According to the census report from the President's Committee on Employment of People with Disabilities Statistical Report (1998a) approximately 49 million Americans reported having a disability and more than 27 million of those people are part of the U.S. working-age population (21 to 64 years of age). Although 27 million people are of working age, only 14.3 million people with disabilities reported being employed. The unemployment rate for people with disabilities is over 50% and is estimated to range from 65% to 75% for disabilities such as blindness or severe visual impairment (Moore & Fireison, 1995). Why is this?

Senator Lowell P. Weicker, Jr. described the history of America's formal methods of dealing with people with disabilities as "segregation and inequality" (National Council on Disability, 1997, p. 2). Historically, persons with physical disabilities were either institutionalized or sent to special schools along with the mentally retarded (Braithwaite, 1990). Others, not as fortunate, were ostracized from their communities or left to fend for themselves as beggars (Jernigan, 1973; Matson, 1990). People with physical disabilities were stigmatized as inept and therefore could not earn a living (Kearney, 1994). The ablebodied community fostered the myth of the disabled as needing help and charity from those who could lend an able-bodied hand and for decades kept millions of people from being accepted into the mainstream workforce.

While certain individuals and organizations continued to champion the rights of those with disabilities, it was not until the 1960s that a grass-roots movement started building coalitions and networks within the civil rights community. In the 1970s, a number of legal precedents advanced the rights of the disabled, including the Rehabilitation Act of 1973 and the

1975 Individuals with Disabilities Education Act (IDEA), which prohibited discrimination on the basis of disabilities to organizations that received federal funds. In 1988, powerful testimonials by numerous individuals documented the need for antidiscrimination legislation during congressional hearings. Stories were told of individuals who were denied student teaching opportunities because they were blind, fired because of the onset of a disability, and impeded from entering public buildings. Based on earlier civil rights legislation and with unified effort by disability advocates, in 1990 Congress finally passed the Americans with Disabilities Act (National Council on Disability, 1997).

Many changes have occurred in the few short years following the passage and implementation of the ADA. The success of physical accommodations in public spaces is easy to see (McFadden, 1997). It is common to see public buildings with automatic doors, reserved parking spaces, and restrooms redesigned to accommodate individuals who use wheelchairs. Other accommodations, such as changes in organizational culture and interpersonal interactions are not as apparent; their successes are not as obvious. The President's Committee on Employment of People with Disabilities chairman, Tony Coelho (1997), states, "laws alone cannot guarantee that discrimination will cease or that people with disabilities will have equal opportunities in the workforce" (p. 1). Braithwaite and Labrecque (1994) pointed out that "the opportunities promoted by the ADA are accompanied by misunderstanding, fear, and uncertainty, all of which still interfere with communication between the ablebodied workers and those with disabilities" (p. 292). This is the type of communication that, when disrupted or used ineffectively, becomes the avenue through which biases are transmitted and conflicts arise. Putnam and Poole (1987) argued that communication braces "the formation of opposing issues, frames perceptions of the felt conflict, translates emotions and perceptions into conflict behaviors, and sets the stage for future conflicts" (p. 553). The ADA is a comprehensive civil rights law requiring businesses and governments to take proactive steps toward offering equal opportunities to persons with disabilities. Its intent is to eliminate blatant discriminatory actions in the workplace. Although the intent of the ADA is clear, the implementation of the act is still a concern for some employers.

Although signs of barriers being removed are evident, there are still issues for employers concerning communication with applicants and newly disabled employees. Apprehension by ablebodied employers and employees who work with individuals with disabilities is often caused by a lack of awareness about disabilities. This apprehension is linked with other concerns surrounding adherence to the ADA and the concept of "reasonable accommodation," the fear of litigation, and the concern for creating a productive work environment (Spechler, 1996). Likewise, apprehension by persons with disabilities regarding entering the workforce is linked with the perceived lack of power due to social stigmatization and fear of job loss. The following section addresses the concerns of employers.

EMPLOYER CONCERNS

Whereas certain laws, like the 1973 Rehabilitation Act, introduced some government agencies and corporations to fair employment practices for people with disabilities, in justifying the ADA in 1990, Congress found that discrimination against individuals with disabilities was a serious and pervasive social problem that extended into the workplace (ADA, 1990, Sec.1). The ADA is a comprehensive civil rights law that requires businesses and governments to take proactive steps toward offering equal opportunities to persons with disabilities and to cease discriminatory actions, but it is not without its faults.

Ambiguity of Accommodation

The framers of the ADA went to great lengths to describe examples of accommodation; however, they were purposefully vague in providing detailed definitions for terms within the Act (National Council on Disability, 1997). This ambiguity of "reasonable accommodation" causes some employers and corporate lawyers to feel uncertain about how to comply with the law (Becker, 1992; Verespej, 1992). For many agencies compliance was and is difficult because of a lack of knowledge and experience with accommodations.

Reasonable accommodation is an ambiguous term used to refer to modifications or changes to the job description, work environment, or manner in which the job is typically performed. According to the code of federal regulations on reasonable accommodation, the ADA assures employees with various functional limitations that accommodations will be made to allow them to work as independently as possible as long as it does not place an undue hardship (defined as significantly difficult or expensive) on the organization (GSA, 1996). Accommodations may include adjustments to the job application and interview process, to the performance of the job's essential functions, and to enable an employee with a disability to enjoy equal benefits and privileges of employment (Vernon-Oehmke, 1994). The vagueness of the ADA is still raising questions for employers concerning what constitutes an undue hardship, when a job accommodation can be requested, how to ask for an accommodation, what constitutes reasonable accommodation, and what is unreasonable.

The ADA requires enforcement in three areas: employment practices, public accommodation, and delivery of programs, services, and activities. This chapter specifically focuses on the first tenet of the ADA, which makes it illegal to limit, segregate, or classify a job applicant or employee in a way that adversely affects the opportunities or status of that person because of a disability (ADA, 1990, Sec. 102). This means that years of asking applicants questions about their health, as a method of screening potential employees, came to an end (West, 1996). Businesses cannot exclude an applicant based on his or her disability or fire an employee who becomes disabled if he or she can perform the duties required in the job description if provided with reasonable accommodations.

The President's Committee on Employment of People with Disabilities (1998b), the committee responsible for creating, implementing, and maintaining the ADA, describes reasonable accommodations as "tools provided by employers to enable employees with disabilities to do their jobs, just as the employer provides the means for all employees to accomplish their jobs" (p. 1). Like the ADA, the President's Committee is vague in describing which "tools" will fix which problems because requests for accommodations must be made on a case-by-case basis. For example, an accommodation for an employee who has a mobility impairment might include managing fatigue during the workday, or restructuring the job to include only essential functions, or providing flexible schedules to allow for medical treatment (Job Accommodation Network, 1998). The point the ADA attempts to express is that solutions for accommodating individuals are as varied as the individuals themselves.

Because of the relative newness of the act, and a lack of knowledge about accommodating employees, employers have been averse to hiring persons with disabilities. They believe the cost of making the accommodations will be too high. Employers have a hard time believing that the benefits outweigh the cost of employing someone with a disability. However, the Job Accommodation Network (JAN) reports statistics based on a 1994 survey showing the actual costs of job accommodations for 68% of workers with disabilities cost $500 or less (1998). The survey also reports significant savings for over 57% of companies who accommodated employees. Lack of knowledge concerning the facts of accommodation and disabilities not only leads to inaccurate information, it can also lead to a fear of litigation.

Litigation

The second concern for employers involves the fear of litigation and the costs that could be incurred. Employers fear being sued for violating any code or policy, whether it is affirmative action, sexual harassment, or violations of the ADA. Employers are apprehensive about hiring a disabled worker because of all the political and legal issues associated with hiring. Jones (1993) argued that a "litigation-avoidance mentality" changes the perspective of managers and stops them from focusing on concerns like performance, productivity, interpersonal dynamics, and responsiveness to customers. Instead of focusing on operational effectiveness and taking a macro-level approach, managers are forced to attend to micro-level details and complying with the letter of the law. As Breslin (1989) warned, eventually all the employer can see is a potential litigant with a problem rather than seeing the person first. After all, if employers do not hire persons with disabilities, they eliminate the worry about reasonably accommodating an employee. Few employers realize that previously ablebodied employees who are temporarily or newly disabled are using the ADA law the most frequently ("ADA Title I Charges," 1992). Long-term employees must be accommodated as well as people who are newly hired. It is difficult for any corporation to avoid compliance with the ADA and those that do are running the risk of litigation.

Bell (1996) emphasized the importance of interactive communication between an employer and a person with a disability who has requested reasonable accommodation because failure to communicate about accommodations increases the potential for ADA liability and destroys the employer's "good faith" defense (p. 240). The fear of not complying with the law and ending up in litigation may negatively frame employer's views on hiring someone with a disability or even keeping someone on board after the onset of a disability. Inaccurate perceptions and ignorance on the part of employers may lead to an uncomfortable work environment for the entire office and social alienation for employees with disabilities.

Social Alienation

A third issue that has the potential to disrupt an organizational culture and is a concern for any manager is the social interactions between disabled persons and ablebodied co-workers. Rehabilitation literature (Elliott & Byrd, 1982; Thomas & Wolfensberger, 1982), popular culture literature

(Pierro, 1995; White, 1996), and communication literature (Braithwaite & Labrecque, 1994; Thompson, 1981; Thompson & Seibold, 1978), explain how uncomfortable interactions between well-meaning ablebodied persons and persons with disabilities can have detrimental outcomes for both parties. When messages are poorly sent, confrontation or its opposite—avoidance—may result. For example, Hart and Williams (1995) found that although the intellect of people with physical disabilities is no different from that of their ablebodied counterparts, physical disabilities do influence the behaviors of ablebodied people when communicating with people who are disabled. In this study teachers tended to overreact as guardians, avoiders, rejecters, or nurturers toward students with disabilities. Teachers focused on compensating for the disability rather than focusing on the student first. Although Hart and Williams studied educational settings, their findings are not unique. Feelings of uneasiness are represented in other organizational settings when ablebodied individuals with limited experience interact with individuals who are disabled (McFadden, 1997). Both parties tend to bring with them long-held biases that were reinforced with observed behaviors rather than bringing with them knowledge about the person making or agreeing to make the accommodation request, the person's disability, or the employer's concerns, and often, knowledge of the ADA.

An important point to note about employers' attitudes toward persons with disabilities is that the ADA does not protect the employer who feels uncomfortable being around a person with a physical disability "nor will the concern that co-workers or customers will not wish to associate with an individual with a disability be an appropriate reason to deny such an individual employment" (Lee, 1996, p. 2). However, the ADA does protect the employers' rights as well. Lee further explained that the ADA does not protect employees who engage in misconduct "even if the conduct is related to the individual's disability" (p. 2). Employers have the authority to hold individuals to the same performance and conduct standards as other employees. Therefore, if an employee is habitually late or does not produce at least average quality work, the employer has the ability to discharge the person.

Dealing with discomfort and ending years of disenfranchisement for persons with disabilities who want to work takes time. Many of the fears managers have about hiring persons with disabilities are shared by applicants/employees. The next section examines the issues of social alienation and job loss for employees.

EMPLOYEE CONCERNS

Clearly, most accommodation research is written from the employer's perspective. However, a select number of researchers are starting to focus on the concerns of applicants/employees with disabilities (Braithwaite, 1996; Johnson & Albrecht, 1996; Kissane, 1997). Kissane (1997) directed her research on the employment interview directly to persons with disabilities. Her work answers the questions that concern applicants including how to talk about their disability, the need for accommodations, and finding the ideal work environment.

For most applicants, disabled or ablebodied, the interview is a nervous experience. However, approaching the subject of one's disability puts the disabled applicant in an awkward situation. Knowing how much to self-disclose about the disability can produce a quandary, and managing privacy boundaries is important (Braithwaite, 1991). A paradox exists for applicants with disabilities. Should they offer information about their disability and necessary accommodations or should they remain silent? Quite often, the applicant must decide whether to remain silent or initiate the conversation about the disability. Trapp (1998) believes that it is essential for persons with disabilities to be prepared to educate employers about their abilities and to take charge during the interview process when it comes to discussing accommodations. The interviewee may alleviate concerns of potential employers by bringing up the subject of the disability in relation to job performance. During an interview it is the applicant's opportunity to make a favorable impression and help the employer feel comfortable. Open dialogue about alternative skills and abilities during the interview can alleviate misunderstandings and conflicts later in the job.

For employees, issues surrounding social alienation and job loss can create strained communication. Johnson and Albrecht (1996) explained that "face, legal, and emotional issues are involved in confronting employment and disability" (p. 439). Some employees are reluctant to ask for special treatment that could further stigmatize them as being dependent on others or other things. Employees are reluctant to mention the onset of a disability or illness because they fear losing their jobs or being treated differently. They do not want to identify themselves as people with disabilities and attempt to hide them. Often they will not mention the pain they are experiencing until it is too late. As a result, the disabled worker is unable to perform up to expectations. Failure to meet job expectations sets in motion cycles of doubt by employers. Employers think disabled employees cannot handle additional work and assign it to others. Employers and co-workers start to alienate themselves from their co-workers with disabilities who, in turn, feel angry because they are alienated from their work groups and start to fulfill prophecies of low productivity. All of these threaten opportunities for upward mobility. Data suggest that social factors such as lack of communication with persons with mild and moderate disabilities is often related to job terminations (Goetz, Certo, Doering, & Lee, 1996).

The concerns of employers and employees are more similar than different. Both parties want the best for the company and a pleasant working environment. Creating a welcoming environment and reducing uncertainty is a process that starts with creating a communication plan. Section four explains components of this plan.

COMMUNICATION STRATEGIES

The primary factor in successfully incorporating persons with physical disabilities into any environment is creating an organizational culture that is receptive to differences. Changing attitudes and stereotypes is a slow process and takes a concerted effort by all levels of the organization. A company's culture reflects the core values and beliefs that drive the actions, behaviors, and relationships, both internally and externally, of employees (Marshall, 1995). Tracy (1995) argued that an organization's culture must communicate the value of a diversified workforce. The culture should reflect the organization's conviction that "regardless of impairments of one sort or another, people have a role to play, talents to deliver, and the capacity to contribute to the attainment of the goals and objectives of the organization" (p. 102).

A key factor in changing the culture and adhering to the ADA requirements for reasonably accommodating employees with disabilities is open dialogue between both employers and employees. Dixon (1996) emphasized that employers must specify performance standards to the applicant/employee making the request for accomodation. Likewise, the person with the disability must "communicate his or her needs, what will and will not work for him or her and realistic expectations" (p. 25). Jones (1993) explained that the "thread of nondiscriminatory attitudes weaves throughout all ADA efforts" (p. 15). Jones argued that for this principle of nondiscrimination to take hold at all levels within the organization, the organization must use training and other methods to communicate the ways in which inaccurate perceptions lead to acts of discrimination. In addition, employees must be forthcoming and willing to help educate colleagues and supervisors about their own abilities.

There are signs that some changes are occurring because of the ADA. The good news is that almost three quarters of the top industries across the United States are reported to be hiring people with disabilities (Presidents Committee on Employment of People with Disabilities, 1998a). Kissane (1997) reported that technology-based industries have the most impressive record of hiring people with disabilities, followed by manufacturing companies and the communications industry. Many organizations that have managed these threads of nondiscrimination for people with disabilities have been successful in implementing the ADA because they focus on managing people and accommodating the disability. Disabilities are simply one cultural category among many that are included in education awareness and training programs. The primary emphasis for companies that have a diverse workforce is on maximizing potential and increasing productivity (Kearney, 1994). Minimizing discriminatory practices starts with companies developing communication strategies and employees educating their co-workers and supervisors about their abilities. For the IBM corporation, the successful integration of people with disabilities involved five key components: a commitment by top management, respect for the individual, a focus on abilities, providing full access to all aspects of employment, and making accessibility a way of life (Tracy, 1995). Each of these components involved the development of a communication plan that helped formulate and disseminate this philosophy of inclusion.

Establishing a Communication Plan

One of the first steps in eliminating false stereotypes and negative attitudes is to develop a communication plan that educates all employees about disabilities. Companies need to send the message that diversity is welcomed by widely disseminating information through newsletters, posters, and training programs and incorporating inclusive language into formal documents. One company leading the way is General Electric. Spechler (1996) described how in 1993 the chairman of the board and chief executive officer at General Electric (GE) issued a "Statement of Integrity" that focused on ADA compliance. The statement asked each employee to make a commitment to follow this code of conduct. It included Equal Employment Opportunity Commission and safety guidelines as well as outlined GE'S commitment to equal treatment. This statement of integrity became a key component in their communication plan and in developing a supporting structure. GE also included videos on compliance issues in their training programs to employees and managers and introduced a series of articles in its newsletters addressing ADA issues. After surveying more than 300 companies and their compliance with the ADA, Spechler described the GE Statement of Integrity as a model example of "corporate responsibility that embodies the spirit of the best of what America is all about" (p. 103).

Like IBM, the strength of GE's program is its proactive approach to establishing a recognized communication plan. This plan establishes procedures for hiring, training, and promoting people with disabilities as well as developing procedures for negotiating accommodations that are mutually satisfactory for all parties involved. Other companies that have actively created strategies for including people with physical disabilities as part of their workforce include Bank of America (Campbell, 1996), Sears (Cameron, 1995), and IBM (Spechler, 1996) to name a few. Jones (1993) explained that the companies that have the "best practices" of ADA implementation are those that use the concept of good management as the key principle. Businesses like Du Pont and AT&T approach employees with disabilities with the same attitudes as they do other employees. When focusing on improving performance, effective managers bring the same concerns to employees with and without disabilities. Jones stated, "as they [managers] respond to limitations and problems with non-disabled employees, so it is with employees with disabilities" (p. 8).

Negotiating Accommodations

Overcoming many of the challenges related to employment are "inherently related to communication and to supportive interpersonal relationships" (Johnson & Albrecht, 1996, p. 443). Training managers and individuals with disabilities in problem-solving techniques like negotiation and establishing support structures to help people make sense of the ADA can be valuable for all parties involved. When accommodations are requested by an employee, it is important to have procedures in place for both the employer and the employee who is requesting accommodations. The process of adjustment comes through a series of question and answer periods for both parties. Appropriately approaching the subject of the disability and how that may affect work styles is essential.

If either party fails to be aware of their role in the adjustment process or fails to understand the importance of reducing uncertainty concerning the perceived differences, conflicts are likely to arise. Since communication, or lack of communication, is responsible for fostering conflict, it also seems reasonable that communication is the tool for managing conflict so relationships can grow and both parties can work from common frames of reference. Mullins, Rumrill, and Roessler (1994) advocated the use of a collaborative approach to reasonable accommodations as the best way to help people with disabilities perform their jobs. In turn, the employer benefits from increased productivity, worker satisfaction, and reduced turnover. According to Borisoff and Victor (1998), a collaborative approach may be highly effective because it is concerned with the relationship between the negotiating parties and requires both parties to remain open-minded and to communicate effectively with one another. The foundations of collaborative negotiation are outlined by Murray (1986), who recognized that integrative negotiation requires the acknowledgment of the interdependence of both parties, common interests are valued, the distribution of resources is seen as a joint process, and mutually agreeable solutions are sought.

The most difficult aspect of working with this model is getting both parties to work for mutual benefits. When an employee with a disability and an employer must negotiate and decide together what constitutes reasonable working conditions, it is important that both parties make sure that they clearly communicate their interests in a particular job function or protocol matter. Fisher, Ury, and Patton (1991) explained that "the basic problem in negotiation lies not in conflicting positions, but in the conflict between each side's needs, desires, concerns, and fears" (p. 42). In the collaborative negotiation, both parties attempt to maximize gains for each other.

One way to maximize the gains for each other is by insisting on an objective criteria (Fisher et al., 1991). When both parties have different positions on a subject, it is important to have common criteria to help in the decision-making processes. In determining objective criteria, the guidelines for reasonable accommodation include, but are not limited to, making facilities accessible and usable by persons with physical disabilities, job restructuring, modified work schedules, acquisition or modification of equipment or devices, appropriate adjustment or modification of examinations, and the provision of readers and interpreters (GSA, 1996). There are criteria to protect the employer as well. When trying to decide whether the request would place an undue burden on the employer, factors considered include the size of the agency, the type of operations performed in the agency, and the cost of the accommodations.

These guidelines are purposefully vague so parties can negotiate their own agreements. Yet, the ADA does ensure that an employee receives the tools that are basic for effectively working alongside ablebodied co-workers. Second, it assures employers that they are not legally responsible for accommodations of a personal nature or for the employee who does not formally acknowledge that a disability exists (Lee, 1996). Successfully negotiated agreements have allowed a person who is deaf to work as a bank teller, students who are visually impaired to use assistive devices while taking entrance exams, and have provided new workstations for persons who use wheelchairs.

Establishing Supports

Finding support in a culture that is slow to adapt to changes in its environment and reluctant to accept others who are different does make it difficult for marginalized individuals to speak out without fear of retribution or further stigmatization. Developing natural supports is an alternative for the physically disabled community that is growing. Although there are many different definitions of natural supports, Butterworth, Hagner, Kiernan, and Schalock (1996), defined natural support systems as the following:

> the assistance provided by people, procedures, or equipment in a given work-place or group that (a) leads to desired personal and work outcomes, (b) is typically available or culturally appropriate in the workplace, and (c) is supported by resources from within the work place, facilitated to the degree necessary by human service consultations (p. 106)

Creating natural supports that provide resources to both parties is crucial. The employee needs to provide the employer with information about the limitations of his or her abilities and the employer needs to provide as much work-related support as is considered reasonable. The same applies to co-workers. Ignoring the disability will not make it go away. Learning about how the physically disabled person uses alternative skills is important. Supports can occur spontaneously, or may be facilitated or imported. The crucial point is that supports become part of the workplace culture. They should not be "exceptions to standard procedures for individual employees" (Butterworth et al., 1996, p. 107). The authors pointed out that "naturalness" is but one criterion for establishing an effective support for the physically disabled, not the only one.

A growing trend in the field of rehabilitation services that appears to support this idea of naturalness is the process of ergonomic interventions. Olsheski and Breslin (1996) explored the use of ergonomics, the scientific study of effectively matching jobs to workers, as a method for increasing worker–job compatibility. The authors explained how collaboration among the ergonomist, the therapist, management, labor representatives, and the worker plays a central role in the disability management model. The data gathered from working together may be presented to management to initiate a process of negotiation where the information is used to "make decisions regarding the reasonableness of specific types of accommodations" (p. 679). For example, in many manufacturing industries, back strains are not uncommon among employees who must stand all day or are involved in heavy lifting. Instead of firing the person because they cannot adequately do the job, the problem is controlled by examining the employee's abilities and the workstation. The solutions may involve altering the movements of the employee, providing cushioned floor mats, adjusting table heights, or replacing problem instruments. Ergonomic interventions address the environmental side of the disability and move the focus away from what employees cannot do and toward an emphasis on what they can do if the workplace is adapted to meet their needs.

Because not all companies have implemented such a comprehensive system of accommodations, and not all jobs involve manual labor, other types of adjustments may need to be requested. The process of requesting accommodations requires both the employee and the employer to be comfortable with confrontation and negotiation strategies.

Follow-Up

Finally, follow-up to any accommodation is important and is usually as simple as a visit, phone call, or E-mail message. It ensures that, if either party is having problems with the accommodation, an opportunity to discuss it exists. The key to a successfully negotiated agreement concerning reasonable accommodation in the workplace is communication. Learning how to put stereotypes into perspective and opening up the channels of communication when uncertainty or discomfort exists can help improve the communication practices of the entire organization and unite the marginalized and mainstream groups of a culture, leading to a culture where differences are recognized and conflicts over those differences are managed with effective communication skills.

For employers, developing a communication plan for the company is essential. The plan should allow for an ongoing review and evaluation of not only ADA compliance issues, but also the effectiveness of disability awareness training. For employees with disabilities, effective communication involves developing support systems and educating others about their abilities in addition to their disabilities. In an effort to reduce uncertainty and dispel false stereotypes, employees need to be willing to discuss with interested colleagues their disabilities and the alternative formats they use to accomplish job functions.

IMPLICATIONS AND CONCLUSIONS

Communication scholars are in unique position to address issues of social interaction and the contexts in which they occur (Duck, 1993). They have the ability to provide applicable information about specific groups of people and the potential to provide information that is usable for those groups (Cissna, 1995). People with physical disabilities are organizing and exercising their rights to be treated as equals in a society that has further limited them through social alienation and stigmatization. Communication scholars have the opportunity to understand individuals who historically have been negatively labeled and stigmatized, and also to conduct research and advance new attitudes toward communicating with them. Trainers need to educate managers and employees about the abilities of workers and to focus on individuals first and their disabilities second. Organizational consultants need to increase awareness of the need for communication plans. Most of all, researchers need to gather the experiences of individuals with disabilities and find out what works for them in educating their co-workers about disabilities.

In this chapter we described the importance of communication in the workplace between applicants/employees with physical disabilities and their interviewers/employers. The first section established the need and significance of the ADA, the next section focused on employer concerns about reasonable accommodation, the ambiguity of language in the ADA, and the fear of litigation. The third section linked those concerns to concerns about job inadequacy and alienation of applicants and employees. The final section discussed how corporate communication strategies and the establishment of employee support structures are working to alleviate these concerns. The ADA is making a difference in the workplace. As the ADA matures, it is hoped that we will see a decline in the unemployment rate for persons with disabilities. It is important to remember that an openness and willingness to talk about disabilities is the first step in reducing uncertainties and establishing an inclusive corporate culture.

DISCUSSION QUESTIONS

1. What concerns would you have if you were to work with someone with a physical disability? How could these concerns be addressed?
2. What barriers might prevent persons with physical disabilities from entering the workforce?
3. Who should be required to enroll in disability awareness training—administrators, supervisors, managers, co-workers? How would these sessions differ for each group?
4. If you were to develop a communication plan that emphasizes "people first" for a company, what specific strategies would you include/exclude?
5. Develop a case study that addresses reasonable and unreasonable accommodations as it applies to persons with disabilities in the workplace. How would you define reasonable accommodation?

REFERENCES

ADA Title I Charges. (1992). *Disability Compliance Bulletin, 3*(24), 9.

Americans with Disabilities Act of 1990, 42 U.S.C.A. §12101 *et seq.* (West, 1993).

Becker, G. S. (1992, September 14). How the disabilities act will cripple business. *Business Week, 283*, 14.

Bell, C. G. (1996). The intersection with workers' compensation. In J. West (Ed.), *Implementing the Americans with Disabilities Act* (pp. 227–262). Cambridge, MA: Blackwell.

Borisoff, D., & Victor, D. A, (1998). *Conflict management: A communication skills approach.* Boston: Allyn & Bacon.

Braithwaite, D. O. (1990). From majority to minority: An analysis of cultural change from ablebodied to disabled. *International Journal of Intercultural Relations, 14*, 465–483.

Braithwaite, D. O. (1991). Just how much did that wheelchair cost? Management of privacy boundaries by persons with disabilities. *Western Journal of Speech Communication, 55*, 254–274.

Braithwaite, D. O. (1996). Persons first: Choices by persons with disabilities. In E. B. Ray (Ed.), *Communication and disenfranchisement: Social health issues and implications* (pp. 449–464). Hillsdale, NJ: Lawrence Erlbaum Associates.

Braithwaite, D. O., & Labrecque, D. (1994). Responding to the Americans with Disabilities Act: Contributions of interpersonal communication research and training. *Journal of Applied Communication, 22*, 287–294.

Breslin, J. W. (1989), July. Breaking away from subtle biases. *Negotiation Journal, 5*(3), 219.

Butterworth, J., Hagner, D., Kiernan, W. E., & Schalock, R. L. (1996). Natural supports in the workplace: Defining an agenda for research and practice. *Journal of the Association for Persons with Severe Handicaps, 21*(3), 103–113.

Campbell, I. A. (1996). Disability management model: A system for managing disability in the workplace (Doctoral dissertation, The Union Institute, 1996). *Dissertation Abstract International, 57*(08), 5323B.

Cameron, D. (1995). Standing up for the act. *ADA Quarterly, 8*, 1–2.

Cissna, K. N. (1995). Introduction. In K. N. Cissna (Ed.), *Applied communication in the 21st century* (pp. i–xvi). Hillsdale, NJ: Lawrence Erlbaum Associates.

Coelho, T. (1997, July). A message from Chairman Tony Coelho. [Online]. Available: http://www.pcepd.gov/pubs/ek97/coelho.html.

Dixon, A. P. (1996). AT & T. In J. W. Spechler (Ed.), *Reasonable accommodation profitable compliance with the Americans with Disabilities Act* (pp. 19–26). Delray Beach, FL: St. Lucie Press.

Duck, S. (1993). *Social context and relationships.* Newbury Park, CA: Sage.

Elliott, T. R., & Byrd, E. K. (1982). Media and disability. *Rehabilitation Literature, 43,* 348–355.

Fisher, R., Ury, W., & Patton, B. (1991). *Getting to yes: Negotiating agreement without giving in* (2nd ed.). New York: Penguin Books USA.

General Services Administration (GSA). (Accessed, 1996, November 5). *Code of federal regulations on reasonable accommodation.* [Online]. Available: http://www.gsa.gov/coca/reas_acc.html, 1–5.

Goetz, L., Certo, N. J., Doering, K., & Lee, M. (1996). Meaningful work and people who are deaf-blind. In D. H. Lehr & F. Brown (Eds.), *People with disabilities who challenge the system* (pp. 283–306). Baltimore: Paul H. Brookes.

Hart, R. D., & Williams, D. E. (1995). Ablebodied instructors and students with physical disabilities: A relationship handicapped by communication. *Communication Education, 14*(2), 1–16.

Jernigan, K. (1973, July 5). *Blindness; Is history against us?* An address delivered at the annual convention of the National Federation of the Blind, New York.

Job Accommodation Network. (1998, June 1). *Ideas for accommodating an individual with a back impairment.* [Online]. Available: http://janweb.icdi.wvu.edu/english/pubs/OtherPubs/BACK.html.

Johnson, G. M., & Albrecht, T. L. (1996). Supportive structure for persons with disability: Smoothing or smothering the way? In E. B. Ray (Ed.), *Communication and disenfranchisement: Social health issues and implications* (pp. 433–447). Hillsdale, NJ: Lawrence Erlbaum Associates.

Jones, T. L. (1993). *The Americans with Disabilities Act: A review of best practices.* New York: AMA.

Kearney, D. (1994). *Reasonable accommodations: Job descriptions in the age of ADA, OSHA, and worker's comp.* New York: Von Nostrand Reinhold.

Kissane, S. F. (1997). *Career success for people with physical disabilities.* Chicago: VGM Career Horizons.

Lee, B. A. (1996, November 5). *Reasonable accommodation under the ADA.* [Online]. Available: http://janweb.icdi.wvu.edu/kinder/519reaso.

Marshall, E. M. (1995). *Transforming the way we work: The power of the collaborative workplace.* New York: AMACOM

Matson, F. (1990). *Walking alone and marching together: A history of the organized blind movement in the United States, 1940–1990.* Baltimore: National Federation of the Blind.

McFadden, M. E. (1997). ADA is the glass half empty or . . . ? *Trial, 33*(12), 28–35.

Moore, J. E., & Fireison, C. (1995). Rehabilitating persons who are blind: 75 years of progress. *American Rehabilitation, 21*(3), 22–27.

Mullins, J. A., Rumrill, P. D., & Roessler, R. T. (1994). Use a collaborative approach to reasonable accommodation. *HR Focus, 71*(2), 16.

Murray, J. A. (1986). Understanding competing theories of negotiation. *Negotiation Journal, 2,* 179–186.

National Council on Disability. (1997). *Equality of opportunity: The making of the Americans with Disabilities Act.* Washington, DC: Author.

Olsheski, J. A., & Breslin, R. E. (1996). The Americans with Disabilities Act: Implications for the use of ergonomic in rehabilitation. In A. Bhattacharya & J. D. McGlothlin (Eds.), *Occupational ergonomics: Theory and applications* (pp. 669–683). New York: Marcel Dekker.

Pierro, C. (1995). Talking with your child about disabilities. *Exceptional Parent, 25*(6), 92.

President's Committee on Employment of People with Disabilities. (1998a, June 6). *Statistical report: The status of people with disabilities* [Online]. Available: http://www.pcepd.gov/pubs/fact/statistic.html, 1–6.

President's Committee on Employment of People with Disabilities. (1998b, June 6). *Workplace accommodation process* [Online]. Available: http://www.pcepd.gov/ pubs/ek97/process.html, 1–3.

Putnam, L. L., & Poole, M. S. (1987). Conflict and negotiation. In F. Jablin, L. Putnam, K. Roberts, & L. Porter (Eds.), *The handbook of organizational communication* (pp. 549–599). Beverly Hills, CA: Sage.

Spechler, J. W. (1996). *Reasonable accommodation: Profitable compliance with the American with Disabilities Act.* Delray Beach, FL: St. Lucie Press.

Thomas, S., & Wolfensberger, W. (1982). The importance of social imagery in interpreting societally devalued people to the public. *Rehabilitation Literature, 43*, 356–358.

Thompson, T. L. (1981). The development of communication skills in physically handicapped children. *Human Communication Research, 7*, 312–324.

Thompson, T. L. (1982). Disclosure as a disability-management strategy: A review and conclusions. *Communication Quarterly, 30*, 196–202.

Thompson, T. L., & Seibold, D. R. (1978). Stigma management in "normal" stigmatized interactions: Test of the disclosure hypothesis and a model of stigma acceptance. *Human Communication Research, 4*, 231–242.

Tracy, W. R. (1995). *Training employees with disabilities: Strategies to enhance learning and development for an expanding part of your workforce.* New York: AMACOM.

Trapp, G. D. (1998). Understanding your rights during the job interview. *Braille Monitor, 41*(1), 21–26.

Verespej, M. (1992, April 6). Time to focus on the disabilities. *Industry Week, 241*, 14–19.

Vernon-Oehmke, A. (1994). *Effective hiring & ADA compliance.* New York: AMACOM.

West, J. (1996). *Implementing the Americans with Disabilities Act.* Cambridge, MA: Blackwell.

White, M. (1996, February 1). Blind wrestler pins his problems. *Pittsburgh Post Gazette* [Newsbank Newsfile/CD]. Record Number. 01245*19960201*00092.

9

Communication Strategies in Employment Interviews for Applicants With Disabilities

Kelly P. Herold
Winona State University

Keywords: Disclosure, interviewing, employment, uncertainty reduction, stigma management

For many applicants with disabilities, successful job interviewing is an all-or-nothing battle with prejudiced, nondisabled employers who often operate in bureaucratic support systems and as a result, may have some acknowledged or hidden prejudices (Stone & Sawatzki, 1980). The frustration of job applicants with disabilities has real significance, especially considering the extraordinary unemployment rate of over 70% for the disabled population (Rubin, 1997). Because persons with disabilities, especially those who have the most visible disabilities such as paraplegia, Down syndrome, or closed head injury, are considered less attractive and less employable, they are often left in a perpetual state of social and economic dependency (Albrecht, 1992). This chapter argues that to break from this state of dependency, the applicant with a disability would benefit from using strategic communication during the employment interview to prove that she or he is employable despite the stigma or stereotypes that his or her disability might evoke.

Employing strategic communication strategies to combat prejudicial thinking is justified. The stakes are high. As disability advocate Billy Golfus (Corbet, 1995) pointed out, gimps without jobs are "as invisible as Caspar [*sic*] the ghost" (p. 42), and without gainful employment are effectively excluded from society. Even though it may seem obvious that employment and personal economic stability are central to disabled persons' ability to be successful in society (Yuker, 1988), it is apparent that the cliché "getting a job is a full-time job" is neither accurate nor appropriate for applicants with disabilities. Instead, gaining employment becomes a matter of societal "life and death" and, consequently, stigma management strategies are imperative.

Not surprisingly, the effort needed to get out of the dependent state of "unemployability" is tremendous and increases with the saliency of the applicant's disability (Herold, 1995; Krefting & Brief, 1976; Stone & Sawatzki, 1980). A study by LaPlante, Kennedy, Kaye, and Wegner (1997) revealed that the unemployment rates for different types and degrees of disability seem to range along a continuum of societal prejudice toward disability. Even though there is evidence to demonstrate a decrease in prejudicial treatment for applicants with the most "acceptable" disabilities such as paraplegia and epilepsy (Royse & Edwards, 1989), employment success for even these applicants is still not comparable with that of their nondisabled counterparts (LaPlante et al., 1997).

In this chapter, saliency is meant to exemplify the societal and prejudicial tolerance of disability the degree to which the disability is defined as relevant and negatively valenced. For example, both a paraplegic who uses a wheelchair and an ambulatory person with spastic cerebral palsy have visible disabilities, but the person with spastic cerebral palsy has the more salient disability and he or she would be considered less socially attractive, and consequently have more stigma management concerns to consider (Goffman, 1963). However, saliency is not limited to the visibility of the disability but also extends to what society might consider threatening, such as manic depression. Johnson, Greenwood, and Schriner (1988) found that potential employers expressed specific concerns about hiring someone with a nonvisible disability such as depression or attention deficit disorder because these types of employees would allegedly require more instruction, might not accept their roles, and might require more supervision.

In this chapter I identify appropriate and effective interviewing strategies for applicants with disabilities, especially considering the impact of the Americans with Disabilities Act (ADA). There are six sections in this chapter: (a) perceptions of employability, (b) stigma management in the employment interview, (c) uncertainty reduction theory and interviewing, (d) self-disclosure strategies and uncertainty reduction, (e) expected employment interviewing behavior and the ADA, and (f) improving employability for persons with disabilities.

PERCEPTIONS OF EMPLOYABILITY

Applicants with visible physical disabilities and nonvisible disabilities are perceived as not being employable and thus experience an unemployment rate of over 70% (Rubin, 1997). According to a January 1994 Harris poll, "79% of persons with disabilities who are not working want to work! Eight out of ten of those surveyed expressed their belief that they would have the kind of job they desire if they did not have a disability" (Rubin, 1997, p. 1). This number is disheartening, especially considering that at least 49 million U.S. citizens are persons with disabilities and that they are the largest minority group ever defined (Rubin, 1997). This minority culture (Braithwaite & Braithwaite, 1997; Wiss, 1997) is both economically troubled and stymied (Albrecht, 1992) by a federal government that spends $200 billion annually to support people who are not working as compared with $5 billion spent on preparing persons with disabilities for employment (Rubin, 1997), and by a public sector that is uncomfortable hiring disabled persons (Gouvier, Steiner, Jackson, Schlater, & Rain, 1991; Stone & Sawatzki, 1980). There are several reasons why many persons with disabilities are dismissed as unemployable.

LaPlante et al. (1997) reported that persons with disabilities may not have jobs for one of at least five reasons. The first two of these are most obvious: the severity of their impairments and the social barriers presented by employers. A third reason why persons with disabilities are precluded from work is because they are not well trained. Fourth, persons with disabilities are not as well educated as their nondisabled counterparts. Nondisabled students' high school graduation rate is 82.4% as compared with only 66.7% for students with disabilities. The disparity in college graduation rates is even more striking: 22.9% for people without disabilities compared with 9.6% for people with disabilities. Fifth, as a consequence of inadequate education, persons with disabilities are three times more likely to live in poverty than are their nondisabled counterparts. For those who are offered an employment interview, the question becomes "what communication strategies will reduce uncertainty and maximize the opportunity for gainful employment?"

STIGMA MANAGEMENT IN THE
EMPLOYMENT INTERVIEW

Early in the employment-seeking process a disabled applicant must consider how to combat unreasonable stigmas and stereotypes. The saliency variable is central in determining which communication strategies need to be utilized. Disabled applicants are in the unenviable position of having to judge whether they should disclose information about their disabilities, just sell their talents, or advocate their right to fair treatment during an employment interview.

Communication research about disclosure as a stigma management strategy that may be generalized to an employment interview has yielded inconsistent results (e.g., Braithwaite, 1991; Grove & Werkman, 1991; Thompson, 1982), as has other atheoretical advice offered to applicants with disabilities (Marks & Lewis, 1983; Witt, 1992). During, and especially, after a successful initial screening, interpersonal communication skills, an attractive appearance, and demonstration of knowledge and skills required for the position applied for influence employers' selection decisions. These qualities apply to any applicant, whether disabled or not (Galassi & Galassi, 1978). However, it is clear that presence of a disability damages the disabled applicant's employability regardless of his or her qualifications (Bordieri & Drehmer, 1987; Gouvier et al., 1991; Herold, 1995; Stone & Sawatzki, 1980). Over the past 30 years, advice generated to help reduce the harmful effects of stigma (Marks & Lewis, 1983; Witt, 1992) and improve the unemployment rate of persons with disabilities has been ineffectual, as evidenced by the consistently high unemployment rate of 70% (Rubin, 1997).

Knowing that the employment interview is always a persuasive event (Einhorn, 1981), the answer may seem obvious; do not disclose information regarding your disability. However, there is evidence to show that if a disabled applicant is hired and does not disclose until after the job is offered, the nondisclosure may contribute to a sense of distrust between the employer and applicant. Witt (1992) provided an example of colleagues looking for deficits they expect to find in a co-worker who has disclosed a disability. Their "need to discover" or find proof of the disability is invasive. For those with a visible disability, there is no choice. The "nonverbal disclosure" has already occurred along with a persuasive appeal that implicitly or explicitly contains one or both of the following arguments: that they are excellent candidates in spite of their disability, or that they are excellent candidates because they overcame their disability (Herold, 1995). Although this type of persuasive appeal may appease the interviewer, it often puts the disabled applicant at odds with her or his personal and cultural identity (Shaprio, 1994). An alternative strategy may be to seek protection against prejudicial hiring practices by evoking the ADA. Unfortunately, this strategy, although viable, has potentially explosive consequences on organizational membership (Kreps, 1993, this volume). What is needed, it seems, is advice regarding what type of communication strategies should be employed by whom and when.

A personal example helps to explain the apparent paradox. I have participated in several employment interviews. After initial screening and telephone interviews, I have had to consider whether it was necessary for me to disclose information about my disability. My hemiplegic cerebral palsy can be considered nonvisible because my left side is completely developed. After a lifetime of overcompensating, my left side is extraordinarily strong, while my right side is slightly atrophied and weak. Because of my weak right hand, I often consider the stigma management strategy of fully or partially disclosing information about my disability during an initial interaction, especially if my handshake leaves a "limp fish" impression. When interviewing, I take an immediate inventory of the interviewer's right hand. I have just an instant to decide whether I have conducted a good shake, and if not, I am prepared to implement my stigma management plan. This is obviously a very conscious process and consequently I am as nervous about the initial handshake as I am about the entire interview process.

Coincidentally, all four of my successful interviews have been with women, while the two face-to-face disappointments have been with men. My right hand generally fits nicely into a woman's hand and has adequate squeeze strength, but it is often consumed and crushed by a male handshake. I do not claim a direct relationship between my interview success with men and my handshake, but since I am a 6 foot 3 in. and 210-lb male, I suspect that my weak handshake did not leave a favorable first impression. For me, the moment of the handshake determined whether I needed to repair any perceived damage. At the time, this seemed to be the logical thing to do, according to what I had read in popular and research-based literature on interviewing. However, I failed to recognize that an interview is not truly an interpersonal communication experience and thus, many rules simply do not apply (Herold, 1995; Krefting & Brief, 1976). My strategy to disclose information about my disability as a way to alleviate perceived stigmas turned out to be flawed. As I have subsequently discovered through disclosure research, the best strategy for myself would be not to discuss my disability during an interview.

In the field of communication there has been little theoretically driven advice that directly addresses disability stigma management in the context of an employment interview. Dahnke (1982) developed a deductive theory to examine initial interactions, including those between a nondisabled interviewer and a disabled interviewee. Using uncertainty reduction theory as one of his premises, he found that during initial interactions between a disabled applicant and a nondisabled interviewer, the disabled applicant was considered less favorable and produced more anxiety than a nondisabled applicant. The applicant's disability dominated the attention of the nondisabled person, the nondisabled interviewer was more ambivalent and formal, and as a result, the disabled applicant was either rated more severely or given an overly favorable rating. In addition, Dahnke found that the nondisabled interviewer sat farther away, exhibited less variation in behavior, and distorted his or her opinions to align with the disabled applicant. Most importantly, the initial interaction was terminated more quickly for the disabled applicant than for the nondisabled applicant. Dahnke's research and my personal experiences with interviewing suggest that the most effective way to approach stigma management is through the use of uncertainty reduction theory.

UNCERTAINTY REDUCTION THEORY AND INTERVIEWING

Berger's (1997; Berger & Bradac, 1982) uncertainty reduction theory (URT) posits that when persons initially meet, they have a need to reduce uncertainty about self and others. Communication research conducted on interactions between persons with disabilities and nondisabled persons (Braithwaite, 1991; Dahnke, 1982; Thompson & Seibold, 1978) indicates that persons who have a visible disability create high levels of uncertainty and may need to concentrate on reducing it. In the initial formulation of URT, Berger and Calabrese (1975) discussed three specific conditions that are especially relevant to interaction with a person with a visible disability: deviation from normalcy, the possibility of future interaction, and the outcome of interaction-related costs and rewards.

It is clear that the saliency of a person's disability determines others' need to confirm or disconfirm stereotypes. When a person encounters the novelty of a visible disability it can be predicted that they will act to reduce uncertainty. For the professional interviewer, the disabled applicant presents stimuli that produce anxiousness and uncertainty. Royse and

Edwards (1989) reported that even professionally trained persons often feel some uneasiness when in the presence of persons with disabilities. Bordieri and Drehmer (1987) found that the more severe the disability or the more the job applicant deviated from the norm, the lower the probability of being offered employment. Stone and Sawatzki (1980) reported that an applicant's disability can be so unnerving to the nondisabled interviewer that he or she may overlook the interpersonal behavior of the applicant and instead focus on the novelty of the disability.

According to Berger's (1997) interpretation of URT, persons more intently monitor their interaction when there is a reasonable expectation that they will interact with the person again. Goffman (1963) argued that a person's physical disability is discrediting to such a degree that when nondisabled persons have to interact with persons with a disability they tend to avoid giving any suggestion of an impending long-term relationship. This means that an offer of employment may be problematic because it suggests the development of a long-term relationship. Sunnafrank's (1986) research demonstrates that future interaction serves as the dominating feature of increased anxiety. In a job interview for an applicant with a disability, this is very important because the decision for offering a second interview or a job may depend on the level of uncertainty of the interviewer.

From the perspective of the disabled communicator, the possible rewards or costs of the interaction during the job interview are quite clear—namely, an offer of employment. Berger and Bradac (1982) argued that when communicators perceive their interaction to be of value, they become more concerned about reducing uncertainties. As Coleman and DePaulo (1991) noted, "because of incoherent communication, a lack of shared information, negative attitudes, stereotypes, or stigma, a disabled or ablebodied person may become frustrated or hostile" (p. 63), and some may ultimately resort to terminating the interaction (Sabsay & Platt, 1985). However, there are strategies available to reduce uncertainty.

Berger and Calabrese's (1975) theory postulates that people use three specific ways to increase information and reduce uncertainty: passive, active, and/or interactive strategies of information seeking. The interactive strategy of self-disclosing may be most effective because the disabled interviewee is best equipped to dispel myths and reduce uncertainty (Race, 1972; Thompson, 1982). This strategy is effective when disclosure is not elicited, but instead is disclosed voluntarily, as the ADA requires in an interviewing situation. The applicant with a disability needs to consider his or her self-disclosure not as part of a reciprocated act, but instead as an offensive strategy (Berger, 1997) that utilizes his or her "information power" (Dahnke, 1982) to reduce an interviewer's uncertainty.

It is important to note that the notion of information sharing is based on an interpersonal model where rules of reciprocity exist. For example, participants in an interpersonal communication situation may feel compelled to share information on an equally intimate level. Braithwaite's (1991) research on disclosure by people with disabilities demonstrated that people who are made uncomfortable by a person's disability want to ask questions to reduce uncertainty and in interpersonal settings many do indeed ask such questions. In response, many persons with disabilities provide information, depending on several situational factors. Although it is extremely useful in interpersonal contexts, URT (Berger, 1997; Berger & Calabrese, 1975) does not explain how anxiousness can be reduced in a setting where the rules of interaction are formalized and restricted, like an employment interview.

Spitzberg (1994) recognized that persuasion and uncertainty reduction are unlikely if a relationship is not coequal; an employment interview is such a context. Based on Spitzberg's findings, it is suggested that the nondisabled interviewer is in a powerful position in an employment interview and, depending on his or her competency and motivation to reduce uncertainty, will seek or expect information to be disclosed by the less powerful and presumably less competent disabled interviewee. However, seeking the desired disability information is restricted by the ADA. As a result, if the questions that the interviewer would use to reduce uncertainty are left unanswered, high levels of uncertainty will persist and the applicant's employability may be jeopardized. Information-sharing behavior may be used to reduce uncertainty and also to persuade or gain influence over the target person (Berger, 1997). This suggests that information sharing may be utilized to help convince the potential employer that a disability is not a liability. An examination of the specific strategy of self-disclosure in relation to URT should provide more helpful information for persons seeking employment.

SELF-DISCLOSURE STRATEGY AND UNCERTAINTY REDUCTION

Numerous studies have shown that participants who disclose information that directly disconfirms stereotypical myths are perceived to be significantly more attractive (Cozby, 1972; Hastorf, Wildfogel, & Cassman, 1979; Kleck, 1968; Thompson & Seibold, 1978; Worthy, Gary, & Kahn, 1969).

Of particular importance to the present essay are several reports that when applicants disclose information to combat stereotypes, their ratings of employability significantly improve (Heilman, Martell, & Simon, 1988; Tosi & Einbender, 1985), and this trend is also observed when the applicant has a disability (Hastorf et al., 1979; Jackson, Peacock, & Smith, 1980; Tagalakis, Amsel, & Fichten, 1988). Self-disclosure as a strategy to reduce uncertainty appears to be promising and in only a few circumstances would it cause damage or create a negative image (Thompson, 1982). There is, however, some evidence to show that self-disclosure may elicit negative reactions in certain situations.

As reported by Worthy et al. (1969), self-disclosure can have negative effects when it is presented in a context where reciprocation is not likely—such as an interview—only adding to uncertainty rather than reducing it. In addition, self-disclosure may serve to crystallize the stereotypes of disability as a sickness and thus increase anxiousness (Glideman & Roth, 1980). Disclosure may also misrepresent to the nondisabled counterpart that the person with a disability is preoccupied with his or her disability (Belgrave & Mills, 1981) and is likely to disclose about the disability to anyone (Derlega & Chaikin, 1977). Other discrediting effects of self-disclosure are that it may lead to loss of self-esteem, possibly alienate others, indicate a loss of control, and project a negative attitude (Steele, 1975).

Inconsistencies about the effects of self-disclosure are puzzling. Thompson and Seibold (1978) found that although disclosure reduced levels of tension and uncertainty, it did not contribute to increasing levels of acceptance. As a result, the central question becomes, what contributes to these inconsistencies in research findings? Without an answer, the confusion as to whether to disclose or not remains.

The following six explanations explore why URT and the self-disclosure strategy may not effectively account for the phenomena that occur in the context of a formal interview. First, URT (Berger, 1997; Berger & Calabrese, 1975) suggests that when attempting to reduce uncertainty communicators need to gather information about the other person. However, in the context of an interview, there are many restrictions on reciprocal information gathering. Even with self-disclosure on behalf of the applicant with a disability, the interviewer may not have enough information to reduce uncertainty.

Second, URT suggests that we attempt to reduce anxieties about whether we can predict or explain another's behavior by asking questions and by disclosing information about ourselves. In the context of an interpersonal interaction, self-disclosure is expected and helps to model reciprocated behavior, whereas in an interview context the interviewer is expected to do virtually all of the questioning and not to model appropriate disclosure behavior. Ironically, a successful applicant is expected to exhibit appropriate self-disclosure behavior without the aid of the interviewer's modeling behavior. As a result, the applicant may exhibit inappropriate behavior and jeopardize his or her credibility in the employment interview.

The third reason why uncertainty reduction may not occur is that interacting with a person with a disability deviates from normalcy. URT suggests that uncertainty increases when behavior deviates from what is considered normal. Interacting with an applicant with a disability in the context of an interview is a unique situation. In the context of the interpersonal setting, awkwardness and discomfort may exist, but the communicators are able to adjust to the situation more effectively. In the interview setting, communicators have more restrictions due to the formality of the interview.

Fourth, previous self-disclosure strategies focused on the simple process of disclosure while ignoring the power of strategic information (Dahnke, 1982). The literature shows that if the disclosure includes information that directly attacks typical stereotypes, the likelihood of reducing uncertainty should improve, and more precisely, it may help to improve ratings of acceptability, something previous studies did not find (Thompson, 1982; Thompson & Seibold, 1978).

Fifth, previous studies have largely ignored the impact of the content of disclosed information. Self-disclosure of messages that specifically address stereotypes about the disability rather than messages that only disclose general personal information is likely to have very different implications. This means that applicants with either a nonvisible or visible disability should control their own personal boundaries by presenting information that depicts them as being "normal," well adapted to their disability, and able to fulfill the job requirements.

Sixth, suggestions for effective interviewing strategies are based on the severity or visibility of the disability or on the context of the interaction event. Very little of this advice has been empirically tested. The inconsistent advice on self-disclosure as a way to reduce uncertainty may be due to the lack of specificity in regard to the intended manipulation of disclosure. For example, in an interpersonal setting, self-disclosure may be used to develop attractiveness or to squelch an inappropriate request for disability information (Braithwaite, 1991), whereas disclosure in an employment interview is almost always meant to create a positive impression (Stewart & Cash, 1997).

EXPECTED EMPLOYMENT INTERVIEWING
BEHAVIOR AND THE ADA

The employment interview is a "play" where both the applicant and interviewer have certain roles (Ralston & Kirkwood, 1995). There are scripts to follow, and these scripts allow for little deviation (Tullar, 1989), so the applicant who engages in risky behavior such as disclosing information about a disability may, in fact, not impress the interviewer. Baron (1989) contended that excessive and risky behavior negatively impacts the interviewer's judgment of the candidate. Disclosure about a disability may also make the interviewer uncomfortable if the high intimacy message indicates that reciprocity is expected (Berger, 1997; Berger & Bradac, 1982; Berger & Calabrese, 1975) or because it emphasizes differences between the nondisabled interviewer and the disabled applicant. The discomfort created by disability-related information may actually contribute to an interviewer judging an applicant more severely, and may even trigger negative information recall about the candidate (Bolster & Springbett, 1961).

When candidates decide to discuss a visible or nonvisible disability, they need to be conscious of the level of intimacy that they may be forcing in the interaction. Formal relationships such as that between the interviewer and interviewee are not conducive to intimate disclosure. Braithwaite (1991) noted that the ablebodied interactant (in this case, the interviewer) will likely not know how to react to disclosure about a disability and will not be able to respond with the same level of intimacy. For example, in one interview where I decided to talk about my disability, the interviewer apparently felt it necessary to talk about his or her sore back, and this caused feelings of embarrassment or inequity for both of us. This interaction is certainly not part of the expected employment interview script. This experience may contribute to a perception that the interviewer is losing control of the interview and result in a subsequent loss of respect for the applicant (Smart, 1989).

Ralston and Kirkwood (1995) wrote that "although each party in an employment interview hopes to gain valid information about the other, the interviewing literature does not advocate authentic self-disclosure by either party" (p. 82). The obvious suggestion is that applicants only provide positive information (Downs, Smeyak, & Martin, 1980). Most important, applicants with disabilities should recognize that any disclosure about their disability will be perceived as negative (Herold, 1995). Krefting (personal communication, March 17, 1995) suggested that the interviewee should never challenge or embarrass the interviewer and should even aim to comfort the decision maker. She contended that it is the obligation of applicants not to show off their credentials, but to pacify and put the interviewer at ease. By introducing the topic of disability, the applicant may be inadvertently raising concerns of compliance with the ADA and contributing to the interviewer's anxiousness and discomfort. Even though it seems reasonable from an interpersonal uncertainty reduction perspective that disclosure may help, in all likelihood it will contribute to an unsuccessful employment interview. Advice based on interpersonal communication appears less appropriate when one considers the rules of the interview. For instance, Thompson (1982) wrote:

> while disclosing information about oneself in general creates positive reactions, disclosing information about one's handicap creates even more favorable reactions for handicapped individuals. Talking about the disability may communicate that the bearer of the disability is comfortable with it, so others can be comfortable too, and *can feel free to ask questions about it.* (p. 199)

Just the opposite may be true in an employment interview. When we consider that interviewers are not to engage in "unnecessary" talk about the candidate's disability, then we should conclude that disability disclosure may actually highlight violations of normative interview behavior, even though it seems reasonable to disclose information about disability. In the context of an employment interview the ADA rules are unclear and bring into question whether the interviewer should ask any questions about disability.

The most subtle reason that disability disclosure may be ineffectual is the confusion created by the ADA law. Ironically, a law aimed at protecting the rights of the disabled may inhibit the search for employment. It appears that disability talk is considered off limits in an interview, and may be seen as unnecessary in the "don't tell, don't ask" mode within which many employers operate. In fact, disability-related disclosure may signal to the interviewer that the disabled candidate is not only knowledgeable about the ADA but may be willing to exercise his or her rights.

Braithwaite and Labrecque (1994) observed that, because of the ADA's intentional vagueness, those mandated to comply feel frustrated and may resent the same disabled community that the law is designed to empower (Shaprio, 1994). On the other hand, for many of us who are disabled, the vagueness of the ADA allows the chance to pursue previously unrecognized discrimination. For example, an interviewer might comment that their company could not offer a traveling sales position to a paraplegic applicant because the position requires a lot of driving, but could offer the same applicant a similar position as a telemarketer based at the home office. The ADA obviously does not address this situation directly. While the employer has attempted to offer a comparable position to accommodate the applicant, the applicant may choose to utilize the ADA to acquire the traveling sales position.

Braithwaite and Labrecque (1994) also argued that the ADA may provide the impetus for change. However, marginal improvements in employment, housing, and education suggest that the political movement is still in its embryonic state (LaPlante et al., 1997). Disability rights and advocacy groups send a clear message that empowerment is a grassroots movement that best gains strength through individual participation (Braithwaite & Labrecque, 1994; Golfus, personal communication, May 18, 1998).

IMPROVING EMPLOYABILITY FOR PERSONS WITH DISABILITIES

This chapter argues that it is the individual with a disability who must learn to effectively assert that he or she is employable based on competencies, and should not include reference to the disability in persuasive messages. Persons with visible and nonvisible disabilities should never disclose their disability until after the job offer has been secured. At that time, requests for reasonable accommodations should be presented. To ask for accommodations or to question a company policy before the job offer is made will likely put your candidacy at risk.

Arguably, an employer may be surprised or even angry that you did not disclose about a disability before being hired. At this point, however, the conversation can be considered an interpersonal communication event. In this context, disclosure is acceptable and could result in an open and honest relationship between co-workers. It may be beneficial to explain the ADA at this point and note that you did not want to cause uneasiness or jeopardize your chances in the interview.

This chapter advances five main points. First, recognize that the interview, no matter how casual, is not an interpersonal communication experience, and so advice stemming from that context does not necessarily apply. Second, it is important to recognize that an employment interview is mostly about keeping the interviewer comfortable. Third, knowing that your disability will likely contribute to the interviewer's discomfort, it is important to realize that you may be violating expected interviewing behavior. Fourth, recognize that disability disclosure is the ADA taboo. As an applicant, you have the power to reduce disability-related anxiousness by engaging in expected interviewing behavior. Fifth, and most important, make certain to align yourself with the organization for which you are applying by arguing that your competencies and talents are what make you a good fit for the particular organization. It seems that it is best to save the talk about awkward handshakes for interpersonal situations after having secured your job.

Future research in this area is needed and strongly encouraged. The lack of generalizability of communication research from the interpersonal context to the interviewing context underlines the need for future research to look at varying types of disabilities in different contexts. A careful look at the unemployment figures shows that employment opportunities for persons with nonvisible and less salient disabilities are improving ever so slightly, while the outlook for persons with severe disabilities continues to be very bleak. I challenge others to contribute to research that will provide answers to the employment challenges being faced by persons with disabilities.

DISCUSSION QUESTIONS

1. Based on Herold's arguments that URT's strategy of self-disclosure as a way to manage stigma is less than effective, what communication strategies would you suggest an applicant with a disability employ?
2. After the job has been offered, what interpersonal and organizational benefits are there for a nonvisibly disabled employee to disclose information about a disability? What are the interpersonal and organizational consequences?
3. Persons with disabilities have an extraordinary unemployment rate. Not surprisingly, those with the most severe and those with developmental disabilities experience the highest rates of unemployment. There has been almost no work in the communication field that examines the phenomena of developmental disabilities. Why? Can macro and micro theories and concepts of communication be generalized to this population?
4. A recent observation advanced by several prodisability constituencies is that persons with disabilities have much improved employment opportunities because of computers. As a matter of fact, some

suggest that the disabled applicant take advantage of computers and sell themselves as essentially "at home" employees. In one sense it is argued that computers have made the playing field even because the disabled employee will not have to worry about commuting and other accessibility issues. On the other hand, while organizations get a great employee and do not have to worry about expensive accommodations, are they not essentially contributing to segregation of disabled employees? What are the concerns on both sides of the issue? What ethical or moral questions should organizations consider?

5. The ADA law is very ambiguous. How do applicants with disabilities and employers benefit or suffer due to this ambiguity?

REFERENCES

Albrecht, G. L. (1992). *The disability business: Rehabilitation in America.* Newbury Park, CA: Sage.

Baron, R. A. (1989). Impression management by applicants during employment interviews: "Too much of a good thing" effect. In R. W. Eder & G. R. Ferris (Eds.), *The employment interview: Theory, research, and practice* (pp. 204–216). Newbury Park, CA: Sage.

Belgrave, F. Z., & Mills, J. (1981). Effect upon desire for social interaction with a physically disabled person mentioning the disability in different contexts. *Journal of Applied Social Psychology, 11,* 44–57.

Berger, C. R. (1997). *Planning strategic interaction: Attaining goals through communicative action.* Mahwah, NJ: Lawrence Erlbaum Associates.

Berger, C. R., & Bradac, J. J. (1982). *Language and social knowledge.* London: Edward Arnold.

Berger, C. R., & Calabrese, R. J. (1975). Some explorations in initial interaction and beyond: Toward a developmental theory of interpersonal communication. *Human Communication Research, 3,* 29–46.

Bolster, B. I., & Springbett, B. M. (1961). The reaction of interviewers to favorable and unfavorable information. *Journal of Applied Psychology, 45,* 97–103.

Bordieri, J., & Drehmer, D. E. (1987). Attribution of responsibility and predicted social acceptance of disabled workers. *Rehabilitation Counseling Bulletin, 3,* 218–226.

Braithwaite, D. O. (1991). "Just how much did that wheelchair cost?": Management of privacy boundaries by persons with disabilities. *Western Journal of Speech Communication, 55,* 254–274.

Braithwaite, D. O., & Braithwaite, C. A. (1997). Understanding communication of persons with disabilities as cultural communication. In L. A. Samovar & R. E. Porter (Eds.), *Intercultural communication: A reader* (pp. 154–164). Belmont, CA: Wadsworth.

Braithwaite, D. O., & Labrecque, D. (1994). Responding to the Americans with Disabilities Act: Contributions of interpersonal communication research and training. *Journal of Applied Communication, 22,* 287–294.

Coleman, L. M., & DePaulo, B. M. (1991). Uncovering the human spirit: Moving beyond disability and "missed" communications. In N. Coupland, H. Giles, & J. M. Weimann (Eds.), *"Miscommunication" and problematic talk* (pp. 61–84). Newbury Park, CA: Sage.

Corbet, B. (1995). Billy Golfus' righteous surprise. *New Mobility, 6*(19), 42–44.

Cozby, P. C. (1972). Self-disclosure, reciprocity and liking. *Sociometry, 35,* 151–160.

Dahnke, G. L. (1982). Communication between handicapped and non-handicapped persons: Toward a deductive theory. In M. L. McLaughlin (Ed.), *Communication Yearbook 6* (pp. 92–135). Beverly Hills, CA: Sage.

Derlega, V. J., & Chaikin, A. L. (1977). Privacy and self-disclosure in social relationships. *Journal of Social Issues, 33*, 102–115.

Downs, C. W., Smeyak, G. P., & Martin, E. (1980). *Professional interviewing.* New York: Harper & Row.

Einhorn, L. J. (1981). An inner view of the job interview: An investigation of successful communicative behaviors. *Communication Education, 30*, 217–228.

Galassi, J. P., & Galassi, M. D. (1978). Preparing individuals for job interviews: Suggestions from more than 60 years of research. *Personnel and Guidance Journal, 57*, 188–192.

Glideman, J., & Roth, W. (1980). *The unexpected minority: Handicapped children in America.* New York: Harcourt Brace.

Golfus, B. (1995, January–February). Righteous surprise. *New Mobility, 9*, 42–44.

Goffman, E. (1963). *Stigma: Notes of the management of spoiled identity.* Englewood Cliffs, NJ: Prentice-Hall.

Gouvier, W. D., Steiner, D. D., Jackson, W. T., Schlater, D., & Rain, J. S. (1991). Employment discrimination against handicapped job candidates: An analog study of the effects of neurological causation, visibility of handicap, and public contact. *Rehabilitation Psychology, 36*, 121–129.

Grove, T. G., & Werkman, D. L. (1991). Conversations with able-bodied and visibly disabled strangers: An adversarial test of predicted outcome value and uncertainty reduction theories. *Human Communication Research, 17*, 507–534.

Hastorf, A. H., Wildfogel, I., & Cassman, T. (1979). Acknowledgment of handicap as a tactic in social interaction. *Journal of Personality and Social Psychology, 37*, 1790–1797.

Heilman, M. E., Martell, R. F., & Simon, M. C. (1988). The vagaries of sex bias: Conditions regulating the undervaluation, equivaluation, and overvaluation of female job applicants. *Organizational Behavior and Human Decision Processes, 41*, 98–110.

Herold, K. P. (1995). *An examination of different levels of self-disclosure for a job applicant with a non-visible or visible disability.* Unpublished doctoral dissertation, University of Southern Mississippi, Hattiesburg.

Jackson, N., Peacock, A., & Smith, J. P. (1980). Impressions of personality in the employment interview. *Journal of Personality and Social Psychology, 39*, 294–307.

Johnson, V. A., Greenwood, K., & Schriner, K. F. (1988). Work performance and work personality: Employer concerns about workers with disabilities. *Rehabilitation Counseling Bulletin, 32*, 50–57.

Kleck, R. E. (1968). Self-disclosure patterns of the non obviously stigmatized. *Psychological Reports, 23*, 1239–1248.

Krefting, L. A., & Brief, A. P. (1976). The impact of applicant disability on evaluative judgments in the selection process. *Academy of Management Journal, 19*, 675–680.

Kreps, G. L. (1993, November). *Disability and culture: Effects on multicultural relations in modern organizations.* Paper presented at the annual meeting of the Speech Communication Association, Miami Beach, FL.

LaPlante, M. P., Kennedy, J., Kaye, S., Wegner, B. L. (1997). *Disability and employment* (Disability Statistics Abstract # 11). Washington, DC: NIDRR.

Marks, E., & Lewis, A. (1983). *Job hunting for the disabled.* Woodbury, NY: Barron's.

Patzer, G. L. (1985). *The physical attractiveness phenomena.* New York: Plenum.

Race, W. (1972). "Social action." *Proceedings Review: Twelfth World Congress of Rehabilitation International, 2*, 221–223.

Ralston, S. M., & Kirkwood, W. G. (1995). Overcoming managerial bias in employment interviewing. *Journal of Applied Communication Research, 23*, 75–92.

Royse, D., & Edwards, T. (1989). Communicating about disability: Attitudes and preferences of persons with physical handicaps. *Rehabilitation Counseling Bulletin, 32*, 203–211.

Rubin, K. (1997). *U.S. Census Bureau: The official statistics*. Washington, DC: Author.

Sabsay, S., & Platt, M. (1985). Weaving the cloak of competence: A paradox in the management of troubled conversations between retarded and nonretarded interlocutors. In S. Sabsay & M. Platt (Eds.), *Social setting, stigma, and communicative competence: Explorations of the conversational interactions of retarded adults* (pp. 95–116). Amsterdam: John Benjamins.

Shaprio, J. P. (1994). *No pity: People with disabilities forging a new civil rights movement*. New York: Random House.

Smart, K. M. (1989). *Selection interviewing for managers*. New York: Harper & Row.

Spitzberg, B. H. (1994). The dark side of (in)competence. In W. R. Cupach & B. H. Spitzberg (Eds.), *The dark side of interpersonal communication* (pp. 25–49). Fort Worth, TX: Holt, Rinehart & Winston.

Steele, F. (1975). *The open organization: The impact of secrecy and disclosure on people and organizations*. Reading, MA: Addison Wesley.

Stewart, C., & Cash, W. (1997). *Interviewing principles & practices* (8th ed.). Madison, WI: Brown & Benchmark.

Stone, C. I., & Sawatzki, B. (1980). Hiring bias and the disabled interviewee: Effects of manipulating work history and disability information of the disabled job applicant. *Journal of Vocational Behavior, 16*, 96–104.

Sunnafrank, M. (1986). Predicted outcome value during initial interactions: A reformulation of uncertainty reduction theory. *Human Communication Research, 13*, 3–33.

Tagalakis, V., Amsel, R., & Fichten, C. S. (1988). Job interviewing strategies for people with a visible disability. *Journal of Applied Social Psychology, 18*, 520–532.

Thompson, T. L. (1982). Disclosure as a disability-management strategy: A review and conclusions. *Communication Quarterly, 30*, 196–202.

Thompson, T. L., & Seibold, D. (1978). Stigma management in "normal" stigmatized interactions: A test of the disclosure hypothesis and a model of stigma acceptance. *Human Communication Research, 4*, 231–241.

Tosi, H. L., & Einbender, S. W. (1985). The effects of the type and amount of information in sex discrimination research: A meta-analysis. *Academy of Management Review, 28*, 712–723.

Tullar, W. L. (1989). The employment interview as a cognitive performing script. In R. W. Eders & G. R. Ferris (Eds.), *The employment interview: Theory, research, and practice* (pp. 233–245). Newbury Park, CA: Sage.

Wiss, K. A. (1997, November). *Redefinition or re-marginalization of people with disabilities?: An analysis of disability as culture*. Paper presented at the National Communication Association, Chicago, IL.

Witt, M. A. (1992). *Job strategies for people with disabilities*. Princeton, NJ: Peterson's Guides.

Worthy, M., Gary, A. L., & Kahn, G. M. (1969). Self-disclosure as an exchange process. *Journal of Personality and Social Psychology, 13*, 59–63.

Yuker, H. E. (Ed.). (1988). *Attitudes toward persons with disabilities*. New York: Springer.

10

Disability and Culture: Effects on Multicultural Relations in Modern Organizations

Gary L. Kreps
National Cancer Institute

Keywords: Stigma, cultural ideologies, valuing diversity, pluralistic integration

The Americans With Disabilities Act (ADA) was passed less than a decade ago as a new federal law requiring all organizations to provide equal access and opportunities for employment to individuals with disabilities. The primary goal of the law is to facilitate equal opportunities for full participation of people with disabilities in virtually all American organizations (Miller, 1997). To conform with the mandates of this new law, avoid potential litigation and fines, and preserve any federal funding, most business, education, and government organizations are developing and implementing new strategies for accomplishing the goals of the ADA. While this act promises to open up many new opportunities for people living with physical challenges, it may appear that in actual practice many of the strategies developed by organizations in response to the ADA have been superficial, focus more on form than on substance, and leave a large communication gap between the work lives and career opportunities of the ablebodied and the physically challenged.

It is my contention that aggressive action must be taken to challenge and diminish the insidious underlying stigma and societal prejudice confronting many people living with disabilities (see the following for a discussion of stigma and people with disabilities: Braithwaite, 1996, 1989; Liachowitz, 1988; Thompson, 1986; Thompson & Seibold, 1978). "People with disabilities face bigotry, stereotyping, and exclusion in the workplace based solely on who they are" (Miller, 1997, p. 11). A recent national survey of the work experiences of a broad cross section of people living with disabilities conducted by *Careers and the disAbled* magazine found that respondents "want co-workers, human resource managers, and top-level executives to become more sensitized to their needs and to lead the way in creating a corporate culture that values their differences" (Schneider, 1996, p. 28). Without taking into consideration many of the engrained cultural barriers that face people with disabilities, modern organizations adapting to the ADA are likely to provide only cosmetic changes in the quality of organizational life and the long-term organizational opportunities available to these people.

To meet the mandates of the ADA, there currently appears to be much greater organizational interest and effort concerning the installation of physically adaptive devices (such as ramps and elevators for individuals who use wheelchairs or the introduction of computers and typewriters equipped with Braille touchpads for individuals with visual limitations) than with effectively integrating disabled individuals communicatively within the mainstream of organizational life. I do not mean to minimize the importance of these adaptive devices for enabling people with physical challenges to have entry into the workplace. The introduction of adaptive devises such as ramps, elevators, curb-cuts, door handles, and so forth have certainly been good additions to organizational life for people living with physical challenges and for many other organizational participants. They increase organizational access and even make it easier for people delivering goods and negotiating offices while carrying packages. I am concerned, though, that many organizations confuse such opportunities for entry into organizations with widespread organizational acceptance and opportunity. While the introduction of adaptive devices is an essential first step in enabling individuals with disabilities to participate fully in organizational life, installation of such devices alone is clearly an insufficient and superficial measure in meeting the far-ranging ADA goals for equal opportunities and involvement in organizational life for people with disabilities (Morrissey, 1992). Paul Steven Miller (1997), the commissioner of the U.S. Equal Employment Opportunities Commission, in a recent article evaluating the progress that has been made since passage of the ADA noted that

> we still have much work to do. Persons with disabilities continue to have the highest unemployment rates and the largest number of people living in poverty of any group in American society. More than 60 percent of working age disabled persons are without jobs. Continued systemic discrimination and segregation have combined to prevent many potential workers with disabilities from entering the American workplace. (pp. 10–11)

Without concerted efforts to change the stereotypic and condescending communication attitudes, values, and expectations about disabled individuals that are evident in modern organizational life (and within the larger society), coupled with the development and implementation of effective communicative strategies for promoting the expression of respect, sensitivity, and caring in organizations that are necessary to facilitate relational development between ablebodied and disabled organizational actors, the noble goals of the ADA will never be attained. As Braithwaite (1986) so elegantly explained, "While many physical barriers associated with disability can be detected and corrected, the social barriers resulting from disability are much more insidious. Nowhere are the barriers more apparent than in the communication relationships between persons with disabilities and ablebodied persons" (p. 1). This chapter examines some of the major barriers and primary cultural issues influencing the promotion of effective communication between organizational participants that must be considered and acted on to fully accomplish the far-reaching goals of the ADA.

DISABILITY, CULTURE, AND COMMUNICATION

Disability is a primary cultural attribute that influences communication between ablebodied and disabled persons (Braithwaite, 1984, 1985, 1986, 1987, 1988, 1989; Dahnke, 1982; Emry & Wiseman, 1987; Fox & Giles, 1996; Padden & Humphries, 1988; Thompson, 1981, 1987; Thompson & Cundiff, 1979; Wiseman & Emry, 1987). Culture is a complex and multifaceted social phenomenon that has powerful influences on all aspects of modern life. Culture refers to the collective sense making of members of social groups; the shared ways they make sense of reality. Culture consists of shared beliefs, values, and attitudes that guide the behaviors of group members (Geertz, 1973; Gudykunst, Ting-Toomey, & Chua, 1988; Kreps, 1990). Brown (1963) explained that culture "refers to all the accepted and patterned ways of behavior of a given people. It is a body of common understandings. It is the sum total and the organization or arrangement of all the group's ways of thinking, feeling, and acting" (pp. 3–4).

People of different ages, educational levels, socioeconomic standing, occupations, sexual orientations, and even of different health conditions can be said to belong to their own cultural groups (Kreps & Kunimoto, 1994). Persons who share specific physical, mental, and health conditions, such as people who are blind, deaf, or paralyzed have their own cultural orientations, as do people who are dying, or who have diabetes, cancer, or AIDS. In this chapter I am particularly concerned with the ways the unique cultural perspectives of people with disabilities have been marginalized and stigmatized within modern organizations and society.

THE CRISIS OF CULTURE
IN MODERN SOCIETY

Modern life is currently in cultural turmoil and transition (Locke, 1992; Schlesinger, 1992). While society is becoming increasingly multicultural, with increasing participation of individuals representing many different national, ethnic, racial, gender, and professional cultures in political, educational, business, and health care settings (Copeland, 1988; Lambrinos, 1992), uncertainty about how to communicate effectively across these different cultures has made modern life increasingly challenging (Geber, 1990). Nowhere is this uncertainty more evident than in communication between ablebodied and disabled persons in modern organizational life (Liachowitz, 1988; Thompson & Cundiff, 1979; Thompson & Seibold, 1978).

An examination of relevant literature and social trends suggests there is a historical pattern to the ways American society has responded to increasing cultural diversity (Schlesinger, 1992). Kreps and Kunimoto (1994) identified three major cultural ideologies that have emerged over time as competing interpretive and behavioral frameworks for guiding the ways people respond to the equivocality of cultural diversity. These ideologies include (a) cultural segregation, (b) naive integration, and (c) pluralistic integration.

The earliest, and unfortunately perhaps the most prevalent, of these perspectives is the ideology of cultural segregation. This ideology emphasizes cultural dominance and separation between the dominant culture (usually the cultural group that has been around the longest or controls the largest share of economic resources) and other "marginal" cultural groups (Schlesinger, 1992). In the ideology of segregation, the group that serves as the dominant culture dictates the cultural standards by which all members are judged. The dominant culture in organizational life is often represented by white, male, well-educated, and wealthy individuals, although this may vary based on which cultures are numerically predominant or influential within the membership of a particular organization (Kanter, 1977). For example, Kreps (1987) reported a study of reverse sexism in health care where female nurses were the dominant culture and male nurses belonged to a "marginal" culture within a large urban medical center.

In the case of disability, the ideology of cultural segregation has led to the ostracization and disconfirmation of disabled people by physically and socially segregating them from the dominant (ablebodied) culture. Mike Ervin explained this perspective so clearly: "After all these years, I suddenly understood what it was about that 'physically challenged' stuff that always made me cringe in pain. We're not challenged! We're oppressed!" (1997, p. 67). Soyster (1993) suggested that disability has negated his personhood by making him invisible or, worse, a target of pity, poignantly illustrating the social disconfirmation that occurs to him now that he is confined to a wheelchair: "People see through me now or over me. They don't see me at all. Or they fix me with that plangent aching stare: sympathy" (p. 12). The stigma surrounding disability disconfirms the social status of disabled persons, reducing disabled persons from whole and fully functioning members of society to nonentities or persons who are the objects of pity (Goffman, 1963).

Society has also segregated people living with the challenges of disabilities by physically separating them from others, institutionalizing disabled persons in special schools, group homes, rehabilitation centers, long-term care facilities, and nursing homes. This segregation of disabled persons from the dominant culture serves to further invalidate and disconfirm people with disabilities, while providing most ablebodied persons with limited opportunities to get to know and develop relationships with disabled persons (Thompson, 1986). Is it any surprise that the ideology of segregation inevitably leads to prejudicial treatment of people with disabilities in society? In organizations that subscribe to the ideology of segregation, prejudicial treatment results in job discrimination, unfair hiring practices, and limited opportunities for people with disabilities. Liachowitz (1988) compared the societal discrimination facing people with disabilities with the prejudice and segregation faced by African Americans:

First, most people who diverge from either racial or physical norms share the problem of evoking unpredictable, but usually negative, responses—from the majority population. Second, whether based on biological ascription or social attribution, minority groups often face a common personal and political dilemma. Many of their members want the same treatment accorded those who meet culturally accepted norms, but think that they may need, and often construct their lives to rely on, the extraordinary treatment that society gives to an abnormal group. Third, members of both groups are often forced to meet their need for belonging, and their need for personal and political recognition, by establishing or joining groups composed of "their own kind." (p. 4)

The similarities in discrimination confronting people with physical challenges and African Americans is indicative of the needs both groups of people have for dignity, equity, and opportunity in society and in organizational life.

Murphy (1987) illustrated the discrimination confronting people living with significant physical challenges even more personally when he describes the ways that he was treated after he became a quadriplegic:

The recently disabled paralytic faces the world with a changed body and an altered identity—which even by itself would make his reentry into society a delicate and chancy matter. But his future is made even more perilous by the treatment given him by the nondisabled, including some of his oldest friends and associates, and even family members. Although this varies considerably from one situation to another, there is a clear pattern in the United States and in many other countries, of prejudice toward people with disabilities and debasement of their social status, which find their most extreme expressions in avoidance, fear, and outright hostility. (p. 112)

The ADA was designed to confront such discrimination and dehumanization by promoting organizational equity and opportunity for people living with disabilities.

The dominant culture establishes normative rules for acceptable behavior within social systems, forcing all members to either adopt these prescribed behaviors, or be isolated, alienated, and punished. Within organizations such punishment often takes the form of limited access to relevant information, as well as decreased social influence and respect. Under this "melting pot" ideology individuals are encouraged to give up their own cultural identities and to the greatest extent possible to adopt the cultural perspective of the dominant culture. Metacommunication is used to clearly demonstrate to members that it is to their long-term benefit to emulate the dominant culture if they want to succeed (Kreps & Kunimoto, 1994). This is a double-bind for people with disabilities, who by virtue of their disabilities can rarely effectively emulate the ablebodied. They can never give up their cultural orientation and adopt the ablebodied culture as their own, nor should they want to. Their very physical beings prevent them from effectively "passing" as representatives of the dominant (ablebodied) culture. Further, this fails to respect the individuality of people with physical challenges and undermines their independence.

The ideology of segregation is based on ethnocentrism, where members of the dominant culture assume that their cultural perspective is "best" and other cultural orientations are inferior. This ethnocentric orientation has caused many problems in society (and in modern organizational life) by alienating individuals who are not members of the dominant culture, decreasing the exchange of relevant information between individuals from different cultural perspectives, and diminishing the extra energy (synergy) that derives from multicultural cooperation. Modern organizations will have to reverse the prejudice, segregation, and disconfirmation that people with disabilities commonly face as a result of ethnocentrism, promoting the development of effective multicultural relations between disabled and ablebodied organizational actors, if they are to achieve the goals established by the ADA. This can only be achieved by changing the underlying attitudes organizational participants have toward people living with physical challenges. Unfortunately, the ideology of segregation reinforces prejudicial attitudes toward people living with disabilities.

The second cultural ideology to emerge is the ideology of naive integration, which purports to accept fully all cultural groups, but, like the ideology of segregation, invariably emphasizes coopting of "marginal" cultures by dominant cultural groups. This ideology publicly espouses respect for different cultural perspectives, yet those in key decision-making positions invariably follow the ethnocentric dogma of the dominant culture. For example, token representatives of "marginal" cultural groups are often hired to visible positions within modern organizations to give the image of organizational pluralism, but are rarely given much authority unless they denounce their cultural roots and adopt the dominant norm system. This naive integration ideology is all too prevalent in modern organizations and causes as many problems as the ideology of segregation because, like the ideology of segregation, it undermines multicultural synergy. Naive integration is even more sinister than the ideology of segregation because it falsely purports to respect cultural diversity, giving the handicapped the false expectation of equity and opportunity. It is my fear that the ADA is being implemented from the ideological perspective of naive integration, where cosmetic "concessions" are being made to people with disabilities, without really providing the respect and opportunities disabled persons need to participate fully in organizational life (see, e.g., the following literature about implementation of the ADA: Blanck & Marti, 1997; Longmore, 1998; U.S. Department of Labor, 1997; Young, 1997).

The newest cultural ideology to emerge, and the one that I advocate to achieve the goals of the ADA, is pluralistic integration. In the ideology of pluralistic integration respect is shown for cultural diversity, members of different cultural groups are encouraged to retain and express their cultural perspectives, and social systems reap the benefits of having members share relevant information, eliciting both cooperation and synergy. This ideology is difficult to implement because it depends on using communication to establish and maintain effective multicultural relations. Therefore, competent and sensitive communication is the key to pluralistic integration and effective multicultural relations in organizational life.

The development and implementation of training programs can help organization members enhance their interpersonal communication skills and increase their sensitivity toward the feelings and aspirations of all people. Interpersonal training might focus on the skills needed for competent and sensitive communication, such as effective listening and the expression of empathy toward others. Participants should learn how to use verbal and nonverbal messages to provide meaningful feedback and develop mutually satisfying interpersonal relationships. Sensitivity training can also help promote greater understanding and empathy among organizational participants. Similarly, the use of films, forums for open discussion, and guest speakers representing unique and provocative cultural perspectives can also help raise consciousness among organizational participants. Such communication interventions can facilitate widespread adoption of pluralistic ideologies within organizations to promote increased equity and opportunity for all organization members.

VALUING CULTURAL DIVERSITY

To achieve the goals set forth by the ADA, I recommend the development and expression of genuine interest and respect for different cultural orientations in organizational life. Not only should organization members be tolerant of different cultural perspectives, they should demonstrate active interest and admiration for the cultural norms of other cultures. They must clearly recognize the great value of cultural diversity. By recognizing that cultural norms do not develop haphazardly, but are developed specifically to help cultural members cope with the many constraints they face in the world, organization members will recognize the information value of learning about other cultures and interacting with members of different cultures.

Cultural exploration can teach us a great deal and help us appreciate the great beauty in the different ways that cultures frame reality, establish social organization, and accomplish different goals. The norms governing different aspects of life develop specifically to help cultural groups accomplish their goals within unique physical, social, and political environments. By examining these cultural norms we learn new ways of interpreting and responding to different environments, increase our sophistication and understanding of the world, enhance our abilities to interact meaningfully with people from different cultures, and learn about the differences and commonalties among different peoples.

The exploration of different cultures can help us learn about new ways of interpreting reality, increasing our understanding of other people, their experiences, and the world they live in. The demonstration of respect and interest in the cultural perspectives of others can also serve as a foundation for developing supportive and cooperative relationships with people from different cultures. The norm of reciprocity is a general rule of human behavior that asserts that we feel obliged to respond to others in a manner that is complementary to the way they act toward us (Gouldner, 1960; Kreps, 1990; Kreps & Kunimoto, 1994). The expression of respect and interest validates the legitimacy and worth of others' cultural backgrounds, encourages their reciprocal interest in our cultural orientation, and provides a basis for communication. Mutual exploration of cultural similarities and differences between members of two different cultures helps to make the implicit norms of these different cultures explicit. By learning about each others' rules, expectations, and motivations for behavior, we can diminish the potential of violating each others' cultural norms and encourage the growth of reciprocal respect and cooperation. We also become more multicultural ourselves by learning about and adopting ideas and rituals from other cultures, increasing our abilities to understand different cultural perspectives, adapt to different situations, and interact effectively with representatives of different cultures.

The theory of weak ties suggests that the information value (new information) to be gained by communicating with others from very different cultural orientations is much greater than the information value of interacting with people who share similar cultural perspectives (Granovetter, 1973; Kreps, 1990; Liu & Duff, 1972; Rogers & Agarwala-Rogers, 1976). People from different cultures have more new information to offer each other then people from similar cultures. People who share similar cultural backgrounds are likely to see the world in very similar ways and develop similar solutions to problems. Although this is comforting and reinforcing for us, it does not provide us with innovative ideas and creative solutions to problems. People who share different cultural backgrounds are likely to see the world very differently and develop different solutions to problems. These differences can be challenging and uncomfortable for us because they question the legitimacy of our own cultural orientations. However, if we recognize that there are many different legitimate perspectives on and interpretations of reality, as well as many different ways to solve problems, we welcome the new information gained from divergent cultural orientations.

Unfortunately, although interaction with people from different cultural orientations is likely to provide us with rich new information, it is also more difficult to communicate effectively with those who are different from us than it is to communicate with those to whom we are similar. We are more likely to understand those who are similar to us. We are less likely to violate cultural norms because we are likely to already understand and conform to the cultural guidelines that govern the behaviors of those who are similar to us. It is easier for us to understand those who are similar to us since we probably use similar vocabulary and communication rituals, and are probably familiar with the ideas and logics culturally similar individuals are likely to espouse. To communicate effectively with those who are culturally dissimilar to us, we must be willing to endure the discomfort of unfamiliarity and uncertainty. We must work to overcome communication barriers, to understand different communication patterns, rituals, logics, and norms. We must be open-minded and receptive. We must be willing to disclose personal information and be open to self-disclosure by others (Thompson, 1982). If we can develop the ability to communicate effectively with those who are culturally dissimilar we can learn a great deal from our interactions.

The systems theory principle of equifinality suggests that the attainment of system goals is not determined solely by the initial conditions confronting the system, but that system goals can be reached by the system from different initial conditions in many different ways (Bertalanffy, 1968; Kreps, 1990). There are many different ways of accomplishing goals, based on different environmental conditions and constraints. Exploration of different cultural perspectives can increase our abilities to achieve our goals by helping to identify different strategies for solving complex problems.

CONCLUSION

People with physical challenges have a lot to offer to modern organizations. "Study after study shows that hiring individuals with disabilities makes good business sense" (Coehlo, 1997, p. 14). Employers must "realize that employees with a disability try harder, and work harder, appreciate having a job, and have a greater level of maturity—all assets to any business" (Schnieider, 1996, p. 30). *Careers and the disAbled* magazine presented a survey of the work experiences of a broad cross section of people living with disabilities. In the conclusion of that report, they offered employers the following suggestions focused on improving organizational communication: speaking to people with disabilities just like any other workers, communicating honestly with people with disabilities, judging employees solely on their qualifications and performance, providing sensitivity and disability training to all members of the organization, and asking disabled employees what can be done to help them feel part of the organization (Schneider, 1996, p. 30). These recommendations reflect a cultural ideology of pluralistic integration, where all organization members are treated with support and respect. Sensitive and effective organizational communication is an essential ingredient to implementing the ADA and achieving its primary goals (Braithwaite & Labrecque, 1994; Nemeth, 1993)

To achieve the far-reaching goals of the ADA, modern organizations will have to go well beyond the introduction of physically adaptive devices. They will have to reexamine and rethink the often provincial cultural ideologies that govern the ways their members think and act toward disabled persons. Only by adopting a cultural ideology of pluralistic integration can organization members overcome the ethnocentrism and resultant prejudice that prevents disabled persons from participating fully in modern organizational life. Adopting a cultural ideology of pluralistic integration involves developing sensitivity, respect, and interest in the different cultural perspectives of organizational participants, establishing an organization-wide propensity toward valuing cultural diversity, and utilizing the unique cultural perspectives of organizational participants to enrich organizational life and guide organizational action.

DISCUSSION QUESTIONS

1. What are the primary goals of the ADA?
2. How effective has the ADA been in achieving all its goals? Give examples.
3. How do cultural ideologies influence the ways people with disabilities are treated in modern organizations?
4. Describe the primary barriers confronting people with disabilities in modern organizations.
5. How can human communication be used to implement the ADA fully and help achieve its primary goals?

REFERENCES

Bertalanffy, L. (1968). *General system theory*. New York: Braziller.

Blanck, P. D., & Marti, M. W. (1997). Attitudes, behavior and the employment provisions of the Americans with Disabilities Act. *Villanova Law Review, 42*(2), 345–407.

Braithwaite, D. O. (1984, February). *Able-bodied and disabled persons' communication: The disabled person's perspective*. Paper presented at the Western Speech Communication Association Conference, Seattle, WA.

Braithwaite, D. O. (1985, November). *Impression management and redefinition of self by persons with disabilities*. Paper presented at the Speech Communication Association Conference, Denver, CO.

Braithwaite, D. O. (1986, February). *Redefinitions of disability and identification as a subculture by persons with physical disabilities*. Paper presented to the Western Speech Communication Association Conference, Tucson, AZ.

Braithwaite, D. O. (1987, November). *If you push my wheelchair don't make car sounds: On the problem of "help" between disabled and able-bodied persons*. Paper presented at the Speech Communication Association Conference, Boston, MA.

Braithwaite, D. O. (1988, November). "Just how much did that wheelchair cost?": Management of boundaries by persons with disabilities. *Western Journal of Communication, 55*, 254–274.

Braithwaite, D. O. (1989, November). *Communicating as "normal" by persons with disabilities: Overcoming stigma or deifying normality*. Paper presented to the Speech Communication Association Conference, San Francisco.

Braithwaite, D. O. (1996). "I am a person first": Different perspectives on the communication of persons with disabilities. In E. B. Ray (Ed.), *Communication and disenfranchisement: Social health issues and implications* (pp. 257–272). Mahwah, NJ: Lawrence Erlbaum Associates.

Braithwaite, D. O., & Labrecque, D. (1994). Responding to the Americans with disabilities act: Contributions of interpersonal communication research and training. *Journal of Applied Communication, 22*, 287–294.

Brown, I. C. (1963). *Understanding other cultures*. Englewood Cliffs, NJ: Prentice-Hall.

Coehlo, T. (1997). Dollars, cents, and sensibility: What businesses should know about employees with disabilities and how to recruit them. *Enable Magazine, 1*(1), 14–16.

Copeland, L. (1988). Valuing diversity, part 2: Pioneers and champions of change. *Personnel, 65*(7), 44–49.

Dahnke, G. (1982). Communication between handicapped and non-handicapped persons: Toward a deductive theory. In M. Burgoon (Ed.), *Communication Yearbook 6* (pp. 92–135). Newbury Park, CA: Sage.

Emry, R., & Wiseman, R. L. (1987). An intercultural understanding of ablebodied and disabled persons' communication. *International Journal of Intercultural Relations, 11*, 7–27.

Ervin, M. (1997). The joy of oppression. *New Mobility, 8*(40), 67.

Fox, S. A., & Giles, H. (1996). "Let the wheelchair through": An intergroup approach to interability communication. In W. P. Robinson (Ed.), *Social groups and identity: The developing legacy of Henri Tajfel* (pp. 215–248). Boston: Butterworth-Heinemann.

Geber, B. (1990). Managing diversity. *Training, 27*(7), 23–30.

Geertz, C. (1973). *The interpretation of culture.* New York: Basic Books.

Goffman, E. (1963). *Stigma: Notes on the management of spoiled identity.* Englewood Cliffs, NJ: Prentice-Hall.

Gouldner, A. W. (1960). The norm of reciprocity: A preliminary statement. *American Sociological Review, 25*, 161–178.

Granovetter, M. (1973). The strength of weak ties. *American Journal of Sociology, 78*, 1360–1380.

Gudykunst, W. B., Ting-Toomey, S., & Chua, E. (1988). *Culture and interpersonal communication.* Newbury Park, CA: Sage.

Kanter, R. M. (1977). *Men and women of the corporation.* New York: Basic Books.

Kreps, G. L. (1987). Organizational sexism in health care. In L. Stewart & S. Ting-Toomey (Eds.), *Communication, gender and sex roles in diverse interaction contexts* (pp. 228–236). Norwood, NJ: Ablex.

Kreps, G. L. (1990). *Organizational communication: Theory and practice* (2nd ed.). White Plains, NY: Longman.

Kreps, G. L., & Kunimoto, E. (1994). *Communicating effectively in multicultural health care settings.* Newbury Park, CA: Sage.

Lambrinos, J. (1992). Tomorrow's workforce: Challenge for today. *The Bureaucrat, 20*(4), 27–29.

Liachowitz, C. L. (1988). *Disability as a social construct: Legislative roots.* Philadelphia: University of Pennsylvania Press.

Liu, W., & Duff, R. (1972). The strength of weak ties. *Public Opinion Quarterly, 36*, 361–366.

Locke, D. C. (Ed.) (1992). *Increasing multicultural understanding.* Newbury Park, CA: Sage.

Longmore, P. K. (1998). Disrespecting disabilities. *California Lawyer, 18*(1), 48–49, 84–87.

Miller, P. S. (1997). Seven years later: Seven years of removing barriers. *Enable Magazine, 1*(1), 10–11.

Morrissey, P. A. (1992). Etiquette, protocol, and the ADA. *Disability Compliance Bulletin, 3*(6), 1–3.

Murphy, R. F. (1987). *The body silent.* New York: Henry Holt.

Nemeth, S. A. (1993, November). *Self advocacy and the Americans with Disabilities Act: A win-win situation for rehabilitation professionals and their clients.* Paper presented at the annual meeting of the Speech Communication Association, Miami, FL.

Padden, C., & Humphries, T. (1988). *Deaf in America: Voices from a culture.* Cambridge, MA: Harvard University Press.

Rogers, E. M., & Agarwala-Rogers, R. (1976). *Communication in organizations.* New York: Free Press.

Schlesinger, A. M. (1992). *The disuniting of America: Reflections on a multicultural society.* New York: W. W. Norton.

Schneider, J. (1996, Winter). Sixth annual readers survey. *Careers and the disAbled, 11*(2), 28–31.

Soyster, M. (1993, October 11). Living under Circe's spell. *Newsweek,* p. 12.

Thompson, T. L. (1981). The development of communication skills in physically handicapped children. *Human Communication Research, 7*, 312–324.

Thompson, T. L. (1982). Disclosure as a disability management strategy: A review and conclusions. *Communication Quarterly, 30*, 196–202.

Thompson, T. L. (1986, November). *Communication between the disabled and able-bodied: The issue of disconfirmation.* Paper presented at the Speech Communication Association Conference, Boston, MA.

Thompson, T. L. (1987, November). *Communication strategies used by the disabled for requesting help.* Paper presented at the Speech Communication Association Conference, Boston, MA.

Thompson, T. L., & Cundiff, B. B. (1979, May). *Communication with the handicapped: Avoidance and uncertainty.* Paper presented at the International Communication Association Conference, Philadelphia, PA.

Thompson, T. L., & Seibold, D. R. (1978). Stigma management in normal-stigmatized interactions: A test of the disclosure hypothesis and a model of stigma acceptance. *Human Communication Research, 4,* 231–242.

U.S. Department of Labor. (1997). *Reasonable accomodation for employees with disabilities.* Washington, DC: Office of the Assistant Secretary for Administration and Management.

Wiseman, R. L., & Emry, R. (1987, November). *Assertion of selfhood and learned helplessness: Disabled and non-disabled persons' reactions to helping situations.* Paper presented at the Speech Communication Association Conference, Boston, MA.

Young, Jonathan M. (1997). *Equality of opportunity: The making of the Americans with Disabilities Act.* Washington, DC: National Council on Disability.

III

Disability and Culture

11

Interability Communication: Theoretical Perspectives

Susan A. Fox
Western Michigan University

Howard Giles
University of California, Santa Barbara

Mark P. Orbe
Western Michigan University

Richard Y. Bourhis
Université du Quebec, Montreal

Keywords: Interability communication, Social Identity Theory, Communication Accommodation Theory, Intergroup Contact Theory, Interactive Acculturation Model

More than 50 years ago, Meyerson (1948) urged researchers to develop theoretical frameworks for studying issues related to disability. These theories were meant to go beyond viewing disability as a biological classification and instead frame disability as a social issue. Subsequently, researchers in the areas of rehabilitation, psychology, special education, and sociology responded with a plethora of disability-related theories. Some examples include systems theory, which examines the effects of disabilities on families (Patterson, 1991; Seligman & Darling, 1997); object relations, which describes personality developments of people with disabilities (Thomas & Garske, 1995); drive theory, which explains reactions to disability (Thomas, 1994); contact theory, which describes attitudes toward people with physical disabilities (Tripp, French, & Sherrill, 1995); and attachment theory, which focuses on the limited exploration of the world by people with disabilities (Clegg & Lansdall-Welfare, 1995). Most recent are attempts to integrate medical and psychological models of disability to explain behavior toward people with disabilities (Johnston, 1996). These theories have guided research and increased understanding of the issues related to persons with disabilities, but only in the last 20 years have theories emerged that specifically target communication between people with and without disabilities. In this chapter, we review the literature related to theories of communication between people with and without disabilities, which we term *interability communication*, and in doing so attempt to explain, via interability communication theory (ICT), how psychological and sociological variables affect communication that occurs in interability situations.

EXISTING THEORETICAL FRAMEWORKS

In the following sections we examine the most important interpersonal and intercultural theories of interability communication. Ultimately, we argue for the value of our intergroup approach (see Fox & Giles, 1997), which we refine by incorporating Bourhis, Moise, Perrault, and Senecal's (1997) model of interactive acculturation into our framework.

INTERPERSONAL THEORIES

Disclosure Theory

Thompson and Seibold (1978) first applied a communication theory to interability communication by using disclosure theory to explain behavior in interability situations. The fundamental premise of this theory is that if an interability situation is tense and people without disabilities are uncertain about the person with a disability, then disclosing about a disability (e.g., the type and cause of the disability) will bring about more acceptance of the person with a disability. If tension and uncertainty are reduced, then the initial focus on the disability will recede and the individual, not the disability, will become the focus (Thompson, 1997). Empirical support for this theory, however, is equivocal. For instance, Thompson and Seibold (1978) failed to find support for the hypothesis that disclosure about a stigma would increase the acceptance of the bearer. Subsequent research focused on the subject of disclosing or acknowledging a disability (Belgrave & Mills, 1981; Braithwaite, 1991; Hastorf, Wildfogel, & Cassman, 1979; Royse & Edwards, 1989; Sagatun, 1985; Thompson & Seibold, 1978; see Thompson, 1982, for a review of earlier studies) and how disclosure affected liking and acceptance. These researchers found moderate support for the acknowledgment strategy in alleviating interability anxiety for the person without a disability. However, as with much of the research at the time, the focus was on the reduction of anxiety for the person without a disability and so failed to acknowledge the needs and feelings of people with disabilities. Furthermore, the responsibility of disclosure rested on the person with a disability, instead of making both parties accountable for reducing interability uncertainty (Braithwaite, 1991). As such, people with disabilities prefer to have others request information about their disability than to offer it outright (Sagatun, 1985). Not surprisingly, nondisabled people prefer to have people with the disability offer the information rather than request information from the person with the disability (Sagatun, 1985). Nonetheless, since the privacy issue most concerns the person with a disability, it is important that the decision to disclose information remain with them.

Thompson's work (Thompson & Seibold, 1978; Thompson, 1982) and the later work by other researchers using disclosure theory is useful in looking at disclosure in initial interpersonal interactions. Where this theory falls short, though, is accounting for preexisting stereotypes and expectations that people without disabilities hold of people with disabilities that can guide people's communicative behavior.

Uncertainty Reduction Theory

Dahnke (1983) adapted uncertainty reduction theory (URT) as a theoretical perspective to assist in the understanding of interaction patterns between people with and without disabilities. URT assumes "that when unfamiliar persons initially interact, they are primarily concerned with reducing their own uncertainty in order to predict, explain, and ultimately control the effects of their respective communication behaviors" (p. 107). Research confirms that atypically high levels of uncertainty exist in interability situations. Therefore, Dahnke assumed that there would be a positive association between uncertainty and information seeking, with affiliation, status, and responsiveness as driving factors in the desire to reduce uncertainty. Dahnke offered 16 axioms and 15 testable theorems related to uncertainty reduction and interability communication. These refer to the high anxiety, high uncertainty, and low interpersonal attraction people without disabilities are predicted to experience when facing an impending interability communication situation. He proposed that contact would increase information and therefore decrease uncertainty. Much like disclosure theorists, Dahnke assumed that increases in verbal and nonverbal affiliation by one person (either with or without a disability) would positively affect both the perceived and actual feelings of certainty, anxiety, and attraction of the other person. These theorems presuppose that one must manipulate affiliative behaviors to lessen the uncertainty and anxiety in initial interability encounters. Unfortunately, this theory did not offer any pragmatic suggestions as to how this can be achieved, and no further development or testing of this theory has been undertaken.

As with disclosure theory, there is research that embraces some of the constructs of URT, but does not specifically test the theory. People with disabilities in interability situations experience a demand for uncertainty reduction about their disability in the early stages of relationships; such issues as the nature, onset, and restrictions of the disability as well as the costs related to the disability may be addressed (Braithwaite, Emry, & Wiseman, 1984). Likewise, Braithwaite (1991) discovered that within the first few interability interactions people with disabilities must manage or fend off requests for information and invasions of privacy boundaries in an attempt to retain individuality and control while at the same time trying to build relationships. If uncertainty about the disability is not reduced, it has a negative impact on interability relationships (e.g., premature termination of the relationship; see Thompson, 1982). Thompson and Seibold (1978), however, did not find support for the URT principle that decreases in uncertainty would lead to more liking. Therefore, it seems that in initial interability contexts the predicted increases in attraction do not result from reducing uncertainty.

URT, and to a lesser extent disclosure theory, assume that the uncertainty an individual feels when involved in an interaction motivates a person to reduce it. The propositions are "associational, rather than lawlike causal statements," (Dahnke, 1983, p. 109), and fail to consider larger social factors (e.g., public policies, community ideologies, vitality) that mediate interability situations. Furthermore, URT fails to acknowledge Thompson's work on disclosure theory and other relevant work in the field of disabilities (Thompson, 1997). Although this was an early development of an interability communication theory and useful as a heuristic, no further development has been undertaken. Moreover, when tested alongside positive outcome value (see the following section), research did not support URT (Grove & Werkman, 1991).

Positive Outcome Value Theory

Positive outcome value theory (POV) is a refinement of URT. After an extensive review of URT, Sunnafrank (1986) concluded that only about half of the 100 studies conducted provided any supporting evidence for the theory. Given this knowledge, he reevaluated and recast the role of uncertainty to a secondary position and used predicted costs and rewards as the driving force for reducing uncertainty. Although other theories (e.g., social exchange theory) focus on costs and rewards, POV uses uncertainty reduction in initial encounters as the focus. Grove and Werkman (1991) applied this theoretical advance to interability situations and also tested it experimentally. Positive and negative predicted outcome values are assumed to "lead to communicative attempts to expand and truncate, respectively, both the conversation and the relationship" (Grove & Werkman, 1991, p. 509). In their study, Grove and Werkman had female confederates (trained to use a wheelchair) feign a disability or remain nondisabled when interacting with a nondisabled participant. The nondisabled respondents sought more information and were more aware of behavior from the nondisabled confederate than the "disabled" confederate. The results that less positive predicted outcomes led to less information seeking behavior supported POV. As Kellerman and Reynolds (1990) asserted, "it is not how much a person knows about others but how much a person wants to know that causes information seeking to occur" (p. 67). As such, it could be the case that many people without disabilities lack the motivation to gather information about their conversational partners with disabilities. This lack of desire could then lead to more awkward, mismanaged interability communication.

POV is an important modification of URT, but it does not consider larger societal factors (e.g., public policy, social norms) that might mediate interability situations. Both URT and POV are unidirectional and do not address the transactional nature of the interactions occurring between persons with and without disabilities. They focus instead on the person without a disability, ignoring the uncertainty and information seeking a person with disabilities may be experiencing. Although POV outcomes are clearly important, these approaches fail to help us understand fully the motivations and behaviors occurring in interability interactions.

The Intercultural Approach

Another theoretical approach to interability communication is based on an intercultural model of communication. Emry and Wiseman (1987) construe interability communication as an intercultural experience in which "conflicting demands and stereotypes result in a series of regressive spirals for both communicators" (p. 8). Using Rohrlich's (1983) three-tier model of intercultural communication, they examine the intrapersonal, interpersonal, and systemic levels (see the following paragraphs) that contribute to interability communication.

The intrapersonal level of Emry and Wiseman's (1987) perspective emphasizes the cultural experiences that lead to a person's attitudes, roles, and values in cognitively experiencing a subjective "reality." Interability communication situations are often comprised of conflicting social demands and norms. One social demand for some might be to treat people with disabilities with kindness; another could be to treat them as equals. People with and without disabilities, therefore, have paradoxical needs to act in ways that are dependent as well as independent. This paradox constrains interability interactions, especially interactions between interability strangers. Emry and Wiseman believe these conflicting social demands and norms may lead persons to experience approach-avoidance feelings in interaction between people with and without disabilities. Also at this intrapersonal level are the social stereotypes of which people with disabilities are aware and must manage. One stereotype many people without disabilities hold is that people with disabilities can be highly sensitive about their disability, can be easily offended, and can communicate anger and resentment (Belgrave & Mills, 1981).

Even though Emry and Wiseman (1987) believe that the intrapersonal level is the most important for explaining specific communicative behaviors, the second, interpersonal level is also important. At this level, interability communication is considered "disabled" given the lack of social skills by both parties. People without disabilities, operating with stereotypes, may be unclear as to what constitutes appropriate behavior (e.g., to help or not to help), and therefore they constrain their behavior. Given that people with disabilities generally may have fewer opportunities for interactions (as compared with people without disabilities), the behavior of people without disabilities could have more impact on the person with disabilities than vice versa.

Third, the systemic level deals with "outcomes beyond the intent of the communicators" (Emry & Wiseman, 1987, p. 17). They use four of

Watzlawick, Beavin, and Jackson's (1967) axioms of communication to describe the ongoing process of communication that takes place in interability interactions: (a) one cannot not communicate; (b) communication has content and relational meaning; (c) communication is organized through punctuation and episode; and (d) communication models the power distribution of its interactants. These four factors contribute to communication patterns that continue to be strained and uncomfortable for both parties.

The systemic level of intercultural communication is concerned with the overriding power structures that mediate interability situations. The power structures in interability situations confer higher social status on people without disabilities. People without disabilities, who have the upper hand in conversations, may misconstrue statements made by people with disabilities and guide behavior in a way that supports negative stereotypes. In this fashion the person without the disability does not have to develop new role-taking skills or increase his or her interpersonal sensitivity. One example would be the statement "please don't do that; it is better if I do it myself." Although this may be an attempt by a person with a disability to assert independence, the person without a disability can interpret this statement as a reflection of bitterness and embarrassment, thus sustaining the latter's negative stereotypes.

The intercultural approach has met with controversy. One reason for this is that there is disagreement as to whether "people with disabilities" as a collection of people constitutes a separate cultural group. Moreover, scholars have employed different definitions of culture, sometimes categorizing all people with disabilities as a culture (Braithwaite, 1990, 1996), but at other times applying it only to a subgroup (e.g., people who are deaf; see Padden, 1996). For people who acquire a disability, the idea of a separate cultural group is especially salient. Braithwaite's (1990) interviews revealed that people who acquire a disability are acutely aware of the change they have experienced in moving from a majority to a minority group status. Although research has shown that such individuals do see themselves as a separate group (Beail, 1983; Braithwaite, 1990; Fichten, Robillard, Judd, & Amsel, 1989), it is unclear whether people with disabilities are a "culture." Fine and Asch (1995) argued that people's fear of acquiring a disability, and the related feelings and stereotypes, revealed more about the nondisabled as a culture than the culture of people with disabilities. Fine and Asch (1995) further emphasized that people with disabilities believe that their disabilities are not salient factors in their definitions of self. This issue of culture highlights the need for further refinement of the intercultural approach.

There are both strengths and weaknesses to Emry and Wiseman's (1987) approach. On the one hand, it takes a much-needed transactional view of interability communication by stressing the contributions of both people with and without disabilities as to the communication event. Furthermore, it addresses the role of stereotypes and social norms in ways that the URT/POV approach does not. On the other hand, culture has been defined vaguely and applied inconsistently to different groups of people. The intercultural approach also fails to assess individual motivations and behaviors that occur when interability interactions are successful and, instead, views most interability communication as strained, awkward, and as reinforcing preexisting stereotypes.

The theories discussed above have been useful in stimulating theoretical thought about communication and disability. Unfortunately, little research has stemmed from these theories and limitations exist. The theoretical approaches discussed above have received little data confirmation, have overlooked factors contributing to interability interactions, or fail to offer communicative predictions about interability communication. Two more recent approaches have incorporated some of the strengths of prior theories and applied them to interability situations. These approaches incorporate broader societal factors contributing to interability situations, as well as proposing communicative strategies that may be occurring in interability situations.

NEW THEORETICAL APPROACHES

Co-cultural Theory

Co-cultural theory (Orbe, 1998b) assists in understanding the ways people who are traditionally marginalized in dominant societal structures communicate in their everyday lives. Grounded in the muted group (Kramarae, 1981) and standpoint theories (Smith, 1987), this theory is derived from the lived experiences of a variety of "nondominant" or co-cultural groups, including people of color, women, persons with disabilities, gays/lesbians/ bisexuals, and those from a lower socioeconomic background. Co-cultural theory is grounded in two assumptions: (a) although representing a widely diverse array of lived experiences, co-cultural group members will share a similar positioning that renders them marginalized within society, and (b) to negotiate oppressive dominant forces and achieve any measure of "success," co-cultural group members will adopt different communication orientations in their everyday interactions. Co-cultural theory has primarily been used to provide insight into the general approaches that underrepresented group members may take in negotiating their societal positioning in organizations (Orbe, 1998a) or intergroup relations (Orbe, 1997).

In its most basic form, co-cultural theory lends insight into the process by which co-cultural group members, like persons with disabilities, negotiate their "differentness" with others (both with or without disabilities) and come to select how they are going to interact with others. Although many existing interpersonal and intercultural theories offer general approaches to study such phenomena, co-cultural theory is grounded in the lived experiences of the persons it seeks to describe.

The early stages of research led to the emergence of a co-cultural communication model, focusing on specific strategies that co-cultural groups used during their interactions with dominant group members (Orbe, 1997). However, once these communicative practices were established, the focal point changed to the ways in which persons came to select certain strategies over others. According to co-cultural theory, a person with a disability will adopt one or more communication orientations depending on six interrelated factors: field of experience, perceived costs and rewards, capability, preferred outcomes, communication approach, and situational context (Orbe, 1998b).

The first factor, field of experience, refers to the fact that, throughout their lifetimes, disabled individuals learn the consequences of certain forms of communication, such as what is "effective" and/or "appropriate" for people with disabilities. Second, based on her or his unique field of experience—which is simultaneously similar to, yet different from, other persons with disabilities—an individual comes to recognize that certain costs and rewards are associated with different communication practices. Third, the capability to enact certain strategies that work to establish a specific communicative stance depends on specific circumstances. For example, people with disabilities can have varying levels of success enacting certain practices (e.g., "passing" as an ablebodied person, networking with other disabled persons, or aggressively confronting others). Finally, there are three preferred outcomes that relate to the ultimate goal of the person with a disability: (a) Is he or she aiming to fit in and not bring any unnecessary attention to the disability (*assimilation*)? (b) Or is the goal to avoid making the disability salient and working with others, both ablebodied and disabled persons, to ensure that all interactants' basic needs are adequately met (*accommodation*)? (c) Or yet still, is the goal to limit the interaction with ablebodied people and attempt to create affirming communities with others who are disabled (*separation*)? It is important to note that the preferred outcome functions on a number of levels (interpersonal, group, organizational) and can change between, or even within, different settings.

The communication approach people select depends on the "voices" that can be enacted by persons with disabilities. A *nonassertive* voice can be used, which is somewhat inhibited and nonconfrontational, and seemingly affords priority to others' needs. An *assertive* voice is also possible. This voice encompasses self-enhancing, expressive communication that takes into account the needs of self and others. A third and more self-promoting and controlling (*aggressive*) voice focuses on self needs. No single approach is most (or always) effective; much depends on how the person with a disability negotiates the other factors.

The situational context is the last factor important to co-cultural theory. Instead of adopting a single communication approach (or orientation), most persons with disabilities will alter their communication based on the specific circumstances of the setting (i.e., where it takes place, who else is present, etc.). In fact, it should be apparent that situational context, like the other five factors, intersect in highly intricate, complex ways as they work to formulate different communication stances of persons with disabilities.

Each communication approach (i.e., nonassertive, assertive, and aggressive) is motivated by a specific preferred outcome (i.e., assimilation, accommodation, or separation) and the approach and outcome result in one of six communication orientations influenced by the field of experience, perceived costs and rewards, capability, and situational context. People with disabilities can assume one or more of these communication orientations during their everyday interactions with family, friends, co-workers, or strangers.

Nonassertive Assimilation.   This involves a person communicating in a voice that is passive to ingroup concerns; the ultimate goal is to reap the benefits that are associated with not drawing any expressed attention to his or her disability. In this regard, the individual's communication focuses on similarities associated with being a human (see Turner, Hogg, Oakes, Rercher, & Wetherell, 1987) and allows others to render their disabilities as "invisible."

Assertive Assimilation.   This involves a form of communication that allows the individual to fit into different situations. This is a more active stance (as compared with its nonassertive counterpart), in that additional measures (i.e., overcompensation in work responsibilities or extensive preparation prior to interaction) are taken to increase an individual's capability to fit in.

Aggressive Assimilation. This orientation is adopted when the benefits of assimilation take priority over other factors. Attempting to be seen as part of the group may involve isolating oneself from other persons with disabilities, or even joking about disability with ablebodied persons.

Nonassertive Accommodation. This challenges the oppressive forces of ableism in subtle ways; it is often enacted using a more assertive or aggressive approach that could cause undesirable consequences and be counterproductive. This orientation includes the use of tag questions or other forms of nonthreatening communication.

Assertive Accommodation. This involves a more active voice in challenging existing practices that work to oppress those with disabilities. This stance is utilized when an individual has the capability to work with others for change in certain situations in which one's efforts are not necessarily penalized (or regarded as less important when implementing change).

Aggressive Accommodation. As with its nonassertive and assertive counterparts, aggressive accommodation focuses on affirming issues of disability. A person with this orientation, however, is willing to do whatever it takes, including assuming personal costs (e.g., confronting dominant others on key issues with little attention to their feelings, needs, or positions) to achieve the ultimate rewards affiliated with changing the status quo.

Nonassertive Separation. This is a communication stance that is adopted when the surroundings allow interaction primarily with other people with disabilities and maintenance of interpersonal barriers that limit any substantial communication with ablebodied persons.

Assertive Separation. This is enacted when persons with disabilities choose consciously to interact primarily with others with disabilities. In certain situations the benefits of intragroup interaction (solidarity, pride, support) may outweigh any other potentially disadvantageous outcomes (i.e., isolation in dominant settings, being viewed as a radical).

Aggressive Separation.   This is geared toward maintaining a distance from ablebodied persons. Often attempted with little regard for others' needs, this stance may be the result of past experiences that include grossly unfair treatment by ablebodied persons or the organizations that they dominate.

Braithwaite, Emry, and Wiseman (1984) highlighted an important advantage of the co-cultural theory approach. Co-cultural theory focuses on the views of people with disabilities instead of relying on the attitudes and behavior of people without disabilities toward people with disabilities. The theory is grounded in the communicative experiences of other marginalized co-cultural group members and therefore contains a framework that legitimizes, validates, and affirms a wide range of standpoints occupied by persons with disabilities. Co-cultural theory not only requires testing in interability situations, but also needs to be adopted interpretively to assess its viability in explaining instances of them through independent data. Moreover, future research and theoretical development could benefit from an approach that addresses the reciprocal communication patterns of the nondominant culture, as well as subsequent management processes between them. Nonetheless, co-cultural theory has heuristic potential for the area of interability communication, especially in its ability to utilize an interpretive approach, an area that has proved insightful in previous interability studies (Braithwaite, 1991).

INTERABILITY COMMUNICATION THEORY: AN INTERGROUP COMMUNICATION APPROACH TO INTERABILITY SITUATIONS

The theories described above have a number of substantial contributions to make to our understanding of interability communication. The interpersonally based theories highlight our need to focus on individual motivations driving the interactants in interability situations. The culturally based theories allow us to incorporate the concept of stereotypes that each "culture" possesses and imposes on others. There is still a need, though, for a more robust "intergroup" framework that can incorporate individual factors, yet retain the idea that interability communication can often be an intercultural, group-driven experience. Toward this end, Fox and Giles (1996) proposed an intergroup approach to interability communication that is an amalgam of social identity theory (SIT), communication accommodation theory (CAT), and intergroup contact theory (IGCT) and contributes to our understanding of the communication occurring within, and the consequence of, interability situations.

SIT assists us with the motivations people with and without disabilities have when confronting interability situations. The theory (Tajfel, 1978) maintains that individuals, through a series of behaviors, derive their social and personal identities by belonging to, maintaining membership in, or differentiating from certain groups. This theory can help explain why some people with disabilities attempt to "pass" as a person without a disability, thereby having a more positive social identity as a member of the dominant nondisabled group. SIT also explains why the fear of acquiring a disability may lead nondisabled people to avoid contact with disabled others, choosing not to have their social identity threatened because of the negative attitudes people have toward disabled people.

CAT explains the communicative strategies people choose to assert a positive identity and fulfill goals and intentions. Through linguistic convergence and divergence, people can attempt to assert a positive social identity. For example, patronizing speech toward a person with a disability may be a way a nondisabled person asserts an identity as a caring, compassionate dominant group member. Likewise, if a person with a disability converges and matches the patronizing speech style, they may be attempting to assimilate to the dominant group speech style.

IGCT is concerned with determining whether contact between different groups will lead to more positive attitudes and, subsequently, more positive interactions and further understanding between groups. The theory contends that unless the person(s) involved in intergroup situations are perceived as typical of the whole group, attitude change will not be generalized to the whole group. This can explain why mainstreaming programs (in which children with disabilities are placed in regular classrooms) may increase interpersonal relationships between people with and without disabilities but negative attitudes toward people with disabilities as a group persist.

To the Fox and Giles (1996) model we now add the recently developed interactive acculturation model (IAM; Bourhis et al., 1997). This framework has value for many intergroup settings and hence we transform it here, for the first time, into the interability arena. Quite briefly, IAM invokes macro-level variables such as public policy changes and acculturation orientations to predict the success of immigrant ethnic communities in acculturating into a host community.

To understand interability communication better at a micro level, we elaborate on SIT, CAT, and IGCT (see Fox & Giles, 1996, for a more in-depth explanation of these theories). Then the IAM is explained, applied to interability situations, and finally, integrated into interability communication theory.

SIT

SIT is based on the premise that individuals derive their identity (either personal or social) by belonging to, and maintaining membership in, certain groups (see Hogg & Abrams, 1988, for a comprehensive overview, and Hogg & Abrams, 1993, for further developments). The theory "maintains that society comprises social categories which stand in power and status relations to one another" (Hogg & Abrams, 1988, p. 14). Social identity is therefore an important part of one's self-concept, and when their identity is threatened people strive to positively differentiate their groups from others as a means of further maintaining positive self-esteem.

SIT can be usefully adopted to interpret interability situations. First, intrapersonal conflicts that persons with and without disabilities feel when interacting with one another can be explained via social identities. Because of the stigma related to disabilities, people without disabilities may feel their social identity threatened and may therefore seek to differentiate from people with disabilities in interability situations. This differentiation may take the form of avoidance, or culturally or psychologically creating a help-recipient position that places people with disabilities in a subordinate position. For example, people without disabilities have no need to assimilate with the subordinate group of people with disabilities, although interability helping situations may cause them to feel and derive a more positive social identity. Being a Special Olympics buddy or opening the door for a person with a disability is a way of maintaining a positive identity. Therefore, if the motive of the person without a disability is to maintain a positive social identity, they can differentiate from the subordinate disabled group by interacting with them in a dominant "help-giving" way.

SIT can also explain the ways people with disabilities maintain a positive social identity. Given research that shows that people with disabilities see themselves as a separate group (e.g., Braithwaite, 1990), they can either reject people without disabilities or compare themselves with other people with even more severe disabilities, thereby increasing their identity by being "better off" than others. Beail (1983) found that people with disabilities described their self-concept by rejecting the dominant group's negative attitudes. For example, there are activist groups (e.g., Jerry's Orphans) who consciously reject the dominant group's attempts to label people with disabilities as needy. Fichten et al. (1989) found that, in general, people with disabilities have positive self-images, although these are unlikely to be maintained when they compare themselves with people without disabilities. Plastic surgery, artificial limbs, and breast implants are all expressions of an attempt to conform to the dominant group's ideal and, historically, people with disabilities have exercised these (and other) measures to lessen their membership in the subordinate group. In this way, people with disabilities secure a positive social identity as part of the nondisabled group.

It is important that researchers recognize the different types of social identities people with and without disabilities are attempting to maintain during interability communication. When nondisabled people adopt a helper role, this may be the best way to maintain a positive identity, as well as the dominant group status, even though there is also a conflicting norm that maintains that people with disabilities should not be treated as different. SIT can therefore aid in framing the motivations of people with and without disabilities as they seek to maintain and reinforce a positive social identity.

CAT

SIT describes individuals as having social identities, and how these social identities are maintained and asserted is explained via CAT (see, e.g., Giles & Coupland, 1992). CAT is based on the premise that

> people are motivated to adjust their speech styles (or accommodate) as a means of expressing values, attitudes, and intentions toward each other. It is proposed that the extent to which individuals shift their speech styles toward or away from those of their interlocutors is a mechanism by which social approval or disapproval, and group loyalty is communicated. (Giles, Mulac, Bradac, & Johnson, 1987, p. 117)

Positive identities, then, can be asserted via communication choices. The communicative strategies of convergence and divergence are the ways in which people adjust their communication to achieve their intentions. Convergence is "a strategy whereby individuals adapt to each other's communicative behaviors in terms of a wide range of linguistic/prosodic/nonvocal features including speech rate, pausal phenomena, utterance length, phonological variants, smiling, gaze, and so on" (Giles & Coupland, 1992, p. 63), whereas divergence refers to the accentuation of these communicative differences between individuals.

CAT suggests that individuals seek to achieve the following goals: (a) social approval; (b) communication efficiency; and (c) maintenance of positive social identities. It also assumes that individuals can converge or diverge to their beliefs or communicative expectations regarding another. For example, researchers have found that people with disabilities demonstrate less communication competence in their interactions with nondisabled people (e.g., shorter interactions, decreased eye contact and verbal immediacy; see Coleman & DePaulo, 1991, for a review). Similarly, researchers have found that disabled people will match the opinions they believe nondisabled people hold (Kleck, 1968), perhaps in an attempt to gain social approval. On the other hand, nondisabled people may be attempting to psychologically diverge (see Thakerar, Giles, & Cheshire, 1982) from disabled people and thus use less communicatively competent speech, thereby maintaining a positive social identity and attempting to at least increase communication efficiency. We might see this occur when a nondisabled person stands at a great distance from a disabled person when talking in an interability situation. While this may appear communicatively incompetent given interpersonal distance norms, the nondisabled person may believe he or she is keeping an appropriate distance when the conversational partner is disabled (Holmes, Karst, & Erhart, 1990). In another example, to meet the goal of social approval, people with disabilities may feel that they have to act cheerful when talking with a nondisabled person to make the nondisabled person comfortable (Elliot & Frank, 1990; Wright, 1983). This can be conceptualized as accommodating to a "happy stereotype" that people without disabilities hold of their disabled counterparts.

CAT assists in understanding the motivations and behaviors of people in different communicative circumstances. Although some interability communication experiments have looked at certain communicative behaviors (e.g., information seeking, opinion convergence), again, these have not been developed from an accommodation viewpoint. This approach can help to explain interability communication, producing a more robust framework yet incorporating the important constructs in uncertainty reduction, positive outcome value, and intercultural theories.

IGCT

Although both SIT and CAT explain the individual motivations and communicative behavior of individuals, IGCT explains how these motivations and behaviors lead to attitude change and future behavior toward groups (see Fox & Giles, 1993, for an application of IGCT to intergenerational contexts). Hewstone and Brown (1986) maintained that, unless those involved in positive intergroup experiences are seen as typical of the outgroup, attitude change will not be generalized to that whole community. Hence, mainstreaming programs (in which children with disabilities are placed in regular classrooms) may not work if the assumption is that mere contact alone will lead to greater understanding and more positive attitudes by people without disabilities. Contact and attitude change studies have failed to support the assumption that mere contact will lead to more perceived similarities between the groups, and subsequently more long-term liking, attraction, and affiliation (see Thompson, 1997; Yuker, 1988).

People in interability situations can use three strategies: noninteraction, consisting of avoidance behaviors; interaction with differentiation, comprised of behaviors in which people seek to assert a positive identity by diverging from another group; or interaction with assimilation, including behavior intended to be convergent with others. People without disabilities, seeking to differentiate from the subordinate group with disabilities, are likely to select the noninteraction and differentiation options. For example, support for this noninteraction choice is found in studies showing that children with disabilities are chosen less often as friends and playmates (Gentry, 1983; Peterson & Haralick, 1977). Moreover, when interability interactions do occur, people may create self-fulfilling prophecies that reinforce stereotypes and override disconfirming evidence, which results in no significant attitude or behavioral change. When nondisabled people are confronted with disconfirming evidence, they can discount this evidence by viewing the person who is disabled as an exception to the rule, rather than change their attitude toward people with disabilities as a social group. Therefore, determining whether the outgroup member is behaving typically or representatively of the stereotype is one important dimension in predicting whether the individual will change his or her attitude about the whole group.

It is important to view interability contact situations using Hewstone and Brown's (1986) framework, which recommends equal status contact in situations that are seen as intergroup and not interpersonal in nature. Some more recent studies support this notion of equal status, although they do not explicitly involve contact theory in their discussion of interability contact situations (see Amsel & Fichten, 1988; Fichten, Robillard, Tagalakis, & Amsel, 1991; Westwood, Vargo, & Vargo, 1981). For example, Donaldson (1980) found that in seven out of eight studies, positive attitude change studies resulted from equal status contact. In situations where participants were not of equal status (such as helping situations), Fichten and Amsel (1986) suggested that reciprocity or a superordinate goal could be used. If disabled people were given the opportunity to reciprocate and act as helpers to nondisabled people, this could create less one-sided status interactions. Likewise, having people work together on a project unrelated to disability issues (e.g., a holiday parade) could serve to highlight the strengths of people with and without disabilities. Because of this, IGCT is an invaluable theoretical lens for studying interability interactions and for determining whether the people involved can achieve a generalized behavior change toward the group as a whole.

IAM

Although much research on interability situations takes place at an interpersonal level, these interactions are embedded within a wider context of variables. IAM (Bourhis et al., 1997) incorporates the views of host and immigrant acculturation orientations to understand when acculturative attempts by nondominant immigrants will be successful. This theory analyzes different groups' orientations to acculturation that affect the ability of groups to interact—the attitudes that groups have toward each other. We use this as a springboard for explaining communication between people with and without disabilities. Unlike the theories described above, this model not only addresses micro-level social psychological issues related to communication, it also uses larger public policy issues as they frame interability interactions. IAM approaches acculturation as a dynamic interplay of issues related to immigrant and host communities. In many settings there are (at least) two important policy issues: state immigration and state integration policies. State immigration policies deal with how many immigrants are allowed into (or, in some cases, required to be in) a certain community. This is relevant for people with disabilities because of integration policies, which include programs designed to help the integration of immigrants. In the United States, mainstreaming of students with disabilities into nondisabled classrooms would be considered a state integration policy—an active attempt to integrate people with disabilities into the dominant community. Likewise, the Americans with Disabilities Act (ADA) is a national mandate designed to eliminate discrimination against individuals with disabilities. ADA outlines ways in which people with disabilities can become integrated into the nondisabled host society of the United States.

Therefore, ADA can be seen as an integration policy resulting from the inability of people with disabilities to lead "normal" lives like those of the host community of nondisabled people and the inability of the nondisabled to accept the different lives they do lead.

IAM then describes four different community ideologies that can pervade a society and impact both the interpretation and implementation of the policies. These four ideologies are pluralist, civic, assimilative, and ethnist. All these ideologies have an expectation that immigrants will adopt the public values of the host society, but will differ in their views of private values. Communities employing a pluralist ideology do not regulate private values and will support, financially and socially, the private activities of their minority groups. Communities practicing a civic ideology believe in a nonintervention approach to private values, but provide no support for the perpetuation of minority group values. Instead, civic communities put their financial and social support into programs that promote integration of the minority immigrants into the host community. They further provide antidiscrimination laws that prevent segregation of the minority communities. Communities utilizing an assimilation ideology expect immigrants to abandon their own cultural distinctiveness and private values for the sake of the host community. An example of this is indicative of the former "melting pot" approach in which immigrants were expected to join the "American way of life" and give up their former customs and practices. Finally, communities operating under an ethnist ideology do one of two things; they either expect immigrant groups to reject the immigrant ethnocultural identity for the host group, or never accept immigrants regardless of any of the actions taken by the immigrant group.

These ideologies are not discrete, unchanging entities. Political tensions, such as those in California where Proposition 209 is attempting to revoke affirmative action laws, can change the ideologies of members of the host society (*USA Today*, 1997). Likewise, changes in ideologies can lead to new immigration and integration policies. The political tensions surrounding the discrimination against people with disabilities led to the passage of ADA, and subsequently there may be—and for some, there may already have been—a backlash of negative attitudes toward people with disabilities because of the policy (Larwood, 1995). Therefore, there is a transactional relationship between the ideologies and policies enacted and enforced.

IAM then discusses two of the main sociopsychological issues related to acculturation. The first deals with the beliefs of the immigrant community and whether the immigrant's values should be retained. The other, orthogonally related to the first, is focused on whether the host values should be adopted. Responses to these lead to feelings of integration, assimilation, separation, anomie, and individualism. The host culture has similar concerns: the acceptability of the notion that immigrants maintain their heritage, and the acceptability of immigrants adopting the values of the host community. The responses to these concerns bring about orientations that suggest the following strategies: integration, assimilation, segregation, exclusion, and individualism. Integration reflects a desire to maintain key features of the immigrant identity, while at the same time adopting features of the host majority culture. Assimilation occurs when immigrants abandon identity for the host identity. Segregation happens when the host community distances itself from immigrants but allows them to retain their identity. Exclusion arises when host communities do not allow immigrants to retain their identity or adopt the host identity. Individualism occurs when host communities define both themselves and others as individuals instead of as group members (i.e., interpersonal rather than intergroup).

Another important issue in IAM is the amount of perceived vitality that the group possess (Giles, Bourhis, & Taylor, 1977; Harwood, Giles, & Bourhis, 1994). Vitality is based on demographic variables (such as number of members), institutional control factors (including decision-making powers in government, business, education, and media), and status variables (social prestige, sociohistorical status). The ability of both host and immigrant communities to achieve the goals associated with their orientations depends on the perceived vitality of the immigrant (as well as that of the host) community.

The combination of the host and immigrant community orientations can create concordant or discordant acculturation profiles that result in consensual, problematic, or conflictual relational outcomes. It is only when host and immigrant community orientations are both integration, both assimilation, or both individualistic that consensual outcomes will result. For example, if a person with and a person without disabilities are both individualistic in orientation, positive and effective verbal and nonverbal communication should occur. Discrepant orientations will bring about problematic or conflictual relational outcomes, which can lead to miscommunication, tensions, retaliation, and acculturative stress between the two communities. This could occur if a person with a disability attempted to assimilate into a nondisabled community that had a segregation orientation.

APPLICATION OF IAM TO
INTERABILITY SITUATIONS

We can apply these theoretical assumptions rather incisively to interability situations. One basic assumption of the IAM theory when applied to interability situations is that people with disabilities are attempting to "immigrate" into the host community. This is especially relevant for people who acquire a disability. Braithwaite (1990) found that people who acquire a disability (e.g., a person who becomes paraplegic after an accident) are acutely aware of their movement from a host community to an immigrant community.

In the past it could be argued that the United States held an assimilation (melting pot) or ethnist ideology (see Taylor, 1991). People with disabilities were segregated and students were given "special education," but ultimately expected to accommodate to a nondisabled environment. Recent developments, since the 1970s, in immigration and integration policies suggest a movement toward a civic, and sometimes pluralistic, ideology. The passage of the Education of the Handicapped Act (20. *u.s.c.* §§ 1401 *et seq.*) in 1975 provided disabled students with the opportunity for education in the least restrictive environment possible. Prior to this act, students with disabilities were assigned to segregated classrooms. More recently, the Americans with Disabilities Act (ADA, 1990) was enacted to provide federally enforced antidiscrimination protection for persons with either physical or mental impairments that limit their life activities. These two policies, although arguably shy of a pluralistic ideology, do provide support for the view that a civic ideology is an accepted norm in the United States today, at least in terms of public policy.

However, we must examine whether the civic ideology is present in practice. In addition to the ideologies of the host community, one must explore the acculturation orientations of the host and immigrant communities. Moghaddam and Taylor (1987) asserted that the host's acculturation orientation mediates the extent to which immigrants feel accepted or discriminated against and determines the obstacles immigrants feel when trying to integrate. The predominantly negative attitudes that people without disabilities hold toward people with disabilities supports the idea that the latter face great challenges in attempting to integrate into the host nondisabled culture. These attitudes and expectations can prohibit people with disabilities from successfully integrating into the host community. Braithwaite's research (1990) would indicate that most people with disabilities would prefer to integrate (i.e., retain their immigrant identity) rather than assimilate (i.e., abandon their immigrant identity) into the nondisabled community. However, the more people with disabilities subscribe to a segregation orientation (not supported by the host community), the more likely it is that the two communities will have divergent acculturation goals.

It is also important to point out the factors that contribute to the "objective" vitality of people with disabilities (Giles, Bourhis, & Taylor, 1977). People with disabilities include close to 43 million Americans with physical or mental disabilities—a population increasing as the population as a whole ages. They have a governmental voice that helped to instigate the passage of the ADA, indicating a certain amount of institutional control. In terms of status variables such as social prestige, having a disability is sociohistorically and currently seen as social deviance (Fox & Giles, 1996; Goffman, 1963). Therefore, given the negative attitudes and beliefs nondisabled people hold about people with disabilities, their vitality is assumed (and hence, perceived) to be medium or low.

The relational outcomes of host and immigrant communities are the final component of the IAM model. Historically, the nondisabled community has possessed a segregation orientation toward people with disabilities. This conflicts with the immigrant community's integration orientation. This can be seen in the backlash of negative attitudes toward children with disabilities since the passage of the Education of the Handicapped Act (Bender, 1985). Bender found that the most prevalent criticisms of the law included negative teacher and peer attitudes, less instructional time for nondisabled students, and a less constructive classroom environment. There is also evidence that nondisabled people make negative attributions toward people with disabilities in hypothetical ADA-related job situations (Larwood, 1995), indicating a negative backlash toward the ADA. However, there are factors, such as knowledge of the ADA and attitudes toward people with disabilities, that moderate this backlash (Chism & Satcher, 1997; Satcher & Hendren, 1991). Likewise, participants who felt they were well prepared for the issues involved in the ADA had more positive perceptions of people with disabilities (Chism & Satcher, 1997). Nondisabled people who held negative attitudes toward people with disabilities were less accepting of the ADA than those who held more positive attitudes (Satcher & Hendren, 1991).

The IAM perspective is useful, then, in underscoring the larger macro-level contextual influences that people with and without disabilities have when they communicate, but it does not adequately explain the actions of specific members of individual interactions when interacting. Yet IAM is an important addition to interability communication theory in focusing on the overriding ideologies and policy changes that can influence the interability situations that take place. In the following section these theories are combined into a cohesive compilation utilizing all four approaches to better conceptualize the complex dynamics of interability communication.

THEORETICAL SYNTHESIS
AND APPLICATION

Interactive acculturation, social identity, communication accommodation, and intergroup contact theories can be interwoven to create an explanatory theory of why situations involving people with and without disabilities result in intergroup rather than interpersonal communication. Public policy issues such as the ADA can significantly affect interactions between people with and without disabilities not only by increasing the frequency of interactions, but also by bettering host and immigrant communities' orientations toward each other. IAM therefore contributes to an understanding of how overarching factors operate to impact the orientations (e.g., attitudes, beliefs, expectations, motivations) of people with and without disabilities. These macro-level orientations, however, impact individuals' behavior and subsequently their social identities. For example, the motivation for a person without a disability may be to promote his or her social identity not only as a fully functioning person without a disability, but also that of a helpful and charitable person toward persons with disabilities. Therefore, people without disabilities may be attempting to differentiate from people with disabilities and assert a positive social identity. This identity can be reinforced via communicative choices that attempt to converge to a stereotype by means of the language they believe that people with disabilities would both expect and like to hear. For example, an expectation held by the person without a disability could be that the person with a disability is worthy of charity. This sentiment can be expressed linguistically through such speech choices as patronizing speech (e.g., baby-talk), which is assumed to be nurturing and considerate. If the nondisabled person views a disabled person as typical of the disabled group, the nondisabled person's attitude will be reinforced, as will their behavior toward others in the future.

It is also important to point out the transactional nature of IGCT. While a nondisabled person is asserting a positive social identity, it is imperative to remember that the disabled person is doing so simultaneously. Using the example from above, patronizing speech from nondisabled to disabled persons places the latter in an identity dilemma. If they find this patronizing behavior nurturing and it helps them maintain a positive social identity, then they may accept and converge to the patronizing behavior. The disabled persons could be using passive and accommodating language, accepting the one-down position that the patronizing speech imposes on them. However, it may be difficult for a disabled person to assert a positive identity if reacting negatively to patronizing speech contradicts his or her need to integrate. For example, Weinberg (1983) found that the most common reaction to inappropriate behaviors was to "let it pass" without comment, attributing the behavior of the patronizer as well-intentioned. Similarly, people with disabilities allow nondisabled others to help even when it is not necessary because they realize that "ablebodied people often feel good if they can help somebody in need" (Weinberg, 1983, p. 367). In this way, people with disabilities may feel they are asserting a positive social identity by supporting a member of the group into which they would like to integrate.

When interability situations are viewed as intergroup in nature, IGCT can predict whether interactants will change their stereotypes and attitudes toward other groups. If the nondisabled interactant considers an interability situation to be intergroup in nature, and sees the disabled person as typical, then his or her attitude, and arguably future behavior, will be generalized toward all members of the group. On the other hand, if the nondisabled person sees the person with a disability as atypical and the situation as interpersonal, the disabled person's behavior will be discounted as being not representative of the whole group. Referring to the patronizing speech example, even if a person with a disability linguistically rejects behavior such as patronizing speech, the assertion will not necessarily have a long-term impact on the behavior of the nondisabled person because the disabled other can be seen as an "exception to the rule."

IAM, SIT, CAT, and IGCT theories can work together in explaining group-oriented immigration objectives, the individual motivations, attitudes, and behavior of interactants involved in interability situations. Future research needs to emanate from an interdisciplinary theoretical foundation. Much of the research since Meyerson's (1948) original call for explanatory theories have produced either descriptive or predictive data and have therefore done little to discover the reasons behind the awkward and strained communication that occurs in interability situations. ADA-related changes in public policy will no doubt decrease the physical barriers faced by people with disabilities, but social barriers are slow to change. Therefore, it is important that future researchers focus on the educational, medical, and work contexts that this public policy seeks to make less discriminatory. It is also important that researchers continue to take a transactional approach to the study of interability communication, focusing not only from the dual perspectives of the people without or with disabilities, but also on how the perspectives of both groups interact to influence communication. It is important that researchers recognize the different types of social identities people with and without disabilities are attempting to maintain during interability situations (with assistance or hindrance from the public policies IAM describes). Work in the area of self-disclosure and the management of privacy boundaries (such as helping situations) can set the stage for future theory-driven research and the negotiation of identities in interability situations (Braithwaite, 1991; Sagatun, 1985; Thompson, 1982; Thompson & Seibold, 1978). Determining when people with and without disabilities feel comfortable discussing disability-related issues and refusing help will increase understanding of the role communication plays in the management of positive and negative identities. It is also important to focus on the communicative expectations and choices both people with and without disabilities select as well as the contexts in which these choices are made. Patronizing speech is reported to be a frequent form of communication directed at people with disabilities (Fox & Giles, 1996) and can be used as a starting point for studies that concentrate on the communication orientations proposed in co-cultural theory. The long-term effects of socially based charitable attitudes and subsequent patronizing communication can inhibit more global public policies rather than help people with disabilities to be more independent and successfully integrate into the dominant culture.

CONCLUSION

Medical, technical, and political advances are continuing to increase the physical abilities of people who are disabled. It is important that the social abilities of interability interactants be investigated so that people with and without disabilities can interact effectively. The field of communication and disabilities is in need of theoretically driven research and a framework for explaining interability communication in ways that include macro- as well as micro-level variables. The theoretical approaches to interability communication addressed in this chapter attempt to explain interpersonal, intercultural, and intergroup motivations for the actions and communication occurring in interability situations. Clearly, the next conceptual step (which space precludes discussing here and is beyond the scope of this chapter) is to provide a schematic integrative model of these processes— an exciting theoretical agenda for the future. The early interpersonal theories, although somewhat lacking in breadth, serve to provide a theoretical point of departure on which research could build. Cultural theories broaden our perspective to include stereotypes and social norms contributing to strained and awkward communication occurring in interability situations. Co-cultural theory provides us with specific communication orientations that can be tested in interability contexts. Interability communication theory creates a complex yet increasingly complete picture of the societal ideologies, ensuing public policies, individual factors, subsequent communication, and overall changes in individual and group attitudes occurring in interability situations. A key to increasing positive interability communication and relationships will be to determine how people with and without disabilities communicate, whether it be in an interpersonal or intergroup context, linguistically convergent or divergent, patronizing or empowering.

DISCUSSION QUESTIONS

1. List your stereotypes of people with disabilities. Now list your beliefs of how people without disabilities treat people with disabilities. Draw connections between how the behavior of nondisabled people can reinforce stereotypes of disabled people.
2. Discuss the challenges people with disabilities face in asserting a positive identity in interability situations.
3. How does viewing a person with a disability as atypical because he or she does not act in a stereotypical way keep stereotypes intact?
4. The Special Olympics are designed to empower people with disabilities. Discuss the possible social identities of people with disabilities and the social identities of the volunteers (i.e., "buddies") who "help" them?
5. What are the strengths and weaknesses of the interability communication theory? Draw a model representing a possible interaction between a person with and without disabilities.

REFERENCES

Amsel, R., & Fichten, C. S. (1988). Effects of contact on thoughts about interaction with students who have a physical disability. *Journal of Rehabilitation, 54*, 61–65.

Beail, N. (1983). Physical disability: The self and the stereotype. *International Journal of Rehabilitation Research, 6*, 56–57.

Belgrave, F. Z., & Mills, J. (1981). Effect upon desire for social interaction with a physically disabled person of mentioning the disability in different contexts. *Journal of Applied Social Psychology, 11*, 44–57.

Bender, W. N. (1985). The case against mainstreaming: Empirical support for the political backlash. *Education, 105*, 279–287.

Bourhis, R. Y., Moise, L. C., Perrault, S., & Senecal, S. (1997). Towards an interactive acculturation model: A social psychological approach. *International Journal of Psychology, 32*, 369–386.

Braithwaite, D. O. (1990). From majority to minority: An analysis of cultural change from ablebodied to disabled. *International Journal of Intercultural Relations, 14*, 465–483.

Braithwaite, D. O. (1991). "Just how much did that wheelchair cost?": Management of privacy boundaries by persons with disabilities. *Western Journal of Speech Communication, 55*, 254–274.

Braithwaite, D. O. (1996). "I am a person first": Different perspectives on the communication of persons with disabilities. In E. B. Ray (Ed.), *Communication and the disenfranchised: Social health issues and implications* (pp. 257–272). Mahwah, NJ: Lawrence Erlbaum Associates.

Braithwaite, D. O., Emry, R. A., & Wiseman, R. L. (1984, February). *Able-bodied and disabled persons' communication: The disabled persons' perspective.* Paper presented at the annual meeting of the Western Speech Communication Association, Seattle. (ERIC Document Reproduction Service No. ED 264 622).

Chism, M., & Satcher, J. (1997). Human resource management students' perceptions of employment and individuals with disabilities. *Journal of Applied Rehabilitation Counseling, 28*, 38–42.

Clegg, J. A., & Lansdall-Welfare, R. (1995). Attachment and learning disability: A theoretical review informing three clinical interventions. *Journal of Intellectual Disability Research, 39*, 295–305.

Coleman, L. M., & DePaulo, B. M. (1991). Uncovering the human spirit: Moving beyond disability and "missed" communications. In N. Coupland, H. Giles, & J. M. Wiemann (Eds.), *"Miscommunication" and problematic talk* (pp. 61–84). Thousand Oaks, CA: Sage.

Dahnke, G. L. (1983). Communication and handicapped and nonhandicapped persons: Toward a deductive theory. In M. Burgoon (Ed.), *Communication yearbook 6* (pp. 92–135). Beverly Hills, CA: Sage.

Donaldson, J. (1980). Changing attitudes toward handicapped persons: A review and analysis of research. *Exceptional Children, 46*, 504–514.

Elliott, R. R., & Frank, R. G. (1990). Social and interpersonal reactions to depression and disability. *Rehabilitation Psychology, 35*, 135–147.

Emry, R., & Wiseman, R. L. (1987). An intercultural understanding of ablebodied and disabled person's communication. *International Journal of Intercultural Relations, 11*, 7–27.

Fichten, C. S., & Amsel, R. (1986). Trait attributions about college students with a physical disability: Circumplex analyses and methodological issues. *Journal of Applied Social Psychology, 16*, 410–427.

Fichten, C. S., Robillard, K., Judd, D., & Amsel, R. (1989). College students with physical disabilities: Myths and realities. *Rehabilitation Psychology, 4*, 243–257.

Fichten, C. S., Robbillard, K., Tagalakis, V., & Amsel, R. (1991). Causal interaction between college students with various disabilities and their nondisabled peers: The internal dialogue. *Rehabilitation Psychology, 36*, 3–20.

Fine, M., & Asch, A. (1995). Disability beyond stigma: Social interaction, discrimination, and activism. In N. R. Goldberger & J. B. Veroff (Eds.), *The culture and psychology reader* (pp. 536–558). New York: New York University Press.

Fox, S. A., & Giles, H. (1993). Accommodating intergenerational contact: A critique and theoretical model. *Journal of Aging Studies, 7*, 423–451.

Fox, S. A., & Giles, H. (1996). Interability Communication: Evaluating patronizing encounters. *Journal of Language and Social Psychology, 15*(3) 265–290.

Fox, S. A., & Giles, H., (1997). "Let the Wheelchair Through!": An Intergroup Approach to Interability Communication. In W. P. Robinson (Ed.), *Social psychology and social identity: Festschrift in honor of Henri Tajfel* (pp. 215–248). Oxford: Butterworth Heinmann.

Gentry, B. (1983). *Does mainstreaming insure integration?* Lawrence, KS: University of Kansas Early Childhood Institute. (ERIC Document Reproduction Service No. ED 231 108.)

Giles, H., Bourhis, R. Y., & Taylor, D. (1977). Towards a theory of language in ethnic group relations. In H. Giles (Ed.), *Language, ethnicity and intergroup relations* (pp. 307–348). London: Academic Press.

Giles, H., & Coupland, N. (1992). *Language: Contexts and consequences.* Pacific Grove, CA: Brooks/Cole.

Giles, H., Mulac, A., Bradac, J., & Johnson, P. (1987). Speech accommodation theory: The first decade and beyond. In M. L. McLaughlin (Ed.), *Communication yearbook 10* (pp. 13–48). Thousand Oaks, CA: Sage.

Goffman, E. (1963). *Stigma: Notes on the management of spoiled identity.* Englewood Cliffs, NJ: Prentice-Hall.

Grove, T. G., & Werkman, D. L. (1991). Conversations with ablebodied and visibly disabled strangers: An adversarial test of predicted outcome value and uncertainty reduction theories. *Human Communication Research, 17*, 507–534.

Harwood, J., Giles, H., & Bourhis, R. Y. (1994). The genesis of vitality theory: Historical patterns and discoursal dimensions. *International Journal of the Sociology of Language, 108*, 167–206.

Hastorf, A. H., Wildfogel, J., & Cassman, T. (1979). Acknowledgment of handicap as a tactic in social interaction. *Journal of Personality and Social Psychology, 73*, 590–593.

Hewstone, M., & Brown, R. H. (1986). Contact is not enough: An intergroup perspective on the contact hypothesis. In M. Hewstone & R. Brown (Eds.), *Contact and conflict in intergroup encounters* (pp. 1–44). Oxford: Blackwell.

Hogg, M. A., & Abrams, D. (1988). *Social identifications : A social psychology of intergroup relations and group processes.* London: Routledge.

Hogg, M. A., & Abrams, D. (Eds.). (1993). *Group motivation: Social psychological perspectives.* London: Harvester Wheatsheaf.

Holmes, G. E., Karst, R. H., & Erhart, S. A. (1990). Proxemics and physical disability: Etiology of interactional barriers. *Journal of Applied Rehabilitation Counseling, 21*, 25–31.

Johnston, M. (1996). Physical disability: Integration of WHO and psychological models. In J. Georgas, M. Manthouli, E. Besevegis, & A. Kokkevi (Eds.), *Contemporary psychology in Europe: Theory, research, and applications* (pp. 260–271). Seattle, WA: Hogrefe & Huber.

Kellermann, K., & Reynolds, R. (1990). When ignorance is bliss: The role of motivation to reduce uncertainty in uncertainty reduction theory. *Human Communication Research, 17*, 5–75.

Kleck, R. (1968). Physical stigma and nonverbal cues emitted in face-to-face interaction. *Human Relations, 21*, 19–28.

Kramarae, C. (1981). *Women and men speaking.* Rowley, MA: Newbury House.

Larwood, L. (1995). Attributional effects of equal employment opportunity: Theory development at the intersection of EEO policy and management practice. *Group and Organization Management, 20*, 391–408.

Meyerson, L. (1948). Physical disability as a social psychological problem. *Journal of Social Issues, 4*, 2–10.

Moghaddam, F. M., & Taylor, D. M. (1987). The meaning of multiculturalism for visible minority immigrant women. *Canadian Journal of Behavioral Science, 19*, 121–136.

Orbe, M. (1997). A co-cultural communication approach to intergroup relations. *Journal of Intergroup Relations, 24*, 36–49.

Orbe, M. (1998a, February). An *"outsider within" perspective to organizational communication: Explicating the communicative practices of co-cultural group members.* Paper presented at the Annual Conference of the Western States Communication Association, Denver, CO.

Orbe, M. (1998b). *Constructing co-cultural theory: An explication of culture, power, and communication.* Thousand Oaks, CA: Sage.

Padden, C. A. (1996). From the cultural to the bicultural: The modern deaf community. In I. Parasnis (Ed.), *Cultural and language diversity and the deaf experience* (pp. 79–98). New York: Cambridge University Press.

Patterson, J. M. (1991). A family systems perspective for working with youth with disability. *Pediatrician, 18*, 129–141.

Peterson, M. L., & Haralick, J. G. (1977). Integration of handicapped and nonhandicapped preschoolers: An analysis of play behavior and social interaction. *Education and Training of the Mentally Retarded, 12*, 235–245.

Rohrlich, P. E. (1983). Toward a unified conception of intercultural communication: An integrated systems approach. *International Journal of Intercultural Relations, 7*, 191–209.

Royse, D., & Edwards, T. (1989). Communicating about disability: Attitudes and preferences of persons with physical handicaps. *Rehabilitation Counseling Bulletin, 32*, 203–209.

Sagatun, I. J. (1985). The effects of acknowledging a disability and initiating contact on interaction between disabled and non-disabled persons. *Social Science Journal, 22*, 33–43.

Satcher, J., & Hendren, G. R. (1991). Acceptance of the Americans with Disabilities Act of 1990 by persons preparing to enter the business field. *Journal of Applied Rehabilitation Counseling, 22*, 15–18.

Seligman, M., & Darling, R. B. (1997). *Ordinary families, special children: A systems approach to childhood disability* (2nd ed.). New York: Guilford.

Smith, D. E. (1987). *The everyday world as problematic: A feminist sociology of knowledge.* Boston: Northeastern University Press.

Sunnafrank, M. (1986). Predicted outcome value during initial interactions: A reformulation of uncertainty reduction theory. *Human Communication Research, 13*, 3–33.

Tajfel, H. (Ed.) (1978). *Differentiation between social groups.* New York: Academic Press.

Taylor, D. M. (1991). The social psychology of racial and cultural diversity: Issues of assimilation and multiculturalism. In A. G. Reynolds (Ed.), *Bilingualism, multiculturalism, and second language learning* (pp. 1–20). Hillsdale, NJ: Lawrence Erlbaum Associates.

Thakerar, J. N., Giles, H., & Cheshire, J. J. (1982). Psychological and linguistic parameters of speech accomodation theory. In C. Faser & K. R. Scherer (Eds.), *Advances in the social psychology of language* (pp. 205–257). Cambridge, UK: Cambridge University Press.

Thomas, K. R. (1994). Drive theory, self psychology, and the treatment of persons with disabilities. *Psychoanalysis & Psychotherapy, 11*, 47–55.

Thomas, K. R., & Garske, G. (1995). Object relations theory: Implications for the personality development and treatment of persons with disabilities. *Melanie Klein & Object Relations, 13*, 31–63.

Thompson, T. L. (1982). "You can't play marbles—You have a wooden hand": Communication with the handicapped. *Communication Quarterly, 30*, 108–115.

Thompson, T. L. (1997, November). *Research on communication and disability: The way we were.* Paper presented at the annual conference of the National Communication Association, Chicago, IL.

Thompson, T. L., & Seibold, D. R. (1978). Stigma management in normal-stigmatized interactions: Test of the disclosure hypothesis and a model of stigma acceptance. *Human Communication Research, 4*, 231–242.

Tripp, A., French, R., & Sherrill, C. (1995). Contact theory and attitudes of children in physical education programs toward peers with disabilities. *Adapted Physical Activity Quarterly, 12*, 323–332.

Turner, J., Hogg, M. A., Oakes, P. J., Reicher, S. D., & Wetherell, M. S. (1987). *Rediscovering the social group: A self-categorization theory.* Oxford: Blackwell.

USA Today. (1997). *Court allows Calif. affirmative-action ban.* [Online]. http://www.usatoday.com/ news/court/nscot684.htm.

Watzlawick, P., Beavin, J. H., & Jackson, D. D. (1967). Some tentative axioms of communication. In P. Watzlawick, J. H. Beavin, & D. D. Jackson (Eds.), *Pragmatics of human communication; A study of interactional patterns, pathologies, and paradoxes* (pp. 48–71). New York: Norton.

Weinberg, N. (1983). Social equity and the physically disabled. *Social Work, 28,* 365–369.

Westwood, M., Vargo, J., & Vargo, F. (1981). Methods for promoting attitude change toward and among physically disabled persons. *Journal of Applied Rehabilitation Counseling, 12,* 220–225.

Wright, B. (1983). *Physical disability: A psychosocial approach* (2nd ed.). New York: Harper & Row.

Yuker, H. E. (1988). The effects of contact on attitudes toward disabled persons: Some empirical generalizations. In H. E. Yuker (Ed.), *Attitudes toward persons with disabilities* (pp. 262–274). New York: Springer.

12

Negotiating Personal Identities Among People With and Without Identified Disabilities: The Role of Identity Management

Gerianne Merrigan
San Francisco State University

Keywords: Autonomy, competence, fellowship face needs, cultural identities, relational identities, intercultural communication competence

The 1990 passage of the Americans With Disabilities Act (ADA) focused national attention on disability issues in the United States. It also provided a historical marker for the disability civil rights movement, which has gained prominence in particular disability communities like Deaf culture and in able and disabled populations more generally (Barnartt, 1996; Longmore, 1995; Scotch, 1988). The ADA broadened the U.S. legal definition of disability considerably, and 43 million persons now fit in the category "Americans with disabilities" (Burnett & Paul, 1996). Furthermore, the ADA gave people with disabilities a bigger role in negotiating their own reasonable accommodations.

Today, people with and without identified disabilities have the opportunity to negotiate disability-related identity issues in their relationships, groups, and organizations. This chapter focuses on the specific contributions of identity-management theory (Cupach & Imahori, 1993) to understanding some ways that people with and without identified disabilities negotiate personal identities. Conflicts arise when the identities held by people with disabilities violate the images others hold of them, or vice-versa. The interactions that result from incompatible identities and images often lead to face-threatening actions for one or more parties.

The first section of this chapter introduces some of the specific, identity-related problems people with disabilities face when interacting with those who have no identified disability. The next two sections describe identity-management theory (IMT) as a way of addressing these problems, first by detailing the ways participants' cultural identities are cued in the relation-ship, and second by describing IMT's three-phase model of developing intercultural relationships. The final section outlines some possible ways to anticipate and resolve potential identity conflicts in interactions between people with and without disabilities.

(DIS)ABILITY-RELATED IDENTITY PROBLEMS[1]

Identity is a self-conception, one's theory about oneself (Cupach & Imahori, 1993). Identity management is accomplished for self-benefit. Impression management describes interlocutors' attempts to influence the images others hold of them (Tedeschi & Reiss, 1981). In this way, the identity of a person with a disability is not isomorphic with the images held of that person by others.

In this section, four identity-related problems are posed, each related to (dis)ability and identity. Goffman's influential (1963) *Stigma: Notes on the Management of Spoiled Identity* aptly characterized the first of these problems. Goffman used *stigma* to mean "an undesired differentness," and he specifically listed "abominations of the body, the various physical de-formities" as a source of stigmatization. Goffman called "those who do not depart negatively from the particular expectations at issue" *normals* (p. 5). Three additional problems discussed in this section arise from the persis-tent application of the stigma model, including face-threats, inadequate and incompetent support, and a lack of cultural cohesion among people with disabilities and between those with and without disabilities.

Stigmatizing Disability

The first identity-related problem for people with disabilities is that most disability research has been conducted under the medical pathology model, in which the definition of disability is rooted in health-related disease or defect (Silvers, 1994). This model reflects a conceptualization of relationships between disabled patients and abled health-care professionals, who know what is best for people with disabilities (Fine & Asch, 1988; Scotch, 1988). Rose (1995) and others have pointed out that the medical pathology model of disability is the source of many cultural conflicts about people with disabilities because it stigmatizes people with disabilities as defective and abnormal.

Bishop's (1986) study of the effects of training on verbal and nonverbal behavior and Sharkey and Stafford's (1990) study of turn-taking cues among congenitally blind adults are examples of communication research informed by this pathology model of disability. The researchers start with the assumption that blind people are unable to communicate competently, due to lack of sight, and then suggest that training may help blind people accommodate their behavior to appear competent in sighted terms.

MacLean and Gannon's (1995) research comparing two scales that measure attitudes of nondisabled people toward people with disabilities further illustrates the relationship of the pathology and stigma models: The authors identify as "highly problematical" their finding that the Interaction with Disabled Persons Scale (IDP) measures not only "discomfort," but also "sympathy" toward people with disabilities. They assert that discomfort underlies a negative attitude toward people with disabilities. Unfortunately, the responsibility of minimizing that discomfort usually falls on people with disabilities (cf. Royse & Edwards, 1989). In fact, Braithwaite and Labrecque (1994) identified seven strategies "persons with visible physical disabilities can use to manage the discomfort of ablebodied persons with whom they interact" (p. 289), such as modeling or using humor. Although such suggestions may help to produce more comfortable interactions for everyone involved, the need for such accommodations is most often prioritized from the perspective of the "whole" or "able" person, in what Silvers (1994) called the "tyranny of the normal" (p. 154).

Face-Threats

Brown and Levinson's (1978) anthropological treatise on the phenomena of politeness behavior provided a theoretic framework for the second (dis)ability-related identity problem, face-threats. Face is a communicator's claim to be seen as a certain type of person: Positive face refers to the desire to be liked and respected (Brown & Levinson, 1978). Lim and Bowers (1991) separated these two needs into fellowship and competence face, respectively. Negative face refers to a person's desire to be autonomous, or to avoid being intruded on (Brown & Levinson, 1978; Lim & Bowers, 1991).

Braithwaite's (1991) title, "Just How Much Did That Wheelchair Cost?" captured one instantiation of the sort of privacy violations, or autonomy face-threats, that are endemic to living with a visible disability. Her study of how privacy boundaries are managed by people with disabilities showed how central face-needs are to establishing personal identity. Braithwaite (1996) extended her argument by analyzing how individuals' identification with health, stigma, and cultural models of disability affected their personal identities. Her development of disability as a cultural category showed how face-threats can be negotiated via cultural competence and need not be essential to interactions between those with and without identified disabilities.

Johnson and Hammel (1994) transcribed in-depth interviews with nine people with spinal cord injuries and analyzed these participants' use of alignment actions, the accounts, disclaimers, and excuses interlocutors employ to present their behavior in culturally acceptable terms (Scott & Lyman, 1968; Stokes & Hewitt, 1976). By their nature, therefore, alignment efforts can be used to locate face-threats, or potential face-threats. Johnson and Hammel analyzed patterns of aligning actions used by the speakers, and concluded that self-disclosure and social critique were two forms of culturally suspect conduct among people with disabilities. When people with disabilities engage in this conduct, they risk threatening their interlocutor's face, so that self-disclosure and social critique become confined to in-group interactions among people with disabilities.

Incompetent and Inadequate Support

The third identity-related problem is the receipt of incompetent or inadequate social support by people with disabilities. Hart and William's (1995) participant-observation study of interactions between ablebodied instructors and physically disabled students in U.S. college classrooms induced "four predominant roles assumed by instructors who teach students with disabilities, including the avoider, the guardian, the rejecter, and the nurturer" (p. 144). Of these roles, only the nurturer's way of relating to students with disabilities was positive and enhanced their educational experience. In contrast, "guardian" teachers gave students with disabilities special intellectual and physical roles that resulted in lower performance expectations for the students. The teachers' attempts to address fellowship face, or belonging, actually threatened the students' competence face. Fine and Asch (1988) published a similarly discouraging report on the state of instructors' interactions with disabled students.

Cultural Cohesion

The fourth identity-related problem is one of cultural cohesion. People with disabilities have to address tensions between group cohesion within their disability-community and integration with nondisabled members of their mainstream cultural group(s).[2] For the past 4 years at San Francisco State University (SFSU), I have worked with a class designed to train students with disabilities in the Americans With Disabilities Act. Each semester, after the training was completed, I interviewed the students involved and asked this question: "What was the most rewarding aspect of the project for you?" The following response, from a student with learning disabilities, addressed the challenges of cultural cohesion:

> Meeting others with disabilities and learning more about their problems and not being so focused on my own. This helped me realize the global importance of the disability movement and that I needed to be more outspoken and responsive to the needs of others . . . . In the past, I had interned with the Association for Retarded Citizens (ARC), and only saw clients as "them" or only saw their "otherness." I now realize that attitude kept me from connecting with them . . . . This class has helped me understand the disability community needs to become united in order to give local, state, federal, and global equality. (I-P-2)[3]

Although this student explicitly addressed the problem of cultural cohesion with the disability community, his comments also implicated the other three disability-related identity problems discussed in this section, stigma, face-threats, and inadequate support. The next two sections show how Cupach and Imahori's (1993) IMT can help to address these problems. First, the distinction between cultural and relational identities is explicated and three cultural identity cues are explored. Then, the IMT's three-phase model of intercultural relationship development is presented.

IMT: CULTURAL VERSUS RELATIONAL IDENTITIES

Cupach and Imahori (1993) conceptualized self-concept as having two facets: cultural identity and relational identity. Relational identity includes the cultural identities of both partners, as when two people from different national origins marry. Similarly, a relationship between someone with a disability and someone with no identified disability includes both partners' separate cultural identities as disabled and nondisabled.[4]

However, the partners' individual cultural identities become more and less situationally salient within the relationship, in part, due to the dynamics of three relational phases: (a) trial and error, (b) enmeshment, and (c) renegotiation. According to Cupach and Imahori (1993), these three phases are sequential necessities in developing intercultural relationships. IMT shows how conflicting cultural identities can threaten actors' competence, autonomy, and fellowship face, and prevent their relationship identity from developing beyond the initial trial-and-error phase. Competence, autonomy, and fellowship face needs exist in dialectic tension with one another and are cued by the scope, salience, and intensity of the participants' cultural identities. Therefore, before we can explore the phases of developing intercultural relationships, the tensions among these face needs and identity cues must be examined in detail.

Scope

The first cultural identity cue described by Cupach and Imahori (1993) is scope, which refers to the number of people who potentially share an identity. For example, scope may account for the ease of in-group communication among deaf people at Gallaudet, where most students, faculty, and staff use sign language. Similarly, Berkeley, California, is the home of the Independent Living Movement in the United States and a place of residence for many people with disabilities. Wheelchair users report that they are stared at less and interacted with more effectively in Berkeley than in other U.S. cities. This may be due to the sheer number and presence of people with visible disabilities: There is comfort in being among similar others, access to necessary services is improved, and the novelty effect of disability is lessened.

Salience

The second cultural identity cue, salience, refers to the relevance of one's cultural identity in a given situation or relationship (Cupach & Imahori, 1993). The fact that I see and my friend does not see becomes more relevant when we travel to areas we have not visited before, compared with negotiating familiar settings. Within a relational identity, the salience of a disability identification may be both diminished as novelty wears off and heightened as the stresses of living without walking, seeing, or breathing independently become progressively more apparent (see the third cultural identity cue, intensity, in the following section).

Furthermore, the salience of some cultural identities may be more flexible than that of a disability identity, which significantly affects daily living activities. For example, some people with nonvisible disabilities like alcoholism, HIV, or some learning disabilities, or who have low-level impairments like a mild hearing loss, can pass as able (Goffman, 1963), even within a relational identity. One blind student who had completed two 15-week classes in my department informed me, after our semester ended, that she had an identified learning disability in addition to being blind. She said she chose not to disclose the learning disability to me because, "that is just too complicated for professors to deal with" (O-P-11). She saw her learning disability as less salient. She felt she could cope with it on her own, whereas the blindness was more obvious and required more direct, apparent forms of accommodation such as carrying a cane and audio-taping lecture notes.

Salience is further highlighted in the following interview quotations from students who completed the ADA training program at SFSU. To one student, the campus was a more *salient* setting for ADA training than were small businesses: "I thought that more attention might be focused on changing campus attitudinal barriers rather than concentrating on 'other' organizations around the Bay Area" (I-P-2). Another student summarized, "Being able to implement this knowledge in my life and career will be the real value of the course to me" (I-P-9). Contrast his perception of the program's "real value" with a third student's view: "The most rewarding aspect for me was being able to have the opportunity to educate others about the ADA" (I-P-8). It is likely a matter of personal identity, rather than cultural category membership, that explains why the salience of the program was so different for these three students.

Intensity

The third cultural identity cue, intensity, "refers to the strength with which a particular aspect of the person's identity is communicated" (Cupach & Imahori, 1993, p. 10). For example, the legal and political aspects of disclosing one's disability in competitive situations like those necessitated by employment and higher education make voluntary self-disclosure of the disability an indicator of intense cultural identification. Likewise, immediate disclosure of one's disability, particularly when the disability is not directly relevant to the present interaction, may communicate that the disability is an intense aspect of an individual's cultural identity. Given the potential costs of disclosure and the option to pass or blend in, a person must identify strongly with their disability to disclose it voluntarily and immediately.

However, obvious markers like wheelchairs, respirators, and white canes can make a disability salient for the nondisabled novice observer, even when it is not an intense cultural identity cue for the person with the disability. People with disabilities are expected to take the perspective of the novice observer and empathize with his or her discomfort, or suffer the consequences of continual identity conflicts in which the disability is framed as more intense or more salient than desired. Obviously, the option to blend in, or pass as able (Goffman, 1963), is constrained for those with visible disabilities, at least during face-to-face interaction. That is one reason computer-mediated communication (CMC), is being lauded as a status-leveling technology by the disability community. With CMC, people with disabilities can interact without revealing their physical state (cf. Eckhouse & Maulucci, 1997; Matthews & Reich, 1993). It may be that CMC advantages people with disabilities by allowing them to manage the rate at which others develop an impression of them and their disability, whereas the impressions gained almost instantaneously during a face-to-face meeting make the disability cues too salient and too intense (see Walther, 1993).

IMT: DEVELOPING INTERCULTURAL RELATIONSHIPS

Cupach and Imahori (1993) theorized that the cultural identity cues of scope, salience, and intensity must be negotiated at each phase of the developing intercultural relationship. This section explores IMT's three relationship phases in detail, and demonstrates how competence, autonomy, and fellowship face needs exist in dialectic tension with one another at each phase.

Phase I: Trial and Error

The initial phase of an intercultural relationship is characterized by the parties' separate-but-salient cultural identities, and as such, challenges the participants to negotiate fellowship, or belonging needs, in balance with autonomy, or separateness, needs (Lim & Bowers, 1991). "A competent relationship emphasizes fellowship face when it is appropriate for the partners to be connected and autonomy face when it is crucial for the partners to be independent" (Cupach & Imahori, 1993, p. 128). Autonomy and independence have been highly valued in U.S. culture and in the disability rehabilitation field, and people with visible disabilities regularly experience being offered assistance when it is neither wanted nor needed; such offers threaten the competence and autonomy face of the person with disabilities, implying that he or she cannot function effectively and cannot be left safely alone.

On the other hand, disabled people who rely on others for assistance are judged as maladaptive or worse if they are seen as electing aid over functioning independently. For example, a person with multiple sclerosis or cerebral palsy might use a wheelchair because it affords greater mobility, in time and distance, than walking with crutches. However, if this person rises suddenly from a seated position and walks across the room, observers are likely to feel surprised and somehow offended. In fact, the observer's competence face has been threatened by the wheelchair rider's expectancy-violation. The sanction for such a face-threat often is to blame the victim, assigning him a less-than-pure motive for failing to behave in the expected fashion. Those with identified disabilities are expected to be independent, but only to a limited degree. If they are seen as too independent, their disability identity may be called into question.

The dialectic between autonomy and fellowship face may be the most salient and difficult tension to manage in intercultural relationships between able and disabled people. For example, leaders of the disability civil rights movement at Gallaudet University made substantive contributions to the development of the ADA and many seek its protection, at the same time attempting to isolate their disability-specific deaf culture (O-S-4). Deaf people's autonomy face needs, in this case, promoted their in-group cohesion, while their fellowship face needs encouraged integration with other disability groups. These conflicting needs make cohesion generally difficult between those with and without disabilities, in part because explicit discussion of potentially conflicting face needs is itself face-threatening. It may only be feasible after the relationship enters the enmeshment phase, when shared rules for discussing such delicate issues have emerged.

Phase II: Enmeshment

Cupach and Imahori's (1993) second phase of intercultural relationship development is enmeshment, in which both partners' separate cultural identities are joined by developing shared rules and symbols. In a January 1995 class at SFSU, I was seated next to a hearing-impaired student I had met in another context, but with whom I was not well acquainted. During our break in the class, he apologized for "sssh-ing" me during the lecture, when I had made a side comment. He said he "was having trouble hearing me and the lecture at the same time." This student reads lips and wears a hearing aid. When I responded by apologizing for not recognizing the problem before he pointed it out to me, he replied that I was, "one of about five people that he could lip-read or otherwise understand when they whisper" (O-P-3). This disclosure of a difference that I saw as positive, between our relationship and the relationships he had with most hearing people, confirmed my autonomy and fellowship face simultaneously. In our subsequent interactions in that class and in other contexts, we have been able to negotiate turn-taking and body orientation more-or-less seamlessly, and to the extent this happens successfully, our shared relational identity is each time confirmed.

Similarly, interlocutors in highly interpersonal, intercultural relationships in which one or both partners has a disability (e.g., a married couple) develop integrated rules systems; sometimes, the needs of the partner with the disability predominate, and at other times, the needs of the nondisabled partner predominate. Taking turns happens in all relationships, and is more of a distribution of justice than a true integration of the partners' separate identities. However, Cupach and Imahori (1993) do not address what happens when relational parties' perceptions of their interactions differ. A nondisabled person might leave an interaction with a person with a disability feeling that he or she has behaved competently, and the disabled person may feel that the nondisabled person has been inappropriate or ineffective. The two people may never even know that their perceptions differed. For example, because of rules accommodation, rather than actual coorientation, students with disabilities may never tell me, a nondisabled professor, that I have behaved incompetently. Accommodation, rather than true coorientation, is not addressed by Cupach and Imahori's second phase, relational enmeshment.

Phase III: Renegotiation

Cupach and Imahori's (1993) third phase extends beyond the development of an enmeshed relational identity based on symbolic and rule convergence: "Competent intercultural interlocutors use their narrowly defined but emerging relational identity from the second phase as a basis for renegotiating their separate cultural identities" (p. 127). In this phase, interactants realize a "truly integrated relationship" (p. 127). They evaluate one another's separate cultural identities positively and regard themselves differently for having participated in that intercultural relationship.

Cupach and Imahori (1993) asserted that renegotiation of individual cultural identities allows more competent management of the dialectical tensions between competence, autonomy, and fellowship face needs. Consider a prevalent face-threat to people with visible disabilities—being stared at in public settings. For people with visible disabilities, staring may be a particularly salient face-threat, based on the inherent dialectic tension between competence and autonomy face. In the case of a temporary disability, autonomy face-threats may be more easily tolerated, because both parties know the face-threat is temporary. However, for someone with a permanent disability, the autonomy face-threat cannot be tolerated indefinitely, due in part to the burden of continuously educating disability-ignorant people.

SOLUTIONS FOR (DIS)ABILITY-RELATED IDENTITY PROBLEMS

Cupach and Imahori's (1993) IMT shows how people from different cultural identities can negotiate the face-threats inherent in their relationships, and go on to develop enmeshed relational identities and renegotiate their separate cultural identities. This section presents three possible solutions for identity-related problems among those who seek to develop (dis)ability intercultural relationships.

Emphasize Relational Identities Over Cultural Identities

To emphasize relational identities means becoming aware of cues like scope, salience, and intensity—perceptual cues that can help to identify others' preferred identities, rather than one's own impression about who they are. Emphasizing relational identities also means treating people and relationships as unique, not as reliable representatives of any cultural category or categories. It means experimenting with the trial-and-error phase if we have had little experience with disability, and it means taking the risks needed to enmesh oneself in this intercultural communication. After all, errors are a requisite cost of initial intercultural interactions, despite the inherent threats they pose to fellowship face. If incompetence, paradoxically, is necessary along the road to competent, enmeshed intercultural relationships, perhaps short-term, local risks in each individual interaction are exchanged for long-term attitudinal change and development.

Finally, emphasizing relational identities means renegotiating one's own self-concept as a result of these interactions.

Relating to others interpersonally, seeing others as "persons first" (Braithwaite, 1996) rather than through category memberships, is desirable and helps us appreciate one another as individuals with complex identities comprised of multiple categories. At a policy or societal level, however, where "people with disabilities are handicapped by attitudes toward them" (Hart & Williams, 1995, p. 151), the dilemma of separate or blended identities is not so easily resolved. Political identification with a cultural category leads to collective power, which is also desirable for those involved in the disability civil rights movement.

Anticipate Face-Needs and Learn to Repair Face-Threats

The second possible solution, face-work related to the salience of a disability, may be more a matter of interpersonal support than of mere cultural knowledge (Cupach & Imahori, 1993). The desire to support another's face by including him or her (fellowship), or by respecting his or her abilities (competence) can help interlocutors anticipate and avoid face-threatening acts. When face-threats do occur, apologies can help repair the damage (Scott & Lyman, 1968).

Some actions that are face-threatening in the trial-and-error phase can be face-supporting in the enmeshment or renegotiation phase of a relationship. For example, when I tease my friend about her mobility problems related to a childhood ankle injury, I support her competence and autonomy face simultaneously. The same verbal and nonverbal messages probably would be seen as face-threatening in an obligatory relationship; but when a friend singles a friend out as unique because she belongs to a particular group, cultural identity becomes salient in a complimentary way. This can and does backfire, of course, when interlocutors misjudge their level of friendship and receptivity to autonomy-face support. From a neutral, unknown, or a negative relational partner, attempts to support autonomy face (i.e., uniqueness) and fellowship face (i.e., belonging) are more likely to be seen as face-threatening.

That the perception of face-threat or degree of threat rests with the disabled person in intercultural relationships is generally assumed (Silvers, 1994). A threat to autonomy or fellowship face is perhaps the most difficult face-threat to repair, especially if the parties fail to recognize what is causing the offense. For example, Adler and Rodman (1991) pointed out that reciprocal, voluntary self-disclosure is most effective in developing interpersonal relationships. Too much self-disclosure, too soon, or disclosures that are not reciprocated, threaten competence face. Yet, people with disabilities often are asked to disclose private information in medical and social settings in which nonreciprocal self-disclosure marks them as belonging to a special category, that is, disabled (Braithwaite, 1991; Thompson, 1982). This requested disclosure also threatens their fellowship face. The disabled person who seems reticent to disclose in great breadth or depth, or nonreciprocally, often is labeled as ill-adjusted or noncompliant. Ironically, that labeling amounts to an additional face-threat.

Allow the Paradox of Cultural Cohesion

A third possible solution to identity-related problems between people with and without identified disabilities is to actively embrace the paradox between cohesion within and across these distinct cultural groups. Those who seek to develop intercultural relationships need to recognize that bonding with similar others, or ingroup members, is as valuable as are interactions with those who are different from oneself, or outgroup members.

One student in the ADA project addressed the tension between cohesion and integration with nondisabled people after conducting a consultation with a campus student-services office: "When I told the lady behind the counter what a wonderful difference the changes made, and how pleased I was, she enthusiastically replied that the office staff is also very pleased with the changes. As a result of the modifications they also have more space and feel more comfortable" (O-P-1). This participant had cerebral palsy, and she walked with crutches or used a wheelchair. Her comment suggested cohesion and fellowship with the ablebodied staff members through expressed identification with similar values, in this case, for space and comfort.

However, the lure of cohesion, or fellowship face, may lead interlocutors to threaten one another's competence or autonomy face. For instance, ingratiating may be used to support another's competence face by giving compliments. Asking questions that promote disclosure of information about the other also may be used to support fellowship face. Both moves threaten autonomy face by freezing the other's cultural identity as a person with disability, thereby blocking other aspects of his or her identity from being realized in that interaction. The face-threat comes in trying to relate interpersonally, but in the process locking onto cultural category differences (Cupach & Imahori, 1993). Similarly, highlighting differences when merging identities is desired can be counterproductive. Inferring that another cannot enact any role outside his or her (autonomous) cultural identity threatens both fellowship and competence face. Cupach and Imahori (1993) noted that balancing these dialectic tensions may only work across multiple encounters, so that episodic incompetence is repaired in the long run.

Gradual implementation of the ADA has exacerbated the fundamental tension between inclusion and respect regarding people with disabilities at work. Some attention to fellowship face in the form of "everyone here is equal" can come at the expense of competence face for the person with disabilities. Avoiding conflict, or "helping" a disabled person keep the job—in other words, inclusion on bases other than competence—eventually becomes a violation of fellowship face, and communicates lack of respect through deceit. However, addressing competence face-needs does threaten fellowship face, in some cases, to the point of relational dissolution.

There are no easy answers. Intercultural competence is a matter of individual and relational adaptation after an initial trial-and-error phase, and presumably, with the accumulated wisdom of multiple intercultural relationships over time (Cupach & Imahori, 1993). Relying on the broad category of "disability knowledge" will not help one interact effectively with an individual disabled person.

DISCUSSION QUESTIONS

1. What is the difference between a person's identity and image?
2. Why is it important to consider the issue of identity for people with disabilities, in addition to considering image?
3. Discuss the scope, salience, and intensity of your own cultural identity in your relationship with one other person (e.g., your significant other). How does your cultural identity impact this relationship?
4. For the relationship you identified in Question 3, identify the relationship stage you have reached with this person: Are you "enmeshed" in a relational identity? Have you experienced renegotiation of self?
5. What [dis]ability identity problems have you experienced? What solutions have you tried? Describe your experiences.

REFERENCES

Adler, R., & Rodman, G. B. (1991). *Understanding human communication* (4th ed.). New York: Holt, Rinehart, & Winston.

Barnartt, S. N. (1996). Disability culture or disability consciousness? *Journal of Disability Policy Studies, 7*(2), 1–19.

Bishop, V. (1986). Effects of training on non-verbal and verbal behaviors of congenitally blind adults. *Journal of Visual Impairment and Blindness, 73*, 1–9.

Braithwaite, D. O. (1991). "Just how much did that wheelchair cost?": Management of boundaries by persons with disabilities. *Western Journal of Communication, 55*, 254–274.

Braithwaite, D. O. (1996). "I am a person first": Different perspectives on the communication of persons with disabilities. In E. B. Ray (Ed.), *Communication and disenfranchisement: Social health issues and implications* (pp. 257–272). Mahwah, NJ: Lawrence Erlbaum Associates.

Braithwaite, D. O., & Labrecque, D. O. (1994). Responding to the Americans with Disabilities Act: Contributions of interpersonal communication research and training. *Journal of Applied Communication Research, 22*, 287–294.

Brown, P., & Levinson, S. (1978). Universals in language usage: Politeness phenomenon. In E. N. Goody (Ed.), *Questions and politeness: Strategies in social interaction* (pp. 56–97). Cambridge, U.K.: Cambridge University Press.

Burnett, J. J., & Paul, P. (1996). Assessing the media habits and needs of the mobility-disabled consumer. *Journal of Advertising, 25*(3), 47–59.

Cupach, W. R., & Imahori, T. T. (1993). Identity management theory: Communication competence in intercultural episodes and relationships. In R. L. Wiseman & J. Koester (Eds.), *Intercultural communication competence* (pp. 112–131). Newbury Park, CA: Sage.

Eckhouse, R. H, & Maulucci, R. A. (1997). A multimedia system for augmented sensory assessment and treatment of motor disabilities. *Telematics and Informatics, 14*, 67–82.

Fine, M., & Asch, A. (1988). Disability beyond stigma: Social interaction, discrimination, and activism. *Journal of Social Issues, 44*, 3–21.

Goffman, E. (1963). *Stigma: Notes on the management of spoiled identity.* Englewood Cliffs; NJ: Prentice-Hall.

Hart, R. D., & Williams, D. E. (1995). Ablebodied instructors and students with physical disabilities: A relationship handicapped by communication. *Communication Education, 44*, 140–154.

Johnson, G., & Hammel, J. (1994). *The negotiation of identity by persons with disability: The role of alignment actions.* Paper presented at the annual meeting of the Western States Communication Association, Portland, OR.

Johnson, G., & Albrecht, T. (1996). Supportive structures for people with disabilities: Smoothing or smothering the way? In E. B. Ray (Ed.), *Communication and the disenfranchised* (pp. 433–447). Mahwah, NJ: Lawrence Erlbaum Associates.

Lim, T., & Bowers, J. W. (1991). Face-work: Solidarity, approbation, and tact. *Human Communication Research, 17*, 415–450.

Longmore, P. (1995, September/October). The second phase: From disability rights to disability culture. *Disability Rag*, 4–11.

MacLean, D., & Gannon, P. M. (1995). Measuring attitudes toward disability: The interaction with disabled persons scale revisited. *Journal of Social Behavior and Personality, 10*, 791–806.

Mathews, J. T., & Reich, C. F. (1993). Constraints on communication in classrooms for the deaf. *American Annals of the Deaf, 138*, 14–18.

Rose, H. M. (1995). Apprehending deaf culture. *Journal of Applied Communication Research, 23*, 156–162.

Royse, D., & Edwards, T. (1989). Communicating about disability: Attitudes and preferences of persons with physical handicaps. *Rehabilitation Counseling Bulletin, 32*, 203–209.

Scotch, R. K. (1988). Disability as the basis for a social movement: Advocacy and the politics of definition. *Journal of Social Issues, 44*, 159–172.

Scott, M. B., & Lyman, S. W. (1968). Accounts: The use of alignment actions. *American Sociological Review, 33*, 46–62.

Sharkey, W. F., & Stafford, L. (1990). Turn-taking resources employed by congenitally blind conversers. *Communication Studies, 41*, 161–182.

Silvers, A. (1994). "Defective" agents: Equality, difference, and the tyranny of the normal. *Journal of Social Philosophy, 25*, 154–175.

Stokes, R., & Hewitt, J. P. (1976). Aligning actions. *American Sociological Review, 41*, 838–849.

Tedeschi, J. J., & Reiss, M. (1981). Verbal strategies in impression management. In C. Antaki (Ed.), *The psychology of ordinary explanations of social behavior* (pp. 271–309). New York: Academic Press.

Thompson, T. L. (1982). Disclosure as a disability-management strategy: A review and conclusions. *Communication Quarterly, 30*, 196–202.

Walther, J. (1993). Impression development in computer-mediated interaction. *Western Journal of Communication, 57*, 381–398.

ENDNOTES

1. The brackets in "[dis]ability" are used here to heighten the reader's awareness of the political nature of this term. The prefix "dis-" means "the opposite of" (Webster's New World Dictionary, 2nd ed.); but in fact, many [dis]abilities are defined more by social and cultural biases about a particular ability than by the lack (or limitation) of the ability, per se. For example, some deaf people do not consider themselves [dis]abled. They simply cannot hear.

2. I believe strongly that people with and without disabilities share this burden. However, when people with no identified disability fail to seek out cohesion with disabled people, it becomes the responsibility of people with disabilities, if they seek the benefits of effective in- and out-group relationships (see Johnson & Albrecht, 1996, for a more detailed discussion of this issue).

3. Each quotation taken from the ADA training project at SFSU was coded to identify the data source (i.e., S = survey; O = observation; or I = interview) and speaker's role (i.e., P = participant; S = staff member), while protecting confidentiality and anonymity. Each speaker was assigned an identification number so that quotes from a single speaker can be identified by the reader. For example, the code "S-S-1" indicates a quote taken from survey data, by staff member 1).

4. The students enrolled in the ADA class demonstrated symbolic convergence around the terms *disabled* and *disability community*, and rejected the term *handicapped*.

13

Intercultural Views of People With Disabilities in Asia and Africa

Miho Iwakuma
University of Oklahoma

Jon F. Nussbaum
Pennsylvania State University

Keywords: Cross-cultural disability studies, family responsibility and disability, folk beliefs and disabilities, "tight" societies, uncertainty avoidance societies, *kegare*

Throughout the world, people live with disabilities regardless of race, gender, religion, ethnicity, and/or class. However, these individuals with disabilities tend to be viewed negatively by others (e.g., Murphy, 1990; Oliver, 1996; Whyte & Ingstad, 1995). Many social scientists have tried to explain the origin of this negative perception toward people with disabilities. A structural anthropologist, Mary Douglas (1966), argued that something that departs from the norm or that is unable to be classified into categories is labeled "ambiguous." According to Douglas, this ambiguousness is analogous to uncleanness or even danger in many cultures; therefore, a person, object, or trend in a marginal state tends to be seen as an object of societal "pollution" to be avoided by others. Douglas' theory seems to be applicable to the situation of people with disabilities. This group has identifiable physical features, which often contradict the "ideal" body image. In addition, people with disabilities are often perceived to be in a transitional state between health and sickness, which is considered as "liminal" (Murphy,

Scheer, Murphy, & Mack, 1988; Turner, 1967). Because of this liminal status and ambiguity, individuals with disabilities are often avoided by others. In a similar vein, Goffman (1963) used the notion of stigma from a sociological standpoint to illustrate the treatment of people with disabilities. According to Goffman (1963), it is marginality or deviance of individuals with disabilities that hampers the interactions between nondisabled people and persons with disabilities.

While common negative perceptions about people with disabilities prevail in different cultures, the intensity of the stigma or degree of "pollution" of the disability seems to vary depending on the culture (Murphy, 1990; Whyte & Ingstad, 1995). Traditionally, disability studies have been conducted predominantly in Western societies, especially in the United States. However, as mentioned, disability issues are shared by all humankind, and are thus world issues, which concern all of us.

By the year 2000, about 80% of the world's population of persons with disabilities will live in either Asian or African countries (Nakanishi, 1997). Therefore, addressing disability issues and situations in those countries will help us understand the "big picture" of people with disabilities throughout the globe. Nakanishi pointed out that malnutrition, unsanitary conditions, wars, natural disasters, and increased traffic accidents due to rapid modernization with the absence of safety regulations are major factors contributing to a drastic increase in the number of people with disabilities in Asia and Africa. Accordingly, between the developing and developed countries, consequences and conditions surrounding people with disabilities are quite diverse (Oliver, 1996). However, literature on communication phenomena as they relate to people with disabilities in non-Western countries is scarce. Communication scholars need to focus their attention more on how people with disabilities are perceived and communicate with others throughout the world. In this chapter, we first present an overview of communication and people with disabilities in Africa and Asia. Second, we provide a detailed description of individuals with disabilities in Japan. We utilize one of the researchers' insights and experiences as a native Japanese with a disability to present a personal view.

PEOPLE WITH DISABILITIES IN ASIA

Kalyanpur (1996) wrote of Indian cultural characteristics and their influences on lives of people with disabilities. With an emphasis on the community rather than on the individual, concepts of harmony and duty govern people's lives. Most interestingly, she pointed out that in India, the notion of independence is interpreted quite differently from the Western interpretation, that is, "only married or working individuals are 'socially responsible'" (p. 256). In other words, unlike individuals in the West, people in India feel less ashamed to be dependent on others. This is especially true for cases of people with disabilities. Family members, due to social obligation, assume and are assumed to be responsible for taking care of their family members with disabilities. Also, just as they do for nondisabled individuals, the parents arrange marriages for their children with disabilities.

China has the largest population of people with disabilities in the world: 51 million people with disabilities live in the country (Oliver, 1996; Tefft, 1993). However, it seems that the Chinese environment for people with disabilities is still far from the ideal in terms of access and perceptions. According to Shimizu (1997), there is only one sidewalk that people with wheelchairs can use in downtown Shanghai. Still, many individuals with disabilities move to metropolitan cities, such as Beijing, from their rural communities for better opportunities and lives (Tefft, 1993). Some of these individuals who move are students with disabilities. One of the prestigious universities in China, Beijing University, has no accommodation for students with disabilities and they are discriminated against by others because of a "tremendous instinctive embarrassment" of having disabilities (Tefft, 1993, p. 15). Due to the embarrassment the Chinese hold, newborns with disabilities in China are at a high risk of being abandoned or taken into orphanages where love and/or stimuli are seriously lacking (Tefft, 1993). On the other hand, another prevailing perception of the nondisabled in China is viewing those with disabilities as people to be protected, instead of people with equal rights (Kobayashi, 1997). Accordingly, Shimizu (1997) notes that in China parents of children with disabilities tend to be overprotective, and they will not let their children with disabilities go out by themselves.

This overprotective or "custodial" tendency of ablebodied others can be witnessed in other Asian countries. Carmen Reyes-Zubiaga in the Philippines still remembers her extraordinary wedding and her family's initial reaction to her marriage decision (United Nations, 1995). She uses a wheelchair to compensate for polio and lived in an atmosphere that mandated she would never marry, and would be guarded by her brothers for the rest of her life. Her mother always tried to protect Carmen from others, and the mother was not happy about Carmen's courtship with her boyfriends. When Carmen met her future husband, Dennis, and decided to marry him, her mother became so fearful about Carmen's future that the mother "tearfully pleaded" with her to change her decision to marry (United Nations, 1995, p. 6). The mother could not accept that Carmen was mature enough to bear children by herself or be loved as a female by someone. The mother seemed to have a strong obligation to look after Carmen's life and this was her way of exhibiting care for a daughter with a disability. Like Carmen's experience, what is problematic is that although they know that their families care and are concerned, sometimes an individual with a disability has to "push them away" to become what he or she desires. Especially because of a collectivistic cultural orientation, Asian people with disabilities face difficulties in either case: oppression of their sexuality and living with the expectations of others or deciding to pursue happiness and meet family disagreement. Fortunately, Carmen could persuade her family and was wed in 1988. In the Philippines a bride in a wheelchair was so rare that her wedding scene was televised throughout the country, and many people in similar situations were encouraged by her pursuit of happiness.

The number of individuals with disabilities in Thailand is less clear. Hosaka (1997) pointed out that, just like the Chinese, Thai families feel so ashamed of their relatives with disabilities that they do not submit their birth certificates (Hosaka, 1997). Similar to many other Asian countries, this phenomenon occurs because people in Thailand tend to believe "a disability is frequently seen as direct evidence of a transgression in a previous life, either on the part of the parent or the child" (Groce & Zola, 1993, p. 1049). This is because the concept of karma is deeply rooted into their cosmology and into Asian people's perceptions of a disability. This belief system, furthermore, results in attitudes of one of two extremes: either overprotectiveness or discrimination (United Nations, 1993). Thus, it is not surprising that the Disabled Peoples' International Thailand emphasizes the enlightenment of society toward people with disabilities and strives to change the negative folklore beliefs about disability (Hosaka, 1997).

A similar perspective is evident in the description below based on an interview with a disabled person from Pakistan. Armad is a doctoral student who uses a wheelchair and lives in an apartment at the University of Oklahoma with his wife and three children.[1] He noted that "the biggest problem is an access situation (in Pakistan)" and "the general awareness (toward people with disabilities) is low." According to Armad, once someone becomes disabled, his or her family or close friends' responsibility is to take care of the person, much like in China. With regard to attribution of disability, Armad told the researcher that Pakistanis do not see disabilities as signs of God's punishment as individuals do in Thailand. On the contrary, he added, "with these difficulties at present, I'll have more comfort in another life." He continued to note that people in his country do not feel ashamed to have a family member or a close friend with a disability and that, "people's attitudes are . . . I would say, better over here [in the United States]. But as far as family and friends are concerned, they [Pakistani people] are more helpful and sympathetic." He observed that after having his disability, "[I got more friends than before [having a disability] . . . They are eager to help me anytime." From his comments, it seemed that he was not "pressured" to be independent while having his disability, and he did not perceive relying on others as necessarily negative. This interview illustrates that "independence" and "dependence" are viewed quite differently in Pakistan. His comment contrasts with the U.S. situation in which people value the notions of "self-reliance," "independence," and "try[ing] harder" (Phillips, 1984, p. 260).

Similar to the situation in India, according to Armad, Pakistani families do arrange marriages for people with disabilities. Females with disabilities tend to be more disadvantaged than males with disabilities in regard to marriage because of the many physical chores that females are expected to perform at home. Governmental support for persons with disabilities in Pakistan is scarce, as are the number of accessible buildings or facilities for people using wheelchairs. Nevertheless, in spite of the inconveniences he would face in his country, Armad has never questioned going back to Pakistan after finishing his degree. For Armad, home is where he belongs.

PEOPLE WITH DISABILITIES IN AFRICA

As stated before, Asia and Africa have similar problematic conditions for individuals with disabilities (Nakanishi, 1997). Nakanishi, however, asserts that African disability activists are more assertive than Asian disability activists because of cultural differences. In this section, the focus is on how African cultures shape unique situations for people with disabilities.

Research by Ingstad (1995) demonstrates how ideologies such as equality or rights, which played a crucial role for improving lives of people with disabilities in the West, have been translated into the Botswana culture. According to Ingstad, because a primary Botswana unit is the family, not an individual, some principles (e.g., integration or normalization) have little meaning for Botswanans; the family and community have already integrated them.

In the educational context in Tanzania before the colonial era, children with disabilities were included with their peers without disabilities within an informal education system by community (Kisanji, 1995). Ironically, according to Kisanji, the introduction of the Western education system with less flexibility resulted in segregation classes for pupils with disabilities from their ablebodied schoolmates. Consequently, many special schools have been built exclusively for these students with disabilities but their parents are often reluctant to send their children far from their communities (Kisanji, 1995). The Westernization or modernization in Tanzania has also changed perceptions of ablebodied people about the causes of disabilities (Kisanji, 1995). Whereas more than 40% of studied tribal "elderlies" in the country attribute having disabilities to God's will, primary school teachers within the Western educational system believe that disabilities are caused by diseases. Only 13% of schoolteachers argue that disabilities are caused by God's will and only 11% of elderlies attribute having disabilities to diseases. Kisanji asserted, however, that people with disabilities in Tanzania are generally accepted and included by society. This acceptance is possible because many ablebodied individuals still believe that having a disability is one's fate or God's will; "Disability is . . . taken as a fact of life" (Kisanji, 1995, p. 119).

Cohort effects interact with educational differences in Tanzania to impact general perceptions about individuals with disabilities (Kisanji, 1995). More than 70% of Tanzanian elderlies believe that people with visual impairments are nonproductive and dependent, whereas only 7% of schoolteachers believe so. On the other hand, 91% of studied schoolteachers think that individuals with visual impairments can perform basketry skills, and with proper education can become schoolteachers; only 25% of elderlies believe this. Although little more than 30% of studied elderlies think a person with hearing impairment is marriageable, 71% of the teachers have this belief.

Interestingly, in many African countries or cultures, people do not even have a term comparable to the word *disability* (Whyte & Ingstad, 1995). The Songye culture in Zaire is one that does not have the term *disability* for children (Devlieger, 1995). Instead of having the term, the Songye have three categories (ceremonial, bad, and faulty) for children who are considered to be "abnormal." Songye people also have a much stronger desire to understand "why" than people in the West, and they tend to attribute the acquisition of disabilities to sorcery, ancestral acts, bride-wealth, or God's punishments.

Another society that does not have a Western notion of disability is the Maasai culture in Kenya (Talle, 1995). Talle asserted that, although the idea of disability connotes stigma or inferiority in the Western societies, this is not necessarily true for the Maasai. The Maasai do not see a clear linkage between physical incompetence and stigma or inferiority. Instead, Maasai people view illness as a "sign or cosmic disorder projected on the human body" (p. 61). Unlike the Songye in Zaire, who are very concerned with understanding the reason for a disability, the Maasai generally accept disabilities as a fact of life caused by God or a curse. Similar to the Songye culture, however, people with disabilities in the Maasai society are integrated into their communities based on the premise of, "A child is a child whatever it looks like" (Talle, 1995, p. 69).

Sentumbwe (1995) described communication between the sighted and individuals with visual impairments. According to Sentumbwe, people in Uganda perceive blindness as the worst disability that one can have. Whyte (1995) mentioned that the Ugandans perceive a person with epilepsy negatively, especially if he or she is a stranger. A person with epilepsy outside of his or her community can be quite isolated and avoided by others because of a common belief that epilepsy is contagious. Within the community, however, the Ugandans integrate an individual with epilepsy and treat him or her as a community member. In other words, the issue of insider–outsider is crucial for Ugandan interpersonal communication with a disabled person (Whyte, 1995). According to Sentumbwe (1995), the "spread" phenomenon impacts the treatment of persons with visual impairments in Uganda. Spread is defined as the "assumption that loss of one function leads to a decrease of capacity in other physical functions" (Sentumbwe, 1995, p. 161). Most significantly, spread tremendously deteriorates interpersonal communication between the sighted and people with visual impairments due to the sick roles attached to blindness. The ablebodied tend to perceive individuals with visual impairments as helpless, incompetent, and unable to live normal lives (Sentumbwe, 1995).

In addition to discrimination and stereotypes based on blindness, the power difference between genders pushes females with visual impairments down to the lowest caste in the society (Sentumbwe, 1995). A similar negative situation for females with disabilities in Asia has been mentioned (United Nation, 1995). Therefore, it is not unreasonable to consider blind females as a group that may face the most extreme difficulty in regard to interpersonal communication.

IMPLICATIONS AND SUMMARY OF LIVES OF PEOPLE WITH DISABILITIES IN ASIA AND AFRICA

From the descriptions already given, it is evident that several unique disability themes emerge when non-Western societies are compared with that of the United States. In many of the Asian or African societies that have been studied, disability issues are family or community concerns, rather than a societal concern. Family members thus tend to feel responsible for looking after kin with disabilities (Lewis, 1995). As a result, from the Western viewpoint Asian or African ablebodied people may appear overprotective or custodial when they are interacting with others with disabilities. This is because some Western concepts, such as individualism, independence, and/or dependence, have different connotations in different cultures. In individualistic societies such as the United States, people, including ones with disabilities, strive for maximum independence. As much as the people in these societies praise the independence of individuals, they are horrified by the idea of being dependent on others. Nevertheless, in other cultures this does not necessarily seem to be true: Persons with disabilities can rely on others without feeling guilty or ashamed.

Additionally, the previous section illustrates that religious systems or the cosmology in a culture have a great impact on how people view sickness, health, and/or the disability. Most important, people's attitudes toward individuals with disabilities and communication between the ablebodied and individuals with disabilities can be tremendously affected by these folk beliefs. In addition, disability issues are not free from gender-based perceptions. Sexism needs to be faced in addition to ableism. Finally, the notion of disability as a universal concept is in question. People in some cultures do not have the term *disability*. The category of "the disabled" is socially constructed. Linton (1998) asserted that the modernization in the West that started in the 17th century has created institutionalization and the medical model of people with disabilities. Along with the tide of modernization, perceptions of ablebodied people about persons with disabilities have changed. Whereas Linton acknowledged industrial advancements such as medical technology, she contends that the industrial revolution, bolstered by the notions of efficiency and productivity, has created a group of the "needy disabled" who "can't keep up, who are thought to drain resources, or who remind us in any way of the limitations of our scientific capacities" (p. 46). The issues raised here help introduce the next section, which focuses on Japanese people with disabilities and their role within Japanese society.

JAPANESE PEOPLE WITH DISABILITIES

Shougaisha: People With Obstacles (shou) and Harm (gai)

Unlike the English alphabet, most Chinese characters, which the Japanese language uses, symbolize a specific meaning. For example, many female names in Japanese contain a Chinese character *mi* connoting "beauty" or "elegance," illustrating that most Japanese people perceive femaleness as something that is closely related to beauty or elegance. Consequently, examining Chinese characters used in a Japanese word uncovers a hidden meaning to the word itself; most important, paying attention to Chinese characters reveals how people perceive a thing, concept, or person.

The term that refers to people with disabilities in Japanese is *shougaisha*. This term consists of three Chinese characters: *shou*, *gai*, and *sha*. The last character *sha* means people or a person. The first component, *shou*, signifies meanings of "obstacles," "illnesses," and/or "bothersome." On the other hand, the second one, *gai*, holds meanings such as "harm," "loss," and/or "disaster." Therefore, it is assumed that, at least when the term *shougaisha* was originated, people chose those Chinese characters to convey perceptions of individuals with disabilities as people of "obstacles," "illness," and/or "loss."

Perceptions of Ablebodied People Regarding People With Disabilities in Japan

In the United States, it is hard not to see handicapped parking spots, ramps, or people with disabilities using them. On the other hand, the line separating the ablebodied and people with disabilities in Japan is much clearer, thicker, and deeper. For example, the majority of bathrooms in Japan that are accessible to those with disabilities have a sign: "The Disabled Only." Most of the time, those accessible bathrooms are built outside of the regular bathrooms used by ablebodied individuals. Because the sign says "The Disabled Only," the majority of ablebodied people hesitate to use those accessible bathrooms. Yashiro (1979) witnessed a mother scolding her child who was about to use "The Disabled Only" bathroom by saying, "No, don't use that one! It's dirty there" (p. 83, our translation), illustrating the stigma attached to this bathroom. As a result, it is rare in Japan to see an ablebodied individual and a person with a disability waiting in line together at the bathroom area. The example of the bathroom illustrates that, compared with people in United States, the Japanese tend to have clearer categories (e.g., "The Disabled Only") and they expect others to keep tightly to this categorization.

Triandis (1994) asserted that people in a relatively homogenous society such as Japan tend to have tighter structures when compared with people in relatively heterogeneous societies. In tight cultures, scripted behaviors (norms and rules) are clearer than in loose cultures, and people in tight cultures tend to follow these unwritten cultural scripts without questioning (Gudykunst & Kim, 1997). In a similar vein, "tightness" of society is closely related to Hofstede's (1984) uncertainty avoidance (UA) scale. He reported that "On the cultural level, tendencies toward rigidity and dogmatism, intolerance of different opinions, traditionalism, superstition, racism, and ethnocentrism all relate to a norm for (in)tolerance of ambiguity" (p. 112). According to Hofstede, therefore, the more UA a society, the lower the level of tolerance for ambiguity of the people. People in a high UA society perceive that "deviant persons and ideas are dangerous" (p. 140). Among the 39 countries surveyed by Hofstede, Japan is the 4th on the list (the United States is the 31st) for being a tight and highly UA society.

What are the consequences of having a tight and highly UA society such as Japan? According to Mosel (1973), these two variables are highly correlated with the notion of predictability. In other words, since people seek predictability of others' behaviors, they create tight and highly UA societies. In these kinds of societies, people tend to feel very uncomfortable when encountering unexpected happenings or situations. There are several ways to obtain a high level of predictability about others' behaviors. One is, as mentioned before, expecting others to know their "place," and expecting others to behave accordingly. This kind of society is not flexible because it relies on a tight category system (e.g., "The Disabled Only").

Kuwana's (1997) experience with people at the train station illustrates this tendency in the Japanese. Kuwana, who uses a wheelchair and lives in the United States, contends that whenever she goes back to Japan to visit, she feels her "role" as "the disabled" changes drastically. According to her, the role of "the disabled" in Japan is the one of "being protected by others [by the ablebodied]" (p. 118, our translation). For Kuwana, going back to Japan requires a cultural adjustment; she must be seen as needing care due to her disability. One day, while staying in Japan, she had to miss her bullet train, which she had used every day to commute. She and her colleagues were having a party. During the party, however, Kuwana was told that people at the train station were so concerned about her, since she did not show up at the station, that they were calling around to find her. People at the station called several places, including her workplace and her destined station, because of the information they had obtained when she made her seat reservation. This behavior is not unlike the treatment of a missing child at the station who needs to be protected by others. In a general sense, nondisabled people in Japan both care deeply about and are overprotective of people with disabilities.[2] Nevertheless, this description illustrates how the Japanese ablebodied perceive people with disabilities—as childlike figures.

Kegare: An Origin of Perceptions of People With Disabilities in Japan

Although societal tightness and UA can be found in other nations, there is another notion that explains the relationship between ablebodied people and persons with disabilities in Japan. This is the concept of *kegare*. According to Matsudaira (1946), *kegare* (impurity or contamination) encompasses everything that is outside the blessings of the gods. This includes that which is unclean or grotesque, death, natural disasters, and anything that disorders social patterns. Accordingly, Matsudaira argued that the category of *kegare* encompasses people with disabilities as well as others who are classified as not "normal."

Hare, Ke, and Kegare

According to Namihira (1977), the concept of *kegare* is part of a triadic mythic cosmos of Japanese folklore. She illustrates the relationship among the three notions as follows (Namihira, 1977, p. 34):

$$hare \longleftrightarrow ke \longleftrightarrow kegare$$

Hare and *kegare* are placed on extreme ends of the continuum. The Western concepts of heaven, earth, and hell are analogous to this Japanese cosmic myth (Namihira, 1977). Thus, although *hare* is closely related to concepts such as purity, order, holiness, and/or cleanliness, it also signifies the spatial placement: the heavenly place where *kami* (gods) belong. The notion of *ke* signifies concepts such as ordinary and/or profane; the earth is also associated with *ke*. Finally, *kegare* connotes opposite themes from *hare*. These include death, pollution, out of order, and/or decay. Also, *kegare* is closely related to the spatial concept of the underground where the dead are kept. In addition, Namihira (1977) asserted that the state of *kegare* is contagious. She emphasized this point:

> It is important to distinguish between those phenomena which are of them-
> selves manifestations of "hare," "ke," and "kegare" and those phenomena
> which are associated with these categories as their markers or symbols. . . .
> That is, contact with death, whether through touch or kinship relation, will
> cognitively extend "kegare" to both the place and person having the contact.
> These are absolute manifestations of the cognitive category. (pp. 15–16)

"After we were told that our child had a disability, I was thinking about killing the child *and myself*" (Youda, 1996, p. 14, our translation; italics added). This type of comment is not unusual in Japan when parents dis-cover their children's disabilities. Nevertheless, what is interesting about the statement above is that this mother was thinking not only about killing the child with a disability (a source of her emotional torment), but also killing herself after murdering the baby. It seems that this is because the "pollution" of *kegare* is expanded through "kinship relation" (Namihira, 1977, p. 15); thus, she felt that she was part of *kegare*. Japanese people still strongly believe that being sick or having a disability is caused by sin in the past or in one's previous life (Namihira, 1990). Family members in Japan, therefore, tend to feel ashamed of having someone with a disability in their families. Consequently, incidents of murder/suicide by the parents of children with disabilities happen once in a while, and the public view tends to be sympathetic for the parents as overburdened victims if their children are disabled (Yokozuka, 1975).

This expansion of *kegare* through kinship illustrates the attitude toward disability in Japan. Nobe (1996), who has worked with a support group for parents of children with physical disabilities, remembers a phone call from a middle-aged woman. The woman told Nobe that her niece had twin babies, but one of them was missing a hand. The woman said that having a sister without a hand would negatively influence her siblings' future, including marital options, because it is not uncommon in Japan for a person with a disability to face family opposition from the fiancé's side. The woman on the phone was so concerned about *sekentei* (public appearances) of having a niece with a disability that she asked Nobe about any institutions for the baby without a hand. Such an example demonstrates that having a fam-ily member with a disability may have an impact far beyond the person's immediate family.

Another common occurrence frequently encountered by Japanese people with disabilities is being asked not to appear at occasions of *hare*, such as a wedding ceremony or any kind of grand occasion. Futsukaichi (1982) shared a story of a male with cerebral palsy. He had four brothers, but he never attended their wedding ceremonies because he was told to stay home. Additionally, when his oldest brother and other family members were having a formal meeting with future in-laws at home, he was put in a room and was told not to come out until everyone left. Ohno (1992) discussed similar experiences of individuals with disabilities who are kept away from grand occasions.

The notions of *hare* and *kegare* also help to explain these isolationist tendencies regarding people with disabilities in Japan. Meeting for an arranged marriage or wedding ceremonies represent occasions of *hare*. Another typical *hare* situation in Japan is New Year's day. People in Japan have a stronger emotional attachment to this day than do people in the United States. On January 1, many Japanese wear new or clean clothes and visit shrines where, people believe, the gods live. All these *hare* occasions are under the gods' blessings. Thus, Japanese people do not dare bring any element hated by the gods to such an occasion; this is *kegare*. The Japanese are fearful, hostile, and avoidant of everything that has *kegare*. The Japanese believe that *hare* and *kegare* should not be mixed together.

As research has illustrated, the concept of *kegare* and Japanese people with disabilities are perceived to be tied together. The mother's remark at the accessible bathroom, "No, don't use that one [the accessible bathroom]! It's *dirty* there" (Yashiro, 1979, p. 83, our translation; emphasis added) makes sense if one understands the close relationship between *kegare*, which means "polluted," and people with disabilities. It also explains why ablebodied people in Japan prefer to draw a clear line between individuals with disabilities and themselves (Murphy, 1990) so they will not to be "polluted" by *kegare*. In addition, the concept of *kegare* helps explain why stigmatization toward people with disabilities is worse in Japan than in the United States.

CONCLUSION

The study of disability presents researchers with the opportunity to observe how people in society view health, personhood, cosmology, and communication within a community. Everyone knows that disabilities are universally unavoidable. However, as this chapter demonstrates, the meaning of "disability" can vary from culture to culture. The meaning of disability is context-dependent, and a relationship between people with disabilities and their societies is culture-bound (Kisanji 1995; Whyte & Ingstad, 1995). From the examples in some African countries, it seems that the meaning of "disability" is less relevant when people are living in a preindustrial society with close community networks. In these societies, persons with disabilities are more likely to participate in activities with others without being labeled as "the disabled." Other evidence about the relationship between modernization and the meaning of "disability" can be noted in Norwegian history (Ingstad, 1995). Until the 19th century, Norwegian people did not have a clear category of "disability," and people with disabilities were assimilated into their communities (Ingstad, 1995). Ingstad states that ablebodied people's perceptions of disability have changed along with "internal economic sources" (p. 188), suggesting that the concept and meaning of "disability" is linked to the economic conditions of a society (Linton, 1998; Oliver, 1996). Similarly, Linton contended that even in the United States, "early in the history of this century [before the industrial revolution started], individuals who would today be labeled mentally retarded were absorbed into communities" (p. 46). It is possible, then, that industrialization makes the concept of "disability" more salient in a society. This point deserves more detailed investigation.

In the second section of this chapter, the study of Japanese people with disabilities illustrated that, like other Asian cultures, Japanese people tend to have a strong sense of shame for having a disability. Also, the "pollution" of the disability spreads not only onto people with disabilities themselves, but also onto other individuals who are close to them, such as family members. This section demonstrated the Japanese treatment of people with disabilities and the meaning of having disabilities in Japan by using key concepts such as UA, tightness of society, and *kegare*. These concepts seem to be powerful in explaining communicative phenomena pertaining to people with disabilities in Japan.

With the development of more advanced modes of transportation, more and more people with disabilities travel to foreign countries. Each year many individuals with disabilities from numerous countries choose to visit Japan, and they often encounter overprotective treatment by the Japanese. A Western athlete with disabilities can be offended by the "child-like treatment" of Japanese officials while visiting for an international competition.[3] Conversely, an enormous number of Japanese people (some with disabilities) travel to the United States and are amazed to see people with disabilities frequent public places and appear in the U.S. media. Both groups of people face different expectations and cultural norms about disabilities, about which they have little knowledge, especially in foreign countries.

It is possible that, whereas Westerners with disabilities feel that they are mistreated by the overprotective attitude of Asians, an individual with a disability from the non-West perceives that he or she is not cared for enough by others because of the individualistic culture in the West. Therefore, it is hoped that people preparing for cross-cultural trips will be helped by understanding the cultural differences in the non-West in terms of meanings of disability, perceptions of ablebodied people about individuals with disabilities, and treatment of persons with disabilities.

Finally, the literature addressing cross-cultural disability studies remains quite small. Although there is literature on disability studies conducted from an anthropological perspective, the literature utilizing a communication framework is very scarce. It is evident that little is known about communication in regard to disability outside of the United States, especially in non-Western contexts. Therefore, it is hoped that this chapter will serve to help communication researchers engage in scholarship on cross-cultural disabilities studies.

DISCUSSION QUESTIONS

1. What does "disability is context-dependent" mean in this chapter?
2. What kinds of folk beliefs do people in various parts of the world have about disability? How do these beliefs influence perceptions toward people with disabilities and communication with people who have disabilities?
3. How does family or community play a role in non-Western societies (e.g., in Africa or Asia) with regard to disability issues? Compare these situations with that of the United States.
4. What constructs are mentioned in this chapter to describe the Japanese disability situation? Explain how these constructs are related to each other.

REFERENCES

Devlieger, P. (1995). Why disabled? The cultural understanding of physical disability in an African society. In B. Ingstad & S. R. Whyte (Eds.), *Disability and culture* (pp. 94–106). Berkeley: University of California Press.

Douglas, M. (1966). *Purity and danger*. London: Routledge.

Futsukaichi, Y. (1982). *Shogaisha sabetsu no rekishi to shogaisha no sei* [History of discrimination toward people with disabilities and their lives]. In Zenkoku-shougaishakaihouundou-renrakukaigi (Ed.), *Shogaisha-kaihoundo no ima*. Tokyo: Gendaishokan.

Goffman, E. (1963). *Stigma: Notes on the management of spoiled identity*. Englewood Cliffs, NJ: Prentice-Hall.

Groce, N. E., & Zola, I. K. (1993). Multiculturalism, chronic illness, and disability. *Pediatrics, 91*, 1048–1055.

Gudykunst, W. B., & Kim, Y. Y. (1997). *Communicating with strangers*. New York: McGraw Hill.

Hofstede, G. (1984). *Culture's consequences*. Newbury Park, CA: Sage.

Hosaka, Y. (1997). Tai shogaisha rehabiliteshon-ho to shogaishaundo [National Plan on Welfare and Rehabilitation for the Disabled and disability advocacy in Thailand]. *Fukusi-rodo, 76*, 27–35.

Ingstad, B. (1995). Public discourses on rehabilitation: From Norway to Botswana. In B. Ingstad & S. R. Whyte (Eds.), *Disability and culture* (pp. 174–196). Berkeley: University of California Press.

Kalyanpur, M. (1996). The influences of Western special education on community-based services in India. *Disability & Society, 11*, 249–270.

Kisanji, J. (1995). Interface between culture and disability in the Tanzanian context: Part I. *International Journal of Disability, Development and Education, 42*, 93–108.

Kobayashi, M. (1997). Chugoku no shogaishajigyou no tenkai to kadai [Developments and assignments of Chinese projects for people with disabilities]. *Asia Kenkyu Warudo Torendo, 24*, 16–17.

Kuwana, A. (1997). Korei: Satogaeri sutoresu [Homecoming stress]. *Fukusi-rodo, 76*, 118–119.

Lewis, C. S. (1995). International aspects of the disability issue. In J. A. Nelson (Ed.), *The disabled, the media and the information age*. Westport, CT: Greenwood Press.

Linton, S. (1998). *Claiming disability*. New York: New York University Press.

Matsudaira, S. (1946). *Matsuri: Honshitsu to shosou* [Matsuri: its essences and aspects]. Tokyo: Nikkoshoin.

Mosel, J. (1973, May 17). *Status and role analysis*. Lecture to Japan and East Asia Area Studies Course, Foreign Service Institute, Washington, DC.

Murphy, R. (1990). *The body silent*. New York: Norton.

Murphy, R., Scheer, J., Murphy, Y., & Mack, R. (1988). Physical disability and social liminality: A study in the rituals of adversity. *Social Science and Medicine, 26*, 235–242.

Nakanishi (1997). Ajia Afurica no shougaisha [People with disabilities in Asia and Africa]. *Fukushi-rodo, 76*, 12–19.

Namihira, E. (1977). *"Hare," "ke," and "kegare": The structure of Japanese folk belief*. Unpublished doctoral dissertation, University of Texas, Austin, Texas.

Namihira, E. (1990). *Kegare*. Tokyo: Tokyodo-shuppan.

Nobe, A. (1996). Shogai wo meguru sabetsukozo [The structure of discriminations toward the disability]. In A. Kurihara (Ed.), *Nihonshakai no sabetsukozo*. Tokyo: Koubun-do.

Ohno, T. (1992). *Shogaisha ha ima* [People with disabilities and their current situations]. Tokyo: Iwanami.

Oliver, M. (1996). *Understanding disability: From theory to practice*. New York: St. Martin's Press.

Phillips, M. J. (1984). *Oral narratives of the experience of disability in American culture*. Unpublished doctoral dissertation, University of Pennsylvania.

Sentumbwe, N. (1995). Sighted lovers and blind husbands: Experiences of blind women in Uganda. In B. Ingstad & S. R. Whyte (Eds.), *Disability and culture* (pp. 159–173). Berkeley: University of California Press.

Shimizu, K. (1997). Kaikakukaihojidai no tyugokuzanpeijin [Chinese people with disabilities in the modern era]. *Fukushi-rodo, 76*, 36–42.

Talle, A. (1995). A child is a child: Disability and equality among the Kenya Maasai. In B. Ingstad & S. R. Whyte (Eds.), *Disability and culture* (pp. 56–72). Berkeley: University of California Press.

Tefft, S. (1993, November 10). China's disabled struggle for better opportunities. *Christian Science Monitor, 85*, 14–15.

Triandis, H. C. (1994). *Culture and social behavior*. New York: McGraw-Hill.

Turner, V. (1967). *The forest of symbols: Aspects of Ndembu ritual*. Ithaca, NY: Cornell University Press.

United Nations. (1993). *Asian and Pacific decade of disabled persons, 1993–2002: The starting point.* New York: United Nations.

United Nations. (1995). *Hidden sisters: Women and girls with disabilities in the Asian and Pacific region.* New York: United Nations.

Whyte, S. R. (1995). Constructing epilepsy: Images and contexts in East Africa. In B. Ingstad & S. R. Whyte (Eds.), *Disability and culture* (pp. 226–245). Berkeley: University of California Press.

Whyte, R. S., & Ingstad, B. (1995). Disability and culture: An overview. In B. Ingstad & S. R. Whyte (Eds.), *Disability and culture* (pp. 3–34). Berkeley: University of California Press.

Yashiro, E. (1979). *Kurumaisu kara mita hihon* [Japan viewed from my wheelchair]. Tokyo: Sanichishobo.

Youda, H. (1996). Shogaiji to kazoku wo meguru sabetsu to kyosei no sikaku [Discriminatory and coexistent situations surrounding children with disabilities and their families]. In A. Kurihara (Ed.), *Nihonshakai no sabetsukozo.* Tokyo: Kobun-do.

Yokozuka, K. (1975). *Hahayo! Korosuna* [Mother! Don't kill]. Tokyo: Suzusawa-shoten.

ENDNOTES

1. To protect a privacy, his name is changed.

2. The first author traveled to New York City once and was stuck in an elevator in the subway for a while. No one at the station was available to help her, and she confesses that she missed the Japanese "overprotective" service then. She felt that in the United States, people with disabilities also pay the price of being on their own.

3. Japanese officials prepared a different hotel for athletes with disabilities, and unlike nondisabled athletes, they were not allowed to leave the hotel after 10 p.m. One of the authors was an interpreter during this international competition and she knew that the Japanese officials made these decisions because other hotels, where nondisabled athletes were staying, were not accessible and because of their "custodial" perception about people with disabilities.

14

Deaf Activists in the Rhetorical Transformation of the Construct of Disability

Kara Shultz
Bloomsburg University

Keywords: Social movements, identity, American with Disability, Deaf culture, instrumental and consummatory rhetoric

In May 1995, actor Christopher Reeves, perhaps best known for his portrayal of Superman, was thrown from his horse during an equestrian competition and was left paralyzed from the shoulder down. Reeves, realizing an opportunity, readily accepted the position of advocate for the rights of persons with disabilities. In his numerous public appearances he honored the Americans With Disabilities Act (ADA) and proclaimed his determination to advocate greater funding for research to bring about a cure for spinal cord injuries. "I am going to get out of this chair, throw it away and walk," he told Larry King in an hour-long interview on CNN February 22, 1996. "We are on the threshold of a cure—maybe in 5, 7, 8, 10 years."

Reeves's goal appeared to be noble; however, there were some in the disabled community who objected to his words. These disabled activists censured Christopher Reeves for his campaign for a cure for spinal injury, arguing that his actions perpetuate prejudice against persons with disabilities and invalidate the pride and appreciation many persons with disabilities have discovered within themselves and the lives they have constructed (Martin, 1997). Perhaps most startling to conventional thinking is that many say they would reject being cured even if it were possible. One disability activist declared, "I would not trade my disability for anything." (Martin, 1997, p. 1). The perspective articulated by this disability activist is, on the surface, confounding for persons who are temporarily ablebodied.[1] Wouldn't anyone if given the chance prefer to be ablebodied?

In this chapter I explore the distinctions and contradictions between these two divergent perspectives on disability. The first perspective, represented by Reeves, is concerned with establishing the rights of persons with disabilities to live the most "normal" life possible given the opportunities science and technology promise in a modern society. The alternative perspective is articulated by disabled activists, such as the one just cited, who are interested in constructing or reconstructing an alternative identity that incorporates disability as a unique and viable way of being within a postmodern society. The perspective of a disabled identity tied to a disabled culture, which is worthy of being both celebrated and protected, is controversial when tied to a disability-rights perspective that demands that society pay for the maintenance of this culture, even if the disabled person rejects medical or technological fixes for her or his disability.

RHETORIC AND THE DISABILITY MOVEMENT

Rhetoric is the study of social influence, in particular, how people use language as a means for achieving social cooperation and fulfilling human potential (Bizzel & Herzberg, 1990; Smith, 1998). Through rhetoric a society perpetuates itself, debates its internal problems, and decides which norms and values it will follow without resorting to violence.

Social movements are primarily a rhetorical process by which a disenfranchised group can fashion a more powerful existence (Cathcart, 1980; Griffin, 1951, 1964; Stewart, Smith, & Denton, 1994; Wilkinson, 1976). The social movement definition offered by Charles A. Wilkinson (1976), focuses on the symbolical elements of social movements and is useful in this analysis:

> Movements, rhetorically defined, are: Languaging strategies by which a significantly vocal part of an established society, experiencing together a

sustained dialectical tension growing out of moral (ethical) conflict, agitate to induce cooperation in others, either directly or indirectly, thereby affecting the status quo. (p. 91)

Edwin Black (1965) in his classic text *Rhetorical Criticism: A Study in Method*, first suggested movement study as "a new and exciting prospect of rhetorical criticism" (p. 22) and since this time the study of social movements has come to constitute a vast and burgeoning area of contemporary rhetorical criticism (e.g., see an extensive summary in Stewart et al., 1994).

Social movements such as the disability movement in the United States are grand rhetorical acts—fascinating and confounding. Persons with disabilities have joined together to engage in a collective effort to challenge both the conditions and the assumptions of their lives. They are united by their desire to improve the quality of their lives; however, they are divided by what they believe constitutes a quality life. Disability-rights advocates, on the one hand, have sought greater access for persons with disabilities to mainstream social life through removal of environmental barriers such as inaccessible workplaces and through greater opportunities to share in the nation's resources as active, contributing, and employed citizens. Disability-power activists, on the other hand, advocate the development of a personal political identity and a radical transformation of societal attitudes toward disability by attempting to eliminate the stigma around disability. They argue that disability is simply a normal variation of human diversity. "We will not change to fit the mold," one disabled-power activist proclaimed, "Instead, we will destroy the mold and change the world to make sure there is room for everyone" (Martin, 1997, p. 1).

This chapter undertakes a rhetorical analysis of these two conflicting goals of the disability movement in exploring the rhetorical interjections and interventions of activists with disabilities in reconceptualizing disability as a lived construct. The category of disability, although politically useful when it comes to legal protection offered by the ADA, is problematic for those persons with disabilities who identify as a cultural group rather than as people suffering from medical conditions (Braithwaite & Braithwaite, 1997). Deaf activists, in particular, have long been engaged in a struggle to reconceptualize rhetorically the meaning of Deaf life,[2] wherein being deaf becomes an unique and valuable, rather than a disabled, way of being (Shultz, 1991, 1997a).

ADA AND THE DISABILITY
RIGHTS MOVEMENT

In essence the ADA is a piece of civil rights legislation aimed at integrating persons with disabilities into the mainstream of the broader society. The ADA was passed in large part because of the collective efforts of disability rights activists (Oliver, 1996). In 1983 the National Council on Disability proposed an amendment of the civil rights law to Congress and thereafter the disability rights movement took on passage of the ADA as its key concern. Disability rights activists, a heterogeneous group of individuals, undertook extensive lobbying and public demonstrations, including the occupation of the Capitol rotunda by the direct-action group ADAPT, which eventually resulted in the passage of the ADA into law.

Despite this achievement, disability rights advocates have been disappointed with the effects of the ADA. According to Laura Koss-Feder (1999), the U.S. industry, although demonstrating an increased openness to hiring people with disabilities, is still far from meeting the initial expectations of disability activists who pushed for the ADA.

> In 1994, the latest year for which U.S. Census Bureau statistics are available, some 3.7 million people with severe disabilities were at work, up from 2.9 million 3 years earlier. As the employment numbers also indicate, a large proportion of America's disabled population still has its nose pressed against the workplace window. Prejudice, lack of adequate transportation and physical barriers to employment are still common, contributing to a sense of discouragement among the disabled themselves. For instance, though exact numbers vary, experts cite a 1998 survey by Louis Harris & Associates that found only 30% of adults with disabilities to be employed full or part time, compared with nearly 80% of adults without disabilities. Nearly 6 out of 10 of those surveyed last year in Louis Harris' annual poll said the ADA had made no difference in their lives.

Mary Johnson (1989), editor of *The Disability Rag*, lamented the passage of the ADA as a separate law rather than an amendment to Title VII of the Civil Rights Act and the failure of Congress to appropriate moneys for enforcing the law. "For years our movement has been fighting the misconception that bias against the disabled is different from other kinds of discrimination... We've got a foot—or a wheel or a cane—in the door" (Johnson, 1989, p. 446).

In addition to the disappointment of disability-rights advocates, there is a growing backlash of criticism emanating from the institutions forced to comply with the ADA (e.g., Allen, 1992; Donlan, 1991; Olsen, 1997; Rockwell, 1992; Shalit, 1997; Weaver & Brady, 1991). Critics, such as Shalit, argue that while modern disability law was "inspired by the most human motive," these "grand aspirations were framed in the fuzziest terms," without adequate limits, and are being taken advantage of by persons with questionable "neodisabilities" rather than those "truly disabled" the law was intended to help (pp. 16–22). Although no flood of ADA suits has been forthcoming (Pelka, 1996; Samborn, 1992), a subsequent backlash against persons with disabilities has resulted (Braithwaite & Labrecque, 1994).

RE/CONSTRUCTING DISABILITY

Both disability activists and scholars argue that society in general will benefit by changing the way we think about and deal with disability (Oliver, 1996). Misconceptions about the ADA might be linked to general misconceptions and prejudice about persons with disabilities. The population of ablebodied persons is generally mystified by and even fearful of persons with disabilities (e.g., Barnes, 1996; Coleman, 1997). According to a Lou Harris poll, more than half of all Americans (58%) feel embarrassed around disabled persons (Wolfe, 1996). Add to this the disturbing realization that persons with disabilities are the only minority group anybody can join at any time and you have a situation ripe for prejudice. Demystifying disability has been one of the central aims of the disability rights movement. According to Scotch and Schriner (1997), "To the extent that society fully accommodates a condition, it ceases to be a disability under this concept" (p. 155). However, what is meant by full accommodation from a rights perspective is quite different from what is meant by full accommodation from a power perspective.

Challenges to the worth of the ADA came not only from the established order, but many disability activists themselves were frustrated with the limitations of a rights perspective (Wendell, 1996). Disability activists discovered a need to redefine themselves as persons whose identity is defined around, rather than in spite of, their disability and to move beyond the boundaries imposed by abnormality (Peters, 1996). They learned the lesson women had learned in the 1970s—that the personal is political and that identities are socially constructed, shifting, unstable, and always open to change. To change the circumstances of their lives they discovered they must begin by transforming the way they viewed themselves.

> The act of conscientization necessitates pushing ourselves beyond discourse and scrutiny to action. . . . Specifically, building the process for creative change, goals and strategies for action must be the end result. However, criticism and vision are not static but are in a continuing process of transformation. This transformation is the essence of liberation pedagogy of disability necessary for teaching ourselves new ways of living through personal and political processes of identity formation. (Peters, 1996, p. 232)

Over time the social construction of disability has shifted perspective (Hahn, 1997). Disability activists and some scholars of disability assert that disability is better understood as a socially constructed condition, rather than a biological one (Morris, 1991; Oliver, 1996; Scotch, 1984; Wendell, 1996). Rather than focus on medical, technological, or economic fixes in ameliorating the deficit of disability, they suggest an alternative focus on identity while recognizing disability as a natural part of human variation (Scotch & Schriner, 1997).

In moving toward this alternative, disability activists have demanded they be accepted as different rather than be rejected as defective. For militant disability activists a rights perspective does not go far enough; they demand a radical transformation in the way disability is conceptualized. Radical disability activists argue that disabled persons are united in a culture (e.g., Braithwaite & Braithwaite, 1997). However, identifying oneself as disabled is frequently a contentious political issue (e.g., Wendell, 1996). According to Martin (1997), disability activists dissatisfied with the ADA are articulating this dissatisfaction in forceful and startling ways:

> Not only do they criticize the Franklin Delano Roosevelt Memorial for omitting a wheelchair, they point out that the Braille is too high up and too large to read. Far from applauding the customers in wheelchairs shown in commercials, they grumble that there are no disabled sales clerks. They castigate Christopher Reeves for his campaign for a cure for spinal injury, saying it is unrealistic and offensive to people who have learned to live with their disabilities and indeed thrive on them. They demonstrate against giving doctors the right to assist in suicide, calling that a slippery slope. They grimly point out that Hitler killed 200,000 disabled people before he got around to other groups. (Martin, 1997, p. 1)

Perhaps no group of disabled persons in society better typify this position than those persons who identify themselves as members of Deaf culture. The opposition between those who seek to cure disability and those who identify themselves as members of disabled culture can be fervent. One of the most heated sites of controversy is taking place between Deaf Power activists and those in favor of cochlear implants for the deaf (Shultz, 1997b).[3] Moreover, many of the lessons and concerns recognized in the Deaf Power movement can be utilized in the disabled activists' quest for recognition of a disabled identity. Although the concept of a disabled culture and the articulation of a disabled identity are relatively recent turns in the disability movement, the struggle to establish the culture and identity of Deaf persons has a much longer history (Gannon 1981; Lane, 1984; Shultz, 1991; Van Cleve & Crouch, 1989).

DEAF CULTURE'S RHETORICAL REJECTION OF THE LABEL "DISABLED"

Perhaps because of the uniqueness of their disability in interfering with communication in an aural/oral modality, Deaf persons have long gathered into a distinct community constructing their own separate and viable culture (Sacks, 1989). As Carol Padden and Tom Humphries (1988) explained in *Deaf in America: Voices from a Culture*:

> Deaf culture is a powerful testimony to both the profound needs and the profound possibilities of human beings. Out of a striving for human language, generations of Deaf signers have fashioned a signed language rich enough to mine for poetry and storytelling. Out of a striving to interpret, to make sense of their world, they have created systems of meaning that explain how they understand their place in the world. That the culture of Deaf people has endured, despite generations of changing social conditions, attests to the tenacity of the basic human needs for language and symbol. (p. 121)

To identify with Deaf culture is to believe that being Deaf involves much more than the absence of sound (Lane, 1993; Padden & Humphries, 1988; Woodward, 1982). Membership within Deaf culture involves identification and participation with others who share a similar experience and a wide variety of interests, a common visual language, and values and goals (Padden & Humphries, 1988). The Deaf Power movement is the attempt by Deaf activists to establish their culture, their language, and their identity as Deaf persons as valid and worthwhile (Shultz, 1991).

Deaf Power advocates argue that deafness as a handicap is much more a social problem than a physiological one and that the "signing community" is more a linguistic minority than a disabled minority (Shultz, 1991,

1997a). M. J. Bienvenu (1989), a radical Deaf activist and cofounder of *The Bicultural Center*, argued against Deaf people identifying themselves as disabled:

> I cannot agree that Deaf people belong in the disabled group. To me, what lies behind this view is the assumption that there is a defect—a broken-ness. But that meaning of Deaf is not "cannot hear." In fact, Deaf people are a distinct minority group with a separate language and culture that has often been overlooked and/or oppressed by the hearing majority. (p. 1)

Thus, Deaf cultural activists set up an internal source of approval for big "D" deaf people who reject hearing people who try to fix or cure deafness, labeling these "biased members of the hearing establishment" as "audists" and "oppressors" and including the rejection of hearing parents who refuse to accept the validity of Deaf culture (Lane, 1993).

Deaf activists proclaim their identity as cultural rather than disabled, rejecting medical and technological efforts to cure deafness as cultural genocide (Shultz, 1997b). Barbara Kannapell (1992), a Deaf community activist, explained:

> It is time to end the hearingization of Deaf people. We are not a pathology waiting to be cured. We see ourselves as a linguistic and a cultural minority. [Cochlear implants] contribute to the destruction of our beautiful American Sign Language and our culture! (p. 2)

In sum, radical Deaf activists are rhetorically rejecting the broader society's attempts to mitigate deafness as an invalidation of the validity of their identities as Deaf people.

DEAF PEOPLE AND THE ADA

Of the 40 to 50 million Americans with disabilities, it is estimated that there are more than 22 million deaf and hearing-impaired persons (DuBow, Geer, & Strauss, 1992). The ADA grants benefits to deaf and hearing-impaired persons in the form of employment opportunities and increased access to interpreters, relay services, 911 TDD access, and closed-captioning of public television. The Deaf community fought alongside other disability activists to ensure the passage of the ADA and has largely embraced the passage of the ADA as an opportunity for Deaf persons to establish their citizenship rights and increase access to the broader society. Moreover, the Deaf community generally views the ADA's influence as primarily positive (Moore, 1995).

This acceptance of the ADA's benefits, however, required a reconciliation with the insistence on deafness as a cultural identity. The tension between a view of deafness as an impediment to success in mainstream society and a view of deafness as a unique and viable way of being has long been evident in Deaf activist rhetoric. Is deafness a disability or a culture? Can it be both? If Deaf people do not consider themselves disabled, then should society be forced to foot the bill for the expensive assistive devices required by the ADA? Moore and Levitan (1992) comment:

> We're not handicapped, just different. Well, then, according to this logic, if we don't have a disability, how can we take recourse in the Americans with Disabilities Act? Aren't deaf people included in its coverage? Doesn't it apply to us, too? Shouldn't we be honest about our needs as disabled persons? (p. 9)

Bonnie Poitras Tucker (1997) a deaf law professor, argued that the "right of deaf persons to receive costly assistance is not unlimited" (p. 34), and that deaf persons must "accept full responsibility for the ramifications of chosen deafness" (p. 35). Therefore, Tucker claimed that the concepts of culture and disability are mutually exclusive:

> Deaf people cannot have it both ways. Deaf people cannot claim to be disabled for purposes of demanding accommodations under laws such as the ADA, yet claim that deafness is not a disability and thus efforts to cure deafness should cease. The two precepts are not reconcilable. (p. 36)

Tucker acknowledged the necessity of current expenditures to allow deaf persons to take their "rightful place in society" (p. 34). However, when deafness becomes "correctable," as she argues it inevitably will, Deaf people have a moral and ethical responsibility to society to be fixed/cured rather than continue to demand that society pay for "costly accommodations to compensate for the lack of hearing of that individual (or his or her child)" (p. 35).

Fully one third of Tucker's essay is spent detailing the costs of accommodating a deaf person in today's society, through special education, college programs for deaf students, relay services mandated by the ADA, and interpreter fees. For instance, she noted that the cost of educating a deaf child in a residential school for the deaf is $35,780. From this "economic" analysis, Tucker concluded that it is unreasonable for deaf persons to choose to remain deaf if technology can correct their deafness.

Tucker briefly explored the controversy over cochlear implants. She acknowledged that "recipients evidence a wide variety of success with use of the implant"; however, she fails to discuss the costs involved in the surgical procedure and follow-up rehabilitation of such scientific fixes for deafness.

In contrast, some Deaf persons argue that the categories of deafness and disability are not mutually exclusive. Moore (1997) noted:

> Is deafness a disability or is it a culture? Does it have to be one or the other? Can it be both? If you want to give the most accurate answer, taking into account the complexities of being medically Deaf, you'll have to be annoyingly vague. You'll have to say in some ways yes, yes; in some ways no. (p. 9)

However, the vast majority of Deaf activists openly reject the notion of deafness as disability and had great difficulty reconciling themselves to the rights perspective advocated by the ADA.

REJECTION OR RECONCILIATION?

Activists within a social movement must struggle internally as well as externally to re/construct their lives. They must negotiate the terms of this re/construction, constantly choosing between reconciliation with and rejection of the established order. On the one hand, to survive they must reconcile themselves to the established order by seeking to gain access to and representation within the broader culture. However, victory in achieving self-determination leads to the inevitable question of how rights interfere with self-actualization and the struggle for a more powerful existence. The struggle for rights, when even marginally achieved, soon reveals its limitations in failing to significantly change the conditions of movement members' lives, thus leading to a re/visioning phase as movement leaders and members attempt to establish the validity of their existence.

The ideology behind these two alternative and conflicting movement goals, self-determination and self-actualization, is expressed in the form of the movement's rhetoric. Randall Lake (1983), in his analysis of Native American movement rhetoric, identified two rhetorical forms—instrumental and consummatory. Instrumental rhetoric is pragmatic and task oriented, its efforts are focused outward, and the users seek external goals such as legislation. Consummatory rhetoric is ritualistic and emotive. Its efforts are concerned with the formation and manifestation of self-suasory (inward) resolution and the users are involved with rhetoric for rhetoric's sake. Consummatory rhetoric serves an ego function, acting to "psychologically refurbish and affirm" the oppressed (Gregg, 1971). Richard B. Gregg's (1971) exploration of "ego-function" argues that "the primary appeal of the rhetoric of protest is to the protestors themselves, who feel the need for psychological refurbishing and affirmation" (p. 74). Lake (1983) argued that consummatory rhetoric succeeds in "provoking the spiritual rebirth" of the movement members' culture.

The argument, then, is that, whereas rights leaders advocate an instrumental goal, power activists advocate a consummatory goal. These two goals serve radically different functions within the life of a movement and produce a tension within the movement and between the movement and the established order.

The tension between a rights perspective and a power perspective is not unique to disability activists. Very much like the transition from civil rights in the early 1960s to Black Power in the late 1960s, disabled activists have shifted from the ADA to a transformation of societal attitudes about disability wherein disabled people are conceived as beautiful and powerful (Brockriede & Scott, 1968). According to Brockreide and Scott (1968), Carmichael used the slogan "Black Power" to imply "personal power in being black, responsibility to other blacks, and power as a group to deal with outsiders" (p. 5).

Disability movement leaders are engaged in a dialectical enjoinment in the moral arena (Cathcart, 1978), mediating reality and mitigating the power relations both within their cultural community and throughout the broader society. Disability, when conceived as the basis for a cultural group, informs an identity constructed through identification with others who are disabled. According to Douglas Martin, in his *New York Times* article on the subject, "hardly self-pitying, disability culture celebrates disability and finds expression in literature, poetry, dance, and, most pointedly, a slashingly dark humor" (Martin, 1997, p. 1). For those who embrace disabled culture, disabilities are something to be celebrated and cures are to be abhorred as cultural genocide. Both the Deaf Power movement and the most recent manifestation of the disability movement are attempts to celebrate disability and to actively counter the prejudice and stigma long directed toward persons with disabilities through a rhetoric best characterized as consummatory.

The Deaf Power movement has been successful in establishing its own culture and a group of people who identify strongly with that culture.

However, to continue to be deaf requires special accommodations (interpreters, telecommunication devices, etc.) when interacting within the broader society. As technological fixes for deafness such as the cochlear implant and closed-captioning devices advance, can Deaf people continue to maintain their culture and identity? The rights perspective, which advocates advances in technology be utilized to assist the disabled person in becoming a full member of the broader society, is viewed by radical Deaf activists as a threat to the continuation of a power perspective.

DISCUSSION QUESTIONS

1. What do you think is meant by the proclamation of disability pride activists that "We will not change to fit the mold. Instead, we will destroy the mold and change the world to make sure there is room for everyone" (Martin, 1997, p. 1)?
2. The ADA is a piece of civil rights legislation aimed at integrating persons with disabilities into the mainstream of the broader society. Do you think integration should be the ultimate goal for persons with disabilities? Why or why not?
3. Why is demystifying disability important and how is this best accomplished? What is the significance of arguing that identities are socially constructed, shifting, unstable, and always open to change?
4. Bonnie Tucker argued that the concepts of culture and disability are mutually exclusive. Is deafness a disability or a culture? Can it be both? If Deaf people do not consider themselves disabled, then should society be forced to foot the bill for the expensive assistive devices required by the ADA?

REFERENCES

Allen, C. (1992, April 13). Disabling businesses. *Insight, 8*(15), 6–13.
Barnes, C. (1996). Theories of disability and the origins of the oppression of disabled people in western society. In L. Barton (Ed.), *Disability and society: Emerging issues and insights* (pp. 43–60). New York: Longman.
Black, E. (1965). *Rhetorical criticism: A study in method.* Madison: University of Wisconsin Press.
Bienvenu, M. J. (1989, April). Disabled: Who? *TBC News, 13*, p. 1.
Bizzel, P., & Herzberg, B. (Eds.). (1990). *The Rhetorical tradition: Readings from classical times to the present.* Boston: Bedford Books.
Braithwaite, D. O., & Braithwaite, C. A. (1997). Understanding communication of persons with disabilities as cultural communication. In L. A. Samovar & R. E. Porter (Eds.), *Intercultural communication: A reader* (8th ed., pp. 154–164). Belmont, CA: Wadsworth.

Braithwaite, D. O., & Labrecque, D. (1994). Responding to the Americans With Disabilities Act: Contributions of interpersonal communication research and training. *Journal of Applied Communication, 22*, 287–294.

Brockreide, W. E., & Scott, R. L. (1968). Stokely Carmichael: Two speeches on Black Power. *Central States Speech Journal, 19*, 3–13.

Cathcart, R. S. (1978). Movements: Confrontation as rhetorical form. *Southern Speech Communication Journal, 22*, 151–160.

Cathcart, R. S. (1980). Defining social movements by their rhetorical form. *Central States Speech Journal, 31*, 267–273.

Coleman, L. M. (1997). Stigma: An enigma demystified. In L. J. Davis (Ed.), *The disability studies reader* (pp. 216–231). New York: Routledge.

Donlan, T. G. (1991, September 23). What price compassion? *Barron's*, p. 10.

DuBow, S., Geer, S., & Strauss, K. (1992). *Legal rights: The guide for deaf and hard of hearing people.* (4th ed.). Washington, DC: Gallaudet University Press.

Gannon, J. R. (1981). *Deaf heritage: A narrative history of deaf America.* Silver Spring, MD: National Association of the Deaf.

Gregg, R. B. (1971). The ego-function of the rhetoric of protest *Philosophy and Rhetoric, 4*, 71–91.

Griffin, L. M. (1951). The rhetoric of historical movements. *Quarterly Journal of Speech, 38*, 184–188.

Griffin, L. M. (1964). The rhetorical structure of the "New Left" movement: Part I. *Quarterly Journal of Speech, 50*, 113–133.

Hahn, H. (1997). Advertising the acceptably employable image. In L. Davis (Ed.), *The disability studies reader* (pp. 172–186). New York: Routledge.

Johnson, M. (1989, October 23). Enabling act. *The Nation*, p. 446.

Kannapell, B. (1992, December). Letter to *60 minutes. Bicultural Center Newsletter, 52*, p. 2.

Koss-Feder, L. (1999, January 25). Able to work: Spurred by the Americans with Disabilities Act, more firms take on those ready, willing and (employing disabled persons). *Time, 153*(i3), p. 82A.

Lake, R. (1983). Enacting red power: The consummatory function in Native American protest rhetoric. *Quarterly Journal of Speech, 69*, 127–142.

Lane, H. (1984). *When the mind hears: A history of the deaf.* New York: Random House.

Lane, H. (1993). *Mask of benevolence: Disabling the Deaf community.* New York: Alfred A. Knopf.

Martin, D. (1997, June 1). Eager to bite the hands that feed them. *New York Times*, Sec. 4, p. 1, 6.

Moore, M. (1995, September). Has the ADA had any impact on your life? *Deaf Life*, p. 30.

Moore, M. (1997, February). Isn't deafness a disability? If it is, why do deaf people consider it a culture? *Deaf Life*, pp. 8–9.

Moore, M. S., & Levitan, L. (1992). *For hearing people only: Answers to some of the most commonly asked questions about the Deaf community, its culture, and the "Deaf Reality."* Rochester, NY: Deaf Life Press.

Morris, J. (1991). *Pride against prejudice.* Philadelphia: New Society.

Niparko, J.K. (1995, May). *Accessing the hearing pathway with the cochlear implant.* Speech presented at the NIH Science Writers Briefing on Cochlear Implants, Bethesda, MD.

Oliver, M. (1996). *Understanding disability from theory to practice.* New York: St. Martin's Press.

Olsen, W. (1997, May 5). Disabling America. *National Review, 49*(8), 40–42.

Padden, C., & Humphries, T. (1988). *Deaf in America: Voices from a culture.* Cambridge, MA: Harvard University Press.

Pelka, F. (1996). Bashing the disabled: The right-wing attack on the ADA. *Humanist, 56*(6), 26–30.

Peters, S. (1996). The politics of disability identity. In L. Barton (Ed.), *Disability and society: Emerging issues and insights* (pp. 215–234). New York: Longman.

Rockwell, L. H. (1992, September 7). Disabilities act goes too far and stifles a free economy. *Insight, 8*(36), 20.

Sacks, O. (1989). *Seeing voices: A journey into the world of the deaf.* Berkeley: University of California Press.

Samborn, R. (1992, March 16). No flood of ADA suits—yet. *National Law Journal, 14*(28), 3, 12.

Scotch, R. K. (1984). *From good will to civil rights: Transforming federal disability policy*. Philadelphia: Temple University Press.

Scotch, R. K., & Schriner, K. (1997). Disability as human variation: Implications for policy. *Annals of the American Academy of Political and Social Science, 549*, 148–159.

Shalit, R. (1997, August 25). Defining disability down. *New Republic, 217*, 16–22.

Shultz, K. (1991). *Breaking the sound barrier: The rhetoric of the Deaf Power movement*. Unpublished doctoral dissertation, University of Denver, Denver, CO.

Shultz, K. (1997a). American Deaf culture: Community through conflict. In C. D. Brown, C. Snedeker, & B. Sykes (Eds.), *Conflict and diversity* (pp. 89–115). Cresskill, NJ: Hampton Press.

Shultz, K. (1997b). *"Every child a star" (And some other failures): Rhetorical trajectories of guilt and shame in the cochlear implant debates*. Paper presented at the National Endowment for the Humanities Grant Seminar, University of Colorado, Boulder, CO.

Smith, C. R. (1998). *Rhetoric and human consciousness: A history*. Prospect Heights, IL: Waveland Press.

Stewart, C., Smith, C., & Denton, R. E., Jr. (1994). *Persuasion and social movements*. Prospect Heights, IL: Waveland Press.

Tucker, B. P. (1997). The ADA and deaf culture: Contrasting precepts, conflicting results. *Annals of the American Academy of Political and Social Science, 549*, 24–36.

Van Cleve, J. V., & Crouch, B. A. (1989). *A place of their own: Creating the Deaf community in America*. Washington, DC: Gallaudet University Press.

Weaver, C. L., & Brady, J. S. (1991). At issue: Will the Americans With Disabilities Act impose excessive costs on society? *CQ Researcher 1*(32), 1009.

Wendell, S. (1996). *The rejected body: Feminist philosophical reflections on disability*. New York: Routledge.

Wilkinson, C. A. (1976). A rhetorical definition of movements. *Central States Speech Journal, 27*, 88–94.

Wolfe, K. (1996). Ordinary people: Why the disabled aren't so different. *The Humanist, 56*(6), 31–34.

Woodward, J. (1982). *How you gonna get to heaven if you can't talk with Jesus: On depathologizing deafness*. Silver Spring, MD: T.J. Publishers.

ENDNOTES

1. The term *temporarily ablebodied* has been utilized by disability activists in an attempt to help those who are not disabled understand that this is at best a temporary condition. Most of us in our lifetimes will experience some form of disability, even if it is only a broken leg or a loss of hearing as we age.

2. Throughout the text I use a convention originated by James Woodward (1972) and adopted by many researchers of Deaf culture. The word *Deaf* capitalized refers to the ethnic minority deaf persons who identify with Deaf culture. The lower case *deaf* refers to the physical, audiological aspects of deafness.

3. The cochlear implant is an electronic instrument that, when surgically implanted and with extensive therapy and rehabilitation, can help to provide some sense of sound to persons who cannot hear (Niparko, 1995). Over the past 20 years, more than 10,000 persons worldwide have received cochlear implants. In June 1990, the U.S. Food and Drug Administration (FDA) approved the use of cochlear implants for deaf children aged 2 through 17. The FDA approval of cochlear implants for children served as an exigence, triggering a volatile debate between persons working within the field of communication disorders and Deaf activists (Shultz, 1997b).

IV

Media and Technologies

15

If They Limp, They Lead? News Representations and the Hierarchy of Disability Images

Beth Haller
Towson University

Keywords: Hierarchy of disability in news images, cultural themes in news images, media models of disability, disability rights narrative, camera angles and wheelchairs

Reinterpreting the old journalism adage, "If it bleeds, it leads" in terms of disability, this chapter examines the news media's values in terms of representing disability in the news, arguing that people who have visually apparent disabilities are valued within the news because of the unspoken visual and emotional cues they provide. Many have argued that, in modern times, U.S. society has moved into a more visual, rather than text-based, culture (Messaris, 1994), meaning that television images and print photographs have taken preeminence over the printed word for media audiences. Therefore, this chapter discusses the representation of people with disabilities in televised, photographic, and print news; however, the bulk of the analysis rests on the visual images because of their higher salience for media audiences. This chapter's analysis is based on a study of 12 major newspapers' and news magazines' coverage of the Americans with Disabilities Act (ADA) from 1990 to 1993, which included 171 news photographs, 26 TV news interviews with people with disabilities, and 525 print stories (Haller, 1995).

First, the preeminence of the news media as a definitional tool in U.S. culture must be understood. Higgins (1992) noted that as a society we "make disability" through our language, the mass media, and other public and visible ways, such as photography, art, and literature. The news media actively "construct" and frame people with disabilities in their stories and images. As Goffman (1963) posited in his development of the concept of stigma, people with disabilities are portrayed as "different" or as people who may not fit within the mainstream. This affects both the public's view of disability, as well as the self concepts of people with disabilities (Nelson, 1996). The ability of mass media to make people aware of and characterize social groups is consistent with McCombs and Shaw's (1972) notion of agenda-setting. In revisiting their seminal work 20 years later, McCombs and Shaw (1993) explained that agenda-setting research on news media has shown us that media not only tell their audiences what to think about but how to think about certain issues and groups. In the 1990s, federal legislation, such as the ADA, and such societal issues as assisted suicide have put disability concerns on the public's agenda and given us more images of people with disabilities in the news. However, media coverage of these issues tends to fall into a framework of "handicapism" (Bogdan & Biklen, 1977), even though the passage of the ADA is an attempt to help end discrimination against people with disabilities. Even in the face of this minority group status conferred on people with disabilities by government legislation, media coverage of disability issues has continued to be spotty and stereotyping, rather than in-depth and empowering.

The way the media frame disability and its issues has real implications in the lives of people with disabilities. Because of numerous societal barriers, much of the general public gets its information about the disability community from media sources rather than through interpersonal contact. "Our televised 'acquaintances' who have disabilities represent a larger portion of all the people with disabilities whom we 'know'" because people with disabilities still have not been fully integrated into society" (Makas, 1993, p. 257). Television viewers "meet" a person with a disability through that medium about every 4.2 hours. A Louis Harris poll (1991) showed that Americans surveyed were less likely to feel awkward around people with disabilities after having viewed fictional television and movie presentations about people with disabilities. However, disability rights activists have long complained that much of the media coverage patronizes and stigmatizes by making people with disabilities seem either like sick, needy invalids or like inspirational superheroes (Clogston, 1989, 1990). In lobbying for the ADA, disability activists advocated a civil rights narrative in the societal representations of disability. This narrative contrasts with what Scotch (1988) said is a reigning rhetoric about people with disabilities, in which disability is seen as a physical problem alone residing within individuals. Disability activists advocate a perspective in which disability is understood as "socially constructed," for example, as a phenomenon created by society, which historically has had architectural, occupational, educational, communication, and attitudinal barriers to prevent people who are physically different from being totally integrated into society (Liachowitz, 1988). In the civil rights narrative, physical difference is acknowledged, and even celebrated as an ethnicity might be by some, but the focus is away from the disabled individual as the problem and on society's structures instead.

PAST MODELS OF DISABILITY IMAGES

In 1990, media scholar John Clogston developed five models of news media representations of disability, which were used to analyze news stories about disability. These models and three more created by Haller (1995) provide eight parameters for analyzing news media representations of disability. Three models fit with what Clogston called the "traditional," or more stigmatizing, representations of people with disabilities. First, is the medical model, in which disability is presented as an illness or malfunction, which causes a state of dependency and passivity. Second, in the social pathology model, disabled people are presented as disadvantaged and must look to the state or to society for economic support, which is considered a gift, not a right (Clogston, 1990). In the third or supercrip model, the disabled person is portrayed as deviant because of "superhuman" feats or as "special" because he or she lives a regular life "in spite of" disability (J. S. Clogston, personal communication, March 8, 1993). The other two models are considered "progressive" because they represent people with disabilities as active, full members of society. The fourth is the minority/civil rights model, in which disabled people are seen as members of the disability community, which has legitimate civil rights grievances (Clogston, 1990). In the fifth model, the cultural pluralism model, people with disabilities are seen as multifaceted and their disabilities do not receive undue attention. They are portrayed as nondisabled people would be (Clogston, 1990).

Haller (1993) applied these models to the presentation of deaf persons in the *Washington Post* and *New York Times* in the years before, during, and after the Deaf President Now protest at Gallaudet University in 1988. The coverage of this student protest of a hearing person being appointed president of a university for deaf persons illustrated how coverage shifted after the deaf community actively lobbied for its rights. The traditional models, medical and social pathology, accounted for 62% of the stories in the 2 years before the Deaf President Now protest. Stories reflecting those models dropped to 24% in 1988, the year of the protest, and stayed lower at 40% in the 2 years following the protest.

To account for the post-ADA media environment after 1989, which saw more lobbying for disability rights, Haller (1995) added three more models to Clogston's typology. The sixth is the business model, in which disabled people and their accessibility to society are presented as costly to society in general, and to businesses especially (Haller, 1995). Seventh, the legal model, in which people with disabilities are presented as having legal rights and possibly a need to sue to halt discrimination (Haller, 1995). The final model is the consumer model, in which people with disabilities are presented as an untapped consumer group; therefore, making society accessible could be profitable to businesses and society (Haller, 1995).

These models were not applied to media images and stories in a mutually exclusive manner. Media representations embody a range of elements and therefore a newspaper photograph, TV image, or news story might contain several models. For example, a television image might contain stigmatizing camera angles that fit within the social pathology model, as well as other shots that might fit within the minority group model.

An analysis of camera angles in news photos illustrated the application of the eight models. Camera angle is a significant component when assessing the television or photographic representations of people with disabilities, because those who use wheelchairs are always seated. Much of the theory on the meaning of camera angles comes from TV and film research. For example, in experiments, Kraft (1987) found that camera angles do influence the physical and personal representation of characters in a story. The overriding opinion is that a high-angle shot (one from above) reduces the importance of a subject, conveying weakness (Berger, 1981); this would fit as an element of the social pathology model. A low-angle shot (one from below) gives power to the subject, making him or her more "godlike" (Berger, 1981); this would fit as an element of the supercrip model. An eye-level shot imparts equality or objectivity (Kervin, 1985), which fits with the cultural pluralism, minority group, or consumer models.

An analysis of photos that accompanied stories about the ADA illustrate this effect. People using wheelchairs were the most prominent disability group depicted in the ADA photos. Fifty-two percent of the photos had a camera angle at equal/eye level, 29% were shot from above, and 16% were shot from below; camera angle could not be determined in about 4% of the cases (Haller, 1995). In the case of the TV shots, 15 of the interviews were shot on the same level as the interviewee, 9 from above, and 2 from below. Based on camera angle then, the majority of the news photos had elements that would place them in the progressive models. However, that does not mean the photos could not also include elements of the traditional models.

In addition to the eight distinct models of media representation, media research on disability representations has found broad cultural narratives about people with disabilities imbedded in U.S. media stories and images. For example, Douglas Crimp (1992) argued that the cultural message in photographs about people with AIDS, especially gay men, is that they are horribly ill, grotesquely disfigured, or wasted into nothingness; these phobia-inducing images are part of the culture because people fear that someone with AIDS will still be sexual. Crimp (1992) noted that media images refuse to show people with AIDS as active, fighting, and controlling their lives because if they are strong, they may be sexual. By creating this image, people can fantasize that AIDS has stopped gay promiscuity and sexuality.

Klobas (1988) asserted that, in general, the stories about people with disabilities in fictional TV presentations use "formula treatment where disability is a personal problem one must overcome" (p. xiii). This screen image is also present in TV news and newspapers, which continually cover people with disabilities as human interest stories, Klobas argued. No matter what the topic of the story, people with disabilities are portrayed as courageous and inspirational. Similarly, British researchers Cumberbatch and Negrine's (1992) study of both fictional and factual television programs found four prominent themes in news programs: fitting into normal life (32%), the physical progress of a person with a disability (30%), the lack of understanding by society/individuals (19%), and fighting for civil rights (17%).

In addition, like other groups that face negative media stereotypes, people with disabilities must overcome a history in which they were either pitied or feared. The prevailing attitude, according to Funk (1987), is that people with disabilities cannot contribute to society. "Thus, a societal attitude developed that this class of persons, viewed as unhealthy, defective, and deviant, required special institutions, services, care, and attention in order to survive" (p. 9). Similarly, British photographer David Hevey (1992) argued that disability has been used in photography to transmit "enfreakment," turning people with disabilities into freaks in visual composition.

Absence from cultural representations is another way in which media define people with disabilities. Historically, studies of television content has shown that although people with disabilities represent about 20% of the population, they represent only a small number of prime-time TV characters, about 3% (Donaldson, 1981; Leonard, 1978; Montgomery, 1989). Those who do appear are depicted as targets of humor and ridicule, as well as victims of verbal and physical abuse. When they are cast in a positive light, the story usually involves an unrealistic miracle cure for their disabilities.

These cultural narratives about disability, which are reinforced by media, fit with Carey's (1989) ritual view of mass communication. He sees news representations not as information dissemination, but as a framing and reinforcement of a specific view of the world. Thus, a society that stigmatizes people with disabilities receives reinforcement of those beliefs from media stories and images. However, as societal attitudes change and government legislation such as the ADA tries to address inequities for people with disabilities, a sliding scale of media images begins to develop. At one end are the images that reinforce past pity and fear of disability, and at the more modern end, media images present an empowered and equal social group.

THE HIERARCHY OF DISABILITY IMAGES

A wide range of media representations of disability exist, but not just because of societal stigma. They are a function both of the norms of journalism as well as biases among people with disabilities themselves. For example, Byzek (1996) explained a so-called pecking order among disability advocates in her article "Chair trumps cane, acquired trumps developmental." She explains that people using wheelchairs rank at the "top" in terms of both activism and obtaining services. Of course, journalists also value people whose disabilities are apparent because they provide visual cues in TV and photographic images. The analysis of news photos, which accompanied stories about the ADA, confirmed both these influences.

These media images depicted wheelchair use as the main symbol of disability. Wheelchair use dominated modern news photographs, as well as popular culture images such as in films (Norden, 1993). Knoll (1987) noted that disability symbols in photographs can also include such things as medical equipment, symbols of impaired mobility, beds, bandages, twisted hands, etc. These allow the person to be labeled as having a disability without it being stated.

In terms of journalistic norms, wheelchairs and other disability-related equipment may pull viewers to news images through the rhetoric of tragedy and a sense of people "coping with adversity," themes that have been shown to win important photojournalism awards (Singletary & Lamb, 1984). Disability in a photo draws on drama and human interest, two long-held values in journalism. Another journalistic news value, oddity, fits squarely with how editors might view photos or video footage of disability. As one prominent college newswriting textbook explains: "Deviations from the normal . . . are more newsworthy than the commonplace" (Fedler, 1997, p. 94).

Although 20% of the U.S. population has some form of disability, as legally defined, media imagery relies on one type of disability—mobility impairments that require wheelchair use. Out of the 171 ADA photos, more than half pictured a wheelchair user. However, only .05%, or about 1.5 million, of people in the United States use a wheelchair (based on a U.S. population of 251.8 million), making disabilities that require wheelchair use one of the smaller segments of disability demographics. In contrast, the National Institutes of Mental Health (1993) estimates that 23.9 million Americans have some form of mental disorder, and the U.S. National Center for Health Statistics (1990) estimates that 23 million Americans have hearing impairments, 7.5 million have visual impairments, and 19.3 million have heart conditions.

There were also racial and gender dimensions to the hierarchy of disability images. News images portrayed disability as caucasian and male. For example, in ADA photos, time and again a young, professional, White, male wheelchair user is depicted. A White lobbyist for the Paralyzed Veterans Administration is pictured on a ramp to a District of Columbia sandwich shop in the *Washington Post* (Herndon, 1990) or a White psychotherapist sat before his accessible van in the *Los Angeles Times* (Barnard, 1992). Only eight Black men with disabilities, nine Black women with disabilities, two Latino men with disabilities, and one Latino woman are presented in the ADA photos. No Asian men with disabilities are depicted, and one Asian woman with a disability is depicted.

In terms of gender, news images also conflict with other sources on the incidence of disability among women. Men with disabilities show up most prominently in the ADA photos, with 46% depicting men alone compared with 40% depicting women alone. A news photo in the *Los Angeles Times* illustrated this phenomenon. In the story about accommodations under the ADA a Latina woman with a disability was quoted extensively in the article, yet the photos that accompanied the story were of a White male wheelchair user who was not even a source in the story (Newton, 1990). However, according to census studies women more often have disabilities than men (Disability Statistics Program, 1991), and there are slightly more women in the U.S. population than men. This gender bias seems to fit with the norms of news photos, which traditionally depict many more men than women (Blackwood, 1983; Miller, 1975), and many more Whites than other racial groups (Singletary, 1978).

Although these images do not represent the racial and gender demographics of disability in America, they do accurately reflect the disability rights movement, which is composed of many white males. Backman (1994) noted the contradiction within the disability rights movement: "While ethnic and racial minority groups are disproportionately susceptible to disability, the leadership of the disability rights movement is mostly white" (p. 24). In fact, many disability researchers currently believe the incidence of disability in minority racial groups has been underestimated in the past. The Disability Statistics Program (1991) reports there are 6.8 million African Americans with disabilities, 2.5 million people of Spanish origin with disabilities, and 1.4 million people with disabilities of other ethnic groups. With heavy reliance on pictures of white people with disabilities, however, news images framed disability as a "White issue." In the post-ADA news media environment, the media told society people of color rarely have disabilities, when, in fact, many have a higher incidence of disability within their ethnic group than do caucasians. This is a similar message to what occurs on fictional TV, where Zola (1985) and Makas (1993) found most people with disabilities on TV to be young, single, White males.

In a "public relations" sense, it may be favorable to ethnic minority groups to be portrayed as disability free, especially considering cultural notions about disability. Actually perpetuating this frame could have dire consequences to groups already oppressed. The National Council on Disability (1993) reported that because of poverty, unemployment, and poorer health, many members of ethnic minority groups may be at higher risk of disability. Consequently, if minorities with disabilities were not shown to exist, they might not receive services equal to those of other persons with disabilities.

Therefore, this hierarchy of images, presenting a monolithic, one-race, one-disability, one-gender news media representation, potentially negates the 46.5 million people with disabilities who do not require wheelchair use, the 26 million people with disabilities who are not male, and the approximately 12 million people with disabilities who are not White.

CULTURAL THEMES
IN DISABILITY IMAGES

Although disability images are still narrow in terms of demographic elements, a focus on cultural elements indicates that media images of disability are in transition because cultural narratives about disability are changing in the post-ADA media environment. Therefore, the cultural messages embodied by the eight models of media representation (J. S. Clogston, personal communication, March 8, 1990; Haller, 1995) merge with the norms of journalism and the demographics of disability activism to create a blending of media images. For example, although stories and photos about the ADA reported one of the most sweeping changes in government and societal treatment of disability, they still embodied some subtle remnants of medicalization and paternalism toward disability.

Barkin (1984) and Bird and Dardenne (1988) explained that journalists transmit the narratives of a culture. The media images of disability in the ADA stories and images presented a cultural narrative that mobility impairment is the "true" disability. Why did they transmit this theme about disability? One study reported that almost one third of people surveyed agreed that wheelchair use is a tragedy (Patterson & Witten, 1987); therefore, photojournalists were able to grab the attention of the media audience with this one media image. Media images are constructed to use techniques of drama to add impact and emotion to elicit strong response from viewers (Schwartz, 1992), and images of people in wheelchairs fit that goal. Because society and journalists still view disability in terms of tragedy, pity, or inspiration, it connects well with journalistic codes.

However, news images of wheelchair users need not be negative or stigmatizing. Showing a wheelchair user in a photo doing something symbolically empowering or confronting barriers could send positive cultural messages about people with disabilities as equal citizens in society. For example, the fact many news images show wheelchair users commuting or working at their jobs sends a positive message about equal employability and the importance of workplace access. The cultural themes embodied in the consumer model, which values people with disabilities' financial contribution to society, or the cultural pluralism model, which sees people with disabilities as multifaceted people, are both found in current media images. However, these models are still in constant battle with negative themes found in the medical, social pathology, and business models.

Another positive cultural message embodied in the media's overuse of wheelchairs to represent disability was one of confronting the barriers to architectural access. Even if wheelchair users have less impairment than other types of disabilities, they still cannot enter the grocery store, post office, factory, and so forth if these places are not accessible. Society "handicaps" wheelchair users with very visible architectural barriers. For journalists, the visual nature of both wheelchair use and these access issues make them most compelling for video or still media images. In addition, disability rights advocates themselves have given architectural access a top ranking in their political agenda. Altman (1994) noted the disability rights movement put wheelchair users in the "front lines" to make a more memorable point about civil rights. She explained it this way:

> Visibility becomes paramount in differentiating the "oppressed" from the oppressors. So, during the civil rights movement we saw black leaders with much darker skins than were generally the case prior to the civil rights movement, when light skin was preferred. In the same way, persons who used wheelchairs became the most effective protestors during the early years of the disability rights movement because of their visibility and because their physical access problems were also visible. (p. 49)

This fight for access put media coverage squarely within the minority group/civil rights model of representation, a positive cultural theme the media have helped spread.

On the other hand, using wheelchairs repetitively as the symbol of disability may stigmatize wheelchair users and negate those who have other, more hidden disabilities. Someone with Tourette's syndrome or mental retardation may confront more attitudinal or educational barriers and have more disabling conditions than a wheelchair user, but the news media's reliance on a more visual narrative meant their barriers were more difficult to represent to an audience. Sadly, many media images could be interpreted as pessimistic views of disability: These images presented notions of what cannot be done because of disability, rather than what can be done. Discussing the cultural notions about the disability experience that pervade U.S. culture, Phillips (1990) explained:

> (1) that society perceives disabled persons to be damaged, defective, and less socially marketable than nondisabled persons; (2) that society believes disabled persons must try harder to overcome obstacles in culture and should strive to achieve normality; and (3) that society attributes to disabled persons a preference to be with their own kind. (p. 850)

It is clear that journalists used cultural stereotypes of disability, both positive and negative, in their image creation. However, negative cultural images conflict with the disability rights movement's message of empowerment and equality for people with disabilities. Therefore, newer cultural narratives about disability are currently in conflict within news media images. The newer civil rights narrative must compete with the more entrenched, and potentially "handicapist," cultural images of disability.

EFFECTS OF THESE REPRESENTATIONS

These representations of disability provided by the news media not only have impact on what the larger society believes about people with disabilities but what people with disabilities think of themselves (Kent, 1988; Morris, 1991; Wendell, 1996). As Nelson (1996) said, for centuries the people of many societies have been taught, through negative stigmatizing portrayals of disability, that "deformity of body [was] usually associated with deformity of spirit" (p. 120). Longmore's (1985) classic essay explained that even the words used within a society to describe people with disabilities can contribute to a social identity that continually forces them into a "sick" or "handicapped" status.

If people with physical disabilities constantly have to confront this status in an "ableist" society, the media images filled with tragedy, pathos, pity, or inspiration would tend only to undermine that fight for a new social identity. Wendell (1996) explained that "stereotypes repeatedly get in the way of full participation in work and social life" (p. 43). For example, when many of the media images of women with disabilities portray them as weak and dependent (Morris, 1991), women with disabilities may internalize this belief and feel like "person[s] of no account" (Kent, 1988). These internalized beliefs could affect the self image of people with disabilities, as well as the larger culture's attitude toward them.

Attitudes toward disability based on media images can develop into a mix of devaluating pity and inspirational respect for coping. Zola (1991) said, on the one hand, stories about the successes of people with disabilities illustrate that they can live full, happy, goal-oriented lives. On the other hand, the message of success sets up expectations that all disabled people must try to meet. This message "states that if a Franklin Delano Roosevelt or a Wilma Rudolph could OVERCOME their handicap, so could and should all the disabled. And if we fail, it is **our** problem, **our** personality, **our** weakness" (Zola, 1991, p. 161).

In addition, mobility impairments are misunderstood by most people to be "dependent" states. This sharply contrasts with American notions of independence and individualism. Longmore (1987) suggested that the televised portrayals of people with disabilities as pathetic or dependent present a stereotype of loss of self control, which frightens ablebodied people. "Suffering caused by the body, and the inability to control the body, are despised, pitied, and above all, feared" (Wendell, 1989, p. 112). Ablebodied people may shudder at the thought that someone might need assistance with daily living tasks. However, they also conveniently forget the interdependent nature of most human tasks these days (D'Lil, 1997). Most of them are dependent on many other people to grow their food, make their clothes, take care of their children, build their transportation systems, or disseminate their societal information. So when journalists believe people are "confined or bound" to a wheelchair, they inaccurately portray and misunderstand concepts of interdependence and disability. Wheelchairs are not binding or confining, but they actually increase mobility, speed, and ability. For many people, wheelchairs increase personal freedom (Kailes, 1988).

In the post-ADA disability rights era, disability activists fought against these negative media images. Nelson (1996) said that the disability rights movement, by protesting and fighting against these stereotyping portrayals, has begun to recast itself in terms of self empowerment and strength. Kathryn Montgomery (1989) said that advocacy groups are extremely concerned with their mass media depictions because these depictions may demean them in the eyes of others. "To minorities, women, gays, seniors, and the disabled, television is a cultural mirror that has failed to reflect their images accurately. To be absent from prime time, to be marginally included in it, or to be treated badly by it are seen as serious threats to their rights as citizens" (Montgomery, 1989, p. 8). Michael Berube (1997) added that cultural representations of disability affect all people because they create definitions of what it means to be human. These definitions have consequences for future social policy about disability issues.

CONCLUSION

As discussed, the problem of stigmatizing representations of disability has not been solved yet. The mass media still act as significant agents in socially constructing images of people with disabilities and disability issues in U.S. culture. The importance of the news media in defining people with disabilities in U.S. society cannot be overemphasized as news media images may create a societal barrier just as formidable as any of the educational, architectural, or communication barriers people with disabilities already face daily. Studying news depictions helps us understand the media's role in re-inforcing a world view of people with disabilities as different and outside the "mainstream." This chapter illustrates that there must be more aware-ness and creativity when telling the news of disability issues. It has become too easy for news images to rely on one visual cue—the wheelchair—to transmit the cultural story. Relying so heavily on one type of disability, one racial group, and one gender to tell the story may distort the message of dis-ability rights as it impacts the public agenda. This becomes the innovative challenge to journalists—how can they represent a diverse group of people accurately without falling into the trap of the stigmatizing representations of the past?

One solution is for photojournalists, who already know numerous tech-nical aspects of image making, to strive to understand the cultural im-plications of their techniques. A simple awareness of camera angle when photographing or videotaping a person with a disability can change the final image that is produced. In addition, journalists must learn to focus less exclusively on wheelchair users to tell the disability story. In contrast, compelling images of people with disabilities who look like everyone else in U.S. society could confront cultural notions about disability and might even grab the attention of viewers.

Another important step for media professionals is to understand and confront their own attitudes about disability. Disability arouses emotional fears for people as they confront the reality that they could one day acquire a disability (known as the "fate worse than death" scenario by disability rights activists). Journalists may not understand the imbedded cultural biases they may carry with them, so they feel outright pity for people with disabilities or associate disability with tragedy or adversity.

Disability studies scholar Frank Bowe (1978) explains that one very incorrect assumption has infected key attitudes: "That disabled people are different from us more than they are like us, that their disabilities somehow set them apart from the rest of us" (pp. 108–109). Journalists, editors, and news directors can confront this problem directly by seeking out their local disability rights organizations and centers for independent living. Through discussions with the activist community, journalists may come away with more understanding of disability issues. They also may learn how to make better decisions about representing people with disabilities. Journalists will still control news decisions, but they will be able to create more accurate and less stigmatizing news images.

Joe Shapiro (1993) at *U.S. News and World Report* is a good model for excellence in journalism about disability issues. He has created one of the few established "disability beats" in America. The existence of this beat tells society and journalists that ending disability-based discrimination and full societal access have become crucial social issues that must be covered vigorously. Shapiro's book (1993), *No Pity, People with Disabilities Forging a New Civil Rights Movement*, illustrates that journalists never need delve into pathos, pity, or tragedy in covering disability issues. Shapiro found the "big story" of disability: that American society is in a unique transition as it tries to empower its citizens with disabilities and treat them as equals.

DISCUSSION QUESTIONS

1. What are some of the ways in which news images represent disability?
2. What is the significance of white male wheelchair users being a dominant news image?
3. How might news images affect attitudes toward people with disabilities?
4. How might news images affect the self concept of people with disabilities?
5. What ways do news image themes of tragedy and coping fit with the norms of journalism?
6. How does ablebodied ideology affect news images?
7. What are some ways journalists can begin to create more accurate representations of disability?

REFERENCES

Altman, B. M. (1994). Thoughts on visibility, hierarchies, politics & legitimacy. *Disability Studies Quarterly, 14*(2), 48–51.

Backman, E. (1994, May). Is the movement racist? *Mainstream*, pp. 24–31.

Barkin, S. M. (1984). The journalist as storyteller: An interdisciplinary perspective. *American Journalism, 1*(2), 27–33.

Barnard, T. (1992, January 26). Psychotherapist Thomas W. Fritz hopes [Photograph]. *Los Angeles Times*, p. D1.

Berger, A. A. (1981). Semiotics and TV. In R. P. Adler (Ed.), *Understanding television*. New York: Praeger.

Berube, M. (1997, May 30). The cultural representation of people with disabilities affects us all. *Chronicle of Higher Education, 43*(38), B4–5.

Bird, S. E., & Dardenne, R. W. (1988). Myth, chronicle, and story. In J. W. Carey (Ed.), *Media, myths, and narratives* (pp. 67–86). Newbury Park, CA: Sage.

Blackwood, R. E. (1983). The content of news photos: Roles portrayed by men and women. *Journalism Quarterly, 60,* 710–714.

Bogdan, R., & Biklen, D. (1977, March/April). Handicapism. *Social policy,* pp. 14–19.

Bowe, F. (1978). *Handicapping America.* New York: Harper & Row.

Byzek, J. (1996, November/December). Chair trumps cane. *Mouth,* p. 14.

Carey, J. W. (1989). *Communication as culture.* Boston: Unwin Hyman.

Clogston, J. S. (1989, August). *A theoretical framework for studying media portrayal of persons with disabilities.* Paper presented at the annual meeting of the Association for Education in Journalism and Mass Communication, Washington, DC.

Clogston, J. S. (1990). *Disability coverage in 16 newspapers.* Louisville: Advocado Press.

Clogston, J. S. (1993, March 8). Personal communication.

Crimp, D. (1992). Portraits of people with AIDS. In L. Grossberg, C. Nelson, & P. Treicher (Eds.), *Cultural studies* (pp. 117–133), New York: Routledge.

Cumberbatch, G., & Negrine, R. (1992). *Images of disability on television.* London: Routledge.

D'Lil, H. (1997, November). Being an "inspiration." *Mainstream,* pp. 14–17.

Disability Statistics Program. (1991, January). People with functional limitations in the U.S. *Disability statistics abstracts, 1.*

Donaldson, J. (1981). The visibility and image of handicapped people on television. *Exceptional Children, 47*(6), 413–416.

Fedler, F. (1997). *Reporting for the print media.* Fort Worth: Harcourt Brace.

Funk, R. (1987). Disability rights: From caste to class in the context of civil rights. In A. Gartner & T. Joe (Eds.), *Images of the disabled, disabling images* (pp. 7–30). New York: Praeger.

Goffman, E. (1963). *Stigma.* Englewood Cliffs, NJ: Prentice-Hall.

Haller, B. (1993) Paternalism and protest: The presentation of deaf persons in the *Washington Post* and *New York Times. Mass Comm Review, 20,* 169–179.

Haller, B. (1995). *Disability rights on the public agenda: News media coverage of the Americans with Disabilities Act.* Unpublished doctoral dissertation, Temple University, Philadelphia, PA.

Herndon, C. (1990, December 29). Lee Page of the Paralyzed Veterans Association uses a ramp [Photograph]. *Washington Post,* p. E1.

Hevey, D. (1992). *The creatures time forgot: Photography and disability imagery.* London: Routledge.

Higgins, P. C. (1992). *Making disability: Exploring the social transformation of human variation.* Springfield, IL: Charles C. Thomas.

Kailes, J. I. (1988). *Language is more than a trivial concern.* Unpublished manuscript.

Kent, D. (1988). In search of a heroine: Images of women with disabilities in fiction and drama. In M. Fine & A. Asch (Eds.), *Women with disabilities* (pp. 80–110) Philadelphia: Temple University Press.

Kervin, D. (1985). Reality according to television news: Pictures from El Salvador. *Wide Angle, 7*(4), 61–72.

Klobas, L. E. (1988). *Disability drama in television and film.* Jefferson, NC: McFarland.

Knoll, J. A. (1987). *Through a glass, darkly: The photographic image of people with a disability.* Unpublished doctoral dissertation, Syracuse University.

Kraft, R. N. (1987). The influence of camera angle on comprehension and retention of pictorial events. *Memory and Cognition, 15,* 291–307.

Leonard, B. K. (1978). Impaired view: Television portrayal of handicapped people. *Journalism Abstracts, 16,* 13–14.

Liachowitz, C. (1988). *Disability as social construct.* Philadelphia: University of Pennsylvania Press.

Longmore, P. K. (1985). A note on language and the social identity of disabled people. *American Behavioral Scientist, 28,* 419–423.

Longmore, P. K. (1987). Screening stereotypes: Images of disabled people in television and motion pictures. In A. Gartner & T. Joe (Eds.), *Images of the disabled, disabling images.* (pp. 65–78). New York: Praeger.

Louis Harris and Associates, Inc. (1991). *Public attitudes toward people with disabilities* (National poll conducted for National Organization on Disability). New York: Author.

Makas, E. (1993). Changing channels. The portrayal of people with disabilities on television. In G. L. Berry & K. K. Asaman (Eds.), *Children & television: Images in a changing sociocultural world* (pp. 255–268). Newbury Park, CA: Sage.

McCombs, M., & Shaw, D. (1972). The agenda-setting function of the press. *Public Opinion Quarterly, 36,* 176–187.

McCombs, M., & Shaw, D. (1993). The evolution of agenda-setting research. *Journal of Communication, 43*(2), 58–67.

Messaris, P. (1994). *Visual literacy.* Boulder, CO: Westview.

Miller, S. (1975). The content of news photos: Women's and men's roles. *Journalism Quarterly, 52,* 70–75.

Montgomery, K. C. (1989). *Targeting prime time.* New York: Oxford University Press.

Morris, J. (1991). *Pride against prejudice. Transforming attitudes to disability.* Philadelphia: New Society Publishers.

National Council on Disability. (1993). *Meeting the unique needs of minorities with disabilities.* Washington, DC: National Council on Disability.

National Institute of Mental Health. (1993, August). *Statistics on prevalence of mental disorders.* Rockville, MD: Information Resources and Inquiries Branch.

National Organization on Disability. (1990). [Brochure]. Washington, DC: Author.

Nelson, J. A. (1996). The individual cultural group: Images of disability. In P. Lester (Ed.), *Images that injure* (pp. 119–126). Westport, CN: Praeger.

Newton, E. (1990, August 15). Disabled: The battle goes on. *Los Angeles Times,* pp. 1, 16.

Norden, M. (1993). Reel wheels: The role of wheelchairs in American movies. In *Beyond the stars III.* Bowling Green, KY: Bowling Green State University Press.

Patterson, J. B., & Witten, B. (1987). Myths concerning persons with disabilities. *Journal of Applied Rehabilitation Counseling, 18*(3), 42–44.

Phillips, M. J. (1990). Damaged goods: The oral narratives of the experience of disability in American culture. *Social Science & Medicine, 30,* 849–857.

Schwartz, D. (1992). To tell the truth: Codes of objectivity in photojournalism. *Communication, 13,* 95–109.

Scotch, R. K. (1988). Disability as the basis for a social movement: Advocacy and politics of definition. *Journal of Social Issues, 44,* 159–172.

Shapiro, J. (1993). *No pity. People with disabilities forging a new civil rights movement.* New York: Times Books/Random House.

Singletary, M. W. (1978). Newspaper photographs: A content analysis, 1936–76. *Journalism Quarterly, 55,* 585–589.

Singletary, M. W., & Lamb, C. (1984, Spring). News values in award-winning photos. *Journalism Quarterly, 61,* 104–108.

U.S. National Center for Health Statistics. (1990). *Vital and health statistics* (Series 10, No. 181). Washington, DC: Author.

Wendell, S. (1989). Toward a feminist theory of disability. *Hypatia, 4*(2), 104–124.

Wendell, S. (1996). *The rejected body.* New York: Routledge.

Zola, I. K. (1985). Depictions of disability—metaphor, message, and medium: A research and political agenda. *Social Science Journal, 22*(4), 5–1.

Zola, I. K. (1991). Communication barriers between "the able-bodied" and "the handicapped." In R. P. Marinelli & A. E. Dell Orto (Eds.), *The psychological and social impact of disability* (pp. 157–164). New York: Springer.

16

Film Images of People
With Disabilities

Kim Wolfson
Communication Consultant, Amherst, MA

Martin F. Norden
University of Massachusetts-Amherst

Keywords: Isolation of movie characters, repulsion-attraction to disability, movie character stereotypes, exploitative, exploratory, incidental portrayals, activities for activists

It should come as no surprise to discover that the Hollywood tendency to construct highly problematic social imagery has extended as much to the portrayal of people with disabilities (PWDs) as to other oppressed subgroups in our society. As film historians Quart and Auster (1982) argued, "Hollywood, hardly noted for its realistic screen treatment of racial and ethnic minorities and women, has not been any more sensitive or illuminating in its portrayal of the disabled" (p. 25). Movies are powerful cultural tools that have helped perpetuate mainstream society's disregard for people with disabilities, and the images conveyed by those movies have often differed sharply from the realities of the disabled experience. This essay examines the movie industry's general approach to creating disabled characters, the common movie stereotypes that have arisen therefrom, and activist strategies for combating those images.

THE STRATEGY OF ISOLATION

One of the most immediately apparent common-denominator aspects of Hollywood's disability depictions is the strong sense of isolation that all but envelopes disabled characters. In other words, Hollywood moviemakers have gone out of their way to separate disabled figures from their ablebodied peers (as well as from each other) and "otherize" them. This long-term strategy has generally coincided with the way that mainstream society has treated its disabled population for centuries. As Grant and Bowe (1990) noted, "Prior to [the late 1960s and early 1970s], being disabled almost assured social, educational, and occupational isolation" (p. 5). While the process of mainstreaming—bringing people with disabilities out of institutions and into the mainstream of society, allowing those with and without disabilities to learn from each other—has by its very nature weakened the trend toward isolation in society and has led to some presumably correlated improvements in the screen portrayals of PWDs, the long-standing moviemaker tendency to isolate disabled people is still relatively strong. Longmore (1985) summed up the usual sense of separation that accompanies most disability depictions in the movies:

> The disabled person is excluded because of the fear and contempt of the nondisabled majority. Still, even when the handicapped character is presented sympathetically as a victim of bigotry, it remains clear that severe disability makes social integration impossible. While viewers are urged to pity [such a character], we are let off the hook by being shown that disability or bias or both must forever ostracize severely disabled persons from society. (p. 33)

The phenomenon of isolation is reflected not only in the typical storylines of the films, but also to a large extent in the ways the filmmakers have visualized the characters interacting in their environments; they have often used the basic tools of their trade—framing, editing, sound, lighting, and set-design elements such as fences, windows, and staircase banisters—to suggest a physical or symbolic separation of disabled characters from the rest of society. Audience positioning within the films becomes a critical issue, for more often than not moviemakers have photographed and edited their works to reflect an ablebodied point of view. This strategy of encouraging audience members to perceive the world depicted in the movies from this perspective and thus associate themselves with ablebodied characters has the effect of further isolating characters with disabilities by reducing them to objects of spectacle for the ablebodied majority.

This latter point deserves further examination, as it is the key to understanding why moviemakers create disabled characters at all. Stubbins (1988) bluntly declared that "the toughest item on the agenda of disability is that modern America has no need for most disabled persons" (p. 22), yet mainstream filmmakers, far from turning their backs on this minority, have constructed hundreds, perhaps even thousands of cinematic portraits of disabled characters that reach back to the earliest years of the medium; it is worth asking why. Henderson and Bryan (1984) provided a partial answer by suggesting that "throughout history, people without disabilities have had a paradoxical repulsion-attraction for those with disabilities" (p. 3). Their observation echoes the work of Fiedler (1978), who has argued that people with genetic disorders (e. g., dwarfs, giants, hermaphrodites, Siamese twins) have always fascinated members of mainstream society because the former, simultaneously "others" and mirrors of the self, are akin to mythic icons that reflect the latter's dreams and fears. Though Fiedler distinguished people with genetic disorders from those with other disabling circumstances (pp. 23–24), a number of his generalizations have particular relevance here.

Chief among them is Fiedler's observation that "human Freaks have, in fact, been manufactured for ritual aesthetic and commercial purposes ever since history began" (p. 251). The majority society has always had a strong desire to gaze on human anomalies, and entrepreneurs have all too willingly catered to that desire by creating "freaks," sometimes through mutilation, always through packaging and promotion. Although Fiedler was referring to people who have been intentionally deformed, his observation easily transfers to the world of movies; filmmakers have quite literally manufactured disabled characters in the name of commercial gain. As Fiedler pointed out, movies have usurped the inglorious function of carnival sideshows, which, despite occasional revivals, have been in decline since the advent of movies: "Human curiosities [have], for most Americans, passed inevitably from the platform and the pit to the screen, flesh becoming shadow" (p. 16). We might argue that moviemakers' treatment of people with disabilities is thus two-tiered: They try to keep the minority isolated and at the same time frequently pander to the rather questionable needs of their ablebodied audience.

POLITICS, MOVIES, AND DISABILITY

Because the practice of isolating disabled people in society as well as in the movies reflects a not-so-hidden political agenda—what better way to control a minority than to divide and quarantine it?—it might be helpful at this juncture to examine the general topic of political issues and their linkage with movies.

Briefly put, a mainstream society will do whatever it can to maintain itself in power, and its strategy of keeping minorities such as PWDs "in their place" and dependent by defining the issues represents a significant part of its self-continuance. Specialists in the rehabilitation field, an area dominated by ablebodied people, have certainly exhibited this perspective, as Stubbins (1988) argued: "[Rehabilitation] professionals define the problems, the agenda, and the social reality of disabled persons in ways that serve their own interests more closely than those of their clients" (p. 23).

The movie industry, so intertwined with other institutions of the dominant culture, has likewise demonstrated such behavior. Its products constitute an important mode of discourse by which the culture perpetuates itself and its perspectives, and they operate on several levels in service to it. Not only do they frequently deal explicitly, if often misguidedly, with contemporaneous social concerns (such as the films of the 1940s and 1950s that examined the lives of disabled World War II veterans), but, more significantly, they also contain submerged ideological perspectives, or what Mast and Kawin (1992) called "the unspoken, assumed cultural values of films—values that seem so obviously true for that culture that they are accepted as inevitable, normal, and natural rather than as constructs of the culture itself" (p. 5). These values, which typically go undetected and unquestioned by mainstream audiences, often assume the form of stereotyped images that, through sheer repetition, eventually take on a ring of truth in that society.

TEN DISABILITY STEREOTYPES

In the case of people with disabilities, the movie industry has perpetuated or initiated a number of exceptionally durable stereotypes that have inspired pity, awe, humor, fear, or some combination thereof and that reflect a theme of isolation. The 10 movie disability stereotypes described here, which Norden (1994) developed from analysis of over 300 films dating from the late 1890s to the early 1990s, represent the most typical types of portrayals.

The Civilian Superstar is a world-class performer in a field such as sports, the arts, politics, or medicine who seldom allows his or her disability to interfere with career goals. The 1975 film *The Other Side of the Mountain* details the life of Olympic contender Jill Kinmont before and after a 1955 skiing accident left her paralyzed from the shoulders down. Although the movie shows the Kinmont character as demoralized after the accident, her perseverance eventually leads her to finish college and embark on a successful teaching career. Other examples of the Civilian Superstar tradition include the internationally famous (and wheelchair-using) diagnostician Dr. Leonard Gillespie of *Dr. Kildare's Crisis* (1940) and 14 other films in the "Dr. Kildare" series; hearing-impaired Thomas Edison of *Edison, the Man* (1940); Marjorie Lawrence King, who refuses to let poliomyelitis stop her operatic career in *Interrupted Melody* (1955); one-legged baseball pitcher Monty Stratton of *The Stratton Story* (1949); and Franklin Roosevelt of *Sunrise at Campobello* (1960).

The Comic Misadventurer possesses a disability that causes self-directed problems, other-directed problems, or both. In the 1964 satire on Cold War relations, *Dr. Strangelove or: How I Learned to Stop Worrying and Love the Bomb*, the title character, a German advisor to the U.S. president, happens to use a wheelchair and have a bionic arm prone to choking its owner or giving Nazi salutes during tense moments. Other Comic Misadventurers are the physically and mentally impaired World War II veteran of *Fire Sale* (1977), the blind Mr. Muckle of *It's a Gift* (1934), the blind and deaf newspaper vendors of *See No Evil, Hear No Evil* (1989), and the laboratory assistant Igor of *Young Frankenstein* (1974).

The Elderly Dupe, a figure limited mostly to silent-era films, is an aged character who because of a disability (almost always blindness) is easily fooled by younger ablebodied types. In *The Four Horsemen of the Apocalypse* (1921), for instance, a blind man is completely unaware of his young wife's rather conspicuous affair with a dashing soldier. Elderly Dupes also appear in such films as *The Jury of Fate* (1917), *The Man and the Woman* (1908), *The Miracle Man* (1919), and *The Show* (1927).

The High-Tech Guru is a wheelchair-using male who proves unusually adept at manipulating computers, communication consoles, and related paraphernalia. *The Anderson Tapes* (1972) shows a sharp-witted boy using a roomful of communications gear to notify police of burglars in his parents' townhouse, while *Three Days of the Condor* (1975) presents a CIA officer known simply as "the Major" who adroitly manipulates a communications console. Both of these characters happen to use wheelchairs. Other films with similar figures include *No Way Out* (1987), *Power* (1986), and *Starman* (1984).

The Noble Warrior, or disabled war veteran, made numerous appearances in movies during the years following World War I, World War II, and the Vietnam War. Exhibiting perhaps the greatest degree of variability among the stereotypes noted in this chapter, the Noble Warrior evolved from a stick-figure level of treatment during the WWI era (in which disabilities were treated as not much more than badges of honor) to the warm and sympathetic portrayals of the WWII era to the bitter, rage-filled characterizations of the post-Vietnam period. Homer Parrish, a veteran who lost his hands in a shipboard accident in *The Best Years of Our Lives* (1946), is one of Hollywood's best-known Noble Warriors. Others include Jim Apperson of *The Big Parade* (1925), Ron Kovic of *Born on the Fourth of July* (1989), Luke Martin of *Coming Home* (1978), Dan Taylor of *Forrest Gump* (1994), Al Schmid of *Pride of the Marines* (1945), and Perry Kincheloe of *Till the End of Time* (1946).

The Obsessive Avenger is an Ahab-like character, usually male, who does not rest until he has wreaked revenge on those responsible for disabling him and/or violating his moral code in some other way. In the 1994 thriller *Speed*, a vengeful disabled man threatens the lives of a busload of passengers by attaching a bomb to the bus, so that the bus will explode if the driver lets the speed drop below a certain point. Other Obsessive Avengers include the title characters of *Freaks* (1932), Captain Hook of *Hook* (1991) and *Peter Pan* (1924, 1952), Quasimodo of the many versions of *The Hunchback of Notre Dame* (1923, 1939, 1957, 1996), Captain Ahab of *Moby Dick* (1930, 1956) and *The Sea Beast* (1926), the legless gangster of *The Penalty* (1920), and the wheelchair-using schemer nicknamed "Dead Legs" of *West of Zanzibar* (1928).

The Saintly Sage, another elderly character, can "see" things sighted people cannot. Especially prevalent in movies of the 1930s and 1940s, the Cassandra-like Saintly Sage dispenses much wisdom to his or her younger colleagues, who ignore it at their peril. *Bride of Frankenstein* (1935) portrays an old, nameless, blind hermit who befriends the Frankenstein monster. The hermit shares his food and lodging with the monster and even begins a modest socialization program for him. His humane treatment leads to a later irony when a man who has been hunting the monster asks the hermit incredulously, "My God, man, can't you see?" Although sightless, the hermit does "see"; he is the only character in the entire film who understands that the monster will behave as a human if treated like one. Other Saintly Sages include a fugitive's blind mother in *The Devil Doll* (1936), the blinded World War I veteran of *The Enchanted Cottage* (1943), "Blind Anna" of *Heidi* (1937), an elderly blind man who befriends a fugitive in *Saboteur* (1942), and the parody of *Bride of Frankenstein*'s Saintly Sage— a combination of the Comic Misadventurer and Saintly Sage stereotypes, in effect—in *Young Frankenstein* (1974).

The Sweet Innocent is a pure, godly, humble, asexual, and exceptionally pitiable figure who often receives a "miracle cure." Typically a child or young woman, the Sweet Innocent seems to bring out the protectiveness of most ablebodied characters that come her or his way. American and British filmmakers have adapted Charles Dickens' classic novel *A Christmas Carol* into movies many times, including *A Christmas Carol* (1901, 1908, 1910, 1912, 1914, 1938, 1951) and *Scrooge* (1913, 1935, 1970), and they all feature that most famous of Sweet Innocents, Tiny Tim. The stereotype also finds expression in the form of the nameless young flower-seller of *City Lights* (1931), the title character of *Forrest Gump* (1994), the child cured by the title character of *The Miracle Man* (1919), Louise of *Orphans of the Storm* (1921), and the title characters of *Pollyanna* (1920, 1960) and *Stella Maris* (1918).

The Techno Marvel is a character whose prosthesis (often a high-tech affair) frequently performs better than the limb, vision, or hearing it has replaced. The "Star Wars" trilogy—*Star Wars* (1977), *The Empire Strikes Back* (1980), *Return of the Jedi* (1983)—includes two characters who fit this description: Darth Vader, whose countless battle injuries have turned him into a walking wonderland of bionic effects; and Luke Skywalker, whose prosthetic hand works better than his original one (which Vader sliced off during the laser-sword duel that concludes *The Empire Strikes Back*). *Blind Date* (1984), *Innerspace* (1987), and *Stephen King's Silver Bullet* (1985) also illustrate this stereotype.

The Tragic Victim is usually a poverty-stricken social outcast who often expires by film's end. The 1947 movie *Kiss of Death*, a gangland tale centering around a criminal who tries to go straight, contains a sequence involving a psychotic killer who verbally harasses a wheelchair-using mother of a "squealer" he has been assigned to find. After calling the woman a "lying old hag" and binding her to her chair with a lamp cord, he wheels her out of the apartment and shoves her down a long flight of stairs. Other Tragic Victims appear in *The Blind Musician* (1909), *The Faithful Dog* (1907), *The Hidden* (1987), and *His Daughter's Voice* (1907).

MOVIES AND SOCIETY

The images described in the preceding section typically bear little resemblance to the actual experiences and lifestyles of people with disabilities. After examining hundreds of disability-related film and television dramas, Klobas (1988) concluded that "an immense chasm exists between disabled

people and their screen counterparts" (p. xi). Her view is shared by Schuchman (1988), a Gallaudet University professor: "The deaf characters I have
seen on movie screens and on television bear little resemblance to the
deaf people or community that I knew as a boy or that I know today as
a professional in daily contact with deaf people" (p. ix). Commentary by
Thomson (1997) on the literary constructions of disability readily applies
to the versions under analysis in this chapter:

> Although such representations refer to actual social relations, they do not of
> course reproduce those relations with mimetic fullness. Characters are thus
> necessarily rendered by a few determining strokes that create an illusion of
> reality far short of the intricate, undifferentiated, and uninterpreted context
> in which real people live. (p. 10)

According to Klobas (1988), the discrepancies between real-life disabled
people and their movie portrayals are traceable to mainstream society's
reluctance to recognize disabled people as a minority group suffering from
discrimination:

> The "cultural" chasm between real-life and screen disability can be graphi-
> cally defined by looking at disability not as a physical/personal problem, but
> as one of human rights. A simplistic parallel argument would be to state that
> the reason black Americans did not vote in previous decades, could not use
> all public bathrooms, and had to sit at the back of the bus was because they
> had not "accepted" the reality they were black. Their anger resulted from not
> "overcoming" their race. Obviously, this was never the case and it sounds
> ludicrous to state the same. However, it is happening to the nation's disabled
> citizens. Their social problems and individual idiosyncrasies are ignored,
> while easy emotional stories of "bitterness," "overcoming," and "courage"
> abound. (p. xii)

Appraising the situation in similar terms, Longmore (1985) noted that
the ablebodied majority views disability as

> primarily a problem of emotional coping, of personal acceptance. It is not
> a problem of social stigma and discrimination. It is a matter of individuals
> overcoming not only the physical impairments of their own bodies but, more
> importantly, the emotional consequences of such impairments. [The films]
> convey the message that success or failure in living with a disability results
> almost solely from the emotional choices, courage, and character of the
> individual. (p. 34)

The people immediately responsible for this and other messages are, of course, the ablebodied folk who dominate the movie industry. Their attitudes toward disabled people as expressed in their films range from mildly insulting to overwhelmingly hostile and are often informed by an esoteric logic. For example, the silent-film director Rex Ingram recruited short-stature performers to play minor characters in many films including *The Prisoner of Zenda* (1922), *Trifling Women* (1922), *Where the Pavement Ends* (1923), *Scaramouche* (1923), *Mare Nostrum* (1925), and *The Magician* (1926), in part because, according to his biographer, he believed they would bring him luck (O'Leary, 1980, pp. 51, 73). A handful of old-line Hollywood directors have had visual or auditory impairments, most notably, John Ford, Raoul Walsh, André de Toth, Tay Garnett, Nicholas Ray, and William Wyler, but little of their work—Wyler's *The Best Years of Our Lives* (1946), Ray's *On Dangerous Ground* (1951), Ford's *The Wings of Eagles* (1957), maybe a few others—suggests any sensitivity to disability issues. People with disabilities occasionally act as advisors on films, but ultimately the authorship of the movie rests with one or more ablebodied people. This is not to say that ablebodied people cannot have insights into the disabled experience, but far more often than not they warp the images to fit preconceived notions. The resulting films often have only the most tenuous connection to the world of people with disabilities.

Though members of the movie industry are obviously the front-line cultivators of these images, it would hardly be appropriate to suggest they have been operating independently of long-standing mainstream values. Movies are intimately tied to the 20th century, but they are informed to a large extent by negative attitudes toward disabled people that predate the cinema by centuries. For example, the Bible, a major defining text for western society, frequently associates disease and disability with sin and punishment and also admonishes its readers to act charitably toward PWDs but not treat them as equals (Weinberg & Sebian, 1908). Such attitudes and values have found their way into a variety of cultural expressions, such as our language ("She's blind to that situation," "Their proposal fell on deaf ears," "That's a lame excuse," "He doesn't have a leg to stand on," etc.) and the rules and regulations that have helped shape our society. In her analysis of pre-20th century laws and public policy statements, Liachowitz (1988) concluded that "the cultural practice of translating physical abnormality into social inferiority is so deeply rooted as to have had an almost certain impact on both the formulation and implementation of later public policy"

(p. 1). These same deeply ingrained attitudes toward people with disabilities have also served as the movie industry's basis for the disabled characters that populate its films.

Consider, for example, a typical moviemaker's use of disability: to suggest some element of a person's character, a tradition that carries back to the earliest days of the medium. Field (1982), the dean of screenwriting teachers, wrote:

> A screenplay, remember, is a story told with pictures. Pictures, or images, reveal aspects of character. In Robert Rossen's classic film *The Hustler*, a physical defect symbolizes an aspect of character. The girl played by Piper Laurie is a cripple; she walks with a limp. She is also an emotional cripple; she drinks too much, has no sense of aim or purpose in life. The physical limp underscores her emotional qualities—*visually*." (p. 27)

Field's (1982) prime justification for admonishing screenwriters to continue this contemptible tendency is its sheer longevity: "Physical handicap—as an aspect of characterization—is a theatrical convention that extends far back into the past. One thinks of *Richard III*" (p. 27). If Field's beliefs are anywhere near the industrial norm, as the authors of this chapter believe they are, there is little mystery as to why such images continue to find their way into the movies.

AN HISTORICAL OVERVIEW

Despite the negative nature of many movie constructions of disability, the film industry has demonstrated a general sense of progress, a sense that is more detectable if we divide the movie depictions into three general historical periods: the late 1890s to the late 1930s, the World War II years into the 1970s, and the 1970s through the end of the 1990s.

Films from the first period tended to gravitate toward highly exploitative portrayals, with Comic Misadventurers, Sweet Innocents, and Obsessive Avengers dominating hundreds of films and Elderly Dupes, Saintly Sages, and Tragic Victims making their appearances as well. Seldom rising above a comic-book level of complexity, these movie constructions defined the disability-movie scene during this time.

After about four decades' worth of such tenuous and unfair images, moviemakers began offering more sensitive and enlightened portrayals during the World War II era. Noble Warriors and Civilian Superstars began displacing the older images as the movies took on more of an exploratory quality. Disability, which during the first period had been used mainly to telegraph a character's inner qualities to the audience or simply propel the plot, was now treated as a major issue to explore and overcome. Such constructions were not without problems (the movies often presented the disabled characters as larger than life and placed the burden of "overcoming" solely on their shoulders while ignoring problems of prejudice and access), but they represented a major step forward.

The third period, which began approximately during the 1970s, began featuring movies that treated disability in more of an incidental fashion. Rehabilitative struggles, which took center stage during the second period, began giving way to other concerns: pursuing a career, fighting for social justice, sexually expressing oneself, simply getting on with everyday life. In other words, filmmakers were now framing the characters as people who happened to be disabled and who have a wide range of concerns like anyone else. Though the period has been littered with rather flat character types, such as the Techno Marvel and the High-Tech Guru, characterizations of a more three-dimensional nature began developing during this time.

Although this general history has been marked by frequent slippage back to the older forms of expression (e.g., the return of Comic Misadventurers and Obsessive Avengers in such relatively late films as *See No Evil, Hear No Evil, Hook*, and *Speed*), the general movement from exploitative to exploratory to incidental treatment does suggest a slowly developing enlightenment on issues of disability.

This gradual improvement may well be related to the increasing level of social interaction among people with disabilities and ablebodied people. Social scientists and other observers have long known that ablebodied people have typically tended to avoid interacting with disabled people (Thompson, 1982; Yamamoto, 1971) and, furthermore, that this avoidance is rooted to a large extent in fear. Mairs (in Berubé, 1997) effectively underscored this point by suggesting that "most non-disabled people I know are so driven by their own fears of damage and death that they dread contact, let alone interaction, with anyone touched by affliction of any kind" (p. B4). As those with and without disabilities continue to dialogue and network, however, this problem appears to be diminishing. Weinberg (1978) suggested that continued intermingling of those with and without disabilities has the general effect of minimizing differences as perceived by the latter group: "As contact between ablebodied and disabled is intensified, the stereotype of the disabled as different diminishes.... There is a positive relationship between contact and perceived similarity: as contact increases, perceived similarity increases" (p. 123). Although Weinberg was commenting on members of society in general, her observations suggest what undoubtedly will be the key to the continuing improvement of movie depictions of people with disabilities: working with ablebodied peers both within and outside the movie industry.

CHANGING ATTITUDES IN HOLLYWOOD

To a limited extent, such collaborations within Hollywood are already underway. Ron Kovic, the disabled Vietnam veteran who cowrote the screenplay for *Born on the Fourth of July*, proclaimed himself "extremely proud" of the movie based on his like-titled autobiography. "I was able to see my story come out the way I wanted to see it and the way I felt it should come out," he said, adding that his ablebodied colleagues on the film "treated me with a great deal of respect" (in Seidenberg, 1990, p. 56). Another disabled person who has enjoyed success in Hollywood is Neal Jimenez, who wrote and codirected a film based partially on his own experiences called *The Waterdance* (1992). An unflinching look at the wide range of issues facing newly disabled males, *The Waterdance* won critical praise. Canby (1992) of the *New York Times* gave it a very favorable review, noting that "though small in scale, it is big in feelings expressed with genuine passion and a lot of gutsy humor" (p. C13). It also won several awards at the Sundance Film Festival that year.

ACTIVIST STRATEGIES

Activists outside the movie industry have also worked to improve the image of PWDs. Disability-related associations ranging from local to international have been concerned about raising public awareness of the imagery and calling for improvements. For example, participants at the 1997 International Leadership Forum for Women with Disabilities held in Bethesda, Maryland, issued a statement demanding a greater use of disabled people in mass media productions and that "these portrayals must be positive, sensitive and life enhancing" (International Leadership, 1997).

Other activists have gone a step further by directly attempting to influence the production and exhibition of Hollywood films. For instance, Levitan (1992) detailed the efforts of a number of Deaf groups to convince the producers of *Calendar Girl* (1993), a comedy about three Nevada boys who trek to Hollywood to meet Marilyn Monroe, to reconsider their decision to hire a hearing actor to play a minor character who is deaf. Though the activists lost that round, they refused to give up the battle and staged a series of protests during the film's premiere.

Similarly, Paul Spudich, a man with kyphoscoliosis, organized a national letter-writing campaign in 1995 to protest the Walt Disney company's plans to produce an animated version of *The Hunchback of Notre Dame* ("Disney Says No," 1995). In addition, the 3,000 delegates who attended the 1997 New Orleans convention of the National Federation of the Blind unanimously passed a resolution asking Disney to abandon production of *Mr. Magoo* (1997), a film about a hapless, nearsighted man (Bannon, 1997).

The creation of films and videos that pose alternative perspectives to those promoted by Hollywood represents yet another strategy. Billy Golfus, a man who sustained brain damage as a result of a traffic accident during the 1980s, wrote and directed an independently produced film called *When Billy Broke His Head...and Other Tales of Wonder* (1994) that details his experiences as a person with a disability in American society. It also explores the lives of many other PWDs, and in the process reveals a world far different from that constructed in most Hollywood films.

SUGGESTED STRATEGIES FOR ACTIVISTS

If you would like to help improve the movie image of disabled people, you might use the examples given here as a guide for developing your own course of action. Following are several suggestions:

1. Join disability-related associations in their campaigns against unfair movie portrayals.
2. Use the Internet to find news groups and mailing-list memberships interested in discussing disability topics. On the World Wide Web, the following site provides links to many websites and "e-zines" (i.e., on-line magazines) devoted to disability research and activism: <www-unix.oit.umass.edu/~norden/dra.html>.
3. Use the *Hollywood Creative Directory* or similar sources to find the names of companies that are in the process of creating what you believe to be questionable movies. Contact the director and the executive producer of the films you are protesting and make your views known. Directors can also be reached through their union, the Directors Guild of America, at <www.dga.org>.

4. Produce your own movie or video that features disabled people. Interview several film/video production companies to find a creative team that will work with your concept (and within your budget). You might premiere the film at a nearby college or on your local-access cable TV station.

Through the combined efforts of activists within and outside Hollywood, the movie image of people with disabilities will undoubtedly reflect refinements. It has been and will continue to be an uphill struggle, but as disability activists' influence over the construction of Hollywood's social imagery continues to grow and as the Americans With Disabilities Act concomitantly brings people closer together, the sense of isolation that has haunted people with disabilities in life and in the movies may well become a thing of the past.

DISCUSSION QUESTIONS

1. What could filmmakers do to make a character with a disability appear isolated from the audience and from other movie characters? Give an example from a movie you have seen.
2. Why do you think moviemakers create disabled characters? Do you agree with the reasons given by Wolfson and Norden?
3. Offer an example of each of the 10 movie character stereotypes offered in this chapter.
4. Contrast exploitative, exploratory, and incidental portrayals of PWDs.
5. Which of the suggested strategies for activists are most useful? Why? If you wanted to help improve movie images of PWDs, how would you go about it?

REFERENCES

Bannon, L. (1997, July 31). The vision thing. *Wall Street Journal*, p. A1.
Berubé, M. (1997, May 30). The cultural representation of people with disabilities affects us all. *Chronicle of Higher Education*, pp. B4-B5.
Canby, V. (1992, May 13). Heroism and humor as paraplegics learn [review of the film *The Waterdance*]. *New York Times*, p. C13.
Disney says no to disability consultants. (1995, January 16). *One Step Ahead, 2*, 4.
Fiedler, L. (1978). *Freaks: Myths and images of the secret self*. New York: Simon & Schuster.
Field, S. (1982). *Screenplay: The foundations of screenwriting* (Expanded ed). New York: Dell.

Grant, A., & Bowe, F. (1990). Watch your language! In R. Eckstein (Ed.), *Handicapped funding directory* (7th ed., pp. 6–7). Margate, FL: Research Grant Guides.

Henderson, G., & Bryan, W. (1984). *Psychosocial aspects of disability*. Springfield, IL: Charles C. Thomas.

International Leadership Forum for Women with Disabilities. (1997, June). *Final statement*. Unpublished manuscript.

Klobas, L. (1988). *Disability drama in television and film*. Jefferson, NC: McFarland.

Levitan, L. (1992, August). Faking it! *Deaf Life, 5*, 21–26.

Liachowitz, C. (1988). *Disability as a social construct: Legislative roots*. Philadelphia: University of Pennsylvania Press.

Longmore, P. (1985, Summer). Screening stereotypes: Images of disabled people. *Social Policy, 16*, 31–37.

Mast, G., & Kawin, B. (1992). *A short history of the movies* (5th ed.). New York: Macmillan.

Norden, M. (1994). *The cinema of isolation: A history of physical disability in the movies*. New Brunswick, NJ: Rutgers University Press.

O'Leary, L. (1980). *Rex Ingram: Master of the silent cinema*. New York: Harper & Row.

Quart, L., & Auster, A. (1982, Fall). The wounded vet in post-war film. *Social Policy, 13*, 24–31.

Schuchman, J. (1988). *Hollywood speaks: Deafness and the film entertainment industry*. Urbana: University of Illinois Press.

Seidenberg, R. (1990, January). To hell and back. *American Film, 15*, 28–31, 56.

Stubbins, J. (1988). The politics of disability. In H. Yuker (Ed.), *Attitudes toward persons with disabilities* (pp. 22–32). New York: Springer.

Thompson, T. (1982, Spring). "You can't play marbles—you have a wooden hand": Communication with the handicapped. *Communication Quarterly, 30*, 108–115.

Thomson, R. (1997). *Extraordinary bodies: Figuring disability in American culture and literature*. New York: Columbia University Press.

Weinberg, N. (1978, December). Modifying social stereotypes of the physically disabled. *Rehabilitation Counseling Bulletin, 22*, 114–123.

Weinberg, N., & Sebian, C. (1980). The Bible and disability. *Rehabilitation Counseling Bulletin, 23*, 273–281.

Yamamoto, K. (1971, March). To be different. *Rehabilitation Counseling Bulletin, 14*, 180–189.

FILMOGRAPHY

Norden (1994) offered production details and narrative summaries for many of the films listed here. Similar information may also be obtained online through the Internet Movie Database <us.imdb.com>. To save space, films with the same title are listed as a single entry with separate dates (e.g., *Peter Pan* [1924, 1952]).

The Anderson Tapes (1972)
The Best Years of Our Lives (1946)
The Big Parade (1925)
Blind Date (1984)
The Blind Musician (1909)
Born on the Fourth of July (1989)
Bride of Frankenstein (1935)
Calendar Girl (1993)
A Christmas Carol (1901, 1908, 1910, 1912, 1914, 1938, 1951)
City Lights (1931)

Coming Home (1978)
The Devil-Doll (1936)
Dr. Kildare's Crisis (1940)
Dr. Strangelove or: How I Learned to Stop Worrying and Love the Bomb (1964)
Edison, the Man (1940)
The Empire Strikes Back (1980)
The Enchanted Cottage (1943)
The Faithful Dog (1907)
Fire Sale (1977)
Forrest Gump (1994)
The Four Horsemen of the Apocalypse (1921)
Freaks (1932)
Heidi (1937)
The Hidden (1987)
His Daughter's Voice (1907)
The Hunchback of Notre Dame (1923, 1939, 1957, 1996)
The Hustler (1961)
Innerspace (1987)
Interrupted Melody (1955)
It's a Gift (1934)
The Jury of Fate (1917)
Kiss of Death (1947)
The Magician (1925)
The Man and the Woman (1908)
Mare Nostrum (1925)
The Miracle Man (1919)
Moby Dick (1930, 1956)
No Way Out (1987)
Mr. Magoo (1997)
On Dangerous Ground (1951)
Orphans of the Storm (1921)
The Other Side of the Mountain (1975)
The Penalty (1920)
Peter Pan (1924, 1952)
Pollyanna (1920, 1960)
Power (1986)
Pride of the Marines (1945)
The Prisoner of Zenda (1922)
Return of the Jedi (1983)
Saboteur (1942)
Scaramouche (1923)
Scent of a Woman (1992)
Scrooge (1913, 1935, 1970)
The Sea Beast (1926)
See No Evil, Hear No Evil (1989)
The Show (1927)
Star Wars (1977)

Starman (1984)
Stella Maris (1918)
Stephen King's Silver Bullet (1985)
The Stratton Story (1949)
Sunrise at Campobello (1960)
Three Days of the Condor (1975)
Till the End of Time (1946)
Trifling Women (1922)
The Waterdance (1992)
West of Zanzibar (1928)
When Billy Broke His Head . . . and Other Tales of Wonder (1994)
Where the Pavement Ends (1923)
The Wings of Eagles (1957)
Young Frankenstein (1974)

17

Invisible No More:
Advertising and People
With Disabilities

Olan Farnall
California State University-Fullerton

Keywords: Ability-integrated advertising, Media Access Office, National Easter Seals Society, EDI Awards, charity advertising, David Ogilvy, National Organization on Disability, persuasion theory, animatics, Maryland Planning Council on Development, minority advertising, advertising content analysis

In the book *Images that Injure*, Jack Nelson (1996) wrote a chapter on physical stereotypes and people with disabilities. He called the chapter, "The Invisible Cultural Group: Images of Disability." In that chapter he argued that societal attitudes toward people who are disabled were in the midst of a significant shift. Since the late 1980s, a similar shift in the advertising industry has transformed the status of people with disabilities. In advertising, people with disabilities are invisible no more.

This chapter tracks the appearance and acceptance of people with disabilities in advertising, a genre often associated only with profit-motivated objectives. It details an often overlooked example of positive portrayals of disability in advertising, outlines the major players in promoting ability-integrated advertising, and makes some observations on the outcomes to marketers, people with disabilities, and society at large.

WHY DON'T ADVERTISERS USE PEOPLE WITH DISABILITIES?

The fact that people with disabilities have not been well represented in advertising is no real surprise to any researcher in media effects. After all, numerous content analyses address the underrepresentation of minorities in the media (Greenberg & Brand, 1994). Why should the minority group defined by disability be any different from African Americans or Hispanics or women? But there are more factors at work in advertising.

One factor limiting inclusion of people with disabilities in advertising is the practice of including only physically beautiful people as representatives of the product. One could argue that what is considered beautiful by society is largely shaped by the media in general and advertising specifically. From the 1930s to the 1980s, media depictions of people with disabilities certainly would not be considered "beautiful." According to Elliott and Byrd (1982), when people with disabilities appeared in entertainment media, the roles were normally "negative images of the disabled as pitiful beggars on the street, patients displaying bizarre symptoms who are forever confined to mental institutions, and dangerous menacing villains" (p. 349).

Another reason marketers were not in any hurry to insert disability issues into their product advertising was the fear that they might be labeled exploitive, as CBS was when the 1983 fall schedule promos included images of disability (Longmore, 1985) or, even worse, alienate their current consumer. The average consumer was perceived by advertisers as not wanting to see someone with a disability trying to sell him or her toothpaste or even insurance. Advertisers may have feared that being confronted with handicapped people might make consumers uncomfortable.

All of this is not suggesting that there were no examples of advertising featuring people with disabilities prior to the passage of the Americans With Disabilities Act (ADA). But the majority of what could be called disability-integrated advertising prior to the ADA was demeaning to people with disabilities and portrayed them as being in need of help.

THE EARLY YEARS

A search of the archives of the National Museum of Advertising History at the Smithsonian Institute uncovered a limited number of examples of ability-integrated advertising. The examples that were found fit into one of two groups. The first group of ads dates back to the 1920s and is definitely the most unflattering portrayal of people with disabilities. It is characterized by line drawings of disfigured bodies just waiting for replacement limbs and raucous posters of sideshow attractions like General Tom Thumb and the Fiji Mermaid (Foster, 1967). Often these same posters exaggerated the physical differences of the celebrity, such as one poster that enlarged the head of the famous general to make his body appear even smaller than his 3-foot frame. Clearly these are not shining examples from advertising history.

The other group of ads could be labeled charity advertising. Typical of this group are the "poster child" print ads for nonprofit organizations and the heart-breaking TV spots aired during the telethons of the 1970s. In these advertising executions, the visuals usually featured a child in a wheelchair or with braces and crutches. The voice-over copy was usually dramatic and poignant. In its boldest form, the copy portrayed a person whose life needed to be changed and who was condemned to a pitiful existence without contributions from viewers.

Fortunately, the trend in some charity advertising has recently shifted away from that approach to a more positive theme. For example, in 1995 the National Easter Seals event moved away from the old-style "telethon" to a 20-hour event featuring more entertainment and theme segments on acceptance of children and family members with disabilities (Brady, 1995). In 1998 the marathon event was dropped completely by the group.

THE MAN IN THE HATHAWAY SHIRT

There is one notable exception to the two classes of ability-integrated advertising mentioned previously. It is probably the most interesting example of pre-1980 advertising featuring a model portraying a disability and it is one of the most often cited works by one of advertising's most important figures. It is the original campaign for Hathaway shirts created by David Ogilvy, founder of Ogilvy and Mather. Ogilvy came up with the idea of using a model with an eyepatch over one eye to give the advertising execution "story appeal." This concept of story appeal in advertising was one of the reasons Ogilvy was credited with being one of a trio who sparked the creative revolution in advertising during the 1960s.

In a taped interview for the American Association of Advertising Agencies (Caravatt, 1977), Ogilvy discussed the idea behind the creation of the eye-patch wearing, distinguished gentleman who became known as the "man in the Hathaway shirt":

> They (the Hathaway company) came to us after not advertising for 106 years and they asked if we would take on the account. . . . Well I had been reading

a book titled "Attitude and Interest Factors in Advertising" by Hal Rudolph and in this book Rudolph said pictures had a certain story appeal and the more story appeal a photo had, the more people would look at your ad. So, I started writing down ideas about how to get story appeal and I wrote 18 and the man wearing the eyepatch was the eighteenth. And that idea lasted 19 years.

Nowhere in his discussion was the concept of disability even mentioned. The model who played the role was not disabled. In fact, in his description of the "man in the Hathaway shirt" Ogilvy used only positive adjectives.

So what did the eyepatch do for Hathaway? According to Bruce Bendinger, author of *The Copy Workshop Workbook* (1993), the man with the eyepatch, "added interest and readership, distinctiveness and memorability" (p. 34). It sold the product.

Two interesting observations can be drawn from this example. The first is that no one—not Ogilvy, not the public, and not the authors who have written about this historic ad campaign—seemed to address the eyepatch as representing a disability. One could argue that wearing an eyepatch does not have the same visual impact as crutches, a wheelchair, or even someone using sign language when representing a disabling condition and therefore might not cause the angst in the viewer that, say, a quadriplegic might cause. This author would argue that the more important issue is how the character was portrayed. The entire mystique of the character was built on admiration and a desire to be just like "the man in the Hathaway shirt." The second observation is that other creatives in advertising in the 1960s did not copy Ogilvy's idea. In advertising one of the best ways to know an idea is good is to see how quickly it is copied. Although this experiment with portrayals of disability was a tremendous success for Ogilvy and the Hathaway shirt company, it was not until the mid-1980s that marketers began to experiment in earnest with advertising executions that included roles for people with disabilities.

1980s MARK THE DEVELOPMENT OF ABILITY-INTEGRATED ADVERTISING

There is some disagreement among experts about which national company was the first to recognize the potential of including people with disabilities in its overall promotional efforts. A curator from the Center for Advertising History at the National Museum of American History said discount retailer Target Stores claims credit for being the first major marketer to insert people with disabilities in its print ads. According to Longmore (1985), the first television execution including disability was the CBS spot featuring the paraplegic wheelchair racer.

No matter who led the charge, the number of print ads and television commercials with disabled roles increased to the point of being noticed in the mid- to late 1980s. By 1985, major manufacturers like Levi's Jeans, McDonalds, Kodak, and Plymouth were including representations of people with disabilities in their advertising campaigns. This previously "invisible minority" was being portrayed in a big way. Marketers were beginning to recognize and address a market estimated in 1985 to be some 43 million strong. The use of actors and actresses with disabilities in the ads also suggested that society might be ready to start to look at people with disabilities as individuals able to lead normal lives and as promoters and consumers of products (Longmore, 1985).

DISABILITY ACTIVISTS/GROUPS SUPPORT ABILITY-INTEGRATED EFFORT

The emergence of ability-integrated advertising was a positive step toward gaining respect for the disability community. But, without promotion and public recognition of the effort by major supporters in the community, the experiment might have come and gone without much fanfare. Two primary players in this support role were the National Easter Seals Society (NESS) and the Media Access Office in New York.

The establishment and success of the NESS Equality, Dignity, and Independence (EDI) Awards has given ability-integrated advertising recognition and respectability. Since 1989, NESS has recognized and encouraged realistic portrayals of people with disabilities by presenting EDI Awards to members of the media, entertainment, and advertising industry. In the advertising category, both print and broadcast executions are judged, with the best receiving recognition at the annual awards banquet.

This award has grown in size and stature. Advertising award winners from the 1996 and 1997 competition include familiar names such as Kellogg, Coca-Cola, Air-Touch Cellular, and Mattel. The number of companies entering the competition has also increased. In 1989 only five entries were received in the advertising category. By 1992, the number of entries had increased by 300%.

Besides the increase in EDI entries, there has also been an increase in the activity of groups like the Media Access Office in Los Angeles and the Non-Traditional Casting Office in New York. In addition to promoting ability-integrated advertising, these groups work with writers, producers, and directors to advocate the use of actors and actresses with disabilities in disabled roles and promote a more positive portrayal of people with disabilities in the entertainment industry (Nelson, 1996).

Although some in the disability community might be content to simply appreciate these positive signs, others continue to search for reasons to explain the increased awareness and attention people with disabilities experienced from marketers in the late 1980s and 1990s. Probably the most logical was that media attention focused on people with disabilities as a result of the push for passage of the ADA. News stories about the ADA, complete with estimates of the size of the potential market, forced companies to look at people with disabilities as a meaningful target group. For almost 20 years advertisers have been looking for narrowly defined target markets, identifiable by some common thread (O'Guinn, Allen, & Semenik, 1998). Information about this undiscovered minority began to circulate in the press. The value of a new group of 43 million people was obvious and fit well into the relationship marketing strategies of the day.

A different theory of success can be derived from the results of a national survey conducted by Louis Harris and Associates and sponsored by the National Organization on Disability in 1991. This survey indicated that nondisabled people held more favorable attitudes toward people with disabilities than in previous years. The data from the survey also indicated that people were seeing more positive images of people with disabilities as a result of the popularity of a number of movies and television programs featuring disabled roles. Byrd (1989) suggested a number of theories relative to the issue of disability portrayal in media that support the connection between positive portrayal of a person with a disability in the media and attitude change. These include expectancy theory, Heider's balance theory and his later attribution theory, Festinger's theory of cognitive dissonance, and an entire body of motivation and persuasive communication theory. Although most of the theories Byrd put forth can play a part in explaining attitude change, the most promising with regard to advertising portrayals are those based in the Yale communication research of the late 1950s that looked at source, message, and audience factors as impacting opinion change.

A less likely theory for the discovery of people with disabilities by marketers is that the creative revolution of the 1990s, combined with the politically correct pressure in business, might have caused advertisers to look at many minority groups in a more socially conscious light. It may be a bit naive to expect advertisers to put social issues before economic potential, but there are examples that infer advertisers are more conscious of the importance of culture today. Consider the reformulation of Betty Crocker as an example. No longer the Anglo-American housewife, Betty Crocker 1996 is a mixture of more than 30 cultural backgrounds (Sivulka, 1997). Suppositions aside, advertisers, brand managers, or even media assistants would be foolish to overlook a market that in 1998 is estimated to be 51.6 million in number and possess $796 billion a year in buying power (Praeger, 1997).

ADVERTISING INTEGRATION AND ITS EFFECTS

In 1964, many advertisers were afraid to integrate African Americans into their product advertising because of possible consumer backlash. At that time a number of different studies demonstrated that White consumers did not show significantly negative reactions to these integrated advertisements except in cases of highly prejudiced individuals (Barban & Cundiff, 1964). In fact, when Black actors were included in ads, Black consumers were better able to recall ad content and showed more positive affect toward the product (Bush, Hair, & Solomon, 1979; Cagley & Cordoza, 1970).

Research on television advertising containing portrayals of actors with disabilities similarly indicates that audiences do not show significant negative reactions to disability-integrated advertising. In fact, if done correctly, there are some indications that attitudes toward the advertising and brand may improve. For example, Farnall (1996) had college undergraduates participate in an investigation on positive stereotypes and attitudes disguised as an evaluation of television commercials. Participants were asked to evaluate three television commercials for national brand products presented in rough, animatic form. The use of still photos, or animatics, allowed for the manipulation of the ad with regard to inclusion of character(s) with disabilities. After exposure, each respondent was asked to indicate on a Likert scale "attitude to the ad, attitude to the brand, and purchase intention" measures for the three different products—an athletic shoe, a bar of soap, and a national discount store.

Results showed no negative effects for any of the products on the three dependent measures as a result of including images of people with disabilities in the ads. In fact, the versions of the soap ad and the athletic shoe spot that included images of people with disabilities received significantly higher scores on at least one of the three dependent measures. In the case of the shoe company, the animatic with the character with a disability received ratings a full point higher on an 11-point scale than the animatic without the disabled character.

The results of this study become even more important to advertisers when one looks at the different creative strategies used by the three hypothetical advertisers. In the two ads that did show significant positive shifts after exposure (athletic shoe and soap), the character with a disabilitiy was the primary figure in the ad instead of an incidental person on the sidelines. Further, these two ads made a point of showing the characters with disabilities succeeding in whatever activities they were attempting. The third ad (the discount store) failed to project a positive image of the person with a disability, who was a woman shopper in a wheelchair, receiving help with her shopping. Specifically, the commercial depicts the woman being handed a box by an employee of the store. Although this may seem very minor on the surface, it actually reinforces the attitude that disability causes helplessness, and stereotypes the character as "one who needs to be cared for, or the burden" (Nelson, 1996, p. 122).

ABILITY-INTEGRATION PITFALLS

It is not surprising that TV commercials such as the discount store ad just described do not always succeed in the area of positive portrayals of persons with disabilities. Even with the best of intentions, it is easy to fall into one of the negative stereotypical portrayals of people with disabilities such as those mentioned by Nelson (1996). When writers, producers, and directors include characters with disabilities just to make sure that the group is represented, there is a greater chance the ad will actually alienate consumers with disabilities instead of embracing them.

In the relatively short history of disability-integrated advertising the faux pas most often cited is the use of nondisabled actors to play disabled roles. Many have been guilty of that error, but no case better illustrates how easily it can happen than the Maryland Planning Council on Developmental Disabilities campaign. In 1988 a Baltimore agency produced a set of 30- and 60-second TV spots for the council featuring a nondisabled actor portraying a man in a wheelchair (Erickson, 1988). The agency said a last-minute rewrite at the request of the council changed the script from one in which the actor got up from the wheelchair to one in which the actor did not reveal his ability to walk. The casting had already been done. The spots brought an avalanche of letters to professional publications and the council from activist groups and individuals who were aware of the production.

The agency had done three previous pro bono campaigns for the council and all of them used people with disabilities for disabled roles. The agency even won a Clio in 1986 for their portrayal of a mentally retarded man. Being conscious of these disability issues is difficult, but advertisers must make the effort.

Another unfortunate trend that holds back the progress of people with disabilities is the failure on the part of marketers and others to include representatives from the disability community when discussions center around minority groups or cultural diversity. *Advertising Age* was chastised when its special 1997 report on diversity did not mention people with disabilities. Jay Chiat, president of Chiat Day advertising, was praised by many for his promotion of a super-fund aimed at recruiting and training minority talent for advertising and marketing. But, as Sandra Gordon, then senior VP of corporate communication for NESS pointed out, his plan did not specifically mention people with disabilities as part of that minority ("Where Sponsorship Lives," 1994).

Academics in the world of advertising have not done much better in their efforts. An investigation of five accepted "principles of advertising" texts failed to discover any coverage of disability advertising, with only a few texts even mentioning people with disabilities as a recognized minority. A new book on advertising and culture completely ignores the subject of integrated disability advertising and does not even mention people with disabilities in its discussion of minority markets, although it did include the gay and lesbian market (Sivulka, 1998).

WHAT LIES AHEAD

At this point sufficient evidence has been presented to conclude that, at least within advertising, people with disabilities are not the invisible minority described by Nelson (1996). Although the percentage of realistic portrayals does not begin to approach a number equivalent to the percentage of people with disabilities in the population, there are still notable realistic and positive examples in advertising. From Nike's use of Olympic wheelchair racer Chris Blanchette to blind actor Rick Boggs as spokesperson for Air-Touch Cellular, the disabled community is beginning to make progress. An increasing number of major companies acknowledge people with disabilities as potential consumers instead of some special segment of the population with special needs. Discounters like K-Mart and Target regularly acknowledge people with disabilities in their catalogs by showing them as shoppers. Fab laundry detergent lets us know that a person in a wheelchair does do laundry. Whiska's cat food lets us know that deaf actress Marlee Matlin loves her cat.

It is hoped advances in portrayal and participation will continue into the millennium, thanks to forces like the Media Access Office, NESS, and the many other coalitions that continue working to ensure that images of the disabled in the media reflect realistic portrayals and not stereotypical roles. The success of media targeted specifically for the disability community, such as *We* magazine and Kaleidoscope Television also can be viewed as positive signs. *We* is a lifestyle magazine for Americans with disabilities and Kaleidoscope Television is a home shopping channel targeted toward people with disabilities. It is received in 15 million households, providing 24-hour-a-day programming.

But one must remember that these positive signs do not mean the battle is won. There is some value in looking at the progress of other minorities in the media. For example, consider the success of African Americans in the past 30 years and the lack of success of Hispanics during that same period. African American roles on television have increased and improved in regard to portraying positive lifestyles during the past 20 years, while portrayals of Hispanics have actually gone down by 1% (Greenberg & Brand, 1994). What are the components that made the difference? What must the minority identified as "the disabled" do to ensure acceptance in society and realistic treatment in the media?

These are broad questions, and certainly encompass much more than just the genre of advertising, but there are applications in advertising that may help answer the overall question. The first component missing in the area of advertising is a major content analysis of disability portrayal in print and television advertising. This content analysis must be more than just an exercise in "bean counting." To be really insightful it is important to know not just how much, but how well people with disabilities are being portrayed. Message content and impact are critical variables that must be examined in addition to mere exposure. Any significant content analysis undertaken to record ability-integrated advertising must be designed to be sensitive to the implications of the representation such as the negative portrayal from the discount store described earlier.

Even more helpful and rarer are field and experimental studies that address the impact of these portrayals. The research included in the present chapter is extremely limited. How much better would it be if communication scholars could describe to advertisers the precise impact of including characters with disabilities in their advertising on product sales among the disabled community? And what about the impact on societal attitudes? How might advertising support a move toward total acceptance of people with disabilities?

While it is easy to point out the areas of research that are missing, doing something to fill the holes is much more difficult. Cooperation from business is paramount here, since the kind of sales information really needed is usually kept proprietary and the cost of gathering the stimulus materials necessary to test different executions of the same strategy are quite expensive. Perhaps the business community could be convinced that an important outcome for them as a result of this kind of cooperation would be demonstrated success on how advertising featuring disabled people should be presented to show the product and the company in the most positive light. If the economic opportunity is there, companies are likely to listen.

Finally, it would be prudent to redouble the efforts of disability rights activists. It is through the continued efforts of these activist groups that much of the advertising trade is made aware of the potential and pitfalls of ability-integrated advertising. The struggle for appropriateness of portrayal is a battle minorities have been fighting for decades. Those who advance in that fight are persistent and make sure they are heard. Those who wonder why are left behind.

DISCUSSION QUESTIONS

1. Why do you think the "man in the Hathaway shirt" was not recognized as being disabled? Would the reception of the ad be different in today's disability sensitive culture?
2. Examples were given of early 1990 movies, television programs, and even commercials that featured ability-integrated characters. Discuss whether you think that trend is continuing or declining. Provide examples to support your contention.
3. Is *ability-integrated* advertising an appropriate term? Why or why not?
4. Do you think the type of disability plays an important part in the advertiser's decision to use ability-integrated creative strategies? Explain.

REFERENCES

Barban, A. M., & Cundiff, E. W. (1964). Negro and white response to advertising stimuli. *Journal of Marketing Research, 1*, 53–56.

Bendinger, B. (1993). *The copy workshop workbook* (2nd ed.). Chicago: Copy Workshop.

Bush, R. F., Hair, J., Jr., & Solomon, P. (1979). Consumers' level of prejudice and response to black models in advertisements. *Journal of Marketing Research, 16*, 341–345.

Brady, J. (1995, February 20). Brady's bunch. *Advertising Age*, 28.

Byrd, K. (1989). Theory regarding attitudes and how they may relate to media portrayals of disability. *Journal of Applied Rehabilitation Counseling, 20*, 36–38.

Cagley, J. W., & Cordoza, R. N. (1970). White response to integrated advertising. *Journal of Advertising Research, 10*, 35–39.

Caravatt, J. (Producer, Director). (1977). *A conversation about advertising with David Ogilvy* [Film]. New York: American Advertising Federation.

Elliott, T., & Byrd, E. K. (1982). Media and disability. *Rehabilitation Literature, 43*, 348–355.

Erickson, J. L. (1988, April 25). Disabling move: Spots fail to use handicapped actor. *Advertising Age*, 36.

Farnall, O. F. (1996). Positive images of the disabled in television advertising: Effects on marketing measures. In G. B. Wilcox (Ed.), *Proceedings of the 1996 conference of the American Academy of Advertising* (pp. 123–130). Austin University of Texas Press.

Foster, G. A. (1967). *Advertising: Ancient market place to television.* New York: Criterion.

Greenberg, B. S., & Brand, J. E. (1994). Minorities and the mass media: 1970s to 1990s. In J. Bryant & D. Zillmann (Eds.), *Media effects: Advances in theory and research* (pp. 273–314). Hillsdale, NJ: Lawrence Erlbaum Associates.

Longmore, P. K. (1985). Screening stereotypes: Images of disabled people. *Social Policy, 16*, 31–37.

National Organization on Disability. (1991). *Public attitudes toward persons with disabilities* (Research Rep. No. 912028). New York: Louis Harris and Associates, Inc.

Nelson, J. (1996). The invisible cultural group: Images of disability. In P. M. Lester (Ed.), *Images that injure: Pictorial stereotypes in the media* (pp. 119–125). Westport, CT: Praeger.

O'Guinn, T. C., Allen, C. T., & Semenik, R. J. (1998). *Advertising.* Cincinnati: SouthWestern College Publishing.

Praeger, J. H. (1997, October 17). Advertising: Disability can enable a modeling career. *Advertising Age*, 1.

Sivulka, J. (1997). *Soap, sex, and cigarettes: A cultural history of American advertising.* Belmont, CA: Wadsworth.

Where sponsorship lives. (1994, June 13). *Advertising Age*, 32.

18

The Uses and Abuses of Computer-Mediated Communication for People With Disabilities

Susan Anne Fox
Western Michigan University

Keywords: Computer-mediated communication, impersonal communication, hyperpersonal communication, computer-based self-help/mutual aid groups

In 1986 it was estimated that in the United States there were 1.7 million "homebound" people with disabilities and eight times that number who were temporarily disabled (Zastrow, 1986). Fifty years ago this could have meant social and personal isolation for these people who had limited physical means to interact with others, especially others with disabilities. Today, assistive technologies are radically changing the lives of people with disabilities (Joslyn-Scherer, 1993), and inexpensive computer technologies have dramatically expanded the economic and social opportunities of people with disabilities (Hood, 1996). The World Wide Web (WWW), the newest addition to the Information Age, also called the Information Superhighway, and computer-mediated communication (CMC), a segment of that highway, are greatly increasing the access of people with disabilities to information and interaction. Given the exponential growth and use of the WWW and CMC, it is important to examine this medium of communication and its impact on people with disabilities. In this chapter, I seek to accomplish four goals. First, I give an overview of the various types of resources presently available to and about people with disabilities on the WWW. Second, I broadly review the area of CMC, the theories used to explain online relationships, and how CMC specifically relates to people with disabilities, arguing that CMC has advantages over face-to-face communication for people with disabilities. Third, I discuss the use of computer-based self-help/mutual aid (CSHMA) groups by people with disabilities and integrate social support literature as it relates to CMC. Finally, I investigate and question the strengths and weaknesses of CSHMA groups as a credible avenue of social support for people with disabilities.

WWW RESOURCES FOR PEOPLE WITH DISABILITIES

The WWW includes a tremendous number of resources for and about people with disabilities. Although some researchers have questioned the possible inability of some groups to access the Information Superhighway, there is reason to hope that disadvantaged groups will have equal political, economic, and social access to the WWW and to CMC (Pingree et al., 1996). Because a thorough review of the WWW resources available to people with disabilities would be voluminous, I discuss only a sampling of these resources, including the following topics: (a) how to understand and utilize the Americans With Disabilities Act (ADA); (b) access to medical libraries and experimental protocols for people with disabilities; (c) assistive software and hardware specifically designed for people with disabilities; (d) employment opportunities for people with disabilities; (e) guidelines for creating accessible WWW pages; and (f) electronic bulletin boards, newsgroups, and listservs that provide participants increased CMC.

Much of the information on the WWW is related to the passage of the ADA. This act has been met with both praise and criticism. The statute is "long and complex and . . . is likely to be the subject of substantial litigation" (Parry, 1990, p. 292). Because of this, many on-line resources seek to demystify some of the issues surrounding the ADA. The ADA Document Center (http://janweb.icdi.wvu.edu/kinder/) includes the Americans with Disabilities Act statute as well as answers to commonly asked questions related to the statute. Moreover, it includes step-by-step instructions people must follow to file an ADA complaint. It also serves as a resource for small businesses, identifying the steps they must take to comply with the ADA and guidelines for working effectively with people with disabilities. People with disabilities and businesses that must conform to the requirements set forth by the ADA save time and money because these ADA resources give them access to information not readily available in print form. The convenience of this information on the WWW also has had an impact on disability legislation in other countries.

A second resource for people with disabilities and researchers is the National Center for the Dissemination of Disability Research (NCDDR; http://www.ncddr.org). The site lists general information related to disability research as well as specific research results. For example, the site recently reviewed results of the most important issues faced by women with disabilities (e.g., caretaker abuse and domestic violence). This site also includes calls for proposals for grants, such as research training grants designed to advance rehabilitation training. The *Research Exchange Quarterly*, a periodical of NCDDR information, is also available online. People with and without disabilities can receive empowerment from these types of resources as they gain access to information about research.

The WWW also gives people with disabilities resources to increase their independence and lessen their reliance on professional agencies for assistance. "Solutions" is a WWW resource that links people with disabilities to "resources, products, and services that promote active, healthy independent living" (http://disability.org). These can include mobility products, aids for daily living, and accessible travel accommodations. It also has a consumer advocacy component that includes reviews by people with disabilities of products and services. This is important given the difficulty consumers face determining the viability and credibility of some WWW sites and the products sold online.

More than just products and services, the National Institute on Life Planning for Persons with Disabilities (NILP; http://www.sonic.net/nilp/) serves as a clearinghouse of information for professionals (e.g., advocates, social workers, teachers, guardians, and lawyers) on aspects of life planning such as guardianship, schools, supported employment, and housing. For example, this site has advice on how to prevent children with disabilities from being abused and what to do about abuse if it does happen. Related to the job aspects with which the NILP can assist, the Job Accommodation Network (http://janweb.icdi.wvu.edu) is also a highly structured resource that provides information about the ADA, job accommodations, and employability for people with disabilities.

Those who develop WWW pages should be aware that a diverse group of people will visit their web pages, including people with disabilities. The

Universal Design for Accessible Web Pages (http://www.inform.umd.edu/ EdRes/Topic/Disability/InternetRes/UniDsgn/) is a useful resource for people attempting to be sensitive to the needs of people with disabilities. This and related pages give guidelines on how to make web pages accessible, taking into account such things as issues related to graphics that cannot be viewed by people with visual impairments or audio files that cannot be heard by people with hearing impairments. These are especially important for WWW pages designed for access by people with disabilities.

Clearly, no single book chapter can include all of the important information relevant to people with disabilities housed on the WWW. Furthermore, this information is constantly expanding and changing. Table 18.1 contains a list of resources, including the sites discussed above as well as directories of disability-related WWW pages. Technologies such as the WWW and the Internet have allowed people with disabilities to create cyber-communities that are spread across the globe and are not restricted by spatial and temporal boundaries and have helped people without disabilities become more informed about disabilities (Mitra, 1997).

The immense body of information the WWW perpetuates is ever changing and growing, giving people with disabilities an avenue from which to retrieve information and interact with others with disabilities. Given that some people with disabilities lack the physical means to interact face-to-face with other people, especially other people who have disabilities, the WWW and CMC allows increased access to information and contact with others through chat rooms and newsgroups that focus on issues related to disabilities. I now turn to these more interpersonal aspects of computer use by people with disabilities.

THE RELATIONSHIP BETWEEN CMC AND PEOPLE WITH DISABILITIES

CMC is especially relevant to people with disabilities because of the social and attitudinal barriers that often are present in interability contexts (see Braithwaite, Waldron, & Finn, 1999; Fox & Giles, 1996) and physical barriers that can restrict communication. The numerous listservs, electronic bulletin boards, and newsgroups allow people with disabilities communicative access to other people with whom they would otherwise have little chance to interact. Having access to a whole world of online users rather than just those in a physically immediate community makes access especially

TABLE 18.1
List of WWW Pages and Addresses Related to Disability Issues

disABILITY Information and Resources—a directory of resources including chat rooms, events, databases, and politics	http://www.eskimo.com/ ~jlubin/disabled.html
Disability Links - Non-Profit Organizations—a directory of non-profit agency home pages dealing with aids to daily living, assistive technology, children/parenting	http://disability.org
Disability Rights Activist information needed to enable anyone interested in the rights of disabled people to work for those rights	Http://www.Disrights.Org/
Discrimination and Abuse of Persons with Disabilities Abuse Personal—resources for the prevention of abuse to people with disabilities	http://www.quasar. ualberta.ca/ddc/ICAD/ icad.html
Job Accommodation Network—a consulting service that provides information about job accommodations (ADA) and the employability of people with disabilities	http://janweb.icdi.wvu.edu/
National Center for the Dissemination of Disability Research— general information on disability research, the results of research carried out by grantees, and links to related information	http://www.ncddr.org/
National Institute On Life Planning For Persons With Disabilities—legal, medical, and educational issues	http://www.sonic.net/nilp/
U.S. Department of Justice Americans with Disabilities Act ADA home page	http://www.usdoj.gov/crt/ ada/adahom1.htm
Universal Design for Accessible Web Pages—information related to how to design web pages accessible to people with disabilities	http://www.inform.umd. edu/EdRes/Topic/ Disability/InternetRes/ UniDsgn/
WebAble—the authoritative web directory for disability-related Internet resources	http://www.webable.com
World Association of Persons with Disabilities	http://www.wapd.org

Note. Given the changes and expansion of the WWW, these resources may no longer be available. Using the key words "disability" and "Americans with Disabilities Act" will get you started.

important for people with less common disabilities. To fully understand the role that CMC fulfills for people with disabilities it is important to build on historical and theoretical perspectives related to computer communication.

CMC was originally thought to be an impersonal communication medium (see Walther, 1996) lacking the richness of face-to-face communication. Others argue that the inaccessibility of nonverbal cues makes CMC less personal and socioemotional than face-to-face communication (Hiltz, Johnson, & Turloff, 1986). Social presence theory (Kiesler, Siegel,

& McGuire, 1984) describes CMC as having very low social presence because of its lowered capacity to communicate information about people's appearance, the environment, and vocalic and nonverbal dynamics of face-to-face interactions. Sproull and Kiesler (1986), using a "social context cues" approach, explain that because of the lack of dynamic nonverbal behaviors (e.g., gestures, vocal cues, personal appearance) and status cues normally available in the physical environment, CMC produces more uninhibited and negative communication, increased self-absorption, and status reduction. An outcome of this decrease in social context cues is more equalized participation (Dubrosky, Kielser, & Sethna, 1991; Kiesler et al., 1984) between communicators. Media richness theory also describes CMC as lower in richness given the absence of nonverbal cues present in face-to-face channels (Trevino, Lengel, & Daft, 1987). These three theories are collectively known as the "cues-filtered out" perspective (Culnan & Markus, 1987; Walther & Burgoon, 1992) given the inability of CMC to transmit the types of nonverbal cues available in face-to-face communication.

Walther (1992, 1993) contended that the cues-filtered out perspective is only appropriate for describing initial CMC interaction among strangers, and his social information processing perspective predicts normal, but slower, interpersonal development for CMC. Essentially, Walther (1996) believes that given sufficient time, CMC interactions can go beyond impersonal to interpersonal relationships that parallel face-to-face relationships. This occurs in part because interactants will substitute or find other textual forms of communication to convey nonverbal information (Jackson, 1996). These can include the use of pictographs such as smiley faces :) (see Thompson, 1982; Thompsen & Foulger, 1996), spelling out of vocalics (hmmm, uhh, ugh, hahaha), or capitalization of words that can denote INTENSITY. In this way, text-based forms are used to compensate for losses in nonverbal richness.

From this social information-processing perspective comes the notion there may be some instances in which greater affection and emotion occurs in CMC interactions than in face-to-face interactions. When CMC becomes more socially desirable than face-to-face communication, Walther (1996) asserted that communication moves from an interpersonal level to a "hyperpersonal" one. This highly intimate on-line communication may take longer to develop than face-to-face communication, but the intimacy people feel on-line can surpass that which occurs face-to-face (Chidambaram, 1996). Likewise, Spears and Lea (1994), using social identity individuation theory, claimed that with insufficient information, people will develop stereotypic overly positive or negative impressions of others. In the case of CMC, computer users may create exaggerated positive impressions of others, which can lead to hyperpersonal communication (Walther, 1996). Adding to this effect is the senders' ability to plan and edit messages, allowing senders to create and manipulate idealized online images. Matheson and Zanna (1990) stated that people in CMC contexts have greater levels of "private self-awareness," including greater awareness of personal feelings, attitudes, values, and beliefs than people experience in face-to-face interactions, thereby increasing the potential for positive outcomes in CMC. In this way, the ability to show a positive face, combined with the increase in positive attributions by others, may make computer-mediated interactions seem more positive than face-to-face interactions.

These perspectives are critical to understanding the importance of CMC for people with disabilities. People with disabilities are often at a disadvantage in face-to-face interability interactions. Although research shows that there are some positive consequences of being stigmatized (Herman & Maill, 1990), research on interability communication is replete with research showing the disadvantages of having a disability in face-to-face interactions (see Coleman & DePaulo, 1991, for an extensive review). For example, interability interactions are normally shorter and terminated abruptly without common leave-taking behaviors (Comer & Piliavin, 1972; Mills, Belgrave, & Boyer, 1984; Thompson, 1982). There is also increased distance (Kleck, 1969; Kleck et al., 1968) and less smiling (Comer & Piliavin, 1972) between interability interactants. Furthermore, there is less eye contact (Kleck et al., 1968), although more staring by the person without disabilities if the person with disabilities is unaware (Houston & Bull, 1994; Sigelman et al., 1986). Banks (1988) asserted that for those people who find face-to-face communication troublesome, CMC can be empowering. Because nonverbal communication often is either not possible or distorted in face-to-face interability communication, online nonverbal markers (e.g., ;)) are equally available for use by people with and without disabilities. Therefore, what may be nonverbally limiting for people without disabilities may actually be more liberating for people with disabilities. Whereas face-to-face interability communication is often unequal, CMC offers a more equal playing field for people with disabilities.

Other nonverbal interpersonal boundaries that people with disabilities confront in face-to-face interactions are reduced in CMC. Many people with disabilities in face-to-face interactions have physical attributes that can make others feel uncomfortable and make interactions awkward and strained (e.g., Stovall & Sedelack, 1983). Physical cues (e.g., a wheelchair) may distinguish ingroup and outgroup members (Mitra, 1997), causing interability interactions to become intergroup, as opposed to interpersonal, in nature (see Fox & Giles, 1996). People with disabilities report being treated as though they are "damaged goods" because of their disability (Goffman, 1963; Phillips, 1990), decreasing their feelings of being treated as a "person first" (Braithwaite, 1991). CMC technologies reduce the social barriers to communication, causing an equalization effect (Dubrovsky et al., 1991; Seigel et al., 1986; Sproull & Keisler, 1986). This equalization is especially relevant for people with disabilities because of the negative attitudes held and lower social standing assigned to them by people without disabilities (see Makas, 1988, for a review of attitudes toward people with disabilities). Because E-mail messages have a very limited amount of information provided nonvoluntarily (e.g., job title, race, and appearance), there are fewer distinguishing social context cues (e.g., wheelchair) and therefore more homogeneity of users and a greater potential for people with disabilities to experience equality with online users without disabilities. Zuboff (1988) quoted a respondent who aptly exemplifies this equalization effect in CMC: "If you are a hunchback, a paraplegic, a woman, black, fat, old, have two hundred warts on your face, or never take a bath, you still have the same chance" (p. 370).

Behavioral expectations that exist in face-to-face situations are also diminished in a computer-mediated context. For example, research shows that persons with disabilities feel that they have to be cheerful to reduce the discomfort of others (Elliot & Frank, 1990; Wright, 1983), but this expectation is removed in online communication. Furthermore, given the ability to plan and edit communication, people with disabilities also have a greater chance of creating or manipulating impressions others have about them so that such impressions are not tainted by a physical disability. People with disabilities may therefore have feelings of liberation because of the comfort they feel expressing their unsuppressed authentic self (Spears & Lea, 1994).

Walther's (1996) hyperpersonal perspective is especially relevant for people with disabilities because of the social stigmas related to having a disability. The decrease in social context cues, along with the anonymity of the CMC medium, can deregulate communication and increase people's participation by reducing inhibition, evaluation anxiety, and feelings of accountability (Dubrovsky et al., 1991; Spears & Lea, 1994). Moreover, because the depersonalizing effects of CMC are limited to initial interactions, and differences between CMC and face-to-face interactions all but disappear with time, many of the difficulties people with disabilities have in face-to-face interactions can be avoided through online communication. Consequently, the combination of asynchronous communication and anonymity brought by the medium may actually increase more positive and open relational communication (Walther & Burgoon, 1992; Matheson & Zanna, 1988). In this way, people with disabilities may prefer on-line communication to face-to-face communication, supporting Walther's hyperpersonal perspective.

In summary, advantages exist for people with disabilities within the context of CMC that do not exist in face-to-face communication. In many ways, CMC assists people with and without disabilities to overcome many of the barriers present in face-to-face interability situations. Organized CMC groups that service different types of disabilities (e.g., people with cerebral palsy, multiple sclerosis, polio, blindness) and discuss disability-related issues (disability services, rehabilitation, ADA law), including listservs, online bulletin boards, and newsgroups are more formal ways that people can interact with others. This type of interaction may yield a sense of community and support—a "Virtual Community" (Nelson, 1995). These online groups have the ability to become online social support networks for people with disabilities, possibly increasing the life satisfaction of those who participate.

USE OF CSHMA GROUPS BY PEOPLE WITH DISABILITIES

Researchers and practitioners have long supported people's involvement in self-help groups for help during life changes and to overcome social and physical adversity (see, for reviews, Green, 1993; Roberts, 1988). Research on the benefits of self-help groups for people with disabilities has been ongoing since the 1970s (e.g., Gussow & Tracy, 1976) and finds that people with disabilities are at an elevated risk for depressive symptoms that can be lessened by social support (Turner & Noh, 1988). Listservs, electronic bulletin boards, and newsgroups are all organized avenues that people with disabilities use to interact with other people who share similar concerns and issues related to their disability. There are more than 50 listservs specifically focused on issues related to people with physical disabilities (Table 18.2 gives a directory of many of these listservs as well

TABLE 18.2
Directory of Listservs and Subscription Addresses Related to Disability Issues

ADA related legislation (ADA law)	listserv@vm1.nodak.edu
AMPUTEE list for information exchange (amputee)	listserv@sjuvm.stjohns.edu
Assistive technology For PWD, including children (Crt-Focus)	crt-focus@list.gatech.edu
Cerebral palsy list (C-Palsy)	listserv@sjuvm.stjohns.edu
Coalition Advocating For Disability Reform In Education (CADRE)	listserv@sjuvm.stjohns.edu
Digest of several on-line resources (L-Hcap)	listserv@vm1.nodak.edu
Disability support of families list (Dis-Sprt)	listserv@sjuvm.stjohns.edu
Discuss adaptive technology issues (Adapt-L)	listserv@auvm
Discussion group for technology for the handicapped (L-Hcap)	l-hcap@ndsuvm1
Discussion list of computers & information technology (Techsym-L)	listserv@listservr.isc.rit.edu
Discussion of disabilities and employment (Able-Job)	listserv@sjuvm.stjohns.edu
Discussion on Americans with disabilities (AWD)	majordomo@counterpoint.com
Fathers of children with disabilities (Dadvocat)	listserv@ukcc.uky.edu
Information—children's amputee network (I-Can)	maiser@hoffman.mgen.pitt.edu
Information & Technology for the Disabled complete journal (Itd-Jnl)	listserv@sjuvm.stjohns.edu
Information about muscular dystrophy (Md-List)	md-list-request@data.basix.com
International Coalition On Abuse & Disability (Icad-L)	listserv@ualtavm.bitnet
International Committee on Accessible Document Design (Icadd)	listserv@asuvm.inre.asu.edu
Mobility disabilities list (Mobility)	listserv@sjuvm.stjohns.edu
Multiple sclerosis (Mslist-L)	listserv@technion.bitnet
Research & disability (Disres-L)	listserv@ryevm.ryerson.edu
Services to students with disabilities in higher education (DST-L)	listserv@ubvm
Travel For the disabled (Travable)	listserv@sjuvm.stjohns.edu

as their subscription address), and hundreds more exist for sensory, cognitive, and learning disabilities. An example of one online support group's description is as follows:

> The AMPUTEE list exists for the purpose of information exchange. Whether you are an amputee, relative, friend, family member, teacher, PE instructor, Doctor, prosthetist or are a lonely soul looking for companionship this listserv is for you. (http://www.inform.umd. edu:8080/ EdRes/Topic/Disability/ InternetRes/Listserv/amputee-issues, 1996).

The objective of many of these listservs is to "be a support list for people who have disabilities and their families" (STUT-HLP, 1996), and these CSHMA groups act as a link for people with disabilities who might not otherwise be able to interact. "People find social support, companionship, and a sense of belonging through the normal course of [CSHMAs]," even though they are composed of people they hardly know (Wellman, Salaff, & Dimitrova, 1996, p. 225). Weinberg et al. (1996) maintained that online support groups provide many characteristics of the more traditional face-to-face support groups. The next section will explore the benefits and possible drawbacks of listservs, electronic bulletin boards, and newsgroups, collectively defined herein as CSHMA groups.

CSHMA groups have unique advantages independent of face-to-face groups (see Braithwaite et al., 1999, for a review). Weinberg et al. (1995) contended that people who may be unable or unwilling to participate in face-to-face support groups may turn to computer-mediated support groups for assistance. The medium permits thoughts and feelings to be expressed in an open forum without many of the interpersonal risks that exist in face-to-face groups. Computer-mediated support groups can bypass mobility and communication difficulties (Fullmer & Walls, 1994), and can elicit information from a large geographical area and diverse population. For example, HIGH-Net, a computer bulletin board designed for families affected by hemophilia (Scheerhorn, Warisse, & McNeilis, 1995), allows people dealing with different cultural barriers and public policy issues access to each other. CSHMA groups also have 24-hour-a-day access (Finn, 1996). CSHMA groups can also be a source of information for "lurkers'" those who gather information without having to participate or become part of the interaction (Finn, 1996). CSHMA groups also can enhance and increase effective communication for those people who have interpersonal or communicative difficulties. This interaction may yield a sense of community and support (Nelson, 1995).

The advantages of this online context have positive effects for the people who subscribe to the listservs, newsgroups, and bulletin boards. Research consistently demonstrates that computer-mediated reciprocal support, mutual aid, and online information exchanges increase self-esteem (Constant, Kiesler, & Sproull, 1994; Constant, Sproull, & Kiesler, 1996; Kollock & Smith, 1996). Psychologically disturbed adolescents feel more comfortable expressing feelings and interpersonal issues in a computer-mediated context than in a face-to-face context (Zimmerman, 1987). Sexual abuse survivors who engage in online self-help groups experience reduced social status cues, encouraged participation from reluctant members, and more open communication by those with interpersonal difficulties (Finn & Lavitt, 1994). Other groups, such as breast cancer patients (Williams, 1996) and prostatitis survivors (Kay, 1996) feel a diminishment of shame and guilt from their online experiences.

There are also positive effects of CSHMA groups for people with disabilities. Braithwaite et al. (1999) reported that the most prevalent type of support exchanged on an electronic bulletin board for people with disabilities is emotional support (40% of support messages), followed by informational support (31.3%), esteem support (18.6%), network support (7.1%), and tangible support (2.9%). In their study, electronic bulletin board participants were able to "validate one another's experience and perceptions and provided great amounts of encouragement, understanding, and empathy to one another" (Braithwaite et al., 1999).

Although the benefits of face-to-face support groups have been documented, little research has been done about the possible negative effects of social support groups (see, however, Galinsky & Schopler, 1994; Schopler & Galinsky, 1981). In face-to-face support groups, negative experiences include embarrassment, distress, obtaining incorrect information, becoming too dependent on the group, learning inappropriate behavior, or finding open communication threatening (Galinsky & Schopler, 1994). From such negative interactions residual feelings may include "such sentiments as humiliation after exposing inadequacies, [and] anger for being 'put down'" (Schopler & Galinsky, 1981, pp. 425–426). Furthermore, Schopler and Galinsky (1981) believe people involved in negative experiences may withdraw from the group and avoid future group involvement, thereby not receiving much-needed support. CSHMA groups are thriving even though negative experiences may actually be more prevalent in computer-mediated support groups than in face-to-face groups (see the following paragraph). Although computer-mediated support groups can facilitate significant social support (as research indicates), there may also be negative messages unique to the online medium.

One potential disadvantage of CSHMA groups is a lack of clear and accountable leadership and strong role models (Finn, 1996). Strong role models are important in face-to-face groups because these people reinforce group norms, provide needed empathy, and promote identification (Peyrot, 1985). Because CMC can create an equalization effect among participants (Dubrovsky et al., 1991), there may be a lack of online leadership. Furthermore, noncredible sources may give inaccurate information, perceived by other group members as accurate. Without professional supervision, which many of these groups lack, receivers may obtain incorrect information from well-intentioned, but misinformed, others that could contribute to negative outcomes. There has as yet been no research on the amount of inaccurate information that is communicated in the CSHMA groups, but future research needs to address this issue both online and in face-to-face support groups.

Another disadvantage of CSHMAs is the possibility that CMC may create an overdependence on computer relationships that leads to a lack of personal contact (Finn, 1996; Gans, 1994). Likewise, users may substitute CSHMA support for other more appropriate forms of professional contact (Finn, 1996). Although "Internet addiction" is debated, it may be that participants become overdependent on the CSHMA groups for social interaction. If this occurs, it may decrease other important forms of interaction and lead to a society of electronic shut-ins. If online impressions are distorted toward overly positive perceptions of others, this could cause people to find face-to-face interactions less rewarding and less appealing than CMC, supporting Walther's (1996) argument that CMC can become hyperpersonal. If this happens, CSHMA group members may choose online relationships over face-to-face ones.

Given the public nature of most CSHMA groups, there is also a potential for confidentiality problems to occur. Although confidentiality problems exist in face-to-face interactions, given that information in newsgroups, bulletin boards, and listservs is archived and can be retrieved easily by those who are not group members, there is a possibility that information posted online could be damaging to the CSHMA members.

The problem of access is especially relevant to people with disabilities. Glastonbury and LaMendola (1992) pointed out that although the number of people using computers and telecommunications is growing exponentially, the poor, undereducated, women, and elderly (and arguably people with disabilities) have been left out of the information revolution. Furthermore, people with disabilities must have not only access and training on computer hardware and software, they also must have the physical means (through their own or others' efforts) to engage in online dialogue. If computer-based resources are accessible to only those people who have computer access and knowledge, the voices of those without access remain silent. It is ironic that the medium that in many ways creates communicative freedom for people with disabilities may also be one that limits communication.

A final problem with CSHMAs may be the debated issue of increased negative online communication. Braithwaite et al. (1999) contended that online communication may cause "harm through negative, hostile, or malicious encounters" (p. 12). Researchers have found that the lessening in social status cues may lead to more uninhibited communication, a reduction of online politeness, and the potential for an increase in negative communication (i.e., "flaming") online (Sproull, 1986; Sproull & Kiesler, 1986). Matheson (1991) believes that because CMC reduces other-awareness, social norms, social pressures, impression management, and public self-awareness, it will result in increases in uninhibited behavior. Feelings of depersonalization and the lack of fear of social sanctions in CMC can also increase negative communication (Kiesler et al., 1984; Sproull & Kiesler, 1986). Researchers have discovered that flaming and negative communication are more frequent in listservs than in person-to-person electronic mail (Thompsen & Ahn, 1992), arguably because participants are sending a group message as opposed to a personal one.

There are researchers who question the amount of negative communication occurring online (Walther, Anderson, & Park, 1994) and believe the incidence of flaming and negative communication is overrated. Others contend negative communication is a necessary evil that promotes effective communication (Wang, 1996). McCormick and McCormick (1992) believe that flames may be viewed as positive and humorous and not as insulting. Perhaps, in the same way that people may depersonalize the messages they send, they may depersonalize the messages they receive. If this is the case, participants may not be as negatively (or positively) affected by them as they would in a face-to-face medium. However, given inconsistent findings regarding negative communication in electronic messages, it is important for researchers to examine the occurrence and outcome of negative messages in CMC. As Finn and Lavitt (1994) concluded:

> There is a paucity of research about the users, helping mechanisms, benefits, and potential harm related to CSHMA groups. If CSHMA groups are indeed found to be useful, it will be important to: promote their development through referral and clearing house activities; encourage public institutions such as the library to provide training and access to computers; understand and facilitate the organizational structures which maintain CSHMA groups; and teach clients when and how to best access and utilize them. If harm or lack of value is associated with aspects of CSHMA group participation, we are obligated to know this so that our clients can be informed consumers. (p. 43)

Ultimately, the possibility of negative communication in CSHMA leads to questions regarding the effectiveness and benefits of online social support groups if in fact more negative affect is present. Likewise, if positive effects exist, CSHMAs should be more accessible to people with disabilities than they are at present.

CONCLUSION

Given possible physical mobility challenges faced by people with disabilities, the WWW and CMC function as conduits to social interactions that were unavailable 15 years ago. The WWW acts as a clearinghouse of information, empowering people with disabilities by providing access to disability-related information that might otherwise be difficult and awkward to obtain. Furthermore, CMC allows people with disabilities access to others to whom they would not normally have access in a medium that equalizes status cues. For people with disabilities, CMC may be one of the few media in which interactions are not mediated by the disability-related stigma and where a person with a disability can truly feel like a "person first." In this way, people with disabilities may find CMC to be more rewarding (i.e., hyperpersonal) because of the advantages of this medium over others. CSHMA groups allow people with disabilities an arena in which to gain social support from an international audience of others. Even with the clear advantages and benefits of this medium, we must be cautious in assuming that it is a panacea for people with disabilities, especially given the access issues that still exist for many people with disabilities. Researchers have a wonderful opportunity to explore (and arguably influence) the WWW and CMC as the burgeoning medium of online communication continues to grow and change.

DISCUSSION QUESTIONS

1. What advantages does CMC provide for people with disabilities?
2. How might the hyperpersonal nature of computer-mediated relationships decrease the quality of face-to-face relationships? What are the social ramifications of such a decrease?
3. Support or refute the following: "CMC is the great equalizer."
4. Discuss the ethics of CSHMA groups.

REFERENCES

Banks, M. (1988). *The modem reference*. New York: Brady.

Braithwaite, D. O. (1991). "Just how much did that wheelchair cost?": Management of privacy boundaries by persons with disabilities. *Western Journal of Speech Communication, 55*, 254–274.

Braithwaite, D. O., Waldron, V. R., & Finn, J. (1999). Communication of social support in computer-mediated groups for people with disabilities. *Health Communication, 11*, 123–151.

Chidambaram, L. (1996). Relational development in computer-supported groups. *Management Information Systems Quarterly, 20,* 143–165.

Coleman, L. M., & DePaulo, B. M. (1991). Uncovering the human spirit: Moving beyond disability and "missed" communications. In N. Coupland, H. Giles, & J. M. Wiemann (Eds.), *"Miscommunication" and problematic talk* (pp. 61–84). Thousand Oaks, CA: Sage.

Comer, R. J., & Piliavin, J. A. (1972). The effects of physical deviance upon face-to-face interaction: The other side. *Journal of Personality & Social Psychology, 23,* 33–39.

Constant, D., Kiesler, S. B., & Sproull, L. S. (1994). What's mine is ours, or is it? A study of attitudes about information sharing. *Information Systems Research, 5,* 400–421.

Constant, D., Sproull, L. S., & Kiesler, S. B. (1996). The kindness of strangers: The usefulness of electronic weak ties for technical advice. *Organizational Science, 7,* 119–135.

Culnan, M. J., & Markus, M. L. (1987). Information technologies. In F. M. Jablin, L. L. Putnam, K.H. Roberts, & L. W. Porter (Eds.), *Handbook of organizational communication: An interdisciplinary perspective* (pp. 420–443). Newbury Park, CA: Sage.

Dubrovsky, V. J., Kiesler, S., & Sethna, B. N. (1991). The equalization phenomenon: Status effects in computer-mediated and face-to-face decision-making groups. *Human Computer Interaction, 6,* 119–149.

Elliott, R. R., & Frank, R. G. (1990). Social and interpersonal reactions to depression and disability. *Rehabilitation Psychology, 35,* 135–147.

Finn, J. (1996). Computer-based self-help groups: On-line recovery for addictions. *Computers in Human Services, 13,* 21–41.

Finn, J., & Lavitt, M. (1994). Computer-based self-help/mutual aid groups for sexual abuse survivors. *Social Work with Groups, 17,* 21–46.

Fox, S. A., & Giles, H. (1996). "Let the wheelchair through": An intergroup approach to interability communication. In W. P. Robinson (Ed.), *Social groups and identity: The developing legacy of Henri Tajfel* (pp. 215–248). Oxford: Butterworth Heinmann.

Fullmer, S., & Walls, R. T. (1994). Interests and participation on disability-related computer bulletin boards. *Journal of Rehabilitation, 60,* 24–30.

Galinsky, M. J., & Schopler, J. H. (1994). Negative experiences in support groups. *Social Work in Health Care, 20,* 77–95.

Gans, H. J. (1994). The electronic shut-ins—Some social flaws of the information superhighway. *Media Studies Journal, 8,* 123–127.

Glastonbury, B., & LaMendola, W. (1992). *The integrity of intelligence.* New York: St. Martin's Press.

Goffman, E. (1963). *Stigma: Notes on the management of spoiled identity.* Englewood Cliffs, NJ: Prentice-Hall.

Green, G. (1993). Editorial review: Social support and HIV. *AIDS Care, 5,* 87–104.

Gussow, Z., & Tracy, G. S. (1976). The role of self-help clubs in adaptation to chronic illness and disability. *Social Science and Medicine, 10,* 407–414.

Herman, N., & Maill, C. E. (1990). The positive consequences of stigma: Two case studies in mental and physical disabilities. *Qualitative Sociology, 13,* 251–269.

Hiltz, S. R., Johnson, K., & Turoff, M. (1986). Experiments in group decision making: Communication process and outcome in face-to-face versus computerized conferences. *Human Communication Research, 13,* 225–252.

Hood, J. (1996). Taking the byte out of disability. *Policy Review, 76* [On-line], http://www.townhall.com/heritage/p_review/mar96/bless.html.

Houston, V., & Bull, R. (1994). Do people avoid sitting next to someone who is facially disfigured? *European Journal of Social Psychology, 24,* 279–284.

Jackson, C. (1996). *The interpersonal nature and effects of computer-mediated communication.* Unpublished manuscript, Western Michigan University.

Joslyn-Scherer, M. S. (1993). *Living in the state of stuck: How technologies affect the lives of people with disabilities.* Cambridge, MA: Brookline Books.

Kay, J. (1996, November). *Health views within internet support communities: Communication, community, culture and technology.* Paper presented at the Speech Communication Association Convention, San Diego, CA.

Kiesler, S., Siegel, J., & McGuire, T. W. (1984). Social psychological aspects of computer-mediated communication. *American Psychologist, 39,* 1123–1134.

Kleck, R. (1969). Physical stigma and task oriented interactions. *Human Relations, 22,* 53–60.

Kleck, R. E., Buck, P. L., Coller, W. L., London, R. S., Pfeiffer, J. R., & Vukcevic, D. P. (1968). Effect of stigmatizing conditions on the use of personal space. *Psychological Reports, 23,* 111–118.

Kollock, P., & Smith, M. A. (1996). Managing the virtual commons: Cooperation and conflict in computer communities. In S. Herring (Ed.), *Computer-mediated communication* (pp. 109–128). Amsterdam: John Benjamins.

Makas, E. (1988). Positive attitudes toward people with disabilities: Disabled and nondisabled person's perspectives. *Journal of Social Issues, 44,* 49–61.

Matheson, K. (1991). Social cues in computer-mediated negotiations: Gender makes a difference. *Computers in Human Behavior, 7,* 137–145.

Matheson, K., & Zanna, M. P. (1988). The impact of computer-mediated communication on self-awareness. *Computers in Human Behavior, 4,* 221–233.

Matheson, K., & Zanna, M. P. (1990). Computer-mediated communications: The focus on me. *Social Science Computer Review, 8,* 1–12.

McCormick, N. B., & McCormick, J. W. (1992). Computer friends and foes: Content of undergraduates' electronic mail. *Computers in Human Behavior, 8,* 379–405.

Mills, J., Belgrave, F. Z., & Boyer, K. (1984). Reducing avoidance of social interaction with physically disabled persons by mentioning the disability following a request for aid. *Journal of Applied Social Psychology, 14,* 1–9.

Mitra, A. (1997). Diasporic web sites: Ingroup and outgroup discourse. *Critical Studies in Mass Communication, 14,* 158–181.

Nelson, J. A. (1995). The Internet, the virtual community and those with disabilities. *Disability Studies Quarterly, 15,* 15–20.

Parry, J. (1990). The Americans With Disabilities Act: Summary, analysis and commentary. *Mental and Physical Disability Law Reporter, 14,* 292–298.

Peyrot, M. (1985). Narcotics Anonymous: Its history, structure and approach. *International Journal of Addictions, 20,* 1509–1522.

Phillips, M. J. (1990). Damaged goods: Oral narratives of the experiences of disability in American culture. *Social Science and Medicine, 30,* 849–857.

Pingree, S., Hawkins, R. P., Gustafson, D. H., Boberg, E., Bricker, E., Wise, M., Berhe, H., & Hsu, E. (1996). Will the disadvantaged ride the information highway? Hopeful answers from a computer-based health crisis system. *Journal of Broadcasting and Electronic Media, 40,* 331–353.

Roberts, S. J. (1988). Social support and help seeking: Review of the literature. *Advances in Nursing Science, 10,* 1–11.

Scheerhorn, D., Warisse, J., & McNeilis, K. S. (1995). Computer-based telecommunication among an illness-related community: Design, delivery, early use, and the functions of HIGHnet. *Health Communication, 7,* 301–325.

Schopler, J. J., & Galinsky, M. J. (1981). When groups go wrong. *Social Work, 26,* 424–429.

Siegel, J., Dubrovsky, V., Kiesler S., & McGuire, T. W. (1986). Group processes in computer-mediated communication. *Organizational Behavior Human Decision Processes, 37,* 157–187.

Sigelman, C. K., Adams, R. M., Meeks, S. R., & Purcell, M. A. (1986). Children's nonverbal responses to a physically disabled person. *Journal of Nonverbal Behavior, 10,* 173–186.

Spears, R., & Lea, M. (1994). Panacea or panopticon? The hidden power in computer-mediated communication. *Communication Research, 21*, 427–459.

Sproull, L. (1986). Using electronic mail for data collection in organizational research. *Academy of Management Journal, 29*, 159–169.

Sproull, L., & Kiesler, S. (1986). Reducing social context cues: Electronic mail in organizational communication. *Management Science, 32*, 1492–1512.

Stovall, C., & Sedelack, W. E. (1983). Attitudes of male and female university students toward students with different physical disabilities. *Journal of College Student Personnel, 24*, 325–330.

STUT-HLP. (1996). [On-line]. Stutter's support list gopher: //SJUVM.STJOHNS.EDU:70/00/disabled/widlist/wid-dis/widx022.wid-dis.

Thompsen, P. A., & Ahn, D. (1992). To be or not to be: An exploration of E-prime, copula deletion and flaming in electronic mail. *Et Cetera: A Review of General Semantics, 49*, 146–164.

Thompsen, P. A., & Foulger, D. A. (1996). Effects of pictographs and quoting on flaming in electronic mail. *Computers in Human Behavior, 23*, 222–243.

Thompson, T. L. (1982). "You can't play marbles—You have a wooden hand": Communication with the handicapped. *Communication Quarterly, 30*, 108–115.

Trevino, L. K., Lengel, R. H., & Daft, R. L. (1987). Media symbolism, media richness, and media choice in organizations. *Communication Research, 14*, 553–574.

Turner, R. J., & Noh, S. (1988). Physical disability and depression: A longitudinal analysis. *Journal of Health and Social Behavior, 29*, 23–37.

Walther, J. B. (1992). Interpersonal effects in computer-mediated interaction: A relational perspective. *Communication Research, 19*, 52–90.

Walther, J. B. (1993). Impression development in computer-mediated interaction. *Western Journal of Communication, 57*, 381–398.

Walther, J. B. (1996). Computer-mediated communication: Impersonal, interpersonal, and hyperpersonal interaction. *Communication Research, 23*, 3–43.

Walther, J. B., & Burgoon, J. K. (1992). Relational communication in computer-mediated interaction. *Human Communication Research, 19*, 50–88.

Walther, J. B., Anderson, J. F., & Park, D. W. (1994). Interpersonal effects in computer-mediated interaction: A meta-analysis of social and antisocial communication. *Communication Research, 21*, 460–487.

Wang, H. (1996). Flaming: More than a necessary evil for academic mailing lists. *Journal of Communication 6* [On-line serial]. www.cios.org/getfile \wang_V6N196.

Weinberg, N., Schmale, J., Uken, J., & Wessel, K. (1996). Online help: Cancer patients participate in a computer-mediated support group. *Health & Social Work, 21*, 24–29.

Weinberg, N., Schmale, J. D., Uken, J., Wessel, K. (1995). Computer-mediated support groups. *Social Work with Groups, 17* (4), 43–54.

Wellman, B., Salaff, J., & Dimitrova, D. (1996). Computer networks as social networks: Collaborative work, telework, and virtual community. *Annual Review of Sociology, 22*, 213–238.

Wright, B. (1983). *Physical disability: A psychosocial approach* (2nd ed.). New York: Harper & Row.

Zastrow, C. (1986). *Social welfare institutions*. Chicago: Dorsey Press.

Zimmerman, D. P. (1987). A psychosocial comparison of computer-mediated and face-to-face language use among severely disturbed adolescents. *Adolescence, 22*, 827–840.

Zuboff, S. (1988). *In the age of the smart machine*. New York: Basic Books.

V

Communication Issues as They Impact Specific Types of Disabilities

19

Reducing Uncertainty Through Communication During Adjustment to Disability: Living With Spinal Cord Injury

Roxanne Parrott
University of Georgia-Athens

Tricia Stuart
University of Georgia Press

Adrian Bennett Cairns
Rehabilitation Counselor, Chattanooga, TN

Keywords: Stages of adjustment to SCI, uncertainty reduction theory, illness uncertainty theory, uncertainty management theory

Due to improvements in health care, including better resuscitation rates and long-term care, the number of persons who survive spinal cord injury (SCI) has been increasing (Frank et al., 1987). Approximately 8,000 SCIs occur annually in the United States, where there are currently 250,000 existing SCI cases (Tyroch, Davis, Kaups, & Lorenzo, 1997). The range of disability associated with SCI can be classified into four groups based on motor and/or sensory function preserved: (a) no motor or sensory function preserved, (b) motor paralysis with deep sensation in feet preserved, (c) massive tetra paresis with affected extremities rendered functionally useless, and (d) pareses of lesser intensity, such that some muscle strength is preserved (Kiwerski, 1993). Causes of SCI are classified as blunt or penetrating injuries. The majority of SCIs (70%) result from blunt trauma, with the most common source (65%) of blunt injury being motor vehicle collisions (MVC); falls and dives constitute a far less common source of blunt injury (Tyroch et al., 1997). The vast majority of penetrating SCIs (95%) are caused by gunshot wounds (Tyroch et al., 1997). Given these most common causes of SCI, not surprisingly, there is a 4:1 male–female ratio for spinal cord injuries, with injury most often occurring at a young age, 80% to people under the age of 40, and 50% to people between the ages of 14 and 24 (Tyroch et al., 1997).

Across classes of SCIs, injured persons move through several stages relating to loss of body function and the extreme physical, psychological, and social uncertainty associated with SCI, as suggested by the following quotation:[1]

> he kicked me with such force with his elbow in the back of my neck, it broke my spinal column, knocked the bones loose. They cut my spinal cord. They had to operate on my neck. The surgery, they took bones out of my hip. They put those in the back of my neck and fused it. I was thinking when that was done, "I'm fixed. A few months, I'm going to walk. . ." It was a big let-down when I see these guys starting to get up and move their legs and things. And I couldn't do it (2:6)

The stages of adjustment to SCI include (a) numb stage, in which the persons with injury feel powerless; (b) initial interventions, in which they establish trust with caregivers; (c) panic stage, in which they learn to control fear and anxiety; (d) egocentric stage, in which they often feel depression and anger; (e) interactive stage, in which they acquire power through education; and (f) directive stage, in which they develop power through others (Mahon-Darby, Ketchik-Renshaw, Richmond, & Gates, 1988). Each phase of adjustment to disability is associated with the need for particular types of information and assistance to reduce uncertainty (Braithwaite, 1990). These issues comprise the focus of this chapter, which includes examples from interviews of persons with SCI to illustrate their perceptions of both the uncertainty associated with SCI and the uncertainty associated with interpersonal relationships during adjustment to living with SCI.

INFORMATION-SEEKING AND
ADJUSTMENT TO SPINAL CORD INJURY

Mishel's (1988, 1990) uncertainty in illness theory (UIT) provides a framework for understanding the trajectory of persons' information-seeking about SCI. UIT represents illness as a multidimensional construct, with uncertainty about the state of an illness, its treatment, diagnosis, and prognosis all comprising elements of individuals' lack of understanding and feelings of confusion about health status (Mishel, Hostetter, King, & Graham, 1984). Studies examining the types of information persons with SCI seek support this perspective, with individuals exhibiting the need for (a) medical information about SCI (Miller, 1988); (b) psychosocial adjustment information, which affords a sense of prognosis for living with SCI (Miller, 1988); and (c) daily living information, which functions to reduce uncertainty about diagnosis and prognosis relating to the injury (Kanellos, 1985).

Competing tensions are associated with information-seeking and the reduction of uncertainty about SCI. Too little information about issues such as treatment options may reduce chances of survival, suggesting that uncertainty may pose a "danger" and motivate persons with SCI to seek information through communication with various sources. Too much information, however, especially early on for persons with SCI, may be devastating to an injured person and the family, destroying hope for the future. This suggests that uncertainty may also function as an "opportunity" for the patient. The existence of these dual realms of uncertainty about health status forms the basic premise of uncertainty management theory (UMT; Brashers, 1995; Brashers & Babrow, 1996), with SCI classically illustrating this premise.

Not all uncertainty experienced during adjustment to living with SCI, however, relates to the injury itself. Uncertainty reduction theory (URT) addresses the fact that when individuals lack knowledge about and ability to predict others' behavior, this relational uncertainty sometimes motivates people to communicate (Berger, 1979; Berger & Bradac, 1982; Berger & Calabrese, 1975). Persons with SCI may experience relational uncertainty in two domains. First, the people who care for persons with SCI will most likely be strangers. Second, SCI itself is likely to increase uncertainty in already established personal relationships. Relational uncertainty is likely to be integrally related to efforts to manage uncertainty about SCI, as will be illustrated in the discussion about health caregivers, family members, and friends.

HEALTH CAREGIVERS' ROLES IN
REDUCING UNCERTAINTY ABOUT SCI

The acute phase of SCI is marked by a person's inability to communicate and, in some instances, dependency on others even to breathe (Wells & Nicosia, 1995). During this phase, UIT (Mishel, 1988) suggests that uncertainty about injury will be extremely high, and physicians are expected to reduce this uncertainty through the provision of medical information. Physicians themselves, however, are often uncertain about patients' ability to regain mobility and may inadvertently create uncertainty about their own professional competence in efforts to promote, in the language of UMT (Brashers & Babrow, 1996), the "opportunity" associated with uncertainty about the injury. The impact of this on perceptions of the relationship may be seen in the following quotation:

> When I landed in the hospital, I wanted to know what was wrong! I wanted to know if I'm gonna be in a wheelchair, or if I'm gonna walk, or whatever. But the doctor couldn't give it to me 'cause they ain't gonna tell if you're gonna walk. They don't know much about spinal cords. You might, you might not. Gotta wait and see. (15:6)

Quite likely, it was not the caregivers' intention to create uncertainty about physicians by conveying that they "don't know much about spinal cords" but, rather, to promote optimism and hopefulness, as the extent of motor and/or sensory function loss revealed itself with the passage of time.

Compounding the likelihood that persons with injury and their families will experience a lack of knowledge about or ability to predict the caregivers' behavior, patients with SCI need care from many medical experts. One physician is unlikely to be familiar with another physician's area of expertise, and failure to communicate among specialists contributes to a lack of continuity in care and patients' uncertainty about caregivers (Donovan, Clifton, & Carter, 1982). The tendency to designate hospitals as either acute or rehabilitation centers further limits the likelihood that physicians will interact with each other, fragmenting the organization and delivery of care to persons with SCI (Donovan et al., 1982). This absence of continuity in care affects assessments of relationships with health caregivers, as observed in the following statement:

> Doctors back in Savannah, I didn't feel like I could trust them too much because they wantin' to do what they wantin' to do and that was that. But here, they listen until they give you an option and everything. (5:6)

The uncertainty associated with SCI trajectories, and the concomitant manner in which this uncertainty is communicated by health caregivers to persons with injury and their families, may provide one explanation of why persons living with disabilities more frequently express dissatisfaction with physicians' communication and preventive teaching than do other patients (Patrick, Scrivens, & Charlton, 1983).

As in other areas of health care, nurses' accessibility, both in terms of availability to give care and similarity in status to persons with injury, make them a vital communication source to reduce uncertainty about SCI. URT asserts that similarity in matters such as societal status and other sociodemographic variables reduces uncertainty about a communication source, increasing the ability to predict the source's behavior (Berger & Calabrese, 1975). Persons with SCI and their families likely feel more confident about what a nurse does than they do about predicting the behavior of the specialists assigned to care for the person who has suffered SCI, as the following quotation illustrates: "When I first got down there, I was scared. Let me tell you something, Karen is probably the biggest help to me there is. She's a nurse. . . . She's there" (13:5). A good communication strategy for the nurse caring for the patient with SCI during the initial intervention stage is a verbal introduction of each experience before it occurs, including X-rays, lab studies, and respiratory treatments, which reduces uncertainty about the injury experience (Mahon-Darby et al., 1988). In the panic phase, when a patient with SCI may feel as though he or she cannot get enough air, the nurse, after ruling out physiological causes, may identify events leading to panic attacks and ward off anxiety before it reaches a panic state, which helps to build confidence in and reduce uncertainty about the nurse as a caregiver. Nurses may also increase patients' feelings of control, thereby helping them to manage their uncertainty about injury, by affording patients a method to communicate during the initial interventions and panic stages. Quadriplegics who are ventilator-dependent, for example, might be told to call the nurse by making clicking sounds with their lips and tongue, or blinking their eyes (VanBennekom, Jelles, & Lankhorst, 1995). Alphabet or phrase boards may be used, with the nurse pointing to letters, numbers, or phrases. Computer-assisted communication systems serve this purpose as well (Hurlburt & Ottenbacher, 1992). Each of these strategies reduces patients' uncertainty about health caregivers' abilities to provide assistance when patients seek it. Once the panic phase has passed, patients gain longer attention spans and are able to integrate more information about their injury, seeking, according to UIT (Mishel, 1988, 1990), understanding about diagnosis and prognosis. They often become angry or depressed about loss, suggesting the need to continue to manage levels of uncertainty, avoiding the danger of knowing too little, while promoting the opportunity associated with some uncertainty about motor and sensory loss, as suggested by UMT (Brashers & Babrow, 1996). During this egocentric stage, persons with SCI need psychosocial information, including reassurance that their fears are common and a natural part of adjustment to living with SCI. To help ward off the potentially debilitating psychological effects associated with medical information, daily living information is needed to cope (Anderle, 1995). Other health caregivers, in addition to physicians and nurses, communicate with persons with SCI during this period, assisting in the progression beyond the initial acute phase of living with SCI. Personal assistants (PAs), caregivers whose responsibilities range from helping patients bathe to assisting with shopping, are a critical link to persons with disabilities' success in attaining personal control and independence in their lives (Anderle, 1995). The following quotations suggest that persons with SCI recognize the value of PAs, called human resource technicians (HSTs) in the organization where the interviews used in this chapter were conducted. One interviewee noted, "The HSTs are probably the biggest help of all. They're the ones that are there for you all the time" (13:1). Another said, "If you need to talk, they (HSTs) listen, cause after they work with you for so long they know when something is wrong" (8:3). These statements emphasize the need for some health caregivers to be constant over time and willing just to listen. Perhaps because the parameters associated with PAs in assisting persons with SCI are so varied, the responsibility for persons with SCI to know their own care needs and communicate them explicitly is critical to successful relationships between persons with SCI and PAs (Anderle, 1995).

Occupational therapists (OTs) also work with patients who have SCI during the interactive and directive stages of adjustment to living with SCI, helping them regain and retain eye–hand coordination, and promoting use of environmental control units (ECUs). As one person interviewed observed, "(OTs) show me different devices I can use to make life easier" (12:1). ECUs are comprised of a control interface or input device, such as a keyboard, joystick, switch, and voice activator, together with a feedback display to show what action is being controlled. ECUs aid persons with SCI in the use of telephones, televisions, household appliances, computers, and even lighting and temperature in their homes (Holme, Kanny, Guthrie, & Johnson, 1997). This further reduces uncertainty about living with SCI, affording information about prognosis, one dimension of uncertainty addressed by UIT (Mishel, 1988, 1990), and averting the danger associated with too little information alluded to in UMT (Brashers & Babrow, 1996). SCI patients' assimilation of information about ECUs and use has been found to be directly related their efforts to seek education and travel, and improved attitudes about living with SCI (Holme et al., 1997). Cost savings also have been associated with use of ECUs, as the need for PA care is reduced by an average of 2 hours per day for persons with SCI who used ECUs an average of 10 times per day (Holme et al., 1997).

While OTs focus on reducing uncertainty about persons with SCI ability to perform tasks associated with daily living, physical therapists (PTs) focus on promoting the ability to retain some body function, offering patients hope for more physical control over their lives. The efforts of OTs and PTs are interrelated, as more physical control grants greater ability to perform tasks associated with daily living. Physical therapy often continues beyond the provision of any other formal health care, as suggested in the following comment, "(PTs) taught me a lot. And what therapy I get at home today, I'm still benefiting" (7:1). Another said, "My physical therapist, he's real patient with me. He's real great. He don't try to work you 'til you're sore and can't move" (14:1). These comments make evident the confidence these persons have developed in their relationships with PTs and the contribution these caregivers make to managing the uncertainty associated with living with SCI. As in many health care situations, however, family and friends are likely to be vital links in efforts to adjust to a new health status, acting as advocates for the person, coordinating communication of information and care among providers, and providing social support through all the stages of adjustment.

FAMILIES' AND FRIENDS' ROLES IN REDUCING UNCERTAINTY ABOUT SCI

Life partners and other family members face the same types of uncertainty as patients with SCI about their loved ones' medical condition, as addressed in UIT (Mishel, 1988, 1990). They also face the same challenges to manage the uncertainty in a positive way, as addressed by UMT (Brashers & Babrow, 1996), stifling the impulse to insist on having information about a loved one's condition when information may only take away hope, but answering the impulse to seek information to promote the loved one's well-being. Moreover, the event that caused the SCI, as foreshadowed in research using URT (Berger & Calabrese, 1975), is likely to introduce uncertainty into these personal relationships. Events that increase uncertainty in personal relationships include changes in personality or values (Planalp, Rutherford, & Honeycutt, 1988), and although one can imagine a wide range of illnesses and changes in health status that may cause shifts in personality, few seem likely to encompass the spectrum of change associated with SCI. A person with SCI suffers from bouts of depression, anger, and fear, all in association with early phases of adjusting to SCI, then bouts of resignation and hopelessness during the rehabilitation period. Families may feel helpless in the face of these displays and confused about what they should do, as persons with SCI reframe their values and purpose for living, adjusting to limits associated with SCI.

Perhaps it is not too surprising that divorce has been found to be higher among couples where one partner sustains an SCI than in the general population (Urey & Henggeler, 1987). Many persons with SCI who divorce, however, already had relational problems before their injury (Carlos, 1978), as this example illustrates: "Before I had my accident, I'd been going through a divorce for two years, so I been in depression. My husband has custody, temporary custody of my two children" (14:1). Thus, divorce is not an inevitable outcome of SCI, as marital satisfaction among couples where one person sustains an SCI derives from the same sources as prior to SCI, including the exchange of positive feelings and behaviors toward one another (Urey & Henggeler, 1987). One person interviewed observed:

> My old lady [patient's wife], she learned all about cathetering [*sic*], she could get me out of bed and into a wheelchair. She learned a lot. She played the main role you know, 'til I got down here [rehab]. She stayed in the hospital every damn night. I'm doin' all this [therapy] for my wife and kids. If it weren't for my wife and kids, I'd say to hell with it. I figured she'd leave me when this happened. But she's been real supportive. (15:2, 4)

This example clearly illustrates how a partner's involvement reduces not only uncertainty about how the person will live with SCI, but how the partner will live with the person with SCI as well, even suggesting that in some cases couples may become closer after the injury than they were before. This is consistent with prior research examining events that increase uncertainty in personal relationships, with less than one third of the individuals in one study labeling such events as negative, less than one tenth terminating a relationship as a result of increased uncertainty, and one fourth indicating that they actually became closer as a result of such an event (Planalp et al., 1988). This is also consistent with past research on the impact of a disability on a marital dyad (Thompson, 1981). Family members' involvement in persons with SCI adjustment to disability has been found to reduce feelings of anxiety, helplessness, and isolation regarding the injury (Rohrer et al., 1980). During the acute phase, family members may place calendars, pictures, clocks, and other familiar objects in positions where the patient is able to view them, and share diversions, such as television, radio, and music (Mahon-Darby et al., 1988). Talking about issues with no relationship to illness or physical care also helps to shift patients' attention from their injuries to other matters. These conversations may help to reestablish the parameters of the relationship, reminding the person with injury and family members of their lives beyond the injury. During the posttraumatic adjustment to SCI, patients whose families talk more openly about the injury, identify specific responsibilities and roles for family members to have in assisting the person with the SCI, and show emotions—both happy and sad—in relation to injury, are more likely to initiate activities on their own, show greater overall independence, and have more involvement socially (McGowan & Roth, 1987). Perhaps this open way of addressing life with SCI makes one another's behavior more predictable, reducing relational uncertainty. Perhaps, too, families who do not discuss these issues and are more closed to conversations about how the SCI affects their lives introduce greater uncertainty about the prognosis of living with injury into the existence of persons with injury.

The belief that family members have been too little involved in rehabilitation efforts for persons with SCI contributed to the development of a program named the "Family Group" designed to provide both information and therapy to family members (Rohrer et al., 1980). A multidisciplinary team comprised of an occupational therapist, nurse, and social worker led the program, which increased communication not only between persons with SCI and family members, but between them and health caregivers, too (Rohrer et al., 1980). In particular, persons with SCI who participated in the program cite the physicians' presentations as being very valuable and highly informational, demonstrating the importance of communicating medical information to persons with SCI and their families (Rohrer et al., 1980). As one respondent reflected:

I had some family members come up to me and say, "If you really want to, can you walk?" I said, "I don't want to hear none of that. If you don't know what you are talking about, don't even come close to me." Family members don't understand. (3:3)

Sustained efforts to help family members to understand are important components of efforts to assist persons with SCI in their efforts to adjust to their disability.

Friends also afford opportunities for persons with SCI to reduce uncertainty about living with their injuries and how injury will impact personal relationships. Obviously, people who provide information to disabled persons interpret that information through their own experiences, knowledge, and bias (Trumble, 1993). Because friends from before injury do not share the experience of being disabled, they have little or no knowledge about SCI and are likely to reflect the friendship through the bias of previous experiences with the friend. As a result, SCI often leads to termination of the relationship, as observed in the following interview excerpts: "My friends . . . there's . . . a lot less of my old friends than there was, I haven't seen a lot of them in a while" (13:1). Another interviewee said, "Right now I have very few friends, whereas before, I had a whole bunch of them, at least I thought they were friends. Some of them came and couldn't deal with it" (2:1). A third participant observed, "Ain't seen none of them since I been down here. Seen a couple of them in the hospital. That was it. They don't care if I walk again or not. We hardly talk" (15:2,4). Efforts to involve friends of persons with SCI in programs similar to the programs developed for families are needed and could perhaps change the too frequent termination of these personal relationships. On the other hand, persons with SCI who share the disability experience often form friendships with one another, as one person noted:

> I've been here a year. I've got friends on the outside that aren't disabled. I can relate to my friends here because they understand. (People with disabilities give) me advice you know, turning me on to other things you know, that people that are disabled can do . . . such as wheelchair sports, for example . . . I didn't know I could do this, wheelchair sports, when I first got hurt till somebody told me I could. (9:5)

Thus, friends with SCI reduce uncertainty about SCI and, at the same time, offer a relationship with seemingly less relational uncertainty owing to the shared injury status and experience.

CONCLUSION

Perceived control, as compared with actual control, significantly impacts a person's adjustment to disability, health information-seeking, and health behavior (Johnston, Gilbert, Partridge, & Collins, 1992). Conversations with health caregivers, family, and friends all have the potential to increase the perceived control of persons with SCI. A number of communication strategies suggested by this discussion and review may contribute to achieving this goal and to reducing uncertainty about SCI and relationships with health caregivers, family, and friends after injury. During the acute period:

1. Physicians should communicate the uncertainty associated with SCI trajectories, but also should not avoid answering the questions of persons with injury or their families and friends.
2. Nurses should communicate reassurance to patients, telling them that their fears are normal and explicitly stating what each test and other activity performed is, but also should not inhibit families' and friends' efforts to be involved.
3. PAs should communicate respect for patients' privacy by, for example, bathing them without others present, but also should not perform tasks that persons with injury can perform for themselves.
4. Life partners and family members should communicate social support by staying with patients during the acute period, coordinating care among physicians, and providing distractions; they also should not expect physicians to provide a long-term prognosis relating to motor and sensory loss.
5. Friends should communicate social support by providing distractions and stay with those who have suffered injuries, but also should not be alienated by others' lack of efforts to involve them.

During the posttraumatic period:

6. Physicians and nurses who work with persons who have SCI should be available to participate in programs like the Family Group.
7. PAs should be willing to listen, but continue to guard against performing tasks that persons with SCI can perform for themselves.
8. OTs should communicate that their purpose is to assist persons with SCI in efforts to retain and regain eye–hand coordination as tools of empowerment and independence.
9. PTs should communicate the need to continue participation in physical therapy activities for the remainder of the patient's life.
10. Life partners and family members should communicate their desire to be involved in rehabilitation.
11. Friends should communicate their desire to continue the relationship and should not be offended when persons with SCI develop new friendships with others who have suffered SCI.

12. Persons with SCI should assume the lead in communicating their needs, but should not reject others' efforts to remain involved in their rehabilitation.

As efforts to increase understanding about communicating about SCI continue, research that directly examines the actual conversations of persons with SCI is needed; presently, only conjecture is possible. Prior published research relies on the recall of persons with SCI. Although perceptions are a vital component of understanding the process, actual conversations may contribute insights about the effectiveness of particular strategies or approaches as compared with others. As a result, efforts to promote the hope associated with some uncertainty about injury and in relationships following injury may be assisted, while the danger associated with having too little information during adjustment to living with SCI is avoided.

DISCUSSION QUESTIONS

1. Compare relational and illness uncertainty. Discuss types of information likely to be used to reduce each type of uncertainty.
2. How could uncertainty about SCI be appraised as opportunity and as danger?
3. What types of communication sources are available to reduce the uncertainty of persons with SCI about their injuries? How might each source work to reduce danger associated with uncertainty about SCI during each stage of adjustment, and to maintain opportunity?
4. How does the organization of health care into specialties and subspecialties contribute to feelings of relational uncertainty about physicians and nurses for persons with SCI and their families? How might this also contribute to illness uncertainty?

REFERENCES

Anderle, C. (1995). Using personal assistance services after spinal cord injury: The role of the nurse. *SCI Nursing, 12,* 77–81.

Berger, C. R. (1979). Beyond initial interaction: Uncertainty, understanding, and the development of interpersonal relationships. In H. Giles & R. St. Clair (Eds.), *Language and social psychology* (pp. 122–144). Oxford: Blackwell.

Berger, C. R., & Bradac, J. J. (1982). *Language and social knowledge: Uncertainty in interpersonal relations.* London: E. E. Arnold.

Berger, C. R., & Calabrese, R. J. (1975). Some explorations in initial interaction and beyond: Toward a developmental theory of interpersonal communication. *Human Communication Research, 1,* 99–112.

Braithwaite, D. O. (1990). From majority to minority: An analysis of cultural change from able-bodied to disabled. *International Journal of Intercultural Relations, 14,* 465–483.

Brashers, D. E. (1995, May). *Communication and the management of uncertainty: The case of persons with HIV/AIDS.* Paper presented at the annual meeting of the International Communication Association, Albuquerque, NM.

Brashers, D. E., & Babrow, A. (1996). Theorizing communication and health. *Communication Studies, 47,* 243–251.

Carlos, V. M. S. (1978). Importance of communication in counseling the spinal cord injury patient. *Paraplegia, 16,* 206–211.

Donovan, W. H., Clifton, G., & Carter, R. E. (1982). Developing a system of comprehensive care for the spinal cord injured patient in Houston, Texas, U.S.A. *Paraplegia, 20,* 174–179.

Frank, R. G., Umlauf, R. L., Wonderlich, S. A., Askanazi, G. S., Buckelew, S. P., & Elliott, T. R. (1987). Differences in coping styles among persons with spinal cord injury: A cluster analytic approach. *Journal of Consulting and Clinical Psychology, 55,* 727–731.

Holme, S. A., Kanny, E. M., Guthrie, M. R., & Johnson, K. L. (1997). The use of environmental control units by occupational therapists in spinal cord injury and disease services. *American Journal of Occupational Therapy, 51,* 42–48.

Hurlburt, M., & Ottenbacher, K. J. (1992). An examination of direct selection typing rate and accuracy for persons with high-level spinal cord injury using QWERTY and default on-screen keyboards. *Journal of Rehabilitation Research, 29,* 54–63.

Johnston, M., Gilbert, P., Partridge, C., & Collins, J. (1992). Changing perceived control in patients with physical disabilities: An intervention study with patients receiving rehabilitation. *British Journal of Clinical Psychology, 31,* 89–94.

Kanellos, M. C. (1985). Enhancing vocational outcomes of spinal cord-injured persons: The occupational therapist's role. *American Journal of Occupational Therapy, 39,* 726–733.

Kiwerski, J. E. (1993). Application of dexamethasone in the treatment of acute spinal cord injury. *Injury: International Journal of the Care of the Injured, 24,* 9–13.

Mahon-Darby, J., Ketchik-Renshaw, B., Richmond, T. S., & Gates, E. M. (1988). Powerlessness in cervical spinal cord injury patients. *Dimensions of Critical Care Nursing, 7,* 346–355.

McGowan, M. B., & Roth, S. (1987). Family functioning and functional independence in spinal cord injury adjustment. *Paraplegia, 25,* 357–365.

Miller, S. B. (1988). Spinal cord injury: Self-perceived sexual information and counseling needs during the acute, rehabilitation, and post-rehabilitation phases. *Rehabilitation Psychology, 33,* 221–227.

Mishel, M. H. (1988). Uncertainty in illness. *Image: Journal of Nursing Scholarship, 20,* 225–232.

Mishel, M. H. (1990). Reconceptualization of the uncertainty in illness theory. *Image: Journal of Nursing Scholarship, 22,* 256–262.

Mishel, M. H., Hostetter, T., King, C., & Graham, V. (1984). Predictors of psychosocial adjustment in patients newly diagnosed with gynecological cancer. *Cancer Nursing, 7,* 291–299.

Patrick, D. L., Scrivens, E., & Charlton, J. R. H. (1983). Disability and patient satisfaction with medical care. *Medical Care, 21,* 1062–1075.

Planalp, S., Rutherford, D. K., & Honeycutt, J. M. (1988). Events that increase uncertainty in personal relationships II: Replication and extension. *Human Communication Research, 14,* 516–547.

Rohrer, K., Adelman, B., Puckett, J., Toomey, B., Talbert, D., & Johnson, E. W. (1980). Rehabilitation in spinal cord injury: Use of a patient-family group. *Archives of Physical and Medical Rehabilitation, 61,* 225–229.

Thompson, T. L. (1981). The impact of a physical handicap on communicative characteristics of the marital dyad. *Western Journal of Speech Communication, 45,* 227–240.

Trumble, S. (1993). Communicating with people who have intellectual disabilities. *Australian Family Physician, 22,* 1081–1082.

Tyroch, A. H., Davis, J. W., Kaups, K. L., & Lorenzo, M. (1997). Spinal cord injury: A preventable public burden. *Archives of Surgery, 132,* 778–781.

Urey, J. R., & Henggeler, S. W. (1987). Marital adjustment following spinal cord injury. *Archives of Physical and Medical Rehabilitation, 68,* 69–74.

VanBennekom, C. A. M., Jelles, F., & Lankhorst, G. J. (1995). Rehabilitation activities profile: The ICIDH as a framework for a problem-oriented assessment method in rehabilitation medicine. *Disability and Rehabilitation, 17,* 169–175.

Wells, J. D., & Nicosia, S. (1995). Scoring acute spinal cord injury: A study of the utility and limitations of five different grading systems. *Journal of Spinal Cord Medicine, 18,* 33–41.

ENDNOTE

1. Two facilities in Georgia specialize in treating acutely injured spinal cord patients. The largest granted permission to the third author to conduct interviews with patients whom the injury prevention and patient/family education specialist solicited to participate in a study of the communication of information and adaptation to disability. Patients who were medically stabilized to the point that they could be available for 1 to 2 hours to be interviewed were eligible to participate. Sixteen SCI patients were interviewed; a secondary analysis of transcripts of these interviews has been used to illustrate the discussion in this chapter. Names of interviewees are not included; they are identified by number with quotations cited by page number of the transcript where the quotation appears.

20

When the Deaf and the Hearing Interact: Communication Features, Relationships, and Disability Issues

Anne McIntosh
Central Piedmont Community College

Keywords: American Sign Language, hard of hearing, hearing-impaired, late-deafened, sign language, speechreading

Scenario 1: A professor sees Curtis in the campus dining hall and asks how he likes the class. The student ignores the tenured faculty member altogether. Perplexed, the professor gets his lunch and returns to the department office. He shares the puzzling incident with a graduate teaching assistant who informs the professor that Curtis is deaf.

Scenario 2: Ana and Conrad are having this phone conversation:
  Conrad: I had a doctor's appointment today; I had to see a urologist.
  Ana: How did it go?
  Conrad: Oh, fine. I have to have a yearly check-up but I still hate to go.
  Ana: It's no big deal. I see one, too.
  Conrad: (laughing) You do not see a urologist.
  Ana: (in an irritated voice) I do, too! Men aren't the only ones who need to see neurologists.
  Conrad: What? (laughing harder) Ana! Urologist, not neurologist.

Scenario 3: Steve, a poised and savvy communicator, recently became violently ill. To save his life, he was administered ototoxic medications. Steve woke up 6 weeks later permanently deaf. Unable to hear the doctors and nurses, he felt cut off from the world. Instantly, he became unable to communicate.

Curtis, Ana, and Steve each experience deafness differently and their communication styles vary. It is estimated that one out of every nine Americans have some degree of deafness affecting their ability to communicate effectively (Trychin, personal communication, May 19, 1988). The 1997 edition of the *Statistical Abstract* indicates that 22,400,000 Americans have impaired hearing.

This chapter focuses on communication features and adaptations common to communicators who are culturally Deaf, hard of hearing, and late-deafened. Communication theory and research as it has been developed is chronicled, including studies on deaf–deaf and deaf–hearing relationships. Finally, the communication discipline is urged to integrate Deaf and hearing communicators into its research and teaching.

People who do not have normal hearing levels are usually part of one of the following subgroups: the culturally Deaf, the hard of hearing, or the late-deafened. Emerging models are presented to give the reader general characteristics of each; however, it is possible that not all characteristics will embody each individual.

COMMON COMMUNICATION FEATURES

Characteristics of Culturally Deaf

Members of the culturally Deaf community identify themselves as *Deaf* with a capital "D" (Higgins, 1980; Humphries & Alcorn, 1995; Nash & Nash, 1981; Schein, 1989; Woodward, 1972). In the United States, these people use American Sign Language (ASL)[1] as their main mode of communication and do not generally benefit from assistive devices such as hearing aids or amplified telephones. They communicate mostly via interpreters, paper/pen, electronic mail, and facsimile machines. Historically, before 34 CFR, the Education for all Handicapped Children Act of 1975, and 34 CFR, the Education of the Handicapped Act Amendments of 1986, most deaf children were educated at residential schools for the deaf where they often lived away from their families and visited home only on holidays.

Characteristics of Hard of Hearing

The hard of hearing represent the majority of people who do not possess normal hearing acuity. It is thought that 28 to 40 million people have a hearing loss that to some extent interferes with communication; however, there is no widely accepted universal standard, which accounts for the numerical disparity. Hard of hearing people predominantly communicate by relying on their residual hearing, hearing aids, speechreading, and bluffing. Generally, communicators who are born with a hearing impairment display dysfluency and misarticulation in their production of speech sounds (Seyfried, Hutchinson, & Smith, 1989) and have difficulty monitoring the volume of their voices. People who are hard of hearing commonly repeat what has already been uttered and interrupt others because they do not hear them talking.

In the example at the beginning of the story, Ana thought she understood Conrad. Ana's deafness is in the high frequencies where most consonant sounds reside. Her brain "guesses" what the consonant might be and checks the "guess" against her vocabulary, the context, and the topic at hand. When the brain gets a "match," it gives Ana an interpretation of what is being said; Ana then responds accordingly. The brain knew something was said and had to "fill in" what would fit the context. "Neurologist" made sense, only it was not the word Conrad used. Unable to speechread over the phone, she could not see the difference between a rounded "u" in "urologist" versus the teeth slightly apart and tongue behind the upper teeth for the "n" in "neurologist." In a face-to-face interaction, Ana probably would have understood Conrad; in a situation where speechreading is not possible (e.g., phone), she depends on Conrad to ensure she accurately understands the messages.

In ideal conditions skilled speechreaders accurately interpret less than 50% of what is being said (Hipskind, 1989; Martin, 1994; Vernon & Andrews, 1990). For communicators who are hard of hearing, the people with whom they are talking may not have the skills to repair communication breakdowns, leaving both parties dissatisfied with the communication encounter.

Characteristics of Late-Deafened

Like Steve, late-deafened adults have had normal hearing all of their lives. A traumatic injury, illness, or ototoxic medication can disable the normal hearing process, sometimes rapidly and without warning. Often characterized as having a "hearing mind with deaf ears," their language skills and thinking process are mapped as a hearing person's, only they can no longer hear. Late-deafened adults can find themselves unable to do tasks they could do before because their brains previously used auditory cues. Neurologically mapped to utilize auditory information, the brain continues to demand auditory cues while the body has become unable to meet the demand. Knutson and Lansing (1990) examined adults who became deaf later in life and found inadequate communication strategies and poor accommodations to the deafness associated with limited communication performance; a few studies show that the late-deafened can function well with their hearing impairments (Pichora-Fuller, Johnson, & Roodenburg, 1998). It appears that, of the three subgroups of communicators who do not have normal hearing thresholds, the late-deafened communicator has a more difficult time adapting new communication strategies. In the following section research specifically related to these subgroups is reviewed.

COMMUNICATION RESEARCH

Inadequacies of Past Research

Comparing Deaf With Hearing in a Hearing Language. Up until the 1980s, research incorporating culturally Deaf people as part of sampling pools consisted mainly of quantitative methods where investigators determined how far school-aged children who are culturally Deaf lagged behind their hearing counterparts in reading (Furth, 1966; King & Quigley, 1985; Moores, 1987). Linguistic research spearheaded by Dr. William Stokoe shows that ASL is a language with its own syntax and grammar separate from English (Flodin, 1994; Sternberg, 1987; Stokoe, 1961; Stokoe, Casterline, & Croneberg, 1965). Furthermore, researchers have learned that, when tested in their native language, the Deaf do not lag behind their hearing counterparts in language per se. Past researchers may not have wanted to confound research results with subjects who have disabilities, but with sophisticated analysis tools such as computerized principal components analysis, scholars are better able to account for diversity in variances. Overall, inclusion of Deaf subjects would make findings more representative of the population at large.

Exclusions in Present Research

Changing Philosophy on ASL Used by the Culturally Deaf. Increasingly, institutions of higher education are moving sign language courses out of programs that focus on disability, special education, and communication disorders into foreign language departments, which is where a cadre of scholars from linguistics and Deaf studies argue ASL belongs. Prior to 1961, consensus was that ASL was ungrammatical, "broken" English done manually on the hands. Poizner, Klima, and Bellugi (1987) examined whether sign language occupies the same area of the brain as spoken language. The researchers reported evidence that, when deaf people have strokes, their sign language is as impaired as hearing people's spoken language after a similar illness. They concluded that the left hemisphere is the site for language regardless of whether the language is signed or spoken.

Shifting Philosophy on Communication Breakdowns and Communicating With the Hard of Hearing. Dedicating his career to researching the hard of hearing communicator, Trychin focuses on identifying and repairing communication breakdowns. Trychin advocates active listening and paraphrasing, so that, if the hard of hearing person has not heard correctly, the hearing party can repair the breakdown.

Trychin and others conduct classes that discuss "Communication Guidelines of Talking with the Hearing-Impaired." Examples of the guidelines include (a) getting the person's attention before speaking to him or her; (b) refraining from overenunciating, which distorts speechreading; and (c) giving clues when changing topics. Follow-up inquiry substantiating how well people benefit from such courses has not been published; meanwhile, authors have offered a plethora of colorful biographical anecdotes of mishaps (e.g., Kisor, 1990) that suggest misunderstandings are a widespread occurrence.

All communicators need to understand that hearing aids do not give a hard of hearing listener "20/20" hearing in a way that eyeglasses restore vision to normal levels. Research from the field of hearing science shows that high frequency consonants carry 95% of the information and yet these sounds are faintly audible, yielding only 5% of the energy. For example, the words *mom, pop, mop, mob, pom,* and *bob* look identical on the lips, and a person with a high frequency hearing loss would not be able to distinguish between the *p, m,* or *b* sounds. Often hard of hearing people speak about being shut off from the outside world because, from their perspective, they are not able to participate as fully as hearing people. This very real sense of isolation is often identified by people who are hard of hearing, as they feel left out of communicative encounters (Foster, 1989).

Emerging Philosophy on Communicating With the Late-Deafened.   Shawn Lovley, a faculty member of theatre and performance studies, suffered from a brain tumor on the auditory nerve in 1987. To save his life, the auditory nerve was severed to remove a cancerous mass. Lovley (1996) wrote an anecdotal handbook, *Now What? Life After Deaf*, explaining the need to address communication coping skills for people who are late-deafened, have English reading skills, and intelligible expressive English speaking skills, but have poor receptive skills for spoken communication.

Future Research: Opportunity for Adequacy and Inclusion

Speech communication scholars learning about gender issues and cultural differences are minimizing the White, college-educated, middle-class male prototype on which much interpersonal communication theory is based (Infante, Rancer, & Womack, 1990; Knapp & Miller, 1985; Wood & Duck, 1995). Deaf, hard of hearing, and late-deafened people are recognizing that their ability to communicate is not any less important, but does differ from mainstream, hearing culture.

It is a common perception for hearing people to think that deaf people are only unable to hear. The inability to hear goes beyond the sense itself and affects a person's sociological, psychological, and emotional well-being (Moore & Levitan, 1992; Vernon & Ottinger, 1989). Subscribing to the systems theory view (von Bertalanffy, 1968), these effects extend to the deaf person's personal, social, and professional relationships (Luey & DiPietro, 1998).

COMMUNICATION ISSUES IN RELATIONSHIPS

Research on Media Information and Technology Affecting Communication

In this century, two important inventions that have facilitated communication beyond all expectations have connections to deafness. It is well-documented that Alexander Graham Bell's mother and wife were both deaf. A teacher of the deaf and an inventor, Bell wanted to help his mother, wife, and students hear. One of his failing attempts to create what might be called a modern-day hearing aid was the invention of the telephone. A second invention that flourishes is the Internet. Describing himself as hard of hearing, Vinton Cerf, widely known as the *"Father of the Internet,"* coinvented the Internet in part in an attempt to equalize the playing field for the deaf in a world that thrives on people's ability to communicate with others.

Hearing communicators extract information from a variety of sources, including radio, newspaper, television, and telephone. Deaf, hard of hearing, and late-deafened people use some of these media in their original forms or slight variations thereof; however, other media integral to keeping hearing individuals oriented is of no use to communicators who do not have normal hearing thresholds.

Radio is not an information source for most culturally Deaf, severely hard of hearing, or late-deafened communicators, as they cannot hear well enough to discriminate the speech sounds nor can they speechread the radio. Before dismissing the radio as an insignificant medium, think about how many hours a hearing person listens to the radio or hears late-breaking news first from the radio. The newspaper is a source available to everyone with usable vision; however, recall that English is a second language to Deaf communicators. Research shows that the average Deaf adults' proficiency in English is at a fifth-grade level (Moores, 1987) and most newspapers are written at a seventh or eighth-grade level. Television is an important source of communication when equipped with closed captioning, which prints in written text what people on the television are saying. The television is not always accessible to people who do not have normal hearing thresholds because not all televisions are caption-ready in spite of several acts of legislation. Telephone use can be modified by amplifiers or placing the handset of the telephone on a device called a TTY (also known as a Telephone Device for the Deaf or TDD). Teletypes (TTY) allow a typed message to be encoded and transmitted through the phone line where it is then decoded by another TTY at the other end. Hearing people have the freedom to stop on the highway or at the airport and pick up the telephone and make a call with no difficulty. TDD users must search for scarce TTYs or pack a personal TTY. The task of using the phone is not a spontaneous, effortless event. Telephone communication can occur between people who do not have TTYs and people who rely on TTYs. Mandated under Title IV of the American With Disabilities Act (ADA), relay allows deaf and hearing people to telephone one another. As stipulated by ADA, each state provides a relay service. Relay agents can relay calls for a speech-impaired (agent becomes their voice) or hearing-impaired caller (agent becomes their ears).

Research on Deaf–Deaf Relationships

Data on deaf–deaf relationships is antiquated (Bell, 1884; Fay, 1897, 1898) and of limited generalizability. Most deaf individuals in the past grew up in closed environments such as residential schools; therefore, findings of past research may not hold true today as deaf individuals live in more open environments. Deaf–deaf relationships are thought to be stable and satisfying due to ease of communication because both deaf partners converse in the same language, ASL.

Deaf–deaf couples have not always had full civil rights, especially regarding romantic relationships. Attempts have been exerted to sterilize them or to prevent them from marrying one another (Moores, 1987). In modern times, the debate of controlling deaf persons' reproduction continues. A. G. Bell (1884) asked Congress to pass a law preventing the deaf from marrying each other; the proposal was not approved. The misguided argument that deaf–deaf marriages produced deaf offspring resurfaced. It has since been demonstrated that 90% of deaf children come from hearing–hearing partnerships, not deaf–deaf partnerships (Higgins, 1980; Schein, 1989). Today, genetic counseling determines the statistical likelihood of passing deafness to one's offspring, which may be desired among some couples who have strong ties to the Deaf community.

Research on Deaf–Hearing Relationships

Winefield (1987) offered an interpretation of Bell's classic 1884 article, arguing that A. G. Bell was not opposed to deaf people marrying if they married hearing people to increase the likelihood of breaking any cycles of genetic deafness. Using himself, Bell was able to show two examples of how his theory of a deaf person marrying a hearing person did break the cycle of deafness. First, Bell was a product of a deaf–hearing marriage, as his father was hearing and his mother was deaf. Second, Bell married a deaf woman and they produced several hearing children.

Not a great deal is known empirically about deaf–hearing relationships. It is estimated that there may be as many as 250,000 deaf–hearing romantic relationships in the United States (McIntosh, 1995a). Fay (1897), in a theoretical essay, asserted deaf–hearing marriages are more unstable and less satisfying than hearing–hearing or deaf–deaf marriages. He did not elaborate on the criteria for relational satisfaction or how it was measured. Since the 1800s, several sources have argued that deaf–hearing marriages were less stable (Cohen, 1994; Schein, 1989; Schein & Delk, 1974) but no recent studies have tested this hypothesis specifically.

I completed a 2-year study on deaf–hearing couples and how their communication patterns, specifically self-disclosure, compare with hearing–hearing and deaf–deaf couples' patterns (McIntosh, 1995a, 1995b). Results indicate that deaf–deaf couples value self-disclosure more highly than do deaf–hearing or hearing–hearing couples. More than 60% of the deaf–hearing couples in my sample report they self-disclose in contexts where they can keep their eyes on their partners to lip-read and use their hands for signing or gesturing.

Another type of deaf–hearing relationship examined more extensively than romantic relationships is parent–child relationships. Hearing children of deaf adults (better known as CODAs) learn sign language (i.e., ASL) as their first language and, later, English as a spoken language. Although these bilingual children can hear, they often feel more comfortable in Deaf culture and consider themselves culturally Deaf (Sacks, 1989; Walker, 1986). Paul Preston (1994), a CODA himself, interviewed 150 CODAs and summarized his findings in an ethnography. Although they are physically hearing, CODAs interact with the Deaf community, have cultural ties with Deaf members, and are accepted as lifetime members of the Deaf community. Reinzi (1990) compared hearing children of deaf parents with hearing children of hearing parents; she finds that hearing children of deaf parents have a greater number and percentage of their ideas and conversation accepted than do hearing children of hearing parents. Chan and Lui (1990) and Charlsen (1990) examined self-concepts of hearing adolescents who had deaf parents; they maintain their results are inconclusive but that generally, these hearing children have a deeper and more intimate understanding of deafness and do not view deafness as a disability.

With legislation mandating mainstreaming, deaf people are increasingly in the proximity of hearing people; consequently, relationships between deaf and hearing communicators are formed. The interaction of two cultures, two languages, and different educational and social experiences plays a heavy role in these relationships. The need to understand deaf–hearing communication encounters better has been recognized and there is an online organization for deaf–hearing couples who want to discuss communication issues. Subscribers repeatedly state that it is their personal and professional experience that counselors and social workers are not trained in deafness and how the dyadic interaction of deaf and hearing individuals affects communication and relationship satisfaction.[2]

Deafness has been considered a disability in the past and is still considered a disability by some; therefore, recent studies comparing the Deaf with their hearing counterparts are reviewed in the following section.

DISABILITY ISSUES

Historical Perspective of Research on Deaf Children

Children have been used heavily as a subject pool for researchers wanting to learn more about differences between the normal-hearing and deaf persons' communication. For example, in one study, three mainstreamed female deaf and hard of hearing students were age-matched with three normal-hearing kindergartners; results were inconclusive (Hulsing, Leutke-Stahlman, Loeb, & Nelson, 1995). In another study, Gaines and Halpern-Felsher (1995) analyzed the development and use of communication between a pair of identical twins in which one sibling was hearing and the other was deaf. Comparisons indicated that, although both twins were able to learn language and communicate with one another, the hearing twin prefers a vocal form of language while the deaf twin shows a preference for sign. Spencer, Koester, and Meadow-Orlans (1994) examined a group of deaf and hearing children in a day care center where children frequently interact with one another and teachers whose hearing status may differ from their own. Spencer et al. concluded that hearing and deaf children show tendencies to initiate communication with children whose hearing status is similar to theirs. Minnett, Clark, and Wilson's (1994) research reinforces Spencer et al's. conclusion that among deaf, hard of hearing, and hearing children, each prefers to communicate with others who are of the same hearing status.

The above research does not offer support for integration, as it appears that the young children willfully segregate themselves. In a similar vein, research is showing that children who are deaf often internalize an image of themselves that is determined by how their parents and/or primary care-givers view deafness. Kolod (1994) examined 15 deaf children with deaf parents and 15 deaf children with hearing parents. Her findings indicate that deaf children with hearing parents had a "damaged sense of themselves" compared with deaf children with deaf parents. It is not surprising that deaf parents, through role-modeling, pass along coping tips on how to communicate and get along in a mostly hearing world, translating into confidence and positive self-image. The stigma of disability is heavily ingrained at the familial level. Hearing parents, undoubtedly, worry about their deaf children and are not in a position to model how the deaf function in an auditory world. Desselle (1994) investigated family communication patterns of deaf children and finds a positive impact on the deaf child's self-esteem if total communication (sign and fingerspelling with speech) is used. Families who choose total communication (sign language used in conjunction with voicing) are usually more accepting of the deafness (e.g., Spradley & Spradley, 1978). Conversely, if a family chooses an oral-only method for communication, deaf children test lower on self-esteem measures (Desselle, 1994).

Current Debate About Deafness: Cultural Trait or Pathological Condition?

Former President George Bush signed the ADA into law in July 1990. Some deaf, hard of hearing, and late-deafened people applauded this piece of legislation, while others were not as thrilled. Why the schism? Padden and Humphries (1988) detailed differences between a "hearing center" and a "Deaf center" arguing that a person must choose one center over the other and that there is no middle ground. Choosing the Deaf center means that self-identified members of the Deaf culture are proud of deafness and do not view it as a handicap (cf. Davis & Silverman, 1960; Martin, 1994) but rather see their deafness as a cultural trait much as a black person might recognize his or her African-American heritage.

Some deaf individuals do not consider themselves handicapped and refuse any government assistance offered based solely on the premise of their deafness (e.g., government Social Security Insurance payments). Others, however, are willing to accept discounts or tax breaks due to their deafness. These issues have kept the disability versus physical (cultural) trait debate alive among scholars in deaf studies and have confused scholars from other disciplines. Lane, Hoffmeister, and Bahan (1996) commented on this issue, saying that members of the Deaf community have suffered the ill effects of receiving government subsidies by living at a lower standard and forgoing such intangible benefits as pride and self-sufficiency derived from gainful employment.

Fine and Ashe's (1988) research portrays a different view of deafness, more akin to how mainstream society has conceptualized disability.

Their deaf subjects share feelings of reduced sex appeal and attribute the loss of sex appeal to the handicap of hearing loss directly. Notice, too, that even the term *hearing loss* connotes a deficit, something missing, a handicap.

Social support for culturally deaf, hard of hearing, and late-deafened communicators varies, depending on how they conceptualize deafness. For culturally Deaf people, there is the National Association of the Deaf (NAD). NAD sponsors conferences, national publications, and a clearinghouse that disseminates information that discusses deafness more positively. The national organization, Self Help for Hard of Hearing (SHHH) at its conventions and in its publications takes the view that hearing loss is a disability and is active in getting legislation passed to increase hearing conservation, neonatal hearing screening, hearing aid awareness, and assistive technology to augment communication. The Association of Late-Deafened Adults (ALDA) meets the needs of those adults who grew up hearing and lost their hearing later in life, and often sees both conceptualizations of deafness. ALDA has conferences and publications and is vocal about asking for more research to be done on late-deafness because most studies overlook the communicator who is late-deafened.

Future Implications: Including Deafness to Learn More About Communication

To extend present theories and research in speech communication, scholars are encouraged to rethink existing communication queries and include subjects with disabilities. The diversity and varied communication patterns noted in one speech community may be extrapolated to another speech community.

The discipline of communication studies has an opportunity to discover how communicators of various backgrounds (Jankowski, 1991; Rose, 1995) adapt to ever-changing communication climates and address communication challenges by employing creative, unconventional, collaborative problem-solving tactics. With workplaces and homes becoming noisier each year with more automation, new medications being developed that may have ototoxic effects, and the general aging of the U.S. population, the communication studies field needs to renew ties with its sister discipline, communication sciences and disorders. Deafness is increasingly affecting more communicators, influencing their communication, and affecting relational satisfaction.

CONCLUSION

Inevitably, there will be scholars from the field of Deaf studies who will be disappointed to find a chapter (let alone two) in a handbook on disabilities, given that Deaf studies advocates are concerned with taking the "disability" out of deafness. Harlan Lane (1984, 1992, 1995), discussed various constructions of deafness and denounces the pathological model by urging readers to view the deaf as a linguistic minority. He argued that the Deaf world has a distinct culture and that a change in how one conceptualizes deafness would highlight the richness of Deaf culture, as opposed to obsessing on the disability.

Other disciplines such as counseling (Sainsbury, 1986), psychology (Rousso, 1988), and medicine (Bradley, 1991; Carbary, 1988; Ekstrom, 1994; Meyer et al., 1997; Smith, 1992) are recognizing the need for deaf awareness and broader definitions of cultural diversity. Henwood and Pope-Davis (1994) have made their colleagues aware of how deafness and its cultural diversities affect counselors working with deaf and hard of hearing clients. Zazove (1997) educated the field of medicine on understanding Deaf and hard of hearing patients to increase the quality of healthcare. The benchmark models on which the communication studies discipline is firmly grounded (e.g., Altman & Taylor, 1973; Berger & Calabrese, 1975; Watzlawick, Beavin, & Jackson, 1967) do not include disability as a possible factor that affects communication. Hypotheses presented about deaf–deaf and deaf–hearing relationships were grounded in stereotypes and hearsay considered "common knowledge" and yet could not be supported (McIntosh, 1995a). Inclusion of disabilities in research can help abolish unsupported assumptions that are inherently formed and subtly reinforced when generating research questions and hypotheses.

DISCUSSION QUESTIONS

1. Prior to the discussion in this chapter, have you considered technology to be integral to communication? What experiences have you had with using interpreters or relay to communicate with a culturally deaf, hard of hearing, or late-deafened person? Discuss.

2. It is clear that many hearing people do not adapt the communication climate when interacting with someone who is not normal-hearing. As a hearing person, how would you communicate in terms of frequency, breadth, and depth with someone who is not able to depend

on spoken language for full information? Would it alter your view of that person in terms of intelligence? Would you consider the person to be disabled?

3.   Being exposed to someone who does not function auditorially in the hearing world is not the same as being immersed in the culture. Provide some insight as to how it might feel to be a CODA who can hear but is raised in a silent world that is heavily dependent on sight and touch.

REFERENCES

Altman, I., & Taylor, D. A. (1973). *Social penetration: The development of interpersonal relationships.* New York: Holt, Rinehart, & Winston.

Bell, A. G. (1884). Upon the formation of a deaf variety of the human race. *National Academy of Sciences Memoirs, 2,* 155–162.

Berger, C. R., & Calabrese, R. J. (1975). Some explorations in initial interaction and beyond: Toward a developmental theory of interpersonal communication. *Human Communication Research, 1,* 99–112.

Bradley, S. (1991, Aug.). The signs of silence: Communicating with deaf and hearing-impaired patients. *Journal of Emergency Medical Services, 16*(8), 26–28.

Carbary, L. J. (1988, Sept.). "What did you say?" Caring for the patient who has a hearing impairment. *Journal of Practical Nursing, 38*(3), 36–39.

Chan, L., & Lui, B. (1990). Self-concept among hearing Chinese children of deaf parents. *American Annals of the Deaf, 135,* 299–305.

Charlson, E. (1990). *Social cognition and self-concept of hearing adolescents with deaf parents.* Unpublished doctoral dissertation, University of CA, Berkeley, and San Francisco State University.

Cohen, L. H. (1994). *Train go sorry.* Boston: Houghton Mifflin.

Davis, H., & Silverman, S. R. (1960). *Hearing and deafness.* New York: Holt, Rinehart & Winston.

Desselle, D. D. (1994). Self-esteem, family climate, and communication patterns in relation to deafness. *American Annals of the Deaf, 139,* 322–328.

Ekstrom, I. (1994). Communicating with the deaf patient. *Plastic Surgical Nursing, 14*(1), 31–35.

Fay, E. A. (1897). An inquiry concerning the results of marriages of the deaf in America. *American Annals of the Deaf, 42,* 97–101.

Fay, E. A. (1898). *Marriages of the deaf in America.* Washington, DC: Volta Bureau.

Fine, M., & Ashe, A. (Eds.). (1988). *Women with disabilities: Essays in psychology, culture, and politics.* Philadelphia: Temple University Press.

Flodin, M. C. (1994). *Signing illustrated.* New York: Perigee.

Foster, S. (1989). Reflections of a group of deaf adults on their experiences in mainstream and residential school programs in the U.S. *Disability, Handicap & Society, 4*(1), 37–56.

Furth, H. G. (1966). *Thinking without language.* New York: Free Press.

Gaines, R., & Halpern-Felsher, B. L. (1995). Language preference and communication development of a hearing and deaf twin pair. *American Annals of the Deaf, 140*(1), 47–55.

Henwood, P. G., & Pope-Davis, D. B. (1994). Disability as cultural diversity: Counseling the hearing impaired. *Counseling Psychologist, 22,* 489–503.

Higgins, P. (1980). *Outsiders in a hearing world.* Beverly Hills, CA: Sage.

Hipskind, N. M. (1989). Visual stimuli in communication. In R. L. Schow & M. A. Nerbonne (Eds.), *Introduction to aural rehabilitation* (pp. 125–180). Boston: Allyn & Bacon.

Hulsing, M. M., Leutke-Stahlman, B., Loeb, D. F., & Nelson, P. (1995). Analysis of successful initiations of three children with hearing loss mainstreamed in kindergarten classrooms. *Language, Speech, and Hearing Services in Schools, 26*(1), 45–57.

Humphries, J. H., & Alcorn, B. J. (1995). *So you want to be an interpreter.* Amarillo, TX: H & H.

Infante, D. A., Rancer, A. S., & Womack, D. F. (1990). *Building communication theory.* Prospect Heights, IL: Waveland Press.

Jankowski, K. (1991). On communicating with Deaf people. In L. A. Samovar & R. E. Porter (Eds.), *Intercultural communication: A reader* (6th ed., pp. 142–150). Belmont, CA: Wadsworth.

King, C. M., & Quigley, S. P. (1985). *Reading and deafness.* San Diego, CA: College-Hill.

Kisor, H. (1990). *What's that pig outdoors?* New York: Hill and Wang.

Knapp, M. L., & Miller, G. L. (1985). *Handbook of interpersonal communication.* Beverly Hills, CA: Sage.

Knutson, J. F., & Lansing, C. R. (1990). The relationship between communication problems and psychological difficulties in persons with profound acquired hearing loss. *Journal of Speech and Hearing Disorders, 55,* 656–664.

Kolod, S. (1994). Lack of a common language: Deaf adolescents and hearing parents. *Contemporary Psychoanalysis, 30,* 634–650.

Lane, H. G. (1984). *When the mind hears: A history of the deaf.* New York: Random House.

Lane, H. G. (1992). *The mask of benevolence: Disabling the deaf community.* New York: Knopf.

Lane, H. G. (1995). Constructions of deafness. *Disability and Society, 10,* 171–189.

Lane, H., Hoffmeister, R., & Bahan, B. (1996). *Journey into deaf-world.* San Diego, CA: Dawn Sign Press.

Lovley, S. (1996). *Now what? Life after deaf.* Fairfax, VA: Association of Late-Deafened Adults.

Luey, H. S., & DiPietro, L. (1998). *An altered world: Living with new deafness.* Gallaudet University: National Information Center on Deafness.

Martin, F. N. (1994). *Introduction to audiology.* Englewood Cliffs, NJ: Prentice-Hall.

McIntosh, R. A. (1995a). *Self-disclosure in deaf-hearing, deaf-deaf, and hearing-hearing married couples: A look at frequency, value, and contexts in relation to marital satisfaction.* Unpublished doctoral dissertation, University of Texas, Austin.

McIntosh, R. A. (1995b). Mixed couples: Mixed communication. *Hearing Health, 11*(3), 23–24.

Meyer, S. G., Gulati, S., King, B., Nesheim, R. S., Sack, W. H., Sonis, W. A., Stuber, M. L., Webster, T. G., & Work, H. (1997). Issues to consider in deaf and hard of hearing patients. *American Family Physician, 56,* 2057–2064.

Minnett, A., Clark, K., & Wilson, G. (1994). Play behavior and communication between deaf and hard of hearing children and their hearing peers in an integrated preschool. *American Annals of the Deaf, 139,* 420–429.

Moore, M., & Levitan, L. (1992). *For hearing people only.* Rochester, NY: Deaf Life Press.

Moores, D. F. (1987). *Educating the deaf: Psychology, principles, and practices* (3rd ed.). Boston: Houghton Mifflin.

Nash, J., & Nash, A. (1981). *Deafness in society.* Lexington, MA: Lexington Books.

Padden, C., & Humphries, T. (1988). *Deaf in America: Voices from a culture.* Cambridge, MA: Harvard University Press.

Pichora-Fuller, M. K., Johnson, C. E., & Roodenburg, K. E. J. (1998). The discrepancy between hearing impairment and handicap in the elderly: Balancing transaction and interaction in conversation. *Journal of Applied Communication Research, 26,* 99–119.

Poizner, H., Klima, E. S., & Bellugi, U. (1987.) *What the hands reveal about the brain.* Cambridge, MA: MIT Press.

Preston, P. (1994). *Mother father deaf.* Cambridge, MA: Harvard University Press.

Reinzi, B. M. (1990). Influence and adaptability in families with deaf parents and hearing children. *American Annals of the Deaf, 135,* 402–408.

Rose, H. M. (1995). Apprehending deaf culture. *Journal of Applied Communication Research, 23,* 156–162.

Rousso, H. (1988). Daughters with disabilities: Defective women or minority women? In M. Fine & A. Ashe (Eds.), *Women with disabilities: Essays in psychology, culture, and politics* (pp. 139–171). Philadelphia: Temple University Press.

Sacks, O. (1989). *Seeing voices.* Berkeley: University of California Press.

Sainsbury, S. (1986). *Deaf worlds: A study of integration, segregation, and disability.* London: Hutchison.

Schein, J. (1989). *At home among strangers.* Washington, DC: Gallaudet University Press.

Schein, J. D., & Delk, M. T. (1974). *The deaf population of the United States.* Silver Spring, MD: National Association of the Deaf.

Seyfried, D., Hutchinson, J., & Smith, L. (1989). Language and speech of the hearing impaired. In R. Schow & M. Nerbonne (Eds.), *Introduction to aural rehabilitation* (pp. 181–239). Boston: Allyn & Bacon.

Smith L. E. (1992). Communicating with patients who are deaf. *Journal of the American Academy of Physician Assistants, 5,* 37–46.

Spencer, P., Koester, L. S., & Meadow-Orlans, K. (1994). Communicative interactions of deaf and hearing children in a day care center: An exploratory study. *American Annals of the Deaf, 139,* 512–518.

Spradley, T. S., & Spradley, J. P. (1978). *Deaf like me.* Washington, DC: Gallaudet University Press.

Sternberg, M. L. A. (1987). *American sign language dictionary.* New York: Harper & Row.

Stokoe, W. C. (1961). *Sign language structure, studies in linguistics.* Silver Spring, MD: Linstok Press.

Stokoe, W. C., Casterline, D., & Croneberg, C. (1965). *A dictionary of American Sign Language.* Silver Spring, MD: Linstok Press.

Vernon, M., & Andrews, J. (1990). *The psychology of deafness.* New York: Longman.

Vernon, M., & Ottinger, P. J. (1989). Psychosocial aspects of hearing impairment. In R. L. Schow & M. A. Nerbonne (Eds.), *Introduction to aural rehabilitation* (pp. 241–269). Boston: Allyn & Bacon.

von Bertalanffy, L. (1968). *General system theory: Foundations, development, applications.* New York: WW Norton.

Walker, L. A. (1986). *A loss for words.* New York: Harper & Row.

Winefield, R. (1987). *Never the twain shall meet: Bell, Gallaudet, and the communications debate.* Washington, DC: Gallaudet University Press.

Watzlawick, P., Beavin, J. B., & Jackson, D. D. (1967). *Pragmatics of human communication.* New York: WW Norton.

Wood, J. T., & Duck, S. (1995). *Under-studied relationships.* Thousand Oaks, CA: Sage.

Woodward, J. (1972). Implications for sociolinguists research among the deaf. *Sign Language Studies, 1,* 1–7.

Zazove, P. (1997). Understanding deaf and hard of hearing patients. *American Family Physician, 56,* 1953–1954.

ENDNOTES

1. Although ASL (Ameslan) is the third most used language in the United States, it is one of many sign languages. There is no universal sign language just as there is no universal spoken language.

2. Deaf-Hearing Couples Communication Enrichment Network (DHC) is free to any E-mail user. Contact the author for more information.

21

Sighting Sound/Sounding Sight: The "Violence" of Deaf–Hearing Communication

Heidi M. Rose
Villanova University

Andrew R. Smith
Edinboro University of Pennsylvania

Keywords: Deaf–hearing communication, ASL, Pierre Bourdieu, symbolic violence

Eyeth, a popular narrative in American Deaf[1] folklore, describes a Deaf child's experience of alienation from the hearing majority. The child attends a school for Deaf children and is discovered crying one Friday afternoon by his hearing teacher—crying because he does not want to go home to a weekend with his nonsigning family. The teacher tells him of a far-away planet called "Eyeth" where he can go someday to feel more at home. The child grows up, studies rocket science, and becomes an astronaut. He travels to this far-off planet and discovers, to his amazement, that on Eyeth everyone signs. There he gets a job teaching hearing/speaking children to sign and, one Friday afternoon, notices a child crying as she sits on the school steps. Recognizing that she feels left out at home because everyone in her family is Deaf, he tells her of a far-off planet called "Earth" where she will feel that she belongs. As the story ends, the viewer is left with a profound image of parallel universes, identical in every way except that in one, speech rules, and in the other, sign.

This narrative provides initial insight into the experience and perceptions of Deaf people living in a predominantly hearing world. How many hearing people have ever noticed that the name of our planet, "Earth," contains the word, "ear"? A mere linguistic fluke but, in this poignant story, it becomes the foundation for the creation of the world, Eyeth, where sight, not hearing, is the primary sense for linguistic perception; where the eyes, not the ears, are the primary organs for communication and language acquisition; and where the hands and face, not the voice, are the basis for linguistic expression.

Eyeth exposes the reality that Deaf and hearing people live in worlds based on different sensory orders of experience. When the two worlds meet, disruption occurs, notable in the story as the majority on both planets tries to make the minority into something it is not. This depiction resonates strongly with Deaf audiences who have been compelled to live in a dominant hearing world that, in general, views deafness as an aberration that must be controlled and "normalized" through the use of hearing aids, cochlear implants, and the mandated teaching of speech instead of sign language. However, in direct contrast to the reality of most interactions between the Deaf and hearing worlds, *Eyeth* suggests the arbitrariness of this power differential; in creating the possibility of worlds that are both separate and equal, the narrative compels its viewers to recognize and question the socially constructed concept of "normal."

Deafness itself may be viewed as a social construction that changes over time (Baynton, 1996). In a cultural critique of 19th-century America's crusade against sign language, Baynton outlined competing and evolving metaphors of that period that defined deaf people and guided hearing actions toward deaf people; these metaphors ranged from the "noble savage" in need of spiritual (Christian) enlightenment, to the "foreigner" whose inability to speak English threatened the national security of the country.

In the ensuing 100 years, the social construction has shifted; at present the competing metaphors of deafness contrast "disability" with "culture." The former is embodied primarily by the medical and some social scientific communities; it conceives of deafness as a deviation from the hearing norm and hence attempts to "cure" or remedy the deaf condition so that deaf individuals may function in society as much like hearing people as possible. The latter metaphor derives from the Deaf community itself as well as disciplines in the humanities and anthropology; it emphasizes the cultural dimensions of deafness, including distinction from the hearing majority in terms of language, values, norms, and artifacts, and works for recognition and acceptance of the Deaf community as an intact linguistic minority that does not need "fixing."

Baynton (1996) argued that we should view deafness both as a social construction and as a physical reality that involves undeniable differences in sensory experience. Any metaphor of deafness, including the culture and disability models, tends to be created by hearing people in an attempt to comprehend and explain deafness and thus tends to sidestep the reality that deaf individuals live in a different sensory world, which necessarily impacts their modes of perception and communication.

In this chapter, we move beyond the unresolved conflict between the two competing metaphors of culture and disability to explore instead the symbolic violence that occurs when two different sensory orders of experience collide. We argue that the symbolic violence of Deaf–hearing interaction is a function of (a) an institutionalized violence embedded in the dominant (hearing) social structure and thus embedded in both hearing and Deaf communicative expectations and practices, and (b) a fear of modal and sensory difference arising from a progressive distancing of hearing people from the deep connections between language and bodily expression. The chapter begins with a discussion of symbolic violence and continues with an in-depth application to Deaf–hearing communication.[2]

SYMBOLIC VIOLENCE

For any violence to occur, there must be some violation of a person's autonomy or dignity. Garver (1968) stated this point most succinctly:

> What is fundamental about violence is that a person is violated. And if one immediately senses the truth of that statement, it must be because a person has certain rights which are undeniably, indissolubly, connected with his [sic] being a person. One of these is the right to his body, to determine what his body does and what is done to his body—inalienable because without his body he would cease to be a person. The dignity of a person does not consist in his remaining dignified, but rather in his ability to make his own decisions. (p. 819)

Making one's own decisions (and feeling free to express them) without any sense of coercion from an external source, and having unqualified control over one's bodily bearing in the world, are perhaps the most fundamental rights of being a person. Violence occurs when these rights are infringed on, whether overtly through physical coercion or covertly through psychological force. In an attempt to understand how contact between Deaf and hearing worlds produces "violence," the authors discuss the nature and function of covert, psychological violence—what Bourdieu (1991) referred to as "symbolic violence."[3]

Symbolic violence may be direct and personal, such as an explicit threat imposed by one person on another, or it may be indirect and impersonal, as when embedded in institutional relations of power. Following Bourdieu (1991), violence may be exercised indirectly through the institutional authority of one who has status and resources that another or others do not. It is important to note that Bourdieu's notion of "institutional" is "not necessarily a particular organization—this or that family or factory, for instance—but is any relatively durable set of social relations which *endows* individuals with power, status and resources of various kinds" (Thompson, 1991, p. 8). Whether symbolic violence is primarily direct or indirect is contingent, then, on interactions in particular institutional contexts, and in context the difference between the two forms becomes more a matter of degree rather than kind.

For example, two hearing-dominated institutions have had extensive influence on the lives—the bodies—of Deaf individuals: the medical community and the educational establishment. To draw, for the moment, from the institution of deaf education, we find evidence of symbolic violence that has been legitimized by the existence of the institution itself—violence manifested primarily in the practices of language instruction. A direct use of symbolic violence may be seen in early models of deaf education in which children lived under the threat of corporeal punishment if they used their hands to sign, instead of communicating through spoken English and lipreading. More indirect symbolic violence is situated within the historic overarching goal of deaf education. With the goal of integrating deaf children into the hearing world, English naturally became the preferred language of classroom instruction and hearing teachers were "legitimately" preferred over deaf teachers, thus establishing a power and status differential between deaf and hearing persons early in the deaf person's life.

Deaf children raised in the hearing-dominated educational institution have thus been socialized into a state of inferiority and indebtedness[4] to their hearing teachers who work steadfastly to "fix" them, and whose mere bodily presence constitutes a threat against potential transgressive behavior (e.g., using one's hands to communicate). Garver (1968) argued that such "institutionalized quiet violence ... operates when people are deprived of choices in a systematic way by the very manner in which transactions normally take place. It is as real and as wicked as a thief with a knife" (pp. 821–822). Forbidding the learning of ASL and mandating speech and lipreading training deprive deaf children of linguistic choice. In addition, these practices establish a condition of Deaf–hearing social relations that inherently endows hearing people with economic as well as educational control and superiority.

Through these examples we can begin to recognize how symbolic violence is immanent in any authorized discourse embedded in institutional relations of power, and how it is enacted covertly through the potential of persons with "legitimate" authority (power, status, resources) to exercise force over those in subordinate positions. Indirect symbolic violence, especially, becomes "scripted" into everyday relationships in such a way that it seems "natural" to both the one who violates and the one who is violated (Bourdieu, 1991; Bourdieu & Passeron, 1990; Hammoudi, 1997). Whereas more direct forms have immediate physical effects (one feels physically confined or displaced by an explicit threat, for example), indirect forms rule physically (or dispose a person bodily) by first dominating psychologically—that is, by first influencing how and under what interpersonal conditions one constructs an image of oneself (Hammoudi, 1997). And one then learns to value oneself according to the extent to which he or she is capable of producing and reproducing linguistic forms and social habits that are "redeemable" in a speech community or "linguistic market" (cf. Ross-Landi, 1983, pp. 48–52).

The impact of internalizing a dominated image of self can be gauged by addressing how those who are subject to symbolic violence are, in effect, complicitous in their own domination. The idea of complicity in this context may seem a bit extreme, since complicity is usually connoted with culpability or passivity. Forms of complicity exist, however—such as children's complicity with their parents' decisions and demands (e.g., Maxwell, 1985; Strong, 1988), many women's economic and linguistic complicity with patriarchal forms of subjugation (e.g., Irigaray, 1993; Kraus, 1993), and workers' complicity with the discourse of the dominant class (e.g., Cronon, 1996; Huspek, 1993)—that are "neither passive submission to external constraints nor a free adherence to values" (Bourdieu, 1991, pp. 50–51). For example, a deaf child is, in many respects, externally constrained when the decision is made to implant a cochlear device in his or her inner ear, but no such constraint exists when a deaf child born to hearing parents is raised in an "oral only" environment both at home and school. Even before improved medical technology, for generations thousands of "oral" deaf people have interacted with the hearing world according to language and social practices that "constructed" them as inferior, yet many deaf individuals still speak and act according to such constructions and would argue that they do so freely and without external constraints. Many deaf individuals indicate tremendous pride in their ability to "overcome the hardships" of deafness.

That people are complicitous (consciously or preconsciously) with their own domination should be addressed critically, however, only if the critic is willing to reflect on his or her own tendencies in this regard. As already suggested, we all participate to various degrees in institutional or organizational practices that "decide for us," "mold our bodies," and endure throughout our life histories in such a way that we learn how to "succeed" in a dominated position as if it were "second nature." Similarly, a person who exercises authority over others may not intend consciously to dominate them, but does so preconsciously by virtue of the fact that he or she has embodied the "legitimacy of the official language" and its attendant social norms in such a way that others who deviate from that language and those norms are devalued or dismissed. That one is complicitous with his or her own domination, or violates the autonomy and dignity of others due to the ostensible demands of his or her position in a particular "field," suggests for Bourdieu how the *habitus*—one's socially learned predispositions— generates and conditions set "practices, perceptions and attitudes which are 'regular' without being consciously co-ordinated or governed by any 'rule'" (Thompson, 1991, p. 12; see also Taylor, 1993). Indeed, devaluing and dismissing others occurs regularly, beyond the conscious following of a rule, in the everyday lives of vast numbers of people.

Just because one is conditioned to accept or otherwise "live with" such regularity, however, does not mean that he or she cannot resist it and engage in emancipatory practices. The habitus enables and disposes us not only to speak, think, feel, and act in ways that perpetuate dominant forms of symbolic violence, but also to resist and experiment with these forms, to learn and learn how to learn in creative if not radical ways (Bourdieu, 1977, 1991).[5] Symbolic domination can, indeed, be resisted and experimented with, but one must do so with care. Sometimes resistance legitimizes and strengthens dominant structure, and experimentation can yield unsavory as well as emancipatory results. In fact, Bourdieu (1991) contended that "resistance" often if not inevitably perpetuates a dualist mode of thought (resistance/submission) and ultimately functions more as a way of impressing one's "fellows" than making any real difference in the workings of the dominant system (cf. Foucault, 1977, 1984; Huspek, 1993).

Although the scope of this chapter does not allow us to cover the depth of Bourdieu's theory of practice, the preceding discussion permits an exploration of the ways in which covert psychological violence alternately silences and indebts Deaf persons in institutional relations of power, and how the legitimation of these "symbolic" forms of domination further rigidifies dominant (institutionally constructed and compensated) images of self and other. In the following sections, we are concerned not only with the degree to which Deaf persons are inculcated (or not, as the case may be) into a linguistic market that values or devalues the ways they communicate and gain knowledge, but also the ways in which they improvise from or "out of" such a "market." To illustrate, the authors turn to literature that has explored conceptions of deafness and Deaf–hearing communication.

DEAF–HEARING INTERACTION

Scholars from related disciplines of communication, sociolinguistics, linguistics, psychology, comparative literature, anthropology, and the more recently developed Deaf studies have contributed to deafness-related research. The last 40 years have produced significant studies of, for instance, the structure and nature of American Sign Language (ASL), ASL-English translation and interpreting, the history and consequences of various educational practices regarding deaf children, the development and nature of ASL literature, and the ongoing conflict between theorizing deafness as pathology/disability or as culture. The breadth of this literature is too vast to review in these pages; since this chapter focuses on the problem of Deaf–hearing communication, the discussion is limited to those studies for which communication is a central component.

The literature reveals both competing and complementary views of deafness as well as of the complex relationship between Deaf and hearing people. Problems of control, the social construction of deafness (identities), language development, and forms of bodily expression become the primary sites of struggle in Deaf–hearing interaction.

Control

Consonant with the cultural model defining the Deaf experience both in the United States and elsewhere, scholars from diverse disciplines have identified the Deaf community with other traditionally marginalized ethnic or racial groups that have experienced oppressive conditions within the dominant culture (e.g., Baynton, 1996; Lane, 1992; Marcowicz & Woodward, 1982; Maxwell, 1985; Padden & Humphries, 1988; Reagan, 1995; Rose, 1995, 1996, 1997; de Saint-Loup, 1996; Strong, 1988; Wilcox, 1989). To resist and, ultimately, to end this oppression requires the assertion of an identity different from the one constructed by the majority group; with this identity comes a voice, the power to be heard. Gaining this voice is equated with autonomy, with taking control of one's sense of self and future, as opposed to acquiescing to the "violence" of the majority.

For example, hearing people have experienced a clear history of discomfort in Deaf–hearing interactions, created in part because hearing people view deafness as an "invisible disability" (de Saint Loup, 1996, p. 3). Except for the occasional person using sign language on television, the Deaf world is removed from, and completely foreign to, hearing people (Reagan, 1995). In a Deaf–hearing exchange, the hearing person does not expect any breach or difference in communication and is uncomfortably surprised when that breach occurs. Rather than approaching the interaction as one of mutual misunderstanding, the hearing person typically blames the Deaf "other" for the communicative failure. Drawing from Bourdieu (1991), this blame derives from the sense of legitimate authority embedded in the hearing person's consciousness since birth, an authority that results in the hearing person's violation of the Deaf person's autonomy and dignity by devaluing his or her language or communication mode.

Clearly alluding to the covert, psychological violence perpetuated by our society, Maxwell (1985) details the unstated social policy designed to remove Deaf adults from any decision making in the education of deaf children, a practice which ultimately desires to eliminate the Deaf community's cultural uniqueness by fully integrating them into mainstream hearing society. This creates complex tensions within the Deaf and hearing worlds in terms of the social–political–emotional meanings behind speaking and signing. As Bourdieu (1991) suggested, "legitimate [communicative] competence can function as *linguistic capital*, producing a profit of distinction on the occasion of each social exchange" (p. 55). The hearing world welcomes a deaf person who speaks because he/she possesses the "legitimate" linguistic and cultural capital to interact successfully with hearing people; the Deaf world shuns this same deaf person as the equivalent of an "Uncle Tom." In contrast, a Deaf person who signs is welcomed by the Deaf world, yet is shunned by the hearing world because he or she is perceived as deviating from what is considered normative (Maxwell, 1985). Choosing how to be linguistically competent essentially "double-binds" the deaf individual; a profit in one mode comes only at the expense of the other.

Despite isolated and fragmented moments of hearing persons' attempts to understand Deaf perspectives, the inevitable minority status of Deaf individuals will not improve until Deaf people "take control of their own destiny" by expressing themselves and their differences to the hearing world (de Saint Loup, 1996, p. 23), and doing so on their own terms. This may be achieved in part by asserting control over education of deaf children through the advocacy of bilingual–bicultural programs in both residential and mainstream schools (Reagan, 1995; Strong, 1988). Bilingual–bicultural education requires hearing educators to relinquish exclusive linguistic control over deaf children and, in so doing, provides children with the means to develop a Deaf identity, to interact more effectively with the hearing majority, and to educate the hearing world about the Deaf world.

Social Constructions of Deafness

Some literature on deafness is guided by an intentional and conscious utilization of either the pathology/disability or culture model of deafness to frame a particular argument, while other studies reveal, in their tacit use of either model, much about the implications of such embedded frames.

Although the focus in this chapter does not include linguistic research on ASL, it is worth noting that the first scholarship to outline ASL as a natural language with the same structures as any spoken–written language was developed by a hearing professor of English and linguistics, William Stokoe (1960), not a Deaf or native user of ASL. Stokoe's work laid the foundation for viewing the Deaf community as a linguistic and cultural minority, yet his work was held highly suspect at first by Deaf and hearing alike, who had been socialized to view ASL as a mere system of gestures or as an inferior form of English. The initial response to Stokoe's work—and the fact that well over 100 years had passed since ASL became standardized in the American Deaf community—demonstrates the depth of symbolic violence committed on Deaf individuals; in Bourdieu's (1991) terms, the internalized dominant image of inferiority is most evident in Deaf people's historically conflicted perception of their language—on one hand, cherishing it as their most natural means of communication and on the other hand, feeling ashamed that it was not a "legitimate" language like English.

Despite the last 40 years of research supporting and extending Stokoe's findings, this internalized image of inferiority, with regard to language specifically, persists in many Deaf high school and college students. Even at a university like Gallaudet (the only liberal arts university for deaf people) where sign language and speech are valued equally, students have demonstrated the impact of institutionalized violence that marks them as inferior because of their preferred language. Fernandes (1983) led Gallaudet students in a project exploring the creation of new languages and found that many students continued to look to English as the foundation from which ASL derived. For example, students assumed that ASL signs refer directly to words from English, as opposed to linguistic concepts. In a diglossic community—one in which two or more languages coexist—the majority language may often assume the position of the "high variety" or "real" language by which all others are judged.

Strong evidence of this internalized dominant image of inferiority comes from Seamans (1996), a deaf person who writes from inside the discourse of the educational institution. Representing the perspective of many "oral" deaf people, he criticizes the Deaf culture movement and promotion of ASL as cop-outs on the part of deaf people, defining these movements as deliberate threats to the abilities of deaf people to be part of "normal" society. In essence, Seamans argues that ASL and the culture model serve to disempower deaf people, because they exist to keep Deaf people separate from the majority culture. Historically, for example, deaf residential schools emphasized vocational training; Seamans asserts that this deprived children of the high academic opportunities and potential for success available in hearing/English school environments. Enmeshed as he is within the institutionalized system of inferiority, however, Seamans cannot recognize that, under the linguistic market valued by the dominant hearing society, residential schools had little choice but to provide students with vocational training; deaf adults had little choice but to take jobs that focused on manual labor and required minimal linguistic exchange. The present movement toward bilingual–bicultural education, which occurs primarily in residential schools, changes the perception of the linguistic market. Bilingual–bicultural programs simultaneously acknowledge ASL as the first language of Deaf children and support the teaching of English as a second language, thus emphasizing the necessity of functioning in a majority English-using society. Seamans' work provides an excellent example of the degree to which deaf people have been inculcated into the practices of a specific linguistic market—a market whose values of turning a "profit" on the event of each exchange are so deeply embedded that Seamans cannot recognize how they construct and market his own image of self and other deaf people.

Similarly, some hearing researchers, who initially may appear either to advocate for deaf people or to assert a neutral view of deafness, in fact reflect the unconscious framing of deafness from within the values of the dominant linguistic market. For example, in an essay pointing out the need for widespread development and availability of television closed captioning for deaf viewers, Austin (1980) argued that the television industry has ignored a large percentage of the viewing market. In identifying this market, however, Austin does not distinguish between "Deaf" and "hearing impaired" individuals, thus ignoring the different linguistic needs of the two. Austin assumed English to be the normative language, and speech–writing to be the normative communication modes. To support his argument concerning the need for English closed-captioning, Austin cited evidence suggesting that deaf people rely far more on facial affect (which does not provide linguistic information) than on lip-reading when watching television, and that lip-reading skills do not improve from watching television. This argument is notable for what it lacks, or omits: (a) it assumes a linguistic market consisting only of English, the dominant language, and ignores the existence of ASL, and (b) this assumption results in devaluing a sensory order of experience (deafness) that is primarily visual and spatial. The only solution presented for deaf viewers is the written form of English, through closed-captioning. Although clearly an improvement in the mass transmission of information to the deaf population, closed-captioning is nonetheless embedded solely within the social construction of deafness that places deaf individuals in a position of inferiority.[6]

Other researchers have attempted to extend communication theories to the deaf population, most notably Booth-Butterfield and Booth-Butterfield (1994) in their study of the relationship between communication anxiety and signing effectiveness. Arguing from within the dominant system, they construct their argument from, at first glance, an innocuous view of deaf communication based in "channel overload." They argue that deaf people may experience channel overload, and hence communication anxiety, because in communicating with hearing people they must rely solely on the visual channel, whereas hearing people gain information from both visual and auditory channels. This argument may have some inherent value, but their study was conducted in a residential deaf high school, a place in which communication occurs between deaf people or between deaf and hearing signers—in other words, a place in which this kind of channel overload should not exist. In not recognizing the inconsistency of their argument,

these researchers reveal their unconscious hearing bias, a bias deeply entrenched in the social constructions of deafness. If no bias existed—if
Booth-Butterfield and Booth-Butterfield had viewed Deaf/ASL as separate and equal to hearing/English—they could have argued persuasively
by analogy; that is, if hearing people manifest communication anxiety
through certain vocal and articulatory problems, then Deaf people may
manifest communication anxiety through complementary manual and facial dysfluencies.[7]

Like so many hearing educators throughout the history of deaf education,
Booth-Butterfield and Booth-Butterfield (1994) perceived the deaf "condition" as unfortunate and abnormal, while the perception of deficiency
is more latent: Deaf people, due to their sensory deficiency, experience
channel and cognitive overload that impedes their ability to communicate.
Yet, in deaf–hearing interaction, why are hearing people not considered to
experience a similar kind of overload as they struggle to comprehend the
facial expressions and gestures of the deaf person, or his or her "different-
sounding" speech? When communicating with a Deaf person, hearing individuals find themselves at the same communicative disadvantage but,
because every linguistic exchange is marked by the institutional power
that grants status and authority to the hearing world, the onus for communicative success or failure is automatically placed on the deaf individual.
Research emerging from this deeply entrenched social construction identifies the deaf experience not as separate and equal, but as separate and
abnormal/deficient.

In fact, the power and status differential between Deaf and hearing people runs so deep that it makes itself known without, or beyond, language; a
Deaf person encounters intimidation the moment he or she enters a predominantly hearing situation, and a hearing person imposes on Deaf persons
(on a preconscious, if not unconscious level) the moment he or she enters
their space. As Bourdieu (1991) stated, "The relation between two people
may be such that one of them has only to appear in order to impose on the
other, without even having to want to, let alone formulate any command,
a definition of the situation and of himself (as intimidated, for example),
which is all the more absolute and undisputed for not having to be stated"
(pp. 51–52; cf. Smith, 1994; Smith & Martinez, 1995). Whether the context involves a hearing waiter taking a food order from a deaf patron, or a
hearing parent visiting a deaf school, the hearing person expects accommodation and the deaf person knows he or she is obligated to adapt to the
hearing person's communicative norms.

The authors have already argued for the usefulness of Bourdieu's (1991) theory to analyze the ways in which institutional structures shape Deaf children at an early age such that their choices are delimited and their identities systemically forged by dominant linguistic, medical, and educational paradigms. Bourdieu's theory can also help if one consciously steps outside the dominant system and explores how the development of Deaf culture and bilingual–bicultural education has created a social and educational milieu through which Deaf persons have learned to expose the taken-for-granted forms of symbolic violence that characterize their encounters with dominant hearing practices.

Bourdieu's work suggests a framework for understanding how Deaf artists, for example, generate new discourse genres that articulate and mitigate the effects of domination for themselves (as artists) and their audiences. Poetic invention may be viewed as a means of demonstrating ownership of language; thus, while the original poetry and narrative of ASL may be slow to impact Deaf-hearing interactions (because the majority of the hearing world is neither exposed to it nor conversant in ASL), these poetic texts enhance Deaf autonomy and dignity and create resistance to hearing "violence" as they reconstruct deafness outside of hearing/English norms and values. Language and identity are inextricably connected, and when Deaf individuals find and assert their "voice" in artistic uses of ASL their senses of self and capacity to take control of their lives are greatly enhanced (Rose, 1996, 1997).

Language Development and Bodily Expression

Thus far the focus of this chapter has been on clashes in Deaf–hearing communication based in expectations and practices that derive from the dominant (hearing) social structure; focus now shifts to the relationship between language and bodily expression to explore another manifestation of symbolic violence in Deaf–hearing interaction.

Researchers of sign language and Deaf culture frequently refer to the generally accepted conclusion that bodily expression and/or gestural communication predates linguistic expression (e.g., Baynton, 1996; Hall, 1989; Haukioja, 1993). This view places spoken language higher on the evolutionary ladder of communicative form than expression through the body, because gesture (ostensibly) does not possess linguistic structure and is thus perceived as a less sophisticated means of communication. One reason for the historic inferior status of sign language, prior to Stokoe's (1960) work, is its association with this limited notion of gesture.

Recently, however, researchers have challenged the separation of spoken-written language and gesture in various ways, resulting in a fresh recognition of inherent similarities between communication through sign and communication through speech (e.g., Daniels, 1994; Haukioja, 1993). Challenging the view that language—whether signed or spoken—is separate from gesture, Haukioja observed the language acquisition of deaf babies and discovered that, initially, lexical signs and gestures were inseparable; babies used both but could neither distinguish between them nor recognize linguistic properties (rules) in the signs until later in their linguistic development. Haukioja suggested this phenomenon to be true of hearing babies as well, concluding that (a) babies naturally possess the inclination to communicate bodily, and (b) bodily expression is inherently linked to linguistic expression, whether the mode is sign or speech.

Furthering this notion, Bouvet (1996) explored the relationship between language and actual bodily experience, suggesting that, "experience of the body and our representations of it [are] at the origin of the development of human language" (p. 27). Bouvet suggested, similarly to Haukioja (1993), that sign languages and spoken languages are far more similar than was previously thought, as both are linked directly to corporeal experience. Using spoken French and French Sign Language (LSF), Bouvet drew attention to the metaphors of the body embedded in spoken language and sign language, which serve to give physical reality to abstract concepts. For example, an LSF sign for "lazy"—expressed as two hands dangling at the end of the forearms, which are held horizontally and move downward twice—directly relates to a French spoken idiom, "to do nothing with one's ten fingers"; and both sign and phrase exist as "representations linked to our corporeal experience" that associate the hand with activity, action, work, abilities (p. 30). Viewed another way, as bodily experience both sign and speech possess iconic and indexical, as well as purely symbolic, elements of meaning constitution (Rose, 1992).

Bouvet's (1996) comparison of spoken French idioms and LSF signs implies that, whether deaf or hearing, humans possess a common perceptual base in bodily expression—and that this is simply made more manifest in signed form:

> even within the abstract lexicon of French Sign Language, we find representations of the body that are also found in the imaged or metaphoric expressions of French spoken language—expressions *very often disembodied from the*

gestural language that created them, but which the medium of a gestural language makes reappear. (p. 37)

Thus, although the sensory experience of Deaf and hearing people is undeniably different, they both "participate in the same culture arising from a way of living and behaving gesturally." (p. 38).

To argue that humans initially perceive the world directly through the body's interaction with the world, and that linguistic expression is linked to bodily expression, permits a provocative recognition of consonance between sign language and spoken language. More salient to this chapter, the authors suggest that it also reconfigures the tensions in Deaf–hearing interaction. The linguistic link to the body is more tacit in the hearing world than in the Deaf world; not only are the spatial and corporeal metaphors conventionalized beyond conscious awareness in spoken English,[8] but much of the body itself is (seemingly) not required for linguistic communication—one needs only the voice. Speech, conceived as a linguistic mode of expression in which gesture is merely an enhancement of communicated meaning, distances hearing people from their bodies. The authors suggest, then, that in general, hearing people have been inculcated into a dualist mode of thinking about language and body that sustains unconsciousness of, and perhaps discomfort with, modes of expression that foreground gesture. This preconceived and hence taken-for-granted separation explains in part why many hearing individuals experience discomfort or even fear when confronted with Deaf people and sign language.

The devaluing of the Deaf communicative mode may be viewed as symbolic violence in the way it has been defined thus far, but the violence derives from more than a judgment based on "difference," "abnormality" or a disability/pathology model. The authors suggest that the symbolic violence derives from a fear of engaging the bodily expression with which many, or most, hearing people have lost affiliation. For example, after being immersed in the language for a while, hearing college students learning ASL frequently reflect on their fear of looking foolish as they make unfamiliar facial expressions or try to use their bodies to punctuate a gesture; often students refer to the discomfort of feeling like they are "acting," where acting means expressing themselves in a "fake" and unnatural manner.

Hearing students will often quickly recognize the metaphor and/or metonymy of sign language; for example, in the sign for "stress" (as in, "I feel stressed") one hand, open with palm facing down, presses down hard on the other hand which is in a fist position in front of the signer's torso. The sign for "hate" or "intense dislike" is made by the thumb and middle finger of both hands "flicking" away from the signer's body. Hearing students take delight in metaphor/metonymy when they observe it in sign language; they have difficulty, however, relaxing enough to engage it in their own bodies, and they have little awareness of its manifestation in spoken language. Bodily expression requires using space assertively and, in turn, requires a kind of vulnerability that makes hearing people uncomfortable. Thus, to avoid the initially disquieting (re)discovery of the relationship between bodily expression and language, the hearing world in general negates the legitimacy of the Deaf language and communicative mode. If hearing and Deaf people could recognize the consonance of their experience—that bodily expression is the foundation of both sign and speech—then Deaf–hearing interactions might proceed from a stronger position of equality and understanding.

CONCLUSION

In this chapter an attempt has been made to reveal the futility of perpetuating the discourse of conflict between the "disability" and "culture" constructions of deafness. As competing metaphors, the discourse is unresolvable; the authors argue instead that the tensions of Deaf–hearing interaction are better conceptualized as manifestations of symbolic violence. This covert, psychological violence is a function of an institutionalized devaluation of gestural language and communicative practices, which derives in part from the ever-increasing but imperceptible distancing of many hearing people from the deep connections between bodily expression and language.

Hearing and Deaf persons alike can benefit from self-reflexively analyzing their assumptions, expectations, and practices when interacting with each other. Hearing persons, especially, can benefit from remembering that Deaf individuals operate from a sensory order of experience that highlights visual perception. It is easier for hearing people to adapt to a visual–spatial communicative mode than it is for Deaf people to adapt to an auditory mode. Thus, if hearing persons utilize direct eye contact, active facial expressions, gestures and even pantomime, in addition to writing, communication will be enhanced.[9]

The value of Bourdieu's work lies in aiding recognition of the hidden, disguised symbolic violence in social exchanges. A hearing person's best of intentions may mask the reality of depriving a Deaf person of his or her autonomy and dignity. Engaging others with respect for difference can create insightful explorations into distinct sensory orders of experience.

DISCUSSION QUESTIONS

1. If you are hearing, what experience have you had with Deaf individuals? What assumptions have you made about them?
2. If you have ever seen or studied ASL, what similarities and/or differences from spoken English have you observed?
3. Do you agree with the authors' contention that hearing people are often disconnected from bodily expression and experience in their communication? Why or why not?
4. How is nonverbal communication different from sign language?
5. Does the term *disability* connote symbolic violence? Why or why not?
6. What other groups in the United States or other parts of the world experience symbolic violence? In what way(s)?

REFERENCES

Arendt, H. (1970). *On violence*. New York: Harcourt Brace.

Austin, B. (1980). The deaf audience for television. *Journal of Communication, 30*, 25–30.

Baynton, D. (1996). *Forbidden signs: American culture and the campaign against sign language*. Chicago: University of Chicago Press.

Booth-Butterfield, M., & Booth-Butterfield, S. (1994). Communication anxiety and signing effectiveness: Testing an interference model among deaf communicators. *Journal of Applied Communication Research, 22*, 273–286.

Booth-Butterfield, M., & Booth-Butterfield, S. (1995). The study of anxiety and signing as social science. *Journal of Applied Communication Research, 23*, 163–166.

Bourdieu, P. (1977). *Outline of a theory of practice* (R. Nice, Trans.). New York: Cambridge University Press.

Bourdieu, P. (1985). The genesis of the concept of habitus and field. *Sociocentrum, 2*, 195–220.

Bourdieu, P. (1991). *Language and symbolic power* (G. Raymond & M. Adamson, Trans.). Cambridge, MA: Harvard University Press.

Bourdieu, P., & Passeron, C. (1990). *Reproduction in education, society, and culture* (2nd ed.). Newbury Park, CA: Sage.

Bouvet, D. (1996). Metaphors of the body in gestural languages. *Diogenes, 175*, 27–39.

Brubaker, R. (1985). Rethinking classical theory: The sociological vision of Pierre Bourdieu. *Theory and Society, 14*, 745–775.

Collins, C. (1993). Determination and contradiction: An appreciation and critique of the work of Pierre Bourdieu on language and education. In C. Calhoun, E. LiPuma, & M. Postone (Eds.), *Bourdieu: Critical perspectives* (pp. 116–138). Chicago: University of Chicago Press.

Cronon, C. (1996). Bourdieu and Foucault on power and modernity. *Philosophy and Social Criticism, 22*, 55–85.

Daniels, M. (1994). The effect of sign language on hearing children's language development. *Communication Education, 43*, 291–298.

de Saint-Loup, A. (1996). A history of misunderstandings: The history of the deaf. *Diogenes, 175*, 1–25.

Fernandes, J. J. (1983). Sign language and "picture-talk": An experiential learning approach. *Communication Education, 32*, 197–202.

Foucault, M. (1977). *Discipline and punish: The birth of the prison* (A. Sheridan, Trans.). London: Allen Lane, Penguin Books.

Foucault, M. (1984). *The history of sexuality* (Vol. 1, R. Hurley, Trans.). New York: Vintage.

Garver, N. (1968, June 24). What violence is. *The Nation*, 819–822.

Hall, E. T. (1989). Deaf culture, tacit culture, and ethnic relations. *Sign Language Studies, 65*, 291–304.

Hammoudi, A. (1997). *Master and disciple: The cultural foundations of Moroccan authoritarianism.* Chicago: University of Chicago Press.

Hanks, W. F. (1996). *Language and communicative practices.* Boulder, CO: Westview Press.

Haukioja, T. (1993). Pointing in sign language and gesture: An alternative interpretation. *Language and Communication, 13*, 19–25.

Huspek, M. (1993). Dueling structures: The theory of resistance in discourse. *Communication Theory, 3*, 1–25.

Irigaray, L. (1993). *je, tu, nous: Toward a culture of difference* (A. Martin, Trans.). New York: Routledge.

Kraus, B. (1993). Gender and symbolic violence: Female oppression in the light of Pierre Bourdieu's theory of practice. In C. Calhoun, E. LiPuma, & M. Postone (Eds.), *Bourdieu: Critical perspectives* (pp. 156–177). Chicago: University of Chicago Press.

Lane, H. (1992). *The mask of benevolence: Disabling the Deaf community.* New York: Knopf.

Marcowicz, H., & Woodward, J. (1982). Language and the maintenance of ethnic boundaries in the Deaf community. In J. Woodward (Ed.), *How you gonna get to heaven if you can't talk with Jesus: On depathologizing deafness* (pp. 3–19). Silver Spring, MD: T.J. Publishers.

Maxwell, M. (1985). Some functions and uses of literacy in the Deaf community. *Language in Society, 14*, 205–221.

Padden, C., & Humphries, T. (1988). *Deaf in America: Voices from a culture.* Cambridge, MA: Harvard University Press.

Reagan, T. (1995) A sociocultural understanding of deafness: American Sign Language and the culture of Deaf people. *International Journal of Intercultural Relations, 19*, 239–251.

Rose, H. (1992). A semiotic analysis of artistic American Sign Language and a performance of poetry. *Text and Performance Quarterly, 12*, 146–159.

Rose, H. M. (1995). Apprehending Deaf culture. *Journal of Applied Communication Research, 23*, 156–162.

Rose, H. M. (1996). Inventing one's "voice": The interplay of convention and self-expression in ASL narrative. *Language in Society, 25*, 427–444.

Rose, H. M. (1997). Julianna Fjeld's "The Journey": Identity production in an ASL performance. *Text and Performance Quarterly, 17*, 331–342.

Ross-Landi, F. (1983). *Language as work and trade: A semiotic homology for linguistics and economics* (M. Adams, Trans.). Boston: Bergin & Garvy.

Seamans, P. (1996). A socio-anthropological perspective of American Deaf education. *Diogenes, 175*, 41–53.

Smith, A. R. (1994). Phrasing, linking, judging: Communication and critical phenomenology. *Human Studies, 17*, 139–161.

Smith, A. R., & Martinez, J. (1995). Signifying harassment: Communication, ambiguity, and power. *Human Studies, 18*, 63–87.

Stokoe, W. (1960). *Sign language structure.* Silver Spring, MD: Linstok.

Strong, M. (Ed.) (1988). *Language learning and deafness.* New York: Cambridge University Press.

Taylor, C. (1993). To follow a rule . . . In C. Calhoun, E. LiPuma, & M. Postone (Eds.), *Bourdieu: Critical perspectives* (pp. 45–60). Chicago: University of Chicago Press.

Thompson, J. B. (1991). Editor's introduction. In P. Bourdieu (Ed.), *Language and symbolic power* (pp. 1–31). Cambridge, MA: Harvard University Press.
Wilcox, S. (Ed.). (1989). *American Deaf culture*. Silver Spring, MD: Linstok.

ENDNOTES

1. According to standard practice, uppercase "Deaf" refers to membership in a culture defined primarily by its use of American Sign Language (ASL) as the preferred and primary language. Lowercase "deaf" refers to the physiological condition of being unable to hear (Padden & Humphries, 1988). Individuals who are deaf (e.g., they speak and lipread) often prefer to self-identify as *hearing impaired*, a term that clearly links them to the hearing world.

2. It should be noted here that we are both hearing persons. Rose has worked with members of the Deaf community for 8 years, and Smith has worked extensively in a variety of intercultural contexts. The fact remains, however, that our perceptions necessarily derive from our experiences as hearing persons.

3. See Arendt's (1970) treatise on (human) violence, which suggests a relation between power and violence that is especially pertinent for this discussion. Although she argued persuasively that violence is a means requiring "implements" or tools, while power is an end in itself that presupposes the collective will of the group, she also suggested that this apparent difference in kind is actually one of degree. Violence resides at the end of power, paradoxically, as both its most extreme form and its loss.

4. Although others have demonstrated how gifts and debts are ways to gain a "hold" on others, Bourdieu is the first to conceptualize such a hold as symbolic violence. In modern industrialized societies, symbolic violence is institutionalized through "objective mechanisms," according to Bourdieu (1977), such that explicit master–servant relations of domination are "euphemized" as "credit, confidence, obligation, personal loyalty, hospitality, gifts, gratitude, piety" and so on — in short, accepted if not necessary forms of hierarchical relations. Discourses that claim not to bind through generous conduct are, in turn, exercising perhaps the most insidious forms of euphemized violence to the extent that "fair exchange" is impossible. Deaf persons become indebted for "generous conduct" that restricts their choices to those valued by the hearing majority.

5. Critics of Bourdieu's theory of symbolic violence claim that the model does not adequately accommodate individual agency and emancipatory potential, and persons are thus condemned to legitimize existing practices and established social positions (Brubaker, 1985; Collins, 1993; Cronon, 1996; Huspek, 1993). We believe this criticism to be misguided for two reasons. First, it circumvents Bourdieu's (1985) conception of the habitus as a "quasi-postural disposition to action" (p. 13) or "embodied inclination of agents to evaluate and act upon the world in typical ways" (Hanks, 1996, p. 239). Second, it ignores how the habitus is also a "generative principle of regulated improvisations" (Bourdieu, 1977a, p.78) through which persons develop a capability to interpret and act on received "scripts" or "scores" in novel and unpredictable ways (see Kraus, 1993, pp. 168–173).

6. Interestingly, in Quebec certain televised programs include a trilingual adaptation: One can watch a Quebecois government debate conducted in French, listen to the voice-over

translation in English, and watch an interpreter signing the ASL translation in a small box in the lower right corner of the screen. We have not seen, however, two screens simultaneously, one with ASL (used by Deaf Canadians) and the other with LSQ (used by Deaf French Canadians)—demonstrating that, even with sign languages, dominant linguistic markets exist.

7. See the exchange between Rose (1995) and Booth-Butterfield and Booth-Butterfield (1995) for additional discussion of differing views in deafness-related research.

8. For example, consider the idioms, "head over heels in love," "keep your chin up," "head strong," "stab in the back," and so forth.

9. When communicating through an interpreter—a three-way communicative challenge that, due to space constraints, cannot be addressed in detail here—the hearing interactant should maintain eye contact with the Deaf interactant, not with the interpreter. Doing otherwise results in a latent form of symbolic violence, as the Deaf person becomes excluded from the very conversation of which he or she is a cocreator.

22

Communication and the Blind or Visually Impaired

John W. Smith
Krishna P. Kandath
Ohio University

Keywords: Blindness, visual impairment, blind culture, organizational diversity

> *Why, in truth, should I not bear gently*
> *the deprivation of sight, when I may hope*
> *that it is not so much lost as revoked and*
> *retracted inwards, for the sharpening rather*
> *than the blunting of my mental edge?*
> —John Milton (1608–1674)

We live in a world of unlike people. Myriad sexes, ethnicities, classes, and nationalities, among other classificatory systems, determine the unlikeness of our world. Within this diverse spectrum are included individuals with disabilities. People with disabilities add an interesting dimension to our social world, in that they adopt a unique set of discursive practices to adapt and construct their social environment.

People who are blind or visually impaired comprise a significant number of individuals with disabilities living in the United States. The study of the communicative experiences of people who are blind or visually

389

impaired is a recent development in the field of interpersonal communication. Even today, scholarship in interpersonal communication portrays individuals as being alike and engaging in similar interaction patterns and processes. The failure to capture the total experience of communication among diverse individuals, and in this case individuals who are blind or visually impaired, is a serious limitation within the study of everyday human interaction. This is particularly relevant for people who are blind or visually impaired, because our everyday stories and narratives are filled with myths and perceptions promoted by individuals with sight (Jernigan, 1965; Monbeck, 1973). Such myths include, but are not limited to, the notion that "the eyes are the window to the soul" and that blindness equals darkness, thus connoting inferiority and second-class citizenship. It is the perpetuation of these myths and the continued distancing of the discursive social worlds of individuals who are blind or visually impaired within the field of interpersonal communication that motivates the present authors and governs the text of this chapter. Additionally, one of the major paradoxes about living with a limitation like blindness and relating with individuals who have sight is disregard for the independence of individuals who are blind or visually impaired, especially because dependence is expected of them (see Emry & Wiseman, 1987b). The authors think that independence is acknowledged, whereas assertiveness is considered to be a limitation and perceived negatively by sighted populations.

Much of the literature reviewed here reflects the experiences of both of us. The first author is totally blind, living in a mostly sighted world, and the second author is sighted and informed by both his U.S. and international experiences in communicative relationships with individuals who are blind or visually impaired. Furthermore, the chapter also testifies to the communicative relationship of both of us.

Specifically, this work is informed by a review of the extant literature on communication and individuals who are blind or visually impaired. First, there is a discussion of what it means to live blind or visually impaired, leading to an exploration of the different types of blindness and visual impairments that individuals like the first author experience in society. Second is a discussion of the communicative experiences of people who are blind or visually impaired. Third, the idea of culture and the dynamics of viewing those who are blind or visually impaired as a cultural group in society are examined. Fourth, we present a review of the communicative strategies of individuals who are blind or visually impaired, followed by a discussion of the research on communication among the blind or visually impaired. This is particularly influenced by the first author's experiences in communicating with others who are blind or visually impaired. Following this is an analysis of the research addressing communication between the blind or visually impaired and those having sight. Once again, our communicative relationships influence this section. This leads us to explore the communicative relationships of individuals who are blind or visually impaired within organizations and their cultures and subcultures. The chapter concludes with a summary of the research, theory, and methods discussed and our suggestions for future research on communication with the blind or visually impaired.

LIVING BLIND OR VISUALLY IMPAIRED

The first author was born blind in one eye due to glaucoma.[1] At the age of 3, he last registered certain communication cues and images of a person with sight, before a very tragic accident removed the sight from his "good" eye. Currently, he is congenitally blind and cannot remember what it meant to have sight before his third birthday. Blindness can either be congenital or adventitious. After the age of 5, congenital blindness differs from adventitious blindness.[2]

Having sight does not translate into perfect vision. When an individual has normal vision it means that such vision is correctable. However, blindness is the loss of normal or correctable vision. According to Heward (1996), blindness has both legal and educational definitions.[3] An individual is considered legally blind when a correction in vision still results in a legally unacceptable vision level or what is identified as visual impairment.[4] An educationally blind person is totally blind, not just visually impaired.

Self-confidence and self-reliance are fundamental considerations for empowering and enhancing the performances of individuals with sight and individuals who are blind or visually impaired. The negotiations and feedback that individuals who are blind or visually impaired receive during communicative experiences with other individuals, especially with sighted populations, determines their social self and self-identity. This is an important issue for individuals who are blind or visually impaired because the behavioral responses of individuals with sight are crucial to their socialization and independence in society (Baker, 1973). Although visual behavior is significant to social interaction among sighted populations (Ellsworth &

Ludwig, 1972), it is not considered a requirement. For instance, Argyle, Lalljee, and Cook (1968) investigated dyadic verbal interaction under conditions of reduced visibility and found that speech synchronization was not significantly affected.

Individuals who are blind or visually impaired are constantly challenged by the attitudes and misconceptions of people with sight, living in a world of coconstructed likeness (Monbeck, 1973). Most of the individuals who are blind or visually impaired have lived with a dichotomy of positive and negative beliefs about blindness. Blank (1957) remarked: "Society is strongly ambivalent towards the blind, about whom the sighted have contradictory and paradoxical beliefs. The blind are both saints and sinners, pariahs and prophets" (p. 1). They are challenged to manage their limitation by devising alternative techniques that facilitate their working experiences and expand their social reach. However, people who are blind or visually impaired deal with the social construction of their identity by learning to cope with these everyday communicative behaviors of a population that is mostly sighted.

COMMUNICATIVE EXPERIENCES OF PEOPLE WHO ARE BLIND OR VISUALLY IMPAIRED

The complexity of our social world poses constant challenges to communication scholars engaged in different kinds of struggles, especially unveiling the intricacies and rules that human beings jointly create in their discursive practices. Often, the outcomes of such scholarship result in a disparity: The experiences and imaginations of people with "normal" sight guide our knowledge about the social worlds of individuals who are blind or visually impaired. It is important to address this gap. As much as the perceptions of people who are sighted is important, it is critical to understand, from their own perspective, the people who are blind or visually impaired. This section, then, focuses on the social worlds and discursive practices of people who are blind or visually impaired.

Blindness has a multitude of symbolic meanings for the individual and for others who are sighted, the most powerful among them being an innate need to make sense of uncontrollable and unpredictable events (Frankl, 1968). This uncertainty is instrumental in the initiation and maintenance of successful communicative relationships. Research on communication between individuals with disabilities and individuals with ablebodies indicates the uncomfortable nature of such relationships (Braithwaite, 1989,

1990; Goffman, 1963; Thompson & Seibold, 1978). Although uncertainty is also characteristic of relational initiation among ablebodied individuals, there is often greater ambiguity and uncertainty in both the initiation and the development of relationships between individuals with and without disabilities (Braithwaite, 1989; Thompson, 1982). Such deterrents make the partners self-conscious and significantly impact their spontaneity (Braithwaite, 1989). However, scholars like Braithwaite (1989, 1990, 1991) have observed the biased nature of research in this area because of the interest toward the feelings and behaviors of ablebodied individuals as opposed to the concerns of individuals with disabilities.

Individuals who are blind or visually impaired report many common experiences when communicating with sighted people. For instance, sighted individuals do not address them as normal people, treating blindness as a characteristic of the human body rather than as just a limitation. People who are blind or visually impaired like to be seen as able communicators in all other respects. Similarly, a common experience of adults who are blind or visually impaired is that they are not treated as adults. They like to be addressed just as are sighted individuals around them, as mature and grown-up adults.

Individuals often speak loudly with them when hearing is not actually a concern. Similarly, individuals who are blind or visually impaired are uncomfortable when they do not know who is around them, especially in a closed space. They prefer hearing the voices of individuals in the room and being apprised about other people or animals around. A common experience is that sighted individuals feel uncomfortable using the word "see." For example, individuals who are blind or visually impaired also use "see" when they say "see you tomorrow." In fact, they are often glad to see others. Finally, individuals who are blind or visually impaired do not mind discussing their blindness although they also have many other interests, just as sighted individuals do.

CULTURE AND INDIVIDUALS WHO ARE BLIND OR VISUALLY IMPAIRED

In the field of interpersonal communication, the word *culture* has taken on myriad meanings. The most common usage of culture stems from its interpretation in intercultural and cross-cultural communication, which is a limited understanding in that nationality, diaspora, and the symbolic meanings and practices attached to them have been identified with culture.

A broader understanding of culture is necessary to consider the communicative experiences and practices of individuals who are blind or visually impaired. Raymond Williams (1976) defined culture as a structure of feeling. Individuals who are blind or visually impaired are a cultural group in many of the ways that Williams defined culture. However, their cultural practices, mostly communicative, are a functional and situational adaptation of their blindness. Therefore, it is reasonable to consider communication between individuals with and without visual impairments as intercultural communication (Braithwaite & Braithwaite, 1997; Emry & Wiseman, 1987a). Many implications stem from such an understanding. Particularly relevant to this chapter is turn-taking in conversations, which depends on the linguistic and cultural organization of communities (Wilson, Wiemann, & Zimmerman, 1984).

Communicative Strategies of Individuals Who are Blind or Visually Impaired

Everyday communicative behaviors depend on both verbal and nonverbal cues, including visual cues. The study of human communication emphasizes the role of visual cues in the ability to engage efficiently in symbolic interaction. Individuals who are blind or visually impaired lack these cues, disadvantaging their communicative experiences in social situations (Erin, Dignan, & Brown, 1991).

Social skills are crucial for individuals who are blind or visually impaired if they are to engage in effective communicative action with sighted people (Erin et al., 1991). This involves both making sense of a world that is visually sensible to individuals with sight and developing strategies that can enhance social behaviors, including such routine needs as seeking assistance (Erin et al., 1991). There are no established standards that determine appropriate social skills for people who are blind or visually impaired, making them dependent on skills used by individuals with sight. In the last two decades there has been an increasing emphasis on interventions to develop the social skills of individuals who are blind or visually impaired. However, these have been governed by the behaviors of individuals with sight (Erin et al., 1991). Erin et al. wrote:

> The little instruction in the area that has been done has been based on the assumption that the most desirable social skills are those in common use by the sighted population or those that provide access to the experiences

of the sighted world. Although this assumption may promote interaction in a sighted world, it is a lofty assumption and may not include all the skills that blind or visually impaired persons need to enjoy satisfying social interactions. (p. 58)

Braithwaite (1989, 1990) identified seven strategies that individuals with disabilities can use to positively influence their social interactions with ablebodied individuals. These include initiation, modeling behavior, establishing normalcy, humor, confrontation, intentional embarrassment, and avoidance. These strategies can also be used by individuals who are blind or visually impaired. For example, a person might use humor to help dissipate discomfort and tension or demonstrate/model for the sighted person how they would like to be treated.

Bonfanti (1979) observed some differences in the communicative behaviors of individuals who are blind or visually impaired compared with individuals with sight. An important conversational strategy used by individuals who are blind or visually impaired is turn-taking. Thus, considering the limitation of individuals who are blind or visually impaired in receiving visual cues, an understanding of turn-taking in conversations can also inform us about their cultural strategies when interacting with sighted counterparts, including the opening, maintenance, and regulation of conversation.

Limited research has been conducted on turn-taking in conversations with individuals who are blind or visually impaired (Sharkey & Stafford, 1990). Sharkey and Stafford wrote: "Due to the fact that the sighted and blind cultures vary in their ability to perceive the world, they function as disparate cultures. Hence, regulatory problems may arise when two persons from these two cultures interact" (p. 161). This corresponds with Kemp's (1980) observation that individuals who are blind or visually impaired employ unusual turn-taking resources during conversations with sighted individuals. Sharkey and Stafford's conversation analysis observed the limited use of nonvocal turn-taking resources in comparison with vocal ones in blind–blind dyads. This provides important directions for understanding the turn-taking resources utilized by individuals who are blind or visually impaired during conversations with sighted individuals. It is likely that individuals who are blind or visually impaired use vocal turn-taking resources while interacting with individuals with sight because of the immense potential to increase their communicative competencies.

COMMUNICATION WITH INDIVIDUALS
WHO ARE BLIND OR VISUALLY IMPAIRED

The integration of individuals with visual impairments into society involves interaction with people who have sight. It entails socializing and seeking out friendships, professional contacts, and, many times, romantic relationships with others. Limited knowledge exists about the communication skills necessary to create effective social discourse in these everyday encounters (Baker, 1973). These discourses are necessary for individuals with visual impairments as a stage in enhancing their communicative competence. Through most conversations, these individuals will frequently monitor how they present themselves and how others reciprocate that presentation.

Many factors and considerations are crucial to ensure effective social interaction between individuals who are blind or visually impaired and individuals with sight. Baker (1973) wrote that individuals with sight have limited understanding about the behavior of individuals who are blind or visually impaired. In communicative situations, "the perceived verbal and physical behavior of blind persons . . . determines what others think and feel about them" (p. 316). This is a hurdle to the development of communicative relationships and also to the social self of individuals who are blind or visually impaired. However, blindness–visual impairment is not a significant deterrent in communicative situations (Argyle et al., 1968). Because blindness and visual impairment are simply limitations, sighted individuals only need to make some adaptations toward the blind and visually impaired.

One of the early assumptions in research on communicative relationships among sighted people is the value of eye contact (Ellsworth & Ludwig, 1972), and many observations have been made to substantiate its importance. For instance, Kendon and Cook (1969) observed a correlation between duration of gaze among friends in dyads and the subsequent evaluation of their partners. Partners involved in longer gazes were evaluated more positively. Similarly, eye contact is considered significant in enhancing communicative relationships (Bonfanti, 1979; Sanders & Goldberg, 1977), especially romantic relationships. Although there is a relationship between eye contact and interpersonal attraction, it is still possible for individuals who are blind or visually impaired to engage in both social and romantic relationships. However, such relationships are outcomes of understanding and mutuality of interests and not necessarily attractiveness. For instance, eye contact is privileged in a physical sense and yet we believe that blind or visually impaired individuals keep eye contact. Here, the contact is at the perceptual level and is crucial to the interaction. (The first author is married to a sighted woman and has a perfectly happy relationship. Attractiveness was never a barrier in the couple's relational initiation and maintenance.)

EMPLOYMENT ISSUES

About 27% of individuals with a severe visual impairment (unable to see words and letters) are employed (McNeil, 1993). Seventy percent of individuals in the 21- to 64-year-old age group who are blind or visually impaired "are either unemployed or underemployed" (Rovig, 1994, cited in Hagemoser, 1996, p. 134). Such a situation has several negative outcomes. Tuttle (1984), for instance, observed that underemployment can severely impact individuals who are blind or visually impaired, affecting self-esteem and personality, increasing hostility, and inducing them into dependency relationships.

Employment outcomes may be affected by factors external to blindness and visual impairment such as the prejudices of employers and lack of appropriate training (Hagemoser, 1996). Individuals who are blind or visually impaired can enhance organizational diversity provided they are trained and sighted individuals understand them. Social relationships can also contribute to work adjustment and promote job satisfaction.

Scholarly interest in organizational diversity is a recent phenomenon and has primarily been studied using Eurocentric frameworks. At a time when there is a need to bridge the gap between theory and praxis in organizational diversity (Corman, Banks, Bantz, & Mayer, 1990), researchers should focus their attention on the communicative performances that both construct and result from organizational experiences of individuals, taking into context their diverse backgrounds. Such backgrounds include culture, race, ethnicity, gender, and disability, among other things.

Organizational diversity, for the most part, is defined in terms of culture and values of different ethnic groups in society. More recently, women have been included in the discourses of cultural diversity. Missing from this scenario is the role and experiences of individuals with disabilities. It is likely that their limited membership in organizations makes them invisible for scholarly investigations. These individuals are rarely heard in scholarly discussions about the communicative experiences of individuals belonging to the "normal" workforce. Specifically, people who are blind or visually impaired are considered as lacking the abilities that are expected of people with sight. However, blindness is just a limitation. In a study conducted by Walls, MacDonald, and Gulkus (1974), both individuals who are blind or visually impaired and individuals with sight reported the vocational aspects of blindness as more serious than the social or personal ones. Job performances are affected mostly by functional limitations of blindness (Roberts, 1992). However, proper training and equal opportunity enables individuals who are blind or visually impaired to work to at least the standards of the average person with sight.

Technology has had a profound impact on the organizational experiences of individuals who are blind or visually impaired, equalizing their abilities with those of individuals with sight. The first author accomplishes his routine organizational tasks with a Braille 'n' Speak, a talking computer, talking clocks, Braille watches, and a number of tape recorders. However, there is a dearth of knowledge about how individuals who are blind or visually impaired use these technologies to remove the barriers to communicative experiences between themselves and their sighted counterparts.

One of the functional limitations of blindness is seen in interpersonal transactions, in that people who are blind or visually impaired are not able to perform adequately on monitoring tasks (Roberts, 1992). Also known as feedback, monitoring is identified as the information-seeking function of visual interaction (Argyle & Dean, 1965). Although training can significantly develop the workplace monitoring abilities of individuals who are blind or visually impaired, colleagues with sight can communicatively and symbolically enhance this process by participating in the normalization of newly adopted practices. This is important because feedback is crucial to communicative situations and facilitates behavioral modifications.

King (1993) provided the following rules of courtesy to enhance the work relationships of individuals who are blind or visually impaired. These are also applicable to regular conversational situations:

♦ When offering assistance to a person who has visual impairments, speak in a normal tone. Address him or her directly; this will help the person locate you. Just ask: "May I be of help?"

♦ When guiding a person who is blind, permit him or her to take your arm. A nice way to offer is to say, "Here is my left (or right) arm." Then the person knows how to take your arm and will respond to your motion much as a dancer follows a partner. Never grab a blind person's arm; he or she cannot anticipate your movements if you do.

+ When walking with a person who is blind, walk at a normal pace and slightly ahead; hesitate slightly before stepping up or down and indicate "up" or "down." After crossing a street or changing direction, make sure the person is started straight in the right direction. Alert him or her to any obstructions ahead.

+ When giving directions, do not point. Give directions in terms of distance and direction. For example, say, "Walk three blocks ahead, cross the third intersection, turn left, and go one block. The building will be on your right." Do not identify intersections by street names; a person with visual impairments might not be able to read the signs that identify them.

+ When showing a blind person who is blind to a chair, place his or her hand on the back of it. Do not try to push the person into the chair. The person will use her or his sense of touch to determine the type, height, and width of the chair.

+ When dining with or serving food to a person with visual impairments, call attention to each item as it is placed on the table ("Here is your water."). In a restaurant, offer to read the menu aloud, including the price of each item. If the person needs any additional help, he or she will ask for it, but it is never bad for someone to offer help.[5]

+ When conversing with a person who is blind, use normal terms as well as normal tones. A person who is blind might greet you by saying "It's good to see you again." Speak directly to the person: If your gaze wanders, your voice follows.

+ Identify yourself when you meet a friend who is blind; a friend might ask for help from you that he or she would not ask for from others.

+ Always alert a blind person before you leave; otherwise, the person might be left talking to no one.

+ Above all, do not pity people who have visual impairments. Thousands are successful, active, and useful citizens.

BLINDNESS, VISUAL IMPAIRMENT, AND HUMAN COMMUNICATION: FUTURE RESEARCH

One of the major issues that needs to be considered in conducting research on communication and the blind or visually impaired is the limitation in different methods of inquiry. Observational methods may not fully capture the communicative experiences between individuals who are blind or visually impaired and those having sight because of limitations in determining human motivations and feelings through mere observation of social action (Baker, 1973). Similarly, surveys may not serve as appropriate instruments because individuals with sight may report attitudes toward individuals who are blind or visually impaired that are not consistent with their social actions (Baker, 1973). Individuals with sight, either due to embarrassment or lack of awareness, tend not to speak openly of their feelings about blindness (Hollins, 1989).

A less acknowledged issue is that both individuals who are blind or visually impaired and individuals with sight hold "unrealistic attitudes" toward blindness (Hollins, 1989). Such attitudes derive from the system of beliefs within the cultural system of sighted individuals; most commonly, a dialectical perception of these individuals is the simultaneous view of the blind as sinners (God's punishment) and saints (special powers of perception).

However, individuals who are blind or visually impaired also contribute to difficulties in analyzing communicative experiences. Often their everyday behaviors are very stereotypical. Although they may or may not engage consciously in such behaviors, they tend to develop a certain fixed sense of space, place, and speech. Baker (1973) observed a tendency among both individuals who are blind or visually impaired and other individuals "to engage in both verbal and physical behavior which is consistent with the personality characteristics the public generally attributes to them and which it generally reinforces" (p. 317). Such continuation of everyday behaviors removes the strategic engagement and dramaturgical emphasis that are crucial concepts in the understanding of communicative relationships and experiences.

Future studies should take the social worlds of individuals who are blind or visually impaired into consideration. Although different methods of inquiry have limitations, interpretive or qualitative methods of inquiry can facilitate discussion, apart from providing the researcher with rich data for analysis and interpretation.

CONCLUSIONS

This chapter has discussed the meanings attached to living blind or visually impaired and the communicative nature of relationships with individuals who are blind or visually impaired. Unlike the deaf culture, not many individuals who are blind or visually impaired see themselves as a culture.

However, they adopt a set of practices that are cultural to the extent that they are able to overcome the limitations posed by blindness or visual impairment. Since this is a new area of study within the communication discipline, there is much to be done here. One of the areas that needs to be researched further is turn-taking, especially between individuals who are blind or visually impaired and sighted people. Similarly, conversational practices within organizations is an area with tremendous potential for application.

DISCUSSION QUESTIONS

1. Based on the information provided in this chapter about the cultural practices of individuals who are blind or visually impaired, do you think a unique blind culture exists in the United States? Why or why not?
2. What are the criticisms relating to the study of individuals who are blind or visually impaired? What are some effective ways to study the communicative relationships and strategies of this population?
3. How can technology be used to further integrate individuals who are blind or visually impaired into organizations and to enhance their everyday experiences?

REFERENCES

Argyle, M., & Dean, J. (1965). Eye contact, distance, and affiliation. *Sociometry, 28*, 289–304.
Argyle, M., Lalljee, M., & Cook, M. (1968). The effects of visibility on interaction in a dyad. *Human Relations, 21*, 3–17.
Baker, L. D. (1973). Blindness and social behavior: A need for research. *New Outlook for the Blind, 67*, 315–318.
Blank, A. R. (1957). Psychoanalysis and blindness. *Psychoanalytic Quarterly, 26*, 1.
Bonfanti, B. H. (1979). Effects of training on nonverbal and verbal behaviors of congenitally blind adults. *Visual Impairment and Blindness, 73*, 1–9.
Braithwaite, D. O. (1989, February). *An interpretive analysis of disabled persons' impression management strategies in response to perceived discomfort and uncertainty of ablebodied others.* Paper presented at the annual meeting of the Western Speech Communication Association, Spokane, WA.
Braithwaite, D. O. (1990). From majority to minority: An analysis of cultural change from able-bodied to disabled. *International Journal of Intercultural Relations, 14*, 465–483.
Braithwaite, D. O. (1991). "Just how much did that wheelchair cost?": Management of privacy boundaries by persons with disabilities. *Western Journal of Speech Communication, 55*, 254–274.
Braithwaite, D. O., & Braithwaite, C. A. (1997). Understanding communication of persons with disabilities as cultural communication. In L. A. Samovar & R. E. Porter (Eds.), *Intercultural communication: A reader* (8th ed., pp. 154–164). New York: Wadsworth.

Corman, S. R., Banks, S. P., Bantz, C. R., & Mayer, M. E. (1990). *Foundations of organizational communication: A reader.* New York: Longman.

Ellsworth, P. C., & Ludwig, L. M. (1972). Visual behavior in social interaction. *Journal of Communication, 22,* 375–403.

Emry, R., & Wiseman, R. L. (1987a). An intercultural understanding of ablebodied and disabled persons' communication. *International Journal of Intercultural Relations, 11,* 7–27.

Emry, R., & Wiseman, R. L. (1987b). *When helping may not be helpful: The development of learned helplessness in disabled persons.* Paper presented at the annual meeting of the Speech Communication Association, Boston, MA.

Erin, J. N., Dignan, K., & Brown, P. A. (1991). Are social skills teachable? A review of the literature. *Journal of Visual Impairment & Blindness, 85,* 58–61.

Frankl, V. (1968). *The search for meaning.* Philadelphia: Westminster Press.

Goffman, E. (1963). *Stigma: Notes on the management of spoiled identity.* Englewood Cliffs, NJ: Prentice-Hall.

Hagemoser, S. D. (1996). The relationship of personality traits to the employment status of persons who are blind. *Journal of Visual Impairment & Blindness, 90,* 134–144.

Heward, W. L. (1996). *Exceptional children: An introduction to special education* (5th ed.). Englewood Cliffs, NJ: Prentice-Hall.

Hollins, M. (1989). *Understanding blindness: An integrative approach.* Chapel Hill: University of North Carolina Press.

Jernigan, K. (1965). *Blindness—Concepts and misconceptions.* Baltimore: National Federation of the Blind.

Kemp, N. J. (1980). Social interaction in the blind. *International Journal of Rehabilitation Research, 3,* 87–88.

Kendon, A., & Cook, M. (1969). The consistency of gaze patterns in social interaction. *British Journal of Psychology, 60,* 481–494.

King, A. S. (1993). Doing the right thing for employees with disabilities. *Training & Development, 47,* 44–49.

McNeil, J. M. (1993). *Americans with Disabilities: 1991–1992 (U.S. Bureau of the Census Current Population Reports P70–33).* Washington, DC: U.S. Government Printing Office.

Monbeck, M. E. (1973). *The meaning of blindness.* Bloomington: Indiana University Press.

Roberts, A. H. (1992). Looking at vocational placement for the blind: A personal perspective. *RE:view, 23,* 177–184.

Sanders, R. M., & Goldberg, S. G. (1977). Eye contacts: Increasing their rate in social interactions. *Visual Impairment and Blindness, 71,* 265–267.

Sharkey, W. F., & Stafford, L. (1990). Turn-taking resources employed by congenitally blind conversers. *Communication Studies, 41,* 161–182.

Thompson, T. L. (1982). Disclosure as a disability-management strategy: A review and conclusions. *Communication Quarterly, 30,* 196–202.

Thompson, T. L., & Seibold, D. R. (1978). Stigma management in normal-stigmatized interactions: A test of the disclosure hypothesis and a model of stigma acceptance. *Human Communication Research, 4,* 231–242.

Tuttle, D. W. (1984). *Self-esteem and adjusting with blindness: The process of responding to life's demands.* Springfield, IL: Charles C. Thomas.

Walls, R. T., MacDonald, A. P., Jr., & Gulkus, S. P. (1974). The disability seriousness scale: Rating the effects of blindness. *New Outlook for the Blind, 68,* 174–177.

Williams, R. (1976). *Keywords: A vocabulary of culture and society.* New York: Oxford University Press.

Wilson, T. P., Wiemann, J. M., & Zimmerman, D. H. (1984). Models of turn taking in conversational interaction. *Journal of Language and Social Psychology, 3,* 159–183.

ENDNOTES

1. Nearly 3 million Americans have glaucoma. If it is not detected and treated properly, glaucoma can lead to blindness. If it is detected before extensive symptoms develop, serious vision loss due to glaucoma can often be prevented.

2. An individual who is congenitally blind does not have any mental references, whereas an individual who is adventitiously blind lost vision beyond the fifth birthday and can still rely on mental references from the earlier experiences that occurred with sight.

3. Jernigan (1995) found limitations in the legal definition of blindness, in that the emphasis is on describing blindness in "medical and measurable terms" (p. 1). He argued that "blindness can best be defined not physically or medically but functionally and sociologically" (p. 3).

4. After correction, a legally blind person has a visual acuity of 20/200 or higher denomination; or a range of peripheral vision under 20 degrees.

5. There is some disagreement about offering help (see chapter by Potts & Roloff, this volume).

23

Invisible Disability

Cynthia K. Matthews
Nancy Grant Harrington
University of Kentucky

Keywords: Invisible disability, impression management, stigma, shame

The population of persons who are disabled constitutes one fifth of the population in the United States (McNeil, 1993), and it has been estimated that at least 40% of this group has disabilities that cannot be seen, or are "invisible" (Asch, 1984). Matthews (1994) defined *invisible disability* as "one that is hidden so as not to be immediately noticed by an observer except under unusual circumstances or by disclosure from the disabled person or other outside source" (p. 7). The category of invisible disabilities includes both physical and mental conditions. Physical conditions include those resulting from chronic illnesses, such as heart disease, or neuromuscular diseases, such as epilepsy; mental conditions include various neuroses and learning disabilities as well as cognitive processing problems like dementia and mental retardation.

TERMINOLOGY

In researching the literature, we found it important to consider usage of the terms *nonvisible* and *hidden* as well as *invisible*, as there has been confusion over how to label these disabilities. The research literature uses all three, although the term *invisible* seems to be most commonly and consistently used (e.g., Goffman, 1963; Jones et al., 1984; Sinnema, 1992), and is the term used here. A more compelling reason to use the term *invisible* is the subtle, yet important, distinction between the meaning of these terms. *Nonvisible* or *hidden* implies that the condition can be seen if only one would look and discover it; *invisible*, however, implies that the condition cannot be seen. This distinction becomes important when considering an individual's motivation to communicate about the disability or keep the disability concealed.

Although terminology used to describe disability is constantly evolving, the World Health Organization (1980, cited in McNeil, 1993) has defined three concepts within their conceptual framework: impairments, disabilities, and handicaps. *Impairments* are abnormalities in system or organ functioning, body structure and/or appearance (e.g., kidney disease, spine deformity, or loss of limb); the functional consequences of impairments are *disabilities* (e.g., the inability to perform light housework or experiencing difficulty in self-care); the disadvantages experienced by individuals with impairments and disabilities are *handicaps* (e.g., the inability to attend a sports event because of second-hand smoke or to attend a class because of lack of adequate access; McNeil, 1993). The distinction among these concepts often is blurred as many scholars and researchers use the terms interchangeably (Susman, 1994). In this chapter the term *disability* is used to place emphasis on the importance of the impact of the impairment on day-to-day functioning.

PREVALENCE

The United States presently is experiencing a dramatic increase in the number of people with invisible disabilities, as evidenced by several factors. First, the number of people with chronic diseases and disabilities has been escalating for the last quarter century (Hayden, 1993; Kaye, LaPlante, Carlson, & Wegner, 1997). Chronic conditions are those that are lasting, as opposed to acute conditions, which are short-lived (Roper, 1988).

In a study by the National Institute on Disability and Rehabilitation Research (LaPlante, 1991), the conditions that most frequently caused activity limitations were chronic, including arthritis, heart disease, diabetes, mental and nervous disorders, and lung disease; these conditions are predominately invisible. Chronic conditions make up two-thirds of the disabling conditions reported in the United States (LaPlante, 1997). Blum (1992) reported that 1 out of every 10 children born in the United States has some type of chronic condition and of those, nearly one-third have activity limiting conditions. Second, new treatments and therapeutic interventions have increased the survival rate for people with chronic conditions and disabilities dramatically. Examples of particularly remarkable changes in survival rate are cystic fibrosis, up 700%; spina bifida, up 200%; and heart disease, up 300% since the early 1970s (Blum, 1992). Third, The National Center for Health Statistics reports a sharp increase in disability rates among people under 45 years of age, accounted for by a greater prevalence in the diagnosis of asthma, mental disorders (e.g., chronic fatigue syndrome, attention deficit disorder), and orthopedic impairments (e.g., back and joint problems; Kaye et al., 1997), conditions that again are predominantly invisible.

RATIONALE

Given these increases in the numbers of persons with invisible disabilities, it is important not only to acknowledge the existence of invisible disability, but also to understand the consequences of the visibility factor on the attitudes and behavior of those living with an invisible disability. Western societies value independence, self-reliance, beauty, and health; the U.S. culture is particularly obsessed with health (Galanti, 1997). People are told that to be healthy is normal and that illness is considered a deviance (Hayden, 1993). This has resulted in the category of invisible disability often being ignored and even receiving widespread public denial (Hassenfeld, 1993). Persons with invisible disabilities, therefore, have great impetus to keep their conditions concealed.

Unfortunately, concealing disabilities can have profound negative implications in terms of relationships and health. This chapter reviews the literature on disability and explores the influence of the visibility factor as it is evidenced in feelings of stigma and shame, and as it influences impression management and self-disclosure, ultimately impacting persons' relationships and health.

REVIEW OF LITERATURE

An examination of the research on communication and disability shows that, whereas persons with disabilities are receiving attention from scholars, the focus of the research is on the perspective of the ablebodied (Braithwaite, 1991; Braithwaite & Braithwaite, 1997). Most researchers seem to believe the key to understanding the power that underlies prejudice and discrimination is the study of the attitudes and behavior of ablebodied persons toward people who are disabled (Asch, 1984). Indeed, in looking at the research that has been done on disability, Braithwaite and Braithwaite (1997) found that three problems emerged:

> First, very little is known about the communication behavior of disabled people ... second ... most researchers talked *about* persons with disabilities, not *with* them ... (and) third, and most significantly, the research is usually conducted most often from the perspective of the ablebodied person (reflecting) an *ethnocentric bias.* (p. 158)

The result is that the research offers little from the perspective of the disabled person (Braithwaite, 1991; Fine & Asch, 1988.)

Furthermore, although the visibility factor is acknowledged in communication research (e.g., Braithwaite, 1991; Braithwaite & Braithwaite, 1997), most of the research into disability typically has focused exclusively on the visibly disabled. This research finds that people with visible disabilities experience hostile feelings, stereotyping, and avoidance from ablebodied others (Hassenfeld, 1993; Mills, Belgrave, & Boyer, 1984; Thompson, 1982). Interestingly, research that did consider invisible disabilities tended to find similar results when the invisible disabilities are revealed (Asch, 1984). For the most part, however, researchers have not focused their investigations solely on the experiences of people who are invisibly disabled.

To address this omission, Matthews (1994) conducted a pilot study to investigate the use of privacy boundaries by persons with invisible disabilities, and Harrington and Matthews (1997) investigated the experience of shame among persons with invisible disabilities. The study by Matthews revealed that most people with an invisible disability did not disclose about their disability unless practical reasons demanded it. Additionally, she found that people with invisible disabilities felt disclosure would elicit unwanted sympathy, invite judgment, and damage existing relationships with people who might not understand their disability and, most significantly, might not find them believable. Harrington and Matthews found that, although invisibly disabled people did not appear to be more prone to the experience of shame than ablebodied people, condition severity was significantly related to feelings of shame and the amount of normal functioning lost by that individual correlated with the amount of perceived shame.

Additional studies can be found that address specific areas of invisible disability, such as chronic disease (Hayden 1993), cancer (Gotcher, 1993), epilepsy (Schneider, 1988), and chronic obstructive pulmonary disease (COPD; Keele-Card, Foxall, & Barron, 1993). Although these studies do address communication issues between patients and their health care providers or families, most do not address the impact of the invisible nature of the disability on communication. Hayden's work is an exception.

Hayden (1993) discussed the need of persons with chronic diseases to redefine their roles in order to maintain positive self-images as productive members of society and partners in relationships. Being a mother, for example, may have to take on a different meaning for the invisibly disabled parent in her attempt to continue to fulfill the responsibilities of that role. A mother with chronic lung disease may not be able to clean the house, but she can redefine her responsibility to be the one who assigns chores to others. If family members do not recognize or understand this redefinition, communication problems can result. A family member might resent being asked to do work that has been considered "mother's." According to Hayden, the redefinition of language used by people with invisible disability leads to diminished shared meaning with ablebodied others.

This potential for misunderstanding is complicated by the fact that chronic diseases frequently are inconsistent in their symptomology. Often, disability onset is progressive (Milliken & Northcott, 1996). One of the most problematic factors that causes misunderstandings between chronically ill people and their families and friends is the ambiguity that arises with the instability of chronic illness. Many conditions (e.g., rheumatic illnesses, lung diseases, intervertebral disk disorders) may produce acute symptoms on one day and few or no symptoms the next (Sinnema, 1992). This produces uncertainty for people with invisible disabilities and for families and friends, who often will develop doubts about the seriousness of the disease, leading to the perception on the part of the people with invisible disabilities that their condition is not believable (Matthews, 1994; Milliken & Northcott, 1996).

The Impact of Invisible Disability

A number of significant issues face people who are either visibly or invisibly disabled. Stigma (Goffman, 1963) and shame (Lazare, 1987) can be a daily part of life. As a result, impression management and strategic self-disclosure (Admi, 1996) become important communication skills for those with disabilities. These issues can be especially salient for people with invisible disabilities because of the visibility factor.

Stigma.   Goffman (1963) distinguished stigma along four criteria: whether it is visible, known about, obtrusive, or relevant. A visible stigma is one that is immediately evident to others (e.g., obesity, paralysis). An invisible stigma is one that is not easily discerned by others (e.g., heart disease, HIV). Stigmas, both visible and invisible, are discerned or not by another depending on circumstances and relationships. A stigma is more or less obtrusive to the degree that it interferes with social interaction (e.g., arthritis would interfere with playing on an athletic team). Finally, a stigma is relevant depending on the context (e.g., one's ability to run laps may be relevant to certain athletic teams, but should not be relevant in an academic setting).

Goffman (1963) clearly recognized the influence of the visibility factor on stigma when he made a distinction between "discredited" and "discreditable" persons. The discredited person believes that the defect is visible and recognized by others; this person must manage the anxiety caused by the knowledge being public. The discreditable person believes that his or her defect is invisible or unrecognized; this person must deal with the information management problem of how to keep the information concealed. Matthews (1994) found that in communicating with ablebodied others, people with invisible disabilities most often engaged in the information management strategy of "passing," a deliberate concealment of a stigmatizing condition (Goffman, 1963). This finding reiterates the importance of the ability to conceal the disability.

Persons with invisible disabilities clearly view information about the existence of their disability as private information. Concealing or controlling the dissemination of private information is implicit in Petronio's (1991) definition of disclosure as boundary regulation (see also, Derlega, Metts, Petronio, & Margulis, 1993). The strategic use of privacy boundaries is basic to the way persons with disabilities use impression management to accomplish stigma management and avoid vulnerability to shame (Braithwaite, 1991). The decision to reveal information about a disability is a primary one involving a great deal of risk on the part of the person with disabilities because of associated stigma and shame (Braithwaite, 1991; Matthews, 1994; Scambler, 1984; Thompson & Seibold, 1978).

Understandably, disabled persons want to be seen as "persons first" (Braithwaite, 1991, 1996; Braithwaite & Braithwaite, 1997). As soon as a disability is recognized, however, the disabled individual becomes "labeled." For those with invisible disabilities, though, as long as their disability remains invisible, it simply does not exist for the other and therefore provides no basis for labeling. This confers a "normal" status to the relationship between the disabled and ablebodied others. The person with the disability, therefore, can be seen as a person not just "first" but "only." This provides strong motivation to keep knowledge of an invisible disability concealed.

Based on the hypothesis that many of the social and psychological barriers faced by persons with disabilities have their foundation in the discomfort experienced by nondisabled people, some researchers have advocated the use of self-disclosure by individuals with disabilities (Hastorf, Wildfogel, & Cassman, 1979; Thompson, 1982; Thompson & Seibold, 1978). This, they assert, would reduce uncertainty on the part of the nondisabled and facilitate interaction. While openness on the part of the person with the disability may be positive in terms of reducing the uncertainty and discomfort of the ablebodied, the costs in terms of self-esteem to the disabled individual can be substantial (Braithwaite, 1991). Braithwaite (1991) found that these costs included feelings of misunderstanding as well as propagation of the diseaselike stereotype many ablebodied people have of disability. Researchers have concluded that while self-disclosure may be adequate to force a momentary interaction and does reduce uncertainty, it is not enough to significantly reduce social avoidance or increase acceptance of the party with disabilities by the nondisabled (Braithwaite, 1991; Mills et al., 1984; Thompson & Seibold, 1978). Therefore, the costs associated with disclosure may outweigh the rewards.

Whereas people with invisible disabilities may deliberate over the conscious decision to disclose about their disabilities, sometimes their conditions will produce symptoms that suggest a disability exists. People with invisible disabilities will expend energy to avoid this "leakage" (Goffman, 1963). They may either attribute the leakage to something other than the disability (e.g., claim to have rushed to a meeting to explain shortness of breath), avoid the presence of others when leakage occurs (e.g., leaving the room until symptoms diminish), or avoid engaging in behavior that would reveal that a disability exists (e.g., claiming to dislike an activity that might bring on symptoms).

Because of their "discreditable" status, people with invisible disabilities endure threats to their self-esteem. The unknown nature of an invisible disability sets up the possibility for negative discovery. It is not surprising, then, that those with disorders that are invisible tend to experience more emotional problems than those with visible manifestations of their disease (Ireys, Gross, Werthamer-Larsson, & Kolodner, 1994). For this reason, people with invisible disabilities are particularly vulnerable to shame.

Shame.   Shame is a painful emotion involving a negative evaluation of the global self (Tangney, Wagner, Fletcher, & Gramzow, 1992; Tangney, Wagner, & Gramzow, 1992). Shame results from the perception that oneself or one's presentation to others has not met with one's personal expectations (Lazare, 1987). It can occur in response to any discrepancy between one's ideal self and one's perception of the actual self (Sidoli, 1988). Shame is also related to the fear of being negatively evaluated by others (Gilbert, Pehl, & Allan, 1994).

According to Lazare (1987), shame results from the interaction of a shame-inducing event, the individual's vulnerability to shame, and the social context. A shame inducing event is one that exposes the self and portrays it as inadequate or defective. Individuals are most vulnerable to shame when they feel rejected, weak, somehow bad or defective, messy/dirty, disgusting, or when they fail at something or lose control of themselves or a situation (Lazare, 1987). Chronic illness and disability are accompanied by a loss of control (Lazare, 1987). Given this definition, it is hard to imagine a time when many people with disabilities, particularly those whose disabilities are invisible, would not be vulnerable to shame.

For people with disabilities, shame-inducing events can be recurrent and arise from several sources. Accessing services necessary for self-maintenance, from health care to personal aid, requires that persons with disabilities focus on those disabilities. Most people experience a disability as a defect or inadequacy of the self (Martin, 1993). Although this is true for both visibly and invisibly disabled persons, those with invisible disabilities face the additional burden of explaining why they need a particular service. This explanation can be a shame-inducing event. The process of determining needed services can also be a source of shame for persons with disabilities (Lazare, 1987). The results of diagnostic evaluations emphasize inadequacies. Medical terminology can exacerbate the problem (e.g., cardiac insufficiency). Hayden (1993) pointed out the pervasive use of negative terminology that defines disease and disability as dark and sinister. Additionally, many health care providers do not realize the extent to which they shame the people whom they treat, either merely by showing too little empathy or by expressing disappointment in progress (Lazare, 1987).

Another potential source of shame for persons with disabilities lies in their conception of their ideal self. An assumption made by ablebodied people is that a disabling condition is central to the self-concept of a person with a disability (Admi, 1996; Fine & Asch, 1988). In fact, physical limitation may be more significant to the ablebodied person than to the person with the condition, who may very well identify more with people without physical limitations (Admi, 1996; Fine & Asch, 1988). This is particularly relevant for people who become disabled at an early age and grow up around others who are ablebodied. Persons with disabilities, therefore, may base their ideal selves on role models that are unattainable with physically limited bodies. As not living up to one's ideal self is a primary shame trigger, it is not surprising that these people experience shame.

A Model of the Impact of Shame

Matthews (1996) proposed a model to explain the role of shame in shaping the communication behavior of persons with chronic illness and disabilities when interacting with ablebodied others. Although still untested, this shame response model offers insight into otherwise unexplained reactions that affect the relationships between disabled and nondisabled individuals. The model is depicted in Fig. 23.1.

Matthews (1996) argues that shame is usually triggered by a single precipitating event. This precipitating event could come in the form of a message (e.g., a direction or request for behavior) given by a health care provider, a family member, or a friend to whom the individual wishes to respond but may not be able to because of his or her disability. When individuals cannot respond because of their disabilities, they perceive their physical or psychological limitations as shortcomings that attack the cherished images of the self (e.g., youth, beauty, strength, stamina, independence, or mental competence) (Lazare, 1987). They then integrate these perceptions, instigated by the message, into their memories. The message is integrated with past experiences and present schemas based on cultural information about the behavior, information gleaned from communication with others, and from past personal experience.

Matthews' (1996) shame response model posits that, when responding to a behavioral request, people with disabilities will assess their own perception of performance success. The choices that people make are strongly

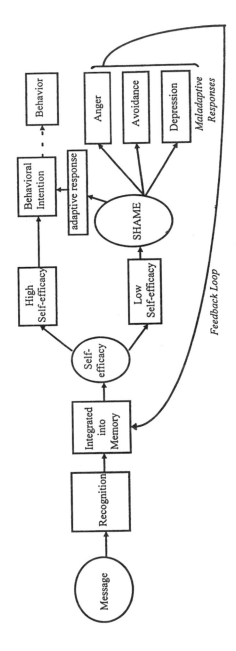

FIG. 23.1. Shame response model.

influenced by their view of their capability to succeed. This performance perception is assessed in terms of their personal self-efficacy, or the ability to represent future consequences cognitively (Bandura, 1977). If self-efficacy is high, it is probable that they will attempt the behavior and, barring outside or unanticipated complications, the behavior will occur. However, when self-efficacy is low and people experience acute uncertainty about their ability to successfully carry out an activity, it is likely that they will avoid even attempting the behavior (Bandura, 1977). Subsequently, they will experience some level of shame resulting from their perceived inadequacy in the eyes of others as well as themselves (Lazare, 1987). Response to this shame experience may be adaptive or maladaptive. An adaptive response allows the person to work on whatever deficiency he or she perceives as preventing the behavior or to make adjustments that could possibly make the behavior attainable. However, most often, because the response to shame is to protect oneself from further exposure, a maladaptive response is more likely to occur (Lazare, 1987). Indeed, shame has been found to be related to anger, resentment, blame externalization, expressions of hostility, and feelings of worthlessness (Tangney, Wagner, Fletcher, & Gramzow, 1992). It is not surprising, then, that people who feel that they are stigmatized and experience shame often will respond maladaptively, with avoidance, anger, or depression. Avoidance reactions can result in behaviors such as lying, deliberately failing to comply with requests, or avoiding contact with those connected with the shame experience altogether. Anger can be directed at the person perceived to be eliciting the shame response or can be turned toward the self (Lane & Hobfoll, 1992). Depression can lead to withdrawal from significant others and feelings of hopelessness, powerlessness, and worthlessness (Niedenthal, Tangney, & Gavanski, 1994; Tangney, Wagner, & Gramzow, 1992). Experiences of these shame responses will be incorporated into memory, intensifying the maladaptive response to the next shame experience, even if not in response to the same behavior request (Matthews, 1996). This can set up a negative spiral of shame that increasingly causes relationship problems for the person with the disability.

This negative shame spiral can be particularly problematic for people with invisible disabilities, as the cause of the response may be concealed. Examples of consequences of shame can be found throughout the literature on conditions related to invisible disability. For example, Lane and Hobfoll's (1992) study on anger found that people with chronic obstructive pulmonary disease experienced a spiraling effect of anger when disease symptoms became apparent. This anger had the effect of bringing on more symptoms. In addition, the anger exhibited by the disabled person resulted in anger reflected by social supporters, increasing the invisibly disabled person's vulnerability to additional stress experiences.

Implications for Relationships and Health

The relationships between health care providers, family and friends, and people who are disabled are complex. Shared meaning is only accomplished through repeated and mutual checking of interpretation (Barnlund, 1976). As we have discussed, however, achieving shared meaning is particularly difficult when invisible disabilities are involved. Impression management, self-disclosure, and issues of shame all affect communication. It is important that health care providers and support system members be sensitive to the implications of stigma and disability, and the possibility of maladaptive shame responses from the person with an invisible disability.

What are the options for health care providers, family members, and friends when interacting with persons with invisible disabilities? First, they need to be aware that the person with an invisible disability is actively engaged in impression management and may be going to great lengths not to appear disabled. This is true even when the invisible disability has in some way been revealed, affecting communication about changes in the condition or the severity of the condition. Health care providers, family members, and friends should not allow themselves to be led to believe that all is well when, in fact, it might not be. Passing behavior on the part of invisibly disabled people may significantly affect adherence to health care providers' instructions, often resulting in serious health decline, sometimes even death. For example, when a diabetic chooses to skip medication because a lack of privacy exists for an injection, serious and life threatening consequences could result.

Furthermore, health care providers, family members, and friends need to be aware of the potential for their messages to initiate a shame response. This is particularly problematic in a medical setting in which physicians may lack both communication training and time. In the world of managed care and the 10-minute encounter (Gordon, Baker, & Levinson, 1995), communicative skills that respect patients' needs and acknowledge their intelligence must be cultivated. Martin (1993) claimed that better physicians and better medical care would result from the inclusion of the study of shame in the medical curriculum. Feeling shame carries a cultural taboo in American society (Martin, 1993); therefore people rarely discuss feelings of shame with their physicians nor do physicians broach this feeling with patients. Insight into shame by physicians would facilitate the accomplishment of the three tasks suggested by Lazare (1987): (a) to decrease the patient's shame, (b) to avoid exacerbating shame responses, and (c) to recognize and manage the health care provider's own shame responses. It should be possible for physicians and other health care providers to adjust their communication strategies to provide better understanding and support, better health care, and ultimately achieve more positive relational and health outcomes (Kaplan, Greenfield, & Ware, 1989). Such patient-centered communication, particularly as it relates to reducing the shame response, traditionally has not been taught as part of the medical curriculum (Lazare, 1987; Scambler, 1984). Understanding the effects of shame could contribute additional evidence in support of such training.

The importance of training should also be recognized for family members and friends. Although it is not common, it is possible for one person to experience shame for another (Lazare, 1987). For example, a spouse, parent, or child may experience shame for the disabled person. Families, then, need to be aware of the shame response on several levels. Awareness is only the first step, however, in the effort to keep shame from interfering in relationships. It is possible that workshops and support groups could be designed to help family members learn to avoid sending messages that are inappropriate or easily misinterpreted. Like health care providers, they could be taught the necessary person-centered communication skills needed to deal with shame.

It is also possible that with education, invisibly disabled people themselves could learn to respond differently to shame-eliciting situations. While a stigmatized person's efforts to think of him- or herself as a worthy human being can lead to resentment of a nonstigmatized person's negative behavior, over time such reactions may become automatic, regardless of the behavior of the nonstigmatized person. Indeed, Lazare (1987) argues that when people feel stigmatized, socially discredited or branded, they actually will begin to anticipate unfavorable reactions from others. This process is described in the model by Matthews (1996). An interesting study by Farina, Allen, and Saul (1968) speaks to this possibility. The study involved a laboratory manipulation designed to explore the changes in behavior and communication when subjects believed they had been stigmatized, when in fact they had not. The study demonstrated that, if an individual believed he or she was perceived in an unfavorable way by another person, his or her behavior in a subsequent interaction was affected independently of the other person's actions in the situation. Simply believing that one is viewed as blemished and degraded, therefore, can alter behavior in such a way as to sometimes cause rejection by others. If invisibly disabled persons can be made aware of this, they may be able to avoid such behavior and enhance relationships with ablebodied others.

CONCLUSION

The conventional clinical model of health care focuses on treating and curing disease (Stewart et al., 1995). In this model, patients adopt the Parsonian "sick role" (Parsons, 1951) that characterizes the responsibilities and privileges of individuals who are ill. One of the responsibilities is to get well. Given the changing landscape of illness at this time, however, this sick role is no longer applicable in many cases (Dietz & Mills, 1998). Unfortunately, expectations of most people in our society is that those who are ill should get well. The role of the permanently disabled is one that health care providers must legitimatize and family and friends must accept, for only then will the communication barriers that presently exist begin to be overcome.

There is a critical need for research directly addressing the issues surrounding invisible disability. As the number of individuals with invisible disabilities continues to increase, the need for greater understanding of relevant communicative behavior and its impact on relationships and health will increase as well. It is important that communication scholars respond to this challenge.

DISCUSSION QUESTIONS

1. You are in a parking lot and you see a person pull into a designated handicap parking place and get out of the car. The person does not appear disabled in any way. What do you think? What do you say to yourself? To others? To the person?
2. Has anyone you know ever revealed to you that they were disabled when you saw no evidence of it? How did you react? Were you asked not to tell anyone? How did you feel about this? Did you honor the request?
3. Are you, or is anyone close to you, invisibly disabled? Would you be willing to share that information and your experiences with the disability with others? If so, with whom and under what circumstances?
4. What impression management strategies might you expect a person with an invisible disability to use? What consequences might this have in a relationship?

5. Can you recall a time when you experienced shame as described in Matthews' shame response model? Did you respond adaptively or maladaptively? Describe your behavior.
6. Have you had an experience when someone failed to respond to you, was illogically angry, or lied to you? Could the behavior have been triggered by shame? If so, how might you have responded to the behavior differently?

REFERENCES

Admi, H. (1996). Growing up with a chronic health condition: A model of an ordinary lifestyle. *Qualitative Health Research, 6*, 163–183.

Asch, A. (1984). The experience of disability: A challenge for psychology. *American Psychologist, 39*, 529–536.

Bandura, A. (1977). Self-efficacy: Toward a unifying theory of behavioral change. *Psychological Review, 84*, 191–215.

Barnlund, A. (1976). Doctor–patient encounters. *Journal of Medical Education, 51*, 716–725.

Blum, R. W. (1992). Chronic illness and disability in adolescence. *Journal of Adolescent Health, 13*, 364–368.

Braithwaite, D. O. (1991). "Just how much did that wheelchair cost?" Management of privacy boundaries by persons with disabilities. *Western Journal of Speech Communication, 55*, 254–274.

Braithwaite, D. O. (1996). "I am a person first": Different perspectives on the communication of persons with disabilities. In E. B Ray (Ed.), *Communication and disenfranchisement: Social health issues and implications* (pp. 257–272). Mahwah, NJ: Lawrence Erlbaum Associates.

Braithwaite, D. O., & Braithwaite, C. A. (1997). Understanding communication of persons with disabilities as cultural communication. In L. A. Samovar & R. Porter (Eds.), *Intercultural communication: A reader* (8th ed., pp. 154–164). Cincinnati, OH: Wadsworth.

Derlega, V. J., Metts, S., Petronio, S., & Margulis, S. T. (1993). *Self-disclosure.* Newbury Park, CA: Sage.

Dietz, J. T., & Mills, M. B. (1998, April). *Personal responsibility and the social experience of illness.* Paper presented at the Kentucky Conference on Health Communication, Lexington, KY.

Farina, A., Allen, J. G., & Saul, B. B. (1968). The role of the stigmatized person in affecting social relationships. *Journal of Personality, 36*, 169–172.

Fine, M., & Asch, A. (1988). Disability beyond stigma: Social interaction, discrimination and activism. *Journal of Social Issues, 44*, 3–21.

Galanti, G. (1997). *Caring for patients from different cultures: Case studies from American hospitals.* Philadelphia: University of Pennsylvania Press.

Gilbert, P., Pehl, J., & Allen, S. (1994). The phenomenology of shame and guilt: An empirical investigation. *British Journal of Medical Psychology, 67*, 23–36.

Goffman, E. (1963). *Stigma: Notes on the management of spoiled identity.* Englewood Cliffs, NJ: Prentice-Hall.

Gordon, G. H., Baker, L., & Levinson, W. (1995). Physician-patient communication in managed care. *Western Journal of Medicine, 163*, 527–531.

Gotcher, J. M. (1993). The effects of family communication on psychosocial adjustment of cancer patients. *Journal of Applied Communication Research, 21*, 176–188.

Harrington, N. G., & Matthews, C. K. (1997, November). *Shame-proneness among the invisibly disabled: Implications for communication with health care providers.* Paper presented at the Annual Convention of the Speech Communication Association, Chicago, IL.

Hassenfeld, I. N. (1993). Chronic disease and disability. In F. S. Sierles (Ed.), *Behavioral science for medical students* (pp. 408–414). Baltimore: Williams & Wilkins.

Hastorf, A. H., Wildfogel, J., & Cassman, T. (1979). Acknowledgment of handicap as a tactic in social interaction. *Journal of Personality and Social Psychology, 37,* 1790–1797.

Hayden, S. (1993). Chronically ill and "feeling fine": A study of communication and chronic illness. *Journal of Applied Communication Research, 21,* 263–278.

Ireys, H. T., Gross, S. S., Werthamer-Larsson, L. A., & Kolodner, K. B. (1994). Self-esteem of young adults with chronic health conditions: Appraising the effects of perceived impact. *Journal of Developmental and Behavioral Pediatrics, 15,* 409–415.

Jones, E. E., Farina, A., Hastorf, A. H., Markus, H., Miller, D. T., & Scott, R. A. (1984). *Social stigma: The psychology of marked relationships.* New York: W.H. Freeman.

Kaye, H. S., LaPlante, M. P., Carlson, D., & Wegner, B. L. (1997). Trends in disability rates in the United States, 1970–1994. [On-line]. *Disability Statistics Abstract, 17.* Available from http://dsc.ucsf.edu.

Kaplan, S. H., Greenfield, S., & Ware, J. E., Jr. (1989). Impact of the doctor-patient relationship on the outcomes of chronic disease. In M. Stewart & D. Roter (Eds.), *Communicating with medical patients* (pp. 228–245). Beverly Hills, CA: Sage.

Keele-Card, G., Foxall, M. J., & Barron, C. R. (1993). Loneliness, depression, and social support of patients with COPD and their spouses. *Public Health Nursing, 10,* 245–251.

Lane, C., & Hobfoll, S. E. (1992). How loss affects anger and alienates potential supporters. *Journal of Consulting and Clinical Psychology, 60,* 935–942.

LaPlante, M. P. (1991). Disability risks of chronic illness and impairments. *Disability Statistics Report, 2,* 1–39.

LaPlante, M. P. (1997). Health conditions and impairments causing disability. [On-line]. *Disability Statistics Abstract, 16.* Available from http://dsc.ucsf.edu.

Lazare, A. (1987). Shame and humiliation in the medical encounter. *Archives of Internal Medicine, 147,* 1653–1658.

Martin, J. T. (1993). Shame and the origin of physician-patient conflict. *Journal of the American Osteopathic Association, 93,* 486, 489–491.

Matthews, C. K. (1994, February). *To tell or not to tell: The management of privacy boundaries by the invisibly disabled.* Paper presented at the annual meeting of the Western States Communication Association, San Jose, CA.

Matthews, C. K. (1996, September). *Understanding the role of shame in interactions involving chronic illness and disability: A shame response model.* Paper presented at the Kentucky Communication Association Annual Convention, Lake Cumberland, KY.

McNeil, J. M. (1993). *Americans with disabilities: 1991–92.* Washington, DC: U.S. Government Printing Office.

Milliken, F. J., & Northcott, H. C. (1996). Seeking validation: Hypothyroidism and the chronic illness trajectory. *Qualitative Health Research, 6,* 202–223.

Mills, J., Belgrave, F., & Boyer, K. M. (1984). Reducing avoidance of social interaction with a physically disabled person by mentioning the disability following a request for aid. *Journal of Applied Social Psychology, 14,* 1–11.

Niedenthal, P. M., Tangney, J. P., & Gavanski, I. (1994). "If only I weren't" versus "If only I hadn't": Distinguishing shame and guilt in counterfactual thinking. *Journal of Personality and Social Psychology, 67,* 585–595.

Parsons, T. (1951). *The social system.* Glencoe, IL: Free Press.

Petronio, S. (1991). Communication boundary management: A theoretical model of managing disclosure of private information between marital couples. *Communication Theory, 1,* 311–335.

Roper, N. (Ed.). (1988). *New American pocket medical dictionary.* New York: Churchill Livingstone.

Scambler, G. (1984). Perceiving and coping with stigmatizing illness. In R. Fitzpatrick, J. Hinton, S. Newman, G. Scambler, & J. Thompson (Eds.), *The experience of illness* (pp. 203–226). London: Tavistock.

Schneider, J. W. (1988). Disability as moral experience: Epilepsy and self in routine relationships. *Journal of Social Issues, 44*, 63–78.

Sidoli, M. (1988). Shame and the shadow. *Journal of Analytical Psychology, 33*, 127–142.

Sinnema, G. (1992). Youths with chronic illness and disability on their way to social and economic participation: A health-care perspective. *Journal of Adolescent Health, 13*, 369–371.

Stewart, M., Brown, J. B., Weston, W. W., McWhinney, I. R., McWilliam, C. L., & Freeman, T. R. (1995). *Patient-centered medicine: Transforming the clinical method.* Thousand Oaks, CA: Sage.

Susman, J. (1994). Disability, stigma and deviance. *Social Science and Medicine, 38*, 15–22.

Tangney, J. P., Wagner, P., Fletcher, C., & Gramzow, R. (1992). Shamed into anger? The relation of shame and guilt to anger and self-reported aggression. *Journal of Personality and Social Psychology, 62*, 669–675.

Tangney, J. P., Wagner, P., & Gramzow, R. (1992). Proneness to shame, proneness to guilt, and psychopathology. *Journal of Abnormal Psychology, 101*, 469–478.

Thompson, T. L. (1982). Disclosure as a disability management strategy: A review and conclusions. *Communication Quarterly, 30*, 196–202.

Thompson, T. L., & Seibold, D. R. (1978). Stigma management in normal-stigmatized interactions: A test of the disclosure hypothesis and a model of stigma acceptance. *Human Communication Research, 4*, 231–242.

24

Communicating With Persons Who Stutter: Perceptions and Strategies

Bryan B. Whaley
University of San Francisco

Mindi Ann Golden
University of Utah

Keywords: Stuttering, perceptions of stutterers, interactive strategies and stuttering

Centuries of social interaction have time-tested stuttering as a dependable source of derision and mockery (Bobrick, 1995; Peters & Guitar, 1991; Van Riper, 1982). Although the severity of ridicule sustained may have eased from previous times, most stutterers still report being regarded as stupid, emotionally troubled, and comic by a majority of the general public (e.g., Van Riper, 1978). Hence, some argue persons who stutter experience the wrath of being different more than persons with other communicative or physical disabilities (Bobrick, 1995; Love, 1981; Neal & White, 1965; Van Riper, 1982).[1]

Differential treatment of stutterers may be founded on the uniform archetype of perceptions fluent persons have of them. Specifically, the negative stereotype for persons who stutter is constituted by descriptors such as shy, nervous, introverted, fearful, inhibited, tense, and quiet. These perceptions follow stutterers through their lives from childhood (Crowe & Cooper, 1977) to their professional careers (M. I. Hurst & Cooper, 1983). Even persons responsible for aiding stutterers in their communicative (Cooper & Cooper, 1985, 1996), educational (Ruscello et al., 1994; Ruscello et al., 1991), and vocational needs (M. A. Hurst & Cooper, 1983) hold this view.

Stutterers know how fluent persons perceive them and this, coupled with the anticipated negative responses to and social penalties for their stuttering, greatly exacerbates the frequency and severity of stuttering occurrences (Bloodstein, 1995). Hence, detailing the nature of fluent persons' perceptions of and their reactions to persons who stutter are key to understanding the social interaction between stutterers and fluent persons. These can help form the bases for suggestions for improving such interaction.

The aim of this chapter is to review the factors essential to communicating with persons who stutter. This chapter discusses the contributions of the communication field to stuttering, addresses attitudes toward stuttering by both fluent speakers and persons who stutter, reviews communication research concerning strategies for interacting with stutterers, and offers suggestions for future inquiry.[2]

Early Contributions from Communication

A consistent pattern of contributions regarding stuttering appears in communication journals published from 1920 through 1970; fewer have been published since this time (e.g., Ragsdale & Dauterive, 1986). The corpus of articles was authored by the early premier stuttering theorists, Jon Eisenson (Eisenson & Pastel, 1936), Wendell Johnson (1933), Joseph Sheehan (Sheehan & Voas, 1954), Lee Edward Travis (1946, 1959), and Charles Van Riper (1937, 1958), and generally focused on the etiology and psychology of stuttering. However, treatises concerning stuttering and interaction authored by speech pathologists or by communication theorists (Devito, 1969) are essentially nonexistent.[3]

There are several reasons for this paucity of contributions. First, stuttering affects only 1% of the populace, or approximately 3 million Americans (Bloodstein, 1995; Guitar & Peters, 1991; National Stuttering Project, 1998). Traditionally, phenomena are judged in terms of worthiness of investigation in relation to the number of people affected. Second, stuttering historically has been viewed as a disorder and, hence, the province of another discipline (i.e., speech pathology/communication disorders). And, once the field of communication disorders created journals, treatises addressing stuttering appeared most frequently in these outlets. Finally, both speech pathology and communication, as fields of study, were in their foundational years in 1930–1940s, and thus were grappling with larger theoretical issues. Early theorizing in both camps focused on etiology and theories of stuttering, rather than on issues of social interaction.

PERCEPTIONS OF PERSONS
WHO STUTTER

Recent research concerning the fluent public's perceptions of stutterers provides a foundation from which to begin investigating issues of social interaction between stutterers and fluent persons. The basis of these perceptions are key to fostering theory and research.

Fluent Speakers' Perceptions

Research designed to ascertain fluent persons' perceptions of those who stutter has typically asked them to "imagine a typical male and female adult stutterer and a typical boy and girl stutterer" and generate the adjectives that they feel best reflect the nature of these four hypothetical individuals. This investigative practice has yielded consistent and robust findings regarding how fluent persons view stutterers. Persons who stutter are regarded as nervous, insecure, shy, tense, anxious, fearful, afraid, introverted, withdrawn, quiet, unsociable, boring, defensive, reticent, guarded, restrained, passive, self-conscious, cowardly, pessimistic, sensitive, frustrated, embarrassed, bungling, hesitant, undecided, and aimless. These descriptors also reflect a global negative and stereotypical perception of those who stutter— that is, the adjectives represent an overwhelming prominence of negative personality traits, and a virtual paucity of such other descriptors as appearance, intelligence, particular talents, or speech characteristics (Woods & Williams, 1976).

This pattern of perceptions of stutterers prevails regardless of fluent perceivers' age, sex, level of education, or profession. Specifically, mothers/parents (Crowe & Cooper, 1977; Fowlie & Cooper, 1978; Yairi & Williams, 1971), elementary/secondary school teachers (Crowe & Walton, 1981; Lass et al., 1992; Yeakle & Cooper, 1986), college students (McKinnon, Hess, & Landry, 1986; Ruscello, Lass, & Brown, 1988; Silverman, 1982; Turnbaugh, Guitar, & Hoffman, 1981), professors (Ruscello et al., 1991), special educators (Ruscello et al., 1994), speech pathology students (Horsley & Fitzgibbon, 1987; Ruscello et al., 1989–90; St. Louis & Lass, 1981), speech clinicians (Cooper & Cooper, 1985, 1996; Cooper & Rustin, 1985; Kalinowski et al., 1993; Lass et al., 1989; Ragsdale

& Ashby, 1982; Silverman, 1982; Turnbaugh, Guitar, & Hoffman, 1979; Yairi & Williams, 1970), vocational rehabilitation counselors (M. A. Hurst & Cooper, 1983), school administrators (Lass et al., 1994), nurses (Silverman & Bongey, 1997), employers (M. I. Hurst & Cooper, 1983; Neal & White, 1965), store clerks (McDonald & Frick, 1954), and the general public (Ham, 1990; Kalinowski et al., 1993) attribute the same characteristics to stutterers. Also, males rate stutterers more severely than females (Burley & Rinaldi, 1986; Silverman & Zimmer, 1979). Moreover, cultural differences exist regarding fluent persons' perceptions of the emotional health of stutterers. Specifically, some cultures attribute more severe traits or psychopathology to persons who stutter than do other cultures (Bebout & Arthur, 1992).

This predominantly negative attitude toward stutterers by fluent speakers has clear interactive consequences. Fluent speakers frequently exhibit impatience, amusement, and minor indications of repulsion, pity, sympathy, curiosity, surprise, and embarrassment when interacting with persons who stutter (McDonald & Frick, 1954). In addition, fluent listeners may try to avoid or limit conversation with stuttering partners (Hubbard, 1965; Rosenberg & Curtiss, 1954; Woods & Williams, 1976), and want more social distance between themselves and those who stutter (Emerick, 1966; McKinnon, Hess, & Landry, 1986).

Foundations of the "Stuttering" Stereotype

There is no empirical evidence to suggest that persons who stutter possess the personality traits attributed to them by fluent speakers, that stuttering is the manifestation of underlying emotional problems, or a personality characteristic that almost all persons who stutter possess (Bloodstein, 1995; Silverman, 1992; Starkweather, 1987). These factors make the fact that fluent persons consistently view stutterers negatively, regardless of the amount and nature of their exposure to stuttering individuals, perplexing.

Attempts have been made to discern the fundamental processes by which fluent speakers create the "characteristic stuttering stereotype." For instance, White and Collins (1984) hypothesized that the stuttering stereotype fluent speakers have of stutterers is formed by inference from beliefs about the internal states that accompany dysfluencies experienced by themselves, which they perceive are akin to stuttering. Specifically, White and Collins posited that because all fluent speakers experience dysfluencies normally under stressful conditions, they may attribute the feelings or responses they experience during these circumstances (e.g., nervousness, tension, embarrassment) to those that stutterers experience during their periods of dysfluency. When investigating this explanation, however, White and Collins found that the basis of the stuttering stereotype may be fluent persons' uncertainty about stuttering and how to interact with stuttering persons and the discomfort associated with this ambiguity, rather than motivational factors or perceived similarity in internal states during dysfluencies.

Stutterer's Self- and Other Perceptions

Kalinowski, Lerman, and Watt (1987) found that dysfluent speakers did not differ significantly from a group of their fluent counterparts when rating themselves on an inventory of 21 personal characteristics. Participants who stuttered perceived themselves just as "open," "secure," "talkative," and "friendly" as did their more fluent peers. However, when asked to characterize each other, significant rating differences occurred. Specifically, stutterers rated fluent speakers higher on such characteristics as "calm," "friendly," and "secure." Conversely, fluent subjects gave lower ratings to stutterers on the same traits (Kalinowski, Lerman, & Watt, 1987).

Stutterers appear to evaluate themselves and others on the basis of the severity of their dysfluencies (Leith, Mahr, & Miller, 1993; Manning, Dailey, & Wallace, 1984). Persons who rate their stuttering as moderate or severe consider themselves as more "friendly" and "attentive" than their peers who stutter mildly. Individuals who stutter moderately also view themselves as better at leaving a good impression after social interaction than those who stutter mildly. Those who identify themselves as stuttering severely are significantly less accepting of their dysfluency than their moderate and mild stuttering colleagues (Leith, Mahr, & Miller, 1993). Despite their common experiences with fluent speakers, individuals who stutter do not consider themselves as belonging to a homogeneous group.

Recent research found that stutterers' perceptions of other persons who stutter coincide with the perceptions of stutterers by fluent persons. For instance, Lass et al. (1995) asked persons who stutter to list adjectives they thought most accurately described the nature of stutterers (i.e., "four hypothetical stutterers" used in much of previous research). Their findings were similar to the pattern of responses of fluent persons toward persons who stutter. Specifically, stutterers primarily produced a majority of negative personality traits to describe persons who stutter.

Apparently, then, persons who stutter tend to view themselves similarly to the way fluent individuals reflect on their own characteristics. Moreover, a stutterer sees him- or herself as being different from persons who stutter, as a group (Fiedler & Wepman, 1951; Fransella, 1968). These perceptions by individuals who stutter, according to Fransella, can be gleaned to suggest, "Yes, of course I stutter, but I am not like the general run of stutterers, as an individual I am unique" (p. 1533).

Factors Affecting Perceptions

The nature of fluent persons' perceptions of stutterers is robust and consistent and appears to be based in fluent persons' uncertainty of how to interact with those who stutter. Specifically, given that stuttering is a communication problem of prosody, fluent speakers are unsure what to expect because of the timing disruption in speech production and flow of conversational exchange. Research has revealed two factors that can enhance fluent persons' perceptions of those who stutter—acknowledgment of one's stuttering and eye contact.

Acknowledgment of Stuttering. Collins and Blood (1990) found that fluent female participants reported a preference for interacting with severe stutterers who verbally acknowledged their stuttering. Moreover, persons with mild and severe stuttering patterns who acknowledged their dysfluency were rated more favorably on intelligence, personality, and appearance scales by fluent speakers.

Another means of acknowledging stuttering is the use of messages printed on T-shirts. Silverman (1988) investigated how university students would react to a stutterer wearing a T-shirt with "I stutter. So what!" printed on it. Significant differences in the perception of persons who stutter were detected. Specifically, stutterers wearing T-shirts were rated as having a better sense of humor; a better self-concept; being less frightened and isolated; and being more aggressive, brave, calm, comfortable, confident, dominant, extroverted, happy, intelligent, interesting, organized, orientated, rash, secure, sociable, soothing, stable, strong, talkative, and uninhibited than the stutterers not wearing the T-shirt. Silverman, Gazzolo, and Peterson (1990) repeated the investigation using store clerks and other business people as research participants, rather than university students. The findings of this study were similar to Silverman's (1988). Persons who stuttered wearing a T-shirt of this sort were perceived more positively than stutterers without such a shirt—specifically, they were considered to have a better self-concept; to be more aggressive, comfortable, confident, content, employable, emotional, extroverted, fluent, industrious, intelligible, interesting, lovable, relaxed, secure, sociable, soothing, stable, talkative, witty, and able to converse with others; and regarded as less afraid, cautious, frustrating, hesitant, inhibited, and isolated.

Stuttering theorists generally agree that when stutterers put their dysfluency "out in the open" (i.e., tell fluent interactants they stutter), the severity of their stuttering is reduced (Silverman, 1988). This practice appears to greatly reduce uncertainty and increase comfort in fluent interactants, which results in more positive attributions of stutterers (White & Collins, 1984). These findings coincide with other works suggesting the benefits of persons with disabilities acknowledging their state to others (Hastorf, Wildfogel, & Cassman, 1979; Thompson, 1982). However, disclosure of a disability can significantly affect a person and should be given strong consideration before being undertaken.

Eye Contact. Sheehan (1970), a notable stuttering theorist and researcher, counseled the stutterer that "interpersonal communication is nearly always facilitated by eye contact" and that "to succeed it is sufficient that *you* look at them." Empirical research suggests that Sheehan's and others' (e.g., Fraser, 1987; Van Riper, 1973) advice was sound. Stutterers' increased eye contact when interacting with fluent persons greatly affects the traits attributed to them by fluent speakers. Tatchell, van den Berg, and Lerman (1983) investigated the role of eye contact and speech fluency concerning communicator credibility using a 2 (high–low eye contact) × 2 (fluent–dysfluent) design. The authors found that eye contact, rather than fluency, was a better predictor of receiver ratings of the stuttering communicator. These findings are further supported by Atkins (1988), and suggest that fostering effective eye contact should be a major objective in stuttering therapy.

STRATEGIES FOR INTERACTING WITH PERSONS WHO STUTTER

Regardless of how fluent persons view stutterers, persons who stutter still have to go about their interactive lives. Because the traditional focus of research has concerned determining etiology, viable interventions, and the traits attributed to persons who stutter, little has been accomplished to suggest to fluent speakers how to interact more effectively with stutterers. However, the frequency and severity of stuttering is greatly influenced by the reactions of fluent persons—this renders stuttering a communicative and interactive issue, in addition to a pathological one. Framed in this manner, stuttering as an interactive concern provides more heuristic promise for communication research.

Foundational Suggestions

There are relatively few sources suggesting strategies for interacting with persons who stutter. Most of the work available, however, has focused on and is limited to helping the stutterer in the educational setting (Amidon, 1958; Barbara, 1956; Knudson, 1940; Krohn & Perez, 1989; Whaley & Langlois, 1996). For instance, the standard strategies to avoid when interacting with a person who stutters include suggesting the stutterer "slow down," "take deep breaths," "think before speaking," "whisper," "stop and start over," or "practice," suggesting distraction techniques (i.e., finger snapping, foot stomping); filling in or supplying a blocked word; and asking the stutterer to use "will power" to keep from stuttering. In addition to avoiding these practices, instructors are encouraged to maintain continuous eye contact with those who stutter during periods of blocking or dysfluencies, avoid facial grimaces, and be patient (Krohn & Perez, 1989; Pindzola, 1985).

As sound and effective as these interactive suggestions may appear, they lack empirical foundations (Amidon, 1958). Specifically, the interactive recommendations are void of empirical generation and scrutiny. Moreover, the sources of these interactive strategies are rarely clear. When the origins of the strategies are offered, it is often an adaptation from "authoritative" sources (Krohn & Perez, 1989; Pindzola, 1985; Whaley & Langlois, 1996). This observation led to an empirical investigation to garner effective interactive strategies for fluent people when speaking with those who stutter.

Empirically Derived Strategies

Whaley and Golden (1998) collected open-ended responses from 357 persons who stutter regarding behaviors that fluent speakers employ when interacting with them that increases their communication satisfaction. Their findings yielded five general categories of communicative behaviors: (a) show acceptance and understanding, (b) show patience, (c) treat the person as a fluent speaker, (d) create relaxed speaking environment, and (e) acknowledge stuttering. These strategies constitute behaviors that should be employed before, during, and after the block, and are not necessarily mutually exclusive. Because this investigation is the single empirical large-scale effort regarding communicative strategies and interacting with stutterers, some detail concerning participants' responses is warranted.

Acceptance and Understanding.   Exhibiting acceptance and understanding can be accomplished by several means. Nonverbally, a fluent interactant should assume a relaxed posture, warm facial expression, and comfortable tone of voice. Sustaining normal eye contact with a stutterer during a block, and avoiding stares of shock or looking away in discomfort, also shows acceptance. A smile of sincerity, rather than mockery or negative facial expressions (e.g., scowl, frown, wincing, flinching, startle, embarrassment) is also valued.

Verbal behaviors offered by participants include not offering advice for overcoming stuttering, giving sweeping suggestions for curing stuttering or blocking (i.e., "just slow down" or "just take your time"), and avoiding criticizing a stutterer's speech (i.e., "Excuse me?!" or "Did you forget your name?"). Reference to relationships a fluent speaker has with others who stutter can aid the situation, as well (i.e., "I understand that it's hard to get the words out sometimes; my sister stutters, too"). Finally, refraining from exhibiting amusement (e.g., laughing, grinning, or smirking; not verbally ridiculing—mimicking his or her speech, or telling stuttering jokes) can show acceptance.

Show Patience.   Persons who stutter provided numerous methods for fluent persons to show patience. Specifically, avoid interrupting a person who stutters (e.g., wait for stutterer to finish speaking and avoid filling in words or sentences during a block); avoid fidgeting and shifting weight from leg to leg; and avoid indicating they want to speak when the stutterer blocks. Rushing the person who stutters will likely worsen the block. Hence, rather than gesturing for the stutterer to hurry up or saying, "I only have a short time," offering, "It's okay; take your time" or "Don't worry; I have time" will prove more beneficial.

Treat the Person as a Fluent Speaker.   Stutterers possess the same traits as fluent speakers, other than occasional dysfluencies. Accordingly, persons who stutter want to be treated like fluent speakers. Stutterers suggest that this requires showing interest when they are speaking (e.g., facing the speaker, listening, nodding head in understanding, not turning away, not doing other things unrelated to the interaction, not looking at others to see their reactions to the stutterer, and focusing on content, not delivery).

Conversationally, fluent speakers should continue the interaction. This means not walking away or starting a conversation with someone else once the stutterer finishes speaking, not changing the subject abruptly under the notion that a different topic will aid the stutterer; if interacting via telephone, not hanging up; not continuing to talk just so a person who stutters cannot speak; asking the stutterer questions, rather than avoiding hearing him or her speak; and asking the person who stutters to repeat something that is not understood.

Stutterers offer four methods of treating them as fluent speakers after an initial interaction in which a block has occurred: (a) acknowledging their presence rather than ignoring them (e.g., welcoming conversations, initiating getting together, and initiating causal conversations), (b) treating them with respect (i.e., not patronizing), (c) treating the individual as an equal (e.g., recognizing his or her abilities, valuing his or her knowledge/authority on a given subject), and (d) offering a stutterer speaking opportunities.

Relaxed Speaking Environment.   Once fluent speakers are aware that an individual stutters, they can engage in specific behaviors that contribute to a relaxed speaking environment. Stutterers offered six means to avert pressure or anxiety that would make dysfluencies more likely or more severe. The initial three focus on speaking traits of a fluent speaker: (a) speak slowly and calmly, (b) ask the stutterer questions carefully (e.g., ask one question at a time; avoid questioning in an aggressive or demanding manner; avoid asking complicated, multifaceted questions), and (c) avoid trying to be a perfect speaker; fluent speakers may be more aware of their own speech when talking with stutterers and often, will try to eliminate natural dysfluencies from their speech.

Three remaining suggestions concern a fluent speaker's reactions to a person who stutters: (a) if a stutterer expresses concern or seems apprehensive about stuttering (which is typical), a fluent speaker can offer reassurance (e.g., "It's okay," "It doesn't bother me," or "Don't worry about it"), (b) a fluent speaker can offer a person who stutters encouragement (e.g., "You can do it"), and (c) a fluent speaker should laugh if stutterers makes jokes about their dysfluencies, which often eases tension and discomfort.

Acknowledge Stuttering.   A final way for fluent speakers to make interaction easier and more satisfying for stutterers is to acknowledge stuttering. Acknowledging involves fluent speakers (a) asking about stuttering in general or specifically about a stutterer's speech, (b) asking if there is anything they can do to help during a block or conversation—and performing it, (c) looking concerned (vs. pityingly) about the person's stuttering difficulty, (d) offering positive feedback immediately after a speech turn (e.g., acknowledging improved fluency) and after a person who stutters has made a presentation or addressed a group (e.g., "You did a good job"), and (e) implicitly acknowledging a person's stuttering by expressing their own weaknesses. When fluent speakers realize the dysfluencies, employing these strategies brings this realization out into the open in a positive and productive manner.

FUTURE INQUIRY

Stuttering has been part of the human condition and, given our present knowledge concerning this disability, will continue to be for many more years (Perkins, 1996). While stuttering is theoretically an intriguing and complex mystery of speech timing, practically it serves as a dependable source of social torment and interactional discomfort. Although research efforts concerning etiology and therapeutic options of stuttering continue, communication theorists can begin to make contributions regarding the interactive aspects of stuttering.

Speech pathologists have provided a body of literature from which to launch systematic inquiry. Specifically, an ample amount of research describes how fluent persons perceive stutterers, and confirms that fluent interactants contribute to the frequency and severity of stuttering and that acknowledgment by a stutterer of dysfluency contributes to more positive perceptions and interactions. These findings are clear indicators that viewing stuttering as interactive and pathological will be a far more productive course for researching the communicative patterns between persons who stutter and those who are fluent.

Stuttering is a fluency and timing phenomenon, and human speech and conversation are micro-coordinated behaviors. As such, improved interaction between fluent persons and stutterers will clearly require more from fluent interactants. However, this will only require fluent speakers to consciously apply the same behaviors to stutterers as they use with fluent interactants. For instance, Whaley and Golden's (1998) findings appear to put considerable responsibility on the fluent public for the interactive satisfaction of stutterers. On closer examination, their data suggest globally that persons who stutter want the fluent public to interact with them in the same manner as they do with fluent persons. More specifically, the communicative behaviors offered by stutterers to fluent interactants clearly, at this point, reduce to core communicative issues of uncertainty (Berger, 1997), politeness (Brown & Levinson, 1987), and accommodation (Giles, Coupland, & Coupland, 1991). Programmatic inquiry into how each of these issues specifically applies to stutterers will surely render pragmatic results. For instance, understanding more specifically how interacting with someone who stutters affects the strategies of "face" employed by fluent persons would clearly be of foundational benefit.

The field of communication has the theoretical foundations to begin systematically unveiling, understanding, and validating competent interactive strategies for stuttering and fluent individuals to employ. After centuries of uncertainty, now would be a good time to begin.

DISCUSSION QUESTIONS

1. What factors contribute to the negative perceptions fluent persons have of stutterers? In what ways do these perceptions impact interactions?
2. Why are persons who stutter more severely regarded than persons with other communicative, physical, or mental disabilities?
3. What can be done to (a) alter existing perceptions of stutterers and (b) foster the development of positive views in children toward persons who stutter?
4. Why are fluent persons impatient with stutterers?
5. Why is it apparently easy for fluent persons to attack the "face" of persons who stutter?
6. Identify and describe specific ways fluent speakers can increase a stutterer's interactive satisfaction.

REFERENCES

Amidon, H. F. (1958). A report on a class for high school stutterers—are we meeting their needs? *Speech Teacher, 7*, 114–117.

Ashton, D. (1997, October). "Stutterer" vs. "people who stutter." *Letting Go*, p. 3.

Atkins, C. P. (1988). Perceptions of speakers with minimal eye contact: Implications for stutterers. *Journal of Fluency Disorders, 13*, 429–436.

Barbara, D. A. (1956). The classroom teacher's role in stuttering. *Speech Teacher, 5*, 137–141.

Bebout, L., & Arthur, B. (1992). Cross-cultural attitudes toward speech disorders. *Journal of Speech and Hearing Research, 35*, 45–52.

Berger, C. R. (1997). *Planning strategic interaction*. Mahwah, NJ: Lawrence Erlbaum Associates.

Bloodstein, O. (1995). *A handbook on stuttering* (5th ed.). San Diego, CA: Singular Publishing Group.

Bobrick, B. (1995). *Knotted tongues: Stuttering in history and the quest for a cure.* New York: Simon & Schuster.

Brown, P., & Levinson, S. C. (1987). *Politeness: Some universals in language use.* Cambridge, U.K.: Cambridge University Press.

Burley, P. M., & Rinaldi, W. (1986). Effects of sex of listener and of stutterer on ratings of stuttering speakers. *Journal of Fluency Disorders, 17,* 329–333.

Collins, C. R., & Blood, G. W. (1990). Acknowledgment and severity of stuttering as factors influencing nonstutterers' perceptions of stutterers. *Journal of Speech and Hearing Disorders, 55,* 75–81.

Cooper, E. B., & Cooper, C. S. (1985). Clinician attitudes toward stuttering: A decade of change (1973-1983). *Journal of Fluency Disorders, 10,* 19–33.

Cooper, E. B., & Cooper, C. S. (1996). Clinician attitudes toward stuttering: Two decades of change. *Journal of Fluency Disorders, 21,* 119–135.

Cooper, E. B., & Rustin, L. (1985). Clinician attitudes toward stuttering in the United States and Great Britain: A cross-cultural study. *Journal of Fluency Disorders, 10,* 1–17.

Crowe, T. A., & Cooper, E. B. (1977). Parental attitudes toward and knowledge of stuttering. *Journal of Communication Disorders, 10,* 343–357.

Crowe, T. A., & Walton, J. H. (1981). Teacher attitudes toward stuttering. *Journal of Fluency Disorders, 6,* 163–174.

Davis, J. (1997, December). Stutterer vs. persons who stutter. *Letting Go,* p. 7.

Devito, J. (1969). Are theories of stuttering necessary? *Central States Communication Journal, 20,* 170–177.

Eisenson, J., & Pastel, E. (1936). A study of the preseverating tendency in stutterers. *Quarterly Journal of Speech, 22,* 626–631.

Emerick, L. (1966). Social distance and stuttering. *Southern Speech Journal, 31,* 219–222.

Fiedler, F. E., & Wepman, J. M. (1951). An exploratory investigation of the self-concept of stutterers. *Journal of Speech and Hearing Disorders, 16,* 110–114.

Fowlie, G. M., & Cooper, E. B. (1978). Traits attributed to stuttering and nonstuttering children by their mothers. *Journal of Fluency Disorders, 3,* 233–246.

Fransella, F. (1968). Self-concepts and the stutterer. *British Journal of Psychiatry, 114,* 1531–1535.

Fraser, M. (1987). *Self-therapy for the stutterer* (6th ed.). Memphis, TN: Speech Foundation of America.

Giles, H., Coupland, N., & Coupland, J. (Eds.). (1991). *The contexts of accommodation.* New York: Cambridge University Press.

Guitar, B., & Peters, T. J. (1991). *Stuttering: An integrated approach to its nature and treatment.* Baltimore: Williams & Wilkins.

Ham, R. E. (1990). What is stuttering: Variations and stereotypes. *Journal of Fluency Disorders, 15,* 259–273.

Hastorf, A. H., Wildfogel, J., & Cassman, T. (1979). Acknowledgement of handicap as a tactic in social interaction. *Journal of Personality and Social Psychology, 37,* 1790–1797.

Horsley, I. A., & Fitzgibbon, C. T. (1987). Stuttering children: Investigation of a stereotype. *British Journal of Disorders of Communication, 22,* 19–35.

Hubbard, D. J. (1965). *The effect of interviewer dysfluency on interviewee speech behavior.* Unpublished masters thesis, University of Iowa.

Hurst, M. A., & Cooper, E. B. (1983). Vocational rehabilitation counselors' attitudes toward stuttering. *Journal of Fluency Disorders, 8,* 13–27.

Hurst, M. I., & Cooper, E. B. (1983). Employer attitudes toward stuttering. *Journal of Fluency Disorders, 8,* 1–12.

Johnson, W. (1933). An interpretation of stuttering. *Quarterly Journal of Speech, 19,* 70–76.

Kalinowski, J. S., Armson, J., Stuart, A., & Lerman, J. W. (1993). Speech clinicians' and the general public's perceptions of self and stutterers. *Journal of Speech-Language Pathology and Audiology, 17,* 79–85.

Kalinowski, J. S., Lerman, J. W., & Watt, J. (1987). A preliminary examination of the perceptions of self and others in stutterers and nonstutterers. *Journal of Fluency Disorders, 12*, 317–331.

Knudson, T. A. (1940). What the classroom teacher can do for stutterers. *Quarterly Journal of Speech, 26*, 207–212.

Krohn, F. B., & Perez, D. M. (1989). Management of classroom stutterers. *Exercise Exchange, 35*, 12–13.

Lass, N. J., Ruscello, D. M., Pannbacker, M. D., Schmitt, J. F., & Everly-Myers, D. S. (1989). Speech-language pathologists' perceptions of child and adult female and male stutterers. *Journal of Fluency Disorder, 14*, 127–134.

Lass, N. J., Ruscello, D. M., Pannbacker, M. D., Schmitt, J. F., Middleton, G. F., & Schweppenheiser, K. (1995). The perceptions of stutterers by people who stutter. *Folia Phoniatr Logop, 47*, 247–251.

Lass, N. J., Ruscello, D. M., Schmitt, J. F., Pannbacker, M. D., Orlando, M. B., Dean, K. A., Ruziska, J. C., & Bradshaw, K. H. (1992). Teachers' perceptions of stutterers. *Language, Speech, and Hearing Services in Schools, 23*, 78–81.

Lass, N. J., Ruscello, D. M., Schmitt, J. F., Pannbacker, M. D., Schmitt, J. F., Kiser, A. M., Mussa, A. M., & Lockhart, P. (1994). School administrators' perceptions of people who stutter. *Language, Speech, and Hearing Services in Schools, 25*, 90–93.

Leith, W. R., Mahr, G. C., & Miller, L. D. (1993). The assessment of speech-related attitudes and beliefs of people who stutter. *ASHA Monographs* (Vol. 29). Rockville, MD: American Speech-Language-Hearing Association.

Love, R. J. (1981). A forgotten minority: The communicatively disabled. *ASHA, 23*, 485–489.

Manning, W. H., Dailey, D., & Wallace, S. (1984). Attitude and personality characteristics of older stutterers. *Journal of Fluency Disorders, 9*, 207–215.

McDonald, E. T., & Frick, J. V. (1954). Store clerks' reactions to stuttering. *Journal of Speech and Hearing Disorders, 19*, 306–311.

McKinnon, S., Hess, C., & Landry, R. (1986). Reactions of college students to speech disorders. *Journal of Communicative Disorders, 19*, 75–82.

National Stuttering Project (1998). National Stuttering Project homepage [On-line]. Available: members.aol.com/nsphome/index.html.

Neal, W. R., Jr., & White, W. F. (1965). Attitudes of selected employers toward the employment of stutterers. *Southern Speech Journal, 31*, 28–33.

Perkins, W. H. (1996). *Stuttering and science*. San Diego, CA: Singular Publishing Group.

Peters, T. J., & Guitar, B. (1991). *Stuttering: An integrated approach to its nature and treatment*. Baltimore: Williams & Wilkins.

Pindzola, R. H. (1985). Classroom teachers: Interacting with stutterers. *Teacher Educator, 21*, 2–8.

Ragsdale, J. D., & Ashby, J. K. (1982). Speech-language pathologists' connotations of stuttering. *Journal of Speech and Hearing Research, 25*, 75–80.

Ragsdale, J. D., & Dauterive, R. (1986). Relationships between age, sex, and hesitation phenomena in young children. *Southern Speech Communication Journal, 52*, 22–34.

Rosenberg, S., & Curtiss, J. (1954). The effect of stuttering on the behavior of the listener. *Journal of Abnormal Psychology, 49*, 355–361.

Ruscello, D. M., Lass, N. J., & Brown, J. (1988). College students' perceptions of stutterers. *National Student Speech Language Hearing Association Journal, 16*, 115–119.

Ruscello, D. M., Lass, N. J., French, R. S., & Channel, M. D. (1989-90). Speech-language pathology students' perceptions of stutterers. *National Student Speech Language Hearing Association Journal, 17*, 86–89.

Ruscello, D. M., Lass, N. J., Schmitt, J. F., & Pannbacker, M. D. (1994). Special educators' perceptions of stutterers. *Journal of Fluency Disorders, 19*, 125–132.

Ruscello, D. M., Lass, N. J., Schmitt, J. F., Pannbacker, M. D., Hoffmann, F. M., Miley, M. A., & Robinson, K. L. (1991). Professors' perceptions of stutterers. *National Student Speech Language Hearing Association Journal, 18*, 142–145.

St. Louis, K. O., & Lass, N. J. (1981). A survey of communicative disorders students' attitudes toward stuttering. *Journal of Fluency Disorders, 6*, 49–80.

Sheehan, J. G. (1970). *Stuttering: Research and therapy.* New York: Harper & Row.

Sheehan, J. G., & Voas, R. B. (1954). Tension patterns during stuttering in relation to conflict, anxiety-binding, and reinforcement. *Speech Monographs, 21*, 272–279.

Silverman, E. M. (1982). Speech-language clinicians' and university students' impressions of women and girls who stutter. *Journal of Fluency Disorders, 7*, 469–478.

Silverman, E. M., & Zimmer, C. H. (1979). Women who stutter: Personality and speech characteristics. *Journal of Speech and Hearing Research, 22*, 553–564.

Silverman, F. H. (1992). *Stuttering and other fluency disorders.* Englewood Cliffs, NJ: Prentice-Hall.

Silverman, F. H. (1988). Impact of a t-shirt message on stutterer stereotypes. *Journal of Fluency Disorders, 13*, 279–281.

Silverman, F. H., & Bongey, T. A. (1997). Nurses' attitudes toward physicians who stutter. *Journal of Fluency Disorders, 22*, 61–62.

Silverman, F. H., Gazzolo, M., & Peterson, Y. (1990). Impact of a t-shirt message on stutterer stereotypes: A systematic replication. *Journal of Fluency Disorders, 15*, 35–37.

Starkweather, C. W. (1987). *Fluency and stuttering.* Englewood Cliffs, NJ: Prentice-Hall.

Tatchell, R., van den Berg, S., & Lerman, J. (1983). Fluency and eye contact as factors influencing observers' perceptions of stutterers. *Journal of Fluency Disorders, 8*, 221–231.

Thompson, T. L. (1982). Disclosure as a disability-management strategy: A review and conclusions. *Communication Quarterly, 30*, 196–202.

Travis, L. E. (1946). My present thinking on stuttering. *Western Journal of Speech Communication, 10*, 3–5.

Travis, L. E. (1959). A theoretical formulation of stuttering. *Western Journal of Speech Communication, 23*, 133–140.

Turnbaugh, K. R., Guitar, B. E., & Hoffman, P. R. (1979). Speech clinicians' attribution of personality traits as a function of stuttering severity. *Journal of Speech and Hearing Research, 22*, 37–45.

Turnbaugh, K. R., Guitar, B. E., & Hoffman, P. R. (1981). The attribution of personality traits: The stutterer and nonstutterer. *Journal of Speech and Hearing Research, 24*, 288–291.

Van Riper, C. (1937). The growth of the stuttering spasm. *Quarterly Journal of Speech, 23*, 70–73.

Van Riper, C. (1958). The speech therapist speaks to the communications' staff. *Communication Education, 7*, 324–331.

Van Riper, C. (1973). *The treatment of stuttering.* Englewood Cliffs, NJ: Prentice Hall.

Van Riper, C. (1978). *Speech correction.* Englewood Cliffs, NJ: Prentice-Hall.

Van Riper, C. (1982). *The nature of stuttering* (2nd ed.). Englewood Cliffs, NJ: Prentice-Hall.

Whaley, B. B., & Golden, M. A. (1998). *Toward more satisfying interactions for persons who stutter: Empirically-generated suggestions for fluent speakers.* Manuscript under review for publication.

Whaley, B. B., & Langlois, A. (1996). Students who stutter and the basic course: Attitudes and communicative strategies for the college classroom. *Basic Communication Course Annual, 8*, 58–73.

White, P. A., & Collins, S. R. (1984). Stereotype formation by inference: A possible explanation for the "stutterer" stereotype. *Journal of Speech and Hearing Research, 27*, 567–570.

Woods, C. L., & Williams, D. E. (1976). Traits attributed to stuttering and normally fluent males. *Journal of Speech and Hearing Research, 19*, 267–278.

Yairi, E., & Williams, D. E. (1970). Speech clinicians' stereotypes of elementary-school boys who stutter. *Journal of Communication Disorders, 3*, 161–170.

Yairi, E., & Williams, D. E. (1971). Reports of parental attitudes by stuttering and by nonstuttering children. *Journal of Speech and Hearing Research, 14*, 596–604.

Yeakle, M. K., & Cooper, E. B. (1986). Teacher perceptions of stuttering. *Journal of Fluency Disorders, 11*, 345–359.

ENDNOTES

1. There is disagreement within the stuttering community concerning terms of reference (Davis, 1997). For example, many *stutterers* prefer to be called *those who stutter*. Here, stuttering is a communicative pattern those who stutter do rather than something they are. Conversely, others prefer *stutterer* because stuttering is what they do and, hence, who they are (e.g., "If I teach, I'm a teacher, if I sing, I'm a singer," etc.; Ashton, 1997). Still others refer to *stutterers* as persons who let stuttering control their lives, and *persons who stutter* as those who have dealt with stuttering in a manner that no longer hinders the quality of their lives. Hence, in an attempt to acknowledge these respective differences and preferences, *stutterer* and *persons who stutter* will be alternated throughout the chapter.

2. The theories regarding the cause of stuttering are too numerous and complex to articulate in this chapter. For an organized and detailed review of the classical and contemporary views concerning stuttering etiology and episodes or moments of stuttering see, for example, Bloodstein (1995).

3. These claims are founded on the first author's review of articles written about stuttering cited in *Communication Abstracts* and *Index to Journals in Communication Studies* (commonly known as the "Matlon index").

25

Children and Adults Who Experience Difficulty With Speech

Mary Ann Romski
Rose A. Sevcik
Georgia State University

Keywords: Augmentative and alternative communication (AAC), talking computers, non-speaking, aided and unaided forms of communication

Ruth Sienkiewicz-Mercer, a woman with severe physical disabilities who has never spoken, wrote, "If I were granted one wish and one wish only, I would not hesitate for an instant to request that I be able to talk if only for one day, or even one hour" (Sienkiewicz-Mercer & Kaplan, 1989). Virtually without giving it an overt thought, we communicate and interact with others through speech. We use speech as a vehicle for self expression. It offers us a window into a person's thoughts, feelings, hopes, needs, and desires. One's "voice" is also a personal signature; we all can easily remember the way in which a special relative or close friend's voice sounds. While these are often abilities and skills that we take for granted, each of us can recall an example of the frustration caused by temporary silence, like that associated with a severe case of laryngitis.

More than 2 million children and adults in the United States experience significant long-term difficulty communicating via speech (ASHA, 1991). This difficulty results in an inability for their communication to be understood by others and affects their relationships, education, employment, and socialization (e.g., Beukelman & Mirenda, 1998; Prizant & Meyer, 1993). Our particular attention to this area of study and practice stems from a more than 20-year focus on the communicative development of children who exhibit severe cognitive and linguistic disabilities and the formulation of interventions to facilitate their ability to communicate (Romski & Sevcik, 1996).

This chapter is about the people who might encounter significant difficulty communicating via speech, the development of means to augment their natural forms of communication, and the effects these augmentative and alternative communication (AAC) means have on the communication process and on the perceptions of others. Finally, we close with a discussion of directions in which the field is advancing and some practical strategies for communicating with persons who do not speak.

WHO USES AAC ACROSS THE LIFESPAN?

Individuals from young children to older adults encounter difficulty communicating via speech. While these children and adults all share a common bond, that is, they can not communicate via speech, their characteristics may diverge significantly.

Children who cannot use speech are either born with some type of congenital disability that hinders their development of speech or acquire an injury or illness that substantially limits their existing speech and language abilities. Congenital disabilities that impede the development of speech and language may include autism, cerebral palsy, dual sensory impairments, genetic syndromes, mental retardation, multiple disabilities (including hearing impairment), and even a stroke at or near birth. A child can also acquire an inability to communicate via speech through a traumatic brain injury caused by some type of accident, stroke, or in a rare instance, severe psychological trauma. Sickle cell anemia, for example, can cause debilitating strokes that, when severe, hinder a child's ability to speak.

Across the life span, children's difficulty with speech often does not dissipate and thus some adults who do not speak were once children who did not speak. In addition, adults may also become nonspeaking for a wide range of reasons such as a stroke that causes aphasia (a loss of language abilities), cancer that may affect the vocal mechanism, traumatic brain injury, or a progressive neurological disease (e.g., Parkinsonism, multiple sclerosis, or amyotrophic lateral sclerosis).

It is also important to note that each of the disorders just described can result in a broad range of communication outcomes, from functional speech and language skills to not speaking at all. Not every child or adult presenting with one of these disorders is, or will be, nonspeaking. Some of the adult onset disorders that are progressive in nature may result in significant difficulty with speech later rather than earlier in the course of the disorder. As with all abilities and disabilities, there are individual differences in communication patterns.

AAC: COMMUNICATING WHEN SPEECH IS NOT FUNCTIONAL

The American Speech-Language Hearing Association (ASHA) defines AAC as an area of clinical practice that attempts to compensate (either temporarily or permanently) for the impairment and disability patterns of individuals with severe expressive communication disorders (i.e., the severely speech-language and writing impaired; ASHA, 1989, p. 107). For more than three decades, the field known as AAC has been addressing the communication needs of individuals who cannot rely on speech for functional communication (e.g., Beukelman & Mirenda, 1998; Zangari, Lloyd, & Vicker, 1994). The AAC field addresses a range of issues from defining approaches to communication and developing interventions directed toward promoting communication, to consumer advocacy and social policy issues related to persons with significant difficulty with speech.

Forms of AAC

There is a wide range of approaches to communication via AAC. Typically, forms of AAC are divided into two broad groups, known as unaided and aided forms of communication. Unaided forms of communication consist of nonverbal means of natural communication (including gestures and facial expressions) as well as manual signs and American Sign Language. These forms of communication can be employed by children and adults who are able to use their hands and have adequate fine-motor coordination skills to make fine-grained production distinctions between handshapes.

Aided forms of communication consist of those approaches that require some additional external support, such as a communication board with symbols (i.e., pictures, photographs, line drawings, printed words) or a sophisticated computer that "speaks" for its user via either synthetically produced speech or recorded natural (digitized) speech. From laptop computers that talk as well as perform a wide range of other operations (e.g., word processing, World Wide Web access) to computerized devices dedicated to communication, technological advances during the 1980s and 1990s have produced numerous opportunities for communication. These boards and devices typically display visual-graphic symbols that stand for or represent what an individual wants to express. Some users create messages via traditional orthography.

Access to aided forms of communication can be via direct selection or scanning. Direct selection includes typing or pointing with a hand, a head stick that is positioned on the user's head or the user's eyes that are directed by the user to indicate symbols from a set of available choices. From an array of four picture choices that represent toys, for example, a child can use a finger to point to the picture of the specific toy with which he or she wants to play (see Beukelman & Mirenda, 1998, for additional detail about aided forms of communication).

For some children and adults, direct selection is not a viable means to access a device because the severity of the individual's physical disabilities limits motor control. In these cases, the items to be selected either are displayed by another person (e.g., a familiar knowledgeable communication partner) or by an electronic communicative device (e.g., a computer that talks for its user) in a predetermined configuration or pattern. The AAC user must wait while a person or the device proceeds through items and reaches the item of choice. The AAC user then chooses the item by indicating a "yes" or "no" answer to a question or by activating a switch. This type of selection is called scanning. There are many types of scanning including those that use vision (e.g., row column scanning, linear scanning) or hearing (e.g., auditory scanning). Although there is limited research evidence, it is generally presumed that scanning requires less motor control but more cognitive skill than direct selection, which, in turn, is believed to require less cognitive skill and more motor control (Beukelman & Mirenda, 1998; Romski, Sevcik, & Sundgren, 1997).

Interpersonal Communication Via AAC Means

Rick Creech, a young man who grew up with cerebral palsy, provides a striking illustration of the adverse effects of speechlessness on communication interaction. He wrote:

If you want to know what it is like to be unable to speak, there is a way. Go to a party and don't talk. Play mute. Use your hands if you wish but don't use paper or pencil. Paper and pencil are not always handy for a mute person. Here is what you will find: people talking; talking behind, beside, around, over, under, through, and even for you. But never with you. You are ignored until finally you feel like a piece of furniture. (Musselwhite & St. Louis, 1998, p. 104)

The most important goal of using AAC is to enable an individual to communicate efficiently and effectively in a wide range of interactions with unfamiliar as well as familiar partners. These communication interactions can vary from interpersonal to group communicative situations (e.g., giving a speech in public). In general, two main issues have been addressed by the scholarly and practice literature: first, learning how to use the AAC system, which can include its physical operation, vocabulary access, and speed of device activation; and second, how one actually communicates with others using the AAC system. Commonly, a slow rate of communication by the AAC user substantially alters the pace and character of the communication interaction (e.g., alters turn-taking). For example, this change can lead to interpretation and guessing on the part of the listener in an attempt to speed the pace of the interaction. It can frequently relegate an AAC user to the role of responder rather than initiator in a conversational exchange. Sometimes AAC users' conversational skills are also limited by the vocabulary that is available to them on their AAC device. Light (1988, 1989) proposed a model of communicative competence for AAC users that outlined four essential dimensions: operational, strategic, social, and linguistic. Operational competence is the ability to operate and maintain aspects of the AAC device or system. Often, family members and/or educational, residential, and vocational staff take on the primary responsibility of maintenance aspects of the AAC device. Linguistic competence involves the functional mastery of the symbol system or linguistic code used on the display. Social competence requires the AAC user to have knowledge, judgment, and skills in both the social–linguistic and social–relational aspects of communication. Finally, strategic competence is the ability to communicate effectively within the restrictions of an AAC system. This model provides a framework in which to consider how AAC forms of communication may alter the communication process in a range of important ways and to develop intervention strategies to improve functional communication.

Finally, the AAC concerns of children and adults can be distinctly different and the literature has usually discussed issues relating to children and adults separately. For children, who are still within the developmental period, communicative skills provide a window through which to observe the social world around them and increase their knowledge and understanding of that world. The primary focus of intervention strategies with children has been on using AAC to foster and/or advance functional language and communication skills at home, at school, and in the community. Attention has also been placed on using AAC with peers and siblings in addition to adults (parents, teachers, caregivers). With the implementation of these instructional strategies over the developmental period, the child who employs AAC can develop communication skills that permit them to communicate their thoughts, wants and needs, and feelings to a range of partners (Beukelman & Mirenda, 1998).

It is often difficult to group adult AAC users together because there are many distinct causes for their AAC needs, from an accident or brain injury to a progressive neurological disorder. For the most part, these are adults who have had many years of communicating via speech. Their speech has now been compromised, and the literature has focused on what types of supports they need to communicate. In some cases an AAC system serves as a temporary bridge during a period in which a person cannot use his or her voice (e.g., Fried-Oken, Howard, & Stewart, 1991). In other instances an AAC system is a supplement to existing speech and aids in restoring functional communicative skills. In still other instances an AAC system provides the only way in which an adult can communicate.

PERCEPTIONS AND ATTITUDES TOWARD CHILDREN AND ADULTS WHO USE AAC

People who cannot use intelligible speech to communicate are often perceived in negative ways. First-person reports suggest that individuals who do not speak are sometimes perceived in degrading ways, such as being less intelligent than their speaking counterparts. Doreen Joseph (1986), who lost her speech following an accident, said "Speech is the most important thing we have. It makes us a person and not a thing. No one should ever have to be a 'thing'."

The available literature suggests that, in general, speech and language impairments negatively affect how others perceive children and adults (e.g., Rice, Hadley, & Alexander, 1993). What effect does AAC have on the perception of an individual's competence? The use of an AAC device may enhance not only a participant's on-going communication with partners but also how competent she or he is judged to be by unfamiliar observers (Romski & Sevcik, 1996). The AAC device may raise expectations of competency, which may influence how positively the participant is viewed as a potential communicative partner. In turn, this view by communicative partners may support and encourage the use of more diverse conversational topics and more elaborate interactions.

For example, in their longitudinal study, Romski and Sevcik (1996) observed that, as one of the school-aged participants with severe cognitive disabilities in their longitudinal study was independently ordering lunch with his speech-output communication device at a local fast food restaurant, the store manager remarked: "If your children can use computers, they must be pretty smart." He went on to say that he would seriously consider hiring them to work at his store. Clearly using an AAC system has the potential to have a powerful outcome, that is, in changing perceptions of competencies. Although they did not explicitly measure partner perception as part of their study, Romski and Sevcik obtained parent and teacher reports about community perception across the course of the study. One participant's mother reported that her son took his communication device to church on Sunday morning. Church members showed an interest in her son's way of communicating and his mother reported an increase in the number of church members who communicated with him since he had his AAC device.

Gorenflo and Gorenflo (1991) specifically examined the attitudes of college-age adults toward adults using AAC devices. They reported that the use of computer-based speech output communication devices, coupled with additional information about the person and his or her disability, increased favorable attitudes of observers toward individuals using augmented communication systems. In a follow-up study, Gorenflo, Gorenflo, and Santer (1994) investigated the effects of four different voice synthesizers on the attitudes of college-age adults toward adult AAC users. When the synthetic voice was considered easier to listen to, more favorable attitudes were noted. Interestingly, a voice appropriate to the sex of the user did not produce significantly more favorable attitudes. Although it appears that high-quality synthetic speech is sufficient to positively influence attitudes about AAC users, a voice appropriate to the sex of the user is a favorable but not necessary addition. Hoag et al. (1994) examined the effects of a number of variables and observer background and experience on ratings of an adult AAC user's communicative competence in a scripted communication scenario with a speaking partner. They found that longer message length (phrase vs. single word) affected observers' rating of the

AAC user's communication skill. Perhaps most important inexperienced or naive observers rated the AAC user's communication more positively than observers with professional experience (i.e., speech–language pathologists), suggesting that everyday communications are often functionally adequate. Speech–language pathologists may rate communication more stringently because their goal is to strive for the "best communication possible."

Another set of studies has examined the attitudes of children toward other children who use AAC devices. Blockberger et al. (1993) examined the attitudes of fourth-grade children toward a nonspeaking peer who used three different types of communication techniques (an unaided technique, an aided nonelectronic technique, and an aided electronic technique). They found no differences in attitude related to the specific communication technique used, suggesting that children valued the communicative message rather than the means by which it was communicated. More positive attitudes were exhibited by females, better readers, and children who had experience with children with disabilities. Beck and Dennis (1996) investigated the attitudes of fifth graders toward a similar-aged peer who was nonspeaking. Their findings, consistent with those of Blockberger and her colleagues, were that females and children who had experience with children with disabilities had more positive attitudes toward the child who communicated through augmented means.

In general, experience with an AAC user appears to facilitate another's favorable perception. It may be that persons without disabilities are fearful of communicating with someone who uses different forms of communication. Positive communicative experience with individuals who do not communicate via speech may reduce that fear and enhance interactions. With the implementation of the Americans With Disabilities Act of 1990, increased visibility of people communicating via a variety of means may begin to change perceptions and attitudes toward AAC users in the general population. For example, in 1998 President and Mrs. Clinton hosted a series of talks about science and the millennium. One of the speakers in the series was noted physicist Dr. Stephen Hawking, who employed a talking computer to communicate with the president and to give his speech to the audience because he has a progressive neurological disease, amyotrophic lateral sclerosis. *USA Today* provided front page coverage for his speech and a description of how he prepared the speech using his "talking computer" as well as some of the accommodations that had to be made so that Dr. Hawking could, for example, answer live questions from the audience (Page, 1998). Dr. Hawking's appearance at the White House was an opportunity for the national media to educate the general public about "talking computers" and the people who use them. Children and adults who communicate via AAC means are finally beginning to be recognized as people first. There are consumer advocacy groups (e.g., "Hear Our Voices") and newsletters with a consumer focus (e.g., *Alternatively Speaking*) that provide avenues for interchange and the exchange of information (see Beukelman & Mirenda, 1998 for a comprehensive list of resource materials).

DIRECTIONS FOR FUTURE RESEARCH

Although the AAC field is still in its relative infancy, it has grown substantially since its beginnings some three decades ago. Research has shown that everyone can communicate (Beukelman & Mirenda, 1998). The field's focus has moved away from assessment of who can use what type of AAC device and concentration on the technology per se to effective interventions and use, along with broader issues of consumer advocacy and social policy. Communication interaction research has focused on specific behaviors, such as communicative functions (e.g., requesting, questioning) as well as enhancement of the rate of interaction. Currently, AAC research is focusing on a broad set of issues including the development of new technologies to facilitate the communication process. Another important area of research, particularly with changes in our health care system, is efficacy or outcomes of intervention strategies for the broad range of individuals who may use AAC. Here research is focused on the development of measurement tools to assess the broad range of functional communication outcomes possible from simply learning a new vocabulary word to communicating with a broad audience in a public speech. AAC research also includes an emphasis on the perceptions of others and how functional communication outcomes can facilitate persons' inclusion in society. Research in the AAC field is answering questions that influence social policy decisions but there is still a substantial amount of uncharted territory to be studied in the future.

STRATEGIES THAT MAY FACILITATE COMMUNICATION

Perhaps the most important strategy to employ when communicating with an AAC user is to talk to the person, not to an accompanying individual. Braithwaite and Braithwaite (1997) reported that being a person first is an important theme for individuals with disabilities who speak. It is certainly one for individuals who encounter significant difficulty with speech. Initially, it may be uncomfortable communicating with someone who uses AAC because it is a new situation with new and different communicative demands. Look for a written explanation of how the individual's AAC device may operate and how the AAC user will communicate with you. Then, let the AAC user guide you in the communicative interaction through the AAC device as well as the individual's natural nonverbal communication (e.g., facial expressions, gestures). As a communicative partner, one may expect a significantly slowed rate of communication when an AAC device is employed. Give the AAC user the time he or she needs to communicate a message or to answer your question. You will find that experience and patience should decrease any hesitation you may have in communicating with individuals using AAC.

DISCUSSION QUESTIONS

1. Describe examples of times you have not been able to communicate with another. What feelings do you associate with not being able to communicate? Why?
2. Why do you think the general public is uncomfortable when someone cannot communicate via speech?
3. How does communicating via a computer alter the course of interpersonal communication with an AAC user? Why?
4. Discuss the strategies you could use that may facilitate communication with an individual who is nonspeaking.

ACKNOWLEDGMENTS

The preparation of this chapter was supported in part by NICHD-06016 and the Department of Communication and College of Arts and Sciences, Georgia State University. Thanks to Nanette Cooper Dieterle and Carol Horsley for their assistance with manuscript preparation.

REFERENCES

American Speech Language Hearing Association (ASHA). (1989). Competencies for speech-language pathologists providing services in augmentative communication. *ASHA, 31*, 107–110.
American Speech Language Hearing Association (ASHA). (1991). Report: Augmentative and alternative communication. *ASHA, 33* (Suppl. 5), 9–12.

Beck, A., & Dennis, M. (1996). Attitudes of children toward a similar-aged child who uses augmentative communication. *Augmentative and Alternative Communication, 12*, 78–87.

Beukelman, D., & Mirenda, P. (1998). *Augmentative and alternative communication: Management of severe communication disorders in children and adults* (2nd ed.). Baltimore: Paul H. Brookes.

Blockberger, S., Armstrong, R., O'Connor, A., & Freeman, R. (1993). Children's attitudes toward a nonspeaking child using various augmentative and alternative communication techniques. *Augmentative and Alternative Communication, 9*, 243–250.

Braithwaite, D. O., & Braithwaite, C. A. (1997). Understanding communication of persons with disabilities as cultural communication. In L. A. Samovar & R. Porter (Eds.), *Intercultural communication: A reader* (8th ed., pp. 154–164). Belmont, CA: Wadsworth.

Gorenflo, C., & Gorenflo, D. (1991). The effects of information and augmentative communication technique on attitudes towards nonspeaking individuals. *Journal of Speech and Hearing Research, 34*, 19–26.

Gorenflo, C., Gorenflo, D., & Santer, S. (1994). Effects of synthetic voice output on attitudes toward the augmented communicator. *Journal of Speech and Hearing Research, 37*, 64–68.

Fried-Oken, M., Howard, J., & Stewart, S. (1991). Feedback on AAC intervention from adults who are temporarily unable to speak. *Augmentative and Alternative Communication, 7*, 43–50.

Hoag, L., Bedrosian, J., Johnson, D., & Molineux, B. (1994). Variables affecting perceptions of social aspects of the communicative competence of an adult AAC user. *Augmentative and Alternative Communication, 10*, 129–137.

Joseph, D. (1986). The morning. *Communication Outlook, 8*(2), 8.

Light, J. (1988). Interaction involving individuals using augmentative and alternative communication systems: State of the art and future directions. *Augmentative and Alternative Communication, 4*, 66–82.

Light, J. (1989). Toward a definition of communicative competence for individuals using augmentative and alternative communication systems. *Augmentative and Alternative Communication, 5*, 137–144.

Musselwhite, C., & St. Louis, K. (1988). *Communication programming for persons with severe handicaps* (2nd ed.). Boston: College-Hill Press.

Page, S. (1998, March 6). Man of the millennium. *USA Today*, pp. 1A–2A.

Prizant, B., & Meyer, E. (1993). Socioemotional aspects of language and social-communication disorders in young children and their families. *American Journal of Speech-Language Pathology, 4*, 56–71.

Rice, M., Hadley, P., & Alexander, A. (1993). Social biases toward children with speech and language impairments: A correlative causal model of language limitations. *Applied Psycholinguistics, 14*, 445–471.

Romski, M. A., & Sevcik, R. A. (1996). *Breaking the speech barrier: Language development through augmented means.* Baltimore: Paul Brookes.

Romski, M. A., Sevcik, R. A., & Sundgren, W. (1997). Augmentative and alternative communication in the schools. In P. O'Connell (Ed.), *Speech, language, and hearing programs in schools* (pp. 289–304). Gaithersburg, MD: Aspen.

Sienkiewicz-Mercer, R., & Kaplan, S. (1989). *I raise my eyes to say yes.* Boston: Houghton Mifflin.

Zangari, C., Lloyd, L., & Vicker, B. (1994). Augmentative and alternative communication: An historical perspective. *Augmentative and Alternative Communication, 10*, 27–59.

26

Overcoming Loss of Voice

Al Weitzel
San Diego State University

Keywords: Voicelessness, larynx, humor, stigma

Except for scholars in communication disorders, communication researchers do not generally use the term literally when they refer to someone "not having a voice." Usually the phrase refers to a person or group of people without the rhetorical power to influence events or without the ability to make a strong statement (e.g., Bell, 1997). However, in addition to those who are born without the ability to speak, there are people who literally had a voice and lost it, imposing oral–verbal silence—that is, a primarily nonvocal state.

Although it is not common, loss of voice after birth is a reality faced by a sizeable number of people. One with a high profile recently was Michael Zaslow, the soap opera Emmy winner who lost his voice due to a neurological disorder known as Lou Gehrig's disease (A Statement From Michael Zaslow, 1998, May 11).

There are a number of causes of voice loss (aphonia). One is psychological trauma. For example, a child might lose his or her voice after a traumatic experience, such as witnessing a violent act. Another is a neurological disorder known as dystonia, estimated to number between 50,000 and 300,000 diagnosed cases; about 10% of the cases affect the voice (known as spasmodic dysphonia, Kaufman, 1997). This particular form of dystonia almost always appears in adulthood, most frequently in people over 40. The cause or specific source of dystonia is not known (Jones, 1991), and even diagnosing it is not a simple matter—patients sometimes have to consult many different doctors several times before receiving a correct diagnosis (NSDA, 1992). Another type of voice loss is dysarthria, which can be caused by a stroke: "The person can understand language, but the muscles in the throat and mouth which control speech have been affected. Speech may come out distorted, slurred or not at all" (Stroke, 1997). Recovery is possible, but rehabilitation progress varies, and it may take many months or years (Stroke: Prevention and Treatment, 1998).

Surgery is another reason for loss of voice, usually due to the presence of cancer (Silverman, 1989). This is not common among those who seek assistance for voice disorders, as only about 4% may be diagnosed as having cancer (Kaufman, 1997), but it may involve removal of the tongue (glossectomy) or the larynx (laryngectomy).

Loss of voice is not generally permanent, as discussed below, but the mere threat of permanent loss is, of course, a major crisis in people's lives, and Gilmore's (1994) description is a poignant one.

> [The voice is] one of the most important and central facets of a person's identity.... Its loss deprives the individual of an organ that has served... important functions since early childhood [including] expression of emotions, defense, [and] gratification.... [Removal of the larynx]... signifies both a mutilation and deprivation of very important functions necessary to adaptation.... [Some maintain] that speechlessness is a psychological devastation for both the patient and the family. (p. 405)

Probably part of the shock is derived from the "suddenness" of the development. People grow accustomed to being very able to engage in casual discourse for, they anticipate, their entire lives. So it seems devastating to them to think that they will no longer be able to do so.

Romski and Sevcik's chapter in this volume addresses some of the unaided and aided forms of communication for those without a voice. The present chapter discusses some of the perceptions and communication experiences of those who have had surgery that removed their larynx, which is commonly known as the voice box. This report is partly based on the author's experiences as an unwitting participant/observer of life as a laryngectomee (a person without a larynx).

LOSS OF VOICE AND REGAINING VOICE

Laryngeal surgery is generally necessitated by the presence of cancer, and approximately 75% of patients survive diagnosis and treatment through radiation therapy, chemotherapy, and/or surgery to subsequently lead productive and meaningful lives. There are about 12,500 new persons diagnosed per year, and they currently number approximately 50,000. Most are over the age of 55 (Lauder, 1994; Spiegel & Sataloff, 1993).

As one might expect, the literature about laryngectomees, most of it medical and therapeutic, generally refers to communication in terms of the anatomical elements—the larynx and related physiology. Some literature refers to communication in abstract terms rather than in terms of strategies and process. For example, communication has been noted as one of the "most frequently mentioned [problems] by cancer patients" (Richardson, Graham, & Shelton, 1989, p. 283). Other literature might offer advice for enhancing communication with laryngectomees. For example, Salmon (1994a) advised spouses: "Try to understand how each other feels"; "Place close attention to attempts to communicate"; and "Phrase conversation for 'yes' and 'no' answers" (p. 142). Elsewhere, she urged: "*Do* use your communication skills to your best advantage"; "*Do* be aware of proximity. . . . loudness varies in inverse proportion to the square of the distance"; and "*Do* allow opportunity for lipreading" (Salmon, 1994b, p. 152).

The experiences of laryngectomees vary a great deal of course, but, like other cancer patients, probably "one of the greatest fears during the early stages of cancer is the fear of being rejected and abandoned" (Sullivan & Reardon, 1986, p. 708). Another fear, losing one's voice, is probably common to all laryngectomees, and it is often regarded with greater concern than the concern for cancer (Gilmore, 1994). Unless people have had personal contact with those who have lost their voices, few ever imagine what the condition means on an hour-to-hour basis as they attempt to engage in human interaction. People learn to take their ability to speak for granted. Learning that it will be lost is immediately recognized as a nightmarish inconvenience. Imagine not being able to answer your phone or call your friends and relatives. What would you do if your house were on fire or if you were stranded in an isolated area on the highway and your car broke down? How would you communicate with your teammates on the softball field or the basketball court? How would you call your dog?

If the cause of voice loss is the existence of cancer, "death may no longer seem abstract and distant" (Feber, 1996, p. 37). In addition, voice loss means taking on the stigma (taintedness) of becoming a person with a disability (Braithwaite, 1990, 1996; Goffman, 1963). Losing one's voice

has been described as having "a unique nightmare quality" with a multitude of uncertainties about the future, including dependence on others,
effects on family life, job loss, and inability to find work or accepting less
satisfactory employment (Gilmore, 1994, p. 405). Self-worth is in doubt.
The stressful results may include anger, depression, guilt, emotional disturbance, and "why me?" One's entire personality may be affected (Gilmore,
1994). In one study, 45% of patients felt that their social acceptability
was reduced (Feber, 1996), and McDaniel et al. (1995) reported that up
to 40% of throat cancer patients experienced depression. Abandonment of
efforts to communicate and social withdrawal can result (Richardson et al.,
1989).

The reality of voice loss is generally not as overwhelming as anticipated.
Help from family is usually available and is a key factor because it is highly
correlated with depression, dysfunction, and communication (Richardson
et al., 1989). In addition to the support of friends and loved ones, enthu-
siastic support may be available through the 300 laryngectomee support
groups located throughout the world, usually called "Lost Chord Clubs"
or "New Voice Clubs" and affiliated with the American Cancer Society
and the International Association of Laryngectomees (Lauder, 1994). To
date, there are also two online listserv support groups and web sites that
republish newsletters from support organizations.

Regaining Voice

In addition to the obvious means of being able to write messages, there
are three alternate means of oral expression that are ultimately possible in
almost all cases. However, none of the three means is an identical replication
of one's natural voice.

Individual experiences of laryngectomee patients vary greatly, as some
need more time than others to heal from surgery and radiation treatments.
Some laryngectomees are able, almost immediately after surgery, to use an
electronic device known as an electrolarynx to simulate the voice with a
sound very much like the stereotypic, computer-generated voice. An electrolarynx simply simulates the sound vibrations that are normally provided
within the larynx, and the sounds are then shaped in the area of the mouth.
Using an electrolarynx is a skill, however, so it may take a good deal of
practice to learn to speak in an intelligible way. For example, one new
laryngectomee did not use the telephone much because his wife usually
answered it.[1] Once, she had to run some errands and asked her husband
to convey some information to a client whom she expected to call. When

she returned home the husband said that the client had called and that he had given him the information and had taken down his phone number. She called the client, and he was impressed that she had a computer that could answer the phone and give out complicated messages. She told him that it was her husband, but he didn't believe her until she broke out in laughter.

Other laryngectomees may be able to choose a voice prosthesis that is surgically implanted in the neck. The prothesis may provide a very adequate replication of a human voice for some people, but for others it may be far less than ideal. One prosthesis user was placing a phone order from a catalog. A young woman on the line interrupted his slurred words with "Pardon me, sir. Do you drink?" "No, I do not!" he replied. She then said "Oh! I am so sorry. I thought you had a drinking problem."

A third option is the development of a simulated voice through what is known as esophageal speech. Esophageal speech is achieved by forcing air into one's throat in an area known as the esophagus as opposed to air coming from the lungs, which is the basis of one's natural voice. For esophageal speech the air is then expelled with sounds shaped in the area of the mouth. It is a feat that youngsters sometimes use playfully to force a belching sound. Like the voice provided by a prosthesis, the quality of an esophageal voice varies a great deal from one person to another.

Because of the need to heal from surgery, the voice prosthesis and esophageal speech options are generally not available for some time. One of the options almost never elected as a major mode of communication is American Sign Language because its effectiveness is severely restricted by the relatively small number of people who know how to use it.

As suggested above, it would be a mistake to conclude that those who adopt these "surrogate" (substitute) modes of speech are orally indistinguishable from laryngeal speakers. Alaryngeal speakers (those without a larynx) are clearly distinguishable, and their voices affect the perceptions of them as persons (Burgoon, Buller, & Woodall, 1996). For example, one electrolarynx user visited a Native American reservation casino and a security guard thought that the electrolarynx was some sort of device to beat the slots; in this case the user's morality was doubted because he used a voice device.

Alaryngeal speakers who do not use an electrolarynx generally have less volume, speak slower and probably less frequently, and their voices are almost always more "hoarse," "throaty," or "gravelly" (Hyman, 1994; Shanks, 1994). All alaryngeal speakers have considerable difficulty in articulation of certain sounds. In addition, because in most cases they will elect to speak less frequently, they may be perceived as asocial, antisocial, or socially inept (McLaughlin & Cody, 1982).

As many as 30% to 40% of laryngectomees develop none of the speech alternatives mentioned here (Gilmore, 1994; Spiegel & Sataloff, 1993) and thus largely forego oral–verbal interactions. Silverman (1989) suggested that there are three reasons for limited desire to communicate: depression, little or no need to communicate, and a lack of positive reinforcement for communicating. There may be other reasons that people would not use one of the surrogate voices just described. They may simply be too ill to have a high desire to communicate, or there may be too much embarrassment, or there may be a lack of confidence that they will be understood or that other people will make enough effort to understand them.

Laryngectomees also can use a device known as a TTY (teletypewriter) to enable them to use the telephone to a limited number of locations that accommodate TTY calls. TTY users also have a voice relay service available through their telephone companies so they can call an operator who will read the typed TTY message to a recipient specified by the caller.[2]

During the period prior to development of the alternative oral means of speaking, communication for the laryngectomee is a frightening experience. Most noteworthy for some is the delightful and reassuring discovery, supported by previous research (Do, 1997), that most people are kind, understanding, patient, accepting, and often supportive of the new relationship with persons with disabilities.

Most laryngectomees will also quickly adapt to their new circumstances. Most probably learn to economize their use of words. For example, research reported by Killworth and Bernard (1976) found TTY users more terse in their communication in order to make an exchange as efficient as possible. My experience as a TTY user is that people are surprisingly receptive and tolerant of this unique form of communication.

In addition, those without a natural voice will probably rely more than others on their use of nonverbal cues and for good reason. I find myself employing subtle gestures to accompany what I say verbally. For example, if I use the word "writing," I will try to be subtle in moving my hand as though it had a pen in it. Research reviewed by Hyman (1994) suggests that nonverbal cues play a significant role for those unable to speak with a "normal" voice, improving understanding 16% to 50%; nonverbal communication research using a channel reliance model confirms this proposition, but it is not possible to partition and measure oral/verbal–nonverbal contributions to overall message impact (Burgoon, Buller, & Woodall, 1996).

THE STIGMA OF BECOMING A PERSON
WITH A DISABILITY

As mentioned earlier, there is a stigma attached to becoming a person with a disability, as discussed by Braithwaite (1990, 1996) in terms of three phases that are based on the work of Deloach and Greer (1981). These phases are adapted in this chapter to the experiences of people who have lost their voice, based on data reported previously (Weitzel, 1998). These data were collected with a written questionnaire delivered to members of a local support group for laryngectomees.

The first phase of becoming a person with a disability is stigma isolation, wherein the persons "perceive events occurring as unrelated to being physically disabled" (Braithwaite, 1990, p. 470). In the second phase, stigma recognition, the individuals realize that being disabled affects their lives, and this phase is an important one in moving to the third phase, stigma incorporation. This final phase "involves integration of the disability into the individual's definition of self" (Braithwaite, 1990, p. 471).

Stigma Isolation and Stigma Recognition

It serves little purpose to divorce stigma isolation from stigma recognition in this discussion. Isolation is a process of denying or repressing reality by a person with a disability (DeLoach & Greer, 1981), so the person does not recognize that he or she is being isolated—it would take a third party to report an act of isolation by a person with a disability. Of more relevance is a focus on stigma recognition by the person, so it is more appropriate to consider isolation and recognition together.

It is easy to imagine laryngectomees not included in activities, especially those in which speech would be an assumed feature. For example, a colleague suggested jogging together. However, the experience of jogging with another person commonly involves chatting, and, like some other laryngectomees, I don't have good access to any of the three options discussed earlier to develop a surrogate voice for my loss of natural speech. I elected to pass on jogging together. It is important to recognize that it is perfectly natural to become isolated in some daily circumstances until a surrogate voice is developed. Indeed, researchers have reported that people with disabilities may see significant changes in their personal relationships after becoming disabled (Braithwaite, 1990). For example, laryngectomees have confided how relationships with friends have changed. One said, "My friends really surprised me. They were supportive during my [radiation] treatments, but after surgery they seemed to be too busy for me.... They aren't anywhere near as friendly as before surgery." Another reported, "Even after almost 10 years there are a few that still cannot accept me because of the manner in which I speak."

More subtle forms of exclusion also take place. One was related by an electrolarynx user: "I hesitate calling a radio talk show. I have no idea if the radio waves would modulate the transmission—I've tried, but the radio host screener put me on hold until the program was over."

In addition to these forms of stigma isolation, researchers have found that there are some common patterns of stigma recognition by those who have lost their voice.

Transference of Perceived Physical Disability to Perceived Mental Disability.   As indicated in the Do and Geist chapter in this volume and by others (e.g., Kleinfield, 1979; Morris, 1991; Shapiro, 1993), people who are not disabled often equate physical disability with mental disability or hearing impairment. For example, Do (1997) noted that "most persons who are not physically disabled will conclude that a person with a physical disability will have a mental disability as well. In other words, people tend to stereotype ... physically disabled [persons] as being unintelligent or 'mentally handicapped'" (p. 5).

This phenomenon is reflected in laryngectomees' perceptions. For example, one person who speaks with a voice prosthesis reported that "*Most* people, especially clerks, treat me like I'm not mentally all there." Electrolarynx users have reported similar behaviors: one said, "When I have tried [talking to people, they] have stared at me as though I am from another planet ... or turn their back on me, which means they don't want to deal with it." Another prosthesis user said, "When some people hear me talk they look at me and say 'that sounds like something from *Star Wars* R2-D2.'"

Telephone Communication.   There are some consistent problems for people with a laryngectomy related to being heard and understood on the phone (Davill, 1983). People commonly refuse to talk to users of an electrolarynx, and hang-ups are frequent. One person described how a recipient of her call said "there's a crazy person calling" and hung up. Another reported that when he called a hotel operator while trying to reach a friend who was a guest at the hotel, "the young male operator giggle[d] in hearing my voice. I could hear him say to a[n] associate—I have 'Dark [*sic*] Vader on the line.'" Additionally, speaking by phone with those who have impaired hearing presents a compounded difficulty.

Communicating by Written Messages.

Virtually all laryngectomees spend at least a few days immediately after surgery with writing as the main means of communication, and the amount of time thereafter varies a great deal, from weeks to years. The immediate postsurgery period is a crucial one, of course, as most patients awake from surgery without a voice for the first time in their lives. One person commented about this crucial time, "My worse [*sic*] experience was trying to get a nurse after surgery. They are asking me what I need, [and] I was not able to get my messages across. I think the nursing staff needs to be taught about our lack of communication."

Several nonspeaking persons noted that others assume that the laryngectomee also cannot hear. For example, one said:

A friend and I were in line for the cashier in a department store. Two young women stepped in front of us. My friend wanted to speak up, I shook my head no. One of the women said, "It's ok" to the other one, "she can't hear anyway."

The assumption of impaired hearing is not uncommon: In the absence of a contrary cue, people are quick to conclude that those who cannot speak are also not capable of hearing, as reported by 67% of laryngectomees in one study (Gilmore, 1994). Another response is that people simply speak much louder. For example, one person without a natural voice said, "I've had people go into [American] sign language or start shouting my name." In addition, it is also not unusual for a clerk or a restaurant server to respond to written notes by similarly writing a note.

Nonspeakers may also have difficulty in casual, social contexts because conversations generally progress rapidly and change topics quickly. It is extremely common for interactants to make no accommodation for nonspeakers to inject a comment, and by the time that they can write a comment, the topic has passed. In a more formal decision-making context, it is not uncommon for a group leader to ask for a voice vote until reminded that a voice vote is not possible for people without a voice.

Similarly, people will often casually ask a question of a nonspeaker that may require a rather complex answer of seven or eight sentences. Speaking people seemingly forget, at least for the moment, that the answer is going to require several minutes of writing by one person and reading by the other. This period of time can be very embarrassing or awkward for the laryngectomee because it emphasizes their disability. Similarly, a nonspeaking laryngectomee might be asked in a meeting or public forum for a spontaneous reaction; however, a response might require a good deal of time for preparation and writing, and the discussion would move on before the person could formulate a thoughtful written response.

Sometimes humorous situations result from the writing of messages. A farcical incident that I experienced was buying gasoline at a small station, and I wrote a message to the clerk that said, "$7 on #2." The clerk stared at it, obviously not understanding it. A third person entered and read the message aloud to the clerk, the transaction was completed, and the third party commented, "Now *that* is a communication problem."

Breaking Visual Contact by Interactants.   Virtually all laryngectomees are able to make at least some sounds that do not require the vibration of the vocal chords (such as hissing, "pop," the "bronx cheer," etc.), and usually even some small portion of the sound of a word is audible. As such, there sometimes seems a natural tendency for interactants to tilt their heads to place their ears closer to the laryngectomee's mouth to hear better. However, tilting one's head is problematic because this action breaks visual contact and thus eliminates the possibility of reading the laryngectomee's lips and also visually receiving some nonoral cues. McIntosh reports in her chapter in this volume that "under *ideal* conditions, *skilled* [italics added] speechreaders will accurately interpret less than 50% of what is being said," but I have found that interactants often seem to have very little confidence in their ability to read lips of nonspeaking laryngectomees. This is an unfortunate assumption, because my experience is that those who make a genuine effort to lip-read become surprisingly adept very quickly. It is probably best to assume that many other variables affect lipreading, including frequency of interaction and familiarity with the persons involved.

Distinct from the concept of lipreading, nonspeaking laryngectomees have expressed frustration about interactants who are fully conscious of a person's disability but will often greet the nonspeaker by asking, "How are you?" They will then inadvertently turn their back or divert their eyes toward some other person or object, thus inhibiting a nonoral response by the nonspeaker.

Stigma Incorporation

As suggested earlier, following stigma isolation and stigma recognition, there is a third phase of adjustment to a disability wherein "the individual comes to recognize both the positive and negative aspects of disability and develops task-oriented strategies to cope with the negative aspects of membership in the disabled culture" (Braithwaite, 1990, p. 471). This phase is represented by several communication strategies that have been reported by laryngectomees (Weitzel, 1998).

Incorporating Optimism. Some persons who have lost their natural voices stress the importance of optimism and stress the positive aspects of their present lives. For example, one said, "I have had many wonderful experiences communicating with people along with a few unpleasant ones. It takes understanding and a real sense of humor to overlook something that happened." Others might express joy about some of their experiences. One man said that he was offered a second chance at life after the discovery of cancer, and another commented that esophageal speech is a "miracle." A prosthesis user talked about the steps that she had taken toward speech: "My communication got on in full speed, and I'm still in charge. Friends, relatives and strangers often comment on the clarity in my speech."

Becoming a Social Advocate. It is extremely common for laryngectomees to become ardent antitobacco advocates. One explained, "If I see a person smoking, I tell them 'look what happened to me.'" A member of my local support group reported encountering a very well-known professional baseball player in a parking lot. He told the player, "you know, there are lots of young people who watch you play and chew tobacco." The player interrupted, "Now I'm going to get a lecture." The advocate said, "No. No lecture. But why don't you tell the TV people not to put the camera on you when you're chewing?" The following season, it appeared that the player was obviously chewing gum and blowing bubbles on the field.

Others participate in opportunities to speak in schools about smoking. One reported that a "young lady bagging the groceries said, 'I know you. You spoke at my school and I quit smoking that very same day.'" Another person reported that she had been invited to speak to doctors and nurses at a hospital: "About 35 in all. They all asked questions and took notes. They were all grateful and pleased." She said that at a church meeting 12 of the 50 smokers in attendance had quit because of her advocacy.

Selecting Social Contexts.   Communicating in social contexts can be very problematic for laryngectomees, and they may become extremely self conscious. Alterations in communication necessitated by a laryngectomy mark them distinctively. Furthermore, social contexts are often loud, and esophageal speakers frequently cannot be heard; users of an electrolarynx must adjust the volume upward, thus making their speech even more conspicuous. As such, laryngectomees often elect to avoid many social situations rather than deal with the challenges or the discomfort of alternative communication modes. Additionally, in an interpersonal or group context they will often forego opportunities to participate orally when they would not have passed up such opportunities prior to their loss of natural voice.

It is challenging to be a casual interactant with laryngectomees. Interactants need to work harder than they are accustomed and become much more patient in receiving a response to a question or comment. The usual, rapid "banter" ceases, and in many cases it is difficult for the speaking party to be comfortable with more silence than usual. A particularly awkward situation results when interactants do not anticipate being thrown into a situation with a person who is unable to speak.

Stigma Incorporation Through Humor.   Humor is a communication strategy used by persons with a disability as a way to put people at ease by showing that the disabled person is not overly sensitive (Braithwaite, 1989, 1996). One way to put people at ease includes making a joke about an electrolarynx-induced voice. One person called it an "easy sex change," and another described it as an excellent means of disposing of telephone solicitors.

Esophageal speakers seem similarly inclined to joke about their new voices. One woman reported talking to a friend in a store, and a bystander commented, "My, you are hoarse [your voice]." "No, I have had my voice box removed and that's how I talk now." The bystander patted her on the shoulder and said, "That's all right honey, it will grow back."

Some humor can be a little dark. A laryngectomee reported a visit by an out-of-town friend during recovery from surgery. The friend was alarmed by the patient's use of a feeding tube, which is standard postsurgery procedure, and some of the other life adjustments that were evident. The visitor asked, "How can you act so calm, be so easygoing, and be so happy?" The patient replied, "it's better than being planted in a box." The humor strategy had the desired effect: "We all laughed, had a few good drinks and enjoyed the holidays."

THE FUTURE

New media, such as computer-mediated communication (CMC) and fax messaging, offer some compensation opportunities for the nonspeaker, but their adoption so far by laryngectomees is not extensive. This is probably partially because most laryngectomees are 50 years old and older and many are beyond 60. For example, only 16% of people above age 55 have computers, whereas 40% of people aged 18 to 34 have them.[3]

However, future laryngectomees and other persons with communication disabilities are likely to be much more inclined to use new media as it is assimilated into society, and this form of communication provides exciting possibilities for people who are voiceless. CMC in the form of E-mail, "chat" modes, listservs, and computer bulletin boards, in particular, can function as excellent surrogate media for a person without a voice. Indeed, TTYs have functioned effectively in this manner for years. Computer conversation certainly has the potential to liberate persons who are voiceless and put them on equal conversational footing with their interaction partners (Braithwaite, Waldron, & Finn, 1999; see also Fox, this volume).

CONCLUSION

Loss of voice can seem to be a devastating development, but it is not generally permanent, and the reality of voice loss ultimately is not as overwhelming as anticipated. There are means of compensating for the loss of one's natural voice, which are made possible by medical and scientific developments. In addition, family, friends, working associates, and even strangers usually are understanding, patient, and helpful. The disability is overcome to a large extent, and communication becomes, as always, a process of adaptation. Those who have lost their natural voices are generally optimistic and seem disposed to seek the lighter side of their disability, when possible.

Like almost all persons with disabilities, those who have lost their natural voices seek lives with dignity. Others can respect the wish for dignity by treating them as we all wish to be treated, while recognizing that persons with disabilities often do not have as many options in leading their lives. As suggested in this chapter, there are a number of procedures that one can follow to facilitate communication with those who have lost their natural voices. For example, it may require extra effort to understand the "surrogate" voice produced by those without a larynx—it will probably help to attempt to read th: person's lips. Similarly, in general, one cannot expect an esophageal speaker or a person with a voice prosthesis to speak louder—doing so is probably not possible, and if it is possible, it will likely be very uncomfortable. In addition, one needs to remember that a nonspeaker needs writing tools and a good deal of time to answer a question that is not posed with a simple set of alternative choices—I'm always a bit exasperated when my hands are indisposed because I am carrying things and someone stops me to ask a question ("What is the assignment for next week?"). Though people are able to overcome their loss of voice, they nonetheless have a disability, and others need to recognize this.

DISCUSSION QUESTIONS

1. What do persons unable to speak have in common with persons with another communication disability, such as an inability to see or hear?
2. What communication experiences do you think would be the most trying if you lost your voice?
3. If you were introduced to someone without a voice and suddenly told that you would be the sole passenger in her car for a 1-hour trip, what communication strategies would you employ?
4. Try carrying on a 3-minute discussion with a classmate without using oral words and without writing. What were the most effective communication strategies and tactics?
5. Which of the following statements is true about persons who are unable to speak and why: (a) They cannot communicate orally, (b) they cannot communicate verbally, or (c) they cannot communicate nonverbally.

REFERENCES

Bell, E. (1997). Listen up. You have to: Voices from "women and communication." *Western Journal of Communication, 61*, 89–100.

Braithwaite, D. O. (1989, February). *An interpretive analysis of disabled persons' impression management strategies in response to perceived discomfort and uncertainty of ablebodied others.* Paper presented at the annual meeting of the Western Speech Communication Association, Spokane, WA.

Braithwaite, D. O. (1990). From majority to minority: An analysis of cultural change from ablebodied to disabled. *International Journal of Intercultural Relations, 14*, 465–483.

Braithwaite, D. O. (1996). "Persons first": Expanding communicative choices by persons with disabilities. In E. B. Ray (Ed.), *Communication and disenfranchisement: Social health issues and implications* (pp. 449–464). Mahwah, NJ: Lawrence Erlbaum Associates.

Braithwaite, D. O., Waldron, V. R., & Finn, J. (1999). Communication of social support in computer-mediated groups for persons with disabilities. *Health Communication, 11,* 123–152.

Burgoon, J. K., Buller, D. B., & Woodall, G. (1996). *Nonverbal communication: The unspoken dialogue.* New York: McGraw-Hill.

Davill, G. (1983). Rehabilitation—not just voice. In Y. Eels (Ed.), *Laryngectomy: Diagnosis to rehabilitation* (pp. 192–217). Beckenham, Kent, UK: Coom Helm Ltd.

DeLoach, C., & Greer, B. G. (1981). *Adjustment to severe physical disability: A metamorphosis.* New York: McGraw-Hill.

Do, T. (1997). *How do you expect me to succeed if you keep telling me how to fail?: Messages encouraging or limiting the trans-formation of persons with disabilities.* Unpublished master's thesis, San Diego State University, San Diego, CA.

Feber, T. (1996). Promoting self-esteem after laryngectomy. *Nursing Times, 92*(30), 37–39.

Gilmore, S. I. (1994). Physical, social, occupational and psychological concomitants of laryngectomy. In R. L. Keith & F. L. Darley (Eds.), *Laryngectomee rehabilitation* (pp. 395–486). Austin, TX: Pro-Ed.

Goffman, E. (1963). *Stigma: Notes on the management of spoiled identity.* New York: Simon & Schuster.

Hyman, M. (1994). Factors influencing the intelligibility of alaryngeal speech. In R. L. Keith & F. L. Darley (Eds.), *Laryngectomee rehabilitation* (pp. 253–262). Austin, TX: Pro-Ed.

Jones, N. G. (1991). *Adductor spasmodic dysphonia.* [On-line]. Available: http://www.bcm.tmc.edu./oto/grand/71391.html.

Kaufman, J. A. (1997, July 21). *What are voice disorders and who gets them?* [On-line]. Available: http://www.bgsm.edu/voice/voice_disorders.html.

Killworth, P. D., & Bernard, H. R. (1976). Informant accuracy in social network data. *Human Organization, 35,* 269–286.

Kleinfield, S. (1979). *The hidden majority: A profile of handicapped Americans.* Boston: Little, Brown.

Lauder, E. (1994). *Self help for the laryngectomee.* (1994–1995 edition). Health Corp. Available from the American Cancer Society. San Antonio, TX: Lauder Pub.

McDaniel, J. S., Musselman, D., Porter, M., Reed, D., & Nemeroff, C. (1995). Depression in patients with cancer. *Archives of General Psychiatry, 52,* 89–96.

McLaughlin, M. L., & Cody, M. J. (1982). Consequences of the conversational lapse. *Human Communication Research, 8,* 299–316.

Morris, J. (1991). *Pride against prejudice: Transforming attitudes to disability.* Philadelphia: New Society.

National Spasmodic Dysphonia Association (NSDA). (1992). Survey. [On-line]. Available: http://www.bgsm.edu/voice/survey_sd.html.

Richardson, J. L., Graham, J. W., & Shelton, D. R. (1989). Social environment and adjustment after laryngectomy. *Health and Social Work, 14,* 283–292.

Salmon, S. J. (1994a). Pre- and postoperative conferences with laryngectomees and their spouses. In R. L. Keith & F. L. Darley (Eds.), *Laryngectomee rehabilitation* (pp. 133–148). Austin, TX: Pro-Ed.

Salmon, S. J. (1994b). Laryngectomee visitations. In R. L. Keith & F. L. Darley (Eds.), *Laryngectomee rehabilitation* (pp. 149–154). Austin, TX: Pro-Ed.

Shanks, J. C. (1994). Developing esophageal communication. In R. L. Keith & F. L. Darley (Eds.), *Laryngectomee rehabilitation* (pp. 205–217). Austin, TX: Pro-Ed.

Shapiro, J. P. (1993). *No pity: People with disabilities forging a new civil rights movement.* New York: Random House.

Silverman, F. H. (1989). *Communication for the speechless* (2nd ed.). Englewood Cliffs, NJ: Prentice-Hall.

Spiegel, J. R., & Sataloff, R. T. (1993). Surgery for carcinoma of the larynx. In W. J. Gould, R. T. Sataloff, & J. R. Spegel (Eds.), *Voice surgery* (pp. 307–337). St. Louis: Mosby.

Statement From Michael Zaslow. (1998, May 11). [On-line]. Available: http://america.net/~gwp/mzexpo/als-stat.html.

Stroke. (1997, July 22). [On-line]. Available: http://www.carers.asn.au/stroke.html.

Stroke: Prevention and Treatment. (1998, July 3). [On-line]. Available: http://www.medscape.com/govmt/DHHS/patient/StrokePrevention.html#5.

Sullivan, C. F., & Reardon, K. K. (1986). Social support satisfaction and health locus of control: Discriminators of breast cancer patients' styles of coping. In M. L. McLaughlin (Ed.), *Communication yearbook 9* (pp. 707–722). Beverly Hills, CA: Sage.

Weitzel, A. (1998, February). *Persons without a voice: An exploratory study of communication by laryngectomees.* Paper presented at the annual meeting of the Western Speech Communication Association, Denver, CO.

ENDNOTES

1. Some of the stories in chapter are taken from "Cancer of the Larynx, The Lighter Side, Laryngectomee Laffers" (http://members.aol.com/FantumTwo/cancer7.htm, April 14, 1998).

2. Telephone companies are required to provide this service by Sec. 401 of the Americans With Disabilities Act of 1990 (http://www.usdoj.gov/crt/ada/statute.html).

3. Don Bauder, "Computer Makers Keying on Middle-Class Households," *San Diego Union-Tribune*, 27 May, 1996: C-1. There is a webpage about cancer of the larynx (http://members.aol.com/fantumtwo/cancer1.htm) that in 1997 had a self-selected sample of 52 persons who were registered as laryngectomees. The average age was 57 years. About one third were over 60, but it is likely that this sample was a skewed one in favor of persons younger than the population of laryngectomees because members of the self-selected sample were among the younger persons in the overall U.S. population of computer owners/users.

27

Interpersonal Roulette and HIV/AIDS as Disability: Stigma and Social Support in Tension

Rebecca J. Cline
University of Florida

Nelya J. McKenzie
Auburn University, Montgomery

Keywords: Disclosure, identity management, stigma, social support, uncertainty reduction

Disability divides the world into "us" and "them." For the disabled, much everyday interaction is driven by interpersonal dynamics associated with stigma. People with HIV/AIDS are more likely to be stigmatized than to be socially supported (Cline, 1989). For most of the course of their disease, people with HIV/AIDS have a disability that is not identifiable by passing observation. Ironically, concealing their stigma obviates potential social support. Given the power of social support in health care and disease prevention (DiMatteo & Hays, 1981), people with HIV/AIDS face a kind of interpersonal roulette, in which they weigh the chances of receiving the benefits of social support against the risks of outright rejection and dehumanizing treatment, in deciding whether to disclose their disability.

This chapter explores the dilemma of disclosure of HIV disease in the context of the tensions between stigma and social support. The literature (a) establishes the stigmatizing nature of interpersonal communication often experienced by those with HIV/AIDS, (b) identifies the socially supportive interpersonal communication potentially available to HIV-infected individuals on disclosure of their disability, and (c) details the processes employed as HIV-infected individuals confront this dilemma.

HIV/AIDS AS STIGMA: INTERPERSONAL CONSEQUENCES

HIV/AIDS as Disability

Arguably the most stigmatizing disease of modern times, HIV/AIDS was not given legal status as a disability until its second decade (Gostin, 1990). It is so stigmatizing that it was the first disease to have a corps of political activists fighting for the rights of the infected (Stoddard & Rieman, 1990). The Rehabilitation Act of 1973 required nondiscrimination based on handicap for programs receiving federal funding. However, HIV/AIDS was not legally determined to be a disability until 1987. In the case of *School Board of Nassau County, Florida v. Arline*, the Supreme Court held that "a contagious disease can qualify as a 'handicapping condition'" (Stoddard & Rieman, 1990, p. 148). Designating HIV/AIDS as a disability provided some protection, but did not extend to private enterprise. Not until the Americans With Disabilities Act of 1990 did antidiscrimination protection for people with HIV extend to the private business sector (Gostin, 1990).

The Nature of Stigma

Goffman (1963) defined *stigma* as an "attribute that is deeply discrediting" (p. 3). More than a personal characteristic, stigma denotes a type of relationship between those defined as "normal" or desirable and those "marked" as deficient and foretells patterns of interpersonal communication between "mixed contacts."

Goffman (1963) did not limit stigma to physical deformities; he included "blemishes of individual character" (e.g., mental illness, homosexuality, suicidal tendencies) and "tribal stigma" (e.g., race, religion, nationality). Furthermore, not all stigmas are directly observable. Although some sources of stigma render individuals "discredited," those less observable yield people who are "discreditable." Among the interpersonal dilemmas experienced by the discreditable is whether to disclose one's stigma. "Passing" as "normal" protects privacy (Gibbons, 1986). Ironically, at the same time, having a "secret" stigma prevents potentially available social support.

As Crandall and Coleman (1992) suggested, stigma "legitimizes treating the bearer in some ways less humanely than those without the mark"

(p. 163). In anticipation of discomfort, often interaction between "mixed contacts" is avoided. Interaction that does occur often is distorted and negative (Jones et al., 1984), characterized by psychosocial as well as physical distance (Kleck, 1968, 1969); talk tends to be briefer and restricted to task (Gibbons, 1986). Typically, people who are stigmatized are treated as "nonpersons" or "not quite human" (Goffman, 1963, p. 5). Thus, some of the most devastating consequences of stigma are found in interpersonal contexts.

HIV/AIDS as Stigma

Disease and disability themselves mark individuals as "different" (de Monteflores, 1993). People with HIV disease are presumed to differ on a number of stigmatizing conditions: sexual orientation, sexual promiscuity, drug use, race/ethnicity, and socioeconomic status. In the United States, the response to HIV disease is so confounded by judgments of already stigmatized groups that it is virtually impossible to separate the two (Cline & McKenzie, 1996).

People with HIV disease are stigmatized for numerous reasons (Alonzo & Reynolds, 1995). Stigma emanates from blame for "choosing" behavior that yields stigma (de Monteflores, 1993), labels of character flaws (e.g., homosexuality, intravenous drug use; Herek & Glunt, 1988), being infectious (Bean, Keller, Newburg, & Brown, 1989), representing an undesirable form of death, and general misunderstanding of the disease that results in unrealistic fears (Herek & Glunt, 1988). Finally, HIV/AIDS typically is seen both by the infected and by others as the "master status" of the infected (Bennett, 1990). So strong is the stigmatizing effect of HIV/AIDS that even many of those most knowledgeable about the disease (e.g., health care workers), stigmatize people with AIDS (Kelly et al., 1987).

Effects of Stigma on People With HIV/AIDS: The Interpersonal Syndrome

Not just a disease of the immune system, HIV/AIDS threatens the very social fabric of lives. Stigma yields an array of interactional disorders that comprises an interpersonal syndrome linked inextricably to health. Due to stigma, people with HIV/AIDS face threats to their functional, social, and psychological well-being that ultimately influence their health.

Functional Effects.   Ironically, availing oneself of legal protection against discrimination requires disclosure and risk of stigmatization. "Legal protections against discrimination do not eliminate stigma, prejudice, or discrimination. They simply make their overt manifestations more difficult" (Pryor & Reeder, 1993, p. 281). Despite the law, people with HIV/AIDS commonly face threats to employment, housing, insurance, and medical care. Further, because stigma is attached to objects used or owned by people with HIV/AIDS (Pryor & Reeder, 1993), their residences, hotel rooms, hospital rooms, and work areas have been shunned.

Social Impact: Direct Effects on Social Support.   AIDS invariably changes social relationships. After disclosing HIV status or a previously hidden stigma such as homosexuality, the person with HIV/AIDS may be rejected by family, old friends, and even lovers (Lang, 1990). Grappling with personal meanings associated with homosexuality, intravenous drug use, disease, death, and the deviancy associated with these, often prevents supportive responses (Cadwell, 1994). Not only does the person with HIV/AIDS experience stigma, so too do their families, friends, and lovers as they internalize homophobia and encounter abandonment and betrayal as part of a process termed "courtesy stigma" or stigma by association (McDonell, Abell, & Miller, 1991).

Recognizing the threat, many people choose to "pass" for as long as they can to avoid blame and potential rejection (St. Lawrence et al., 1990). Thus, potential social support for people with HIV/AIDS is threatened directly by stigma. Undermined psychological well-being follows.

Psychological Well-Being.   Because the stigmatized tend to take on society's view of their mark, the person with HIV/AIDS may experience self-rejection. Thus, many people with HIV/AIDS have enhanced risks to their mental well-being, including greater risks of anxiety, depression, and suicide (Crandall & Coleman, 1992). In addition to concerns about their health, people with HIV experience the strain of passing and avoiding suspicion as well as fear of hostility from others when finally told (Alonzo & Reynolds, 1995).

People with HIV/AIDS are at enhanced risk for depression. Typical studies report about 40% of people with HIV/AIDS to be clinically depressed (e.g., Belkin, Fleishman, Stein, Piette, & Mor, 1992), but many report substantially higher rates (e.g., McClure et al., 1996; Ritchie, Radke, & Ross, 1992).

Given high rates of depression among people with HIV/AIDS, enhanced risk of suicide is not surprising (e.g., Ritchie et al., 1992). Cote, Biggar, and Dannenberg (1992) found the suicide rate among men with AIDS to be four times greater than in the general population. A New York City study showed suicide risk among people with HIV/AIDS to be 35 times that of the general population (see Marzuk et al., 1988).

THE POTENTIAL ROLE OF SOCIAL SUPPORT AND HEALTH: THE CASE OF HIV/AIDS

The Nature of Social Support

Although theorists define social support in varied ways, at their heart is a consensus: Social support functions to address multiple interpersonal needs (e.g., Cutrona & Russell, 1990). These include needs for relational (i.e., emotional support, attachment), confirmational (i.e., reassurance of worth, esteem support), and instrumental (i.e., tangible aid, information) care.

Stressful conditions enhance interpersonal needs for care. Stress is "a relationship between the person and the environment in which the individual perceives that something of personal value is at stake and judges that his or her resources are taxed or overwhelmed by the situation" (Cutrona & Russell, 1990, p. 324). Thus, stress and the resulting need for social support is a function of the person's perceptions regarding ability to control or influence the situation.

Albrecht and Adelman (1987b) observed that nearly all concepts of social support include elements of "functional effect," that is, social support does something to facilitate uncertainty management and communication (p. 24). They defined social support as "verbal and nonverbal communication between recipients and providers that . . . functions to enhance a perception of personal control in one's life experience" (p. 19). Thus, social support is manifest in communication processes that reduce stress by facilitating uncertainty management.

Social Support and Health

Formal study of the health consequences of social support began in the 1970s when scholars theorized a link between susceptibility to disease and social relationships (Cassel, 1976). Illness promotes uncertainties: ambiguity, complexity, lack of information, and unpredictability (Mischel, 1988). The senses of helplessness and hopelessness engendered serve as an impetus for engaging in communication to manage uncertainty (Albrecht & Adelman, 1987b).

Early research on the health consequences of social support can be characterized as "uniformly positive" (Cohen & Syme, 1985, p. 20). Later research revealed potentially negative consequences of social support (e.g., Albrecht & Adelman, 1987a). Although social support may disrupt family equilibrium, result in caregiver burnout, interfere with compliance, and promote dependence, most critics agree that social support likely has some causal relationship with health status. Evidence associates social support with coping with and recovery from serious illness and injury (DiMatteo & Hays, 1981). Social support has been linked with symptom change, enhanced recovery, responses to the diagnosis of terminal illness, and greater compliance with medical regimens (DiMatteo & Hays, 1981).

HIV/AIDS and the Need for Social Support: A Disease of Uncertainty

HIV/AIDS is a disease of uncertainty that renders helplessness a common experience (e.g., Demas, Schoenbaum, Wills, & Doll, 1995). Both the unpredictability of the disease and of social reactions induce anxiety and decree the need for social support.

Stressors of HIV/AIDS.   From the moment of diagnosis, the person with HIV/AIDS faces a multitude of stressors rooted in uncertainty (Andrews, 1995). Uncertainties surround the disease itself: how one contracted the disease, the course of the disease, and impending multiple illnesses (Longo, Spross, & Locke, 1990), physical dependence, and dying. Uncertainties include lifestyle changes: the ability to work (Longo et al., 1990), housing, finances, insurance, and poverty (Nichols, 1985). Uncertainties abound regarding functional roles (e.g., an array of caretaker roles; Andrews, 1995). Uncertainties about the nature of self and identity add to the struggle: jeopardized self-esteem, internalized homophobia, guilt and fear regarding infecting others (Abrams, Dilley, Maxey, & Volberding, 1986; Andrews, 1995). Uncertainties dominate relational concerns: coming out, stigma, rejection, withdrawal, and abandonment (Lester, Partridge, Chesney, & Cooke, 1995; Longo et al., 1990).

Uncertainty regarding how others will respond becomes dominant (Kimberly & Serovich, 1996) and leads to a dilemma in many interpersonal relationships: to disclose or not disclose one's illness. Two primary outcomes result: social stigma, in itself a major source of uncertainty and stress (Demas et al., 1995) or social support, the central need of people with HIV/AIDS. Ironically, the choice not to disclose one's HIV-positive status is made in an attempt to maintain a greater sense of control. Although secrecy can function to maintain privacy, reduce embarrassment, and protect one's self-esteem (Petronio, 1991), that temporary choice to control one's privacy boundaries virtually ensures loss of potential social support.

The Need for Social Support.   Evidence differs regarding the types of social support most needed by people with HIV. Separate studies have identified emotional, instrumental, and informational support as most significant. However, the stage of the disease may account for differences.

Although people with HIV often identify emotional support as their greatest need, instrumental support most often correlates with physical and psychological well-being (Abrams et al., 1986; Namir, Wolcott, & Fawzy, 1989). Needs for assistance in getting groceries, preparing meals, doing laundry, conducting business, and transportation increase as the disease progresses. Whereas one half of people with HIV disease report needing practical assistance, more than one third of these report unmet needs (Hedge, 1990). However, from the patient's perspective, particularly earlier in the disease, emotional support often is most valued (e.g., Pakenham, Dadds, & Terry, 1994; Stewart, Hart, & Mann, 1995). Finally, due to the tremendous uncertainty associated with the disease, informational support is particularly valuable and may be more important for HIV than for other serious illnesses (Hays, Magee, & Chauncey, 1994).

When asked to identify "helpful" and "unhelpful" behaviors (Hays, Magee, & Chauncey, 1994), responses from people with HIV crystallize the social support–stigma dynamic. Helpful behaviors reflect emotional, informational, and instrumental support (e.g., encouragement, concern, and sharing feelings; information; practical and material assistance). Unhelpful behaviors deny support and manifest stigmatization (e.g., judgment, avoidance, insincerity, and breaking confidentiality).

HIV/AIDS and the Experience of Social Support

Health care workers, partners, family, and friends, as well as social support groups are potential sources of support for people with HIV/AIDS. Research focusing on the presence and absence of social support provides a mixed picture that highlights the uncertainty of people with HIV/AIDS regarding social support.

Sources of Support.   When asked the most important sources of social support, most people with HIV identify either family or peers. However, HIV-infected women (Bor, 1990) identify health care professionals as their main source of social support (75%), while 69% reported relying on a partner or family, and 44% on friends. Only 41% expressed interest in social support groups. When HIV-infected men were asked what would be most helpful from health care workers, they identified empathy and acceptance (Longo et al., 1990).

HIV-infected women reported having fewer close friends in their support networks than HIV-negative women (Persson, 1994). Likewise, HIV-positive gay men are less likely to be in primary relationships than HIV-negatives and thus may have less access to support (Hoff et al., 1996).

The family is a potentially powerful source of social support in most crises (Eggert, 1987). In addition to stigma, a number of social barriers limit families' social support to people with HIV/AIDS: lack of geographic access, lack of intimacy, and the interpersonal costs to the person receiving support (e.g., fear of physical and financial burden, loss of independence; Smith & Rapkin, 1995). As a result, often families are perceived as less supportive than peers (Hays, Catania, McKusick, & Coates, 1990), particularly for gay men.

Among HIV-discordant couples (one infected, the other not), one fourth of the infected partners and one half of the negative partners reported having no support from their families (Foley, Skurnick, Kennedy, Valentin, & Louria, 1994). Although most of the infected partners reported having at least one aware and supportive relative, often that support was meager. Similarly, 52% of homosexual/bisexual men with AIDS reported having one or no family members in their social support networks (Namir et al., 1989).

Social support groups offer an alternative to traditional sources of support. Potential benefits include reduced stigma (Cadwell, 1994), emotional support through identification and openness, enhanced self-esteem from helping others, encouragement of healthy lifestyle changes (Grant, 1988), and information about treatments and care (Kalichman, Sikkema, & Somlai, 1996), as well as a means for reducing burnout among family and friends (Abrams et al., 1986).

Satisfaction With Support.   Levels of satisfaction vary with types of social support. More satisfaction is reported with emotional support (72%) than with informational (64%) and practical support (67%; Stewart et al., 1995). Ironically, support tends to become less available as the prognosis worsens (e.g., Namir et al., 1989) and disclosure becomes less of a choice. Unlike other diseases, such as cancer, social support from friends and family may actually diminish due to fear, exhaustion, and anticipatory grieving as symptoms worsen (e.g., Stewart et al., 1995).

HIV/AIDS and the Value of Social Support

While the actual value of social support for people with HIV/AIDS likely remains underestimated due to difficulties in conducting research, ample evidence argues an array of benefits that include both mental and physical well-being. In effect, stigma and social support are a type of yin and yang; where stigma destroys, social support heals.

Evidence of the mental health benefits of social support for people with HIV is compelling. Social support functions to reduce depression (e.g., Andrews, 1995; Grant & Ostrow, 1995) and anxiety (e.g., Grant & Ostrow, 1995). Perceived social support is associated with reduced psychological stress (Zich & Temoshok, 1987) enhanced self-esteem (e.g., Linn, Lewis, Cain, Kimbrough, 1993), and use of effective coping strategies (Hays, Chauncey, & Tobey, 1990).

Some evidence indicates that the strongest predictor of depression is perceived availability of social support, which in turn is associated with symptomatology (McClure et al., 1996). While increased symptoms lead to depression, and in turn to the need for social support, evidence also indicates that increased social support is predictive of fewer symptoms being reported. Regardless of the specific causal relationship(s), clearly the ability to tolerate the consequences of this disease depends on the availability of constructive social support (Holland & Tross, 1985).

Evidence indicates that social support is correlated directly with number of symptoms and CDC4 cell counts; however, these factors may be reciprocally influential (Pakenham et al., 1994). People with less social support tend to be slower to seek treatment (Katz, Bindman, & Komaromy, 1992). In addition, healthier lifestyle changes may be facilitated by social support (e.g., getting off drugs, safer sex; Nyamathi, Flaskerud, Leake, & Chen, 1996).

In summary, when the individual with HIV/AIDS experiences social support rather than stigma, the health consequences of social support function to ameliorate both deteriorating social and immune systems.

MANAGING THE DILEMMA OF DISCLOSURE: THE RISKS OF STIGMA VERSUS THE VALUE OF SOCIAL SUPPORT

The dilemma faced by persons with HIV/AIDS is this: risk becoming stigmatized by disclosing their condition to take a chance on potential health benefits of social support or avoid being stigmatized by engaging in concealment, thereby losing potential health benefits of social support. Research identifies two patterns of response to the dilemma, avoidance and seeking support, with responses varying based on the individual's social characteristics.

The Dilemma

Potential supporters cannot provide social support unless they know a person's HIV status (Foley et al., 1994). People with HIV are reluctant to disclose their status in an attempt to maintain control. Reasons for failure to disclose invariably center around stigma. For example, many postnatal HIV-positive women's attempts to communicate with their partners led to denial, anger, and abandonment, reinforcing the risk of disclosure (Lester et al., 1995). Not telling family and friends correlates with a feeling of a lack of social support and, in turn, with depression (Ritchie et al., 1992).

People with HIV (particularly women) report the desire for social support as a primary reason for choosing to disclose their HIV status (Simoni, Mason, Marks, & Ruiz, 1995). Women reported that, on disclosure, parents typically responded by providing support, only rarely by becoming angry or withdrawing. In contrast, lovers frequently were angry and withdrew; 20% indicated that in response to the disclosure, their partners left them. However, some evidence indicates that gay men with HIV received more favorable reactions than expected in response to their disclosure, with most lovers and friends being supportive (Mansergh, Marks, & Simoni, 1995). Thus, responses indicate that women are more stigmatized by HIV than are men (Cline & McKenzie, 1996) and thus may differ both in their disclosure patterns and in responses to disclosure. Evidence also indicates ethnic differences in disclosure, with Spanish-speaking Latinos being less likely to disclose their HIV status than English-speaking Latinos or Whites, likely due to the cultural value of protecting their families from the adverse consequences of their disclosure (Mason, Marks, Simoni, & Ruiz, 1995).

Strategies for Managing the Dilemma

The dilemma of disclosure is just one more stressor in the lives of people with HIV (Demas et al., 1995). Research indicates that people with HIV tend to respond with one of two major coping strategies: concealing their status through avoidance or seeking social support. The strategy chosen appears to vary to some extent on the basis of social characteristics.

Avoidance.   People with HIV who engage in denial of their disease are more likely to respond with avoidance. Avoidance strategies are more likely to be used by the disadvantaged: minorities, intravenous (IV) drug users, and those with lower incomes (Fleishman & Fogel, 1994). IV drug users are more likely than gay men to rely on avoidance (Fleishman & Fogel, 1994) and gay men use avoidance more than women (Semple et al., 1996). Further, HIV-positive women more often use avoidance as a general coping strategy than HIV-negative women (Catalan et al., 1996). However, when poverty is a factor, women often employ denial as a coping strategy when diagnosis occurs before symptoms emerge. As Andrews (1995) argues, "for some women, the diagnosis of HIV disease may appear to be a relatively minor stressor within the context of poverty and the demands of family life" (p. 39). Some research also indicates that blacks more often than whites respond with denial and avoidance (Leserman, Perkins, & Evans, 1992). Ironically, as people with HIV become sicker, they may be more likely to withdraw from interaction and thus obviate social support (Katoaka-Yahiro, Portillo, Henry, & Holzemer, 1996).

Seeking Social Support.   An alternative and generally deemed healthier coping response is to seek social support (e.g., Leserman et al., 1992). Generally, women seek social support more than men (Fleischman & Fogel, 1994), perhaps reflective of differences in gender socialization regarding the value of relationships and independence. Blacks report seeking social support less than Whites, due in part to less satisfaction with their social support networks (Leserman et al., 1992).

In addition to other benefits of social support, the strategy of seeking social support is associated with other health behaviors. For example, women with multiple partners report less use and efficacy of social support than those with one or no partners (Nyamathi et al., 1996). Although women who report using IV drugs report greater availability of social support than those denying drug use, these women actually use their available social support less and find it less efficacious (Nyamathi et al., 1996). In fact, the only coping strategy among IV drug users to correlate with psychological adjustment is seeking social support (Grummon, Rigby, Orr, Procidano, & Reznikoff, 1994).

CONCLUSION

People with HIV/AIDS face the predictable dilemma of whether, when, and to whom to disclose what, for much of the course of the disease is an invisible "mark." A self-fulfilling prophecy often emerges whereby the person with HIV disease anticipates rejection and so withdraws from potential sources of support, thereby ensuring the absence of social support (Crandall & Coleman, 1992). In fact, when questioned about changes in relationships due to HIV/AIDS, about 17% of respondents reported a loss of social support, whereas 43% reported increase in social support (Crandall & Coleman, 1992). Thus, both actual rejection due to stigma and withdrawal due to anticipated stigma result in reduced social support among people with HIV disease. The multiple stigmas experienced by people with HIV/AIDS often function to preclude them from the social support requisite to coping and survival. As one's social worth is threatened by stereotypes associated with the disease, so is one's health and well-being.

Future research needs to focus on interpersonal communication and relational issues, particularly as they relate to the effectiveness of social support and the reduction of stigma. Not only do individuals need strategies for reducing their own sense of stigma, they need strategies for facilitating stigma reduction on the part of those with whom they interact. Also, research needs to clarify the role of disclosing one's HIV status on subsequent disclosure decisions. Disclosure is not a singular all-or-none phenomenon. Most people with HIV disease disclose selectively; little is known about the sequencing of disclosures or the cumulative effects of multiple disclosure decisions and responses. Similarly, little reference is made in the literature to how a person's responses to another's HIV disclosure may change over time from stigma to social support or vice versa. Although extant research emphasizes the positive effects of social support in the case of HIV/AIDS, some anecdotal evidence refers to negative effects;

potentially destructive effects of social support need to be understood as well. Finally, although some evidence (e.g., Braithwaite, Waldron, & Finn, 1999) suggests the potential for on-line social support networks for the disabled, this potential needs to be explored specifically for people with HIV disease.

What constitutes efficacious stigma management strategies in interpersonal relationships remains largely unknown. In the interim, practitioners, family, and friends face their own dilemmas of yielding to the pressures of stigma or providing social support. Choosing to provide social support is choosing to be health promoting to someone whose life is in jeopardy. Those who encounter people with HIV can be helpful by recognizing several factors. First and foremost, people with HIV disease desire to be treated as individuals with identities beyond their disease, as they were prior to their HIV disclosure. People with HIV disease experience many stressors, including how others will respond to their disclosure. Initial acceptance and maintaining consistent, accepting, and supportive contact can reduce that stress. The primary social support needs of people with HIV are emotional, instrumental, and informational support. Individuals might assess which of these they are capable of and willing to provide. Identifying informational and institutional resources is in itself supportive. People supportive of those with HIV disease also need to recognize that needs change over the course of the disease; emotional support is a high priority among family and friends, particularly early in the disease. As the disease progresses, needs for instrumental support grow. Rarely can one person provide for the growing needs; caregivers need to be aware of their own needs for social support.

DISCUSSION QUESTIONS

1. Discuss the uncertainties experienced by people with HIV/AIDS compared with (a) people with other forms of stigma, and (b) people with other diseases and disabilities.
2. What are the personal and relational risks of making one's HIV-positive status known?
3. How can social support help in managing uncertainty and reducing stress for individuals with HIV/AIDS?
4. Discuss the relationships between information control and uncertainty management. Specifically, how can both information control and disclosure of stigma enhance perceptions of personal control?

5. In what ways does the experience of being HIV-positive affect both personal relationships and personal identity?

6. Awareness and fear of stigma affects disclosure of a stigma, and in turn influences the degree of social support one is likely to receive. Brainstorm about (a) how an individual with HIV/AIDS might best manage this dilemma, and (b) how a person who wants to be supportive can overcome his or her own fears and stigma.

REFERENCES

Abrams, D. I., Dilley, J. W., Maxey, L. M., & Volberding, P. A. (1986). Routine care and psychosocial support of the patient with the acquired immunodeficiency syndrome. *Medical Clinicians of North America, 70*, 707–720.

Albrecht, T. L., & Adelman, M. B. (1987a). Dilemmas of social support. In T. L. Albrecht, M. B. Adelman, & Associates (Eds.), *Communicating social support* (pp. 240–254). Newbury Park, CA: Sage.

Albrecht, T. L., & Adelman, M. B. (1987b). Rethinking the relationship between communication and social support: An introduction. In T. L. Albrecht, M. B. Adelman, & Associates (Eds.), *Communicating social support* (pp. 13–39). Newbury Park, CA: Sage.

Alonzo, A. A., & Reynolds, N. R. (1995). Stigma, HIV and AIDS: An exploration and elaboration of a stigma trajectory. *Social Science and Medicine, 3*, 303–315.

Andrews, S. (1995, October). Social support as a stress buffer among human immunodeficiency virus-seropositive urban mothers. *Holistic Nursing Practice, 10*, 36–43.

Bean, J., Keller, L., Newburg, C., & Brown, M. (1989). Methods for the reduction of AIDS social anxiety and social stigma. *AIDS Education & Prevention, 1*, 194–221.

Belkin, G. S., Fleishman, J. A., Stein, M. D., Piette, J., & Mor, V. (1992). Physical symptoms and depressive symptoms among individuals with HIV infection. *Psychosomatics, 33*, 416–427.

Bennett, M. J. (1990). Stigmatization: Experiences of persons with acquired immune deficiency syndrome. *Issues in Mental Health Nursing, 11*, 141–154.

Bor, R. (1990). The family and HIV/AIDS. *AIDS Care, 2*, 409–412.

Braithwaite, D. O., Waldron, V., & Finn, J. (1999). Communication of social support in computer-mediated groups for persons with disabilities. *Health Communication, 11*, 123–157.

Cadwell, S. A. (1994). Twice removed: The stigma suffered by gay men with AIDS. In S. A. Cadwell, R. A. Burnham, & M. Forstein (Eds.), *Therapists on the front line: Psychotherapy with gay men in the age of AIDS* (pp. 3–24). Washington, DC: American Psychiatric Press.

Cassel, J. (1976). The contribution of the social environment to host resistance. *American Journal of Epidemiology, 104*, 107–123.

Catalan, J., Beevor, A., Cassidy, L., Burgess, A. P., Meadows, J., Pergami, A., Gazzard, B., & Barton, S. (1996). Women and HIV infection: Investigation of its psychosocial consequences. *Journal of Psychosomatic Research, 41*, 39–47.

Cline, R. J. W. (1989). Communication and death and dying: Implications for coping with AIDS. *AIDS & Public Policy, 4*, 40–50.

Cline, R. J. W., & McKenzie, N. J. (1996). HIV/AIDS, women, and threads of discrimination: A tapestry of disenfranchisement. In E. B. Ray (Ed.), *Communication and disenfranchisement* (pp. 365–386). Mahwah, NJ: Lawrence Erlbaum Associates.

Cohen, S., & Syme, S. L. (1985). Issues in the study and application of social support. In S. Cohen & S. L. Syme (Eds.), *Social support and health* (pp. 3–22). New York: Academic Press.

Cote, T. R., Biggar, R. J., & Dannenberg, A. L. (1992). Risk of suicide among persons with AIDS: A national assessment. *Journal of the American Medical Association, 268*, 2066–2068.

Crandall, C. S., & Coleman, R. (1992). AIDS-related stigmatization and the disruption of social relationships. *Journal of Social and Personal Relationships, 9*, 163–177.

Cutrona, C. E., & Russell, D. W. (1990). Type of social support and specific stress: Toward a theory of optimal matching. In B. R. Sarason, I. G. Sarason, & G. R. Pierce (Eds.), *Social support: An interactional view* (pp. 319–366). New York: Wiley.

de Monteflores, C. (1993). Notes on the management of difference. In L. D. Garnets & D. C. Kimmel (Eds.), *Psychological perspectives on lesbian and gay male experiences* (pp. 218–247). New York: Columbia University Press.

Demas, P., & Schoenbaum, E. E., Wills, T. A., & Doll, L. S. (1995). Stress, coping, and attitudes toward HIV treatment in injecting drug users: A qualitative study. *AIDS Education & Prevention, 7*, 429–442.

DiMatteo, M. R., & Hays, R. (1981). Social support and serious illness. In B. H. Gottlieb (Ed.), *Social networks and social support* (pp. 117–148). Beverly Hills, CA: Sage.

Eggert, L. L. (1987). Support in family ties: Stress, coping, and adaptation. In T. L. Albrecht & M. B. Adelman (Eds.), *Communicating social support* (pp. 80–104). Newbury Park, CA: Sage.

Fleishman, J. A., & Fogel, B. (1994). Coping and depressive symptoms among people with AIDS. *Health Psychology, 13*, 156–169.

Foley, M., Skurnick, J. H., Kennedy, C. A., Valentin, R., & Louria, D. B. (1994). Family support for heterosexual partners in HIV-serodiscordant couples. *AIDS, 8*, 1483–1487.

Gibbons, F. X. (1986). Stigma and interpersonal relations. In S. C. Ainley, G. Becker, & L. M. Coleman (Eds.), *The dilemma of difference: A multidisciplinary view of stigma* (pp. 95–122). New York: Plenum Press.

Goffman, E. (1963). *Stigma: Notes on the management of spoiled identity*. Englewood Cliffs, NJ: Prentice-Hall.

Gostin, L. A. (1990). The AIDS litigation project: A national review of court and human rights commission decisions, Part II: Discrimination. *Journal of the American Medical Association, 263*, 1086–2093.

Grant, D. (1988). Support groups for youth with the AIDS virus. *International Journal of Group Psychotherapy, 38*, 237–251.

Grant, I. M., & Ostrow, D. B. (1995). Perceptions of social support and psychological adaptation to sexually acquired HIV among white and African American men. *Social Work, 40*, 215–224.

Grummon, K., Rigby, E. D., Orr, D., Procidano, M., & Reznikoff, M. (1994). Psychosocial variables that affect the psychological adjustment of IVDU patients with AIDS. *Journal of Clinical Psychology, 50*, 488–502.

Hays, R. B., Catania, J., McKusick, L., & Coates, T. J. (1990). Help-seeking for AIDS-related concerns: A comparison of gay men of various HIV diagnoses. *American Journal of Community Psychology, 18*, 743–755.

Hays, R. B., Chauncey, S., & Tobey, L. A. (1990). The social support networks of gay men with AIDS. *Journal of Community Psychology, 18*, 374–385.

Hays, R. B., Magee, R. H., & Chauncey, S. (1994). Identifying helpful and unhelpful behaviours of loved ones: The PWA's perspective. *AIDS Care, 6*, 379–392.

Hedge, B. (1990). The psychological impact of HIV/AIDS. *AIDS Care, 2*, 381–383.

Herek, G. M., & Glunt, E. K. (1988). An epidemic of stigma: Public reactions to AIDS. *American Psychologist, 43*, 886–891.

Hoff, C. C., Coates, T. J., Barrett, D. C., Collette, L., & Ekstrand, M. (1996). Differences between gay men in primary relationships and single men: Implications for prevention. *AIDS Education & Prevention, 8*, 546–559.

Holland, J. C., & Tross, S. (1985). The psychosocial and neuropsychiatric sequelae of the acquired immunodeficiency syndrome and related disorders. *Annals of Internal Medicine, 103*, 760–764.

Jones, E. E., Farina, A., Hastorf, A. H., Markus, H., Miller, D. T., Scott, R. A., French, R. (1984). *Social stigma: The psychology of marked relationships.* New York: W. H. Freeman.

Kalichman, S. C., Sikkema, K. J., & Somlai, A. (1996). People living with HIV infection who attend and do not attend support groups: A pilot study of needs, characteristics and experiences. *AIDS Care, 8,* 589–599.

Katoaka-Yahino, M. R., Portillo, C. J., Henry, S., & Holzemer, W. L. (1996). Physical and social correlates of perceived psychological support among hospitalized AIDS patients. *Journal of Advanced Nursing, 24,* 167–173.

Katz, M., Bindman, A. B., Komaromy, M. S. (1992). Coping with HIV infection: Why people delay care. *Annals of Internal Medicine, 117,* 797.

Kelly, J. A., St. Lawrence, J. S., Smith, Jr., S., Hood, H. V., & Cook, D. J. (1987). Stigmatization of AIDS patients by physicians. *American Journal of Public Health, 77,* 789–791.

Kimberly, J. A., & Serovich, J. M. (1996). Perceived social support among people living with HIV/AIDS. *American Journal of Family Therapy, 24,* 41–53.

Kleck, R. E. (1968). Effects of stigmatizing conditions on the use of personal space. *Psychological Reports, 23,* 111–118.

Kleck, R. E. (1969). Physical stigma and task oriented interactions. *Human Relations, 22,* 53–60.

Lang, N. G. (1990). Sex, politics, and guilt: A study of homophobia and the AIDS phenomenon. In D. A. Feldman (Ed.), *Culture and AIDS* (pp. 169–182). New York: Praeger.

Leserman, J., Perkins, D. O., & Evans, D. L. (1992). Coping with the threat of AIDS: The role of social support. *American Journal of Psychiatry, 149,* 1514–1520.

Lester, P., Partridge, J. C., Chesney, M. A., & Cooke, M. (1995). The consequences of a positive prenatal HIV antibody test for women. *Journal of Acquired Immune Deficiency Syndrome Human Retrovirol, 10,* 341–349.

Linn, J. G., Lewis, F. M., Cain, V. A., & Kimbrough, G. A. (1993). HIV-illness, social support, sense of coherence, and psychosocial well-being in a sample of help-seeking adults. *Aids Education and Prevention, 5,* 254–262.

Longo, M. B., Spross, J. A., & Locke, A. M. (1990). Identifying major concerns of persons with acquired immunodeficiency syndrome: A replication. *Clinical Nurse Specialist, 4,* 21–26.

Mansergh, G., Marks, G., & Simoni, J. M. (1995). Self-disclosure of HIV infection among men who vary in time since seropositive diagnosis and symptomatic status. *AIDS, 9,* 639–644.

Marzuk, P. M., Tierney, H., Tardiff, K., Gross, E. M., Morgan, E. B., Hsu, M. A., & Mann, J. J. (1988). Increased risk of suicide in persons with AIDS. *Journal of the American Medical Association, 259,* 1333–1337.

Mason, H. R. C., Marks, G., Simoni, J. M., & Ruiz, M. S. (1995). Culturally sanctioned secrets? Latino men's nondisclosure of HIV infection to family, friends, and lovers. *Health Psychology, 14,* 6–12.

McClure, J. B., Catz, S. L., Prejean, J., Brantley, P. J., & Jones, G. N. (1996). Factors associated with depression in a heterogeneous HIV-infected sample. *Journal of Psychosomatic Research, 40,* 407–415.

McDonell, J. R., Abell, N., & Miller, J. (1991). Family members' willingness to care for people with AIDS: A psychosocial assessment model. *Social Work, 36,* 45–53.

Mischel, M. H. (1988). Uncertainty in illness. *Image: Journal of Nursing Research, 20,* 225–232.

Namir, S., Wolcott, D. L., & Fawzy, F. I. (1989). Social support and HIV spectrum disease: Clinical and research perspectives. *Psychiatric Medicine, 7,* 97–105.

Nichols, S. E. (1985). Psychosocial reactions of persons with the acquired immunodeficiency syndrome. *Annals of Internal Medicine, 103,* 765–767.

Nyamathi, A., Flaskerud, J., Leake, B., & Chen, S. (1996). Impoverished women at risk for AIDS: Social support variables. *Journal of Psychosocial Nursing in Mental Health Service, 34,* 31–39.

Pakenham, K. I., Dadds, M. R., & Terry, D. J. (1994). Relationships between adjustment to HIV and both social support and coping. *Journal of Consulting and Clinical Psychology, 62,* 1194–1203.

Persson, E. (1994). The threat of AIDS to the health of women. *International Journal of Gynecology & Obstetrics, 46*, 189–193.

Petronio, S. (1991). Communication boundary management: A theoretical model of managing disclosure of private information between married couples. *Communication Theory, 4*, 311–335.

Pryor, J. B., & Reeder, G. D. (1993). Collective and individual representations of HIV/AIDS stigma. In J. Pryor & G. Reeder (Eds.), *The social psychology of HIV infection* (pp. 263–286). Hillsdale, NJ: Lawrence Erlbaum Associates.

Ritchie, E. C., Radke, A. Q., & Ross, B. (1992). Depression and support systems in male army HIV+ patients. *Military Medicine, 157*, 345–349.

Simoni, J. M., Mason, H. R. C., Marks, G., Ruiz, M. S. (1995). Women's self-disclosure of HIV infection: Rates, reasons, and reactions. *Journal of Consulting and Clinical Psychology, 63*, 474–478.

Smith, M. Y., & Rapkin, B. D. (1995). Unmet needs for help among persons with AIDS. *AIDS Care, 7*, 353–363.

St. Lawrence, J. S., Husfeldt, B. A., Kelly, J. A., Hood, H. V., Smith, Jr., S. (1990). The stigma of AIDS: Fear of disease and prejudice toward gay men. *Journal of Homosexuality, 19*, 85–101.

Stewart, M. J., Hart, G., & Mann, K. V. (1995). Living with hemophilia and HIV/AIDS: Support and coping. *Journal of Advanced Nursing, 22*, 1101–1111.

Stoddard, T. B., & Rieman, W. (1990). AIDS and the rights of the individual: Toward a more sophisticated understanding of discrimination. *Milbank Quarterly, 68*(Suppl. 1), 143–174.

Zich, J., & Temoshok, L. (1987). Perceptions of social support in men with AIDS and ARC: Relationships with distress and hardiness. *Journal of Applied Social Psychology, 17*, 193–215.

28

The Margins of Communication: Coping With Adult Dementia

Joachim Knuf
University of Kentucky

Keywords: Alzheimer's disease, dementia, senile, communication competence, caregiving

There are many margins to communication. They come with the social environment and make some of us less accessible than others. History, geography, and fate slot us into communities that preserve their identities at such margins. Language itself is marginal, as we struggle to overcome, despite the ambiguities of our words and the gaps they leave, the interpersonal spaces that separate distinct selves. So, what could be more central to human experience than these margins? Isn't that which is furthest from the center also the outer boundary at which we open up, expand our horizons, negotiate our senses of reality? Center and margin define the ancient dialectic of belonging and exclusion; the potential to be truly human, of fellowship, does not exist deeply buried within us. It must be fulfilled by venturing to the edge of comfort, by reaching beyond our grasp, by turning our own margins and those of others into a commons for us all. In a scholarly sense, this is also what is undertaken in this chapter.

Margins, then, present vital opportunities—but only to those who go there. Those who do find many rewards, yet in the process they also come to face some basic truths: All margins are raw, for the fundamental dichotomy of inside and outside, of I and you, of self and other, is constantly contended, sometimes because we wish, more often because we must. Any sojourn at our own margins, however, invariably extracts a price on the center, and justification for that expense can only be made in terms of the resources of the commons that have to be claimed. As humans, we become increasingly sufficient, then, not by retreating into the innermost strongholds of selfhood, but by making ourselves uncomfortable, by engaging others, by risking the rawness of life.

Communication theory, as it has been formulated over the past half-century or so, has been, in the main, a theory of agency. In numerous versions, diligently listed in recent compendia (e.g., Infante, Rancer, & Womack, 1993; Littlejohn, 1996), theorists have conceived of the communication process roughly like this: An individual who wants to communicate with another realizes this goal in the process of encoding a message, commonly into spoken language, which is then received and decoded by the communicative partner. Some kind of understanding results from this, allowing the two to coordinate their actions in a purposeful manner. Moreover, the experience of the process affects the participants' perceptions of their relationship and selfhood, as well as creating expectations for the future.

When understanding fails to result from communication, sources of interference are sought. They affect, among other factors, accessibility, attention, message processing, interpretation, and retention, and they range widely. Some are associated with the biological substrate, others explain filters and distractions at the emotional or cognitive level, or describe message effects resulting from social influence and power. Interferences are conceived of as subtractive: The integrity of communication is defined by their absence.

The family resemblance between spoken, written, and gestural forms of messages; between audiences of one or of many; and between face-to-face and mediated encounters are strong, although some uniqueness exists. Whatever format and circumstance, the literature advises that communication should be both appropriate and effective, so that its impact on socio-cultural, including ethical, systems, as well as on the emotions of audiences must be judged. Effectiveness implies that messages are not without their purposes; those producing responses commensurate with what (notwithstanding the exhortations of linguistic philosophers and postmodern social theorists) is simply referred to here as their "intent," are judged to be higher in effectiveness. In interpersonal communication theory, for example, this sense of purpose, of appropriate and effective communicative agency, is reflected in the central notion of competence (e.g., Spitzberg & Cupach, 1984).

In truth, however, communication is much more precarious, even under the best of circumstances. As explained elsewhere (Knuf, 1992) and briefly in sections of this chapter, any level of understanding is a collaborative achievement whose highest debt is to the social bonds that extract, at some point in human interactions, the necessary acknowledgment that communication was successful—and this despite the fact that thoughts are locked exclusively in individual minds and conveyed to others by only the most imperfect means: words. The effectiveness of communication is then commensurate with our courage to visit the margins mapped.

This argument is presented with only one purpose in mind: to persuade the reader that, given the multiple marginality of all communication, any margins that derive from physical and cognitive disabilities may certainly appear more raw, but they are not at all special. Although they present their own forms of challenge, the same means that help us create a satisfactory sense of communicative accomplishment should serve us here equally well. Unfortunately, this realization is not generally shared. Therefore, this chapter puts forward the case by discussing some communicative dimensions of adult dementia, especially Alzheimer's disease.

INTRODUCTION

Approximately 4 million Americans are afflicted with Alzheimer's disease and related disorders (ADRD), and at least 20 million U.S. families are directly affected (Alzheimer's Association, 1998). ADRD is the leading cause of dementia in the aging population (Merriam et al., 1988), insidious in onset, and without known cure. The disease is often not recognized by family members, who may be engaged in care for considerable time before a diagnosis is made. Those with ADRD, their family members, and their other caregivers face a barrage of challenges directly attributable to the disease. ADRD brings with it many behavioral changes, including, most profoundly, memory impairment, restlessness and agitation, as well as shifts in mood and personality. The afflicted individual experiences an irreversible deterioration of cognitive and physical abilities and the desperation and emotional trauma associated with this. Family members and significant others take on escalating emotional, physical, and financial burdens that may make them, in turn, dependent on additional support, indeed, turn them into "hidden victims" (Zarit, Orr, & Zarit, 1985).

As the disease progresses, supervision and care needs increase, and more and more of the activities of daily living depend on support. Often, caregivers struggle on many fronts: The person they care for may not recognize them or their surroundings; become incontinent, confused about time, space, and identities; resist and abuse those around them and exhibit other behavioral patterns difficult to manage, such as agitation, hiding things, and wandering. Simultaneously, those not involved in direct contact and care may engage in denial and avoidance, often driven by the fear that they might share a genetic or demographic predisposition to the disease. This withdrawal increases the isolation of caregivers and adds to their burden, especially since frequently the primary caregiver is an elderly spouse or daughter. Not surprisingly, caregivers report having fewer social resources and contacts with friends and family (George & Gwyther, 1986; Johnson & Catalano, 1983; Reese et al., 1994). Finally, caregivers bring to their task unspoken assumptions and fears, insufficient knowledge of the disease, and open emotional agendas that affect them, their care, and the person for whom they care. The rawness at the social and emotional margins of care for another is hence very much in evidence.

Query and Flint (1996) described this situation in terms of a symbolic crisis in which adequate coping skills are difficult to obtain. One obstacle is the faulty assignment of meaning. Persons with ADRD and their family members and caregivers may construe alternative meaning around the disease that inhibits a full understanding of the diagnosis and its consequences. Denial plays a considerable role here. Second, coping skills are especially difficult to develop in an environment where social relationships are challenged all the time. Caregivers review their commitment to kin and friendship bonds according to perceived levels of disease acuity and received support. The illness may invert or redefine parent–child or husband–wife roles, and may eventually turn inherently reciprocal roles into nonreciprocal ones. Comprehensive readjustments in established routines, such as moving the cared-for family member into the caregiver's home or sacrificing careers to the care task, add to the burden. Finally, ADRD forces persons to adjust their own sense of self, an impoverished self, as the grasp on the mundane world and crucial relationships begins to slip.

LANGUAGE AND COMMUNICATION

What does research tell us about the role of language and communication in all this? Forms of senile dementia such as ADRD erode the capacity of persons to speak and understand language and to communicate effectively by linguistic means with their environment, and most important, of course, with their caregivers (Miller, 1989). A deterioration process that may differ individually both in the length and nature of the impairment (see, e.g., Filley, Kelly, & Heaton, 1986; Seltzer & Sherwin, 1983) precedes the complete cessation of speech.

The neurolinguistic and psycholinguistic literature has addressed such issues mostly from a cognitive perspective, for example, in studies of semantic memory (Gewirth, Schindler, & Hier, 1984; Ober et al., 1986; Pietro & Goldfarb, 1985). Since the 1970s, many studies have assessed forms and stages of aphasia, of the partial or complete inability to use and understand words, by a variety of instruments (see, e.g., Appell, Kertesz, & Fisman, 1982; Cummings et al., 1985; Kertesz, Appell, & Fisman, 1986; Murdoch et al., 1987). Although results differ, all these studies report language impairment of some sort in Alzheimer's patients, mostly of semantic aspects, such as naming and word fluency (see, e.g., Ober et al., 1986), including declining oral and reading comprehension and writing competence (Faber-Langendoen et al., 1988). Phonology and syntax appear more resistant to degeneration (Appell et al., 1982; Bayles, 1982; Bayles & Kazniak, 1987; Cummings et al., 1985). Paradigmatic functions then succumb to the disease much more readily than syntagmatic functions, so that sentences result that appear to be relatively well-formed grammatically, but that contain words or expressions that do not necessarily reflect the purposes of the speaker. However, these studies focus nearly exclusively on cognitive and linguistic competencies. They are informed by a theory of language that focuses on meaning as residing in words and sentences (i.e., in text) rather than in the integration of utterances and their context, (i.e., in messages). Hence, they tell us less than one would believe about the ability of those with ADRD to communicate with people in their environment. Indeed, despite a nascent interest in this area, a communicative perspective in dementia research, especially one interested in naturally occurring behavior, remains rare (some exceptions include Bohling, 1991; Hamilton, 1994; Kemper & Lyons, 1994; Knuf, 1994a, 1994b, 1996; Knuf, Gillotti, & Colon, 1993; Lubinski, 1991; Ulatowska, Allard, & Donnell, 1988) but is beginning to supersede earlier work primarily based in nursing experience (e.g., Dawson et al., 1986; Farran & Keane-Hagerty, 1989).

Communicative Competence

Communication is a highly complex phenomenon to which language and cognition are only partial constituents. Semantic proficiency, then, must not be equated with the ability to communicate—it is only one among several factors contributing to the outcome of the communication process. Beyond cognitive and linguistic competencies, communication is the interactive accomplishment of mutual understanding in situated encounters through the use of largely conventional sign systems. Communication competence hence cannot be measured individually but only interstitially, between communicators. Although the expressive capabilities of a speaker clearly matter, the most eloquent phrase will remain enigmatic unless adequately interpreted and acted on by a listener. Note that complete understanding remains an elusive ideal: The content of another's thought remains forever hidden from us.

Communication processes are both fallible and collaborative. Language is by nature elliptic, vague, and ambiguous, so that both speaker and listener must incorporate situational information to make sense of the messages that are exchanged. Words carry meaning not in complete independence from their context of use but rather serve to cue meanings both referentially and indexically (Knuf, 1992), that is, by accessing both knowledge and the salient spatio–temporal, personal, and social parameters of the situation in which they are uttered. Vagueness and ambiguity, necessary features of any natural language, are problems in every instance of communicative interaction. Indeed, the social nature of interactions, the rules people respect and enact, take precedence over the propositional content of mundane talk, so that understanding does not simply depend on the semantic meaning of words and phrases but results from the social contract inherent to any encounter.

The communicative approach taken in this chapter deemphasizes the importance of purely cognitive and linguistic capabilities of persons with ADRD. Rather than measuring their deficiencies, it places the investigation of their competencies in the interpersonal framework of care recipient and caregiver, in which mutual understanding is negotiated and achieved. As the disease progresses, communication outcomes will naturally come to depend more and more on the contributions of the caregiver rather than on those of the person with ADRD. However, both partners continue to benefit from situational factors, that is, from manifest clues the environment makes available for use as conversational resources, as well as the conventional clues they develop in their relationship. In these special encounters, then, ancillary private codes, historically established between the communication partners, achieve a viability they do not have in public (Knuf, 1992).

Paradigmatic and Syntagmatic Language Features

As a consequence of the fallible and collaborative nature of communication, syntagmatic features of language assume a particular importance for the mutual construction of meaning. These include morphological, syntactic, and lexical elements that create coherence in talk and that introduce into sentences and utterances features properly belonging to the external communication situation, which will be described in the following sections.

In particular, successful communicative understanding depends on a class of functional lexemes that affect the overall meaning of utterances. Members of this class serve to point out the relationship between utterance constituents and their textual, social, and physical contexts. Such indicating expressions are know as *deictics*. They anchor utterances in the spatial, temporal, personal, social, and textual frameworks in which they occur: the here and now, the you and I, and the context of what already has been said and will be said. The use of deictic elements is hence the single most important key to understanding the relationship between a sentence and its words and their referents in the world; these relationships are not stable but require ongoing interpretation in changing contexts and, in view of the mechanics of conversation, especially in turn taking.

This feature of the linguistic code system is then of particular importance for understanding the discourse of persons with ADRD and their caregivers. Clearly, a loss of, say, 25% of the referential lexemes of a language, the words used to name things, actions, qualities, and so forth, constitutes an incapacitation. It does not, however, affect the success of communication as much as a commensurate loss of syntagmatic features, of the rules by which words are connected into sentences, as the work on senile dementia (Bayles, 1982; Fromm & Holland, 1989) and on aphasia has shown (e.g., Jakobson, 1968, 1971). Personal vocabularies differ by at least this factor, and basic English operates adequately with a set of about a thousand words. Moreover, Bohling (1991) showed quite convincingly how, in the naturalistic talk of persons with ADRD, their conversational partners as actively interpretive and context-aware listeners are able to substitute defective utterances with more appropriate items from the respective paradigmatic set (e.g., recognizing that talk about a "button" is talk about a "shirt"), and how conversations then come to make sufficient sense. This is accomplished through careful attention to clues imbedded in the immediate communicative context or available from encyclopedic knowledge. Whereas the ability to access referential lexemes then plays a considerable role in communication, but one that can be partially compensated for through interpretive listening, indexical lexemes as well as indexical morphemes establishing the essential deictic reference frame in a conversation are at least as important for its successful outcome.

Persons with ADRD are clearly challenged in the communicative area. Their lexicon deteriorates, obstructing access to words roughly in proportion to their frequency of use. Fortunately, deictic words have a special status in this respect. Pronouns, demonstratives, temporal and spatial adverbs, and other deictics, the elements that establish the semantic relationships among utterance elements and between utterance elements and their contexts, are among the most frequent words and morphemes in language. Their use in communicating with persons with ADRD and close attention to their production in these individuals' talk is hence of greatest importance not only from a scholarly perspective but also in the everyday practice of interacting with patients.

DEICTIC ELEMENTS IN THE TALK OF PERSONS WITH ALZHEIMER'S

Deictic elements encode the speaker's reference framework designed to instruct the listener to decode the relationship between phrases themselves and between phrases and their external referents (Anderson & Keenan, 1985; Fillmore, 1971, 1975). Deixis is a common phenomenon in language. It is "the single most obvious way in which the relationship between language and context is reflected in the structures of languages themselves" (Levinson, 1983, p. 54). Deictic elements such as pronouns and demonstratives serve as indexical signs to circumstances outside language and enable their integration into messages in a direct manner. At the same time, they depend on a mutual awareness of the material and social circumstances of a conversation that provide it with an obligatory, though negotiable, reference framework. Clearly, the message: "Meet me here a week from now with a stick this big" (Levinson, 1983) lacks all appropriate reference when found in a bottle washed up on a beach.

Several kinds of deixis can be distinguished. Person deixis encodes the role of the participants in a conversation, place (or spatial) deixis locations, time (or temporal) deixis temporal points and spans, discourse (or textual) deixis segments of text, and social deixis the relative status of interactors. In actual utterances, however, many deictic elements exhibit more than one such nature. They serve not only to establish the deictic center, the "I" and "you," the "here" and "now," as the interpretation framework for the conversation but also accomplish the respective shifts in deictic projection necessitated by the consecutive arrangement of speaking turns. As Spekman (1983) wrote, "the correct/incorrect usage of deictics would thus appear to reflect an individual's ability to establish this shared perspective" (p. 170).

In an early stage of language acquisition, children acquire a single deictic element that serves simply to draw attention to some referent. Lyons (1977, p. 648) assumed that this deictic is initially quasi-referential and not truly referential, since it is still relatively unfocused and does not select the referent very clearly (e.g., it could refer to an agent, say, a dog, or the agent's behavior, or both). Not much later it begins to reference features of children's environment that arouse their interest. In the two-word and then the three-word stage, children learn to combine this deictic with a small number of words to form utterances that express some attitude toward their referents. Hence, a combination of deictic and word can serve to identify ("This is an X") or express a need ("I want X") or an interest ("Look, an X"). Thereafter the usage of deictics becomes more complex, until in its full development speakers routinely bring about alignments in rapidly shifting spatio–temporal and social reference frameworks that change with every new speaking turn and conversational topic in discourse.

Clearly, there are differences between the acquisition process of deictic elements and the erosion process leading to dementia, although we do not understand the second process very well at this stage. In acquisition, the conceptual association of space and, to a lesser degree, of person and time, precede their full instantiation in language. Adults with dementia, on the other hand, appear to lose conceptual associations before the language disappears. However, very little is known about this crucial aspect of impairment.

As mentioned, persons with ADRD encounter specific problems in using deixis in communication to access the connection between the linguistic system and the external world. Disorientation is particularly evident in their encoding of space, time, and personal identity.

Deictics support the recognition of such relationships on two levels. Gestural or indexical deictics ("The milk is *over there*"), acquired first, point at referents that are common objects of perception in a shared reference frame, and, from case to case, verbal messages may be complemented by the production of appropriate nonverbal signals. In the more complex case, deixis is effected symbolically. A phrase such as "The milk is *in* the refrigerator" can only be understood in reference to encyclopedic knowledge (such as, what does a refrigerator look like, is it a container, can it be opened). Indexical deictics are hence much more immediate, directly support acts of perception, whereas symbolic deictics do so only indirectly. Note, however, that deictics probably always combine symbolic and indexical qualities, although in each given context one will tend to be dominant.

In view of the nature of this form of senile dementia, it is safe to assume that as their disease progresses, the talk of persons with ADRD will evidence an increasing reliance on the use of indexical deictics, whereas the capacity for symbolic deixis will slowly erode. This assumption is supported circumstantially by studies of nominal dysphasia, of the inability to properly name things (e.g., Skelton-Robinson & Jones, 1984), which found that introduction of objects to be named into the visual field of persons with ADRD improved their naming ability.

A related issue important to understanding communication between patient and caregiver is marking. In English, many deictic elements come in converse pairs, one member of which is marked, the other unmarked. The demonstrative "this," for example, is marked (or more specific), whereas "that" is unmarked (and less specific). The differentiation on which marking is based develops later than the single deictic. An understanding needs to be gained, therefore, of whether deictic pairs conflate into single terms at some point in the disease process and how such conflated terms then function in conversations. This question matters in the attempt to understand the cognition of persons with ADRD, since their use of marking provides evidence for a reconstruction of the way in which their discourse sorts elements of the world into oppositional, proximal, and nonproximal patterns.

In sum, attention to deictic elements in the conversations persons with ADRD conduct with their caregivers minimizes a problem associated with past linguistic research in this field. Whereas the present psycholinguistic, especially semantic, focus of studies on memory and knowledge has made it extremely difficult to isolate features of language use from cognitive functions affected by dementia, the attention to deixis highlights explicitly the ways in which linkages of utterance–internal elements and their context of production are accomplished. Compared with current concerns with paradigmatic or lexical features of language impairment, this new syntagmatic focus provides a much more sophisticated picture of how language is used to construct the elementary pragmatic relationships between speaker and listener in which both cooperate in the construction of meaning, aided by mutual reference to the concrete communication context. Let us look at some examples next, especially of person and spatial deictic usage. These data were excerpted from an interview with an older woman with advanced Alzheimer's;[1] please note how these conversations exceed the expectations linguistic deficiency studies would suggest, and how they could be even more productive through the observation of both commonsensical conversational rules and of additional interpretive listening efforts.

PERSON DEIXIS

On the whole, it appears that persons with ADRD have little difficulty determining and applying the correct pronominal form for speaker and addressee in a conversation, that is, for the first and second person pronoun, particularly in its singular form. Both are considered given information in linguistic pragmatics, since in most talking situations speaker and addressee are visually (or at least audibly) salient to participants in the conversation, who take turns at filling these complementary roles. In particular, the first person singular is indexically deictic when the speaker is thus conspicuous and tangible (Knuf, 1993). Under the conditions of such concrete, face-to-face encounters, the conversations of persons with ADRD do not differ from those of healthy adults ("I" is the interviewer, "W" the person with ADRD)[2]:

1. I: Do you like chicken?
2. W: I like- I like fried chicken.

An adequate representation of third parties poses greater problems. For as Lyons (1977) noted, third person is fundamentally different from first or second person. First person carries the principal speaking role, second person a subsidiary role, but third person does not correlate with any positive participant role. Logically, third parties can be present in the situation, hence salient, or absent, hence nonsalient. Situational salience normally allows speakers with ADRD to handle pronominal reference adequately, which can be called a *situational reference*:

1. I: And who's this? Over here- with you.
2. W: That's Nancy.

3. I: She's your daughter, right?
4. W: Yeah.
5. I: How many- how many kids do you have? Is Nancy your baby?
6. W: (Laughs) I don't know when she was my baby or not! I guess
      so (laughs again).

Some of the confusion in this instance results from packaging two distinct information requests into the same utterance (5); the substitution of "when" for the more logical "if" in (6) results from a break in the temporal frame of the conversation (Bohling, 1991; Goffman, 1974), transporting W into a frame defined by the birth of her daughter. Obviously, attention to careful frame management, particularly an avoidance of introducing more than one frame at a time, is of great benefit in such conversations.

Much more challenging to persons with ADRD is pronominal reference to absent, nonsalient third parties, particularly to third parties featured in narrative passages, that is, to those remote in time or space. This usage can be called *narrative reference*. The English pronominal system differs in its representation of third parties in the singular and plural forms. The third person plural pronoun ("they") is the default lexeme capturing any plurality of persons; it is ambiguous in gender and actual number (larger than one). This makes it relatively vague, and incorrect usage becomes less obvious. In contrast, the third person singular pronoun is more specific. Because English does not express relative status in this (or any other) pronominal form (unlike, e.g., German, Russian, or Spanish), errors arise primarily from a confusion or conflation of gender in narrative reference. Gender is most easily confused or conflated when the noun replaced in the narrative by the pronoun carries no clear gender information, as is the case with "teacher":

1. W: When I was in schoo:l . I'd have to hold my book up here right
      here?
2. I: Uhu-
3. W: An' uh . teacher would hold it . back like this, you know? You
      know how . teachers . do.
4. I: Uhum-
5. W: And . uh (4) and I would cry.
6. I: (How old?)
7. W: Oh, I don't remember when that- how old I was. But . I
      start(ed) cryin.' (.8) And uh . she looked up to me and she said, uh,

"Lucille, why are you crying for?" And I said (imitating girl's crying voice) "Well, when you take the book away from me, I can't *see*." (chuckles) And, and . uh. I never will forget that. And, uh, he said- she said . uh . "Why I ain't gonna take it- take that away from you." And I said, "We:ll," I says, "I can't *see*." 'N' he says, "Whaddya mean you can't see?" And I said, (speeding up and getting louder) "Well," I said, "I can't see out of my *e::yes!*"

8. I: (chuckles)
9. W: 'N' I- And I let her know . what=
10. I: =What the problem was, yeah.

In (7), W describes an encounter with a teacher in her youth. She introduces the teacher as female. She later switches to the male pronoun but self-corrects immediately. Still, her error persists, for the next pronoun referring to the teacher is again male, and this time there is no correction. After an unproductive interruption by I, who attempts to break the frame of the narrative, W concludes her telling and returns to the female pronominal form. The teacher is never identified by name, an element of salience that would have helped gender discrimination. W's account is complex, well organized in its narrative elements, and funny; it is an accomplishment of high order and deserves respect. Interruptions (6) and collaborative closings (10) may have brought the telling to an untimely end.

Unfortunately, depending on the progress of the disease, even visual salience may not suffice in a given situation. In the following passage, W looks at a picture of some persons she is asked to identify:

1. I: Well, I wanted to take a look at some of these pictures you have over here. Pictures you have around your around.
2. W: There?
3. I: Uhuh. This one. Do you know who that is?
4. W: Yeah.
5. I: Who is that?
6. W: That's her and that's him. (laughs)
7. I: (laughs) That's Toni
8. W: Uhuh.
9. I: and her husband.
10. W: Uhuh, yeah.

We see here how pronouns are used to signify the proper names of the individuals (W's daughter and her husband). W's positive answer to the request to name the individuals in (4) may indicate that she is aware of these identities, even if unable to put a name against the images. Alternatively, this may be a gambit to escape the naming task, since she uses the third person pronoun in an anaphoric sense, suggesting to I that the two individuals are prior topics of conversation—thereby invalidating the naming task (Knuf, 1994a).

SPATIAL DEIXIS

Spatial deixis poses greater challenges to persons with ADRD. Personal reference is relatively simple, whereas references to spatial phenomena can be much more challenging, and some languages have developed systems much more complex than English (Anderson & Keenan, 1985).

Research on the linguistic competency of persons with ADRD reports that they progressively abandon full reference in their language. The capacity to use symbolic referential terms is gradually lost. Such speakers depend, much more than healthy adults, on the situational presence of the referents of the words they use, and we can see how word realism, overcome in youth, reasserts itself.

Lack of capacity to use deictics in a symbolic sense ("on top of the dining table") and the dependence on more indexical elements ("there"), including an ancillary gestural code (Knuf, 1992), is evident in cases where normally symbolic deictics devolve into their indexical function. In the following passage, W describes a locality:

1. W: And then the road goes like down this way.
2. I: Uh huh.
3. W: And uh, then you go back over here on this side.
4. I: (quietly) OK.

The videotape makes it obvious that nonverbal gestures compensate for a description that could have been provided with respect to some abstractly describable point of reference. As Tanz (1980) remarked about spatial deictics:

> In their symbolic sense, the relationship is defined in terms of attributes inherent in the reference object, its permanent directional features. In the indexical sense of these expressions, the spatial relationship is defined jointly

by the position of the reference object and by the position of a participant in the speech act. (p. 6)

Let us look at the exemplary case of the common English spatial demonstratives, "this" and "that," both indices of entities that "contrast along a dimension that is defined with respect to a deictic variable: proximity to the speaker" (Tanz, 1980, p. 6).

In English "this" is a marked demonstrative, "that" is unmarked (Lyons, 1977; Tfouni & Klatzky, 1983). "This" and "that" form a converse pair, and their appropriate distributive usage in brief exchanges is not problematic for speakers with ADRD (and W's response makes it clear that she perceives such a banal topic of conversation as disparaging her sense of self-worth):

1. I: What's this? Right here.
2. W: That's your watch, ain' it?

How do these demonstratives differ? Simply, unmarked lexemes require less cognitive processing than marked ones. Although one might conclude that the unmarked demonstrative "that" is more prominent in the talk of persons with ADRD, such reasoning does not take into consideration the nature of this form of dementia. Since the temporal span of these speakers' memories is restricted, they have instead a greater need for marking—more precisely, to renew marking—in their talk. Indeed, in some 25 transcript pages of the conversation between I and W, W used the marked demonstrative ("this") 41 times, the unmarked demonstrative ("that") 81 times—a ratio of 1:2. The interviewer produced 27 marked demonstratives and 94 unmarked demonstratives—a ratio of 1:3.5. This finding suggests that there is considerably less need for marking in unimpaired discourse.

Linguists suggest that, in contrast to "that," a distal spatial deictic referring to things removed from the present discourse, "this" is a proximal spatial deictic that introduces new information. Clearly, persons with ADRD, who depend much more on situational rather than narrative reference, should not be able to match unimpaired speakers' usage of deictics that point to things removed from the present discourse. Moreover, "this," because of its conversation-initial position, also marks the topic of a conversation. Speakers with ADRD then have to introduce topic (or, from the perspective of their conversational partners, reintroduce topic) more often than unimpaired speakers. For the latter, active listening for topic

introductions can then provide much better understanding; active placement of topic markers in commensurably short sequence by unimpaired
speakers should also improve the ability of their impaired listeners to stay
focused on the topic of the ongoing conversation. The preference for proximal, marked demonstratives also speaks, in the author's opinion, to a
concern of persons with ADRD with following conversational rules. In
other words, they prefer to err on the side of conversational fluency or to
"oversuppose and understate" (Schegloff, 1979, p. 50). This, indeed, is in
keeping with the normal rules of conversation.

OPPORTUNITIES

Although this chapter is not a complete survey of discourse features of those
with ADRD, it offers valuable information that applies to a wider range
of cognitive disabilities. Paramount is the need for active and interpretive
listening. As Bohling (1991) suggested, incorrect words in impaired talk
provide cues to related words that do make sense, missing words may be
fragments of common idioms, contextual horizons may be limited, some
expressions archaic, and reference to old memories may be easier than that
to recent ones. Consistently, identification of such ruptures is made easier
by attention to the active reference frames of the discourse in terms of time,
space, identity, topic, context, and external situation.

The examples discussed above reinforce this advice. They point especially to the need for caregivers to keep the topic of the conversation clearly,
unambiguously, and actively in the awareness of the impaired speaker, to
avoid narrative reference of low salience, to choose specific and repeated
references to identities, time, space, and other external elements over complex deictics. A name, for example, is always a richer cue than a pronoun,
"after lunch" more substantive than "later." Caregivers should also keep in
mind that topical coherence in talk is predicated on a temporal competence
that progressively eludes persons with ADRD.

Most of all, though, it must be understood that impaired speakers struggle
with the same challenges, albeit on a larger scale, that everyone faces:
ambiguity, elision, forgetfulness, vagueness, and the humbling experience
that what was so clear in our own minds ends up as a jumble of words
that strain comprehension. Impaired speakers should never be judged by
a casual assessment of their communications; they retain a keen sense of
their predicament and struggle for control in their lives—yet they contribute

to the commons in defiance of adversity. By facing the rawness of our communication margins with those whose abilities come at a greater cost, we all have an opportunity to give dignity and receive wisdom.

REFERENCES

Alzheimer's Association. (1998). Understanding Alzheimer's. [On-line]. http://www.alz.org/facts/ index.htm.

Anderson, S. R., & Keenan, E. L. (1985). Deixis. In T. Shopen (Ed.), *Language typology and syntactic description. Vol. 3. Grammatical categories and the lexicon* (pp. 259–308). Cambridge, UK: Cambridge University Press.

Appell, J., Kertesz, A., & Fisman, M. (1982). A study of language functioning in Alzheimer's patients. *Brain and Language, 17,* 73–91.

Bayles, K. A. (1982). Language function in senile dementia. *Brain and Language, 16,* 265–280.

Bayles, K. A., & Kaszniak, A. W. (1987). *Communication and cognition in normal aging and dementia.* Boston: College Press.

Bohling, H. R. (1991). Communication with Alzheimer's patients: An analysis of caregiver listening patterns. *International Journal of Aging and Human Development, 33,* 249–267.

Cummings, J. L., Benson, D. F., Hill, M. A., & Read, S. (1985). Aphasia in dementia of the Alzheimer type. *Neurology, 35,* 394–397.

Dawson, P., Kline, K., Wiancko, D. C., & Wells, D. (1986). Preventing express disability in patients with Alzheimer's disease. *Geriatric Nursing, 7,* 298–301.

Faber-Langendoen, K., Morris, J. C., Knesevich, J. W., LaBarge, E., Miller, J. P., & Berg, L. (1988). Aphasia in senile dementia of the Alzheimer type. *Annals of Neurology, 23,* 365–370.

Farran, C. J., & Keane-Hagerty, E. (1989). Communicating effectively with dementia patients. *Journal of Psychosocial Nursing and Mental Health Services, 27*(5), 13–16.

Filley, C. M., Kelly, J., & Heaton, R. K. (1986). Neuropsychological features of early- and late-onset Alzheimer's disease. *Archives of Neurology, 43,* 571–576.

Fillmore, C. J. (1971). Towards a theory of deixis. *The PCCLLU Papers, 3,* 219–241.

Fillmore, C. J. (1975). *Santa Cruz lectures on deixis.* Indiana University Linguistics Club, Bloomington, Indiana.

Fromm, D., & Holland, A. L. (1989). Functional communication in Alzheimer's disease. *Journal of Speech and Hearing Disorders, 54,* 535–540.

George, L. K., & Gwyther, L. P. (1986). Caregiver well-being: A multidimensional examination of family caregivers of demented adults. *The Gerontologist, 26,* 253–259.

Gewirth, L. R., Schindler, A. G., & Hier, D. B. (1984). Altered patterns of word association in dementia and aphasia. *Brain and Language, 21,* 307–317.

Goffman, E. (1974). *Frame analysis: An essay on the organization of experience.* Cambridge, MA: Harvard University Press.

Hamilton, H. E. (1994). *Conversations with an Alzheimer's patient. An interactional sociolinguistic study.* Cambridge, UK: Cambridge University Press.

Infante, D. A., Rancer, A. S., & Womack, D. F. (1993). *Building communication theory.* Prospect Heights, IL: Waveland Press.

Jakobson, R. (1968). *Child language, aphasia, and phonological universals.* Paris: Mouton.

Jakobson, R. (1971). Two aspects of language and two types of aphasic disturbances. In R. Jakobson & M. Halle (Eds.), *Fundamentals of language* (2nd ed., pp. 67–96). (Janua Linguarum, Series Minor, 1). Paris: Mouton.

Johnson, C. L., & Catalano, D. J. (1983). A longitudinal study of family supports of impaired elderly. *The Gerontologist, 23*, 612–618.

Kemper, S., & Lyons, K. (1994). The effects of Alzheimer's dementia on language and communication. In M. L. Hummert, J. M. Wiemann, & J. F. Nussbaum (Eds.), *Interpersonal communication in older adulthood. Interdisciplinary theory and research* (pp. 58–82). Thousand Oaks: Sage.

Kertesz, A., Appell, J., & Fisman, M. (1986). The dissolution of language in Alzheimer's disease. *Canadian Journal of Neurological Science, 13*, 415–418.

Knuf, J. (1992). "Spit first and then say what you want!": Concerning the use of language and ancillary codes in ritualized communication. *Quarterly Journal of Speech, 78*, 466–482.

Knuf, J. (1993, May). *This and that, here and there: Some thoughts on deictic elements in telephone openings.* Paper presented at the annual conference of the International Communication Association, Washington, DC.

Knuf, J. (1994a, November). *Deixis and paradeixis in the talk of Alzheimer's patients.* Paper presented at the annual convention of the Speech Communication Association, New Orleans, LA.

Knuf, J. (1994b, December). *Some thoughts on deixis in the talk of Alzheimer's patients.* Paper presented at the First International Colloquium on Deixis, Lexington, KY.

Knuf, J. (1996, November). *Salience and reference in the talk of Alzheimer's sufferers.* Paper presented at the annual convention of the Speech Communication Association, San Antonio, TX.

Knuf, J., Gillotti, C., & Colon, S. E. (1993, November). *Communicating with Alzheimer's patients: A pragmatic perspective on nonverbal and verbal sign systems.* Paper presented at the annual convention of the Speech Communication Association, Miami Beach, FL.

Levinson, S. C. (1983). *Pragmatics.* Cambridge: Cambridge University Press.

Littlejohn, S. W. (1996). *Theories of human communication.* Belmont, CA: Wadsworth.

Lubinski, R. (Ed.). (1991). *Dementia and communication.* Toronto, Canada: B. C. Decker.

Lyons, J. (1977). *Semantics* (Vols. 1–2). Cambridge, UK: Cambridge University Press.

Merriam, K. M., Aronson, M. K., Gaston, P., Wey, S., & Katz, I. (1988). The psychiatric symptoms of Alzheimer's disease. *Journal of the American Geriatric Association, 36*, 7–12.

Miller, E. (1989). Language impairment in Alzheimer type dementia. *Clinical Psychology Review, 9*, 181–195.

Murdoch, B. E., Chenery, H. J., Wills, V., & Boyle, R. S. (1987). Language disorder in dementia of the Alzheimer type. *Brain and Language, 31*, 122–137.

Ober, B. A., Dronkers, N. F., Koss, E., Delic, D. C., & Friedland, R. P. (1986). Retrieval from semantic memory in Alzheimer-type dementia. *Journal of Clinical and Experimental Neuropsychology, 8*, 75–92.

Pietro, M. J. S., & Goldfarb, R. (1985). Characteristic patterns of word association responses in institutional elderly with and without senile dementia. *Brain and Language, 26*, 230–243.

Query, J. L., Jr. & Flint, L. J. (1996). The caregiving relationship. In N. Vanzetti & S. Duck (Eds.), *A lifetime of relationships* (pp. 456–483). Pacific Grove, CA: Brooks/Cole.

Reese, D. R., Gross, A. M., Smalley, D. L., & Messer, S. C. (1994). Caregivers of Alzheimer's disease and stroke patients: Immunological and psychological considerations. *The Gerontologist, 34*, 534–540.

Schegloff, E. A. (1979). Identification and recognition in telephone conversation openings. In G. Psathas (Ed.), *Everyday language: Studies in ethnomethodology* (pp. 23–78). New York: Irvington.

Seltzer, B., & Sherwin, I. (1983). A comparison of clinical features in early- and late-onset primary degenerative dementia. *Archives of Neurology, 40*, 143–146.

Skelton-Robinson, M., & Jones, S. (1984). Nominal dysphasia and the severity of senile dementia. *British Journal of Psychiatry, 145*, 168–171.

Spekman, N. J. (1983). Verbal communication and role-taking: An analysis of the use of deictics. In R. J. Di Pietro, W. Frawley, & A. Wedel (Eds.), *The first Delaware symposium on language studies. Selected papers* (pp. 168–184). Newark: University of Delaware Press.

Spitzberg, B. H., & Cupach, W. R. (1984). *Interpersonal communication competence.* Beverly Hills, CA: Sage.

Tanz, C. (1980). *Studies in the acquisition of deictic terms*. Cambridge, UK: Cambridge University Press.

Tfouni, L. V., & Klatzky, R. L. (1983). A discourse analysis of deixis: Pragmatic, cognitive and semantic factors in the comprehension of "this," "that," "here" and "there." *Journal of Child Language, 10,* 123–133.

Ulatowska, H. K., Allard, L., & Donnell, A. (1988). Discourse performance in subjects with dementia of the Alzheimer type. In H. Whitaker (Ed.), *Neuropsychological studies in nonfocal brain damage* (pp. 108–131). New York: Springer.

Zarit, S. H., Orr, N. K., & Zarit, J. M. (1985). *The hidden victims of Alzheimer's disease: Families under stress*. New York: New York University Press.

ENDNOTES

1. I am grateful to D. Danner, W. Friesen, and W. Markesbery of the University of Kentucky Sanders-Brown Center on Aging for making these data available.

2. Of the special symbols used in the transcriptions, "-" denotes a break in the sentence, "." a short pause, (3) a pause of 3 seconds, ":" a lengthening of the preceding sound, and "=" marks places in which the utterances of two speakers follow one another without gap.

VI

Setting a Future Agenda for Communication and Disability Research

29

Communication and Disability Research: A Productive Past and a Bright Future

Dawn O. Braithwaite
University of Nebraska-Lincoln

Teresa L. Thompson
University of Dayton

Not long ago, Dawn was reading a manuscript for a journal. It was a disability-related study, so it was not surprising that the editor would send it to her. The author(s) started out with the claim that the communication discipline was not yet involved with disability research. Experienced scholars know that this type of claim is always risky because, even if generally true, the manuscript will be sent to the one person doing some research in that area. Dawn gently told the author that it was probably best not to leave the dock on a manuscript while simultaneously missing the boat! It was easy to refute this author's claim by pointing to the work of a large group of scholars, all of whom are represented in this volume. The editors are glad to see this book come out so that scholars and practitioners inside and outside of the discipline of communication studies can see the significant scholarly contribution available. The editors see this volume as a very meaningful contribution by members of a discipline to an important area of research. However, it would be negligent to see this volume as an endpoint, rather than a starting place. There is still much work to be done. Following is an idea of where the editors think communication scholars need to go from here as they make a contribution to the lives and experiences of those people who are disabled and those with whom they live, work, and play.

INTERPERSONAL RELATIONSHIPS

Most of the early work on communication and disability focused on the interpersonal realm, emphasizing such issues as self-disclosure, verbal and nonverbal behaviors of and toward people with disabilities, and how people with disabilities reduce uncertainty and communicate in helping situations. An examination of the research literature shows that most of the research is on strangers in early stages of relational formation. This is important, of course, but there is a serious need to understand how disability affects the communication of people with disabilities and their relational partners over the life of the relationship. How does becoming disabled affect an ongoing relationship, and how do those who are disabled form and maintain healthy relationships?

Communication scholars also need to increase their sophistication theoretically. They need to move beyond the use of Goffman's stigma theory. This was groundbreaking and important work, yet it is now well established by scholars across many disciplines, including communication, that people with disabilities are part of the group of stigmatized persons. Revisiting this territory is not all that fruitful. Some progress has begun, as is reflected in this volume. For instance, the editors are very excited about the work of those looking at disability from a feminist perspective, looking at such issues as embodiment and otherness. In particular, they see some very promising work coming from the authors in this book. Other researchers are finding dialectical theory to be a rich and fruitful perspective from which to view the relationships of people who are disabled.

There has been little work regarding social support and people with disabilities. When such work has been done, the assumption has been that support is one-way, from ablebodied to disabled others. Researchers need to look at support as an exchange relationship between people with disabilities and others and maximize what people with disabilities have to bring to personal relationships. For example, people who are not working outside the home may have one commodity that many others do not have—time. They may have significant time to invest in supporting others. Additionally, they may have developed a level of empathy that many others do not have. These issues are relevant to social support.

Interpersonal attraction and relational formation is another useful way to view the experiences of people with disabilities. Barriers to forming relationships by people with disabilities, need to be better understood, to assist them in their interpersonal interactions. This is especially important for women, as disabled men are much more likely to find and maintain intimate relationships than are women.

Likewise, research is needed in relational maintenance by people with disabilities, as research has demonstrated a high divorce rate among people with disabilities. This is especially true for those who have later onset disabilities and, again, this statistic is higher for women with disabilities. Interpersonal scholars have done some very fine work in relational maintenance and relational repair strategies, and communication scholars need to start applying those strategies to the relationships of people with disabilities. Similarly, continued work in disclosure and boundary management should prove to be insightful.

CULTURAL ISSUES

Although the idea of disability as a culture has been discussed for a number of years and there have been great strides in this area, there is still a great distance to go. The work in identity management, as emphasized in the writing of Geri Merrigan and others, is one useful starting place. Dawn has argued elsewhere that being part of the disabled culture occurs when individuals have integrated being disabled into their definitions of self—their identities. Communication scholars have a lot to contribute to understanding this process of identity formation of persons with disabilities and the interpersonal communication strategies people with disabilities can use to communicate.

Scholars have moved beyond the early work on disability as a culture. Fox, Giles, Bourhis, and Orbe have categorized the communication between ablebodied and disabled people as "intergroup" communication, arguing that this is a more fruitful perspective. Their continuing work is very important. Several authors in this book are moving this work forward in very positive directions. Additionally, Susan Fox has been using the term "interability" communication to talk about interactions between people who are disabled and those who are ablebodied. Some feminist scholars have also critiqued the inadequacy of the culture metaphor for these interactions. The editors of this book expect to see giant strides forward that will advance understanding in very concrete ways and hope to see much more work on intercultural views and communication of people with disabilities. Iwakuma and Nussbaum's chapter shows the broad cultural variability regarding how people with disabilities are viewed and treated and how much this differs cross-culturally. Current society is increasingly global, and people with disabilities need to know the barriers and facilitators they will encounter as they travel and work in different geographic regions and form relationships with people from other ethnic and geographic cultures. There is a need for much more research in this area.

In addition, we hope to see more about how American cultural groups view disability. Living in a multicultural country necessitates these understandings. For example, how do Native American, Asian American, or Hispanic views of health and disability affect interactions and behaviors? There is much work to be done in the area of disability and culture.

ORGANIZATIONAL CONTEXTS

Especially given the Americans With Disabilities Act (ADA), scholars need to examine the organizational life of people with disabilities. John Smith, Krishna Kandath, Kelly Herold, and David Worley are all doing important work that looks at students with disabilities on college campuses. Gary Kreps, Audra Colvert, and John Smith are also focusing on broader organizational issues, and Kelly Herold's work on interviewing and applicants with disabilities is very important. There is still a lot of work to be done in this area.

Early data on the implications of ADA legislation indicated that ADA claims were being filed more by people with what Dawn and Denise Labrecque have called "New Age disabilities," such as back trouble, and much less by people with more "traditional" severe disabilities, such as spinal cord injuries, blindness, deafness, and so forth. The editors would like to see research that looks into ADA cases more fully.

Now that people with disabilities are more mainstreamed and are working in many more organizations, researchers should focus on communication and relationships in these contexts. There was a lot of hysteria in the business world after the ADA was passed; businesses feared they would be forced to spend considerable sums of money making adaptations for people with disabilities, for very little return. Evidence indicates that these fears were largely unfounded. However, it is necessary to learn more about communication between disabled and nondisabled people in organizations, especially in long-term work relationships.

There are many other issues about which communication researchers could contribute in the future. For example, how do people with disabilities get mentors in an organization? What needs might they have that are not being met? How have successful people with disabilities in the organizational realm gone about communicating to form and maintain successful relationships with co-workers and clients?

CONCEPTUAL ISSUES

Another intriguing area is the research on "nonvisible" or "invisible" disabilities, such as breathing disorders or epilepsy. Cynthia Matthews and Nancy Grant-Harrington are doing work in this area and researchers have even spent some time arguing about the descriptiveness and emotional loading of those two labels. There has been little research on this topic. Cynthia's early work indicated that people with nonvisible disabilities often fail to disclose them for fear of being stigmatized, and that they seldom invoke their ADA rights or take advantage of available adaptations, even to the point of refusing to park in a handicap parking space when walking is difficult for them. More scholars should take on this research.

Related to this, communication scholars have been broadening the definition of disability. For example, Rebecca Cline and Nelva McKenzie highlighted the need to include people with AIDS in a concept of disability. Kathryn Greene at East Carolina University is also conducting work in this area. The editors applaud their efforts and look forward to new insights.

As the concept of disability is broadened, it becomes necessary to consider when research applies and may be generalized to all people with disabilities and when the work should be focused on particular types of disabilities. Ann McIntosh and Heidi Rose have many years of experience studying people who are deaf. John Smith is studying people who are blind, and Thuy Do, Miho Iwakuma, Roxanne Parrot, and Dawn are all studying those with spinal cord and other mobility-related disabilities. There are scholars studying speech difficulties, including Mary Ann Romski and Bryan Whaley, and Joachim Knuf is studying cognitive disabilities. Al Weitzel approaches the work from personal experience and has begun some very powerful research on "the voiceless," the communication of those people who have lost the ability to speak. Communication scholars have just begun to scratch the surface there, and it is hoped that future researchers will study the unique and shared aspects of different types of disabilities. Goffman argued that people react similarly to all stigmatized groups. Is generalization this indeed valid?

Two other aspects of the communication discipline have been underrepresented in the work on disabilities and have much to offer in the present and the future. Scholars are urged to look for the work of those focusing on performance studies, such as C. Turner Streckline. Within the study of rhetoric, scholars such as Kara Schultz are providing insight into the rhetoric of social movements of people with disabilities. Wade Kenny is writing about how physician-assisted suicide redefines our views of disability. It was not possible to include all of this work in the present volume, but the editors hope that these scholars and others will continue to take up that mantle in the future, as well.

EDUCATIONAL CONTEXTS

Apart from the work on college students mentioned, few communication scholars have yet looked at disability issues within the classroom. It is likely that experiences with persons with disabilities in the earlier years of schooling will have some affect on developing patterns of communication, but currently very little is known about this. Teri's early work on the impact of mainstreaming has not been continued. The chapter by Malian and Nevin in the present volume mentions the paucity of work from within the communication discipline in the area of special education. Surely future scholars can make contributions in this regard.

Other types of disabilities, also invisible but traditionally more associated with the classroom, such as learning disabilities, have yet to be the subject of any communication inquiry. Some of these, and associated issues such as attention deficit disorder (ADD), affect interaction patterns in significant ways. Learning disabilities and ADD undoubtedly affect interaction between teachers and students and among students. ADD also affects parent–child relationships and the development of intimacy between adults. Similarly, intellectual impairment is a disability about which communication scholars know little. It would certainly be important and interesting to examine these concerns from a communication perspective.

HEALTH COMMUNICATION

Although health communication is referred to briefly in chapter 1, communication scholars have yet to contribute much on the impact of disability in the health care context. Although quite a bit is known about health communication, the editors could not uncover any research concerning interaction between a care provider and a patient with a disability. Personal experience leads the editors to feel very strongly that the health care received by persons with disabilities focuses exclusively on health problems caused by the disability, and other health issues are ignored. It may be that quality of life issues are not considered for those with disabilities. It may even be that their lives are not valued as much. This speculation is certainly not out of the realm of possibility in light of the recent evidence indicating the deep racism in medicine (see *New England Journal of Medicine*, Feb. 22, 1999). This line of research has indicated that health problems of African Americans are much less likely to receive medical attention compared with the same problems in Euro-Americans. This finding is true even holding constant virtually every other demographic, nonverbal, and verbal variable. Racism is one variety of stigmatization. The stigmatization experienced by those with disabilities and concomitant assumptions regarding disability also are likely to affect the medical care they receive.

Beyond the impacts on medical care, very little is known about the communicative experiences of those with disabilities in the health care context. There is an awareness of the significant communicative impacts of disability in other contexts, and the import of communication processes in health care is known, so it seems important to study communication and disability within this context, as well. Anecdotal evidence implies that health care workers are often no more comfortable around people with disabilities than are others, and that they are often woefully unprepared to deal effectively with people with disabilities.

These issues all focus on health communication concerns when the patient is disabled. What about when the health care worker is a person with a disability? That concern can be broadened significantly, of course, to focus on the impact of disability on any person in a professional role. How does a disability affect life for an attorney, judge, CEO, politician, professor, and so forth? There are obviously many, many questions of interest in this area.

MEDIA STUDIES OF PEOPLE WITH DISABILITIES

This area was saved for last because it is critical to the discipline's future, but one where the editors' knowledge is perhaps the most limited. Everyone is aware of the power of the media to shape interpersonal attitudes and behaviors as well as facilitate cultural change. Many have noticed that people with disabilities are becoming a bigger part of media images in America. There is fine work being done regarding media and people with disabilities by Beth Haller, Martin Norden, Kim Wolfson, and Olan Farnall. We look to these people and others to set an agenda and lead us into the future. Although their chapters in this volume focus on newspapers (primarily photographs), films, and advertising, there are many other media that affect our daily lives that have yet to be examined. The pervasiveness of television in modern life cannot be ignored, but little is known about the presentation of disabilities on that medium apart from a few commercials. (See Cumberbatch & Negrine, 1992, for a summary of the work that is available on this topic.) What about dramas, situation comedies, news, cartoons, and sporting events? Are persons with disabilities presented in these forums? Can they be? What would be the likely viewer response and impact?

Books are also an important medium, especially for children. Some children's books have introduced characters with disabilities, such as the popular "Little Critter" series by Mercer Mayer. How do children react to these characters? Does early contact with those with disabilities in books lessen the stigma associated with disabilities? What about books for older children and young adults?

The questions just posed lead to a more general concern. Even more important than content analyses or criticisms of the presentation of disability in the media are studies of the effects of such presentations. Media theories such as social cognitive theory or cultivation theory would argue for such effects, but little empirical work has yet tested these assumptions in regard to disability. It does little good to argue for the presentation of people with disabilities in the media if little is known about the impact of such presentations. Although some assume positive effects, that is a very simplistic assumption. How those with disabilities are represented will be crucial.

Several scholars are looking at computer-mediated communication by people with disabilities, most notably Susan Fox, who has been studying the topic for some time. Dawn and her colleagues' study of computer-mediated support groups simply supplements a fertile area for research and practice, as the Internet can help to tear down physical and mobility barriers as well as the stigmatizing social barriers faced by people with disabilities.

Along with this work, the editors believe that some of the greatest challenges and contributions will come in the area of technologies. The great number of assistive technologies available for people with disabilities is staggering and will significantly impact their abilities to live increasingly independent lives. Machines that read printed material for people who are blind are becoming more sophisticated every day. Some universities now offer whiteboards that will print out for deaf students and those who have trouble taking written notes whatever the teacher writes on the board. Voice activated computers provide great freedom for those who cannot type. Transportation advances coupled with medical technologies make it possible for people with very severe disabilities to drive a car and achieve heretofore impossible levels of mobility and independence. Jennings Bryant argued persuasively for the inclusion of a chapter on this topic in the present volume, but the editors were unable to find a scholar to write it. They look for work on this issue in the future.

Technology and medicine will combine for more staggering developments in the future that cannot even be imagined right now. Although communication scholars will not be doing that kind of pioneering research themselves, they have much to offer in looking at how those technologies affect the identity and relational life of people with disabilities, their place in organizations, and how they live and are treated in the culture.

CONCLUSION

Although much research has been summarized in this volume, it is obvious that there are many more questions yet to be answered related to communication and disability than scholars have even begun to ask. We hope that this volume will provoke much of that research. We look forward to future volumes and the attempt to answer more of the critical questions. Taking all this together, the future is bright, and communication scholars have their work cut out for them!

REFERENCE

Cumberbach, G., & Negrine, R. (1992). *Images of disability on television*. London: Routledge.

Author Index

Subject Index